Reference Library of

BLACK

AMERICA

Reference Library of

BLACK AMERICA

VOLUME
V

Edited by
Jessie Carney Smith
Joseph M. Palmisano

Distributed exclusively by:

African American Publications
Proteus Enterprises

Staff

Jessie Carney Smith and Joseph M. Palmisano, *Editors*
Patrick J. Politano, *Assistant Editor*
William Harmer, Ashyia N. Henderson, Brian J. Koski, Gloria Lam, Jeffrey Lehman, Allison McClintic Marion, Mark F. Mikula, David G. Oblender, Rebecca Parks, Shirelle Phelps, Kathleen Romig, *Contributing Staff*
Linda S. Hubbard, *Managing Editor, Multicultural Team*

Maria Franklin, *Permissions Manager*
Margaret Chamberlain, *Permissions Specialist*
Keasha Jack-Lyles and Shalice Shah-Caldwell, *Permissions Associates*

Justine H. Carson, *Manager, Vocabulary Development and Indexer*
Rebecca Abbott Forgette, *Indexing Specialist*

Mary Beth Trimper, *Production Director*
Wendy Blurton, *Senior Buyer*
Cynthia Baldwin, *Product Design Manager*
Gary Popiela, *Graphic Artist*
Barbara J. Yarrow, *Imaging/Multimedia Manager*
Randy Bassett, *Image Database Supervisor*
Pamela A. Reed, *Imaging Coordinator*
Robert Duncan, *Imaging Specialist*
Christine O'Bryan, *Desktop Publisher*

Victoria B. Cariappa, *Research Manager*
Barbara McNeil, *Research Specialists*
Patricia Tsune Ballard, *Research Associate*

ISBN 0-7876-4363-7 (set)
ISBN 0-7876-4364-5 (volume 1)
ISBN 0-7876-4365-3 (volume 2)
ISBN 0-7876-4366-1 (volume 3)
ISBN 0-7876-4367-X (volume 4)
ISBN 0-7876-4368-8 (volume 5)

Printed in the United States of America

10 9 8 7 6 5 4 3 2 1

Advisory Board

101458

Contributors

Donald F. Amerman, Jr.
Editorial Consultant, A & M Editorial Services

Stephen W. Angell
Associate Professor of Religion, Florida A & M University

Calvert Bean
Associate Editor, *International Dictionary of Black Composers*

Lean'tin Laverne Bracks
Editorial Consultant

Rose M. Brewer
Morse Alumni Distinguished Teaching Professor of Afro-American and African Studies, University of Minnesota-Minneapolis

Christopher A. Brooks
Professor of African American Studies, Virginia Commonwealth University

Paulette Coleman
General Officer, African Methodist Episcopal Church

DeWitt S. Dykes, Jr.
Professor of History, Oakland University

James Gallert
Vice President, Jazz Alliance of Michigan

Joseph Guy
Jazz and Touring Coordinator, Southern Arts Federation

Tracey Desirnaí Hicks
Membership and Volunteer Services Coordinator,
Charles H. Wright Museum of African American History

Phyllis J. Jackson
Assistant Professor of Art and Art History, Pomona College

Kristine Krapp
Editor, *Notable Black American Scientists* and *Black Firsts in Science and Technology*

Kevin C. Kretschmer
Reference Librarian, Blazer Library, Kentucky State University

Bernadette Meier
Editorial Consultant

Hollis F. Price, Jr.
Professor of Economics, Tennessee State University

Guthrie P. Ramsey Jr.
Assistant Professor of Music, University of Pennsylvania

Houston B. Roberson
Assistant Professor of History, University of the South

Gil L. Robertson IV
Founder, The Robertson Treatment

Audrey Y. Williams
Professor of Management, Zicklin School of Business, Baruch College, City University of New York

Raymond A. Winbush
Director, Race Relations Institute, Fisk University
Benjamin Hooks Professor of Social Justice, Fisk University

Michael D. Woodard
President, Woodard & Associates

Linda T. Wynn
Assistant Director of State Programs, Tennessee Historical Commission
Adjunct Professor, Department of History, Fisk University

Contents

Introduction

The *Reference Library of Black America* is based on the eighth edition of *The African American Alamanac*, first published in 1967 as *The Negro Almanac* and subsequently cited by *Library Journal*, in conjunction with the American Library Association, as "Outstanding Reference Source." It offers a comprehensive and accurate survey of black culture in the United States and around the world.

New Features in This Edition

All material was extensively reviewed by the editors and a board of prominent advisors and, where appropriate, updated and/or expanded; in many instances completely new topics were added to the existing essays. As a result, most chapters have been rewritten and focus on issues facing African Americans as we enter a new millenium.

African American women and their significant contributions have been given greater emphasis in the reference work than ever before. Examples of this expanded coverage include: speeches and writings of Sojourner Truth, Ida B. Wells-Barnett, Mary McLeod Bethune, and Barbara Jordan (Chapter 3); genetic evidence of a link between Sally Hemings and Thomas Jefferson (Chapter 6); biographical profiles of historic female activists of the black nationalist and civil rights movements (Chapters 8 and 9); female leadership in African American churches (Chapter 17); prominent women artists in the musical fields of gospel, blues, and jazz (Chapters 23, 24, and 25); and the increasing presence of female athletes in professional sports (Chapter 28).

The tremendous impact of the Internet is also reflected in the content of the *Reference Library of Black America*. Many entry listings in such sections as "National Organizations" (Chapter 9); "Historically and Predominantly African American Colleges and Universities" and "Research Institutions" (Chapter 16); "African American Media in Cyberspace" and "Magazines and Journals" (Chapter 19); "Museums and Galleries Exhibiting African American Art" (Chapter 26); and "Popular African American Internet Sites" (Chapter 27) now include website addresses. In addition, the promising effects of information technology on the African American community are discussed in "Entrepreneurship" (Chapter 14), "Media" (Chapter 19), and "Science and Technology" (Chapter 27).

Important African American towns and settlements are described for the first time in "African American Landmarks" (Chapter 4) and "Population" (Chapter 12). Included are listings of such historic sites as Nicodemus, Kansas; Boley, Oklahoma; the Sea Islands in South Carolina and Georgia; and Eatonville, Florida. In addition, expanded, up-to-date profiles of African and Western Hemisphere nations are offered in "Africa and the Black Diaspora" (Chapter 5).

Two new chapters have been added that significantly enhance the broad coverage of the *Reference Library of Black America:*

- "Film and Television" (Chapter 20) offers an overview of African Americans in the film and television industries, a selected filmography of more than two hundred films and documentaries depicting African American themes and issues, and biographical profiles of actors, filmmakers, and industry executives both current and historical.

- "Sacred Music Traditions" (Chapter 23) provides an essay that thoroughly describes the important periods and styles of African American sacred music, as well as concise biographical profiles of notable sacred music composers, musicians, and singers.

Approximately thirty new statistical charts compiled by the Bureau of the Census for the *Statistical Abstract of the United States* appear in pertinent chapters. Finally, a completely revised name and keyword index provides improved access to the contents of the *Reference Library of Black America*.

Content and Arrangement

Information in this edition of the *Reference Library of Black America* appears in 29 subject chapters. Many chapters open with an essay focusing on historical developments or the contributions of African Americans to the subject area, followed by concise biographical profiles of selected individuals. Although the listees featured here represent only a small portion of the African American community, they embody excellence and diversity in their respective fields of endeavor. Where an individual has made a significant contribution in more than one area, his or her biographical profile appears in the subject area for which he or she is best known.

Nearly seven hundred photographs, illustrations, maps, and statistical charts aid the reader in understanding the topics and people covered in the reference work. An expanded appendix contains the names and contributions of African American recipients of selected awards and honors.

24

Blues and Jazz

◆ The Blues Tradition ◆ The Jazz Tradition ◆ Women in Blues and Jazz
◆ The Future of Blues and Jazz ◆ Blues and Jazz Composers, Musicians, and Singers
by Joseph Guy and James Gallert

In a time span of less than a century, the remarkable American music called jazz has risen from obscure origins to become the most original form of musical expression of our times—loved, admired, and played throughout the globe. Jazz has a long and rich ancestry. Its roots go back to the arrival of the first Africans on American soil and the encounter between African and European musical traditions. Black music in America took many forms including work songs, gospel and spirituals, and many and varied kinds of music for dancing popularized by brass bands and traveling minstrel/medicine/vaudeville shows.

◆ THE BLUES TRADITION

Ragtime and Blues

By the late nineteenth century, a dance music called ragtime became very popular. Typically played on piano or by brass bands, its heavily syncopated rhythms and sprightly melodies had a distinctly African American flavor. Its greatest exponent was Scott Joplin (1868–1917), a pianist known as "the king of ragtime composers." About the same time, a form of African American folk music called the blues began coalescing into a 12-bar pattern with three line verses sung in a so-called AAB rhyming pattern that made it adaptable to popular song writing. The blues also displayed a unique harmonic quality derived from a "flattening" of the third and seventh notes of the tempered scale, which while seemingly simple, lends itself to infinite variation. The blues had an impact not only on jazz, but later on such styles as rock and soul music, both of which would be unthinkable without the blues element.

Blues History and Styles

The true origins of the blues as a musical style remain somewhat murky, seeming to have sprung up simultaneously in many places across the South around the turn of the century. From there, the blues more or less accompanied Southerners of African descent to wherever they migrated, evolving and incorporating whatever musical influences were encountered along the way. While the music clearly came from the country, this musical style became known as the blues in the city of Memphis, Tennessee.

W. C. Handy (1873–1958), an African American bandleader of a minstrel orchestra often credited with "inventing" blues, did not invent blues, but he may have been the first individual to achieve commercial success playing it. Although the word "blues" was already being widely used to describe an assortment of work songs, field hollers, and folk tunes by around 1910, it was Handy's publication of "Memphis Blues" in 1912 that established the genre as a readily identifiable musical style. Handy's "discovery" of the blues aside, it was three rural areas—the Mississippi Delta; Texas; and the Piedmont region (Georgia and the Carolinas)—that were the most important developing grounds for the blues.

Mississippi Delta Blues

It was in 1903 at a train station in the sleepy Delta town of Tutwiler, Mississippi, that Handy claimed to have discovered the blues. The style that emerged in Mississippi has also been the one most instrumental in shaping the blues sound over the decades. The Mississippi Delta blues consisted primarily of a singer accompanying himself on a guitar, which is played in a highly

W.C. Handy (Corbis Corporation [Bellevue])

percussive manner. The vocal style of the early Delta bluesmen was the most speech-like, as well as the most passionate, of the early regional styles. String bending and slides or bottlenecks were frequently used as a guitar effect, one that Handy connected with Hawaiian guitar playing.

Charley Patton (1887–1934) was probably the most influential of the early Mississippi blues practitioners. His growling vocal style, descendent from field hollers, work songs, and gospel singing, was emulated by countless other blues singers over the years. Patton's work influenced his contemporaries including Willie Brown, Eddie "Son" House, Johnny Shines, and Robert Johnson. Johnson, perhaps the biggest name to come out of the Delta blues tradition, in turn went on inspire yet another generation of blues artists, which included Chicago bluesmen Muddy Waters, Elmore James, John Lee Hooker, and Howlin' Wolf.

Also in the early 1900s in Memphis, the Beale Street jug band style emerged, made popular by the likes of Furry Lewis and Memphis Minnie. Played on homemade instruments such as kazoos, washboards, washtubs, spoons, and all manner of percussion devices, jug band music is an early example of the blues prior to its

solidification as a guitar-based music relying on the 12—bar format.

Texas Blues

Meanwhile in Texas, Blind Lemon Jefferson (1897–1929) was the undisputed king of the blues. The blues style that developed in Texas, with Jefferson as its main proponent, contrasted with the Delta style in a number of ways. The guitar accompaniment was less percussive and made more frequent use of melodic lines and embellishments. Texas blues singers tended to enunciate their lyrics more clearly than their Mississippi counterparts, often in a high-pitched voice.

The Texas blues bloodline that begins with Jefferson can be traced through such well-known names as Lightnin' Hopkins, Clarence "Gatemouth" Brown, and T-Bone Walker, all the way to such modern blues stars as B.B King, Johnny Copeland, and Albert Collins. From Texas blues, the contemporary blues inherited much of its improvisational element, and jazzy electric guitar soloists owe much to the Texas line of blues heredity.

Piedmont Blues

The Piedmont blues style varied considerably within the region but its most common differences from other blues styles is its more rhythmic base and an emphasis on the finger-picking style of guitar playing. Highly syncopated, the style connects closely with earlier string band traditions integrating ragtime and country dance styles. Early practitioners included Blind Boy Fuller and Blind Willie McTell. Heirs to this tradition include Brownie McGhee and Sonny Terry.

Early Blues Recordings

The commercial success of the female blues performers (see section titled Women in Blues and Jazz) eventually led the record companies to begin recording some of the male artists, who until that time had been completely ignored by the industry. In 1924, Okeh made what may have been the first record by a male country blues singer, a performer named Ed Andrews. The first male blues recording star, however, was Papa Charlie Jackson, a talented banjo player who performed some of the earliest recorded versions of many country blues standards. Over the next several years, a number of record companies produced field recordings, so named because they were recorded not in Northern studios, but on location in the rural South with portable equipment.

Migration of the Blues

During the Great Depression of the 1930s, millions of African Americans left the rural South for the cities of the North, and the blues traveled with them. The majority of the bluesmen who made the trek were of the younger generation. These performers adapted their traditional music to their new surroundings, incorporating the concerns of urban life into their lyrics. Blues scenes began to emerge in Chicago, St. Louis, Detroit, and elsewhere.

Older musicians, on the other hand, tended to stay put in the South. Skip James and Mississippi John Hurt were among the many bluesmen who did not migrate until later, if ever, and whose sounds remained countrified. Even today, blues can still be heard in the Delta that sounds much more like Charley Patton's brand than Buddy Guy's.

The blues players of each region tended to relocate to a particular area as they fled the South. Musicians in the Piedmont region of North Carolina drifted toward New York. Many of the Texans meanwhile headed westward to California. T-Bone Walker was one of the most important representatives of this migration, which led to the development of the West Coast blues sound, including use of the electric guitar after 1940, through a lineage that included a number of important piano bluesmen as well as guitarist B. B. King.

Chicago Blues

As blues artists in the Mississippi Delta and other parts of the Deep South headed to several Northern cities, a fertile blues scene developed in Chicago. The evolution of Chicago blues can reasonably be described as the amplification and small-band arrangement of traditional solo Delta blues. Taking their cue from the work of such Mississippi legends as Robert Johnson and Lonnie Johnson, arrivals from the South had begun to establish a blues scene in Chicago even before the onset of the Depression.

Popular Chicago blues performers during the 1920s and 1930s included Memphis Minnie, Tampa Red, Big Bill Broonzy, and Sonny Boy Williamson. A new wave of blues musicians after World War II solidified Chicago's position as the center of the blues universe. This generation of artists included Howlin' Wolf, Little Walter, and Muddy Waters.

Eventually, Chicago blues began to incorporate elements of blues styles from other areas. The most obvious input came from the Texas/West Coast guitar soloist line, following in the T-Bone Walker vein. This new emphasis on electric lead guitar improvisation was demonstrated in the work of such modern blues stars as Otis Rush, Magic Sam, and Buddy Guy.

The Varied Sounds of Blues

Like jazz, blues is a label that covers an incredibly diverse body of music. It defies convenient classifica-

Muddy Waters (Archive Photos, Inc.)

tion systems. Nevertheless, a number of recognizable styles and movements have emerged within the blues idiom over the years. Some of them are associated with the geographical areas in which they blossomed, while others transcend the boundaries of time and location.

Jump blues developed during the 1940s and 1950s, primarily in California. Jump was a jazzier, horn-driven style that relied less on guitar than many other blues forms. Its proponents have included Amos Milburn, Johnny Otis, and Big Joe Turner. In Louisiana, a laid-back "swamp" style was championed by Lightnin' Slim, Slim Harpo, and Lazy Lester. Louisiana also produced the blues offshoot called "zydeco," whose main proponents have included Clifton Chenier, Boozoo Chavis, and Rockin' Dopsie. The folk-flavored blues of the Carolina Piedmont region spawned the highly underrated Brownie McGhee, who influenced rock and roll, folk, and blues musicians. The term "piano blues" captures a wide variety of music spanning most of the continent and century including the entire progression from barrelhouse to boogie-woogie to hard rocking Chicago blues. Important piano bluesmen include Big Maceo Merriweather, Sunnyland Slim, Albert Ammons, Professor Longhair, and Otis Spann.

Two paths that blues have taken in recent years include modern acoustic blues and modern electric blues. Modern acoustic blues is essentially a movement for the revival of the older country blues sounds. Taj Mahal is one of its major proponents. Modern electric blues simply refers to the most contemporary trappings placed on urban blues. Robert Cray has been its most commercially successful practitioner.

◆ THE JAZZ TRADITION

New Orleans Jazz

It was when ragtime—primarily an instrumental music—and blues—at first primarily a vocal style—came together that jazz was born. Although this process was taking place simultaneously in many parts of America, it was in New Orleans that the basic language of jazz was first widely recognized.

This was due not only to the rich musical tradition of this port city with its international climate, but also because social conditions in New Orleans, while certainly not free from racist elements, were less restrictive and more open than in other large American cities of the time. Thus, there was much contact between musicians of varied ethnic background including those with traditions rooted in the rhythms of West Africa and Latin America, the harmonic structures from European classical music, the melodic and harmonic qualities from nineteenth century American folk music, religious music, work songs, and minstrel show music.

Many histories of jazz mistakenly over-emphasize the importance of the New Orleans red light district called Storyville. While early jazz certainly was performed there, and the word jazz is derived from jass or jas, a reference to this type of district, many other outlets for music making existed. These included dances, picnics, parades, carnivals, and the traditional New Orleans funerals, for which a band would accompany the casket from church to cemetery with mournful strains and then lead the march back to town with lively, peppy music including ragtime and early jazz.

Musicians from New Orleans began to tour the United States from about 1907 onward and had a significant influence wherever they went. Some of them visited Europe, notably the great clarinetist and soprano saxophonist Sidney Bechet (1897–1959), who has been called the first great jazz soloist. However, their intricate style of collective improvisation, in which each instrument in the band had its own specific role, was not so easily absorbed. It is another myth of jazz history that most of these early jazz players were a special breed of self-taught "naturals;" in fact, almost all of them had good

basic musical training, and many could read music well. But it was a somewhat younger New Orleanian, Louis Armstrong (1901–1971), who would have the biggest impact on the future of jazz.

Armstrong was brought to Chicago—by then a center of jazz activity—in 1922 by his mentor and fellow New Orleans trumpeter Joe "King" Oliver (1885–1938) and made his first records there. Two years later he moved to New York to join the band of Fletcher Henderson (1897–1952), the first musically significant big band in jazz.

Early African American Jazz Recordings

Jazz developed almost simultaneously with the phonograph, and without dissemination on records, it is unlikely that jazz would have spread as quickly as it did. Ironically, the first New Orleans jazz group to be recorded was a white group, the Original Dixieland Jazz Band in 1917. By then, African American musicians had already made records, but they were not in a jazz idiom. It would take approximately five more years before the best African American players from New Orleans were able to make records.

By studying recorded performances, musicians anywhere could learn at least the rudiments of jazz, a spontaneous music in which improvisation played a considerable role. "Improvisation" is a much misunderstood concept. It does not mean inventing music on the spot without guidelines. Shared foreknowledge of musical concepts, particularly harmonic and chordal outlines, to which one's own personal ideas are added to fit within a shared framework are the hallmarks of improvisation. In addition, a jazz musician's personal style on their chosen instrument will be based on tonal qualities, a distinctive approach to rhythm and phrasing, and a vocabulary of melodic and thematic characteristics. Taken together, these ingredients are what makes it possible for a seasoned listener to almost immediately identify who is playing in a jazz performance, provided that the musician has developed his own personal style.

The Swing Era

Most early New Orleans jazz bands used an instrumentation of trumpet, trombone, and clarinet for lead instruments and piano, guitar (or banjo), bass (string or brass) and drums for a rhythm section. The early "big bands" in contrast used three trumpets, one or two trombones, three reeds (saxophonists doubling clarinet), and the same rhythm section instruments. As larger ensembles, they more commonly employed writ-

Louis Armstrong performs in Germany in 1952 (AP/Wide World Photos, Inc.).

ten scores called arrangements, but gave the soloists freedom to "improvise" their contributions.

Louis Armstrong's 1924 arrival was a revelation to Henderson's New York big band. His first solos on its records stand out like diamonds in a tin setting. What Louis brought to jazz was, first of all, his superior sense of rhythm that made other players sound stiff and clumsy in comparison. He discovered the rhythmic element called "swing" that sets jazz apart from other music; a kind of rhythmic thrust that seems to float and soar. In addition, his sound on the trumpet was the biggest and most musically appealing yet heard, and he had exceptional range and powers of execution. Furthermore, his gifts of melodic invention were so great that he can well be said to have laid the foundation for jazz as a medium for personal expression by an instrumental soloist.

One of Armstrong's first Henderson colleagues to get the message was tenor saxophonist Coleman Hawkins (1904–1969), who soon created the first influential jazz style on his instrument. Also greatly affected was the band's chief arranger, Don Redman (1900–1964), who was the first to translate Armstrong's discoveries to big

band arranging. Many others followed suit, especially after Louis, now back in Chicago, began to make records with his own studio groups, the Hot Fives and Hot Sevens from 1925 to 1928.

By the late 1920s, jazz had become a mainstay of American popular dance music and had spread to Europe as well. African American musicians were touring worldwide, even in such exotic places as China and India, and wherever they went, their music left an imprint. Yet there was still quite a gap between jazz at its best and its more commercially acceptable versions. Not until the advent of the so-called "swing era" in the mid-1930s did unadulterated jazz reach a level of popular acceptance which, thus far, remains unmatched.

This acceptance was due primarily to the big bands that had reached a new height of artistic maturity. Duke Ellington (1899–1974), rightly called the greatest American jazz composer, was partly responsible for this success. His unique band, for which he gradually created a perfect balance between written and improvised elements, included such great soloists as Johnny Hodges (alto sax), Harry Carney (baritone sax), Barney Bigard (clarinet), Cootie Williams, and Rex Stewart (trumpets). This band began a most important engagement at

Harlem's famous Cotton Club in late 1927 and via appearances there, regular network radio broadcasts, and many recordings, Ellington's music was widely disseminated. His band visited Europe for the first time in 1933.

Other important work was done by Don Redman and Benny Carter (b.1907), a brilliant multi-instrumentalist and arranger-composer. Fletcher Henderson himself had not previously arranged for his band, but began to do so in the early 1930s and soon became one of the best. Such efforts laid the foundation for the success of Benny Goodman (1909–1986), a white clarinetist and band leader, who commissioned the best black arrangers (including Fletcher Henderson) and also was the first white band leader to hire black musicians (i.e, pianist Teddy Wilson in early 1936 and vibraphonist Lionel Hampton later that year).

By 1936, the swing era was under way. African American dance styles set at such places as Harlem's Savoy Ballroom swept the nation, and young people jitterbugged to the sounds of an astonishing number of excellent bands. Those bands led by Jimmie Lunceford (1902–1947) and Count Basie (1904–1984) stood out among the many others. The big bands spawned a host of gifted young players and also brought into the limelight many giants with established jazz reputations such as Armstrong who led his own big bands from 1929 to 1947.

World War II brought economic and social changes that affected the big bands. Gasoline rationing impaired the constant touring that was one of their mainstays. The singers, whose popularity was first established through their work with the bands, became stars in their own right. A nearly year long ban on all recording imposed by the musician's union in August 1942 further hurt big band popularity. After the war, the advent of television wrought fundamental changes in the ways people entertained themselves. Among the chief victims of the new stay-at-home trend was ballroom dancing. The big bands went into rapid decline, and only a handful maintained themselves, among them Ellington and Basie.

Meanwhile, the music itself had also undergone fundamental changes. The new generation of players who had come to maturity by way of big band experiences were eager to express themselves at greater length than most big band work permitted, and they were also developing new and potentially radical musical ideas.

The most advanced soloists of the swing era—Roy Eldridge (trumpet), Lester Young(tenor sax), Art Tatum(piano), and Sid Catlett (drums)—had been extending the rhythmic, harmonic, and technical resources of their instruments. Two young geniuses, both doomed to early death by tuberculosis, guitarist Charlie

Duke Ellington (The Granger Collection Ltd.)

Christian (1916–1942), featured with Benny Goodman, and bassist Jimmy Blanton (1918–1942), featured with Duke Ellington, revolutionized the language of their respective instruments.

Christian was among the many notable players who participated in jam sessions (i.e, informal musical get-togethers) at Minton's Playhouse, a night club in Harlem, in the early 1940s. Here, where pianist Thelonious Monk and drummer Kenny Clarke were in the regular house band, experimentation took place that fed into the new jazz mainstream and led to the advent of modern jazz in 1944–1945.

Bebop Gives Jazz a New Voice

The chief creators of this new jazz language were trumpeter and band leader-composer Dizzy Gillespie and alto saxophonist-composer Charlie Parker, both of whom had put in time with leading big bands. While working together in the band of pianist Earl Hines—the father of modern jazz piano style—in 1943, they began to solidify their mutually compatible ideas. When they joined forces in a small group in 1945, on records and in person, bebop, as the new jazz style soon was called, came into first flowering.

Dizzy Gillespie (AP/Wide World Photos, Inc.)

Though bebop was solidly grounded in earlier jazz styles, it did not seem that way to the public, which often was unable to follow the intricate rhythmic and harmonic elaboration of the boppers. Furthermore, the bop musicians, unlike most of the jazz players who preceded them, were not interested in pleasing the public, but more concerned with creating music that fulfilled their own artistic ambitions. Gillespie, however, was something of an exception, perhaps because his irrepressible sense of humor made him a natural entertainer.

A New Audience for Bebop

In any case, the advent of bop, which had its beginnings in the swing era, went hand in hand with a change in the audience for jazz. By the mid-1930s, small clubs catering to jazz connoisseurs had begun to spring up in most of the larger urban areas. The biggest and most famous concentration was in New York, in two blocks on West 52nd Street, which soon became known as "Swing Street." In such clubs, musicians could perform for knowledgeable listeners without making musical compromises; most of them were too small for dancing, so people came strictly to listen. By this time also, many people all over the world had become seriously interested in jazz. Some studied and documented its origins and history, while others collected, researched, and classified jazz records. Such publications as *Downbeat* and *Metronome*, which catered to musicians and serious fans, sprang up. These magazines conducted polls and presented awards, as was also done by 1944 by the prestigious *Esquire* magazine, which presented these awards at a huge all-star jazz concert on the stage of the Metropolitan Opera House in New York.

Jazz concerts had been a rarity in the 1920s. Then in 1938, Goodman staged one at Carnegie Hall and, from 1943, Duke Ellington gave an annual concert there. By the late 1940s, jazz concerts were regular events, among them the famous Jazz at the Philharmonic (JATP) all-star tours. Thus, in many ways the stage was set for the acceptance, albeit in a limited way, of jazz as a music that no longer could be considered mere entertainment or music primarily meant for dancing, but music having parity with "classical" music in its claim to serious artistic consideration.

The movement towards more "serious" appreciation for jazz, combined with the ascendancy of new forms of the blues, laid the foundation for the advent of rock and roll music. This new music filled the need for young people to have their own music to dance to at a time when jazz was perceived to have largely abandoned them. Nevertheless, the advent of rock music was resented by many jazz musicians and fans. Eventually, of course, rock itself spawned its own constituency of "serious" performers, commentators, and magazines.

Cool Jazz Is Developed

Toward the end of the 1940s, a reaction against the nervous energy of bop began to take form. This movement, spearheaded by trumpeter Miles Davis (1926–1991), came to be known as cool jazz. In contrast with the frenzied pace of bop solos, improvisers in the "cool" camp sought a more relaxed sound. The energy was sensual rather than frenetic and focused on a smooth laggato pace rather than the staccato feel of bop.

While cool jazz began to take root primarily on the West Coast, largely among white musicians, black musicians on the East Coast in the 1950s were pioneering the "hard bop" style. Hard bop built on the harmonies and the fiery approach of bop, while adding a bluesy, hard-edged element. Tenor saxophonist Sonny Rollins, trumpet player Donald Byrd, pianist Horace Silver, and drummer Art Blakey were among the major shapers of hard bop in the second half of the 1950s.

Post-Bop and the Avant-Garde

The trumpeter Miles Davis, who had worked with bop pioneer Charlie Parker and also led his own very influential cool jazz groups, hired a then little-known tenor saxophonist, John Coltrane (1926–1967), in 1956. With Coltrane, who also worked with Thelonious Monk, and pianist Bill Evans, Davis introduced a modal approach (i.e., based on scales rather than harmonies) to jazz improvisation in 1958. Sometimes called simply "modal jazz," this new style came to be known most frequently as "post-bop." It was practiced by many of the same musicians who had been hard boppers a few years earlier including Donald Byrd and drummer Max Roach, as well as such younger performers as Wayne Shorter and McCoy Tyner.

While bop and post-bop continued to develop, they were in turn succeeded by even more radical forms of jazz. In 1959, a young Texas-born alto saxophonist, Ornette Coleman (b. 1930), brought his adventurous quartet to New York, setting off a huge controversy with music that seemed to have abandoned most of the harmonic and structural principles of jazz as it had hitherto been known. In fact, Coleman's music was deeply rooted in the blues and in well-established improvisational jazz procedures, and in time his music was accepted as part of the jazz tradition.

John Coltrane (Down Beat)

By the 1960s, many people viewed the history of jazz as a linear progression toward maximum freedom for the player. Avant-garde jazz was very much in evidence, in many and varied forms. Just as bop had opened new windows of creative opportunity to soloists, each new emerging style that followed stripped away additional layers of constraint. Some saw this trend as the return of African American music to the complete freedom of the field holler; released from the rhythmic and harmonic limitations that had been imported from the classical music of white Europe.

Having left the Miles Davis group in 1960, Coltrane soon formed his own group, which took modality much further and extended improvisation, both in length and intensity, to a point of near ecstasy. The pianist Cecil Taylor (b. 1930), a virtuoso of the keyboard, further stretched the boundaries of jazz with inventive combinations of post-bop jazz, modern classical music, and experimental noise. Meanwhile, the bassist and composer Charles Mingus (1922–1979), deeply influenced by Ellington and Parker, found new and imaginative ways of combining written and improvised jazz. Tenor saxophonist Sonny Rollins (b. 1930), while remaining rooted in traditional harmonic ground, expanded solo improvisation dramatically. And by the end of the 1960s, Albert Ayler (1936–1973), a tenor saxophonist who stripped R&B music to its essentials and played it in "free-form," brought another new and intensely personal voice to jazz.

Over the course of the 1960s, many others contributed to the dismantling of the melodic rulebook. Pharoah Sanders, Archie Shepp, and Sonny Sharrock were among those who learned their art toward Coltrane's side. Ornette Coleman spawned a line of jazz innovators that has included trumpeter Don Cherry, bassist Jamaaledeen Tacuma, and guitarist James "Blood" Ulmer. Don Pullen, Sun Ra, and Anthony Braxton are also among the countless notable proponents of "free jazz," as avant-garde jazz was then beginning to being called, and its various offshoots. When John Coltrane died suddenly in 1967, jazz was at the height of its experimental, expansionist stage, much of it inspired by the social and political upheavals of the time. But within a few years of Coltrane's passing, the storm began to quiet.

Soul Jazz

The most commercially popular jazz style of the 1960s was not bebop, hard bop, or free jazz, but rather soul jazz. While the other more critically acclaimed styles were being recognized as an "art form" suitable for concert halls, soul jazz was thriving in bars and clubs and enjoying success with the record buying public. Soul jazz or funky jazz differs from bebop and hard bop in that the emphasis is on the rhythmic groove. The music's baselines focus on dance rather than sticking to four-to-the-bar walking pattern, with the melodies and solos focused on enhancing and extending the central groove. The focus of soul jazz on being danceable is a common element shared with the earlier swing jazz style.

Often cited as the first soul jazz practitioner, pianist Horace Silver emerged from the hard bop movement of the mid-1950s and began infusing his brand of jazz with blues, gospel, soul, and R&B elements. Other pianists to follow Silver's lead include Bobby Timmons, Les McCann, Gene Harris, and Ramsey Lewis. In 1956 organist Jimmy Smith exploded onto the jazz scene playing the Hammond B-3 organ. His foot-pedal baselines, percussive left-hand chords, and fiery right-hand solo lines revolutionized his instrument and expanded the genre. Smith's 1960 release *Back at the Chicken Shack* is considered a classic of the style. Those following in Smith's footsteps include Brother Jack McDuff, Shirley Scott, Jimmy McGriff, Big John Patton, and Lonnie Smith. But pianists and organist were not the only jazz players to find the style appealing. Saxophonists Stanley Turrentine, Eddie "Lockjaw" Davis, and David "Fathead" Newman

along with guitarists Grant Green, George Benson, Wes Montgomery, and Kenny Burrell all enjoyed tremendous success with soul jazz endeavors.

Fusion and Free Funk

Jazz did not stand still, and the 1970s saw the development of another school called jazz/rock fusion. The groundwork had been laid one decade earlier by Miles Davis on such albums as *In a Silent Way* and *Bitches Brew*. Fusion was essentially a marriage between the rhythms of rock and the virtuosity of the jazz soloist. Other champions of fusion included Wayne Shorter (founder of the group Weather Report), drummer Jack DeJohnette, and keyboardist Herbie Hancock. Another type of fusion that gained popularity in the 1970s was world fusion, which incorporated rhythmic and melodic elements from a variety of international music, most notably Brazilian and other Latin musical styles. Advocates have included Yusef Lateef, Don Cherry, and Ronald Shannon Jackson.

Beginning in the 1980s and building on the jazz/rock fusion model, free funk incorporated the rhythms and sounds of urban funk into a horn-driven, free improvisational framework. Ronald Shannon Jackson, James "Blood" Ulmer, and Jamaaledeen Tacuma—all one-time Ornette Coleman disciples—have been among its best practitioners.

The Return to Traditionalism

In the early 1980s, a goodly number of younger musicians began turning back to the rich tradition of jazz for inspiration. These included the gifted trumpeter Wynton Marsalis (also an expert classical player) and several other remarkable musicians from New Orleans, among them Wynton's older brother Branford Marsalis (tenor and soprano saxophones), trumpeter Terence Blanchard, and alto saxophonist Donald Harrison. These players rejected both "fusion," with its elements of electronics and rock, and the practices of "free jazz" and looked to the bebop tradition and, more importantly, to Louis Armstrong and Duke Ellington for inspiration.

As a way of highlighting their return to earlier jazz traditions, these younger players developed the so-called "repertory jazz" in the late 1980s. This refers to the institutional resurrection and performance of big band compositions and arrangements. The most notable of these ensembles are the Lincoln Center Jazz Orchestra with Wynton Marsalis as artistic director, which specializes in the music of Ellington, and the Smithsonian Jazz Masterpiece Ensemble, jointly directed by David Baker and Gunther Schuller, two master musicians with classical as well as jazz training.

Wynton Marsalis (center) performing with Wycliffe Lincoln (left) and Wes Anderson (right) at the JVC Jazz Festival in 1991 (AP/Wide World Photos, Inc.).

The proponents of traditionalism, the so-called "young lions" of jazz, persisted in their return to jazz roots during the first half of the 1990s, with Wynton Marsalis serving as a sort of godfather figure to the group. Perhaps the most commercially successful "young lion" has been tenor saxophonist Joshua Redman, son of well-known saxphonist Dewey Redman. The younger Redman brought his style of hard bop to its largest audience ever—an audience that worships him as a rock star. Other successful players from this school include: trumpeter Roy Hargrove; alto saxophonist Antonio Hart; the drum and trumpet playing brothers, Winard and Phillip Harper; bassist Christian McBride, guitarist Mark Whitfield, saxophonist James Carter, and pianist Marcus Roberts. These performers have brought jazz to the attention of its broadest audience in decades; in fact, the resurgence of the traditional form led to the first-ever, all-jazz music cable channel, BET Jazz, in 1996. Yet some older jazz artists worry that the reluctance of the younger generation to innovate or challenge the musical status quo does more harm than good to the genre. At the same time, many of these older musicians are seeing their careers revitalized, largely thanks to those same up-and-comers that they criticize.

Neoclassicism

While their origins are vastly different from those of the "young lions," the many gifted players who emerged from Chicago's 1960s Association for the Advancement of Creative Music (AACM) have also arrived at a similar approach to preserving the accomplishments of their "traditions." In such groups as the Art Ensemble of Chicago, the World Saxophone Quartet, and Lester Bowie's Brass Fantasy, musicians from the AACM school continued to refine their take on free jazz through the 1970s and 1980s, eventually creating a style often called neoclassicism. Neoclassicism applies the freedoms gained through the free jazz movement to more structured compositions. Important neoclassicists have included David Murray, Don Pullen, and Henry Threadgill. The AACM scene has remained vital into the 1990s, led by, among others, composer and saxophonist Edward Wilkerson.

Acid Jazz

In the mid-1980s disc jockeys (also known as DJs) in the British dance club scene resurrected classic soul jazz grooves through "rare groove" dance clubs. Utilizing the more obscure cuts from soul jazz and other such "dismissed" jazz explorations as Miles Davis's electric albums, Donald Byrd's *Black Byrd*, and Herbie Hancock's *Headhunters*, DJs such as Gilles Peterson spawned what became known as the acid jazz movement. The return to groove-oriented music was furthered by album releases of the British Hammond B-3 player James Taylor in the late 1980s and the formation of Acid Jazz Records in 1988. The label released a series of compilation albums titled *Totally Wired*, featuring soul jazz obscurities with updated tracks from newly termed acid jazz artists. In turn other acid jazz artists emerged, including Galliano, Young Disciples, Urban Species, the Stereo MCs, MC Solaar, and Courtney Pine. Acid jazz broke into the mainstream in 1991 when the Brand New Heavies released their first album and was followed by several hit singles, which in turn triggered acid jazz communities around the world.

Jazz Vocalists

Although thought of as primarily an instrumental art form, jazz has a strong vocal tradition. Although they primarily made their mark as instrumentalists or bandleaders, Louis Armstrong and Billy Eckstine both enjoyed considerable success as crooners over the course of their careers. Joe Williams, a true vocal giant, got his start in the 1930s, later working with Coleman Hawkins, Lionel Hampton, Count Basie, Henry "Sweets" Edison, and Cannonball Adderley, among others, before going on to lead his own groups beginning in the 1960s. In the late 1950s the vocal trio of Dave Lambert, Jon Hendricks, and Annie Ross rose to national prominence with their recording *Sing a Song of Basie*. The trio perfected and popularized vocalese, the art of putting lyrics to a previously recorded jazz solo. In the 1980s, an artist with a similar vision, Bobby McFerrin, blasted on to the scene. His 1984 release *The Voice* made history as the first major label jazz album recorded entirely without accompaniment or overdubbing. A vocal improviser in the truest sense of the word, McFerrin veered away from jazz later in his career. Will Downing, Jon Lucien, and Kevin Mahogany picked up the slack in the 1990s, with Mahogany being touted as the leading figure among them. Vocal sextet, Take 6, known for mixing elements of jazz, gospel, and pop, have also enjoyed popular success.

However, it has always been the women vocalists who have left the most lasting marks on the jazz vocal tradition. Such giants as Billie Holiday and Ella Fitzgerald emerged in the 1930s, building upon the success of the big band and swing movements. The crop of female vocal stars that followed as bebop took over included Sarah Vaughn, Carmen McRae, Nancy Wilson, and Betty Carter. Dee Dee Bridgewater was one of the few jazz

singers to break out of obscurity in the 1970s. In the 1980s, however, jazz vocals made a bit of a comeback with the emergence of Diane Schuur and Dianne Reeves. Cassandra Wilson, Nnenna Freelon, Shirley Horn, and Rachelle Farrelle have been among the leading jazz vocalists of the 1990s.

Spoken Word Jazz and Jazz Rap

As previously discussed, the roots of jazz include work songs, gospel songs, field hollers, and other vocal traditions. While most histories of jazz have focused on the music's instrumental aspects and mainstream jazz vocalists, little attention has been given to the use of spoken word in jazz.

One of the first persons to combine the more modern forms of jazz music with the spoken word was Langston Hughes (1902–1967). An early leader of the African American movement in the first half of the twentieth century, Hughes wrote eloquently about both the jazz and the blues. In 1958 jazz musician Charles Mingus released *Weary Blues*, an album that featured Hughes performing his poetry. Hughes was also a songwriter, and his songs have been performed by such jazz performers as Betty Carter, Eric Dolphy, Abbey Lincoln, Taj Mahal, and Nina Simone.

While primarily known for his 1960s essays about jazz and his poetry, Amiri Baraka has also been an active participant in the spoken word and jazz movement, contributing his voice and poetry on albums by Malachi Thompson and David Murray. With a focus on Afrocentric social commentary and feminism, poet and percussionist Jayne Cortez has released a number of fine albums from the 1970s through the 1990s. Similar in approach but aligned more with the avant-garde movement is Amina Claudine Myers. A pianist with ties to the AACM in Chicago, Myers's vocal work draws heavily from the spoken word tradition.

A poet who has considerable success in jazz, rap, and R&B, Gil Scott-Heron has released numerous albums featuring his poetry and music. Beginning with his 1970 release *Small Talk at 125th & Lennox*, which was fashioned with legendary jazz producer Bob Thiele, to his mid-1990s albums, Scott-Heron work is always revealing and poignant. Similar to Scott-Heron but with a focus on African American evolutionary prose and poetry in combination with Latin-flavored jazz is Ishmael Reed.

In the 1990s two other spoken word and jazz artists emerged on the New York scene. Sekou Sundiata, a Harlem native who teaches English literature at the New School for Social Research, combines his African American consciousness poetry with soulful and jazzy music on his 1997 debut *The Blue Oneness of Dreams*. In a similar vein, Yonkers poet Sha-Key released her jazz and soul-tinged debut album *A Headnaddas Journey to Adidiskizm* in 1994.

The hip hop world was discovering jazz as well. Initially focused on vocalizations or "raps" over beats "scratched" from vinyl records and later through electronic samplers, rap music began linking with jazz in the late 1980s. In 1988 the band Stetsasonic sampled fusion pianist Lonnie Liston-Smith for a track called "Talkin' All That Jazz," and the band Gang Starr issued their debut single "Words I Manifest" with a Charlie Parker line as the main melody. In 1990 Gang Starr, along with Branford Marsalis, Terence Blanchard, and Kenny Kirkland, contributed the spoken word/jazz track "Jazz Thing" for the soundtrack to Spike Lee's movie *Mo' Better Blues*.

The late 1980s also saw the rise of Afrocentric/native tongue movement led by hip hop pioneer Afrika Bambaataa. The Jungle Brother's 1988 release *Straight out the Jungle* featured several jazzy textures, and the following year, the release of the group De La Soul's debut album *3 Feet High and Rising* further showcased the molding of jazz and rap influences. These two early groups were followed by A Tribe Called Quest whose album *The Low End Theory* featured jazzy moods and textures along with samples from guitarist Grant Green and the bass playing of Ron Carter. By 1993 the trio known as Digable Planets released their album *Reachin' (A New Refutation of Time and Space)*, which featured samples from Eddie Harris, Sonny Rollins, and Art Blakey. Following this release the group mounted a tour that featured live jazz musicians in place of the sampling, one of the first such efforts.

Responding to the prevalence and popularity of hip hop artists using jazz samples in their music, in mid-1993 Blue Note Records granted a British production duo named US3 exclusive license to use samples from its catalogue. In early 1994 the duo had a top ten hit with "Cantaloop (Flip Fantasia)," based on samples from Herbie Hancock's piece "Cantaloupe Island." The most successful fusion of live jazz and rap came in mid-1993 on an album called *Jazzmatazz*. Featuring Roy Ayers, Courtney Pine, and Lonnie Liston-Smith and the stylings of Gang Starr's rapper Guru, the album was a true synthesis of the two styles. Other such projects followed, including *Stolen Moments: Red Hot + Cool*, Branford Marsalis's *Buckshot Lefonque*, and work by the rap band The Roots.

◆ WOMEN IN BLUES AND JAZZ

While most of singers and musicians playing the blues on the rural porches and in the taverns of the South were men, women were fulfilling a large role in blues history through other channels. In fact, the first big recording stars of blues were women, performing a style that eventually came to be known as "classic blues." The first blues recording made by a blues singer was "Crazy Blues" recorded in 1920 by Mamie Smith for Okeh Records. Another pioneering woman blues singer was Gertrude "Ma" Rainey, a blues belter from Columbus, Georgia, who recorded more than one hundred songs over six years.

Perhaps the greatest of the classic blues singers was Bessie Smith, whose popularity stretched from the rural South all the way to the booming metropolises of the North. By the mid-1920s, several record companies such as Columbia (Smith's label) and Paramount (Ma Rainey's) had caught on to the sales potential of so-called "race" records. Other classic blues singers included Ida Cox and Victoria Spivey. Before achieving widespread fame, all of these women got their start in the tent shows of the South.

During the heyday of classic blues from the mid-1920s to the early 1930s, the female singers were usually backed by big jazz combos, and the style maintained a much closer connection to mainstream pop music than to anything that could be called blues until that time. Alberta Hunter, the last of the great classic blues singers, as Bessie Smith before her, performed with Louis Armstrong and Fletcher Henderson in the 1920s. Dinah Washington, who rose to prominence with Lionel Hampton's jazz band in 1943, was often called the "Queen of the Blues."

Etta James, who counts Billie Holiday as one of her idols, and Koko Taylor, who developed her style after that of Bessie Smith, are among the prominent blues vocalists of the last few decades. As the blues sound percolated into other forms of pop music, its traces could be heard in the gospel-inspired voices of such soul and rock artists as Chaka Khan, Tina Turner, and most notably, Aretha Franklin.

Some of the earliest women in jazz, Edythe Turnham and Lil Hardin Armstrong, both led their own jazz bands in the 1920s. Trumpeter Ernestine "Tiny" Davis in the 1930s along with trumpeter Clora Bryant and trombonist Melba Liston in the 1940s and 1950s were all active and admired players. In 1943 pianist and composer Dorothy Donegan became the first woman, as well as the first African American, to play Chicago's Orchestra Hall, sharing the bill with Vladimir Horowitz. In 1992 Donegan was honored with the NEA's American Jazz Master award following Liston's receipt of the award in 1987.

Perhaps the most successful female jazz instrumentalists was pianist and composer Mary Lou Williams, a musician who adapted her style through every jazz era from ragtime to avant-garde. In 1930 Williams was chief emerge in the early 1980s was drummer Cindy Blackman, a classically-trained percussionist who has worked with Jackie McLean, Sam Rivers, and Joe Henderson, in addition to releasing four of her own albums.

Finally, violinist Regina Carter has continued to enjoy considerable success in the 1990s after her involvement with the highly respected, Detroit-based, all-female group Straight Ahead. A talented player with a beautiful tone, it has been suggested that Carter has the potential to become the most significant new violinist in jazz since Jean-Luc Ponty in the late 1960s.

◆ THE FUTURE OF BLUES AND JAZZ

According to many blues scholars and musicians, contemporary blues music has witnessed a progressive decline in popularity among young African American audiences whose interests lie in more identifiable musical forms, notably contemporary R&B, rap, and hip hop. At the same time, blues has enjoyed a revival among white, middle-class audiences that frequently attend music festivals and urban nightclubs. Furthermore, despite the emergence of talented newcomers such as Robert Cray, Lucky Peterson, Corey Harris, and Keb' Mo', there are fewer apprentices for the many veteran artists to pass on their knowledge and skills. Thus, the future of contemporary blues music will be determined by the practitioners's—both old and new—ability to gain greater popularity, notably among African American audiences, and train and inspire emerging artists, while not sacrificing the rich traditions of this important American musical form.

Jazz continues to influence many forms of music and is now accepted alongside classical music as one of the world's great art forms. After a long and remarkable period of intense innovation, the music seems to have reached a point where it is taking stock of its past while looking to the future with such dynamic styles as acid jazz, spoken word jazz, and jazz rap. Whatever that future may bring the story of jazz is one of the most remarkable chapters in the history of the twentieth century artistic creativity, and such names as Armstrong, Ellington, and Parker are bound to loom large when that history is finally written. Born in the crucible of slavery, jazz has become the universal song of freedom. Perhaps, Thelonious Monk put it best when he said "jazz and freedom go hand in hand."

◆ BLUES AND JAZZ COMPOSERS, MUSICIANS, AND SINGERS

(To locate biographical profiles more readily, please consult the index at the back of the book.)

Bessie Smith dancing in costume.

composer and pianist for Andy Kirk's Kansas City big band and was also composing for Benny Goodman, Earl Hines, and Tommy Dorsey. In the early 1940s she had her own band featuring a young Art Blakey and was composing for Dizzy Gillespie and Duke Ellington. During her long career Williams founded a foundation to assist musicians, ran her own record label, and was a university professor, all while continuing to compose and perform.

Detroit's Dorothy Ashby, brought the sounds of the harp to bebop, making her first record as a leader in 1956, and recording nine more albums as leader over the next 14 years. Along similar lines, Alice Coltrane played in husband John Coltrane's last group and then went on to record several albums in the late 1960s and 1970s that featured her distinctive piano, harp, and composing skills.

Having launched her recording career in 1982, pianist and composer Geri Allen has since released a dozen albums featuring such players as Oliver Lake, Ornette Coleman, Lester Bowie, Betty Carter, Ron Carter, and Dewey Redman. As an indication of her artistic excellence, Allen became the first woman to win the Danish Jazzpar Award in 1996. Another fine instrumentalist to

Muhal Richard Abrams (1930–)
Pianist, Composer, Bandleader

Born September 19, 1930 in Chicago, Abrams began his professional career in 1948, playing with many of the city's best musicians and bands. In 1961, he formed the Experimental Band with Roscoe Mitchell, Eddie Harris, and Donald Garrett, which soon became an informal academy for Chicago's most venturesome players. Under Abram's quiet but firm guidance and with the addition of Henry Threadgill, Joseph Jarman, Fred Anderson, and Steve McCall, the academy grew into the Association for the Advancement of Creative Music (AACM). The AACM helped young musicians perform and promote their own music, which could not be presented through established venues. Mitchell and Jarman, along with Lester Bowie, Malachi Favors, and Don Moye, later achieved worldwide prominence as the Art Ensemble of Chicago.

Though he never so appointed himself, Abrams was the recognized leader and moral and spiritual force behind the AACM. In 1976, Abrams moved to New York where he performed with Anthony Braxton, Leroy Jenkins, and others and began a long term relationship with the Italian Black Saint label with whom he released 16 albums as leader or co-leader, bringing him national and international recognition. In 1990, he was the first recipient of the prestigious Danish Jazzpar Award.

Henry "Red" Allen, Jr. (1908–1967)
Trumpeter

Born in New Orleans January 7, 1908, "Red" Allen learned to play trumpet in his father's brass band at an early age, moving on to play in such famous Crescent City bands as that of George Lewis (1923), John Handy (1925), and the riverboat bands of Fate Marable (1926). Allen joined King Oliver's band in St. Louis in 1927, traveling with Oliver to New York, before returning to Fate Marable's Band in 1928, where he was discovered by representatives of the Victor recording company looking for a performer to compete with Louis Armstrong. Through this association Allen recorded with the Luis Russell band (1929–1932) as lead trumpeter before moving to the bands of Fletcher Henderson (1933–1934) and the Mills Blue Rhythm Band (1934–1937).

After a solo career in which he, along with Louis Armstrong, set the standard for the swing era style of trumpet playing, Allen returned to Russell's band in 1937 before leaving again to record New Orleans style traditional music with Jelly Roll Morton and Sidney Bechet. In the 1940s and 1950s, Allen adapted his style to play with Coleman Hawkins, Pee Wee Russell, J.C. Higginbotham, and others.

Red's early playing, like Armstrong's, over time developed into a fluid, light style that took advantage of the trumpet's timbral range. In early years he used trills, smears, growls, and splattered notes that later inspired free jazz players. His later playing reflected a movement away from traditional and swing styles to tight knit combo style playing with blues influences. The hallmark of Red's playing was that he always sounded "modern" in whatever context he was playing as aptly demonstrated on his 1957 LP *World on a String*.

Lilian "Lil" Hardin Armstrong (1898–1971)
Pianist, Singer, Composer

Lil Hardin Armstrong was born in Memphis, Tennessee, in 1898 but her family moved from Memphis to Chicago somewhere around 1914 or 1915. Hardin was a classically trained musician who received her music education at Fisk University. One of her first jobs was selling sheet music in Jones music store in Chicago. Legend has it that she met Jelly Roll Morton while working there, and it was Morton who influenced her style of hitting the notes "real heavy." She joined Freddy Keppard's band while still in her teens and joined King Oliver's Creole Jazz Band in 1920, where she met her husband Louis Armstrong, who was then second trumpet. Lil and Louie were married in 1924. She led her own band with Louis in 1925 and went on to play and write music for many of Armstrong's Hot Five and Hot Seven concerts and recordings from 1925 to 1928.

The Armstrongs were divorced in 1932, but Lil continued working as an accompanist with such players as Red Allen and Zutty Singleton until she led a series of all-star groups for Decca Records from 1937–1940. In 1952 she went to Europe, appearing with Sidney Bechet and as a solo artist. She returned to the United States in the early 1950s and continued playing until her death. Two of her songs "Bad Boy" and "Just For a Thrill" became big hits in the 1960s. While playing at a tribute to Louis Armstrong at Chicago's Civic Center Plaza, Lilian Armstrong collapsed and died of a heart attack on July 7, 1971, one day after Louis's death.

Louis Armstrong (1901–1971)
Trumpeter, Singer

Born August 4, 1901, in New Orleans, Louis Armstrong was not only the most influential instrumentalist and vocalist in jazz history, but quite simply, one of the most famous people of the twentieth century.

Raised by his mother in New Orleans's Third Ward, Armstrong was arrested on December 31, 1913, for firing a pistol in the street and was sent to the Colored Waifs Home. It was there that he first learned to play the cornet. His skill increased with the experience that he gained from playing in the Home's band. When he was finally released from the institution, he was already proficient enough with the instrument to begin playing for money.

Befriended by his idol and mentor Joe "King" Oliver, Armstrong quickly began to develop his jazz skills. When Oliver left for Chicago in 1919, a place opened for Armstrong as a member of the Kid Ory band in New Orleans. In 1922, Oliver asked Armstrong to join him in Chicago as second cornet with his Creole Jazz Band, and it was here that Louis made his first appearance on a jazz recording in 1923.

With his skills and reputation growing, Armstrong left Chicago in 1924 to join the Fletcher Henderson band at the Roseland Ballroom in New York City. After a long tour with Henderson, he returned to Chicago in late 1925 to play with the Erskine Tate Orchestra, switching from cornet to trumpet, the instrument he played from then onward. During the next four years he made a series of recordings titled Louis Armstrong's "Hot Five" or "Hot Seven," which showcased his brilliant technique, swinging style, and improvisational ability. These recordings also featured other great players such as pianist Earl Hines, trombonist Kid Ory, and drummer Baby Dodds.

In 1929, Armstrong returned to New York and, in the revue *Hot Chocolates*, scored his first triumph with a popular song Fats Waller's "Ain't Misbehavin'." This success was a turning point in his career, leading Armstrong to begin fronting big bands and to play and sing popular songs rather than blues or original instrumentals.

With his fame growing Armstrong returned to New Orleans in 1931 and in 1932 headlined at the London Palladium, where he acquired the nickname "Satchmo" as a result of the garbling of a previous nickname in a review in London's *Melody Maker* magazine. From 1933 to 1935 he toured Europe returning to the United States to film *Pennies from Heaven* with Bing Crosby. He continued to evolve from the status of musician to that of personality-entertainer, and his singing soon became as important as his playing. In 1947, he formed a sextet that was an immediate success, and he continued to work in this context for the rest of his career, touring throughout the world.

Armstrong continued to develop his multi-faceted career appearing in numerous movies, at Newport and other major festivals, and scoring highly in a new phenomenon, music polls. He scored a tremendous success in 1964 with his recording of "Hello Dolly," which bounced the Beatles from the top spot on the Top 40 list, a great feat in the age of rock. His style, melodically and harmonically simple compared to those of avant-garde

and then free jazz, evolved little, and his improvisations grew more infrequent. Yet his warmth and genuine appeal never faded. Though his health began to decline, he kept up his heavy schedule of international touring. When he died in his sleep at home in Corona, Queens, two days after his seventieth birthday, he had been preparing to resume work in spite of a serious heart attack suffered some three months prior. "The music—it's my living and my life" was his motto.

Louis Armstrong's fame as an entertainer in the later stages of his extraordinary career sometimes made people forget that he remained a great musician to the end. More than any other artist, Louis Armstrong symbolized the magic of jazz, a music unimaginable without his contribution. "You can't play a note on the horn that Louis hasn't already played," said Miles Davis. "I mean even modern." In addition, such contemporary musicians as Wynton Marsalis echo that opinion. As evidence of his lasting influence, in 1988, on the strength of its use in the film *Good Morning Vietnam* Armstrong's recording of "What A Wonderful World" became a surprise hit, climbing to number eleven on the Billboard chart.

William "Count" Basie (1904–1984)
Pianist, Bandleader

Born August 24, 1904, in Red Bank, New Jersey, William Basie received his musical training from his mother and by picking up rudiments watching the pit bands at Harlem movie theaters. He later took informal organ lessons from Fats Waller (often crouching beside Fats in the Lincoln Theater in Harlem) before debuting in the early 1920s as an accompanist to various vaudeville acts. In 1927 Basie was stranded in Kansas City when the vaudeville act he was touring with disbanded. Remaining in Kansas City in 1928 he joined Walter Page's Blue Devils with Jimmy Rushing as the vocalist, melding his New York stride style to the hard-riffing Kansas City sound. After this Page's band broke up, Basie joined the Bennie Moten band, and after Moten's death in 1935, formed his own band around the core of the Moten group. While playing at the Reno Club in Kansas City, William was soon dubbed "Count" by a local radio announcer.

At the urging of critic John Hammond, Basie brought his group to New York City in 1936, and within a year he had cut his first record and was well on his way to becoming an established presence in the jazz world. The Basie trademark was his rhythm section, which in the early years featured Basie's own clean, spare piano style, the drumming of "Papa" Jo Jones, and the bass work of Walter Paige. Outstanding soloists such as

Count Basie (AP/Wide World Photos, Inc.)

saxophonist Lester Young and trumpeter Harry "Sweets" Edison and original arrangements by Basie and other band members added to the band's distinctive sound.

Throughout the 1940s Basie maintained his big band that featured a steam of outstanding soloists including Illinois Jacquet and J.J. Johnson. Financial constraints led Basie to a small band format with Clark Terry, Wardell Gray, and Buddy DeFranco for the years 1950 and 1951 before he returned to the big band format that he maintained for the rest of his career. In addition to maintaining a rigorous and successful international touring schedule, the Basie band scored two hits in 1955 with "April in Paris" and "Everyday I Have The Blues," featuring the vocals of Joe Williams. In 1957 his band became the first American band to play a royal command performance for the Queen of England and the first African American jazz band ever to play at the Waldorf Astoria Hotel in New York City, completing a 13-week engagement at the hotel. Basie and his band remained active and popular until his death on April 26, 1984.

The legacy of the Count Basie band is far reaching. His rhythm sections keep the pulse strong and propulsive yet uncluttered, providing the perfect springboard for soloists. Basie's own spare piano style laid the groundwork for modern jazz pianists, and the light, airy, and swinging sound of Lester Young's saxophone influenced virtually all jazz players to follow.

Sidney Bechet (1897–1959)
Saxophonist, Clarinetist

Born May 14, 1897, in New Orleans, Sidney Bechet began playing clarinet at age six and by his late teens had played with many of the early New Orleans bands including those of Freddie Keppard and "King" Oliver. After a short stay in Chicago, Bechet relocated to New York where he eventually joined Will Marion Cook's Southern Syncopated Orchestra for a tour of Europe. About this time Bechet began playing the soprano saxophone, which became his signature sound and allowed him to standout in ensembles as only trumpet players had prior been capable. The group received rave reviews, and one such review by conductor Ernest Ansermet resulted in Bechet becoming the first individual jazz player to be seriously accepted as a distinguished musician.

During the early 1920s Bechet made a series of records with Clarence Williams's Blue Five, worked briefly with Duke Ellington (one of his great admirers), Mamie Smith, and others before returning to Europe in the mid-1920s. By this time Bechet's virtuosity and presence as a soloist was unmatched by any other reed player, with Louis Armstrong on trumpet being his only equal. From 1928 to 1938 he worked primarily with Frenchman Noble Sissle, both in Europe and the United States, but saw his popularity decline as the bands of Ellington, Basie, and Armstrong gained popular attention. After a Dixieland revival in the late 1930s, Bechet was being hailed once again by critics as a jazz luminary, and in the 1940s he made several records with Louis Armstrong, Jelly Roll Morton, and Earl Hines.

In 1949, Bechet permanently moved to France, where he enjoyed the greatest success of his career and enjoyed celebrity status. He died there of cancer in 1959.

Art Blakey (1919–1990)
Drummer, Bandleader

Born October 11, 1919, in Pittsburgh, Pennsylvania, Art Blakey was not only one of the greatest drummers in jazz, he was also one of the music's foremost talent spotters and nurturers. After early experience with Fletcher Henderson (1939) and Mary Lou Williams (1940), he joined Billy Eckstine's (1944–1947) band, where along with Dizzy Gillespie, Charlie Parker, and Miles Davis he took part in the early stirrings of bebop. Known up to that time as a shuffle drummer, Blakey adapted his style to the complex velocities and patterns of bebop and began using triplet figures over 4/4 time. After

Eckstine's band dissolved, Blakey worked as a sideman and in his own groups, further developing his style by incorporating African and Afro-Cuban tunings and techniques into his playing.

In 1954 he formed the Jazz Messengers, which met with immediate success. For the next 36 years, Blakey hired and helped to stardom a vast number of gifted players, among them Horace Silver, Lee Morgan, Freddie Hubbard, Benny Golson, Woody Shaw, Wayne Shorter and Wynton Marsalis, to name but a very few. Blakey had one of the most distinctive sounds in jazz, possessed a near photographic memory for arrangements, and a gift for nurturing talent that produced some of the finest recordings in jazz history.

Jimmy Blanton (1918–1942)
Bassist

Born in St. Louis, Missouri, in 1918, Blanton played with Jeter Pillars and Fate Marable before joining Duke Ellington in 1939. During his short life Blanton made a incalculable contribution in transforming the use of the string bass in jazz. Until his emergence, the string bass rarely played anything but quarter notes in ensemble or solos. By playing the bass more as a horn, Blanton began sliding into eighth- and sixteenth-note runs, introducing melodic and harmonic ideas that were totally new to the instrument. His skill put him in a different class from his predecessors, making him the first true master of the bass and demonstrating the instrument's unsuspected potential as a solo vehicle. Tragically, Blanton died of tuberculosis in 1942.

Buddy Bolden (1868–1931)
Cornetist

Buddy Bolden, a barber by trade, was perhaps the first jazz legend known for his drinking ability, his success with the ladies, and his flamboyant showmanship. Because his career predates the recording of jazz, the evidence of his talent as a cornet player lies in the oral tradition. By 1895 he was leading his own band playing dances, parties, picnics, and by the turn of the century his clear, ringing tone and his use of "blue" phrases and notes was so popular that he was often called upon to sit in with several bands on a single evening. It is unknown whether he applied improvisational techniques to his playing or simply heightened the rhythmic coloring and added melodic embellishments to the jigs, rags, and brass band tunes of the day. What is certain is that his playing and his performance style greatly influenced the players of his day and virtually all of those to follow.

In 1906, Bolden began suffering periods of derangement, perhaps brought on by heavy drinking, and was committed by his family to East Louisiana State Hospital in 1907, where he remained for the last 24 years of his life.

William Lee Conley "Big Bill" Broonzy (1893–1958)
Guitarist, Singer

Born Jun 26, 1893, in Scott, Mississippi, Broonzy was one of a family of seventeen who first learned to fiddle on a homemade instrument. Taught by his uncle, he was performing by age ten in church and at social functions before working as a preacher. After a stint with the Army, he moved to Chicago, switched to guitar, and began playing with Papa Charlie Jackson before beginning his recording career with Paramount in 1927. By the early 1930s he was recording hokum and blues and touring with Black Bob and Memphis Minnie as well as working sessions where the powerful new Chicago sound was being developed. He appeared at Carnegie Hall in 1938 for John Hammond's "Spirituals to Swing" series and appeared the following year with Benny Goodman and Louis Armstrong in the film *Swingin' the Dream*. He spent the 1940s barnstorming the South with Lil Green's road show and working in Chicago with Memphis Slim before touring Europe in the early 1950s and developing a worldwide following. He continued to tour and record into the mid-1950s before dying of cancer on August 15, 1958, in Chicago.

Broonzy's impressive musical skill, size and variety of musical repertoire, and influence on contemporaries and their followers make him one of the most important players in blues history. He wrote hundreds of songs including the classics "All by Myself" and "Key to the Highway," and his contributions to the formation of the Chicago blues sound were immense.

Clarence "Gatemouth" Brown (1924–)
Guitarist, Singer

Born April 18, 1924, in Vinton, Louisiana, and raised in Orange, Texas, Clarence "Gatemouth" Brown may have earned his nickname due to his "big as a gate" voice, but it is his guitar wizardry that has earned him a place in the blues pantheon. The son of a Cajun singer who could play accordion, banjo, fiddle, and mandolin, Brown himself became a multi-instrumentalist at an early age. As a youth Brown preferred his father's lively Cajun tunes and the jazz being produced by such musicians as Count Basie and Louis Jordan over the blues. His attitude changed, though, when he was introduced to the jazz-inspired blues of guitar pioneer T-Bone Walker.

Brown's first big break came in 1947, when he was called in as a last-minute replacement for the ailing Walker at a prominent Houston nightclub. The club's owner immediately offered Brown a long-term contract to record for his newly formed label, Peacock Records.

Brown recorded more than fifty sides of music for Peacock by 1960, his blistering riffs of string-bending fury inspiring a legion of Texas players such as Albert Collins, Johnny Copeland, and Johnny "Guitar" Watson. Brown's music did not fare well on the rhythm and blues charts though, and only one of his singles "Mary is Fine"/"My Time is Expensive" (1949) had nationwide success. But his furious instrumentals, low-down Texas blues, and horn-powered tunes became a foundation of the Texas post-war era. The early 1960s proved to be a difficult time for Brown, so in 1964 he went to Europe, where he toured and recorded widely and attained a sizable following. Rebuilding his career, he returned to the United States when blues began to show signs of resurgence. Despite winning a Grammy Award in 1981 for *Alright Again*, he has never quite become a household name in the United States, although his releases have continued to receive acclaim.

Clifford Brown (1930–1956)
Trumpeter, Composer, Bandleader

Born October 30, 1930, in Wilmington, Delaware, Clifford Brown received a trumpet from his father while in high school and studied harmony, theory, trumpet, piano, vibes, and bass with a private teacher. Brown studied mathematics in college, graduating from Maryland State University in 1950. During his college years he often sat in with musicians visiting nearby Philadelphia including Miles Davis and Fats Navarro, both of whom were heavy influences on Brown. He suffered a near fatal car crash in the summer of 1950, but recovered and was soon touring with the R&B band of Chris Powell. He appeared with Tad Dameron and toured Europe with Lionel Hampton's band in 1953. In 1954 he recorded with Art Blakey and so impressed peers and audiences that he soon formed and co-led a group with drummer Max Roach, which included Sonny Rollins on tenor saxophone.

The now legendary Brown-Roach ensemble recorded and performed extensively in 1954–1955, during which Brown's individual style emerged. Often cited for his ability to construct intricate solos akin to those of Dizzy Gillespie, Brown's playing also displayed a bouncy jubilance and soulfulness that defines the post-bop/hard bop sound. Not just a hot soloist, some of Brown's most compelling work is his masterful feel on ballads. Unfortunately, just as Brown was reaching his creative zenith, he was killed, along with Richie Powell and Powell's wife, in a car crash in the early morning of June 25, 1965.

Raymond Matthews Brown (1926–)
Bassist

Born October 13, 1926, in Pittsburgh, Ray Brown studied piano and bass while in high school before

playing with Jimmy Hinsley and Snookum Russell in 1944. He moved to New York in 1945 where he played with Dizzy Gillespie, Charlie Parker, and Bud Powell, eventually joining Dizzy Gillespie's big band and making several recordings. In the late 1940s Brown was part of the great Jazz at the Philharmonic (JATP) tours playing with Lester Young and Buddy Rich, among others. In 1948 Ray married Ella Fitzgerald and led a trio for her for a short period of time (Ray and Ella divorced in 1952). In 1951 Brown recorded with Milt Jackson and John Lewis, in what would later become known as the Modern Jazz Quartet, before joining Oscar Peterson's Trio, an association that lasted 15 years. During this time, he and Peterson produced award-winning records and were in constant demand for concerts.

Brown continued to appear on Jazz at the Philharmonic (JATP) recordings, and after leaving Peterson in 1966 he settled in California and began a successful career managing and producing other jazz acts including the Modern Jazz Quartet and Quincy Jones. Brown continued to perform and record, notably a duet with Duke Ellington in 1972, and formed the LA Four in 1974 with Bud Shank and Shelley Mann. Brown continues to be regarded as one of the finest jazz bassist in history and has recorded as a leader throughout the 1970s, 1980s, and 1990s. Brown received a National Endowment for the Arts American Jazz Master Fellowship in 1995.

Cab Calloway (1907–1994)
Singer, Dancer, Bandleader, Author

Born Cabell Calloway, III, on December 25, 1907, in Rochester, New York, the second of six children born to an attorney and his teacher-wife. Calloway grew up in Baltimore where he sometimes sang with the Baltimore Melody Boys, and after moving to Chicago with his family, he enrolled in pre-law at Crane College. He appeared in *Plantation Days* at the Loop Theatre with his sister Blanche, who along with older brother Elmer also became bandleaders, and also worked as master of ceremonies and relief drummer at the Sunset Caf . In 1928 he took over leadership of an 11-piece band, the Alabamians, which promptly disbanded when its first New York booking at the Savoy Ballroom was a failure. Calloway stayed in New York landing a role in the all-African American revue *Connie's Hot Chocolates*.

In 1929, Calloway took over as leader of another band, the Missourians, where Cab's energetic stage presence ignited the band and its audiences. This group, renamed Cab Calloway and His Orchestra, replaced Duke Ellington's band at the Cotton Club. It was here in 1931 that Calloway, during a radio broadcast, swung into a recently written song called "Minnie the Moocher." According to Calloway, he realized he had forgotten the lyrics and filled in the blanks by scat-singing the first thing that came into his mind: "Hi-de-hi-de-hi-de-ho. Ho-de-ho-de-ho-de-hee." The band played along, the audience hollered back raucously, Calloway had a hit, and his band remained at the Cotton Club for nine consecutive years. It was during this period that Calloway created many of his other signature songs including "Reefer Man" and "Kicking the Gong Around," and he developed his famous scat style of singing. Over the years his band included many great players such as Milt Hinton, Doc Cheatham, Dizzy Gillespie, Ben Webster, Cozy Cole, Mario Bauza, and Chu Berry, all of whom Cab helped in advancing their careers.

After his run at the Cotton Club, Calloway continued to lead his big band, and he also appeared in the 1943 film *Stormy Weather* with Lena Horne. Changing times forced Calloway to disband his orchestra in 1948, and he fronted smaller groups until 1952, when he played the breakthrough role of Sportin' Life in the Broadway revival of *Porgy and Bess*. In addition to continually appearing with jazz bands, Calloway went on to star with Pearl Bailey in the late 1960s all-African American production of *Hello Dolly*, published his autobiography *Of Minnie the Moocher and Me* in 1976, and appeared in the movies *Cincinnati Kid* and the *Blues Brothers*.

Calloway died on November 18, 1994. His official honors include a National Medal of Arts presented by President Clinton. However, his legacy is that of one of the greatest entertainers of all time and as a man who not only withstood the indignities of blatant racism, but inspired, nurtured, and helped promote those with whom he worked.

Benny Carter (1907–)
Saxophonist, Trumpeter, Composer, Bandleader

Bennett Lester Carter, born August 8, 1907, in New York City, is largely a self-taught musician having learned music primarily from his mother. Enrolled in 1925 at Wilberforce College in Ohio to study theology but soon left to join Horace Henderson's traveling band. Late in 1928, he formed his own band which appeared at the Arcadia Ballroom in New York before serving short stints with Fletcher Henderson, Chick Webb, and Charlie Johnson, with whom he recorded in 1929. In 1931 he took the position of musical director for McKinney's Cotton Pickers and wrote tunes for Benny Goodman before launching his own big band in 1933, which helped shape the language of big band jazz. Alumni of this band include Sid Catlett, Chu Berry, and Teddy Wilson. In addition to his influential work scoring for saxophone sections, Carter had few peers as a trumpeter, appearing as a sideman with Willie Bryant in 1934 before moving to Paris and then London in 1936, where he worked as staff arranger for BBC radio. In 1937 he played a session at a Dutch resort leading an interracial and international big band, the first successful unit of its kind in jazz history.

Returning to New York in 1938, Carter again led his own large and small ensembles including work with Dizzy Gillespie, and in 1944 he moved to Los Angeles where his West Coast band included Max Roach, J.J. Johnson, and Buddy Rich. Carter was the first African American composer to break the color barrier in the Hollywood film studios. He scored many major films including *The Snows of Kilimanjaro*, as well as television shows including "Mod Squad." During the 1950s and 1960s Benny wrote and arranged for Sarah Vaughn and Abbey Lincoln while continuing to record and perform with his own projects. Carter received an honorary doctorate in music from Princeton University in 1974, and in 1988, he toured Europe, visited Japan with his own band, performed in Brazil for the first time in his career, and recorded three albums. Carter's recorded legacy documents his talents as a composer-arranger and his alto sax playing, along with that of Johnny Hodges, remains as one of the most important influences of the 1930s.

Clifton Chenier (1925–1987)
Singer, Accordionist

Born on June 25, 1925, in Opelousas, Louisiana, Clifton Chenier is generally regarded as the "King of Zydeco," the dance music that combined Cajun two-step and waltzes with blues licks that arose from Louisiana's black French-speaking Creoles. The son of accordionist John Chenier, Clifton took up the instrument at an early age and by the time he was 17 years of age, he and his brother, Cleveland, who played the rub board, were playing weekend gigs.

By the early 1950s Chenier had formed the Hot Sizzlers, a seven-piece combo with electric guitar, piano, tenor sax, bass, and drums added to the brothers' instruments, drastically changing the direction of the music. Chenier was eventually discovered by a talent scout and signed to the Elko record label in 1954. The first session yielded "The Louisiana Stomp" which had some success, but Chenier moved to the Specialty Records label a year later. His first big hit was "Ay, 'Tit Fille" in 1955, which sold well throughout the South and made it to the rhythm and blues charts. Chenier quickly became a big attraction in the Gulf Coast region and toured with Etta James and Jimmy Reed, but elsewhere remained relatively unknown.

Chenier moved to Houston in the early 1960s, where he was "rediscovered," this time by Chris Strachwitz of Arhoolie Records. He released his first album *Louisiana Blues and Zydeco* on Arhoolie in 1964 and recorded a number of dates for Arhoolie and other labels. In the 1970s and 1980s, Zydeco suddenly experienced something of a renaissance, and Chenier was its point man. He became a fixture on college campuses across the United States and eventually toured Europe as well. Although his health began failing in the 1980s, Chenier continued to work until his death on December 12, 1987.

Charlie Christian (1916–1942)
Electric Guitarist

Born in Dallas, Texas, and raised in Oklahoma City, Charlie Christian studied with his father and played in combos around Oklahoma. Jazz critic John Hammond heard Christian in 1939 and recommended him to Benny Goodman (Hammond's brother-in-law), and Christian soon joined Goodman's sextet. Charlie Christian did for the electric guitar what Jimmy Blanton did for the bass, achieving great fame as the first electric guitarist to play single-string solos. For the first time in jazz, a guitar could be heard over the other players and could move from being strictly a rhythm section instrument to a lead instrument. He revolutionized jazz in other ways as well, where sitting in after hours at such Harlem clubs as Minton's with Charlie Parker, Dizzy Gillespie, Kenny Clarke, and Thelonius Monk, Christian participated in the birth of bebop. Tragically, he did not live to enjoy the huge success of the bebop style that he helped create, for in 1941 Christian was hospitalized with tuberculosis and died on March 2, 1942, at the age of 25.

Kenneth Spearman "Klook" Clarke (also known as Liaqa Ali Salaam) (1914–1985)
Drummer

Born January 9, 1914, Clarke was part of a musically inclined Pittsburgh family. Clarke studied vibes, piano, and trombone, as well as musical theory and gained his early professional experience with Roy Eldridge and Edgar Hayes, traveling to Finland and Sweden with Hayes in 1937. In 1939–1940, Clarke played with Teddy Hill before the remnants of that band became the house band at Minton's in Harlem. There, working with Dizzy Gillespie, Charlie Parker, Thelonious Monk, Bud Powell, and Charlie Christian, Clarke helped develop the early sounds of bebop. It was during this time that Clarke developed his influential style, shifting the basis of timekeeping from the bass drum to the ride cymbal, then using the bass drum and snare to interject accents against the beat, earning him the nickname of "Klook" or "Klook-mop." In addition to his work at Minton's, Clarke also toured with Louis Armstrong and Ella Fitzgerald, played with Benny Carter in 1941–1942, spent a year and a half in Chicago with Red Allen, and led his own band fronted by Coleman Hawkins.

After a stint in the military beginning in 1943, Clarke returned to New York and recorded with virtually all of the bebop players, notably with Dizzy Gillespie in 1946. In 1951, he toured with Billy Eckstine, and in the following year he helped organize the Modern Jazz Quartet, where he remained for the next three years. He moved to France in 1956 where he worked with visiting American talents like Bud Powell and Miles Davis, and co-led a fine "big band" with Belgian pianist and arranger Frency Boland from 1961 to 1972. In addition to his influence on jazz drumming, Clarke is known for co-writing the bop classics " Salt Peanuts" with Dizzy Gillespie and "Epistrophy" with Thelonius Monk. Clarke died on January 26, 1985 in Paris, France.

Nathaniel A. "Nat King" Cole (1917–1965)
Singer, Pianist

Nathaniel Adams Cole was born on March 17, 1919, in Montgomery, Alabama (The family name was Coles, but Cole dropped the "s" when he formed the King Cole Trio years later.). When he was five, the family moved to Chicago, and he was soon taking piano lessons and playing organ and singing in the church where his father served as minister. While attending Phillips High School, Cole formed his own band and played with other small combos. He made his recording debut in 1936 with Eddie Cole's Solid Swingers, headed by his bassist brother Edward with accompaniment by two other brothers, Fred and Isaac.

Cole soon joined the touring revue *Shuffle Along* and, after the show folded, he found work in small clubs in Los Angeles. In 1939 he formed the King Cole Trio with guitarist Oscar Moore and bassist Wesley Prince. The trio played radio shows, worked nightclubs and recorded for Decca, increasing its popularity with the recording of "Sweet Lorraine" in 1940.

Moving to Capital Records in 1943, the trio recorded "Straighten Up and Fly Right," a national hit selling more than 500,000 copies. The trio's popularity was soaring and in addition to their success with recordings they appeared in two movies and in the first Jazz at the Philharmonic (JATP) concert. Starting with the hit "The Christmas Song" in 1946, Cole begin adding string sections to his records, diminishing his piano playing and focusing on his singing. In 1948–1949 his trio was the first African American jazz combo to have its own sponsored radio series. By the time "Mona Lisa" hit number one in 1950, Cole was an international star.

Over the next decade Cole appeared in a number of movies, toured the world, and in 1956–1957 hosted his own television show. Sadly, the show was canceled due to the lack of a national sponsor in a time of pervasive racism. Cole's career continued to soar until his death of lung cancer in 1965.

Nat "King" Cole (AP/Wide World Photos, Inc.)

Ornette Coleman (AP/Wide World Photos, Inc.)

Ornette Coleman (1930–)
Saxophonist, Trumpeter, Violinist, Composer

Born on March 9, 1930, in Fort Worth, Texas, Ornette Coleman began his musical career in carnival and R&B bands. Fired by R&B guitarist-singer Pee Wee Crayton for his unconventional style of playing, Coleman eventually settled in Los Angeles, making his living as an elevator operator while studying harmony and theory textbooks on his own time. He began to compose, sat in jam sessions, and made his first album in 1958. Encouraged by John Lewis, who recommended him for a scholarship to Gunther Schuller's Lennox School of Jazz in the summer of 1959, Coleman and his quartet— Don Cherry, pocket cornet; Charlie Haden, bass; Billy Higgins, drums—opened at the Five Spot in Manhattan in the fall of 1959. The appearance stirred up a firestorm of debate among jazz musicians, critics, and fans. These debates were so furious, some resulting in Coleman being physically threatened, that in 1962 he withdrew from public appearances.

Coleman's music, while abandoning traditional rules of harmony, tonality, and the basing solos on chord changes, obviously was not the senseless noise as some heard it. In fact, the music of the first Coleman quartet,

which made many recordings, was very melodic, had a strong blues feeling, and, in retrospect, sounds not so startling. He continued to go his own way in music, teaching himself to play trumpet and violin (the latter left-handed and amplified) and in 1965 his "comeback" saw the unveiling of a system he called "harmolodic," which gave equal weight to harmony, melody, and "the instrumentation of the movement of forms." Eventually, Coleman was accepted by many of his peers, evidenced by his being named a Guggenheim fellow in 1967, and some of his compositions are now considered jazz standards.

In the 1970s, Coleman composed and performed a long work for symphony orchestra and alto sax, "The Skies of America," and debuted Prime Time, a kind of jazz-fusion band with two electric guitars and two drummers. The original quartet was triumphantly reunited at the 1989 JVC Jazz Festival and also recorded again that year.

Coleman's music has influenced many players, most notably Dewey Redman, Steve Coleman, Miles Davis, and James Ulmer. Yet, his music remains a very personal means of expression; as such, it has much beauty and feeling to offer the open-minded listener. In 1993, a box set of Coleman's works entitled *Beauty Is a Rare Thing* was issued. The following year, Coleman, the father of free jazz, received a prestigious MacArthur fellowship, the so-called "genius award." He continues to release recordings and makes infrequent performance appearances.

John William Coltrane (1926–1967)
Saxophonist, Bandleader

Born September 23, 1926, in Hamlet, North Carolina, John Coltrane was taught to play clarinet by his father before studying alto saxophone in high school. After graduating, he moved to Philadelphia and studied music at the Ornstein School and played cocktail gigs. After playing in a Navy band in Hawaii in 1945–1946, he started his professional career with R&B bands, joining Dizzy Gillespie's big band on alto saxophone in 1949. When Gillespie broke up the band in 1950 and scaled down to a sextet, he had Coltrane switch to tenor sax and kept him.

After stints with two great but very different alto saxophonists, Earl Bostic and Johnny Hodges, Coltrane was hired by Miles Davis in 1955. At first, some musicians and listeners did not care for what they felt was Coltrane's "harsh" sound, but as the Davis Quintet became the most popular jazz group of its day, Coltrane was not only accepted but began to influence younger players, recording his first albums as leader. Coltrane's mounting drug problems forced Davis to release Coltrane in 1957. Returning to Philadelphia, Coltrane underwent a spiritual reawakening and kicked his drug habit, returning to New York later that year to work with Thelonious Monk. It was during this brief period with Monk that Coltrane began being admired as an innovator as his sound became harmonically "dense." Coltrane began inserting ever more complex chord progressions every two beats as opposed to every measure or two, playing sixteenth notes in the process, and his famous "sheets of sound" style emerged.

Rejoining Miles Davis in 1958, Coltrane participated in the influential *Kind Of Blue* record date, and Miles's experiments with modal improvising (i.e., playing on scales rather than chord changes) set the stage for Coltrane's future work as a leader. In 1959 Coltrane composed and recorded "Giant Steps" from the album of the same name, a piece so harmonically intricate and fast that it staggered most of his fellow saxophonists and propelled Coltrane into superstardom. Coltrane left the Davis group in the spring of 1960 and formed his own group that included pianist McCoy Tyner, bassist Steve Davis, and drummer Elvin Jones. In 1961 this group released the album *My Favorite Things*, featuring the show tune of the same name in a performance that featured his soprano sax and lasted nearly 14 minutes,

sparking an renewed interest in the soprano sax and modality. The quartet, with rotating bassists, became one of the most tightly knit groups in jazz history; the empathy between Coltrane and Elvin Jones was astonishing, and in their live performances, the four musicians would sometimes play a single tune for more than an hour, creating music so intense that some listeners compared it to a religious experience.

Still eager to explore new and more challenging territory, Coltrane began experimenting with African and Middle Eastern song forms, unusual instrumentation, and complex arrangements by Eric Dolphy. Two albums from this period, *Africa/Brass* and *Live at the Village Vanguard* feature "Trane," as he was now being called, improvising over bass and drums (no piano) and incorporating braying, squawking, and split tones to convey the emotion of the tunes. Just as Ornette Coleman, Coltrane was moving away from the constraints of melody, steady rhythm, and chord progressions in favor of primal drones and vamps that required his rhythm sections to rethink their roles. He continued to explore these themes, along with more traditional renderings of popular tunes, on numerous releases throughout the early 1960s.

Coltrane was himself a deeply spiritual man and in 1964 he released one of his masterpieces, the suite *A Love Supreme*, an offering of music and poetry that reflects Coltrane's inner peacefulness in the face of the storm of his other musical offerings. But by mid-1965 Coltrane was fully immersed in the avant-garde, free—jazz movement, and albums from this period such as *Ascension* feature three and four saxophonists where minimal thematic material is interspersed with long stretches of collective improvisation. Coltrane had carried the music to where the point was not the notes, but the sounds with which they were voiced. Seemingly on the cusp of breaking further musical ground, Coltrane died of liver cancer on July 17, 1967.

Turiya Alice Coltrane (1937–)
Pianist, Harpist, Composer, Bandleader

Born August 27, 1937 in Detroit Michigan, McLeod began studying classical music at age seven, learning to play both piano and harp. She expanding her skills playing organ in church and playing with R&B bands while in high school before becoming a member of local groups led by Kenny Burrell and Yusef Lateef. McLeod traveled to Paris in 1959 to study with Bud Powell followed by a stint recording and touring with Terry Gibbs. She met saxophonist-composer John Coltrane in 1962, and they were married in 1965. She then replaced McCoy Tyner as pianist in John Coltrane's group the following year and played with Coltrane until his death in 1967.

Coltrane continued her investigation of composition and arrangement and after converting to Hinduism, she began combining classical Indian instrumentation with jazz and classical musical forms. She collaborated with such jazz veterans as Pharoah Sanders, Joe Henderson, Ornette Coleman, and Rashied Ali and released several albums as leader in the late 1960s and throughout the 1970s. With her recording output and performance appearances diminished, Coltrane has since retired from the music industry.

Miles Dewey Davis, Jr. (1926-1991)
Trumpeter, Fluegelhorn, Composer, Bandleader

Born May 25, 1926, in Alton, Illinois, Davis's family moved to East St. Louis in 1927 where his father, a prominent dentists and substantial landowner gave him a trumpet for his thirteenth birthday. Davis played in the high school band and studied with Elwood Buchanan, who encouraged him to develop the warm, vibrato free tone that later became Miles's trademark. In the early 1940s Davis met local star Clark Terry and sat in with his idols Charlie Parker and Dizzy Gillespie when they passed through St. Louis with the Billy Eckstine Band. In 1945, his father sent Miles to the Juilliard School of Music in New York, but within a short time Davis was working the 52nd Street clubs with Charlie Parker and Coleman Hawkins, recording with Parker for the first time in November 1945. In 1946 Parker and Davis left for California where they split (Parker ended up in a sanitarium) and after playing with Charles Mingus, Davis joined the band of Billy Eckstine, bringing him back to New York.

Davis recorded again with Charlie Parker upon Parker's return to New York in 1947, but Davis and drummer Max Roach left in 1948 to pursue a new approach. The new project, a nine–piece band including Lee Konitz, Gerry Mulligan, and John Lewis was short lived, but its recordings had great impact on musicians. Employing such non-traditional instruments as french horn and tuba and using arrangements of rich, complex harmonies and a "cooler" less frenetic sound, the group launched the "cool jazz" movement. The project had no commercial success and the sessions that were recorded were not released in full until years later.

In 1950–1951 Davis recorded his first records for the Prestige label, the first free from the restrictions of the four minute 78 rpm disc and also featuring the playing of both Sonny Rollins and Jackie McLean. Around this time, Davis's addiction to heroin began hampering his career and resulted in erratic behavior that forced his release from the label. He recorded for Blue Note and again with Prestige before kicking his habit in 1953 by moving home, locking himself in a room, and going cold turkey for two weeks. He returned to New York in early

Miles Davis (Corbis Corporation [Bellevue])

1954, recording two dates with Horace Silver, Percy Heath, and Art Blakey and with a slightly different group a few weeks later that introduced a new Davis style. By infusing his "cool" playing with the hard drive of the blues, these recordings signaled the beginnings of the "hard bop" style of jazz.

More success followed when in 1955 Davis formed a quintet with John Coltrane, Philly Joe Jones, Red Garland, and Paul Chambers that released a flurry of classic records for both Prestige and Columbia Records. Unfortunately drug problems resurfaced, this time with other members of the band, and the group disbanded for good in 1957. Meanwhile, Davis changed his focus again and he made his first record with arranger Gil Evans, *Miles Ahead.* This was followed by two other collaborations with Evans, *Porgy and Bess* and *Sketches Of Spain*, both landmarks in jazz for their lush and innovative arrangements that set off Miles's haunting trumpet solos. In 1958 Davis formed a sextet with Cannonball Adderley on alto sax, Bill Evans on piano, and the return of John Coltrane on tenor. The group recorded several sessions highlighted by the album *Kind Of Blue*, which established modal improvisation in jazz and set the stage for Coltrane's later explorations on his own.

Over the ensuing six years, Davis continued to introduce new ideas and give exposure to new talent. By 1964, he had Wayne Shorter on saxophones, Herbie Hancock on piano, Ron Carter on bass, and the sensational 18-year-old Tony Williams on drums. This group, Miles's second great quintet, introduced many new ideas, mostly in the realm of rhythmic and harmonic freedom, and over the next three years released a slate of classic albums, most notably *Miles Smiles*. However, in 1968 Davis got restless again, and attracted by the possibilities of electronic instruments, incorporated three electric pianos played by Hancock, Chick Corea, and Joe Zawinul. New bassist Dave Holland, along with John McLaughlin on electric guitar, filled out the ensemble resulting in the albums *In a Silent Way* and *Bitches Brew*, which ushered a new style—jazz fusion. Davis continued to experiment with this style through 1975 when poor health forced a six-year retirement. He returned to performing in 1981, followed shortly by experiments with hip hop and rap before dying on September 28, 1991.

Miles Davis changed the style of his music more often than any other jazz musician of his stature, influencing the course of jazz history and creating controversy with each change. Yet his instrumental abilities, his eye for talent, and his unique personal vision mark him as one of the greatest jazz musicians in history.

Willie Dixon (1915–1992)
Guitarist, Singer, Songwriter

Born July 1, 1915, in Vicksburg, Mississippi, Willie Dixon was selling his songs to local bands by the time he was a teenager, singing with the Union Jubilee Singers. Afterwards he moved to Chicago, won the Illinois State Golden Gloves Championship, and recorded for Bluebird with his group, the Five Breezes, before being jailed for a year as a conscientious objector for refusing military service. By 1945 he was playing bass guitar for late night jam sessions with Muddy Waters and others and was hired as a session bassist by Chess Records in 1948.

As staff writer, arranger, and bass player, Dixon's work was primarily featured on other artists's cuts. When Muddy Waters recorded "Hoochie Coochie Man," followed by Howlin Wolf on "Evil," and Little Walter on "My Babe," Dixon's career as a songwriter was launched. Dixon became the label's tunesmith, recording manager, and bassist until the mid-1960s. Dixon also worked as musical director for a series of American folk-blues festivals in Europe, and Dixon's music caught on with British rock bands such as the Yardbirds and the Rolling Stones. After his association with Chess ended in the late 1960s, Dixon recorded *I Am the Blues*, a collection of his best-known songs, and organized the Chicago Blues All-Stars for tours of Europe, achieving fame in his own right. In the mid-1970s, realizing that he was not receiving his share of song royalties, he sued ARC Music (Chess's publishing company) and artists such as Led Zeppelin for copyright infringement and regained the rights to his songs as well as financial compensation. During the 1980s Dixon helped other artists regain rights to their songs, was the first producer/songwriter honored with a boxed-set retrospective of his career, and published his autobiography. He suffered from poor health later in the decade, losing his leg to diabetes, before dying on January 29, 1992 in Burbank, California.

Willie Dixon's life and enormous body of work are a cornerstone of the blues. He is one of the first professional blues players to gain recognition and success as a songwriter, producer, and performer. His songs and style inspired generations of American and European artists in both the blues and rock and roll genres. Quite simply, Willie Dixon is one of the most important figures in blues history.

Eric Dolphy (1928–1964)
Alto Saxophonist, Clarinetist, Flutist

Born in Los Angeles June 20, 1928, Dolphy took up alto sax in high school. After a 1950–1953 stint in the army, Dolphy first gained recognition with the Chico Hamilton quintet of 1958 to 1959, playing with the band at the 1958 Newport Jazz Festival. In 1960 he moved to New York where he collaborated with Charles Mingus and played club dates with trumpeters Booker Little and Freddie Hubbard. Dolphy was featured on Ornette Coleman's groundbreaking 1960 album *Free Jazz* before his 1961–1962 stint with John Coltrane, where his arranging skills were featured on Coltrane's *Africa/Brass* release. While on tour with Mingus in 1964, Dolphy decided to stay in Europe, where he recorded with Dutch, Scandinavian, and German rhythm sections. He died suddenly in Berlin on June 24, 1964, of a heart attack possibly brought on by diabetes.

Although he died at age 36, Dolphy's impact on jazz was substantial. He was greatly admired by fellow musicians and was honored with numerous awards including *Down Beat* magazine's New Star award for alto, flute, and miscellaneous instruments in 1961. Dolphy produced a sizable body of work due to a prolific recording schedule—from April 1960 to September 1961 he played on 13 recording sessions—while creating a style that extended bop into new harmonic territory leading to free jazz. As well, his mastery of bass clarinet and flute legitimized them as jazz instruments.

Theodore "Teddy" M. Edwards (1924–)
Saxophonist, Composer

Born April 26, 1924, in Jackson, Mississippi, Theodore "Teddy" Marcus Edwards came from a musical family, his father and grandfather both musicians. Edwards began as an alto player, bouncing between Tampa, Florida, and Detroit, and touring with Ernie Field's orchestra before joining Roy Milton's band in Los Angeles in 1945. Shortly thereafter, he joined Howard McGhee's group and switched to tenor sax. On such classic McGhee recordings as "Up In Dodo's Room," Edwards's helped to define the sound of tenor saxophone in the emerging bebop movement.

During the 1940s and early 1950s, Edwards played with many different artists including Benny Carter, Max Roach, Clifford Brown, Dodo Marmarosa, Dexter Gordon, and Gerald Wilson, helping fashion the West Coast bop sound. In the early 1960s he made some outstanding recordings as leader, playing with Howard McGhee and Phineas Newborn, Jr. In the late 1960s and 1970s he composed and arranged for television, radio, and film before reviving his career in the 1990s through work with Tom Waits. Edwards is known for his big, warm sound that work well with bluesy ballads and on soaring solo flights.

David Roy "Little Jazz" Eldridge (1911–1989)
Drummer, Trumpeter, Singer

Born January 30, 1911, in Pittsburgh, Roy Eldridge played his first "job" at the age of six on drums. When he was fifteen and had switched to trumpet, he ran away from home with a carnival band. After playing with some of the best bands in the Midwest, he arrived in New York in 1930, impressing the locals with his speed and range and finding jobs with good bands. He made his first record in 1935 with Teddy Hill, and by the next year he was starring in Fletcher Henderson's band. In 1937 he put together his own group and recorded as leader for the first time, introducing a trumpet style influenced by Louis Armstrong, but which assimilated the longer lines and fluid articulation of reed players such as Coleman Hawkins and Benny Carter. Eldridge's style would have a profound influence on the bop players to follow, Dizzy Gillespie in particular.

In 1941, Roy, now known in the world of music as "Little Jazz," joined Gene Krupa's big band as trumpeter and singer, becoming the first black musician to be a featured player in a white band (Teddy Wilson and Lionel Hampton were member's of Benny Goodman's band, but not as featured players). Eldridge's duet of "Let Me Off Uptown" with singer Anita O'Day scored a smash hit for Krupa while his instrumental feature "Rockin' Chair" was hailed as a jazz classic. When Krupa's band dissolved in 1943 Eldridge led his own big band for a while, but joined Artie Shaw in 1944. In the late 1940s he was starring in the Jazz at the Philharmonic (JATP) tours, playing with Charlie Parker, Lester Young, and Buddy Rich. A 1950 tour with the Benny Goodman sextet brought Eldridge to Paris, where he stayed for 18 months. During this time his career was stalled due to the advent of bebop and the trumpet innovations of his former disciple Gillespie.

In the 1950s Eldridge backed Ella Fitzgerald and toured with Jazz at the Philharmonic (JATP) and enjoyed a long association with Coleman Hawkins in addition to making a number of solid recordings throughout the 1960s. A full decade, from 1970 and onward, found Eldridge leading the house band at Jimmy Ryan's club in New York City, but a heart attack in 1980 put an end to his trumpet playing, though he still worked occasionally as a singer and gave lectures and workshops on jazz. He died on February 26, 1989. Often thought of as a stylistic bridge between Louis Armstrong and Dizzy Gillespie, Roy Eldridge's innovations and virtuosity on the trumpet qualify him as an equal.

Edward Kennedy "Duke" Ellington (1899–1974)
Bandleader, Composer, Pianist

Edward Kennedy Ellington, nicknamed Duke in his teens for his dapper dress style and courtly manners, was born into a middle-class family in Washington, DC, on April 29, 1899. Duke began playing piano at 7 years of age and by age 18 had formed his first band, Duke's Serenaders, and written his first composition "The Soda Fountain Rag." Duke was offered an art scholarship at Pratt Institute in New York, but he already had a taste of band leading and preferred to stay with music. Although he had some success in his hometown by 1923, he felt the urge to go to New York, where careers were made. Initially he did not succeed, but by 1924 he was leading his band renamed the Washingtonians at Club Hollywood and appearing on weekly radio broadcasts. In 1927 the young pianist-composer opened a five-year stint at the Cotton Club, the most famous Harlem night spot.

It was at the Cotton Club that the unique Ellington style evolved as Duke began composing in earnest, producing "Mood Indigo," "Tiger Rag," "The Mooche," and "Black and Tan Fantasy." Their outrageous "Jungle Nights," arranged and overseen by Duke, brought in huge crowds. Unlike most other bands, Ellington's band played mostly his own music and kept the same players with him. He had a great sense for their potential—almost as a great coach knows how to develop an athlete's skills—and many of Duke's bandmates who joined him during this time stayed with him for decades (none longer than baritone saxophonist Harry Carney, in the band from 1927 until 1974). Many became stars in their own right (ex., Johnny Hodges, alto sax; Cootie Williams, trumpet; and Barney Bigard, clarinet), but somehow they always sounded better with Ellington, who knew just what to write for what he called their "tonal personalities."

In 1932 the Ellington band left the Cotton Club and began touring, and in 1933 a larger version of the band completed their first European tour, where they were enthusiastically received. Back home, the band continued to record (Duke being one of the first musicians to truly understand the importance of records, and the fact that making good ones required something different than playing in public) and released such hits as "Solitude," "Sophisticated Lady," and "In a Sentimental Mood." In 1935, deeply touched by the death of his mother, Ellington composed "Reminiscing in Tempo," his longest work to date; most of his output, however, was tailored to the time limit of a little over three minutes imposed by the 78 rpm technology.

In 1939 the addition of three key players, tenor Ben Webster, bassist Jimmy Blanton, and associate composer-arranger Billy Strayhorn (who would stay with Duke until his death in 1967), propelled the band to new heights. With these additions and until a recording ban went into effect in August 1942, the Ellington band produced a string of classics including Strayhorn's "Take the A Train" and "Chelsea Bridge," along with Ellington's "Jack the Bear" and "Bojangles." In 1943 Ellington initiated what would become an annual appearance at Carnegie Hall where he presented his first extended work "Black, Brown and Beige." The end of the war and the close of the big band era caused the orchestra to struggle with many personnel changes, but Ellington's royalty money kept the band on the road and by the early 1950s the band was back in top form.

A second peak was reached in 1956, when the band gave a tremendous performance at the Newport Jazz Festival. The show, which was recorded, was highlighted by "Crescendo and Diminuendo In Blue," featuring twenty-seven choruses by tenorman Paul Gonsalves, and the seven thousand strong audience nearly rioted. Ellington once again enjoyed renewed popularity appearing on television, touring Europe in 1958 and 1959, playing all the major jazz festivals, and scoring for film. In the 1960s, buoyed by U.S. State Department tours, Ellington again began unveiling such compositional masterworks as "Money Jungle" (1962), "The Far East Suite" (1966), and "The Afro-Eurasian Eclipse" (1971).

Ellington and his astonishing creations have been an inspiration to generations of musicians. Most recently, Wynton Marsalis who both in his own composing and in his efforts to get Ellington's music performed live (as with the Lincoln Center Jazz Orchestra) has done much to keep the Elllington legacy in the forefront of Ameri-

James Reese Europe standing in front of a U.S. Army band (National Archives and Records Administration).

can music. There can be no doubt that Duke Ellington, who was also a brilliant pianist, will stand as one of the greatest composers of the twentieth century. Duke died of cancer on May 24, 1974, four weeks after his 75th birthday.

James Reese Europe (1881–1919)
Bandleader

James Reese Europe was born in Mobile, Alabama, on February 22, 1881, but later moved to Washington, DC, where at ten years of age he studied violin with the U.S. Marine Band. In 1904, he moved to New York and worked as a pianist before organizing the New Amsterdam Musical Association. In 1910 Europe formed the Clef Club, a clearinghouse for African American musicians which also had an orchestra that served as an important incubator for future jazz players. Europe had a concert at Carnegie Hall in 1914 that featured 125 singers and musicians, 25 years before Duke Ellington would debut there. During World War I, Europe directed the 369th Infantry Regimental Band, which performed throughout France and was a major force in the development of jazz in that country. Following his return to the United States, Europe toured the United States with his band. In 1919 he was stabbed to death by a member of his band while on tour.

Ella Fitzgerald (1918–1997)
Singer

Born April 25, 1918, Ella Fitzgerald was discovered in 1934 by drummer-band leader Chick Webb at an amateur contest at Harlem's Apollo Theater in New York City. She cut her first single with Webb, now her legal guardian, a year later. In 1936 she recorded her first efforts at "scat" singing. In 1938 she recorded "A Tisket, A Tasket," a novelty number that brought her her commercial success and made her name widely known among the general public. She soon became the first jazz vocalist to hold more popularity than the band with which she sang. Webb died in 1939, and Ella led the band for the next year. Among musicians, however, her reputation rested on her singular ability to use her voice as an instrument, improvising effortlessly in a style filled with rhythmic subtleties. Her bell-like clarity and flexibility of range were equally effective on ballads and up-number tunes.

In the mid-1940s Ella worked with Dizzy Gillespie, witnessing the birth of bop, and recorded with Louis Jordan and Louis Armstrong. In 1948 she married bassist Ray Brown, with whom she worked and recorded "Airmail Special" (1952), which featured a mature scat style. In 1955 Ella began working exclusively with Norman Granz. Given more suitable material and better playing opportunities her career soared. She appeared in several films including *Pete Kelly's Blues* (1955) and *St. Louis Blues* (1958), presented her own concert at the Hollywood Bowl and, in celebration of the release of their four LP collaboration, played Carnegie Hall with Duke Ellington in April 1958.

In the 1960s and the early 1970s, Ella toured the world, playing with more than forty symphonies in the United States alone, until poor eyesight forced her into semi-retirement. In 1995, Fitzgerald was inducted into the National Women's Hall of Fame. Other career highlights include 11 Grammy Awards, Kennedy Center Honors (1979), Whitney Young Award (1984), National Medal of Arts (1987), France's Commander of Arts and Letters (1990), and the Medal of Freedom (1992), in addition to winning *Downbeat* magazine's best female jazz singer poll for 18 consecutive years.

Since the 1970s, she had been in steadily declining health and had been hospitalized for various ailments. In 1993, her legs were amputated below the knees as the result of complications from diabetes. Ella Fitzgerald died on June 15, 1997. No other vocalist has been so unanimously acclaimed. Fondly known as "The First Lady of Song," she was the leading jazz interpreter of popular song for more than fifty years.

Tommy Flanagan (1930–)
Pianist

Born in Detroit in March 16, 1930, Tommy Flanagan traveled to New York in 1956 as part of the "Motor City" invasion of gifted jazz musicians and soon was playing with Charlie Parker, Dizzy Gillespie, and Ben Webster, who recognized his understated but catchy melodic talents. He was much in-demand as a sideman, recording such classic sessions as *Saxophone Colossus* with Sonny Rollins and *Giant Steps* with John Coltrane. Long stints (1962–1965 and 1968–1978) as Ella Fitzgerald's accompanist and musical director (a role he also filled, much more briefly, with Tony Bennett) kept Flanagan out of the limelight. Since the mid-1970s, as leader of his own fine trios and recording prolifically in the United States, Europe, and Japan, his work has met with critical acclaim including his receipt of the 1993 Jazzpar Award. Flanagan is widely known as a modernist with a love of lyricism who can also play bluesy lines that swing.

"Blind Boy" Fuller (1908–1941)
Singer, Guitarist

Born July 10, 1908, in Wadesboro, North Carolina, "Blind Boy" Fuller was one of the most recorded early blues artists in the Piedmont blues tradition. Unlike his contemporaries, Big Bill and Memphis Minnie, who recorded for decades, Fuller's recordings were completed over a period of six years prior to his premature death at age 33. Fuller was a fine and expressive vocalist and a masterful guitarist who could play in multiple styles including slide, ragtime, pop, and delta blues. Although his career was spent as a street musician and house party favorite, Fuller's National steel guitar can be heard on such hits as "Rag Mama Rag," "Trucking My Blues Away," and "Step It Up and Go." Much of Fuller's repertoire remains a vital part of the Piedmont tradition still played to this day.

Erroll Garner (1921–1977)
Pianist, Composer

Born in Pittsburgh June 15, 1921, Garner grew up in a musical family and began picking out piano melodies before he was three years old. He started taking piano lessons at six but played all his assignments by ear instead of learning to read notes. At seven, he began playing regularly on Pittsburgh radio station KDKA. He dropped out of high school to play with a dance band and soon arrived in New York in 1944, playing the famous clubs of 52nd Street. From 1945–1949 Garner freelanced recording for numerous labels. It was in that

Jazz greats Ella Fitzgerald (vocals), Oscar Peterson (piano), Roy Eldridge (trumpet), and Max Roach (drums) performing in a jam session (Corbis Corporation [Bellevue]).

same year that he recorded "Laura" which sold a half million copies, and his fame began to grow. By 1950 he had recorded with Benny Carter, Charlie Parker, Coleman Hawkins, Teddy Edwards, and others. On March 27, 1950, he gave a solo recital at Cleveland's Music Hall, and in December he performed a concert at New York's Town Hall. Garner's most famous composition "Misty" was a big hit in 1959. During the 1960s and 1970s, Garner appeared with orchestras, scored for film, and toured France, South America, and Asia.

A keyboard artist who played and composed by ear in the tradition of the founding fathers of jazz, Erroll Garner won the international acclaim of jazz lovers, music critics, and the general public. Strong and bouncy left-hand rhythms and beautiful melodies are the trademarks of his extremely enjoyable music. Garner was diagnosed with lung cancer, and he died at age 55 on January 2, 1977.

John Birks "Dizzy" Gillespie (1917–1993)
Trumpeter, Bandleader

Born October 21, 1917, Gillespie received his early musical training in his native South Carolina, studying at the Laurinberg Institute from 1932–1935. After moving to Philadelphia in 1935, he joined Frankie Fairfaxes Orchestra before moving to New York and joining the Teddy Hill band, where he replaced his early idol, Roy Eldridge. He stayed with Hill until 1939 when he joined Cab Calloway's band with whom he remained until 1941. Hill became manager of Minton's Playhouse, and Gillespie was soon sitting in with Kenny Clarke, Thelonius Monk , and Charlie Christian for after hours jams where his bop experimentation was already beginning to develop and his career as an arranger began to emerge. In 1942 Gillespie recorded his first "bop" solo with Les Hite before joining Earl Hines's band in 1943. Shortly he and Charlie Parker joined Billy Eckstine's band, with Parker as lead altoist and Gillespie as musical director. After leaving Eckstine's band in 1945, Parker and Gillespie recorded Gillespie's compositions "Shaw Nuff," "Salt Peanuts," and "Hot House," sounding the first salvo of bebop. In 1946 Gillespie, having split with Parker, formed his own big band. The following year he hired Cuban drummer Chano Pozo, integrating Pozo's Latin clave feel into the bands rhythmic framework and virtually creating Afro-Cuban jazz.

By 1948 Gillespie's trademark goatee, horn-rimmed glasses, and beret were the personifications of bebop, but Gillespie continued to move into new directions. Famed musicians including pianist John Lewis, drummer Kenny Clarke, trombonist J.J. Johnson, and saxophonist John Coltrane all worked with Dizzy until he dissolved the big band in 1949. He then toured the world with smaller ensembles and steadily increased his repu-

tation until by the 1970s and 1980s he was the puckish elder statesman of jazz. Through it all Dizzy's dazzling speed, harmonic ingenuity, and rhythmic flair marked him as genius of the trumpet. His skills as composer, his use of trans-African clave in swing, and his ability to improvise made him one of the true giants of jazz, with many of his compositions now jazz standards. Dizzy died January 6, 1993, in Englewood, New Jersey.

Dexter Keith Gordon (1923–1990)
Saxophonist, Bandleader

Born in Los Angeles on February 27, 1923, the son of a prominent physician whose patients included famous jazz musicians, Dexter Keith Gordon began playing clarinet at seven, switching to alto and then tenor. He joined Lionel Hampton's newly formed big band in 1940. Section work with Louis Armstrong and Fletcher Henderson followed, and in 1944 Gordon cut his first side with Nat Cole. Later that year, he joined the Billy Eckstine band. After freelancing in New York, he returned home and in 1946 recorded a "tenor battle" titled "The Chase" with Wardell Gray, which became one of the biggest modern jazz hits. He sporadically continued to team up with Gray until 1952, when he was imprisoned for two years for heroin possession. His addiction plagued him for much of the next 15 years.

Gordon made a major comeback in the early 1960s with a series of much-acclaimed recordings. His association with the hard bop movement at Blue Note Records, where he worked with Herbie Hancock, Bobby Hutcherson, Sonny Stitt, and Bud Powell, asserted his role as the premier bop tenor stylist. In 1962, he settled and remained in Copenhagen, Denmark, for the next fourteen years, although he released two well-received records in the United States in 1969, and he made brief playing visits to his homeland. In 1977, he permanently moved back to the United States, forming his own group and winning many new fans. In 1986, he starred in the French feature film *'Round Midnight*, in which his portrayal of a character based on Lester Young and Bud Powell won him an Oscar nomination as best actor.

Gordon was one of the prime movers behind the hard bop revolution of the 1960s and his rich, robust tenor sound never faltered. He never succumbed to straying into fusion or pop, choosing instead to be an expatriate to play for audiences who appreciated pure jazz. Dexter died April 26, 1990, in Philadelphia.

John Arnold "Johnny" Griffin III (1928–)
Saxophonist

Johnny Griffin was born in Chicago in 1928 and played his first gigs with Lionel Hampton's big band

Dexter Gordon (AP/Wide World Photos, Inc.)

(1945–1947) and in the armed services. Griffin moved to New York and in 1956 recorded his first album for Blue Note Records followed by two more records in 1957, establishing his fast and exuberant bop style of playing. Later in 1957 he joined Art Blakey's Jazz Messengers where he met Thelonius Monk with whom he recorded the next year, followed by collaborations with Eddie "Lockjaw" Davis on "tenor battles." In December 1962, he moved to Europe and played all over the continent. He lived in Paris in the late 1960s and later moved to the Netherlands, where he owned a farm. In the late 1970s, Griffin moved back to the United States, celebrating the occasion with outstanding concerts and recordings with his friend, Dexter Gordon. Sometimes called "The Little Giant" because he is a small man with a very big sound, Griffin remains dedicated to the bop and hard bop styles.

Buddy Guy (1936–)
Guitarist

For the generation of 1960s British rock guitarists such as Eric Clapton, Jeff Beck, Keith Richards, and others who learned their techniques listening to blues in the early 1960s, Buddy Guy was the real thing. Although it was not until the 1990s that his playing was adequately captured on tape, Guy represents a direct link between the earlier generation of Chicago blues musicians that included his mentor, Muddy Waters, and the crop of blues and rock and roll guitarists, both black and white, that presently dominate the genre.

Born on July 30, 1936, in Lettsworth, Louisiana, Guy began playing acoustic guitars as a teenager, emulating the work of Southern blues artists Lightnin' Slim and Guitar Slim, before working his first gigs in Baton Rouge in the 1950s with Big Poppa John Tilly. He left the South for Chicago in 1957, and quickly made his mark on the local club scene. Before Guy's arrival, blues guitarists usually played sitting down. Guy not only played while standing, but would throw chairs off the stage, abuse his guitar, and wander outside with the aid of a 150-foot cord, increasing his profile immensely. Guy cut two singles for Cobra Records in 1958, followed by a number of singles for Chess between 1960–1967, where he also backed Muddy Waters and other blues legends such as Howlin' Wolf, Sonny Boy Williamson, and Little Walter. His singles from this period, including "Let Me Love You Baby" and "Stone Crazy," are some of the most popular blues of the period.

Guy's first album for Vanguard, *A Man & the Blues*, in 1968 followed in the same vein, but his following albums failed to do well. As a live act, however, he became a legend, both in the clubs of Chicago and at festivals around the world. In the 1970s Guy began his long and successful collaboration with harmonica player Junior Wells. In 1983 Guy opened his own blues club, the Checkerboard Lounge, on Chicago's South side. He sold the Checkerboard in 1985, then opened another club called Buddy Guy's Legends in 1989. In 1991 Guy issued his first domestic release in ten years, *Damn Right I've Got the Blues*, which won a Grammy Award, as did his next album *Feels Like Rain*. Buddy Guy is indeed Chicago's blues king.

Lionel Hampton (1908–)
Vibraphonist, Pianist, Bandleader

Born on April 20, 1908 in Louisville, Kentucky, Lionel Hampton was the first jazz musician to feature the vibraphones or "vibes," an instrument that has since maintained a vital role in jazz. Raised in Chicago, Lionel moved to California in 1928 and played drums with the Paul Howard Orchestra. His first recorded effort on vibes was on the 1930s recording "Memories of You," which featured Louis Armstrong, then fronting the Les Hite band in California. Hampton later left Hite's band to form his own Los Angeles group. When Benny Goodman heard him in 1936, he used him on a record date, along with Teddy Wilson and Gene Krupa, and then persuaded him to join on a permanent basis. This decision established Goodman's band as the first to have an interracial lineup, a practice Goodman would maintain.

Hampton continued to play with the Goodman Quartet until 1940, the year he formed his own orchestra. In 1942 the band scored its first big hit "Flyin' Home," which featured a screaming brass section over a driving

Lionel Hampton (AP/Wide World Photos, Inc.)

rhythm section and "Illinois" Jacquet's rhythm and blues solo, creating a whole new school of tenor playing. By the mid-1940s the band adopted elements of the bop sound, but Hampton's style has remained essentially one of swing. His bands have featured the best of jazz including Dinah Washington, Betty Carter, Dexter Gordon, Clark Terry, Art Farmer, Clifford Brown, and Johnny Griffin. In addition to his long-standing big band, Hampton has run his own record labels, publishing house, and other businesses. In 1981, he became a professor of music at Howard University, and he was honored in 1995 at the Kennedy Center Concert Hall with a tribute to his work as a United Nations music ambassador. Even though he is now past 90 years of age, Hampton continues to tour the world.

Herbie Hancock (1940–)
Keyboardist, Composer, Bandleader

Herbie Hancock was born in Chicago on April 12, 1940, and received early training as a classical pianist. After he graduated from college in 1960, he played his first Chicago jazz gigs with Coleman Hawkins and Donald Byrd. Moving to New York he recorded two albums with Byrd before getting his own sessions in 1962 with

Blue Note. Hancock's world class compositional skills, "soul bop" style, and excellent sidemen (i.e., Tony Williams, Ron Carter, Freddy Hubbard, and Grant Green) define the "experimental" side of Blue Note in the mid-1960s. Concurrently Hancock became a part of Miles Davis's band (1963–1969), considered one of the top rhythm sections (again with Williams and Carter) and jazz groups of all-time, a tenure that imprinted heavily on Hancock's artistic development.

From 1969–1972 Hancock's sextet cut three fusion albums, recording two influential "electric jazz" albums with Davis (i.e., *Jack Johnson* and *On the Corner*) before releasing his own groundbreaking *Headhunters* (1974), where his blend of pop, funk, and jazz sets the standard for fusion. In his career Hancock has released numerous albums, many which are considered classics (ex., *Takin' Off* and *Maiden Voyage*), and has become one of the most commercially successful and famous jazz musicians ever, although many consider his music more pop than jazz. Hancock has won Grammys both for jazz composition and rhythm and blues performance, a handful of MTV Video Music Awards for the video of his 1984 hit "Rockit" and an Academy Award for best original score in 1986 for the film *'Round Midnight.*

His commercial success aside, Hancock is one of the all-time best jazz pianists who works with integrity, creativity, and is consistently attuned to his audience. In addition to his piano and compositional skills, his use of electronics to communicate his vision firmly establishes him as a major jazz figure.

William Christopher "W.C." Handy (1873–1958)
Trumpeter, Composer, Bandleader

Although he began as a cornetist and bandleader in the 1890s, W.C. Handy's fame as the "Father of the Blues" rests almost entirely on his work as a composer. Handy was born on November 16, 1873, in Florence, Alabama. After studying at Kentucky Musical College, Handy toured with an assortment of musical groups, becoming the bandmaster of the Mahara Minstrels in 1896. During his travels Handy came into contact with many African American music traditions, and the melodies and song forms from work songs and gospel were then merged into his own brass band compositions. Popular legend has Handy "discovering" the blues in a train station in Tutwiler, Mississippi, in 1903 when he heard a singer accompanying himself on guitar and reciting three-line rhyming verses.

In 1909, during a political campaign in Memphis, Handy wrote "Mr. Crump," a campaign song for E.H. "Boss" Crump. Three years later, the song was published as the "Memphis Blues," establishing the blues as

Herbie Hancock (AP/Wide World Photos, Inc.)

an identifiable category of music. In 1914, Handy published his most famous song "St. Louis Blues" and that same year also wrote "Yellow Dog Blues." Others songs that have become perennial favorites are "Joe Turner Blues" (1915), "Beale Street Blues" (1916), "Careless Love" (1921), and "Aunt Hagar's Blues" (1922).

In the 1920s, Handy became a music publisher in New York. Despite his failing eyesight, he remained active until his death on March 29, 1958. His songs extended beyond the world of jazz to find their way into the general field of popular music in many forms. Their popularity continues unabated today.

Coleman Hawkins (1904–1969)
Saxophonist

Hawkins was born on November 21, 1904, in St. Louis, Missouri. When Hawkins took up the tenor at the age of nine, he had already had four years of training on piano and cello. He continued his studies at Washburn College in Topeka, Kansas, and in 1922 toured with

gig ended, and from 1948 to 1951 Hines worked again with Armstrong before his career slumped. In 1964, a series of New York recitals revitalized his career, and he enjoyed great success in Europe, Japan, and in the United States until his death on July 22, 1983.

Milton J. "Milt" Hinton (1910–)
Bass

Milt Hinton was born in Vicksburg, Mississippi, on June 23, 1910, and is considered one of the greatest of bass players. He has played with many top jazz artists including Cab Calloway, Count Basie, Louis Armstrong, Teddy Wilson, and Benny Goodman. Hinton has appeared in concerts throughout the world and on numerous television shows, and he has recorded prolifically. Known for his warmth of tone and vitality, Hinton is a master of "slapping" the bass and soloing in a thoroughly modern manner. He is also an accomplished photographer and writer whose autobiography *Bass Lines* appeared in 1988. *Over Time: The Jazz Photographs of Milt Hinton* was published in 1992, and due to the diversity and longevity of his career, it is a valuable glimpse into jazz history.

Billie "Lady Day" Holiday (1915–1959)
Singer

Born Eleanora Harris in Baltimore, Maryland, on April 7, 1915, the daughter of jazz musician Clarence Holiday who later abandoned her, Billie was singing in Harlem nightclubs by the time she was 15 years old. Discovered by talent scout John Hammond, she was recommended to Benny Goodman with whom she cut her first recordings in 1933, and from 1935 to 1939 she established her reputation with a series of records made with Teddy Wilson. She also sang with her own band and those of Count Basie and Artie Shaw, and her recordings of the late 1930s with Lester Young—who dubbed her "Lady Day"—and Buck Clayton underscore how much her singing resembled the playing of an instrumentalist.

Holiday's voice was sweet, sexy, and full of the blues. Her distinctive behind-the-beat style of singing and the way she let her voice trailed off for emotional impact set her apart from all other singers. Her landmark 1939 recording of "Strange Fruit," a protest against lynchings, was released despite her own label's, Columbia Records, refusal to even record the tune. In her song "God Bless the Child," she departed from popular material to depict the personal alienation that she had experienced. By the time of her 1944 release of "Lover Man," she had moved from jazz to a more orchestrated pop setting, and the song is often referred to as the definitive sound of Holiday. By the late 1940s, her long-term addiction to heroin had landed her in jail. Although she returned to performing throughout the 1950s, the effect of her hopeless battle with addiction had greatly diminished her voice, if not her expressiveness.

Holiday brought all of her worldly experience to the stage, and her songs display the vulnerability of a woman who had been betrayed by an unjust and harsh world and herself. Holiday died on July 17, 1959, in New York City, less than a month after her appearance at a benefit concert.

John Lee Hooker (1920–)
Singer, Guitarist

John Lee Hooker was born in Clarksdale, Mississippi, on August 17, 1920. He first learned his "Delta licks" from his stepfather, Will Moore, and his colleagues, James Smith and Coot Harris. He traveled to Memphis, Cincinnati, and Detroit, where in 1948 he cut a demo for Bernie Besman, owner of the Sensation label. "Boogie Chillen" and "Sally Mae" were on the first single he recorded for the Sensation label. It became a hit on the rhythm and blues chart in 1948. He followed this record with "Crawling King Snake" in 1949 and "In the Mood for Love" in 1951, both of which were chart toppers. Hooker then recorded for several labels under a number of pseudonyms including Delta John, Johnny Lee, and Birmingham Sam and his Magic Guitar Hooker, before landing at Vee Jay Records under his own name from 1955 to 1964. At Vee Jay Hooker recorded with a full rhythm section that included Eddie Taylor and Jimmy Reed, and he had several successes including "Baby Lee" in 1956, "I Love You Honey" in 1958, and "Boom, Boom" in 1962. Hooker was idolized by British blues bands and was also popular on the folk coffeehouse circuit.

In the 1970s and 1980s, Hooker collaborated with such popular performers as Canned Heat, Bonnie Raitt, and Van Morrison. He also appeared in the film *The Blue Brothers,* starring John Belushi and Dan Ackroyd in 1980. Long recognized as one of the primary contributors to the blues genre, the prolific Hooker has made more than forty albums, many of which Chess Records has reissued in the 1990s. Rhino released *The Ultimate Collection (1948–1990)* in 1991.

Sam "Lightnin'" Hopkins (1912–1982)
Singer, Guitarist

Born March 15, 1912, in Centerville, Texas, Sam "Lightnin'" Hopkins was one of the most prolific blues artists of all time, both in the recording studio and on stage. Inspired by Texas predecessor Blind Lemon Jefferson, Hopkins built his first guitar out of a cigar box and chicken wire at the age of eight. While still very young, he left home for a life on the road, singing and playing for money throughout Texas. In 1920 he reunit-

Billie Holiday singing in a recording studio (Columbia Records).

ed with Jefferson, serving as his guide and learning his musical licks.

During the late 1920s and much of the 1930s, Hopkins played the Houston bar circuit as a duo with his cousin, legendary Texas blues musician Texas Alexander. After working as a sharecropper near Dallas for a few years, he returned to Houston in 1946 and resumed his beer hall career with Alexander. He was soon discovered by a scout from Aladdin Records and teamed with pianist Wilson "Thunder" Smith to create the duo, Thunder and Lightnin'. They recorded "Katie May" in 1946, which became a regional hit, and scored another hit with "Shotgun Blues" in 1948.

Hopkins made the rhythm and blues charts several times in the early 1950s for a variety of labels, but Hopkins's popularity declined over the course of the decade as his rustic style did not compete well with rock and roll. In 1959, however, folklorist Mack McCormick rediscovered him. Introduced to a new audience consisting largely of whites, Hopkins was reinvented as a "folk-blues legend," and he quickly attained a level of acclaim that had previously eluded him. Hopkins recorded and toured constantly across the United States, Canada, and Europe throughout the 1960s and 1970s,

and he was featured in a number of books and film documentaries. He died of throat cancer on January 30, 1982. As one of the last great country blues musicians, Hopkins style bridged the gap between rural and urban styles.

Eddie James "Son" House, Jr. (1902–1988)
Singer, Guitarist

Born on March 21, 1902, in Riverton, Mississippi, House was preaching the gospel in Baptist churches by the time he was 15 years old, as his family wandered between plantations looking for work. He did not pick up a guitar until he was 25 years of age, once saying he did not even like the sound of a guitar. However, after playing a few house parties, earning some money, and discovering corn whisky, he became a blues musician. His new career was interrupted, however, when he was sentenced to a prison term for killing a man during a drunken party. Released two years later though, he hit the road and soon played with Charley Patton. Although the men were completely dissimilar in style and personal attributes, they shared a love for alcohol and the blues, and by the early 1930s Patton had given House entree to a recording opportunity with Paramount. The sides House cut, including "My Black Mama," "Preachin' the Blues", and "Dry Spell Blues," are some of the darkest, gut-wrenching, and rawest as any blues ever recorded. The recording hardly sold at the time but those who heard them were enthralled, and in 1941 Library of Congress folklorist Alan Lomax visited House to once again record his music. These recordings, mostly solo, but some with a backing string band, where a glimpse into the future of blues as well as rock and roll.

House moved to Rochester, New York, and did not record again until 1964, when guitarist Alan Wilson (later of the blues-rock group Canned Heat) "rediscovered" House. House began touring again, recorded his work, appeared at Carnegie Hall in 1965, and was the subject of a documentary. House fell ill from Parkinson's and Alzheimer's diseases in the mid-1970s, retired from performing in 1975, and died on October 19, 1988, in Detroit, Michigan.

Son House was a major innovator in the Delta blues tradition and, along with his playing partner Charley Patton, he stands at the top of the blues hierarchy. He was a primary inspiration to both Muddy Waters and Robert Johnson, and was one of the most powerful performers in blues, at once spiritual and demonic in delivery and emotional impact.

Howlin' Wolf (Chester Arthur Burnett) (1910–1976)
Singer, Harmonica Player

Blues singer and harmonica player Howlin' Wolf was born Chester Arthur Burnett in West Point, Mississippi, on June 10, 1910. When he was 18 years of age, he met guitarist Charley Patton and, although he never matched Patton's prowess on guitar, Patton's influence was seen in Burnett's later growl of a voice and entertaining ability. He learned to play the harmonica from blues musician Aleck "Rice" Miller (Sonny Boy Williamson II) who married his half-sister Mary, and by the end of the 1930s he was playing local juke joints. After a four year stretch in the Army he settled down as a farmer and by 1948 was a radio personality in West Memphis, where he and guitarist Willie Johnson debuted their electric band. He made his first recording in 1951 for Sam Phillips where his baying style of singing won him the name Howlin' Wolf, and by 1953 he was picked up by the Chess label in Chicago.

At Chess Howlin' Wolf was paired with guitarist Hubert Sumlin, and the two cut several hits including "Evil" and "Smokestack and Lightning" in 1956. The two were then paired with Willie Dixon, who was Chess's staff writer, and over the next several years the trio had major hits with "I Ain't Superstitious," "The Red Rooster," "Back Door Man," and "Wang Dang Doodle." Most of these songs became blues classics but were also picked up by such British bands as the Rolling Stones. Wolf and Dixon parted ways in 1964, and Wolf recorded his own songs including "Killing Floor." By the end of the decade, such rock and roll idols as the Doors, Cream, and Jeff Beck were recording his material. Throughout the 1970s, Wolf was increasingly ill, suffering several heart attacks. He died from complications of an operation on January 10, 1976.

Alberta Hunter (1895–1984)
Singer

Born April 1, 1895, in Memphis, Tennessee, Alberta Hunter debuted as a club singer in Chicago at around 1912, making her first recording in 1921. She wrote "Down Hearted Blues" which became Bessie Smith's first hit, and on her early 1920s recordings she used such prominent sidemen as Fletcher Henderson, Eubie Blake, Fats Waller, Louis Armstrong, and Sidney Bechet. She starred in the stage show *Showboat* with Paul Robeson in London from 1928–1929 and worked in Paris for many years. After returning to the United States, she worked for the USO in World War II and the Korean War before retiring in 1956 to become a nurse at age 61. She was forced to retire from nursing in 1977 when it was discovered that she was 82 years old—not 65 years of age as she had reported. She made a comeback as a jazz singer, appearing regularly at the Cookery in New York City, until her death in 1984.

Jean-Baptiste "Illinois" Jacquet (1922–)
Saxophonist, Bandleader

Jean-Baptiste Jacquet was born in Broussard, Louisiana, on October 31, 1922, and raised in Texas. Jacquet began playing drums as a teenager before learning soprano and alto saxophones. He began his career as an altoist, but when he joined Lionel Hampton's band in 1942 he switched to tenor. Soon thereafter, Jacquet recorded his famous 64-bar honking solo on Hampton's "Flyin' Home" and made both his own and the Hampton band's name.

After stints with Cab Calloway (1943–1944) and Count Basie (1945–1946), Jacquet joined the Jazz at the Philharmonic (JATP) touring group in which he starred in tenor "battles" with Flip Phillips and others. He soon formed his own swinging little band and became a mainstay in the international jazz circuit. He formed a fine big band, Jazz Legends, in 1984 with which he continues to tour and record.

Jacquet was one of the first to "overblow" the tenor sax, reaching high harmonics that were dismissed by some as a circus stunt but really got to audiences; eventually, of course, such overblowing became part and parcel of the instrument's vocabulary, as in the later work of John Coltrane and the style of David Murray.

But Jacquet is also a warm ballad player and is always a swinging tenor.

Elmore James (1918–1963)
Singer, Guitarist

Born on January 27, 1918, in Richland, Mississippi, James adapted to music at an early age, learning to play bottleneck on a homemade instrument made from a broom-handle and a lard can. By the age of 14, he was a weekend musician working diners and juke joints under the names "Cleanhead" or Joe Willie James. He worked with visiting players such as Robert Johnson, Howlin' Wolf, and Sonny Boy Williamson before forming his first band in the late 1930s. He served for three years with the Navy in Guam during World War II, and after his discharge he moved to Memphis where he became one of the first "guest stars" on the "King Biscuit Time" radio show in Helena, Arkansas. James's first recording came in 1951 with "Dust My Broom," which became a surprise top ten rhythm and blues hit and James's signature tune. He then moved to Chicago where over the course of the 1950s he assembled his famous band, the Broomdusters, and recorded numerous sides that made the charts and became blues classics. A regular performer in Chicago's blues clubs and on the radio, James's health began to decline in the late 1950s. After a return to Mississippi, he traveled back to Chicago to record "The Sky is Crying" before legal troubles with record labels and the musicians's union forced him back to Mississippi. He returned again to Chicago in 1963 where on May 24 he suffered a fatal heart attack.

Elmore James was the most influential slide guitarist of the post-war period. His attitude and tone on the guitar updated the sound of Robert Johnson, and his signature guitar licks are a foundation in blues guitar. A radio repairman by trade, James reworked his guitar amplifiers to produce raw, distorted sounds that would inspire the rock and roll movement of the 1960s. His voice was loud, forceful, and prone to break in the high registers, conveying a sense of hysteria. His bands were as loud and powerful as any blues band in Chicago, helping to launch the Electric Chicago Blues movement.

Nehemiah Curtis "Skip" James (1902–1969)
Singer, Guitarist, Songwriter

Although Skip James became much more popular during the blues revival of the mid-1960s than ever before, it makes little sense to speak of his "rediscovery." The fact is that he had barely been discovered in the first place. James was born on June 21, 1902, in Bentonia, Mississippi, home to a thriving Delta blues tradition. His father, a Baptist minister, was competent on both organ and guitar. When James became interested in blues—an interest sparked primarily by local player Henry Stuckey—at about age seven, his father was happy to become his first guitar teacher.

In his teens, James moved to Memphis to play dance hall and barrelhouse music. He returned to Mississippi, settling in Jackson in the 1920s. There his unique falsetto vocal stylings and from-the-heart presentation earned him regional fame. In 1931 James was brought North to record 26 songs for Paramount Records. Only a handful of the songs were ever released, and James gradually withdrew from performing.

By the 1940s, James was out of the music business. In addition to becoming an ordained minister, he worked at a variety of non-music jobs during the next couple of decades. He was "rediscovered" from out of nowhere by blues revivalists John Fahey and Bill Barth in 1964, and by the following year he was earning standing ovations at blues festivals from audiences larger than any he had played for during his prime. James's highly personal style had an air of untarnished authenticity, completely devoid of commercial awareness, that was well accepted by the folk purists who made up his new generation of fans. James died on October 3, 1969, in Philadelphia, Pennsylvania.

"Blind" Lemon Jefferson (1897–1929)
Guitarist, Singer

Blind Lemon Jefferson was one of the pioneers of Texas blues. Born poor and blind, music was one of the few career options open to Lemon—which was his given name, not a nickname. Jefferson's performing career began when he was 14 years old. He would make a daily trek on foot into the nearest town, Wortham, where he would sit in front of some store and begin to play for money. He eventually acquired a sizable local following and was invited to play at country picnics and other such events. At 20 years of age, Jefferson moved to Dallas, where he made money playing in brothels and taverns. Among the local adolescents that he hired as guides during this period were the young Lightnin' Hopkins and T-Bone Walker.

In 1925 and 1926, Jefferson made a series of recording trips to Chicago, home of the Paramount record label. His Records sold well coast to coast, and he became possibly the very first country blues-recording star. He made a total of about eighty Records over the next couple of years. In 1929, the heavy-drinking Jefferson got lost in a blizzard after leaving a party in Chicago and froze to death.

Jefferson was a serious showman who balanced a driving guitar style with a booming two-octave voice. A brilliant improvisor, he often halted at the end of vocal lines to play guitar solos and could play in unusual meters. Too many budding blues musician to mention learned their first licks from these early Jefferson recordings. Long a favorite of American folk fans, Jefferson's songs have since been covered by countless folksingers and rock and roll artists over the years as well, and he was honored in the naming of the rock group Jefferson Airplane in the 1960s.

James Louis "J. J." Johnson (1924–)
Trombonist, Bandleader

Born January 22, 1924 in Indianapolis, Indiana, J. J. Johnson is the unchallenged master of the modern jazz trombone. He is the first musician to have adapted this instrument to the demanding techniques called for by the advent of Bop. Early in his career, Johnson displayed such skill in performing high speed and intricate solos that those who knew him only from records found it hard to believe that he was actually using a slide—and not a valve—trombone.

Johnson started playing the trombone in 1938 and within three years was playing with "Snookum" Russell where he met Fats Navarro who was an early influence. By 1942 he joined Benny Carter where he began arranging before joining Count Basie in 1945. Relocating to New York he played with Dizzy Gillespie, Bud Powell, Miles Davis, and Charlie Parker where participated in the bop movement. During those years, his trombone was as widely imitated as the trumpet and alto of Gillespie and Parker. In 1952, Johnson retired for a time, only to return in 1954 as partner of fellow trombonist Kai Winding's in the popular Jay and Kai Quintet which released several popular recordings.

Johnson's ability as a composer took over and by the late 1960s he had quit performing and concentrated on writing for film and television. Despite his absence from the stage in 1995 *Down Beat* readers and critics both voted him into the magazine's hall of fame and he is now considered the greatest jazz trombonist.

James Price Johnson (1891/94–1955)
Pianist, Composer

James P. Johnson was born on February 1, 1891, in New Brunswick, New Jersey, and studied with his mother and private teachers beginning in childhood. The family moved to New York in 1904, and Johnson was soon working professionally during school breaks. He was soon leading a band at the Clef Club, working vaudeville and cabaret shows, and making piano rolls before releasing his first recordings in 1917. He was musical director for road shows and toured England with *Plantation Days*, before moving to Hollywood to write the classical score for Bessie Smith's *Yamacraw*. In 1928 he appeared at a Carnegie Hall concert before retiring to Jamaica, New York, in the 1930s to concentrate on writing concert music based on traditional

African American themes. He completed a tone poem in 1930, the "Symphony Harlem" in 1932, and a symphonic jazz treatment of "St. Louis Blues" in 1936. Johnson was partially paralyzed by a stroke in 1940 and was semi-active until 1951 when another stroke left him bedridden until his death in New York on November 17, 1955.

Johnson's more serious works were neglected due to the lack of respect accorded to African American composers at the time by the classical world. He is more famously known as the master of the "stride piano," an instrumental style which derives its name from the strong, striding, left hand of the player playing bass notes and chords while the right hand plays melody. "Stride piano" came into its own during the 1920s in conjunction with the phenomenon known as the "rent party." Such a party was held for the purpose of raising rent money and involved the payment of an admission fee which entitled a patron to food, drink, conviviality, and a stride piano session. Johnson, along with Fats Waller and Willie "the Lion" Smith, were among the many who sharpened their skills in the rent party training ground.

Lonnie Johnson (1899–1970)
Guitarist, Singer

Johnson was born February 8, 1899, in New Orleans. By 1912 he was playing on the streets with his father who was a violinist. He began developing his unique jazzy style almost from the start. During World War I, Johnson played with a theater troupe that entertained Allied soldiers. In 1920, after 13 members of his family had died in an influenza epidemic, he moved to St. Louis, where he played in theaters and on riverboats. Johnson signed a recording contract with OKeh Records in 1925 after winning a blues contest, and he quickly attained a sizable following among African American buyers of OKeh's "race" Records.

In addition to his blues work, Johnson made recordings with a number of top jazz artists in the 1920s including Louis Armstrong, Duke Ellington, and Eddie Lang. He also played behind several of the classic female blues singers over the next several years. Altogether, Johnson made about 130 recordings between 1925 and 1932. He moved around quite a bit, eventually settling in Chicago, where he began working the bustling nightclub scene around 1937. He recorded for Bluebird during a five-year stint beginning in 1939 before joining King Records in 1947 where he soon had such hits as "Tomorrow Night," So Tired," and "Confused." In the early 1950s, Johnson toured endlessly, both in the United States and abroad, and recorded regularly.

In spite of his tremendous activity, however, Johnson never achieved major stardom. By the early 1950s, his career was going nowhere, and he took a job as a janitor at a Philadelphia hotel. He was rediscovered in 1960 by jazz scholar Chris Albertson who arranged a new recording contract with the Prestige label. Although Johnson became quite popular with young white audiences in the United States and Europe during the blues revival of the 1960s, these listeners preferred the raw country blues of Skip James, Son House, and others, so major stardom again eluded him. In 1969, Johnson was hit by a car in Toronto, Canada, and he died on June 16, 1970, from the effects of the accident.

It would not be unreasonable to say that Lonnie Johnson was the single most influential guitar player in the history of blues. Johnson not only invented the guitar solo: he invented just about everything else a guitar does in blues, as well as jazz, country, and rock and roll.

Robert Johnson (1911–1938)
Singer, Guitarist

Born on May 8, 1911, in Hazelhurst, Mississippi, Johnson played a bit of harmonica as a teenager but had no real talent, and attempts to sit in with local legends Charley Patton and Son House were at first unsuccessful. He married young and wandered the Delta looking for work, committing himself to being a full-time musician after his wife died during childbirth. After approximately one year of studying with Ike Zinneman, an unrecorded blues musician, Johnson emerged with the astounding abilities to play guitar in a variety of styles and to write carefully constructed songs with original lyrics. These abilities were further honed by his constant work as a street musician and party circuit player that required him to play blues, pop, and hillbilly songs. His quick rise to virtuosity were the source of much of the legend and myth surrounding Johnson. Astounded by his newly found ability, listeners circulated the rumor that Johnson had met the devil at a crossroads, trading his soul for the ability to play guitar.

Johnson did not record as much as his contemporaries Charley Patton, Lonnie Johnson, or Blind Lemon Jefferson, but he traveled more than all of them. After his first recordings were released and "Terraplane Blues" became his signature work, he toured the Delta, Chicago, Detroit, and St. Louis. However, in August 1938 at a juke joint in Three Forks, Mississippi, he was reportedly poisoned by a jealous husband whom had given him a jug of tainted liquor, and he died several days afterwards. Johnson's legend remained only among devotees and British rock and roll stars that covered his songs. However, a retrospective of his work was released by Columbia in the mid-1960s. Later, a complete boxed set including the only two known pictures of Johnson was released in 1990, and it became the first blues record-

ings to sell more than a million units, evidence of Johnson's stature as a blues pioneer.

Johnson's most enduring contribution in style was his ability to accompany himself by playing a boogie bass line on the bottom strings, while playing melody on the top strings. His use of rundowns, turnbacks, and repeats were all new in his day, and his playing inspired many other great blues musicians to follow in his path including Jimmy Reed, Elmore James, and Lightnin' Slim. His recordings of "Love in Vain," "Crossroads," and "Sweet Home Chicago" are blues standards that place Johnson at the top of the blues genre.

Elvin Ray Jones (1927–)
Drummer, Bandleader

Born September 9, 1927, in Pontiac, Michigan, the youngest of the remarkable Jones Brothers developed his style in the vibrant jazz scene of Detroit where he cut his first records in 1953 that displayed his already remarkable style. Arriving in New York in 1955, he worked with such notables as J. J. Johnson, Sonny Rollins, and Donald Byrd before joining John Coltrane's quartet in 1960.

With this group—the most influential of its time—Elvin Jones astonished musicians and listeners with his awesome independence of limbs (keeping four rhythms going at once), amazing drive, and ability to respond within mini-seconds to Coltrane's furious flow of ideas. Elvin Jones left Coltrane in 1965 and soon led his own groups that have featured such fine saxophonists as Frank Foster, George Coleman, and Coltrane's son, Ravi. One of jazz's master drummers, Elvin Jones integrated the drums with the frontline (melody) players to a farther extent than anyone had done before, always maintaining the pulse while featuring complex cross-rhythms and atypical resolutions to phrases.

Henry "Hank" Jones (1918–)
Pianist

The eldest of the three extraordinary Jones brothers, Hank was born on July 31, 1918, and raised near Detroit, where he began his professional career as a jazz musician. He traveled to New York City in 1944 and recorded with the great trumpeter and singer Hot Lips Page. His brilliant keyboard technique and skill as both soloist and accompanist soon found him in the company of such giants as Coleman Hawkins and Charlie Parker. He toured with Jazz at the Philharmonic (JATP) and became Ella Fitzgerald's accompanist.

Settling into studio work in New York, Hank Jones became one of the most recorded jazz musicians—he is to piano what Milt Hinton and George Duvivier were to the bass—in all sorts of contexts. From the 1970s onward, Hank Jones began to do more work in clubs and on tour and to record more as a soloist and trio leader, often billed as "The Great Jazz Trio," with various star bassists and drummers. In the 1990s, Jones remains at the head of the pack when it comes to great jazz pianists.

Thaddeus Joseph "Thad" Jones (1923–1986)
Cornetist, Composer, Arranger, Bandleader

Born March 28, 1923, the middle brother of the gifted Jones family, Thad played in a band led by brother Hank during his teen years before working with Sonny Stitt and a stint in the Army (1943–1946). Thad played with Billy Mitchell in Detroit and cut his first records there in 1953. Traveling to New York in 1954, he was quickly discovered by Charles Mingus, who recorded him for his Debut label, and then joined Count Basie's band that same year, staying for almost a decade. During this time he honed his writing skills, contributing numerous arrangements and original tunes for the band and providing the solo on Basie's biggest instrumental hit "April In Paris."

In New York in 1963, Thad Jones joined forces with the great drummer Mel Lewis to co-lead what began as a rehearsal band but soon became the most talked about new big band in jazz. As the Thad Jones-Mel Lewis Jazz Orchestra, it gave new life to the language of big band jazz, as Thad Jones blossomed as a composer and arranger of music that was swinging but fresh. Perhaps his best-known composition, however, is the beautiful ballad "A Child Is Born." The band held together until 1979, when Thad Jones moved to Denmark and Mel took over, keeping much of Thad's "book" alive. Thad led his own bands in Scandinavia, then traveled back to the United States briefly in 1984 to take on leadership of the Count Basie Band, returning to Denmark in ill health six months prior to his death on August 20, 1986. Thad possessed great skills as both a trumpeter and a composer-arranger making him one of the few "complete" jazz musicians. A player of great agility and melodic invention, Jones's playing displayed a tart and razor sharp sound.

Riley B. "B. B." King (1925–)
Singer, Guitarist, Bandleader

B. B. King is one of the most successful artists in the history of the blues. Riley B. King was born on September 16, 1925, in Indianola, Mississippi. He was first exposed to the blues through an aunt who owned a phonograph. While a teenager, King purchased his first guitar for eight dollars—money he earned working in

B.B. King (Jack Vartoogian)

the cotton fields. At nineteen he hitchhiked to Memphis where his cousin, country blues guitarist Bukka White, taught him the basics of blues guitar. After returning home for a while, King returned to Memphis in 1948, playing at the 16th Street Grill for twelve dollars a night. He then found a spot on a newly opened radio station in Memphis called WDIA, where he played for ten minutes each afternoon and later became a disc jockey. The station named him "The Boy from Beale Street" and, thereafter, he was known as B. B. King.

King cut his first record in 1949 for the Bullet label titled "Miss Martha King," named after his wife he had left in Mississippi. He then signed with RPM Records and cut several sides for them in Memphis under the supervision of Sam Phillips. Soon King had his first rhythm and blues chart topper in 1951 with "Three O'Clock Blues." King hit the road to promote the song, and it was during this era that he first named his guitar Lucille, after a woman who had inspired a barroom brawl and fire that almost cost King his life. For the course of the 1950s, King was a hit-making force in the rhythm and blues field, with more than twenty of his songs scoring on the charts. He continued his success into the 1960s with his release "The Thrill Is Gone," which received the first of King's nine Grammy Awards. Soon King won international success, influencing such artists as the Rolling Stones.

In addition to an average of three hundred performances around the world each year, King has opened two jazz clubs—one in Memphis and the other in Universal City, California—and co-founded the Foundation for the Advancement of Inmate Recreation and Rehabilitation with lawyer F. Lee Bailey. King's many prestigious honors include an honorary doctorate from Yale University (1977), induction into the Rock & Roll Hall of Fame (1987), the Lifetime Achievement Award from the National Academy of Recording Arts and Sciences (1987), and the Presidential Medal of the Arts (1990). In 1995 King was one of the recipients of the Kennedy Center Honors.

Ronald Theodore "Rahsaan Roland" Kirk (1936–1977)
Composer, Flutist, Saxophonist

At first called "gimmicky" by critics, Roland Kirk proved to be one of the most exciting jazz instrumentalists. His variety of instruments was matched only by the range of his improvisational styles, often switching in the middle of a number from a dissonant exploration to a tonal solo based on a conventional melody.

Born in Columbus, Ohio, on August 7, 1936, Kirk was technically blind, having been able to see nothing but light from infancy. Educated at the Ohio State School for the Blind, he began picking up horns at the age of nine. At 19 years of age, while touring with Boyd Moore, he started experimenting with playing more than one instrument at a time. Finding obscure horns such as the stritch and the manzello, he worked out a technique for playing three-part harmony (on three horns simultaneously) through the use of false fingering. In 1960, Ramsey Lewis helped Kirk get his first important recording date with Argo Records, and in 1961 he played with Charles Mingus's group, going on the international circuit later that year. Kirk employed whistles, gongs, and toys as improvisational tools, often vocalizing melody lines and encouraging audience participation and providing amusing commentary from the stage. He reached his greatest popularity in the early 1970s before a stroke caused his left side to be paralyzed. He then switched to playing tenor sax with one hand and continued to tour, although in a more smooth jazz form. Kirk died on December 5, 1977, an icon and visionary of post-bop jazz and individual expression. Among his many compositions are "Three for Dizzy," "Hip Chops," "The Business Ain't Nothin' But the Blues," "From Bechet, Byas, and Fats," and "Mystical Dreams."

John Aaron Lewis (1920–)
Pianist, Composer, Bandleader

Born May 3, 1920, in La Grange, Illinois, Lewis was raised in a middle-class environment in Albuquerque, New Mexico. Lewis studied music and anthropology at the University of New Mexico until 1942. After three years in the Army, he went to New York City and soon became pianist and arranger with Dizzy Gillespie's band. Two years later at Carnegie Hall, Gillespie's band performed Lewis's first major work "Toccata for Trumpet and Orchestra."

After a European tour with Gillespie, Lewis returned to the United States to play with Lester Young and Charlie Parker and to arrange for Miles Davis. In 1952, after having finished his studies at the Manhattan School of Music, Lewis founded The Modern Jazz Quartet (MJQ) along with drummer Kenny Clarke, vibes master Milt Jackson, and bassist Percy Heath. After Clarke was replaced by Connie Kay in 1956, the group stayed together until 1974 with occasional reunions thereafter. With the MJQ, Lewis developed his trademark spare, cool sound with a strong classical presence and wrote many compositions including his classic "Django." Lewis has also composed film scores, collaborated with other "Third Stream" proponents including Gunther Schuller, taught jazz, and co-founded the American Jazz Orchestra. Lewis continues to perform and record, and his economical piano style recalls that of Count Basie in its perfection of note selection and retention of the blues form.

Abbey Lincoln (1940–)
Singer

Born Anna Marie Wooldridge on August 6, 1930, in Chicago, Lincoln graduated from Kalamazoo Central High School in Kalamazoo, Michigan, and later studied music for a number of years in Hollywood under several prominent vocal and dramatic coaches. She began her professional career in Jackson, Michigan, in 1950, after winning an amateur singing contest. After performing in nightclubs, she began recording in 1956. Throughout the late 1950s and 1960s, she sang in a group led by drummer Max Roach whom she married in 1962 (the couple divorced in 1970). Their recording *Freedom Suite* mingled social and political theory with jazz and entered strongly into the collective mindset of the Civil Rights movement.

As a soloist, Lincoln toured in Africa, Asia, Europe, and the Far East before becoming an assistant professor of African American theater and Pan-African studies at California State University. Lincoln made several film appearances including *The Girl Can't Help It* (1956),

Nothing But a Man (1964), and *For the Love of Ivy* (1968), earning several awards and induction into the Black Filmmakers Hall of Fame in 1975. That same year, she produced her own play *A Pig in a Poke*. Just as importantly, however, Lincoln has been hailed by many outstanding African American jazz performers, including Coleman Hawkins, Benny Carter, and Charles Mingus, as a singer with nuance who can shift accents and rhythmic delivery as well as notes, while maintaining a conversational feel to her delivery. Fairly inactive in the 1980s, Lincoln regained her prominence in 1993 via a television documentary entitled *You Gotta Pay the Band: The Words, the Music, and the Life of Abbey Lincoln*, which aired on PBS. Throughout the 1990s, however, Lincoln contributed to and produced numerous lauded albums including her 1999 release *Painted Lady*.

Melba Liston (1926–)
Arranger, Trombonist

Melba Liston, who has played with the greatest names in jazz, is one of the very few jazz female trombonists. Liston was born in Kansas City, Missouri, on January 13, 1926, but her family later moved to California. Her musical history began in 1937, in a youth band under the tutelage of Alma Hightower. Liston continued her trombone studies, in addition to music composition, throughout high school. She found work with the Los Angeles Lincoln Theater upon graduation. She met band leader Gerald Wilson on the night club circuit, and he introduced her to Dizzy Gillespie, Count Basie, Duke Ellington, Charlie Parker, and Dexter Gordon, with whom she recorded some outstanding work in the mid-1940s. By the late 1940s, Liston was playing alongside John Coltrane and John Lewis in Dizzy's band at different times, and she later toured with Billie Holiday as her assistant musical director and arranger. When the big band era waned, Liston jumped off the music circuit and returned to California, where she passed a board of education examination and taught for four years.

During the late 1950s, she was coaxed back into performing by Dizzy for his great State Department band (1956–1957) and then toured with Quincy Jones (1959–1961). During the next twenty years she led an all-female jazz group and performed freelance arrangements for Ellington, Basie, Dizzy, and Diana Ross. In 1974, she went to Jamaica to explore reggae. When she returned to the United States in 1979, she formed Melba Liston and Company, in which she revived swing, bebop, and contemporary compositions, many of which were her own until a stroke forced her to give up performing in 1985. She subsequently began composing with the aid of a computer and, since the early 1990s, she has worked with Randy Weston, Abbey Lincoln, and T.S. Monk. She

is regarded as a brilliant and creative arranger and an exceptional trombonist who possesses a beautiful, polished tone.

James Melvin "Jimmie" Lunceford (1902–1947)
Bandleader

Born on June 6, 1902, in Fulton, Missouri, Lunceford grew up in Denver and played alto sax with George Morrison in 1922. He received his B.A. at Fisk University, where he met Willie Smith, Ed Wilcox, and Henry Wells, all of whom would eventually work in Lunceford's band for many years. He later studied at City College in New York. After having become proficient on all reed instruments, clarinet, flute, guitar, and trombone, Lunceford began teaching and launched his career as a band leader in Memphis from 1926–1929. By 1934, Lunceford's band was playing at the Cotton Club in Harlem, hosting nightly radio broadcasts, and recording for Decca Records. During the next decade, the Lunceford band was as well known as those of Basie and Ellington. His powerhouse swing/dance band featured flashy costume uniforms, choreographed dance moves by the musicians, and a host of brilliant instrumentalists playing original charts of high-energy jazz. The Lunceford vogue faded after 1944, around the time the band was experiencing changes in personnel. Lunceford died of a heart attack on July 13, 1947, while the band was on tour. Although he hardly ever played an instrument while recording with his band —except flute in his recording of "Liza"—the Lunceford style was one which influenced many band leaders and arrangers up to the 1950s. Furthermore, Lunceford's band stands as one of the leading and most influential of the big jazz orchestras in the 1930s.

Howard "Maggie" McGhee (1918–1987)
Trumpeter

Born on March 6, 1918, in Tulsa, Oklahoma, McGhee was raised in Detroit where he played clarinet in high school before switching to trumpet. His early band dates included stints at the Club Congo in Detroit followed by work with Lionel Hampton and Andy Kirk, with whom he made his first recording *McGhee Special* in 1942. During this time, McGhee also participated in the bop experiment at Minton's Playhouse before a 1945 tour with Coleman Hawkins, which took him to California where he recorded his influential dates with Charlie Parker for Dial Records. After returning to New York, McGhee recorded some classic work with both Milt Jackson and Fats Navarro that helped him become one of the most acclaimed trumpeters by the end of the 1940s. In the 1950s McGhee suffered from drug addiction and became obscure, but returned in the early 1960s to make some very good recordings. Inactive again until 1975 when he recorded another set of solid efforts, McGhee remained relatively unknown due to his lack of sustained exposure during his career. McGhee died on July 17, 1987, in New York City.

Howard McGhee was one of the most recorded and important trumpeters of the bop era, forging a hard bop trumpet style that would be built upon by Fats Navarro and Clifford Brown. His solo efforts were known for their flow of ideas and hard-blowing style that were always swinging.

Carmen McRae (1922–1994)
Singer, Pianist

Born in Brooklyn on April 8, 1922, Carmen McRae's natural talent on the keyboards won her numerous music scholarships. During her teen years, she carefully studied the vocal style of Billie Holiday and incorporated it into her own style. An early highlight came when Holiday recorded "Dream of Life," one of McRae's compositions. After finishing her education, McRae moved to Washington, DC, and worked as a government clerk by day and a nightclub pianist/singer by night. In the 1944, she worked with Benny Carter and then with Mercer Ellington and Count Basie through the 1940s. She recorded her first solo record in 1954 for Decca, gaining enough attention to be dubbed a "new star" by *Down Beat* magazine.

In 1967, McRae appeared in the film *Hotel*, thus beginning a string of periodic television and film appearances that extended into the 1980s, when she had a part in the 1986 film *Jo Jo Dancer, Your Life Is Calling*. McRae had a flurry of activity in the 1990s, recording six albums between 1990 and 1991 alone. *Carmen Sings Monk* was nominated for a Grammy Award. In 1994 McRae was honored with a National Endowment for the Arts American Jazz Masters Award. Later in the year she suffered a stroke that eventually led to her death on November 10, 1994. McRae was best known for her witty interpretations of songs, smoky voice, and her behind the beat phrasing that reflected the influence of Billie Holiday.

Branford Marsalis (1960–)
Saxophonist, Bandleader

Branford Marsalis was born on August 26, 1960, in New Orleans. A very gifted player, he got his start as a member of Art Blakey's Jazz Messengers in 1980. From 1982 to 1985, he played in his brother Wynton's quartet. He has since performed with a multitude of artists from Mile Davis and Dizzy Gillespie to Tina Turner and Public Enemy. Only 14 months older than his brother, Wynton, Branford has gained equal fame, not least due to his wide exposure as band leader for the "Tonight Show" from 1992 to 1995. An inventive soloist and an imagina-

tive leader-organizer, Marsalis won a Grammy in 1993, formed the group Buckshot LeFonque, a hip hop and jazz ensemble in 1994, and has hosted "JazzSet" on National Public Radio.

Branford's interests beyond jazz include mid-1980s touring stints with pop/rock acts Sting, Bruce Hornsby, and the Grateful Dead which brought him increased exposure. Marsalis's forays into acting have included parts in several feature films including *Throw Momma From the Train* (1987) and director Spike Lee's motion picture *School Daze* (1988). Marsalis's quartet provided the music for Lee's *Mo' Better Blues* in 1990. More outgoing than his brother, Wynton, Branford is an open-minded neo-traditionalist who is willing to nurture rather than preserve jazz.

Wynton Marsalis (1961–)
Trumpeter, Bandleader

Born on October 18, 1961, into a musical family in New Orleans—his father, Ellis Marsalis, is a prominent pianist and teacher and brothers, Branford and Delfeayo, are both musicians in their own right—Wynton Marsalis was well-schooled in both the jazz and classical traditions. At 17 years of age, he won an award at the prestigious Berkshire Music Center for his classical prowess; one year later, he left the Juilliard School of Music to join Art Blakey's Jazz Messengers.

After touring and recording in Japan and the United States with Herbie Hancock, he made his first LP in 1981, formed his own group, and toured solo extensively. Soon he made a classical album, and became the first instrumentalist to win simultaneous Grammy awards as best jazz and classical soloist in 1984. He received the Pulitzer Prize in 1997 for his oratorio *Blood on the Fields*—the first jazz-based work to win this coveted prize. *Standard Time, Vol. 5: The Midnight Blues* followed a year later. In 1999, he released *Marsalis Plays Monk: Standard Time, Vol. 4* to coincide with the popular PBS special. Beyond recordings, Marsalis has composed music for films and ballet and co-founded the Lincoln Center Jazz Orchestra.

A brilliant virtuoso of the trumpet with total command of any musical situation in which he chooses to place himself, Marsalis has also made himself a potent spokesman for the highest musical standards in jazz, to which he is firmly and proudly committed. He has urged young musicians to acquaint themselves with the rich tradition of jazz and to avoid the pitfalls of "crossing over" to pop, fusion, and rock. His own adherence to these principles and his stature as a player have made his words effective. In 1994, the same year his septet disbanded, Marsalis published *Sweet Swing Blues on the Road*, a collection of essays about the jazz life. Not content with simply playing, Marsalis also teaches with educational outreach program Project Discovery and at such places as the New England Conservatory of Music.

Memphis Minnie (1897–1973)
Guitarist, Singer

Born Lizzie Douglas on June 3, 1897, in Algiers, Alabama, and raised in Walls, Mississippi, Memphis Minnie learned to played banjo and guitar and moved alone to Memphis in 1910—at the age of 13. She played on the streets, toured the South with medicine shows and circuses, and lived with Casey Bill Weldon who tutored her. In 1929, she married guitarist "Kansas" Joe McCoy, with whom she formed a marvelous, inventive duo with a rural flavor. She recorded some master-pieces of guitar playing such as "Hoodoo Lady," and her style became more urbanized. Her style continued to evolve, and in 1938 she formed a duo with her new lover, guitarist Ernest "Little Son Joe" Lawlars, whose compo-sitions "Digging My Potatoes," "Me and My Chauffeur," and "I'm So Glad," and delicate accompaniment com-bined with stunning guitar interplay helped to increase Minnie's popularity and success. In the late 1940s and early 1950s, Memphis Minnie tried several comebacks, but asthma and new trends in African American music forced her to retire in 1957. She died on August 6, 1973, in Memphis.

Memphis Minnie earned the respect of her peers throughout her long career with solid musicianship and more than 250 blues recordings over four decades, some of which are still widely performed by contemporary artists. Undoubtedly, she was the most popular and prolific female blues artist outside the vaudeville tradition.

Charles Mingus (1922–1979)
Bassist, Composer, Bandleader

Born on April 22, 1922, in Nogales, Arizona, Mingus grew up in the Watts area of Los Angeles. Starting on trombone and cello, he settled on the bass and studied with Red Callender, a noted jazz player, and Herman Rheinschagen, a classical musician. He also studied composition with Lloyd Reese. Early in his professional career, he moved to San Francisco and worked with Barney Bigard in a band that included the veteran New Orleans trombonist Kid Ory, and toured briefly in Louis Armstrong's big band. He also led his own groups and recorded with them locally. After a stint in Lionel Hamp-ton's band, which recorded his interesting composition "Mingus Fingers," he joined Red Norvo's trio with which he traveled to New York in 1951.

Settling in New York, he worked with many leading players including Dizzy Gillespie and Charlie Parker and founded the record label Debut with Max Roach. He also formed his first of many so-called jazz workshops in which new music, mostly written by himself, was re-

Charles Mingus (AP/Wide World Photos, Inc.)

hearsed and performed by four to eleven musicians taking verbal cues from Mingus. Mingus believed in spontaneity as well as discipline and often interrupted public performances by his band if the playing did not meet his standards, sometimes firing players on the spot. Although controversial, Mingus inspired loyalty with drummer Dannie Richmond, playing with Mingus from 1956 to 1970 and again from 1974–1977. Other longtime associates include trombonist Kimmy Knepper, pianist Jaki Byard, and the saxophonists Eric Dolphy, Booker Ervin, and John Handy in the earlier years; later, saxophonist Bobby Jones and trumpeter Jack Walrath.

Mingus's music was as volatile as his temper, filled with ever-changing melodic ideas and textures and shifting, often accelerating, rhythmic patterns. He was influenced by Duke Elllington, Art Tatum, and Charlie Parker, and his music often reflected psychological states and social issues—Mingus was a staunch fighter for civil rights and wrote such protest pieces as "Fables of Faubus," "Meditations On Integration," and "Eat That Chicken." He was also steeped in the music of the Holiness Church ("Better Git It In Your Soul" and "Wednesday Night Prayer Meeting") and in the whole range of the jazz tradition ("My Jelly Roll Soul," "Theme

For Lester Young," "Gunslinging Bird," and "Open Letter To Duke"). Himself a virtuoso bassist, he drove his sidemen to their utmost, often with vocal exhortations that became part of a Mingus performance. He composed for films and ballet and experimented with larger forms; his most ambitious work, an orchestral suite called "Epitaph," lasts more than two hours and was not performed in full until years after his death from amyotrophic lateral sclerosis or Lou Gehrig's disease—a disease with which he struggled valiantly, composing and directing from a wheelchair until almost the end of his life. Though he was often in financial trouble and once was evicted from his home, he also received a Guggenheim fellowship in composition and was honored by President Carter at a White House jazz event in 1978.

At its best, Mingus's music—angry, humorous, always passionate—ranks with the greatest in jazz. He also wrote a strange but interesting autobiography *Beneath the Underdog* (1971). A group, Mingus Dynasty, continues to perform his music into the 1990s.

Keb' Mo' (1952–)
Guitarist, Banjo Player, Singer, Songwriter

Born Kevin Moore on October 3, 1951, in Los Angeles, Keb' Mo' was exposed to gospel at an early age. At 21, he joined a rhythm and blues band that was later hired for a tour by Papa John Creach, playing on three of Creach's albums. Keb' Mo' later opened for such jazz and rock and roll artists as the Mahavishnu Orchestra, Jefferson Starship, and Loggins and Messina. These experiences helped broaden Keb' Mo's musical horizons and abilities. In 1980 he recorded a rhythm and blues-based solo album *Rainmaker* for Casablanca, which promptly folded. In 1983, he joined Monk Higgins's band as a guitarist and met a number of blues musicians who collectively increased his understanding of the genre. He subsequently joined a vocal group called the Rose Brothers and worked around the Los Angeles area.

The year 1990 found Moore portraying a Delta blues musician in a local play titled *Rabbit Foot* and later playing Robert Johnson in a docudrama called *Can't You Hear the Wind Howl?* He released his self-titled debut album as *Keb' Mo'* in 1994, featuring two Robert Johnson covers, eleven songs written or co-written by Moore, and his guitar and banjo work. Keb' Mo' performed a well-received set at the 1995 Newport Folk Festival. Keb' Mo's second release on Okeh Records, *Just Like You*, was one of the best-selling blues albums in 1996. The album *Slow Down* followed in 1998 on Sony Records.

Keb' Mo' draws heavily on the old-fashioned country blues style of Robert Johnson, but writes much of his own material, keeping his sound contemporary with touches of soul and folksy storytelling.

Thelonious Sphere Monk (1917–1982)
Pianist, Composer

Born on October 10, 1917, in Rocky Mount, North Carolina, Thelonious Monk's family moved to New York in his infancy. By his early teens, he was providing piano accompaniment for his mother in church. He later toured with an evangelist before studying at Julliard and then working with the Lucky Millender Band (1942), Coleman Hawkins (1943–1945), and Cootie Williams (1945) who first recorded Monks's "Round Midnight." In addition to these bands and Dizzy Gillespie's big band, Monk was in the house band at Minton's Playhouse, the primary breeding ground for the bop movement. Monk recorded his first dates as a leader in 1947, many of which are considered classics. Monk's career was seriously harmed when he was arrested on drug charges and lost his cabaret card, losing his ability to play in New York clubs for the next six years and forcing Monk to survive on session and out-of-town work. After he regained his right to work in New York in 1957, he had a long run at the Five Spot featuring a quartet that included John Coltrane, and his recordings from this period are often considered to be his best. Monk's fame began to grow and he appeared at numerous festivals, on television, and by the mid-1960s was featured on the cover of *Time* magazine. By the end of the decade, health problems cut into his activities, and his last major tour was in 1971–1972. When he died on February 17, 1982, he had not played in public for six years.

Although associated with the bop movement and that genre's harmonic advancements, Monk stood apart from bop in his approach to structure, rhythm, and style of improvisation. His lightening fast right-hand figures and compositions that featured unusual and hard to learn changes made him thoroughly modern. He insisted that improvisations should be derived from the melody rather than the chord changes as practiced in bop. Monk has been called the first jazz post-modernist and most important jazz composer since Duke Ellington. Many of his compositions including "Round About Midnight," "Ruby My Dear," "Off Minor," and "Epistrophy" have become jazz standards.

Ferdinand Joseph Lementhe "Jelly Roll" Morton (1890–1941)
Composer, Pianist, Bandleader

Born October 20, 1890, in New Orleans, Morton was playing piano in New Orleans's Storyville brothels by 1902. Restless and ambitious, he hit the road, working in vaudeville and minstrel shows, hustling pool, running gambling halls, and traveling as far as Alaska and Mexi-

Theolonius Monk (AP/Wide World Photos, Inc.)

Ferdinand "Jelly Roll" Morton (Corbis Corporation [Bellevue])

co. He finally settled in Chicago in 1923, where he then recorded with his Red Hot Peppers in 1926–1928. These recordings feature his own compositions and arrangements, and they showed that he was a major talent, quite possibly the first real composer in jazz, if not the inventor of the music as he would later claim. These recordings also came just as Louis Armstrong was changing the shape of jazz, and Morton's style which emphasized collective improvisation and polyphony clashed with Armstrong's virtuoso performances and big band-ensemble playing. The result was that Morton was consistently overlooked.

In 1928 he moved to New York and made some very good recordings, but he was considered out-of-date when big band swing came to the fore, although Morton's composition "King Porter Stomp" became a swing anthem. In 1938 he was discovered living in Washington, DC, managing an obscure night club by Library of Congress musical folklorist Alan Lomax who recorded a series of solo performances and reminiscences that revived Morton's career and resulted in a few more sessions. Failing health and restlessness led Morton to drive to California, where he had a lady friend. But the trip made him ill, and he died in his fiftieth year, just

before the revival of interest in traditional jazz, which would have given him the break he needed.

Few musicians in jazz were as colorful or talented as Jelly Roll Morton. Morton may not have invented jazz but he certainly was an important bridge between ragtime and jazz. A pool hustler, pimp, and tireless self—promoter, Morton's ego and attitude alienated many people. But his compositions, which were often constructed in three distinct sections and displayed unison melody lines, time choruses, instrumental breaks, and group improvisations are undeniably brilliant. His piano playing influenced many players after him including Earl "Fatha" Hines.

Theodore "Fats" Navarro (1923–1950)
Trumpeter

Fats Navarro was born in Key West, Florida, in 1923. He started on trumpet at age thirteen and also played tenor sax around Miami. Navarro was first heard nationally in 1943–1944 as a member of Andy Kirk's band until Dizzy Gillespie recommended him to Billy Eckstine, with whom he played for eighteen months. In 1946 Navarro was established as a top soloist, and he left Eckstine to work with Illinois Jacquet, Lionel Hampton, and Coleman Hawkins and to record with smaller and less constraining groups, first as a leader in 1946–1947 and then with Tadd Dameron, Bud Powell, and Howard McGhee in 1948–1949. These sessions set the course for jazz trumpeting, as Navarro's fat, full sound and rich, melodious solos would later influence the styles of Clifford Brown and Lee Morgan. Inactive for the last year of his life, Navarro died on July 7, 1950, from the effects of drug addiction and tuberculosis.

Herbie Nichols (1919–1963)
Pianist, Composer

Born January 3, 1919 in New York City, Nichols studied with a private teacher as a youth before serving in the Army until 1943. Most of Nichols's experience was with rhythm and blues and Dixieland groups, which were in sharp contrast to his modern and complex composing style. He made his first records for Blue Note in 1955, featuring numerous original compositions and some excellent sidemen such as drummers Art Blakey and Max Roach. Notably lacking in self-promotion and major support, his work did not sell well and Nichols remained unknown. Although his music is quite accessible to listeners, it was difficult for musicians to play, owing to his frequent extension of the 32-bar AABA form that required rehearsal, rather than jam session blowing. Often compared to Thelonius Monk for their similarity in harmonic language and angular melodies, Nichols composing style was distinct and his piano playing, suggestive of Art Tatum's, was virtuosic.

Most jazz fans know Herbie Nichols through his tune "Lady Sings the Blues," which was recorded by Billie Holiday. During his lifetime, though, only four of Nichols's albums, all in trio settings, were released before his death at age 44 from leukemia. It was only after he had died that his work was discovered and promoted by younger New York musicians such as Roswell Rudd, Cecil Taylor, and Steve Lacy. However, the work that has been documented reveals Nichols to be one of the great unsung legacies of jazz.

Joseph "King" Oliver (1885–1938)
Cornetist

Born May 11, 1885, in Abend, Louisiana, Joe Oliver started on trombone but switched to cornet and began playing with the Melrose Brass Band in 1907 before joining the Olympia Brass Band. Oliver first earned the sobriquet "King" in 1917 in Kid Ory's band after establishing himself as the best cornet performer as compared to Freddie Keppard, Manuel Perez, and a host of others. During the Storyville era, Oliver met and befriended Louis Armstrong, becoming Armstrong's mentor. With the closing of Storyville, Oliver left for Chicago in 1919, and Armstrong replaced him in Ory's band. By

1922, Oliver had a steady gig at Lincoln Gardens and summoned Armstrong to Chicago to play in his Creole Jazz Band as second cornetist. In 1923, the Creole Jazz Band made the first important recordings by an African American jazz group. Other sidemen in Oliver's band included Baby Dodds, Johnny Dodds, Barney Bigard, and Lil Armstrong. From 1925–1927 Oliver led the Dixie Syncopators at the Plantation Caf and constructed a new type of jazz that combined the skills of well-trained musicians with more spontaneous players associated with the earlier New Orleans styles, placing Chicago at the head of the jazz movement.

However, changing tastes, a disastrous tour, business errors, and failing health caused Oliver's career to decline, and he moved to New York in 1928. Continued dental problems forced him to give up playing, and beginning in 1932 Oliver toured mainly in the South before poor health forced him to end his musical career. He died in Savannah, Georgia, where he worked in a poolroom beginning in 1936 until his death on April 8, 1938. Oliver was one of the major inventors of early jazz who used mutes and buckets to alter the sound of his horn and often imitated vocal sounds with his cornet. His distinctive licks and phrases formed the early vocabulary of the great trumpeters who followed him.

Edward "Kid" Ory (1886–1973)
Trombonist, Bandleader

Kid Ory's musical career is in many ways emblematic of the story of New Orleans jazz itself. They both reached a high point during the first two decades of this century. They both moved north during the 1920s, only to lapse into obscurity in the 1930s before being revived in the next two decades.

Ory was born on December 25, 1886, in La Place, Louisiana. He was the best known of the so-called tailgate trombonists—a style that used the instrument for rhythmic effects, fills, and glissandi, and in which solos were played in a rough, forceful style. He led his own bands in New Orleans and Los Angeles, where in 1922 he led Spike's Seven Pods of Pepper as the first African American band to record in the New Orleans style. In 1925 he moved to Chicago to play with King Oliver, Jelly Roll Morton, and with Louis Armstrong's Hot Fives and Hot Sevens with whom he recorded his famous composition "Muskrat Ramble" in 1926.

He returned to the West Coast in 1929 and, after playing for a time with local bands, retired to run a successful chicken ranch from 1930–1939. In the 1940s, he gradually returned to music with Barney Bigard, Bunk Johnson, and other New Orleans notables. He toured Europe successfully in 1956 and again in 1959, and he spent his final years living comfortably in Hawaii before his death on January 23, 1973.

Charlie Parker (Archive Photos, Inc.)

Charles Christopher "Bird" Parker, Jr. (1920–1955)
Saxophonist

Charlie Parker was born in Kansas City, Missouri, on August 29, 1920, and took up alto sax, a present from his mother in 1931. Parker left school at sixteen to become a professional musician. After an initial lack of success, which some attribute to his early drug use and lack of technique, he found work with pianist Jay McShann and others. Parker first visited New York in 1939, and on return in 1941 he recorded his first sides with McShann and met Dizzy Gillespie who was developing parallel ideas that would emerge in the bop movement some four years later.

In the early 1940s, Parker played with the bands of Earl Hines, Cootie Williams and Andy Kirk, as well as the original Billy Eckstine band—the first big band formed expressly to feature the new jazz style in both solos and arrangements. In 1945, Parker cut a series of remarkable sides under Gillespie's name that became definitive sides of the bebop style. Although Parker was revered by a host of younger musicians, his innovations, at first, were met with a great deal of opposition from traditionalist jazz musicians and critics.

Moving to California in 1945, Parker, addicted to heroin, suffered a breakdown and was confined to a state hospital in California in 1946. Six months later he recorded two sessions with Erroll Garner for Dial Records that stand as pinnacles of his career—as influential in Parker's day as Armstrong's Hot Fives sides were in the 1920s. From that point onward, he confined most of his activity to working with quintets, at times featuring Miles Davis, Kenny Dorham, Al Haig, Max Roach, and Roy Haynes. Parker also recorded and toured with a string section and visited Europe in 1949 and 1950. During the last five years of his life, Parker went through cycles of illness brought on by his addictions. He made his final appearance in 1955 at Birdland, the club which had been named in his honor, and died a week later of heart seizure at a friend's apartment.

Parker's influence on the development of jazz has been felt not only in the realm of the alto saxophone, which he dominated, but on the whole spectrum of jazz ideas. The astounding innovations that he introduced melodically, harmonically, tonally, and rhythmically made it impossible for any jazz musician from the mid-1940s to present time to develop without reflecting some of Parker's influence, with or without acknowledgment

Charlie Patton (1887–1934)
Singer, Guitarist

Charley Patton was one of the very earliest practitioners of the Delta country blues style. As such, he profoundly influenced succeeding generations of blues artist, as the Delta sound evolved into the genre's modern recognizable form. His hoarse and impassioned singing and his fluid guitar style made him the original king of the Delta blues. Born in 1887 in Edwards, Mississippi, Patton received his musical education from members of the Chatmon family, some of whom went on to forge their own recording careers in the 1920s and 1930s.

At around 1897, Patton moved to the plantation of Will Dockery, where music was a constant part of the sharecropper lifestyle. At local juke joints, Patton became one the earliest composers of songs in the 12-bar pattern that came to be recognized as the standard blues form.

For the next thirty years or so, Patton played wherever he could—at picnics, on the street, or at other plantations. He gradually developed a sophisticated guitar style that helped lay the groundwork for what eventually coalesced into the Delta style. Although his musical skills were polished, his performance style was not. On the stage, Patton was a clown, performing guitar tricks, singing unintelligibly at times, and improvising at will. He was almost as well-known for his hard-drinking ways and constant womanizing as he was for his raw baritone singing voice. But the sound of his whiskey and cigarette voice would inspire a young Howlin' Wolf, and his propulsive guitar beat and keen rhythmic sense would plant the seeds for John Lee Hooker's boogie style.

In 1929 Patton was brought North to record for the Paramount label. He recorded approximately sixty sides for both Paramount and Vocalion over the next few years, but the surviving quality of the recordings makes it difficult to know how Patton really sounded. He is regarded as one of the first to tie the blues to a strong, syncopated rhythm and to utilize the slide for vocal-like effects. In addition, he is thought to have pioneered the popping of his bass strings and using the guitar like a drum to reinforce beats or make counter rhythms. Patton died in Indianola, Mississippi, on April 28, 1934, of heart disease.

Oscar Pettiford (1922–1960)
Bassist

Pettiford was born on September 30, 1922, in Okmulgee, Oklahoma, on a Native American reservation and raised in Minneapolis. Until he was 19 years old, he toured with the family band (father and eleven children) and was well known in the Midwest. In 1943, Charlie Barnet heard him in Minneapolis and hired him to team up with bassist Chubby Jackson. Pettiford left Barnet later that year, frequenting Minton's Playhouse and playing with Roy Eldridge, before he and Dizzy Gillespie led the first bebop group to perform on 52nd Street. Pettiford cut his first sides in 1943 and played with Coleman Hawkins and Duke Ellington, with whom he recorded "Swamp Fire," a fine example of Pettiford's power and attack.

Pettiford's fame grew during the 1950s through his recordings and his tours of Europe and Asia, and he continued to lead his own sextet and big band. In 1958, he settled permanently in Europe, where he continued to work until his death in Copenhagen in 1960. During his peak in the 1940s, Pettiford was a unique bassist who was melodically inventive and technically agile on both bass and cello. Building on the concepts first explored by Jimmy Blanton, Pettiford extended the range and complexity of jazz bass. Pettiford was also a fine composer who wrote "Bohemia After Dark" and "Blues in the Closet."

Earl Rudolph "Bud" Powell (1924–1966)
Pianist, Composer

Born on September 27, 1924, in New York City into a family of musicians. A piano prodigy, he had his first big-time job with trumpeter Cootie Williams's big band in 1943 and became involved in the "birth of bebop" at Minton's Playhouse in Harlem and on 52nd Street.

In 1945 he was severely beaten about the head by Philadelphia police in a racially-motivated incident, and he suffered the first of several nervous breakdowns that plagued him for the rest of his life. He continued to work with Gillespie and took part in bop combo sessions for Savoy Records in the late 1940s, although he was often in the care of a mental hospital. He lived in Paris from 1959 to 1964, frequently working with his old friend Kenny Clarke. He died in New York on August 1, 1966, and reportedly more than five thousand people attended his funeral in Harlem.

Powell is considered to be the first to transfer the melodic, harmonic, and rhythmic innovations of bop to the piano keyboard, setting the style for modern jazz piano. Although he was greatly influenced by Art Tatum and Teddy Wilson, his rapid right-handed melody lines played to match the horns combined with his random and dissonant left-hand chords were completely his own style.

Sun Ra (1914–1993)
Pianist, Composer, Bandleader

Born Herman Blount on May 14, 1914, in Birmingham, Alabama, Sun Ra spent the early part of his career in Chicago, where he played rhythm and blues, jazz, and blues. A highlight was playing in Fletcher Henderson's band in 1947 at the Club DeLisa. During the 1950s, while Ornette Coleman, Cecil Taylor, and Miles Davis were carving out niches for their musical visions and personalities, Blount changed his name to Sun Ra and assembled a band to play his unorthodox and challenging music.

Ra's Arkestra had three distinct periods: big band/hard bop in the 1950s; free jazz in the 1960s; and swing from the mid-1970s onward. It fused African-style polyrhythms, unusual harmonies, and audacious stage performances to create an often spectacular event. The group, which counted more than one hundred members over its history, lived communally, first in Chicago and later in Philadelphia, and released records on Ra's own Saturn label.

Ra's music pushed into mystical abstraction and theater, and audiences often participated in the experience. An admirer of American popular music, Ra often incorporated compositions by Ellington, Gershwin, and others into his performance. His interpretations—arrangements, tempos, and unique instrumentation—gave these works a different sound. Sun Ra died on May 30, 1993, following a series of strokes.

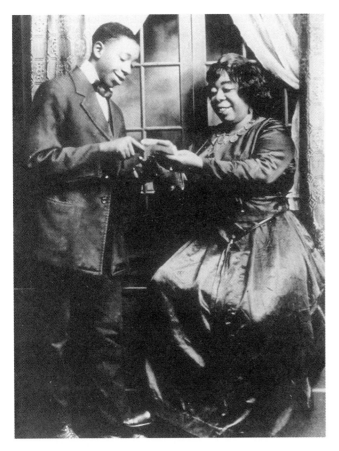

Ma Rainey performing in the musical production *The Rabbit Foot Minstrels* with an unidentified actor (AP/Wide World Photos, Inc.).

Gertrude "Ma" Rainey (1886–1939)
Singer

Ma Rainey, the "Mother of the Blues" who enveloped the 1920s with her powerful, message-oriented blues songs, is remembered as a genuine jazz pioneer. Born Gertrude Pridgett in Columbus, Georgia, on April 26, 1886, she gave her first public performance as a 12-year-old at the local Springer Opera House. In 1904 she married singer/dancer William "Pa" Rainey, and the duo embarked on a long entertainment career, touring around the South with minstrel shows, circuses, and tent shows.

Around 1912, Rainey introduced a teen-aged Bessie Smith into her act, a move that was later seen as having a major impact on the blues/jazz singing styles. She made her first recording in 1923 for Paramount Records and was soon recording with Fletcher Henderson, Louis Armstrong, and Coleman Hawkins. Between 1923 and 1928 when she stopped recording, she has released over one hundred songs including the blues classics "C.C. Rider" and "Bo Weavil Blues." Though she continued to tour the South for a few more years, blues singing by females was less popular than by her male counterparts.

She retired in 1935 and, until her death on December 22, 1939, managed the two theaters that she owned in Georgia. Similar to other classic blues singers of her time, Rainey sang pop, minstrel, and blues tunes, but she delivered them with a heavier, tougher, and earthier delivery than the cabaret blues singers that followed her.

Dewey Redman (1931–)
Saxophonist

Born in Fort Worth, Texas, on May 17, 1931, he started playing the clarinet when he was 12, taking private lessons briefly for six months before he turned to self-instruction. At 15, he earned a job with an eight-piece band that performed in church as the minister passed the collection plate. At Prairie View A&M College, Dewey teamed up with a piano and bass player to work in local clubs, found a spot in the Prairie View "swing" band, and graduated in 1953 with a degree in industrial arts and a grasp on a new instrument on which he had experimented—the saxophone. After a stint in the Army, Dewey obtained a master's degree in education at North Texas State University and taught school and directed school bands in western and southern Texas.

In 1959, Redman moved to Los Angeles, where he found the music scene to be very cliquish, and then to San Francisco, where he remained for seven years, studying music, working on his own theories of chord progressions, improvisation, and technique. In 1967, Dewey went to New York City and joined Ornette Coleman who brought him into his group with Dave Izenson on bass and Denardo Coleman on drums.

By 1973, Dewey was dividing his playing time between solo efforts, gigs with Ornette Coleman and Keith Jarrett, and the composition of "Peace Suite" dedicated to the late Ralph Bunche. Later he co-founded the group, Old and New Dreams. Dewey Redman has spent most of his life in search of a greater knowledge of his instrument—the tenor saxophone—constantly reevaluating his relationship to his music. His son, Joshua, emerged as one of the finest young tenor saxophonists of the early 1990s.

Don Redman (1900–1964)
Saxophonist, Composer

Born in Piedmont, West Virginia, on July 29, 1900, Redman was a child prodigy who played trumpet at the age of three, joined a band at six, and later studied harmony, theory, and composition at Boston and Detroit conservatories. In 1924, he joined Fletcher Henderson's band as lead saxophonist and staff arranger and also recorded as accompanist for such leading blues singers as Bessie Smith, Ma Rainey, and Alberta Hunter. When Louis Armstrong joined the Fletcher band, Redman adopted Armstrong's sense of swing, and in 1928 he became leader of McKinney's Cotton Pickers, having built both of these bands into two of the best in jazz history.

During most of the 1930s, Redman led his own band, regarded as one of the leading African American orchestras of its time and the first to play a sponsored radio series. He also wrote for many other prominent bands, black and white. In 1951, Redman became musical director for Pearl Bailey. From 1954 to 1955, he appeared in a small acting role in *House of Flowers* on Broadway. He continued to arrange and record until his death on November 30, 1964. Redman was the chief architect of the integration of popular orchestral dance music and jazz, using both written and improvised parts to create a swing feel.

Jimmy Reed (1925–1976)
Singer, Guitarist

Born September 6, 1925, in Dunleith, Mississippi, on a plantation, Reed learned the basics of guitar and harmonica from Eddie Taylor, a semi-professional musician. In 1943 Reed moved to Chicago but was soon after drafted into the Navy. After a two-year stint, he moved back to Mississippi to marry before relocating to Gary, Indiana, where he found work in a meat packing plant. In the early 1950s he was working with John Brim's Gary Kings as a harmonica player before the drummer in the band, future guitar legend Albert King, introduced him to Vee Jay Records where he made his first recordings. He was reunited with Taylor—a partnership that lasted the rest of Reed's life—and their third single "You Don't Have to Go" made number five on the rhythm and blues charts. Unfortunately, Reeds severe drinking problem became legendary, and he struggled to even perform or record, often requiring assistance to remember the lyrics or when to play his instruments. With the help of his wife and Taylor, Reed managed to function, even in spite of being diagnosed with epilepsy in 1957, and he placed 11 songs on the Hot 100 chart and 14 on the rhythm and blues charts in the 1950s and 1960s. Reed worked sporadically during the 1970s before becoming a recluse and obtaining treatment for his illnesses. He died in Oakland, California, on August 29, 1976.

Reed's best known songs "Big Boss Man," "Bright Lights, Big City," and "Baby, What You Want Me to Do" are part of the standard blues repertoire and have been played by everyone from garage bands to Elvis Presley. His bottom-string boogie rhythm guitar patterns, two-string turnarounds, country harmonica, and mush mouth vocals served as the first introduction to the blues for many people. While lacking the technical proficiency on his instruments as Son House and Elmore James and also lacking a voice as powerful as Muddy Waters and Howlin' Wolf, Jimmy Reed's simple tunes and laid back feel were a popular contrast, making aspiring players worldwide feel that they could participate in the blues.

Maxwell "Max" Roach (1924–)
Percussionist, Composer

Born on January 10, 1924, in New Land, North Carolina, and raised in Brooklyn, New York, Max Roach is one of the key figures in the development of modern jazz. He made his record debut in 1943 with Coleman Hawkins and was part of the first group led by Dizzy Gillespie to play bebop on 52nd Street in New York (1943–1944). He later worked with Charlie Parker's finest group (1947–1948). In 1954, he joined the brilliant young trumpeter Clifford Brown as co-leader of the Clifford Brown-Max Roach Quintet, an ensemble that defined the hard bop sound. After Brown's untimely death in a car crash, Roach began to lead his own groups of various sizes and instrumentation including interesting work with solo and choral voices, an all-percussion band, and a jazz quartet combined with a string quartet. His many compositions include "We Insist-Freedom Now," a suite written with his wife at the time, singer Abbey Lincoln, which was one of the first jazz works with a strong and direct political and social thrust.

A phenomenally gifted musician with a matchless percussion technique, Roach developed the drum solo into new heights of structural refinement; he has been an influence on every drummer to come along since the 1940s. Along with Kenny Clarke and Art Blakey, Roach is considered to be one of the founding fathers of bop drumming. Over his career Roach has played with Bud Powell, Miles Davis, Thelonius Monk, and Sonny Rollins. A professor of music at the University of Massachusetts since 1972, Roach became the first jazz artist to receive a MacArthur Fellowship in 1988—the most prestigious and lucrative award in the world of arts and letters.

Theodore Walter "Sonny" Rollins (1930–)
Saxophonist, Bandleader

Born on September 9, 1930, in New York City, Rollins took piano lessons when he was nine but lost interest in music until learning to play the alto sax in 1944. He was soon playing gigs on tenor and made his recording debut at 19 years of age with Babs Gonzalas for Capitol Records. Soon afterwards, he made sessions with trombonist J. J. Johnson, who recorded his first composition "Audubon," and pianist Bud Powell. Distinctively personal from the outset, his style developed through work with pianist Thelonious Monk, Powell, drummer Art Blakey, and trumpeter Miles Davis. In 1956 he voluntarily entered the federal penitentiary at Lexington, Kentucky, to kick his drug habit before joining the Clifford Brown-Max Roach Quintet, where he came into his own

Sonny Rollins (Jack Vartoogian)

style. Later that year he recorded *Saxophone Colossus*, marking a major breakthrough with songs such as "St. Thomas" and "Blue 7" that featured his thematic improvisational abilities. Employing a piano-less trio, a form he pioneered, he followed with two more records *Way Out West*, which showcased his love for off-beat pop and show tunes, and *Freedom Suite*, which was built around meditations on the lack of integration of the races in American society. Also during this period, he cut several albums for Blue Note Records that featured his own compositions along with oddball cover tunes made fresh and unique by the quality sidemen (i.e., Philly Joe Jones, Max Roach, J.J. Johnson, Horace Silver, and Thelonius Monk) and Rollins's early hard bop stylings.

In 1959, he took two years off from active playing, studying, and practicing. When he reappeared at the helm of his own quartet in 1961, he surprised even those who already knew the quality of his work with the power and conviction of his playing on *The Bridge*. A string off excellent albums on several labels followed until another "retirement" at the end of the 1960s. He was named a Guggenheim fellow in 1972 and continued to release strong offerings throughout the 1970s and

1980s. Rollins maintained an active schedule into the 1990s. Known for his impressive endurance and stamina, Rollins has often been called a force of nature akin to a volcano.

Rollins has written many fine tunes in his career, but it is as an instrumentalist and improvisor that he is best known. His robust, almost hard tone, use of grace notes, and the ability to create harmonically imaginative but melodic statements, even at amazingly fast tempos, is unmatched. He is recognized as the first jazz soloist to improvise in terms of a complete pattern of a solo, or as Thelonius Monk once said, "play the melody, not the changes." Rollins stands as one of the most commanding musical voices in jazz history.

Otis Rush (1934–)
Guitarist, Singer

Otis Rush has been a mainstay of the Chicago blues scene for more than forty years. A pioneer of the "West side" style of blues guitar work, Rush's sound combines the best elements of the South side, delta-influenced approach with the smoother, modern, urban stylings that B.B. King and T-Bone Walker brought to the blues.

One of seven children, Rush was born on April 29, 1934, in Philadelphia, Mississippi. Although he was attracted to the country blues guitar of Lightnin' Hopkins and others, Rush started out as a harmonica player. In 1948 he moved to Chicago, where he continued to develop his harmonica skills while working a day job in the stockyards. He did not begin studying guitar until 1953. Initially, his guitar role model was Muddy Waters, but he gradually began to infuse the more modern phrasing and jazzier feel of Walker and King into the deep Mississippi foundation that he had inherited from Waters.

Rush was noticed playing in the clubs by bassist Willie Dixon, who got him a contract with the newly established Cobra label. His first record for Cobra, "I Can't Quit You Baby," became a hit in 1956, and his work over the next few years was generally well-received. In 1959, Rush signed with Chess Records and recorded the successful single "So Many Roads, So Many Trains." He was unable to sell consistently for Chess, however, and his career slumped badly in the first half of the 1960s. He signed with the Houston-based Duke Records in 1962, but saw only one single released by that company. Meanwhile, he continued to perform regularly on the Chicago club circuit and occasionally in other cities.

Rush's appearance on the 1966 compilation album *Chicago: The Blues Today* revived his flagging career. It gained him a new generation of fans including a number of white rock musicians, and he was much in demand for blues festival gigs. Nevertheless, large scale stardom continued to elude Rush, with the exception of a wildly enthusiastic reception in Japan in 1975. Discouraged, Rush stopped performing for a short spell in the early 1980s. By the middle of the decade, however, blues was enjoying another revival, and a revitalized Rush finally managed to establish himself as a true giant of the modern blues scene.

James Andrew "Jimmy" Rushing (1903–1972)
Singer

Born on August 26, 1903, in Oklahoma City, Oklahoma, into a musical family (his father played trumpet and brother and mother were singers), Rushing played piano and violin as a youth, but entered music professionally as a singer in the Californian after-hours world in 1925. After that, Rushing was linked with leading bands and musicians: Walter Page (1927–1928); Bennie Moten (1929); and as a mainstay of the famed Count Basie band (1936–1949), where his intense, high-pitched style of blues singing propelled the band to new heights.

Rushing formed his own small group when he left Basie and , in the ensuing years, worked most often solo. Following the upsurge in popularity of the blues in the mid-1950s, Rushing appeared at all the major jazz festivals and made several successful European tours with his own and Benny Goodman's bands, earning him critical acclaim and commercial success. His style endured for more than four decades of jazz, largely due to its great warmth, a sure, firm melodic line, and a swinging use of rhythm. Rushing died of leukemia on June 8, 1972, in New York City. The song "Mister Five by Five," written in tribute to him, is an apt physical description of Jimmy Rushing who was one of the greatest male jazz and blues singers.

Bessie Smith (1894–1937)
Singer

Bessie Smith was born on April 15, 1894, in Chattanooga, Tennessee. Called "The Empress of the Blues," she had no peers. Her magnificent voice, sense of the dramatic, clarity of diction, and incomparable time and phrasing set her apart from the competition and made her appeal as much to jazz lovers as to lovers of the blues. Her first recording, Alberta Hunter's "Down Hearted Blues," sold approximately 750,000 copies in 1923—figures that only Caruso and Paul Whiteman were achieving at that time.

By the earlier 1920s, Bessie Smith had been singing professionally for some fifteen years. However, records by African American singers had only been made since 1920, and only by much less earthy voices. She already had a sizeable following and had appeared in large shows, so the timing was right—not the least for Columbia Records, whom she pulled out of the red. Before long, she was backed by the best jazz players including Louis Armstrong, and by 1925 she starred in her own touring show that traveled in its own private Pullman car. By 1927, she was the highest paid African American artist in the world. In 1929 she made a short film *St. Louis Blues* that captures for posterity some of her magnetism as a stage performer.

But tastes in music were changing rapidly, and though Bessie Smith remained with the times by adding popular songs to her repertoire, the Depression nearly ended the jazz and blues record business. In 1931, Columbia dropped her, and she soon began touring as a "single." John Hammond brought her back to the studios in 1933. Her singles were wonderful, her singing as powerful and swinging as ever, but they did not sell well and turned out to be her last recordings. She still found plenty of work on the traveling circuit, but it proved to be less financially rewarding. Early one morning on a road in Mississippi, she was fatally injured in a car collision. She died on September 26, 1937, at the age of 42.

William "Billy" Strayhorn (1915–1967)
Composer, Arranger, Pianist

Born in Dayton on November 29, 1915, and raised in Pittsburgh, Strayhorn early on showed an unusually sophisticated gift for songwriting, both in terms of music and lyrics. While still in his teens, he wrote "Lush Life," a song he demonstrated to Duke Ellington in 1938. A short time later Ellington recorded the Strayhorn tune "Something to Live For" and by 1939 Strayhorn joined the Ellington entourage in New York. Duke first thought of Strayhorn as a lyricist—something for which he was always searching—but soon found out that Strayhorn had a knack for arranging and was a talented pianist as well.

Before long the two musicians had established a working relationship that remains unique in the history of music. From 1940–1942 Strayhorn contributed many standout tunes to the Ellington repertoire—"Take the A Train," "Passion Flower," "Chelsea Bridge," and "Rain Check." After the mid-1940s, Ellington and Strayhorn began sharing credit for their compositions, and Strayhorn led small group sessions drawn from Ellington's larger band. Strayhorn also co-composed and arranged hundreds of tunes and extended works including "The Deep South Suite," "A Drum is a Woman," "Such Sweet Thunder," and "The Perfume Suite." Strayhorn rarely recorded on his own, and his death from cancer on May 31, 1967, inspired Ellington's great album *And His Mother Called Him Bill*.

A sensitive, swinging pianist Strayhorn is remembered for his great harmonic sophistication and beautiful touch that perfectly complemented Ellington's more percussive and expansive vision.

Arthur "Art" Tatum (1909–1956)
Pianist

Born on October 13, 1909, in Toledo, Ohio, Art Tatum was blind in one eye and partially sighted in the other. Although he could read some music with the assistance of braille, he learned primarily by ear. He made his professional debut on radio in Toledo before going to New York City in 1932 as accompanist for singer Adelaide Hall, with whom he cut his first records. He was soon making his own records and appearing on 52nd street. He settled in Chicago, and by the mid-1930s his reputation was international. Known primarily as a soloist, Tatum began working in a 1943 trio patterned after Nat King Cole's group, with Slam Stewart on bass and either Tiny Grimes or Everett Barksdale on guitar. While he maintained this format for most of the rest of his career, in 1953 he began working with Norman Granz, with whom he recorded a monumental 121 unaccompanied solos, and a series of small group sessions with Benny Carter, Buddy DeFranco, and Ben Webster. It is these recordings on which his reputation was built among both critics and musicians. Though he enjoyed a full career and recorded quite prolifically, Tatum lived too soon to benefit from the acceptance that came to jazz as concert hall music, which would have been an ideal medium for him. He died on November 5, 1956, in Los Angeles, California, from uremia.

For sheer technical mastery, Tatum had few peers—perhaps only Earl Hines and Cecil Taylor have come close to matching Tatum's skill. A child prodigy, Tatum seemed to have all the elements of his style in place by early adulthood. His harmonic and linear invention, unusual phrase lengths, radical leaps in logic, lush tone, and relaxed swing were his trademarks. Tatum exerted a strong influence on the bop movement and all who followed. His left-hand figures were reminiscent of such early stride players as Fats Waller, while his intricate right-hand lines and habit of playing with the tempo suggest the technique of Earl Hines. His ability to never abandon the melody line but to change, obscure, and reharmonize it at will are legendary.

Koko Taylor (1935–)
Singer, Songwriter

As the undisputed "Queen of the Chicago Blues," Koko Taylor has become one of the few women to achieve legendary status in a genre dominated by men wielding electric guitars. Taylor's raspy vocal style is a throwback to the early Delta blues tradition, and she has credited her success to her refusal to dilute her singing to conform to modern fads.

Taylor was born Cora Walton on September 28, 1935, on a farm near Memphis. After her mother died in 1939, her sharecropper father raised her, along with her five older siblings. Working in the cotton fields, the entire family would sing the blues, influenced most strongly by the classic songs played by B.B. King on his radio show. At about the age of 18, she married Robert "Pops" Taylor and moved with him to Chicago, where he had landed a job in a slaughterhouse.

In Chicago, Taylor worked as a domestic during the day and haunted South side blues clubs by night. She frequently joined such legendary Chicago blues musicians as Howlin' Wolf, Buddy Guy, and Junior Wells. Taylor was soon "discovered" by blues star Willie Dixon, who introduced her to Chess Records and wrote three songs for her. One of them, "Wang Dang Doodle," released in 1964 became a huge hit on the rhythm and blues chart.

Taylor quickly became a prominent member of the Chicago blues community. After Chess folded, she signed with Alligator Records, playing a large role in that label's transformation into a major blues outfit. Taylor continued to maintain a hectic tour schedule into the 1990s, and her albums have been regularly nominated for Grammy Awards, winning one in 1984. In addition, she has won numerous Handy awards.

Cecil Percival Taylor (1930–)
Pianist, Composer

Born March 15, 1930, in Long Island City, New York, Cecil attended the New England Conservatory, but said that he learned more from listening to Ellington; another early influence was Bud Powell. Early gigs include work with Hot Lips Page and Johnny Hodges before he made his first recording with Steve Lacy on soprano sax in 1956. The following year he appeared at the Newport Jazz Festival and was also recorded there. Settling in New York City, Taylor often struggled with lack of work and acceptance, but continued to go his own musical way. He worked mostly in live settings with drummer Sonny Murray and alto saxophonist Jimmy Lyons in the early 1960s before releasing a breakthrough album *Unit Structures* in 1966 on Blue Note Records. In the late-1960s, he experimented with larger frameworks for his playing, recording with the Jazz Composers Orchestra. In the early 1970s, he briefly taught at various universities. Meanwhile, he had gained a following in Europe and Japan, and in the 1980s there was more frequent work and a spate of recordings including some brilliant solo efforts. He also teamed for concerts with Mary Lou Williams and Max Roach. In 1988, he was featured in a month-long festival of concerts and workshops in Berlin; some of the results were issued in a lavish eleven-CD boxed set. In that decade, Taylor, always fascinated by dance which he sometimes included in his performances, teamed with the famous ballet star Mikhail Baryshnikov in concert. Despite his lack of acceptance in the mainstream, Taylor received a MacArthur Fellowship in 1992.

Taylor has set his own path in music, combining post-bop, contemporary classical music, and experimental noise into a unique and powerfully personal statement. As one of the leaders of creative-improvised music, Taylor's place in jazz is somewhat similar to John Cage's place in modern classical music. Influenced by Bud Powell, Thelonius Monk, and Duke Ellington, Taylor creates fierce and elegant soundscapes of shifting textures and accents. He once said "approach the keyboard as if it were 88 tuned drums." Taylor continues to stand as a unique force in jazz.

William "Billy" Taylor, Jr. (1921–)
Pianist, Composer, Educator

Born in Greenville, North Carolina, on July 24, 1921, Taylor's career started shortly after graduating from Virginia State College in 1942 with a B.A. in music, when he was employed in Ben Webster's group. He quickly established himself as a pianist on the New York scene, becoming a regular on "Swing Street" and playing with Billie Holiday, Ella Fitzgerald, Coleman Hawkins, Roy Eldridge, and others. A protegee of Art Tatum and Teddy Wilson, Taylor worked with Machito's Afro-Cuban band, toured Europe with Don Redman, and replaced Errol Garner in the Slam Stewart trio. After a 1949–1951 stint as house pianist for the famed Birdland club where he backed visiting stars, Taylor played a year-long engagement at Club Le Downbeat with a trio that included Charles Mingus.

Taylor made recordings with a variety of jazz artists for numerous labels during the 1950s and started his own publishing company before embarking on a campaign to educate the public through radio, television, and print. In 1958, he hosted "The Subject Is Jazz" on the Educational Television Network. He also hosted radio programs on two New York City stations and garnered a Peabody Award for his work. In the 1960s, Taylor served as musical director for Tony Brown's "Black Journal Tonight," and in 1965 he founded Jazzmobile as part of the Harlem Cultural Council's summer programs. Starting out as an idea for a parade float, Jazzmobile eventually developed into a service that seasonally brought major jazz artists out to poor urban areas for free performances.

From 1968 to 1972, Taylor led an 11-piece band for television's "David Frost Show." He returned to school, earning a doctorate in music education from the University of Massachusetts in 1975; his dissertation was later published as "Jazz Piano: History and Development"

Billy Taylor (AP/Wide World Photos, Inc.)

and became the text for a course offered on National Public Radio (NPR). Taylor directed "Jazz Alive!" for NPR from the late 1970s to early 1980s. He also became a regular on "CBS Sunday Morning," serving as the program's jazz correspondent since 1980; in 1983 he earned an Emmy Award for a segment on Quincy Jones. Taylor has served on numerous boards and panels including a position with the prestigious National Council on the Arts. In 1994, he was named the Kennedy Center artistic advisor.

Taylor was won several honors in his career. Among them have been recognition for lifetime achievement (1984) from *Down Beat* and induction into the magazine's Hall of Fame; a Jazz Masters Fellowship from the National Endowment for the Arts (1988); induction into the International Association of Jazz Educators Hall of Fame (1991); a Tiffany Award from the International Society of Performing Arts Administrators (1991); a National Medal of the Arts (1992); and Man of the Year from the National Association of Jazz Educators. Few musicians have done more for the cause of jazz than Dr. Billy Taylor, who has been properly credited with obtaining proper respect and recognition for African American music since the 1950s.

McCoy Tyner (1938–)
Pianist, Composer, Bandleader

Born on December 11, 1938, in Philadelphia, pianist McCoy Tyner attended the Granoff School of Music and then joined the Art Farmer-Benny Golson Jazztet. Moving to New York, Tyner joined John Coltrane's quartet in 1960. During his five years with Coltrane, Tyner developed a unique two-handed, densely harmonic style that matched Coltrane's model approach and could also stand up to Elvin Jones's polyrhythmic drumming. While with Coltrane, he participated in the recordings of such milestone albums as *My Favorite Things, Crescent, A Love Supreme,* and *Ascension.* He left Coltrane's group in 1965 after the addition of second drummer Rashied Ali and saxophonist Pharoah Sanders, which resulted in his playing being drowned out.

After leaving Coltrane, he made a number of albums as leader of his own groups in various sizes—from trios to a unique big band—for Blue Note, Milestone (1972–1980), and Columbia Records, before signing with Impulse Records in 1995. Undergoing a resurgence of popularity in the 1990s, Tyner's band was named Jazz Big Band of the Year by *Down Beat* readers in 1994. Their recording *Journey* featured such players as vocalist Diane Reeves and trombonist Slide Hampton. Tyner is one of the most distinctive and influential pianists in jazz as well as a superb composer and arranger whose own work is often unfairly overshadowed by his work with Coltrane.

Sarah Lois Vaughan (1924–1990)
Singer

Sarah Vaughan was born on March 27, 1924, in Newark, New Jersey. She sang in church, accompanied the choir on the piano, and tried a few pop songs at high school parties. As part of a dare, she entered the Wednesday night amateur contest at Harlem's famed Apollo Theater. Billy Eckstine happened to be backstage, ran out front as soon as he heard her voice, and recommended the young woman to his boss, band leader Earl Hines, who promptly hired her. In the Hines's band at that time were Charlie Parker and Dizzy Gillespie. They and Vaughan left Hines when Eckstine decided to start his own big band, the first to feature the new sounds of bop. By 1945, she made her first recordings under her own name including the classic "Lover Man" with Bird and Dizzy, the only singer to record with the two together.

A year later she started her solo career, gained wide recognition as part of the Jazz at the Philharmonic (JATP) tour in 1948, and signed with Columbia in 1949, helping to launch her to international fame. Though she had some big pop hits during her long and rich career, she never strayed from jazz for long, and her 1950 jazz session with Miles Davis is a classic. Between 1954 and

1967, she cut an amazing array of pop and jazz recordings with Clifford Brown, Count Basie, Roy Haynes, Benny Carter, and Gerald Wilson. In the 1970s and 1980s, she continued to record prolifically, exploring Brazilian songs and the Duke Ellington songbook, but rarely working in the jazz format.

Incredibly, as she aged, she got better, losing none of her amazing top range and adding to the bottom, while her mastery of interpretation also increased. Vaughn was a virtuoso who had complete control of pitch, timbre, and dynamics. Able to use her contralto voice as a horn, she embellished melodies with the leaps and structure of an instrumentalist, leading her fans to call her "the Divine One." Sarah died on April 3, 1990, in Los Angeles, California, a mere six months after he last performance.

Aaron Thibeaux "T-Bone" Walker (1910–1975)
Guitarist, Songwriter

The electric guitar is now the predominant solo instrument in American pop music, largely due to T-Bone Walker. Walker was the first blues artist to use amplification as a music-making tool, and his playing represents a bridge between early jazz and modern, guitar-driven rock. He is cited as an important influence by countless guitarists, blues and rock and roll musicians alike.

Walker was born on May 28, 1910, in Linden, Texas, and grew up in Dallas. Both of his parents were working musicians, and Walker was exposed to many different instruments as a youth. Walker also worked for a time as Blind Lemon Jefferson's guide, escorting the legendary guitarist around town. By the time he was 16 years old, T-Bone (a corruption of his middle name) was himself a working professional guitarist.

Recording as Oak Cliff T-Bone, Walker released two singles for Columbia Records in 1929. In 1934 he relocated to Los Angeles, leaving his steady guitar gig to his soon-to-be-famous pal Charlie Christian, who revolutionized the role of guitar in jazz. In Los Angeles, Walker played in small combos at jazz clubs before joining Les Hite's Cotton Club Orchestra as a singer, guitarist, and composer in 1939. With Hite, Walker established himself as one the pioneers of the electric guitar, which he used to successfully compete on equal terms with the band's horn section.

Having established his own reputation, Walker went solo in 1940, recording for Capital Records on such tunes as "Mean Old World" (1942) and "I Got a Break Baby," which featured his fluid, elegant riffs and mellow vocals. Walker signed with Black & White Records in 1946. A year later, he recorded his most famous hit "Call It Stormy Monday," which quickly became a blues standard of the highest order. His jump blues single "T-Bone Jumps Again" from the same session is an up-tempo instrumental that displays his dexterity playing at faster speeds.

Walker continued to record impressive work for a number of labels for most of the 1950s. He toured tirelessly during the 1960s, living the rugged, hard-drinking lifestyle that often goes with touring. However, as so many other of his peers from the post-war rhythm and blues ranks, he had difficulty competing with the advent of rock and roll. His 1970 release *Good Feelin'* won a Grammy Award, but stomach ailments and a stroke in 1974 slowed him down. He died of pneumonia on March 16, 1975, in Los Angeles.

An incurable showman, Walker dazzled audiences with an arsenal of tricks such as behind-the-back guitar playing while doing the splits, that may have influenced rock and roll performer Jimi Hendrix. Modern day electric blues guitar can be traced directly back to Walker, who was its first innovator.

Thomas Wright "Fats" Waller (1904–1943)
Composer, Pianist, Singer, Bandleader

Born in Greenwich Village in New York City on May 21, 1904, Waller's father wanted him to follow in his footsteps as a preacher. However, the younger Waller liked the good times that came with playing the piano well, which he did almost from the start. At fifteen, he turned pro, backing singers in Harlem clubs and playing piano for silent movies at the Lincoln Theatre. In the early 1920s he became a protegee of stride pianist James P. Johnson who helped him get jobs cutting piano rolls. Waller also accompanied a number of classic blues singers such as Bessie Smith and Alberta Hunter, and began writing songs. By the end of the 1920s Waller was a force in New York, performing on a regular radio broadcast and recording with Fletcher Henderson and Sidney Bechet. A talent for writing songs soon became evident. His first and biggest hit was "Ain't Misbehavin" from 1929; others include "Honeysuckle Rose," "Blue Turning Gray Over You," and "The Jitterbug Waltz." He also wrote "London Suite" for solo piano.

With his own small group and occasional big band, he cut more than five hundred sides between 1934 and his untimely death at thirty-nine in 1943. His style really came across on records, and no matter how trite the tune, he transformed it into a jazz gem. He also appeared in films including *Stormy Weather* with Lena Horne, and toured Europe. He also enjoyed playing Bach, especially on the organ, which he was the first to make into a jazz instrument. In 1932, the world-famous Marcel Dupre invited Fats to play the organ at the Notre Dame Cathedral in Paris. On a return train trip from Hollywood,

Thomas "Fats" Waller (Corbis Corporation [Bellevue])

where he had played the Zanzibar Room, to New York City, Waller died of pneumonia on December 15, 1943.

Waller was one of the greatest showmen of jazz, a terrific organist, fine singer, and talented songwriter. Weighting in at over three hundred pounds and standing more than six feet tall, Waller came by his nickname naturally. Wherever he went people loved him and his terrific style.

Dinah Washington (1924–1963)
Singer

Washington was born Ruth Lee Jones on August 29, 1924, in Tuscaloosa, Alabama, and got her start singing gospel music at St. Luke's Baptist Church on Chicago's South side. She toured churches with her mother, playing the piano and singing solos, until another opportunity beckoned—an amateur talent contest at Chicago's Regal Theater. Her triumphant performance led to performances at local nightclubs, and in 1943 the nineteen year-old singer successfully auditioned for a slot in Lionel Hampton's band. She was soon discovered by composer and critic, Leonard Feather, and Washington and Feather together created several chart toppers including "Baby Get Lost," "Salty Papa Blues," "Evil Gal

Waters moved to Chicago in 1943, where he played in clubs during the evening and worked as a laborer during the day.

In 1946 Waters cut sides for Columbia Records, but his urban sound was not well-received, and they were not released. Appearing as a sideman in 1947 with Sunnyland Slim, Waters also cut two sides for Chess Records before recording "I Feel Like Going Home" in 1948, which became his first national rhythm and blues hit. On the single, he fronted his own band that included Little Walter on harmonica. In the 1950s, Waters produced such masterpieces as Willie Dixon's "I'm Your Hoochie Coochie Man," "Got My Mojo Working," "Tiger in Your Tank," and "Mannish Boy." Popularized by white British youth, Muddy Waters eventually played on stage with many of them including Eric Clapton and Mike Bloomfield, both of whom considered Waters a guitar master and a living legend.

In the late 1960s and into the 1970s, Waters began receiving the kind of widespread recognition he deserved, including winning three Grammy Awards and a Trendsetter Award and being inducted into the *Ebony* Readers' Poll Black Hall of Fame. The post-war Chicago blues scene would have been incomplete without Muddy Waters. His aggressive, swaggering, Delta-rooted vocal sound and piercing slide guitar attack made him the "Father of Electric Blues." Waters died on April 30, 1983.

Dinah Washington (Corbis Corporation [Bellevue])

Blues," and "Homeward Bound." She then worked with Milt Jackson and Charles Mingus in 1945, and over time her singing moved from the blues to more jazz-oriented material. By the 1950s she was a successful crossover artists, gaining legendary status with "What A Difference A Day Makes" and "Unforgettable." Washington died of an overdose of alcohol and diet pills on December 14, 1963, in Detroit.

Washington's popularity as a blues singer in the tradition of Bessie Smith and her ability to cross over into jazz and pop genres have won her many fans in the decades since her death. Able to sound seductive and tough at the same time, Washington was an immensely talented vocalist.

Muddy Waters (1915–1983)
Guitarist, Harmonica Player, Singer

Waters was born Morganfield McKinley in Rolling Fork, Mississippi, on April 4, 1915, and grew up in nearby Clarkesdale on Stovall's plantation. He began playing guitar at the age of 17, performing at parties and fish fries. Waters, who idolized Son House, was first captured on tape in field recordings by Alan Lomax in 1941. After running a juke house in the early 1940s,

Benjamin Francis Love "Ben" Webster (1909–1973)
Saxophonist

Born in Kansas City, Missouri, on March 27, 1909, Ben Webster was at first a pianist, but switched to saxophone in his late teens. He worked with the family band led by Lester Young's father and with many other Midwestern bands. Ben traveled to New York in 1931 with Bennie Moten and was a featured performer on the landmark recording of "Moten Swing." After gaining a name among musicians as one of the most gifted disciples of Coleman Hawkins, he made many records and toured with many prominent bands including those of Fletcher Henderson, Cab Calloway, Benny Carter, and Teddy Wilson.

When Webster joined Duke Ellington in 1940, along with Jimmy Blanton and Billy Strayhorn, he really blossomed as a tenor soloist and soon became an influence in his own right. When he left Ellington in 1943, he mainly led his own small groups, recorded prolifically, and became one of the first African American musicians to join a network radio musical staff in 1944 with CBS. By the 1950s Webster moved to the West Coast and recorded with Art Tatum, Coleman Hawkins, and Billie Holiday. In 1965, he left on what had been planned as his first brief visit to Europe, but he never returned home. Due to a lack of work in the United States and changing trends in the jazz industry, Webster settled in Copenhagen, Denmark, where he spent the final decade of his life as a revered and beloved elder statesman of jazz. During this period, his always masterful ballad playing ripened to full maturity, and his sound, ranging from a whisper to a gruff roar, became one of the unsurpassed landmarks of classic jazz. He died on September 20, 1973, in Amsterdam, Netherlands. One of the big three tenor saxophone players of the 1930s and 1940s, along with Coleman Hawkins and Lester Young, Webster's full-bodied tone, warm vibrato, and bluesy melodies made him an icon.

Mary Lou Williams (1910–1981)
Pianist, Composer, Arranger

Most women who have achieved fame in jazz have been singers, from Bessie Smith to Betty Carter. An exception to this rule was Mary Lou Williams, dubbed the "First Lady of Jazz." Born in Atlanta on May 8, 1910, and brought up in Pittsburgh, Mary Elfrieda Scruggs had already performed in public at the age of six and was a pro by thirteen. Three years later she married saxophonist John Williams, with whom she made her record debut. When John joined Andy Kirk's band, she took over his old group. Soon, however, she was writing arrangements for Kirk, and in 1931 she became the band's pianist and musical director.

Though she also wrote for Benny Goodman, Earl Hines, and Tommy Dorsey, she stayed with Kirk until 1942, helping to make the band one of the swing era's best. After a return home to Pittsburgh in 1942, where she formed her own band that included a young Art Blakey, she settled in New York. A champion of modern jazz, she gave advice and counsel to such rising stars as Dizzy Gillespie and Thelonious Monk and contributed scores for Gillespie's big band. Williams joined Duke Ellington's band and served as staff arranger, contributing some 15 pieces during 1946. She led her own groups (sometimes all female) and began to compose longer works including the "Zodiac Suite," performed at Town Hall in 1946 by the New York Philharmonic Orchestra.

Williams lived in England and France from 1952 to 1954. After returning to the United States, she retired from music for approximately three years, forming a charitable organization to assist musicians with dependency and health problems. Resuming her career, she toured widely including a 1957 appearance at the Newport Jazz Festival with Gillespie, ran her own record label (1955–1963), and wrote several religious works including a jazz mass performed at St. Patrick's Cathedral. In 1977, she became artist-in-residence and teacher of jazz history and performance at Duke University, a

position that she held until her death on May 28, 1981, in Durham, North Carolina.

Williams was a highly regarded instrumentalist, primarily in the swing idiom, and a gifted composer. Most importantly, she was the only major jazz artist who lived and adapted her playing style throughout all of the jazz eras including spirituals, ragtime, blues, Kansas City swing, boogie woogie, bop, and avant-garde.

"Sonny Boy" Williamson (1899–1965)
Singer, Harmonica

Most sources have the man who was to become Sonny Boy Williamson as being born on December 5, 1899 in Glendora, Mississippi. However absolutely nothing is known of his early childhood, and even his real name, believed to be Aleck Ford "Rice" Miller, cannot be verified. What is known is that by the mid-1930s, he was traveling the Delta working under the alias of Little Boy Blue with such blues legends as Robert Johnson, Robert Nighthawk, and Elmore James. By the early 1940s he was appearing on "King Biscuit Time," the first live blues radio show. (The sponsor of the show had Miller pose as John Lee "Sonny Boy" Williamson, an established Chicago blues star, in order to increase sales of their product. Apparently the ruse succeeded and when John Lee was murdered, Miller became "the original Sonny Boy.") The show was an immediate hit, but Miller did not record his work until the period of 1951–1954 when his first single "Eyesight to the Blind" became a hit. Miller also participated in Elmore James's "Dust My Broom" session before recording his first session for Chess Records in August 1955, releasing "Don't Start Me To Talkin." In 1963 he headed to Europe and enjoyed tremendous success, recording with British blues-rock groups, the Yardbirds and the Animals, before releasing the hit "Help Me." Two years later, he returned to the United States, where he died of a heart attack in Helena, Arkansas, on May 25.

Sonny Boy Williamson was one of the great blues legends who enjoyed tremendous popularity among blues purist and rock and roll fans. He wrote and played some of the best blues songs ever. His sly, world-weary vocal delivery, combined with his powerful harmonica playing, made his sound unique.

Teddy Wilson (1912–1986)
Pianist, Bandleader

Born on November 24, 1912, in Austin, Texas, Theodore Wilson's father taught English and his mother was head librarian at Tuskegee Institute. Teddy studied music theory at Talladega College before moving to Detroit in 1929 where he played in local bands before moving to Chicago in 1930. From 1931–33 he played in

Louis Armstrong's big band and with others, before he was brought to New York by Benny Carter in 1933.

Two years later, Wilson began to make a series of records with Billie Holiday, Ben Webster, and Johnny Hodges. Meanwhile, he became famous as the first black jazz musician to be featured with a white band when he was hired in 1935 to play with the Benny Goodman Trio and Quartet with whom he stayed until 1939. His marvelously clear, harmonically impeccable piano style was a big influence on the pianists of the swing era. His own big band formed in 1939 was excellent but not a commercial success. From 1940 onward, he mostly led small groups or appeared as a soloist, touring worldwide and making hundreds of records. Though seriously ill, he continued to perform until a week before his death on July 31, 1986, in New Britain, Connecticut. Two of his three sons are professional musicians.

Wilson's style evolved from the early influence of Earl Hines, Art Tatum (who befriended him early in his career), and Fats Waller, but became a neat and quietly swinging style that featured single note lines that was revolutionary at the time. Wilson was also a fine but little known arranger and writer.

Lester Willis "Prez" Young (1909–1959)
Saxophonist

Born August 27, 1909, in Woodville, Mississippi, Young was instructed on trumpet, violin, alto sax, and drums by his father who was a trained musician that studied at Tuskegee. His family moved to New Orleans during Lester's infancy, and by age ten Lester was playing drums in the family band. He spent his youth on the carnival circuit in the Midwest, choosing to concentrate on the saxophone at age 13 (i.e., the C melody saxophone after his idol Frankie Trumbauer). Young's first major job was as baritone with the Bostonians in 1929–1930, before touring all over the Midwest with the bands of King Oliver and Walter Page.

After a brief stint with Count Basie, Young was offered Coleman Hawkin's chair in Fletcher Henderson's orchestra, but he was criticized for not having the same style as his predecessor and he soon left. He returned to Kansas City to play with Andy Kirk, and then with Count Basie from 1936 to 1940. During the Basie years, Young surpassed Hawkins as the vital influences on the tenor. Hardly a tenor man from the mid-1940s through the 1950s achieved prominence without building upon the foundations laid by Lester Young. After leaving Basie's band, Young worked in several small combos in the early 1940s before entering the Army in 1944. During his 15-month service, Young suffered what many characterized as traumatic racial prejudice that affected him for the rest of his life. After his return to civilian life, he worked in numerous small combos and toured with the Jazz at the Philharmonic (JATP) units. He suffered a complete emotional breakdown in 1955, but made a comeback the next year. He died from a combination of mental problems, alcoholism, and malnutrition on March 15, 1959, within hours of returning from a long engagement in Paris.

It was Lester Young who gave Billie Holiday the name "Lady Day" when both were with Count Basie, and it was Holiday, in turn, who christened Lester Young "President" (later shortened to "Prez"). Young is remembered for his style which formed the bridge from hot and swing jazz to bebop and cool jazz. Young transformed the big, full-tone, and dotted eighth- and sixteenth-note phrasing to a moodier, laconic sound utilizing a series of evenly placed eighth notes played legato.

25

Popular Music

◆ The Rise of Rhythm and Blues ◆ "Crossovers" into Country Music
◆ Sweet Soul Music and Social Revolution ◆ Psychedelic Soul to Disco
◆ Rap: From Subculture to Mass Appeal ◆ New Directions: From Nuevo Soul to Pop–Hip Hop
◆ Popular Music Composers, Musicians, and Singers
by Guthrie P. Ramsey Jr.

◆ THE RISE OF RHYTHM AND BLUES

The appearance of rhythm and blues or "R&B" marks one of the most important developments in American popular music. The term "rhythm and blues" describes a number of historically specific styles that have grown out of the African American vernacular music tradition since mid-century. Rhythm and blues laid the foundation for numerous subsequent styles including rock and roll, soul, disco, funk, jazz fusion, rap and, most recently, "smooth" or contemporary jazz. Rhythm and blues artists combined the conventions of several popular music styles: swing jazz, boogie woogie, gospel blues, blues, and, in some cases, novelty pop. From the swing tradition, rhythm and blues musicians adopted the riff-based horn arrangements and driving rhythms of groups such as Count Basie and His Orchestra. Gospel and blues music provided a system of dramatic vocal techniques, which were crafted by artists into highly stylized personal mannerisms. Gospel, jazz, and blues also provided musical forms such as 32-bar songs and 12-bar blues patterns to the new style. Unlike the swing era big bands, rhythm and blues (or "jump blues") groups featured fewer horns and a heavy rhythmic approach marked by a walking boogie bass line, honking saxophone solos, and a two-four drum pattern. Among the greatest exponents of postwar jump blues were guitarist T-Bone Walker, saxophonist Eddie "Cleanhead" Vinson and blues shouter Big Joe Turner.

Singer and saxophonist Louis Jordan fronted a supremely popular jump blues ensemble that featured his singing, which was a smooth gospel-influenced vocal style. In 1949, the popularity of the style championed by Jordan and others led producer Jerry Wexler, who was working at *Billboard Magazine*, to change its African American pop chart title to rhythm and blues, thus coining the name of this new music. The new sound, originally dubbed "jump blues" and later rhythm and blues, proved extremely popular beyond the African American community, marking one of many important "cross-over" moments in American popular music history. The melding of musical techniques that distinguished rhythm and blues is related to the specific socio-historical context of mid-century America. Due to an ample supply of jobs caused by World War II, black and white Southerners flooded the North seeking new opportunities and life chances. This migration created a dramatic shift in the demographics of major cities in the North, Midwest, and West. The burgeoning U.S. economy during the war provided these migrants with the resources to seek different kinds of entertainment in their new locales.

The lyrics of rhythm and blues songs reflected ways in which some migrants negotiated these changes. Many rhythm and blues lyrics speak of life in the South through a nostalgic lens; others use metaphors that reference country living; and others speak of hardships associated with life in the urban North. As African Americans pressured the U.S. government to end Jim Crow and the laws of the land that denied them equal rights, the color line between the races became less rigid, and as a result, white and black Americans gained greater access to each other's cultures, especially music. Much as jazz music already was, rhythm and blues was an important source of cultural exchange. In fact, the popularity of rhythm and blues paved the way for rock and roll's replacing jazz as the America's quintessential popular music in the 1950s. But the music remained rooted in the sound of the African American church, though not exclusively. Some of the early recordings exemplifying the gospel influence on rhythm and blues were Cecil Grant's 1945 hit "I Wonder," Roy Brown's 1947 classic "Good Rocking Tonight," and Wynonie Harris's 1949 disc "All She Wants To Do Is Rock."

Dinah Washington was one of the earliest female rhythm and blues singers to make a mark on the entertainment industry during the 1940s. Her song stylings combined jazz, blues, gospel, and pop ballads. During her childhood, Washington honed her musical skills in the Baptist churches in Chicago, although she, as many others, was born in the South. After scoring hits with "Evil Gal Blues" and "Salty Papa Blues" early in her career, she recorded a string of hits for the Mercury label, with which she began an association in 1948. Washington's recorded work sprawls over several categories including rhythm and blues, pop, jazz, and country.

Louis Jordan, however, is considered the most important jump blues or rhythm and blues performer during the 1940s. He formed his group Louis Jordan and His Tympani Five in 1938 with an eye toward entertaining and capturing some of the white market. His repertoire was eclectic: jump blues, ballads, and novelty songs. With titles such as "Beans and Cornbread," "Saturday Night Fish Fry," and "Ain't Nobody Here but Us Chickens," the group's chart busting songs, as writer Nelson George has noted, "suggest country life, yet the subject of each is really a city scene."

It was not long before this kind of raw-edged rhythm and blues emerged from hundreds of independent recording labels that appeared across the country in the postwar era. With the increased availability of rhythm and blues recordings, a handful of African American radio disc jockeys became locally famous as the first promoters and salesmen of this music. Bringing their colorful street language to the airwaves, pioneer African American DJs such as Al Benson and Vernon Winslow not only helped to popularize rhythm and blues, but set the trend for modern pop and African American radio programming.

Rhythm & Blues and the African American Church

In the early 1950s, numerous gospel quartets and street corner singing groups set out to establish careers in the African American popular music scene. Influenced by gospel music groups such as the Golden Gate Quartet and the Harmonizing Four and the secular singing of groups such as the Inkspots, vocal groups appeared that performed complex harmonies in *a capella* style. As they would for rap artists in decades to come, street corners in urban neighborhoods became training grounds for thousands of young aspiring African American artists. This music, known as doo wop, first arrived on the scene with the formation of the Ravens in 1945. Not long afterward, there followed a great succession of doo wop "bird groups" including the Orioles who, in 1953, scored a nationwide hit with "Crying in the Chapel"—a song which, for the first time in African American popular music, walked an almost indistinguishable line between gospel and mainstream pop music. In the same year, Billy Ward formed the Dominoes, featuring lead singer Clyde McPhatter, the son of a Baptist minister.

In the wake of the success of these vocal groups, numerous gospel singers left the church to become pop music stars. In 1952, for example, the Royal Sons became the pop group Five Royales. They later changed their name to the Gospel Starlighters (with James Brown), and finally the Blue Flames. Five years later, a young gospel singer named Sam Cooke landed a number one pop hit with "You Send Me," a song which achieved popularity among both black and white audiences.

The strong relationship between gospel and rhythm and blues was evident in the music of more hard-edged rhythm and blues groups such as Hank Ballard and the Midnighters. Maintaining a driving blues-based sound, Ballard's music, while featuring gospel-based harmonies, retained secular themes, as evidenced in his 1954 hit "Work With Me Annie." However, the capstone of gospel rhythm and blues appeared in the talents of Georgia-born pianist and singer Ray Charles, who in 1954 hit the charts with "I Got a Woman," which was based upon the gospel song "My Jesus Is All the World to Me." Charles's 1958 recording "What I'd Say" is famed for its call-and-response pattern which directly resembled the music sung in Holiness churches.

Rock and Roll

The rise of white rock and roll around 1955 served to open the floodgates for thousands of black rhythm and blues artists longing for a nationwide audience. A term applied to black rhythm and blues and its white equivalents during the mid-1950s, rock and roll represented a label given to a music form by the white media and marketplace in order to attract a mass multi-racial audience. Alan Freed, a white DJ from Ohio is credited with being the first to air radio programming dubbed

Louis Jordan and his Tympany Five Band performing in 1946 (Archive Photos, Inc.).

"rock 'n roll," and thus he is remembered in some circles as the "Father of Rock and Roll." While the term itself had been used in black vernacular language for years, it was used by white promoters of rock and roll to distinguish it from rhythm and blues, which was, of course, closely associated with black music culture. Many Southern whites expressed outrage at the growing interest in rhythm and blues and rock 'n roll among white teenagers, and various authorities mounted "Don't Buy Negro Records" campaigns. As African American music writer Nelson George explained, naming this music rock and roll, "dulled down the racial identification and made young white consumers of Cold War America feel more comfortable." Taken from a term common among the Delta and electric blues cultures, rock and roll was actually rhythm and blues rechristened with a more "socially acceptable" title. Of course, the term "rock and roll" had sexual connotations as well; this, along with its roots in black culture, allowed white cultural conservatives of the time to demonize the form.

Thus, the majority of rhythm and blues performers never made the distinction between rhythm and blues and rock and roll. Ike Turner, a talent scout for the pioneering Sun Studios record label, was a formidable

bandleader and guitarist; his 1951 cut "Rocket 88" has been considered by some to be the very first rock and roll record. The song's distorted guitar tone was achieved by accident—coming from a broken amplifier speaker—but would influence the gritty sound of many subsequent rock and blues guitarists. Turner achieved mainstream success in collaboration with his wife, singer Tina Turner, whose fame would later eclipse him. One rhythm and blues artist who established a prosperous career in rock and roll was New Orleans-born pianist Antoine "Fats" Domino. Although he had produced a great amount of strong rhythm and blues material before his career in rock and roll, Domino did not hit the charts until 1955 with "Ain't That A Shame," followed by the classics "Blueberry Hill," "I'm Walkin," and "Whole Lotta Loving." Another rhythm and blues pianist/singer to enter the rock and roll field was Little Richard Penniman, a former Pentecostal gospel singer whose career in pop music began in 1956 with the hit "Tutti Frutti." Little Richard's fiery vocalizations featuring screams, hollers, and falsetto whoops was only matched for intensity by his very explosive and rhythmic piano playing, which drew on blues and gospel traditions. Before entering a Seventh Day Adventist seminary in

Chuck Berry (Jack Vartoogian)

1959, Little Richard produced a string of hits: "Long Tall Sally," "Rip It Up," "The Girl Can't Help It," and "Good Golly Miss Molly."

In 1955, as Fats Domino's New Orleans style rhythm and blues tunes climbed the charts, a young guitarist from St. Louis named Chuck Berry achieved nationwide fame when his country-influenced song "Maybelline" reached number five on the charts. Backed by bluesman Muddy Water's rhythm section, "Maybelline" offered a unique form of rhythm and blues, combining white hillbilly, or rockabilly, with jump blues; Berry revolutionized rhythm and blues by featuring the guitar as a lead, rather than a rhythm instrument. Modeled after his blues guitar mentor T-Bone Walker, Berry's double string guitar bends and syncopated up-stroke rhythm created a driving backdrop for his colorfully poetic tales of teenage life. A very eclectic and creative musician, Berry incorporated the sounds of urban blues, country, calypso, Latin, and even Hawaiian music into his unique brand of rhythm and blues. His classic "Johnny B. Goode" recorded in 1958 became a standard in almost every rock and roll band's repertoire including 1960s rock guitar hero Jimi Hendrix. According to popular music scholar Timothy D. Taylor, many African Ameri-

can early rockers like Berry made a concerted effort to court an integrated audience, a notion that is evident in changes he made to a later recording of the song "Johnny B. Goode."

◆ "CROSSOVERS" INTO COUNTRY MUSIC

African American musicians did not remain consigned to styles closely associated with African American culture. Dinah Washington, for example, recorded several pop tunes beginning with the mainstream title "What a Difference a Day Makes" in 1959, her first major hit. She also recorded what were known as "reverse crossovers," songs that originally appeared in the country or pop category but which Washington performs in her patented jazz-blues-gospel manner. In addition, Chuck Berry was not the only African American to take an interest in country music. Ray Charles's crossover into country music in the early 1960s caused controversy in many circles. In 1959, Charles recorded "I'm Moving On," a country tune by Hank Snow. Despite opposition, Charles went on to record a fine collection of songs in 1962 entitled *Modern Sounds in Country Music*. Filled with soulful ballads and backed by colorful string sec-

James Brown (AP/Wide World Photos, Inc.)

tions, the session produced two classic numbers "You Don't Know Me" and "I Can't Stop Loving You." Its popularity spawned a 1963 sequel *Modern Sounds in Country Music Volume 2*, producing several more hits including Hank Williams's "Your Cheating Heart" and "Take These Chains From My Heart."

Unlike other mainstream African American country artists, Charles's renditions remained immersed in his unique gospel blues sound. Before Charles's entrance into the country music field there had been many African American country artists such as Dedford Bailey, a partially disabled harmonica player who became a regularly featured performer on the Grand Ole Opry from 1925 to 1941. However, it was not until 1965, when Charley Pride arrived on the country music scene with his RCA recordings "Snakes Crawl at Night" and "Atlantic Coastal Line" that an African American artist emerged as a superstar in the country tradition. Pride's songs were so steeped in the country tradition that many radio listeners were astounded when they found out his racial identity. With the arrival of Pride, there appeared other African American country artists such as Linda Martel from South Carolina, O. B. McClinton from Mississippi, and Oklahoma-born Big Al Downing and Stoney Ed-

wards. The most noted of these artists, Edwards recorded two nationwide hits in 1968 with Jesse Winchester's "You're On My Mind" and Leonard Cohen's "Bird on a Wire."

◆ SWEET SOUL MUSIC AND SOCIAL REVOLUTION

The tremendous social upheavals of the 1960s—including but not limited to the Civil Rights, Black Power, and women's movements and the coalescence of a youth-based counterculture—were paralleled by numerous new musical forms. Perhaps no single genre of popular song encapsulated the highs and lows of this period more than soul music. Soul music drew on several idioms of African American music including gospel, jazz, and blues. According to music scholar David Brackett, gospel vocal techniques that signified spiritual ecstasy in the religious context were transplanted by soul singers into the secular context with important results. The most prominent of these is a sense of raw passion that identified the singers with the songs and the songs with the African American community. Thus, being born in the African American church, where testifying preachers and harmonizing choirs shepherded their congregations to weekly ecstasy, the form was escorted into the secular world by a handful of artists schooled simultaneously in gospel, jazz, country blues, rhythm and blues, and rock and roll.

Although he had precursors such as vocalist Clyde McPhatter, who recorded with the Dominoes and the Drifters, singer keyboardist Ray Charles has been credited as one of the founders of the soul genre. His earliest hits—notably, "What'd I Say" and "I Got a Woman"—brought the emotional testifying and call-and-response arrangements associated with gospel music into a nonreligious context. He added the earthy pull of the blues and a jazz-influenced harmonic complexity to his distinctive musical blend. This hybrid of blue groove and spirit was the secular gospel known as soul music. Such innovations were controversial, but the sounds of soul sweetened and enriched rhythm and blues music from then on. Blind "Brother Ray" became a cultural icon in the ensuing decades.

While rhythm and blues had functioned for some time as gospel's sinful, worldly counterpart—focusing largely on the concerns of the body while church music addressed the spirit—soul refused to deny either side of human experience. Even so, the young genre's exuberance and ambition made it ideal for reflecting the growing aspirations of America's black population. Inspired by the teachings and nonviolent organizing of Dr. Martin Luther King, Jr. and other civil rights leaders, African Americans also responded to songs that trumpeted change. "People Get Ready" and "We're a Winner" by Curtis Mayfield and the Impressions were early anthems as soul grew and drew many more listeners.

Singer-bandleader James Brown, meanwhile, combined uplift and hard groove, gradually moving from heady soul/rhythm and blues into a new territory called funk with hits such as "I Got You (I Feel Good)" and "Cold Sweat." Brown ran one of the tightest ships around, alternately inspiring and browbeating his musicians; turnover was high, but the ensemble was always a well-oiled machine. Though he would refine the funk style—driving rhythms emphasizing the "one" or first beat of each measure; repetitive vocal phrases and improvised, "churchy" shouts; and minimal, almost dissonant, instrumental figures—during the early 1960s, its content remained largely sexual for some time. Brown's mid-1960s work began laying the musical foundation for funk, and his music primarily celebrated the dynamic tradition of African American social dancing in song's such as "There Was A Time" and "Licking Stick," often naming popular dances such as the "boogaloo" and the "funky chicken" in songs. Brown's political message did not fully materialize until the end of the decade. By then, his funky sermons championed African American eco-

nomic independence and freedom from addiction. Brown had a seismic affect on pop; not only funk artists but also scores of rock and rap musicians took his work as a point of departure.

Following Brown's lead, Sly and the Family Stone—led by Sylvester "Sly Stone" Stewart, a Northern California DJ and producer—lent a psychedelic rock tinge and communal good vibes to the bedrock funk groove. Featuring musicians black and white, male and female, the group offered one of the most inclusive visions in pop history. While "Dance to the Music" mapped out their utopia in musical terms, they trumpeted tolerance and equality in happy hits such as "Everyday People," "Everybody Is a Star," and "You Can Make It If You Try." Stone's vision would darken substantially later on, however.

The syncopated rhythms of New Orleans were also fundamental to the development of modern funk. The Meters began as an instrumental foursome and eventually backed up acts as diverse as singer Lee Dorsey, vocal group The Pointer Sisters, and British popster Robert Palmer. During the 1960s they scored some instrumental hits—notably "Cissy Strut"—before adding vocals in the 1970s. Though they eventually disbanded and were partly subsumed by soul survivors the Neville Brothers, the Meters were profoundly influential.

Soul North and South: Stax/Volt, Atlantic, and Motown

Soul music's increasing hold on the public imagination during the 1960s had a great deal to do with two record companies, the Atlantic Records subsidiary Stax/Volt in the South and Motown in the North. Stax/Volt was a Memphis-based label that introduced the world to the rough-hewn "funky" sound of Southern soul and rhythm and blues. The company's greatest successes came during the 1960s, thanks to a roster of powerful artists, gifted songwriters, and one of the greatest "house bands" in music history. The band in question, led by keyboardist Booker T. Jones, was a formidable mixed race groove machine that not only backed the whole Stax roster and numerous acts on its parent label, Atlantic, but also achieved success as an instrumental recording act, Booker T. and the MG's. Their smoldering workouts "Green Onions" and "Hip Hug-Her" became signature themes of the era.

Stax's roster included vocal duo Sam and Dave, Rufus and Carla Thomas, Eddie Floyd, and Otis Redding. House songwriters Isaac Hayes and David Porter wrote hits such as "Soul Man" and "Hold On, I'm Coming" for Sam and Dave; Hayes himself would later become a pop/soul superstar. Redding was both an extraordinary singer and a gifted tunesmith; he penned the luminous "Dock of the Bay" and the righteous "Respect." The latter song was transformed into an anthem of nascent feminism and African American dignity thanks to the alchemy of Atlantic Records's Aretha Franklin, a gospel-bred singer turned pop maven; Franklin would become the "Queen of Soul" and one of the most enduring figures in popular music. While Franklin made "Respect" and other celebrated recordings—tracks such as "Chain of Fools," the incandescent "(You Make Me Feel Like a) Natural Woman," and "I Never Loved a Man" at the Fame studios in Muscle Shoals, Alabama, other Atlantic soul stars came to Memphis to make their hit records. The Stax crew collaborated with Wilson Pickett on hugely successful singles such as "In the Midnight Hour" and "Land of 1,000 Dances." Ultimately, however, Stax lost its commercial momentum and by the 1970s was struggling to compete with a panoply of rivals.

As soul music gained a mass following in the African American community, an African American-owned and family-run Detroit record company emerged as one of the largest and most successful African American business enterprises in the United States. In 1959, Berry Gordy, a Detroit entrepreneur, songwriter, and modern jazz enthusiast, established the Motown Record Corporation.

With its headquarters located in a modest two-story home, the company proudly displayed a sign on its exterior reading Hitsville USA. Taking advantage of the diversity of local talent, Gordy employed Detroit-based contract teams, writers, producers, and engineers. Motown's studio became a great laboratory for technological innovations, advancing the use of echo, multi-tracking, and over-dubbing. In the studio, Gordy employed the city's finest jazz and classical musicians to accompany the young singing talent signed to the company.

Unlike the soul music emerging in studios such as Stax and Muscle Shoals, Motown's music was also marketed at the white middle class; Gordy called his music "The Sound of Young America" and sought to produce glamorous and well-groomed acts. "Blues and R&B always had a funky look to it back in those days," explained Motown producer Mickey Stevenson. "We felt that we should have a look that the mothers and fathers would want their children to follow." Indeed, a meticulously controlled and glamorous image was an extremely important component in Berry Gordy's Motown ideology. He required artists signed to the label to attend classes on etiquette, stage presence, and choreography. In fact, the strict division of labor that Gordy established in this company might be compared to the

Berry Gordy (AP/Wide World Photos, Inc.)

automobile assembly lines for which Detroit is well-known.

Thus, Motown set out to produce a sound, which it considered more refined and less "off-key" than the music played by mainstream soul and blues artists. In its early years of operation, Motown retained a rhythm and blues influence as evidenced in songs such as the Marvelettes's "Please Mister Postman" (1961), Mary Wells's "You Beat Me to the Punch" (1962), and Marvin Gaye's "Pride and Joy" (1963).

One of the main forces responsible for the emergence of a unique "Motown sound" appeared in the production team of Brian and Eddie Holland, and Lamont Dozier, or H-D-H, as they came to be known. Utilizing the recording techniques of Phil Spector's "wall of sound," the H-D-H team brought fame to many of Motown's "girl groups" such as Martha and the Vandellas, and the Supremes, featuring Diana Ross.

During 1966 and 1967, H-D-H began to use more complex string arrangements based upon minor chord structures. This gave rise to what has been referred to as their "classical period." As a result, many Motown songs reflected the darker side of lost love and the conditions of ghetto life. This mood was captured in such songs by the Four Tops as "Reach Out, I'll Be There," "Bernadette," and "Seven Rooms of Gloom."

After the Holland-Dozier-Holland team left Motown in 1968, the company, faced with numerous artistic and economic problems, fell into a state of decline. A year later, Gordy signed the Jackson Five, the last major act to join the label before its demise. The Jacksons landed 13 consecutive hit singles including "ABC" and "I'll Be There," championing a style that might be called "bubblegum soul"—African American music directed at a preteen and young adolescent audience, a legacy that was seen in 1980s and 1990s groups such as New Edition and Boyz II Men. In 1971, Gordy moved the Motown Record Corporation to Los Angeles, where the company directed its efforts toward filmmaking. Through the late 1970s and early 1980s, Motown continued to sign such acts as the Commodores, Lionel Richie, and DeBarge. But in 1984, Gordy entered into a distribution agreement with MCA records and eventually sold Motown to an entertainment conglomerate.

◆ PSYCHEDELIC SOUL TO DISCO

Disillusionment after the deaths of civil rights champion Dr. Martin Luther King, Jr. and black power advocate Malcolm X, along with the lingering trauma of the Vietnam War and the worsening plight of America's inner cities, had a marked influence on soul's direction. Curtis Mayfield projected a vision of wary hope in his early 1970s work. His landmark soundtrack for the "blaxploitation" film *Superfly* reflected the new soul paradigm: at once gritty and symphonic, encompassing soul's far-reaching ambition and funk's uncompromising, earthy realism. Isaac Hayes's theme from *Shaft*, another urban action film, earned an Academy Award. Much of the funk and soul of this period drew not only on the percolating rhythms developed by Brown but also on the trailblazing guitar work of Jimi Hendrix.

Hailed by many as the greatest electric guitarist of all time, Hendrix had toiled as a sideman for numerous rhythm and blues acts but emerged as a rocker of the first order during the mid-1960s. By the time of his death in 1970, he had revolutionized lead guitar playing forever; his use of the wah-wah pedal, an effect that lent a powerful percussive dimension to the instrument, became a staple of funk. His melding of psychedelic rock, hard blues, and soul tropes, meanwhile, influenced the "psychedelic soul" that emerged in his wake.

Commercial soul addressed the tenor of the times. Trailblazers Sly and the Family Stone focused less on the rainbow-colored sentiments of the preceding era

Jimi Hendrix (AP/Wide World Photos, Inc.)

and more on urban turmoil with their landmark album *There's a Riot Going On*, as did Marvin Gaye with hits such as "Trouble Man" and "What's Goin' On." The O'Jays enjoyed chart success with such anxious singles as "Backstabbers" and "For the Love of Money," and the Temptations wrapped their prodigious vocal chops around inner-city woes on "Papa Was a Rolling Stone," among other smashes.

These commercial laments were outstripped in daring—though not in sales—by the work of Detroit's Funkadelic. Fronted by singer and hairstylist George Clinton, who led a doo wop group called The Parliaments in the 1950s, Funkadelic mixed acid rock's cosmic guitar excursions with funk's relentless grooves; a danger existed in their work that limited its commercial appeal, but profoundly influenced rock and rap.

Eventually, Clinton established another group, Parliament, which focused on horn-driven funk and elaborate, fantasy-oriented concept albums. Funkadelic and Parliament, though manifestly different at first, gradually moved into similar territory as "P. Funk"; the "P" meaning "pure." Soon P. Funk was the umbrella term for a family of bands that included Bootsy's Rubber Band, The Brides of Funkenstein, and Parlet. Clinton

George Clinton (Ken Settle)

rhythm and blues radio programming. Each drew on jazz, rhythm and blues, and funk in their recordings, some of them featuring piano solos that extended them beyond the length of typical rhythm and blues recordings.

During the mid-1970s, club dance floors were increasingly dominated by the pulsating sounds of disco. With its thumping beat and lush arrangements, the music was viewed by many as a saccharine and escapist form that betrayed the mission of funk and soul. While a number of powerful performers emerged from the disco scene, few could approach the star power of diva Donna Summer, who enjoyed a wave of hits before a religious conversion moved her into gospel. Though disco's "crossover" success meant that a number of artists who scored in that format were white, several all-African American acts, notably Chic, Kool and the Gang, and LaBelle, flourished during this period.

◆ RAP: FROM SUBCULTURE TO MASS APPEAL

While funk sold millions of records and received extensive radio airplay in the mid-1970s, rap music emerged within a small circle of New York artists and entertainers in neighborhoods in Upper Manhattan and the South Bronx. Rap music belongs to a larger cultural system known as hip hop, which comprises graffiti writing and breakdancing (and its derivatives) together with rapping itself. Disc jockeys at private parties discovered how to use "little raps" between songs to keep dancers on their feet. From behind the microphone, DJs created a call and response pattern with the audience. Rapping consists of a vocalist performing non- to semimelodic oral declamations over a rhythmic background, which can be as sparse as a single drum track or an elaborate, multi-textured, multiple instrumental track Taking advantage of their master of ceremonies status, they often boasted of their intellectual or sexual prowess. "Soon a division of labor emerged," explained Jefferson Morley. " DJs concentrated on perfecting the techniques of manipulating the turntables, while master of ceremonies (MCs or rappers) concentrated on rapping in rhymes." Through the use of a special stylus, rappers moved records back and forth on the turntable in order to create a unique rhythmic sound, known within the rap culture as needle rocking and later as "scratching." In its short history, both the MC and DJ aspects of rap music having undergone significant changes, and the genre has exploded in many artistic directions and satellite idioms such as hip hop soul, New Jack Swing, and gangsta rap, among other approaches. The subject matter addressed in rap music has been equally eclectic, covering many topics includ-

scored in the 1980s as a solo artist, most notably with the mega-hit "Atomic Dog." P. Funk was so influential that for a time Parliament found itself competing with acts that appropriated its sound and themes including hitmakers such as the Ohio Players, Rick James, George Duke, and Earth, Wind and Fire. Though funk declined during the 1980s, artists such as Prince took it in a new, eclectic direction.

The decade did not lack for more traditionally romantic performers, however. Apart from Marvin Gaye, the period's most seductive male vocalists were arguably Al Green and Barry White. Green's rich falsetto and intimate phrasing on hits such as "Let's Stay Together" and "Love and Happiness" quickly established him as a visionary in the genre; though he left pop music to sing gospel music and preach, he remained a beloved figure in the soul world and returned to the fold for a 1995 album. White's bedroom soundtracks, meanwhile, kept lovers in thrall with an intoxicating blend of his baritone vocals and symphonic arrangements. Another funk direction coalesced in the work of jazz-based artists such as Herbie Hancock and Patrice Rushen, both of whom scored hits in the 1970s and 1980s that coincided with the appearance of the so-called "Quiet Storm" format in ing male and female braggadocio, highly sexualized content, gender relationships, race politics, partying, and youthful leisure.

Long before the modern rap, or hip hop, culture appeared, however, there were African American artists who performed in a rap style idiom. In 1929, for instance, New York singer-comedian Pigmeat Markham gave performances representative of an early rap style.

Rap music is also rooted in the talking jazz style of a group of ex-convicts called the Last Poets. During the 1960s, this ensemble of African American intellectuals rapped in complex rhythms over music played by jazz accompanists. Last Poet member Jalal Uridin, recording under the name Lightning Rod, released an album entitled *Hustler's Convention*. Backed by the funk band Kool and the Gang, Uridin's recording became very influential to the early New York rappers.

Among one of the first New York rap artists of the early 1970s was Jamaican-born Clive Campbell, aka Cool Herc. A street DJ, Herc developed the art of sampling, the method of playing a section of a recording over and over in order to create a unique dance mix. Others to join the New York scene were black nationalist DJ Africa Bambaataa from the southeast Bronx and Joseph Saddler, known as Grandmaster Flash, from the central Bronx. Flash formed the group Grandmaster Flash and The Three MCs (Cowboy, Kid Creole, and Melle Mel). Later he added Kurtis Blow and Duke Bootee who founded the Furious Five.

However, rap music did not reach a broad audience until 1980 when the Sugar Hill Gang's song "Rapper's Delight" received widespread radio airplay. Small record companies began to affect the development of pop for the first time in years. Def Jam spearheaded the rise of influential rappers LL Cool J, Run-DMC, and Public Enemy, while Tommy Boy Records contributed to the rise of electro-funk. As rap groups assembled during the decade, they began to use their art to describe the harsh realities of inner city life. Unlike early rap music which was generally upbeat and exuberant in tone, the rap style of the 1980s exhibited a strong sense of racial and political consciousness. Grandmaster Flash's "The Message" was the first blatantly political rap hit; its yearning and desperation recalled the angst-ridden soul records of the preceding decade and hinted as rap's potential. Toward the end of the decade, rap came to express an increasing sense of racial militancy. Inspired by the Nation of Islam and the teachings of martyred race leader Malcolm X, rap groups such as Public Enemy turned their music into voice supporting black power. Public Enemy's second LP *It Takes A Nation of Millions to Hold Us Back* sold over one million copies. Their song

Queen Latifah (AP/Wide World Photos, Inc.)

"Fight the Power" appeared in director Spike Lee's film *Do the Right Thing*. The group's third album *Fear of a Black Planet* was released in 1990. While it is a statement against "western cultural supremacy," explained group member Chuck D., it is also "about the coming together of all races" in a "racial rebirth." Rapper KRS-One of Boogie Down Productions provided eloquent, barbed political commentary as well.

Women have also played a role in the shaping of rap music. Rap artists such as Queen Latifah, MC Lyte, and the group Salt-N-Pepa represent a growing number of female rappers who speak for the advancement of black women in American society. Queen Latifah has emerged as critic of male dominance in the music industry and the sexist image of women presented by some male rap artists.

The late 1980s also saw the birth of the "Native Tongues" school of rap, the graduates of which employed an eclectic array of samples and more heavily relied on humor and baroque rhymes than did their hardcore and political counterparts. The best known groups of this school were De La Soul, A Tribe Called Quest, and The Pharcyde; Digital Underground, meanwhile, openly aspired to be "Sons of the P." and wove elaborate Parliament-esque concepts. Artists with a more bohemian bent began to rely heavily on jazz; some, such as Digable Planets and US3, sold briskly. A few, such as Arrested Development and Spearhead, stayed close to their soul and funk roots.

The biggest story in rap during the 1990s was the rise of "gangsta" rap, which utilized old school funk beats and dwelt on hustling and violence—usually without soul's veneer of guarded optimism. The group N.W.A. (Niggaz With Attitude) upset social conservatives with their megahit "F__ Tha Police," and its alumni Dr. Dre, Ice Cube, and Eazy E would all become major solo artists. Ice-T put a slightly more deliberative spin on his gangster tales, but it was Dre's protégés, Snoop Doggy Dogg and former Digital Underground member Tupac Shakur, who would become the biggest crossover acts of all. Snoop's laid-back style in particular earned him pop status with cuts such as "Gin and Juice," "Murder Was the Case," and "Doggy Dogg World." The crossover success of these recordings was so worrisome to aforementioned conservatives that gangsta rap lyrics became a staple in political speeches, and politicians and activist groups threatened to take action against record companies that released such material. Shakur, The Notorious B.I.G. (a.k.a. Biggie Small), and his protégé, Lil' Kim, all made impacts on hip hop culture with powerfully explicit lyrics. The untimely deaths of Shakur and the Notorious B.I.G. from gunshots sent shock waves throughout the entertainment industry and inspired passionate pleas from insiders to tone down some of the more violent lyrics in some artists's work.

Some pop rappers, such as MC Hammer (who eventually dropped the "MC") and DJ Jazzy Jeff and the Fresh Prince, enjoyed periodic success and then faded from the charts. Those who retained a bit more street-level credibility, on the other hand, such as Naughty By Nature, who had a mega-smash with "O.P.P.," and Coolio, who ruled the charts and scored a Grammy Award for his "Gangster's Paradise," enjoyed a longer reign. Beginning in the mid-1980s and into the 1990s, rap artists such as Will Smith (the Fresh Prince), Ice Cube, Ice-T, Tupac Shakur, and Queen Latifah crossed over successfully into film and television projects (some of them with hip hop themes), confirming the widespread acceptance of these artists throughout American culture. Some of these films such as *Do the Right Thing* and *Boyz N the Hood* enjoyed critical acclaim and popularity.

In the mid-1990s, creative rhyme style and techniques were perpetuated by Das Efx, Fu-Schnickens, Mystikal, Bone Thugs-N-Harmony, Busta Rhymez, and the Fugees, among others. With its array of styles and points of view, rap has emerged as a primary cultural form for young African Americans. Similar to the music of its predeces-

Erykah Badu performing at the 1998 Soul Train Awards (Archive Photos, Inc.).

sors, rap is filled with artistic energy and descriptions of the human experience. As a 1999 *Time* magazine cover story exclaims, rap music and hip hop rose in twenty short years from a subcultural expression to one that has changed the course of American popular culture in profound ways.

◆ NEW DIRECTIONS: FROM NUEVO SOUL TO POP-HIP HOP

Perhaps in part to counter the increasing dominance of hardcore hip hop in the marketplace, rhythm and blues and soul moved in a softer direction during the 1980s; as bands were replaced by sequenced keyboards and drum machines, recordings in this genre were increasingly dominated by producers and vocalists. Even longtime soul legends such as Aretha Franklin and Chaka Khan moved in a glossier direction. This period saw the rise of a handful of phenomenally successful singers, notably Whitney Houston, whose mother Cissy had sung with Franklin and others. Following a monster debut, Houston collected a string of hits and awards; her apotheosis came with the gargantuan sales of the soundtrack to the film *The Bodyguard* in which she also had a starring role. Houston's athletic vocal chops paved the way for a number of other new soul divas including Toni Braxton, Mariah Carey, and Mary J. Blige. Producers L.A. Reid and Babyface were among the preeminent hitmakers of this era; like Babyface, R. Kelley was successful both as producer and recording artist. Special mention should be made here of producer Teddy Riley, whose "New Jack Swing" combined the soul singing, hip hop grooves, and intermittent rap performances captured dance audiences in the late 1980s and early 1990s. The Minneapolis-based producing team Jimmy Jam and Terry Louis, also important innovators in the "New Jack Swing" idiom, helped to define the sound of pop-hip hop in the early 1990s. The duo is credited with crafting pop entertainer Janet Jackson's extremely popular sound as her career matured. Perhaps the most successful producer/performer in the pop-hip hop arena has been Sean "Puffy" Combs, who almost singlehandedly defined the sound of mainstream hip hop in the mid- to late 1990s.

While the soft-edged trend continued through the 1990s, some artists within the fold, such as the smash groups TLC and En Vogue, flirted with old school soul. Meanwhile, "alternative" or "nuevo" soul emerged at the margins, thanks to artists such as bassist/singer-songwriter Me'Shell Ndgeocello, Arrested Development refugee Dionne Farris, and Marvin Gaye-disciple D'Angelo. Artists such as Erykah Badu, Lauryn Hill, and Faith Evans enjoyed popularity and critical success, with their unique blends of hip hop sensibilities and soul singing styles. Boyz II Men, Brandi, and Monica updated the bubblegum soul style of previous decades.

◆ POPULAR MUSIC COMPOSERS, MUSICIANS, AND SINGERS

(To locate biographical profiles more readily, please consult the index at the back of the book.)

Nicholas Ashford (1943–)
Valerie Simpson (1948–)
Singers, Songwriters

One of the most enduring songwriting teams to emerge from Motown is the duo of Nicholas Ashford and Valerie Simpson. For over a quarter of a century, the team has written hit songs for artists from Ray Charles to Diana Ross.

Nick Ashford was born in Fairfield, South Carolina, on May 4, 1943, and Valerie Simpson was born in the Bronx section of New York City on August 26, 1948. The two met in the early 1960s while singing in the same choir at Harlem's White Rock Baptist Church. With Ashford's gift for lyrics and Simpson's exceptional gospel piano and compositional skills, the two began to

write for the staff of Scepter Records in 1964. Two years later, their song "Let's Go Get Stoned" became a hit for Ray Charles.

In 1962, Ashford and Simpson joined Motown's Jobete Music, where they wrote and produced hit songs for Marvin Gaye and Tammi Terrell including "Ain't Nothing Like the Real Thing," "Good Loving Ain't Easy to Come By," and the "Onion Song." Next, they worked with Diana Ross who had just set out to establish a solo career producing such hits as "Remember Me," "Reach Out (and Touch Somebody's Hand)," and an updated version of "Ain't No Mountain High Enough."

Ashford and Simpson's success as songwriters led them to release their own solo recording *Exposed* in 1971. After signing with Warner Brothers in 1973, they recorded a number of hit LPS: *Is It Still Good To Ya* (1978); *Stay Free* (1979); *A Musical Affair* (1980); and their biggest seller *Solid* in 1985. The duo temporarily retired from recording in the late 1980s but they returned to the recording scene in 1996, when they launched their own label Hopsack and Silk. Their first release was a collaboration with renowned poet Maya Angelou titled *Been Found*.

Anita Baker (1958–)
Singer

One of the most sophisticated soul divas to emerge in the 1980s, Baker considers herself "a balladeer" dedicated to singing music rooted in the tradition of gospel music and jazz. Inspired by her idols Mahalia Jackson, Sarah Vaughan, and Nancy Wilson, Baker brings audiences a sincere vocal style which defies commercial trends and electronic overproduction.

Born on January 26, 1958, in Toledo, Ohio, Baker was raised in a single-parent middle class family in Detroit. She first sang in storefront churches, where it was common for the congregation to improvise on various gospel themes. After graduating from Central High School, Baker sang in the Detroit soul/funkgroup Chapter 8. Although Chapter 8 recorded the album *I Just Want To Be Your Girl* for the Ariola label, the group's lack of commercial success caused it to disband, and for the next three years, Baker worked as a receptionist in a law firm.

In 1982, Baker, after signing a contract with Beverly Glen, moved to Los Angeles, where she recorded the critically acclaimed solo album *Songstress*. Following a legal battle with Glen, Baker signed with Elektra and recorded her debut hit album *Rapture* in 1986. As the album's executive producer, Baker sought "a minimalist approach" featuring simple recording techniques which captured the natural sounds of her voice. The LP's single "Sweet Love" brought Baker immediate crossover suc-

Anita Baker (AP/Wide World Photos, Inc.)

cess. Baker's follow-up effort, the multi-platinum selling *Giving You the Best I Got* is considered one of the finest pop music albums of the 1990s. Her third effort *Compositions*, recorded in 1990, featured a number of backup musicians including Detroit jazz guitarist Earl Klugh.

After a nearly four-year hiatus, Baker released the double platinum *Rhythm of Love* in 1994. In 1996, Baker filed lawsuits against Elektra, her management and her legal staff. She subsequently joined the Atlantic label, but as of mid-1999 has yet to release an album on that label. Winner of five Grammys, two NAACP Image Awards, two American Music Awards, two Soul Train Awards, and a star on Hollywood's Walk of Fame, Baker has brought her audiences music of eloquence and integrity that sets her apart from most of her contemporaries.

Chuck Berry (1926–)
Singer, Songwriter, Guitarist

The first guitar hero of rock and roll, Chuck Berry's jukebox hits of the 1950s remain some of the most imaginative poetic tales in the history of popular music. Influenced by such bluesmen as Aaron T-Bone Walker and the picking styles of rockabilly and country musicians, Berry's solo guitar work brought the guitar to the forefront of rhythm and blues. His driving ensemble sound paved the way for the emergence of bands from the Beach Boys to the Rolling Stones.

Born on October 18, 1926, in San Jose, California, Charles Edward Anderson Berry grew up in a middle-

class neighborhood on the outskirts of St. Louis. Berry first sang gospel music at home and at the Antioch Baptist Church. Although Berry was drawn to the sounds of bluesmen such as Tampa Red, Arthur Crudup, and Muddy Waters, he did not become serious about music until he was given a guitar by local rhythm and blues musician Joe Sherman. Taken by the sounds of rhythm and blues, Berry formed a trio with Johnny Jones on piano and Ebby Harding on drums. Hired to play backyard barbecues, clubs, and house parties, the trio expanded their repertoire to include Nat "King" Cole ballads and country songs by Hank Williams.

By 1955, the 28-year-old Berry had become a formidable rhythm and blues guitarist and singer. While in Chicago, Berry visited a club to hear his idol, Muddy Waters, perform. At the suggestion of Waters, Berry visited Chess Studios where he eventually signed with the label. Berry's first hit for Chess was "Maybelline," a country song formerly entitled "Ida May." In 1956 Berry continued on a path toward superstardom with the hits "Roll Over Beethoven," "Oh Baby Doll," followed by "Rock and Roll Music," and the guitar anthem "Johnny B. Goode."

Released from the Indiana Federal Prison in 1964 after serving a sentence for violating the Mann Act, Berry resumed his musical career, recording "Nadine" and "No Particular Place to Go." Since the 1970s, Berry has continued to record and tour. Berry's 1972 release of the novelty tune "My-Ding-a-Ling" became his best-selling single. In 1988, Taylor Hackford paid tribute to the guitar legend in his film *Hail! Hail! Rock 'n Roll.* Berry was also a featured performer at the opening of Cleveland's Rock and Roll Hall of Fame and Museum in 1995.

Mary J. Blige (1971–)
Hip Hop Singer

Born in 1971 in Yonkers, New York, Blige was raised in the Schlobohm housing projects. In her youth, Blige was influenced by the rhythm and blues, soul, and funk albums that her mother played, as well as the early lessons her father, a professional jazz musician, gave her. She landed a record deal when Andre Harrell of Uptown Records heard a karaoke tape which she had recorded at age 16.

Called the inventor of "New Jill Swing" by *Stereo Review*, Blige's debut album *What's the 411?* (1992) sold more than three million copies and her second album *My Life* (1994) went multi-platinum, establishing her career as an international recording star. She won a Grammy Award in 1996 for "You're All I Need," which was a duet with the rapper Method Man. Her third

Mary J. Blige (AP/Wide World Photos, Inc.)

project *Share My World* (1997) was also granted multi-platinum status. Blige has also been dubbed the "Queen of Hip Hop Soul," a designation that characterizes the hallmarks her style: soulful melodies over hip hop rhythm tracks.

Bobby Brown (1966–)
Singer

Savvy and street smart, singer Bobby Brown possesses a charismatic charm which has earned him numerous million-selling records. Born in Boston in 1969, he was a founding member of the successful group New Edition. Brown remained with the group from 1984 to 1987. His solo debut album *Kind of Strange* featured the single "Girlfriend." Brown's second release *Don't Be Cruel* produced the single "Don't Be Cruel," and the video hits "My Prerogative" and "Every Little Step."

In 1990, Brown embarked on a worldwide tour after releasing a successful single from the soundtrack to the hit movie *Ghostbusters II*. In July of 1992 Brown married singer/actress Whitney Houston in a star-studded ceremony. Two years later, the two solo artists performed together for the first time on the televised 1994

Soul Train Music Awards program. Aside from maintaining a burgeoning music career, Brown is the owner of B. Brown Productions, as well as his own private recording studio. Brown's violent temper and brushes with the law were the subject of much publicity in the 1990s, even eclipsing the release of his 1993 recording *Remixes in the Key of B* and the album *Forever* in 1997.

James Brown (1933–)
Singer, Bandleader

James Brown's impact on American and African popular music has been of seismic proportion. His explosive onstage energy and intense gospel music and rhythm and blues-based sound earned him numerous titles such as "The Godfather of Soul," "Mr. Dynamite," and "The Hardest Working Man in Show Business." During the 1960s and early 1970s, Brown's back-up group—called the Flames, the Famous Flames, and then the JBS—emerged as one of the greatest soul bands in the history of modern music, one that served as a major force in the development of funk and fusion jazz.

Born in Barnell, South Carolina, on May 3, 1933, Brown moved to Augusta, Georgia, at the age of four. Although he was raised by various relatives in conditions of economic deprivation, Brown possessed an undaunted determination to succeed at an early age. When not picking cotton, washing cars, or shining shoes, he earned extra money by dancing on the streets and at amateur contests. In the evening, Brown watched shows by such bandleaders as Louis Jordan and Lucky Millinder.

At 15, Brown quit school to take up a full-time music career. In churches, Brown sang with the Swanee Quartet and the Gospel Starlighters, which soon afterward became the rhythm and blues group the Flames. During the same period he also sang and played drums with rhythm and blues bands. While with the Flames, Brown toured extensively, performing a wide range of popular material including the Five Royales's "Baby Don't Do It," the Clovers's "One Mint Julep," and Hank Ballard and the Midnighters's hit "Annie Had a Baby."

In 1956, Brown's talents caught the attention of Syd Nathan, founder of King Records. In the same year, after signing with the Federal label, a subsidiary of King, Brown recorded "Please Please Please." After the Flames disbanded in 1957, Brown formed a new Flames ensemble, featuring former members of Little Richard's band. Back in the studio the following year, Brown recorded "Try Me" which became a Top 50 pop hit. On the road, Brown polished his stage act and singing ability, producing what became known as the "James Brown Sound." His 1965 hit "Papa's Got a Brand New Bag" earned him a Grammy for best rhythm and blues recording, a feat he repeated in 1986 with "Living in America," a song that appeared on the soundtrack of the film *Rocky IV.*

After the release of "Out of Sight," Brown's music exhibited a more polyrhythmic sound as evidenced in staccato horn bursts and contrapuntal bass lines. Each successive release explored increasingly new avenues of popular music. Brown's 1967 hit "Cold Sweat" and the 1968 release "I Got the Feeling" not only sent shock waves through the music industry, they served as textbooks of rhythm for thousands of aspiring musicians. In 1970 Brown disbanded the Flames and formed the JBs, featuring Bootsy Collins. The group produced a string of hits such as "Super Bad" and "Sex Machine." *Universal James* (1993) was Brown's seventy-ninth album.

Despite the negative publicity generated by the oft "in trouble" performer, Brown's career remained effervescent in the late 1980s to 1990s. Inducted into the Rock and Roll Hall of Fame in 1986, the ever popular Brown received the Ray Charles Lifetime Achievement Award from the Rhythm & Blues Foundation as part of the organization's Pioneer Awards program in 1993. Later that year, he was awarded for his lifetime achievements at the Black Radio Exclusive awards banquet in Washington, DC. Also, Steamboat Springs, Colorado, voted to name a bridge after the soulster and Brown's hometown of Augusta, followed suit by naming a street after him. Perhaps the sweetest tribute paid to Brown has been the naming of the James Brown Cookeez by a Georgia-based cookie company. Many of his recordings were reissued in the 1990s, and hundreds of his records have been sampled by those in rap and hip hop circles, illustrating Brown's continuing musical influence.

Ruth Brown (1928–)
Singer

Born Ruth Weston on January 30, 1928, in Portsmouth, Virginia, Ruth was initially influenced by jazz greats Sarah Vaughn, Dinah Washington, and Billie Holiday. She ran away from home in 1945 with trumpeter Jimmy Brown whom she soon married. Initial career frustrations including a serious car accident that hospitalized her for nine months from 1948–1949, delayed her debut. However, her first recording for Atlantic in 1949, "So Long," was a torch ballad hit. In the early 1950s her seductive vocal delivery placed her on the rhythm and blues charts with such tunes as "Teardrops in My Eyes," "I Know," "5-10-15 Hours," and "He Treats Your Daughter Mean." By 1960 she had a dozen rhythm and blues chart hits before her career declined.

Brown raised two sons and worked a nine-to-five job before reviving her career in the mid-1970s with television, movie, and stage appearances including her 1989 Broadway show *Black and Blue* for which she won a Tony Award. In the 1990s Ruth has issued some fine recordings, hosted radio shows on National Public Radio, and formed the nonprofit Rhythm & Blues Foundation, an organization that helps musicians recoup their share of royalties (Ruth has personally endured a nine-year fight with Atlantic to win back her royalties). Ruth's hit-making reign during the 1950s helped establish the prominence of the blues as a market force.

Ray Charles (1930–)
Singer, Pianist, Bandleader

Ray Charles Robinson was born on September 23, 1930, in Albany, Georgia. Blinded by glaucoma at the age of six, Charles received his first musical training at a school for the blind in St. Augustine, Florida. His parents died while he was in his teens, and after playing with local bands Charles moved to Seattle in 1947 where he formed a trio. Influenced by the smooth pop/rhythm and blues style of Charles Brown and Nat King Cole, Charles scored a top ten rhythm and blues hit with "Baby Let Me Hold Your Hand." In the early 1950s he teamed with Guitar Slim and Ruth Brown before scoring a number two rhythm and blues hit with "I Got a Woman" in 1955. This recording was the first to capture Charles's gospel moan and horn-driven arrangements that became his trademarks.

Throughout the 1950s Charles released a string of rhythm and blues hits that combined sophisticated arrangements with the emotional grit of rhythm and blues that would become known as "soul" music. Charles also scored his first top ten pop hit with "What'd I Say," which highlighted Charles's pleading church vocals with a rock and roll piano line. His singing and piano playing drew on many sources including jazz, and he cut pure jazz sides with David "Fathead" Newman and Milt Jackson, helping to imbibe a sense of "soul" and instrumental "funkiness" to the jazz idiom.

By the end of the 1950s, Charles switched to ABC Records and gained artistic control of his work. His pop success was assured with "Hit the Road Jack" followed in 1962 by "I Can't Stop Loving You," a country and western song that topped the charts. Charles was immensely popular through the mid-1960s before his career was halted in 1965 by his involvement with drugs. He emerged with more hits in the late 1960s, although he had begun to focus almost entirely on pop music.

Charles was inducted into the Rock and Roll Hall of Fame in 1986, received a National Medal of Arts in 1993, and took part in the 1995 JVC Newport Jazz Festival. Recipient of more than ten Grammy awards and honorary life chairman of the Rhythm and Blues Hall of Fame,

Ray Charles (AP/Wide World Photos, Inc.)

Charles is also an inductee to the Pop Hall of Fame and the Songwriters Hall of Fame.

George Clinton (1942–)
Singer, Songwriter, Bandleader, Producer

The father of "P. Funk," (i.e., "pure") George Clinton spun the funk formula refined by James Brown into an institution. His groups Parliament and Funkadelic and a panoply of offshoots kept the rest of the rhythm and blues world straining to keep up during the 1970s; by the 1990s, the prodigious body of work recorded under the P. Funk moniker exercised a huge influence on rap, soul, and rock. Though he relied heavily on a group of talented musicians to bring his visions to life, Clinton was the visionary behind the legendary "Parliafunkadelicment Thang."

Born in North Carolina, Clinton moved with his family to New Jersey during his adolescence; there he helped form a doo wop group called The Parliaments. After years of struggling and a move to Detroit, the group managed to sell some songs to other artists, but never achieved success on its own. With the advent of psychedelic rock in the mid-1960s, The Parliaments began to change in form; they morphed into Funkadelic by 1968, adding hard rock guitar and spacey grooves. The early Funkadelic albums, notably *Maggot Brain*, became classics of untamed funk rock.

Clinton deployed Parliament as a slightly more conventional funk vehicle in the early 1970s, emphasizing horns and more dance-oriented arrangements. By the middle of the decade, Parliament had become a major hitmaker with its fantasy-themed concept albums and its circus-like performances. Songs such as "Flash Light," "Bop Gun (Endangered Species)," "Mothership Connection," and "Aqua Boogie" became funk staples.

Funkadelic began to take a more commercial turn, particularly after signing with Warner Bros. Records; its biggest hits came with the albums *One Nation Under a Groove* and *Uncle Jam Wants You*. Clinton helped his bassist Bootsy Collins become a funk legend in his own right, and oversaw albums by such P. Funk enterprises as The Brides of Funkenstein, Parlet, and the P. Funk All-Stars, among many others. He also released a slew of solo recordings; his biggest hit in this capacity was the boisterous "Atomic Dog." Though business declined for these acts during the 1980s, Clinton's influence was constant in African American pop; by the 1990s, P. Funk recordings were among the most sampled in hip hop. Clinton went so far as to set up an easy licensing system for rap artists who wanted to lift from his work. Thanks to the adoration of everyone from Dr. Dre to rockers such as the Red Hot Chili Peppers, Clinton became a ubiquitous figure on the pop culture scene. He fronted the P. Funk All-Stars at the Lollapalooza Festival and appeared in numerous films and television commercials.

Natalie Cole (1950–)
Singer

With five gold records and her star on Hollywood Boulevard, Natalie Cole has emerged since the 1980s as a major pop music star. Born on February 6, 1950, in Los Angeles, Natalie was the second daughter of jazz pianist and pop music legend Nat "King" Cole. During the early 1970s, Cole performed in nightclubs, while pursuing a degree in child psychology at the University of Massachusetts. In 1975, she recorded her first album *Inseparable* at Curtis Mayfield's Custom Studios. Her other albums include: *Thankful* (1978); *I'm Ready* (1983); *Good to Be Back* (1989); *Take a Look* (1993); and *Holly and Ivy* (1994), which coincided with her PBS special "Natalie Cole's Untraditional Traditional Christmas."

In 1991, Cole released a 22-song collection of her father's hits. The album, which contains a remixed version of the original title track "Unforgettable," fea-

tures a duet between Cole and her father and earned her "Record of the Year" and "Album of the Year" Grammys, complementing the Grammys she won in 1976 for best new artist and in 1976 and 1977 for best rhythm and blues female vocal performance. Cole also won two NAACP Image Awards in the mid-1970s and an American Music Award in 1978.

Sean "Puffy" Combs (1969–)
Music Company Executive, Entrepreneur

Sean Combs was born in New York, New York, in 1969. His ear for rap and hip hop combined with his production skills are a proven combination. He began to be noticed at the age of 19 in New York's hip hop scene. As an intern at Uptown Records, Combs's talents earned him a permanent position. He headed Uptown's Artist & Repertoire department where his primary responsibilities were signing and developing new talents.

In 1991 Combs's luck took a turn for the worst. Anxious fans for a charity basketball game rushed the entrance, killing nine people. The event, staged by Combs, put a black mark on his young career. Media attacks and mayoral investigations pushed Combs into a depression. Unable to work, Combs confined himself to his Mt. Vernon, New York, home. Within a year, Combs was fired from Uptown.

Frustration and rejection inspired Combs to pursue his life's dreams. Comb's talent had earned him a reputation, prompting Arista Records to sign him to a deal. Combs called this division of Arista Records Bad Boy Entertainment. Success soon followed as Bad Boy released hits by rappers Craig Mack and the Notorious B.I.G., both of whom Combs is credited for discovering.

The ability to find such talent sets Combs apart from most other hip hop producers. The success of Bad Boy's hip hop artists led to the development of new artists. Various projects including the 1996 release of singer Faith Evans's debut kept Combs busy. After the shooting death of his friend, Notorious B.I.G., on March 7, 1999, Combs rewrote some of the lyrics on his own debut album *No Way Out*. The album produced three hit singles including "I'll Be Missing You," a tribute to Notorious B.I.G. Combs continues to be driven to succeed, opening up a soul food restaurant in Manhattan and a clothing label in the late 1990s.

Sam Cooke (1931–1964)
Singer, Songwriter

Sam Cooke's sophisticated vocal style and refined image made him one of the greatest pop music idols of the early 1960s. One of the first gospel music artists to

Sam Cooke (AP/Wide World Photos, Inc.)

crossover into popular music, Cooke produced songs of timeless quality, filled with human emotion and spiritual optimism.

Born in Clarksdale, Mississippi, on January 2, 1931, Sam Cooke grew up the son of a Baptist minister in Chicago, Illinois. At the age of nine, Cooke, along with two sisters and a brother, formed a gospel group called the Singing Children. While a teenager, he joined the gospel group the Highway QCs which performed on the same bill with nationally famous gospel acts.

By 1950, Cooke replaced tenor Rupert H. Harris as lead singer for the renowned gospel group the Soul Stirrers. Cooke's first recording with the Soul Stirrers, "Jesus Gave Me Water," was recorded for Art Rupe's Specialty label. Although the song revealed the inexperience of the twenty-year-old Cooke, it exhibited a quality of immense passion and heightened feeling. Under the pseudonym Dale Cooke, Sam recorded the pop song "Loveable" in 1957. That same year, in a session for producer Bumps Blackwell on the Keen label, Cooke recorded "You Send Me" which climbed to number one on the rhythm and blues charts. On the Keen label, Cooke recorded eight more consecutive hits including "Everyone Likes to Cha Cha Cha," "Only Sixteen," and

"Wonderful World," all of which were written or co-written by Cooke.

After his contract with the Keen label expired in 1960, Cooke signed with RCA, and was assigned to staff producers Hugo Peretti and Luigi Creatore. In August, Cooke's recording "Chain Gang" reached the number two spot on the pop charts. Under the lavish production of Hugo and Luigi, Cooke produced a string of hits such as "Cupid" in 1961, "Twistin' the Night Away" in 1962, and "Another Saturday Night" in 1963. Early in 1964, Cooke appeared on the "Tonight Show," debuting two songs from his upcoming LP which included the gospel-influenced composition "A Change Is Gonna Come." On December 11, Cooke checked into a three-dollar-a-night motel where he demanded entrance into the night manager's room. After a brief physical struggle, the manager fired three pistol shots which mortally wounded Cooke. Despite his tragic death, Cooke left behind a catalogue of classic recordings and over one hundred original compositions including the hit "Shake," which was posthumously released in 1965.

Fats Domino (1928–)
Singer

Antoine Domino was born on February 26, 1928, in New Orleans. As a teenager, Domino received piano lessons from Harrison Verret. In between playing night clubs, Domino worked at a factory and mowed lawns around New Orleans. At age 20, he took a job as a pianist with bassist Billy Diamond's combo at the Hideaway Club. At some point in his early career, his five foot-five-inch, two-hundred-pound frame led to the nickname "Fats."

In 1949, while playing with Diamond's group, Domino was discovered by producer and arranger David Bartholomew, a talent scout, musician, and producer for the Imperial label. During the following year, Domino hit the charts with the autobiographical tune "Fat Man." After the release of "Fat Man," he played on tour backed by Bartholomew's band.

Although Domino released a number of sides during the early 1950s, it was not until 1955 that he gained national prominence with the hit "Ain't That A Shame." In the next six years, Domino scored 35 top hits with songs such as "Blueberry Hill" (1956), "Blue Monday" (1957), "Whole Lotta Lovin" (1958), and "I'm Walkin" (1959). Domino's recording success led to his appearance in several films in the 1950s including *The Girl Can't Help It*, *Shake Rattle and Roll*, *Disc Jockey Jamboree*, and *The Big Beat*.

After Domino's contract with Imperial expired in 1963, he signed with ABC where he made a number of commercial recordings. In 1965 Domino moved to Mercury and then to Reprise in 1968. In the early 1970s, Domino began to tour with greater regularity than he had during the peak of his career. In 1995, while on tour in England, Domino was hospitalized for infection and exhaustion. Despite suggestions his health is in decline, Domino continues to work on new material, and honors flow his way. These honors include a Rhythm and Blues Foundation Pioneer Award in 1995 and a National Medal for the Arts in 1998.

Dr. Dre (1965?–)
Rap Singer, Producer

From the time he was four years old, Dr. Dre, born Andre Ramelle Young, was playing DJ at his mother's parties. In 1981, he heard a song by Grandmaster Flash that inspired him to change his name in honor of basketball star Julius "Dr. J." Erving and become a DJ. Dr. Dre began spinning records at a Los Angeles nightclub, producing the dance tapes in the club's four-track studio. In addition to using the rap trademarks of sampling, scratching, and drum machines, he added keyboards and vocals.

In 1982, when Dre was 17 years old, he formed the World Class Wreckin' Cru with another DJ. Their first independently released single sold 50,000 copies. The following year, Dre graduated from Compton, California's Centennial High School. He was offered a mechanical drafting position with an aircraft firm, but he turned it down to devote himself to music. In 1985, Dr. Dre joined the newly formed group, N.W.A. (Niggaz With Attitude), along with Ice Cube, Eazy E, Yella, M. C. Ren, and Arabian Prince. That year he also produced Eazy E's first platinum album *Eazy-Duz-It.*

N.W.A's successful yet controversial body of work included the multi-platinum *Straight Outta Compton,* released in 1989 on Eazy E and Dr. Dre's Ruthless Records. Dr. Dre produced the D.O.C., a rapper he had discovered in Texas. The result was that the album *No One Can Do It Better* went to number one on *Billboard's* R&B album chart. Dre also produced a platinum album for Michel'le, another number one recording.

In January of 1990, Ice Cube left N.W.A. over a financial dispute; N.W.A. recorded the last of their four recordings without him in 1991. Later that year, Dre left Ruthless to co-found Death Row Records with Suge Knight. Dre's first solo effort *The Chronic* was released in 1993. The work, featuring such budding rap artists as Snoop Doggy Dogg, sold three million copies. He went on to produce Snoop's debut *Doggystyle.*

In 1994, Dre received a Grammy Award for best rap solo performance. At the *Source* Awards, he was named best producer, solo artist, and *The Chronic* was named best album. The following year he was named "One of

Dr. Dre (Interscope Records, Inc.)

the Top 10 Artists That Mattered Most, 1985–1995" by *Spin*. In 1996, Dre stunned the hip hop community by announcing that he was leaving Death Row. He had hoped that the label would spread into other genres such as jazz and reggae, but rap continued to bring in the money, and others did not share his vision. Instead, Dre started his own label, Aftermath Entertainment. He continues to edit videos, in addition to penning his biography. He also appeared in small acting role in the 1996 film *Set It Off*.

Eazy E (1963–1995)
Rap Singer

Born Eric Wright in 1963 in Compton, Louisiana, Eazy E was a former drug dealer who founded Ruthless Records. He was co-founder of the innovative and controversial group N.W.A. (Niggaz With Attitude) that is credited with establishing the gangsta' strain of rap music in the early 1990s. N.W.A. included Eazy, Dr. Dre, Ice Cube, and DJ Yella. The group released clean and explicit versions of their recordings.

Between 1988 and 1991, N.W.A. had many commercial successes despite (and perhaps because of) their

Eazy E (Corbis Corporation [Bellevue])

Kenneth "Babyface" Edmonds holding two Grammy Awards (AP/Wide World Photos, Inc.).

hardcore image including the project *Straight Outta Compton* (1989), which went multi-platinum. Eazy also excelled at production, launching groups such as J.J. Fad, Above the Law, the D.O.C., Michel'le, the Jewish rap group Blood of Abraham, H.W.A (Hoez With Attitude), and Bone Thugs N Harmony. He died of complications from AIDS in 1995.

Kenneth "Babyface" Edmonds (1958?–)
Songwriter, Producer

Edmonds was born in the late 1950s in Indianapolis, Indiana, and spent his high school years finagling interviews with pop star idols such as the Jackson 5 and Stevie Wonder. After performing in a number of rhythm and blues bands, Edmonds began a collaboration with Antonio "L.A." Reid in 1981; they were then members of an act called the Deele, but soon gained acclaim writing and producing songs for other artists such as Shalamar and Bobby Brown.

In 1989, Edmonds and Reid formed their own company, LaFace Records, backed by the Arista label. They continued their success in writing and producing pop,

soul, and rhythm and blues hits for such artists as Paula Abdul and Whitney Houston, and Edmonds and Reid are also credited with giving considerable start to the careers of TLC and Toni Braxton. The duo has won numerous Grammy Awards including one for producer of the year for the 1993 soundtrack to the Eddie Murphy film *Boomerang* and have shared several songwriter of the year honors from Broadcast Music Inc. (BMI).

Edmonds is also a popular solo artist and performer in his own right, with three well-received releases to his name including the 1993 release *For the Cool in You*, a platinum seller whose hit "When Can I See You" brought him the 1993 Grammy for best male rhythm and blues vocalist. For several months between 1994 and 1995 Edmonds was on the road, performing as an opening act for Boyz II Men, yet another one of the enormously successful groups he has written for and produced. In late 1995 he gained further accolades for producing for the soundtrack to the acclaimed film *Waiting to Exhale*. In 1997 Edmonds released the recording *Babyface: MTV Unplugged* and followed it up with a Christmas album in 1998. Edmonds continues to flourish as a record mogul, performer, and movie producer.

Roberta Flack (1939–)
Singer, Pianist

Born in Black Mountain, North Carolina, on February 10, 1939, Roberta Flack moved to Washington, DC, with her parents at the age of nine. Three years later she studied classical piano with prominent African American concert musician Hazel Harrison. After winning several talent contests, Flack won a scholarship to Howard University, where she graduated with a bachelors degree in music education. During the early 1960s, Flack taught music in the Washington, DC, public school system.

While playing a club date in 1968, Flack was discovered by Les McCann whose connections resulted in a contract with Atlantic Records. Flack's first album *First Take* appeared in 1970 and included the hit song "The First Time Ever I Saw Your Face." Throughout the 1970s, Flack landed several hits such as "Killing Me Softly With His Song" and "The Closer I Get to You," a duet with Donny Hathaway; both songs earned Grammys, and "Killing Me Softly" was remade in 1996 by the rap group The Fugees. In the early 1980s, Flack collaborated with Peabo Bryson to record the hit "Tonight I Celebrate My Love For You." In 1991, Flack enjoyed another Top 10 hit "Set the Night to Music," a duet with Maxi Priest. More recently, Flack has been involved in educational projects, and in 1994, she recorded the album *Roberta*, a Grammy nominated recording of jazz, blues and pop classics.

Aretha Franklin (1942–)
Singer, Pianist, Songwriter

During the 1960s, the collaboration of Aretha Franklin and Atlantic Records producer Jerry Wexler brought forth some of the deepest and most sincere popular music ever recorded. As "Queen of Soul," Franklin has reigned supreme since the late 1960s. Her voice brings spiritual inspiration to her gender, race, and the world.

Daughter of the famous Reverend Charles L. Franklin, Aretha was born on March 25, 1942, in Memphis, Tennessee. Raised on Detroit's east side, Franklin sang at her father's New Bethel Baptist Church. Although she began to study piano at age eight, Franklin refused to learn what she considered juvenile and simple tunes. Thus, she learned piano by ear, occasionally receiving instruction from individuals such as the Reverend James Cleveland. Franklin's singing skills were modeled after gospel music singers and family friends including Clara Ward and rhythm and blues artists such as Ruth Brown and Sam Cooke.

At 14, Franklin quit school to go on the road with her father's Franklin Gospel Caravan, an endless tour in which the family traveled thousands of miles by car.

After four years on the road, Aretha traveled to New York City to establish her own career as a pop artist. In 1960, she signed with Columbia Records talent scout John Hammond. Her six year stay at Columbia Records, however, produced only a few hits and little material that suited Franklin's unique talents.

In 1966, Franklin signed with Atlantic Records, and, in the following year, recorded a session for Wexler that resulted in the hit "I Never Loved a Man (The Way That I Loved You)." That same year, Franklin's career received another boost when her reworking of Otis Redding's song "Respect" hit the charts. Franklin's first LP *I Never Loved a Man* was followed by a succession of artistically and commercially successful albums: *Aretha Arrives*, *Lady Soul*, *Aretha Now!*, and *This Girl's In Love With You*. Her prominence grew so great that Franklin appeared on the cover of *Time* magazine in 1968. That year she performed at Martin Luther King, Jr.'s funeral and at the Democratic National Convention.

During the 1970s, Franklin continued to tour and record. In 1971, she released the live LP *Aretha Live at the Fillmore West*, backed by the horn and rhythm section of Tower of Power. Her next release *Amazing Grace* featured Reverend James Cleveland and the Southern California Community Choir. In 1977, she performed at President Jimmy Carter's inauguration, later doing the same for U.S. president Bill Clinton in 1993.

In 1980, Franklin appeared in the film *The Blues Brothers*. No stranger to television, she appeared in the specials "Aretha," "Aretha Franklin: The Queen of Soul," and "Duets," in 1986, 1988, and 1993, respectively. The 1980s also saw Franklin score her first big commercial success in more than a decade with the album *Who's Zooming Who?*, featuring the single "Freeway of Love." In 1988, she released a double-live LP *One Lord, One Faith*—an effort dedicated to her father who passed away the previous year.

Franklin has won 15 Grammy Awards in her career including the lifetime achievement award, which was bestowed upon her in 1995. Other of her honors include an American Music Award and an *Ebony* magazine American Black Achievement Award, both in 1984; declaration as a "natural resource" of the state of Michigan in 1985; induction into the Rock and Roll Hall of Fame in 1987; an Essence Award in 1993; and a Kennedy Center Honors Award in 1994. Only Janet Jackson has matched Franklin's record of 14 gold singles, the most by a female solo artist.

Franklin has stayed active in the 1990s, a decade in which many of her classic recordings were reissued. She was a headliner at the 1994 New Orleans Jazz and Heritage Festival and lent a track to the 1995 *Waiting to*

Aretha Franklin (AP/Wide World Photos, Inc.)

Exhale soundtrack. In 1995, Franklin embarked on a new venture, launching her own label, World Class Records. Franklin also performed on the 1998 VH-1 concert special "Divas Live," along with Gloria Estefan, Celine Dion, Mariah Carey, Shania Twain, and others. The concert raised money to fund music education in elementary schools. Finally, in a celebrated July 17, 1999 concert of the "Three Tenors"—Luciano Pavarotti, José Carreras, and Placido Domingo—in Detroit, Franklin performed the national anthem.

The Fugees
Hip Hop Singing Group

With a sound most often described as "eclectic," the Fugees landed on the hip hop charts in 1993 with their Ruff House debut *Blunted on Reality*. Initially known as the Tranzlator Crew, Lauryn Hill, Prakazrel "Pras" Michel, and Wyclef Jean have been working together since teenagers in northern New Jersey. They were forced to change their name when a 1980s new wave band called Translator filed a legal protest.

Released under the name Fugees, their first album *Blunted on Reality* (1993) received rave reviews. Sales

for the album were moderate, while critics announced that Hill should pursue a solo career.

With sales of 17 million, the trio's second release *The Score* (1996) made them the biggest selling rap act in history. Produced by Jean and Hill, the album included covers of Roberta Flack's "Killing Me Softly with His Song" and Bob Marley's "No Woman, No Cry." The band made great strides in bringing hip hop with a positive attitude to a new generation.

The Fugees remained together and planned future releases as a group at the end of 1997, but each member also embarked on individual projects. Jean released his multi-platinum solo debut *The Carnival* (1997). The album was well-received in the United States and in his native Haiti. Michel's solo efforts culminated in *Ghetto Superstar* (1998). Also in 1998, Hill released her debut solo album *The Miseducation of Lauryn Hill*, which brought her an unprecedented five Grammy Awards.

Marvin Gaye (1939–1984)
Singer, Songwriter

The son of a Pentecostal minister, Marvin Gay was born on April 29, 1939, in Washington, DC (the final "e"

Lauryn Hill of The Fugees (Corbis Corporation [Bellevue])

Marvin Gaye holding a Grammy Award in 1982 (AP/Wide World Photos, Inc.).

on his surname was not added until the early 1960s). Raised in a segregated slum-ridden section of Washington DC, Gaye experienced a strict religious upbringing. As Gaye later recalled: "Living with my father was like living with a king, a very peculiar, changeable, cruel, and all-powerful king." Thus Gaye looked to music for release. Around the age of three, he began singing in church. While attending Cardoza High School, Gaye studied drums, piano, and guitar. Uninspired by his formal studies, Gaye often cut classes to watch James Brown and Jackie Wilson perform at the Howard Theatre.

Soon afterward, Gaye served a short time in the Air Force, until obtaining an honorable discharge in 1957. Returning to Washington, DC, Gaye joined the doo wop group the Marquees. After recording for Columbia Record's subsidiary label, Okeh, the Marquees moved to the Chess/Checker label where they recorded with Bo Diddley. Although the Marquees performed their own compositions and toured regularly, they failed to gain popularity. It was not until they were introduced to Harvey Fuqua, who was in the process of reforming Moonglows, that the Marquees attracted notice in the pop music world. Impressed by their sound, Fuqua hired the Marquees to form a group under the new name

Harvey and the Moonglows. Still under contract at Chess, Fuqua brought the Moonglows to the company's studio in Chicago to record the 1959 hit the "Ten Commandments of Love."

In 1960, Fuqua and Gaye traveled to Detroit where Fuqua set up his own label and signed with Motown's subsidiary, Anna. After a stint as a backup singer, studio musician, and drummer in Smokey Robinson's touring band, Gaye signed a contract with Motown as a solo artist. Released in 1962, Gaye's first album was a jazz-oriented effort entitled *The Soulful Moods of Marvin Gaye*. With his sights on a career modeled after the ballad singer Frank Sinatra, Gaye was not enthusiastic when Motown suggested he record a dance record of rhythm and blues material. Nevertheless, Gaye recorded the song "Stubborn Kind of Fellow" in 1962; it entered the Top 10 R&B charts. This was followed by a long succession of Motown hits, such as "Hitch Hike," "Pride and Joy," "Can I Get a Witness," and "Wonderful One."

Motown's next projects for Gaye included a number of vocal duets, the first of which appeared with singer Mary Wells on the 1964 album *Together*. In collaboration with singer Kim Weston, Gaye recorded the 1967 hit LP *It Takes Two*. His most successful partnership, however, was with Tammi Terrell. In their two-year association, Gaye and Terrell recorded, under the writing and production team of Ashford and Simpson, such hits as "Ain't No Mountain High Enough" and "Your Precious Love" and "Ain't Nothing Like the Real Thing" in 1968.

Back in the studio as a solo act, Gaye recorded the hit "Heard It Through the Grapevine." With his growing success, Gaye achieved greater creative independence at Motown, which led him to co-produce the 1971 hit album *What's Going On*, a session producing the best selling singles "What's Going On," "Mercy Mercy (the Ecology)," and "Inner City Blues (Make Me Wanna Holler)."

After his last LP for Motown *In Our Lifetime*, Gaye signed with CBS Records in April 1981, and within the next year released the album *Midnight Lover*, featuring the Grammy Award-winning hit "Sexual Healing." On Sunday, April 1, 1984, after a heated argument, Gaye was fatally shot by his father in Los Angeles, California. Despite his public image, Gaye had suffered from years of inner conflict and drug abuse. "This tragic ending can only be softened by the memory of a beautiful human being," described long-time friend Smokey Robinson. "He could be full of joy sometimes, but at others, full of woe, but in the end how compassionate, how wonderful, how exciting was Marvin Gaye and his music."

Berry Gordy, Jr. (1929–)
Music Company Executive

From assembly line worker to impresario of the Motown Record Corporation, Berry Gordy, Jr. emerged as the owner of one of the largest African American-owned businesses in American history. A professional boxer, songwriter, producer, and businessman, Gordy has been a self-made man. Through his determination and passion for music, the living legend helped create one of the most celebrated sounds of modern music.

The seventh of eight children, Berry Gordy was born on November 28, 1929, in Detroit. Berry Gordy, Sr., the owner of a grocery store, a plastering company, and a printing shop, taught his children the value of hard work and family unity. Despite his dislike for manual labor, Berry possessed a strong desire to become commercially successful. After quitting high school to become a professional boxer, Berry won several contests before leaving the profession in 1950. A year later, Gordy was drafted into the U.S. Army, where he earned a high school equivalency diploma.

Upon returning from a military tour of Korea in 1953, Berry opened the 3-D Record Mart, a jazz-oriented retail store. Forced into bankruptcy, Berry closed the store in 1955, and subsequently took a job as an assembly line worker at the Ford Motor Company. His nightly visits to Detroit's thriving jazz and rhythm and blues scene inspired Gordy to take up songwriting. In 1957, one of Gordy's former boxing colleagues, Jackie Wilson, recorded the hit "Reet Petite," a song written by Berry, his sister Gwen, and Billy Davis. Over the next four years,

the Berry-Gwen-Davis writing team provided Wilson with four more hits: "To Be Loved," "Lonely Teardrops," "That's Why (I Love You So)," and "I'll Be Satisfied."

By 1959, Billy Davis and Gwen Gordy founded the Anna label, which distributed material through Chess Records in Chicago. Barret Strong's recording of "Money (That's What I Want)," written by Gordy and Janie Bradford, became the label's biggest selling single. With background as a writer and producer with the Anna label, Gordy decided to start his own company. In 1959, he formed Jobete Music Publishing, Berry Gordy, Jr. Enterprises, Hitsville USA, and the Motown Record Corporation. Employing a staff of local studio musicians, writers, and producers, Berry's label scored its first hit in 1961 with Smokey Robinson's "Shop Around." By the mid-1960s, Gordy assembled a wealth of talent including The Supremes, The Four Tops, The Marvelettes, Marvin Gaye, and Stevie Wonder.

In 1971, Gordy relocated the Motown Recording Corporation to Los Angeles. Although most of the original acts and staff members did not join the company's migration to the West Coast, Gordy's company became one of the country's top African American-owned businesses. Throughout the 1970s and 1980s, Motown continued to produce artists such as the Jackson Five, the Commodores, Lionel Richie, Rick James, and DeBarge. Gordy also tried his hand at producing feature films. *Lady Sings the Blues* (1972), *Mahogany* (1975), and *The Last Dragon* (1985) were not critical successes, but attracted the participation of such celebrities as Diana Ross, Billy Dee Williams, Richard Pryor, and Vanity. Faced with financial problems, Gordy signed a distribution agreement with MCA in 1984 and sold the label in entirety to the giant six years later.

Gordy's induction into the Hall of Fame in 1988 brought recognition to a giant of the recording industry who helped transform the sound of popular music. He was honored with a lifetime achievement award at the 1993 Black Radio Exclusive awards banquet ceremony. Among *Forbes*'s four hundred richest Americans in the mid-1980s, Gordy authored his autobiography *To Be Loved: The Music, the Magic, the Memories of Motown* in 1994.

Al Green (1946–)
Singer, Songwriter, Preacher

Possessing one of the supplest voices in popular music, Al Green launched a series of hits up the soul charts during the 1970s. But the Arkansas native turned his back on pop later in that decade, singing gospel and preaching in a Memphis church. His influence on the development of soul was such, however, that he was tempted back to the secular realm for a 1996 album.

Green spent his early years singing gospel in the South, but switched to pop and scored a hit "Back Up Train" in 1967. It was not until he hooked up with producer Willie Mitchell, however, that he found his niche. Recording for Mitchell's Hi Records in Memphis with an ace band, Green managed a remarkable synthesis of intimate, romantic pop and gritty soul. The fruits of this happy union included "Tired of Being Alone," "Love and Happiness," "Let's Stay Together," and "I'm Still in Love With You." His smoldering "Take Me to the River" was covered by numerous other artists.

Though he was "born again" into Christianity in 1973, Green continued to record largely secular music—albeit with a religious tinge—for several years. After founding his own church, the Full Gospel Tabernacle, in Memphis, he returned to gospel music. His recordings won regular honors in gospel circles and even a Grammy Award, but his presence continued to be felt in the soul/rhythm and blues world. Apart from the occasional duet, however, he steered clear of pop until his return in 1995 with *Your Heart's In Good Hands*.

M.C. Hammer (1963–)
Rap Singer

Born Stanley Kirk Burrell in 1963 in East Oakland, California, M.C. Hammer began his career with a group he formed called "The Holy Ghost Boys," in which he performed religious raps during the mid-1980s in Oakland clubs. Hammer recorded his first song "Ring 'Em" in his basement and sold the 12-inch copies out of his car trunk. The song rose to number one in the San Francisco Bay area.

In 1988 Capitol Records re-released his first album, renaming it *Let's Get It Started*. It produced three Top 10 singles and went double platinum. Hammer's second album *Please Hammer, Don't Hurt 'Em*, released in 1990, remained on *Billboard*'s pop chart for 21 weeks. Hammer became internationally known for a "crossover" style rap, colorful costumes, and showy style of dance. His "Can't Touch This" single produced a hit video hailed for its innovative production and Hammer's energetic dancing. Hammer's 1991 *Too Legit to Quit*, which went multi-platinum, leveled a critique at the use of samples in hip hop music, using live musicians and vocalists. Hammer's star rose quickly, and he became a veritable cottage industry in the early 1990s.

Hammer turned to the production end of the business and launched the careers of 3.5.7., Angie B., and Special Generation; he also managed Heavy D. & the Boyz, Troop, Ralph Tresvant., and boxer Evander Holyfield for a short time. Hammer's music has been featured in such films as *Rocky V, Teenage Mutant Ninja Turtles*, and *The Addams Family*. He has won many honors including three Grammy Awards, seven American Mu-

M.C. Hammer (Corbis Corporation [Bellevue])

sic Awards, three Soul Train Awards, and two MTV Awards. After a slump in popularity, mounting criticism from the hip hop critics about his blatant commercialism, and ensuing financial problems, Hammer returned to Christian music in 1997, proclaiming a new music ministry of evangelism with the project *Family Affair*.

Andre Harrell (1962?–)
Music Company Executive, Producer, Musician

Andre O'Neal Harrell was born in the Bronx, New York. While growing up with hard times in the housing projects there, young Harrell developed a desire to succeed. As a teenager, Harrell teamed up with Alonzo Brown to form the playful rap duo Dr. Jekyll (Harrell) and Mr. Hyde (Brown). Before long, they had three Top 20 hits under their belts and were carving a niche for themselves in rap.

Despite the his early rap success, Harrell enrolled in classes at the Bronx's Lehman College. After three years of study in communications and business management, Harrell met Russell Simmons in 1983. Simmons lured Harrell to come work for him at Rush Management, a company that helped define the hip hop of the day. Within two years, Harrell had worked his way to vice president and general manager and was instrumental in building the career of such rap icons as LL Cool J, Run-DMC, and Whodini.

Success continued to follow Harrell wherever he went. He left Rush Management to begin his own record company, Uptown Records. In 1988, the achievements of Uptown Records prompted a $75,000 record deal from music mega-company MCA. Artists such as Al B Sure!, Guy, and Heavy D all prospered under Harrell's direction. By 1992, Uptown and their artists had blazed a shiny trail of gold and platinum albums and had landed an unprecedented $50 million multimedia agreement with MCA. Soon projects such as the television show "In Living Color" and a showcase of Uptown recording artists including Mary J. Blige and Jodeci on MTV's "Unplugged" were in the works. In 1995, Harrell left the reins of Uptown to become the new president/CEO of Motown Records.

Issac Hayes (1942–)
Singer, Pianist, Producer

Born on August 20, 1942, in Covington, Tennessee, Issac Hayes moved to Memphis at age seven, where he was introduced to the sounds of blues, country western, and the music of idol Sam Cooke. Through the connections of saxophonist Floyd Newman, Hayes began a career as a studio musician for Stax Records in 1964. After playing piano on a session for Otis Redding, Hayes formed a partnership with songwriter Dave Porter. Together they were responsible for supplying a number of hits to Carla Thomas, William Bell, and Eddie Floyd.

The first real break for the Hayes-Porter team came when they were recruited to produce the Miami-based soul duo Sam and Dave. In the span of four years, Hayes and Porter succeeded in making Sam and Dave Stax's hottest selling act, producing such hits as "Hold On I'm Coming," "Soul Man," and "I Thank You!" During this period Hayes and Porter continued to perform in a group that established them as an underground legend in the Memphis music scene.

In the late 1960s, Hayes's solo career emerged in an impromptu fashion, when a late night session with drummer Al Jackson and bassist Duck Dunn prompted Stax to release his next effort. *Hot Buttered Soul* went double platinum in 1969. Featuring a soul version of the country song "By the Time I Get to Phoenix," Hayes's rendition set a trend for the disco/soul sound of the 1970s. Following the release of the albums *To Be Continued* and *Issac Hayes Movement*, Hayes recorded the soundtrack for the "blaxplotation" film *Shaft* and the album *Black Moses*. In 1971, "Theme from *Shaft*" won an Academy Award for best song in a motion picture and

Grammy Awards for best instrumental and best original score for a motion picture. *Black Moses* earned a Grammy, too, this one for best pop instrumental performance.

Hayes left the Stax label to join ABC in 1974. Hayes recorded a series of disco albums. In 1977, the commercial downturn in Hayes's career forced him to file bankruptcy. Though he composed Dionne Warwick's "Déjà Vu,"—nominated for a Grammy in 1978—his last gold record "Don't Let Go" was released on the Polydor label in 1979. Hayes moved into the 1980s and 1990s appearing on television shows and in such films as the futuristic thriller *Escape From New York* (1981) and the comedy spoof *Robin Hood: Men in Tights* (1993).

Winner of a 1994 Georgy Award, as bestowed by the Georgia Music Hall of Fame, Hayes has heavily influenced the music of the late 1980s and early 1990s; together with James Brown, Hayes has been one of the most frequently sampled artists by purveyors of rap. Choosing not to jump ship, however, Hayes has stuck to his own brand of "hot buttered soul." In 1995, he issued his first new recordings in seven years—*Branded* and *Raw and Refined*—and contributed a track to the Hughes brothers' film *Dead Presidents*. Hayes has also lent his voice to the role of "Chef" on the Cable Ace Award-winning animated show *South Park*, a role that has introduced him to a new generation of fans.

Jimi Hendrix (1942–1970)
Guitarist, Songwriter

When Jimi Hendrix arrived on the international rock music scene in 1967, he almost single handedly redefined the sound of the electric guitar. Hendrix' extraordinary approach has shaped the course of music from jazz fusion to heavy metal.

On November 27, 1942, in Seattle, Washington, Johnny Allen Hendrix was born to an enlisted U.S. Army soldier and a teenage mother. Four years later, Johnny Allen was renamed James Marshall Hendrix. Because of his mother's fondness for night club life and his father's frequent absences, Hendrix was a lonely, yet creative, child. At school he won several contests for his science fiction-based poetry and visual art. At the age of eight, Hendrix, unable to afford a guitar, strummed out rhythms on a broom. Eventually, he graduated to a fabricated substitute made from a cigar box, followed by a ukelele, and finally an acoustic guitar that was purchased by his father.

By the late 1950s, Hendrix began to play in local bands in Seattle. While a teenager, he played along with recordings by blues artists such as Elmore James and John Lee Hooker. After a 26-month stint (1961–1962) in the 101st Airborne Division, Hendrix played in the Nashville rhythm and blues scene with bassist Billy Cox. For the next three years, Hendrix performed under the name Jimi James, backing up acts such as Little Richard, Jackie Wilson, Ike and Tina Turner, and the Isley Brothers.

In 1964 Hendrix moved to New York City where he performed in various Greenwich Village clubs. While in New York he formed the group Jimi James and the Blue Flames. After being discovered by producer and manager Chas Chandler, the former bassist with the Animals, Hendrix was urged to leave for England. Arriving in England in 1966, Hendrix, along with bassist Noel Redding and drummer Mitch Mitchell, formed the Jimi Hendrix Experience. In 1967, after touring Europe, the trio hit the charts with a cover version of the Leaves song "Hey Joe." In the same year, the group released the groundbreaking album *Are You Experienced?*

In 1968 the Experience recorded *Axis Bold As Love* which led to extensive touring in the United States and Europe. On the Experience's next LP *Electric Ladyland*, Hendrix sought to expand the group's trio-based sound. A double record effort, *Electric Ladyland* featured numerous guest artists such as keyboardists Steve Winwood and Al Kooper, saxophonist Freddie Smith, and conga player Larry Faucette. The record also contained "All Along the Watchtower," a song written by Hendrix's musical and poetic idol Bob Dylan.

After the Experience broke up in 1969, Hendrix played the Woodstock Music and Arts Festival with the Gypsy Sons and Rainbows, featuring bassist Billy Cox. Along with drummer Buddy Miles, Hendrix and Cox formed the Band of Gypsys, and in 1970 the group released an album under the same title. Months later, Mitchell replaced Miles on drums. In August, the Mitchell-Cox lineup played behind Hendrix at his last major performance held at England's Isle of Wight Festival. On September 18, 1970, Hendrix died of a sleeping pill overdose in a hotel room in England. Despite his short career, Hendrix established himself as a major figure in pop music history. In 1992, Hendrix was inducted into the Rock and Roll Hall of Fame.

Whitney Houston (1963–)
Model, Singer, Actress

A multiple Grammy Award winner whose face has graced the covers of magazines from *Glamour* to *Cosmopolitan*, Whitney Houston emerged as one of the most vibrant popular music talents during the 1980s. A talented singer, model, and actress, Houston dominated the pop charts into the 1990s. Her biggest successes were associated with two motion pictures in which she had major roles.

Born on August 9, 1963, Houston grew up in East Orange, New Jersey. As a member of the New Hope

Whitney Houston (Arista Records, Inc.)

Baptist Choir, she made her singing debut at age 11. Later, Houston appeared as a backup singer on numerous recordings, featuring her mother, Cissy Houston, and cousin Dionne Warwick. Despite her success as a fashion model, Houston found the profession "degrading," and, subsequently, quit in order to seek a career in music. She backed up the likes of Chaka Khan, Lou Rawls, and the Neville Brothers.

By age 19, Houston had received several recording contract offers. In 1985, she released her debut album on the Arista label entitled *Whitney Houston*, which produced four hits: "Saving All My Love for You," which won the Grammy for best female pop performance; "You Give Good Love"; "How Will I Know," which earned an MTV Video Music Award for best female video; and "The Greatest Love of All." The album won seven American Music Awards, a feat she would duplicate in 1994. Houston's second LP *Whitney* appeared in 1987, and just as her first effort, the work spawned a number of hits including "I Wanna Dance With Somebody," "Didn't We Almost Have It All," "So Emotional," "Where Do Broken Hearts Go?," and "Love Will Save the Day." The album received four American Music Awards. Following the success of her second record, Houston released *One Moment In Time* (1988) and the slickly produced *I'm Your Baby Tonight* (1990).

In 1992, Houston married singer Bobby Brown and made her acting debut in the film *The Bodyguard*, co-starring Kevin Costner. The first single from the soundtrack, a remake of Dolly Parton's "I Will Always Love You," spent 14 straight weeks on top of the pop singles chart; according to statistics from *Billboard* magazine, Houston set a record for the most time spent at the top of the charts, edging out Boyz II Men's "End of the Road" (13 weeks) and Elvis Presley's "Don't Be Cruel" (11 weeks). Her vocal performance on the soundtrack won her seven American Music Awards including the 1994 Award of Merit; four Grammy Awards including record of the year, album of the year, and best female pop performance; two Soul Train Music Awards including the Sammy Davis, Jr. Entertainer of the Year Award and the Female Rhythm and Blues Single Award for "I Will Always Love You;" four NAACP Image Awards; and the National Association of Black Owned Broadcasters's lifetime achievement award. Later in the year, AT&T signed Houston as the spokesperson for the corporation's "True Voice" campaign; Houston sang in two of the company's commercials.

Houston's next offering was not long in coming. With Angela Bassett, Lela Rochon, and Loretta Devine, Houston co-starred in the 1995 film adaption of Terry McMillan's *Waiting to Exhale*. A box office winner, the movie's soundtrack was written by producer Babyface and featured, in addition to Houston, such performers as Aretha Franklin and Toni Braxton. Houston sang the very successful first single "Exhale (Shoop Shoop)." Her most recent film *The Preacher's Wife* allowed Houston to return to her gospel roots. Her latest album *My Love is Your Love* was released in the fall of 1999.

Phyllis Hyman (1949–1995)
Singer

Phyllis Hyman was a singer of the heart and was appreciated by connoisseurs of both romantic jazz and rhythm and blues singing. She was born in Philadelphia on July 6, 1949, and raised in Pittsburgh. An elementary school teacher noticed and nurtured her vocal talents, but she grew up poor and prepared for a career as a legal secretary.

Nevertheless, Hyman reached New York in her early twenties and soon began working as a vocalist. By 1974 she formed her own band, Phyllis Hyman and the PH Factor. She became a regular at the toney Upper West Side clubs, Rust Brown's and Mikell's. In 1976 she was discovered by percussionist and producer Norman Connors and was a featured performer on his album *You*

Phyllis Hyman (Corbis Corporation [Bellevue])

Are My Starship singing the ballad "Betcha By Golly Wow," which helped Hyman meet the co-writer of the song and her longtime good friend, Linda Creed.

Hyman signed with the record label Arista in 1977, and one of her first releases "Somewhere in My Lifetime" was produced by vocal star Barry Manilow and rose high in the rhythm and blues charts. Her signature hit was the ballad "You Know How to Love Me." Personally, her marriage to manager Larry Alexander in the late 1970s ended in divorce.

Her career took an upswing in the late 1970s when she signed on with the Broadway cast of *Sophisticated Ladies*, a revue of Duke Ellington's music. She sang in the show for three years and earned a Tony nomination for her performance in 1981. Her rendition of "In a Sentimental Mood" is on the original cast album. In 1986 Hyman moved to the Philadelphia International label and made some of her best recordings. *Living All Alone* was soon released and featured her signature lush, sad romantic ballads including a new song written by her friend, Linda Creed. Hyman herself began writing songs that reflected her life story, which is why her songs were so emotionally true and compelling. The 1991 *Prime of My Life* contained songs with such titles as "It's Not

About You (It's About Me)," "It Takes Two," and "Why Not Me?"

In 1988, she appeared in the Spike Lee film *School Daze*. She also toured the USA, Europe, and Japan in the late 1980s with a successful show that played the Harlem Apollo, Oakland's Paramount, and the Fox Theatre in St. Louis. She was a stunning performer, tall and dressed in African clothing.

On talk shows though, Hyman was open about her lifelong search for love and admitted to being lonely. When her friend, Linda Creed, died in 1993, it was rumored that Hyman was struggling with alcohol and drugs. On June 30, 1995, before a performance at the Apollo, she died from an overdose of pills. Not forgotten though, her legend continues to grow as five albums have been released since her death including *We Love You Phyllis: A Tribute to Phyllis Hyman* (1998), featuring Norman Connors and Jean Carne.

Ice Cube (1969–)
Rap Singer, Actor

Behind his oft-misogynistic and racist gangster image, rapper Ice Cube is a serious artist. Dedicated to black pride, he is a staunch spokesperson for black nationalism. Ice Cube looks upon his music as a means of launching a "mental revolution" in order to awaken African American youth to the value of education and the creation of private African American economic enterprises.

Born Oshea Jackson, Ice Cube grew up in the west side of South Central Los Angeles. While in the ninth grade Jackson wrote his first rhyme in typing class. Prompted by his parents to pursue an education after high school, he attended a one-year drafting course at the Phoenix Institute in 1988. In the following year, Ice Cube achieved great commercial success as a member of N.W.A. (Niggaz With Attitude). One of the group's founding members, along with Dr. Dre and Eazy E, Ice Cube wrote or co-wrote most of the material for N.W.A.'s first two albums. *Boyz N the Hood* was released in 1986. Ice Cube's authoritative baritone won him a legion of fans for his N.W.A. rap anthem "Gangsta Gangsta." He also scripted much of Eazy's first solo work *Eazy-Duz-It*, followed by N.W.A.'s platinum *Straight Outta Compton*, which included the controversial single "F__ Tha Police."

Though he still worked sporadically with Dr. Dre after leaving N.W.A., Ice Cube released his 1990 solo album *AmeriKKKa's Most Wanted*, produced with Public Enemy's Chuck D. and the Bomb Squad—the recording went gold within three months. He then formed Street Knowledge, a record production company, and

Ice Cube (AP/Wide World Photos, Inc.)

produced female rapper Yo Yo's *Make Way for the Motherlode*. During the same year, Ice Cube also made his acting debut in director John Singleton 's film *Boyz N the Hood*. The rapper-actor went on to star in a number of films including *Trespass* (1992) with Ice-T; *Higher Learning*, Singleton's vehicle of 1994; the 1995 comedy *Friday*, which he co-wrote and co-produced; Charles Burnett's 1995 work *The Glass Shield*; *Anaconda* in 1997; and *I Got the Hook Up* in 1997. He is set to appear in two new films *Next Friday* and *Shadow Man* in 2000.

Having recorded his own *Kill at Will* and *Death Certificate* in 1991, Ice Cube remained active in Yo Yo's career, serving as executive producer of her *Black Pearl* in 1992, and worked with other artists, directing videos including one for blues-rock artist Ian Moore in 1993. Ice Cube stayed on top of his own music game as well, releasing *The Predator* in 1992; the recording debuted at number one on two *Billboard* charts—pop and rhythm and blues—at the same time, the first to do so since 1976 and Stevie Wonder's *Songs in the Key of Life*. In 1992, Ice Cube figured in the lineup of Lollapalooza II, an annual traveling rock festival. 1993's *Lethal Injection* featured the smash single "It Was a Good Day." Ice Cube also issued *Bootlegs & B-Sides*, and, in 1995, he contributed to the *Streetfighter* motion picture soundtrack.

Janet Jackson (1966–)
Singer, Actress

The youngest child of a family of talented children, Janet Jackson is a tremendously energetic performer, whose singing and dance styles have reached immense popularity around the world. She is one of the most successful of a family of highly talented performers including her brother Michael, the so-called "King of Pop." In the 1990s, she has fully emerged from his shadow and has become a full-fledged sex symbol and role model.

Born on May 16, 1966, in Gary, Indiana, Janet Jackson began performing with her brothers at age six, doing impressions of famous stars such as Mae West and Cher. She made her first professional singing debut at one of the Jackson Five's shows in the Grand Hotel in Las Vegas. Before she was ten years old, Jackson was spotted by television producer Norman Lear, resulting in her appearances on such television shows as "Good Times," "Different Strokes," and "Fame."

In 1982, Jackson's debut album for the A&M label, *Janet*, contained only a few minor hits. Teamed with producers Jimmy Jam and Terry Lewis, Jackson released her more commercially successful LP *Dream Street*. Her 1986 release *Control* scored six hit singles including "What Have You Done For Me Lately," "Nasty," "When I Think of You," "Control," "Let's Wait Awhile," and "Pleasure Principle." Under the direction of Jam and Lewis, Jackson released the dance-oriented album *Janet Jackson's Rhythm Nation 1814* in 1989, which went quadruple platinum. Among the record's numerous singles were "Miss You Much," "Come Back To Me," and "Black Cat."

After an extensive world tour in 1990, Jackson left the A&M label to sign a contract with Virgin Records in 1991. The four-album contract was worth an estimated $80 million with $50 million guaranteed up front. Two years later, she starred alongside Tupac Shakur in John Singleton's *Poetic Justice.* Jackson played a soul-searching hairdresser prone to writing poetry; Maya Angelou, who was also featured in the film, provided the poems Jackson's character read. In 1994, Jackson released *janet.* Critically acclaimed, the album did well commercially, too. The single "Any Time, Any Place" earned Jackson her fourteenth gold single, the most by any female solo artist other than Aretha Franklin. The following year, Jackson collaborated with her brother Michael on a track entitled "Scream." The visually stunning video associated with the single was one of the most expensive ever made. Later in 1995, her *Design of a Decade: 1986–1996* made a splashy debut. She also contributed a song to the soundtrack for *Ready to Wear*. Her follow up album to *janet*, *The Velvet Rope*, debuted at the number one position in The Billboard 200 chart, a testament to her star power.

Jackson has earned much recognition throughout her career. Between 1986 and 1992, she garnered four *Billboard* Awards; seven American Music Awards; two MTV Video Music Awards; one Grammy Award; three Soul Train Awards; a BMI Pop Award; and the 1992 Sammy Davis, Jr. Award for entertainer of the year. In 1990, she acquired a star on Hollywood "Walk of Fame," and, in 1992, the NAACP gave her its Chairman's Award. Three years later, she received an Essence Award. Jackson is also the recipient of the Lena Horne Award for outstanding career achievements (1997).

Michael Jackson (1958–)
Singer, Composer

From child singing star with the Jackson Five to his success as a solo performer in the 1980s, Michael Jackson has amassed the largest following of any African American singer in the history of popular music. Jackson has an audience that transcends the boundaries of nations and bridges the gaps brought about by generational differences. Despite some missteps in the early 1990s, the "King of Pop" reigns supreme.

The fifth of nine children, Michael Jackson was born on August 29, 1958, in Gary, Indiana. As a child, Michael, along with his brothers Tito, Jermaine, Jackie, and Marlon, comprised the Jackson Five. Under the tutelage of their father, Joe, the five boys learned to sing and dance. On weekends the family singing group traveled hundreds of miles to perform at amateur contests and benefit concerts.

After two years on the road, the group landed an audition with Motown records. Upon signing with the label in 1969, the Jackson Five hit the charts with the number one hit "I Want You Back," a song arranged and produced by Berry Gordy, Jr. On recordings and television shows, Michael's wholesome image and lead vocal style attracted fans from every racial and age group. During the group's six-year stay at Motown, the Jackson Five scored 13 consecutive Top 20 singles such as "ABC," "The Love You Save," and "I'll Be There."

While lead vocalist for the Jackson Five, Michael had signed a separate contract with Motown in 1971, formalizing a solo career that produced the hits "Got to Be There" in 1971, "Ben" in 1972, and "Just a Little Bit of You" in 1975. When cast in the role of the scarecrow in the 1975 Motown film *The Wiz*, Jackson met producer Quincy Jones who later collaborated with him to record the 1979 hit LP *Off the Wall* on the Epic label. Two years later, Jackson, guided by the production skills of Jones,

Michael Jackson (Corbis Corporation [Bellevue])

recorded the biggest selling album of all time, *Thriller.* The seven hit singles included "Beat It," "Billie Jean," "Wanna Be Startin' Something," and the title track, which featured a voice over by horror cult figure Vincent Price. The video for the song was almost a mini-movie, starring Jackson as a dancing werewolf run amok, with special effects that rivaled any full-length feature film.

In 1985, Jackson co-wrote the song "We Are the World" for the U.S.A. for Africa famine relief fund. After joining Jones to produce *Bad* in 1987, Jackson led the most commercially successful tour in history. Four years later, Jackson released *Dangerous*, which included the hit single "Black or White."

In 1993, Jackson announced that the progressive lightening of his skin has been the result of a skin disorder known as vitiligo and not from intentional bleaching. The public declaration was one of many Jackson would find himself making about various topics in the ensuing years. Scandal-ridden, Jackson hit a backslide in his career following allegations of child molestation—charges that were dropped—and the coming to light of a pain medication addiction brought about by poor health.

Coming on the heels of such devastating disclosures, *HIStory: Past, Present, and Future, Book I* (1995) featured hits from the past as well as new works. Compared to his previous recordings, sales were disappointing and the recording was not considered a commercial success. Fan loyalty to the gifted musician, however, drove some of the new songs into chart contention including "The Earth Song," the controversial "They Don't Care About Us," and the lilting ballad "You Are Not Alone." The compilation also gave Jackson a chance to work with his sister Janet, when the two collaborated on the duet "Scream," the first single to be released. The ensuing video for "Scream" cost $7 million, making it one of the most expensive and eye-catching videos ever produced. Jackson's follow up album to *HIStory, Blood on the Dance Floor* was released in 1997, and is a partly new, partly remixed recording.

Jackson had made headlines in 1994, when he announced his betrothal to Lisa Marie Presley, daughter of the late rock legend Elvis Presley. The marriage of Jackson and Presley was considered highly unusual, and many critics dismissed it as a publicity stunt. On June 14, 1995, Jackson and Presley were interviewed by Diane Sawyer on ABC's *Prime Time Live.* During the interview, the two insisted they were deeply in love and planned to eventually have children. However, in January of 1996, Lisa Presley announced that she was divorcing Jackson. Jackson remarried later that year to long time friend Debbie Rowe. A son was born to them in early 1997, followed by a daughter in the spring of 1998.

Jackson's business ventures have had more staying power. An astute business man, he entered into a $600 million joint publishing deal with Sony in 1995. The deal combined Sony's music publishing division with Jackson's ATV Music Catalog, which once owned the rights to the entire collection of The Beatles's work.

More importantly, Jackson continues to garner acclaim, despite his setbacks. In 1993, he received three American Music Awards including the first-ever International Artist Award, and was recognized at the World Music Awards ceremony in Monte Carlo, Monaco. In addition, he received special Grammy honors that year. Two years later, he won three MTV Video Awards. While many argue that his work has been uneven, his contribution to modern pop has been enormous. Indeed, Jackson redefined stardom for the video era. Popular culture will never be the same.

Etta James (1938–)
Singer

Born Jamesetta Hawkins on January 25, 1938, Etta James was a child prodigy, singing gospel music on the radio in Los Angeles by the time she was five. As a teenager in 1950, she formed a singing group called The

Etta James

Creolettes with two friends. The trio was discovered by rhythm and blues star Johnny Otis in 1954. Otis changed the group's name to The Peaches and took the girls on the road with him. The Peaches recorded their first song "Roll with Me, Henry" which topped the charts in 1955, along with "Good Rocking Daddy." The success of that record led to a tour with rock and roll star Little Richard and studio backup vocal jobs with Marvin Gaye, Minnie Riperton, and Chuck Berry. James signed with Chess and cranked out ten chart-making hits between 1960 and 1963 including "At Last," "Trust in Me," and "Something's Got a Hold on Me." In 1967 she traveled to the famous Muscle Shoals, Alabama studio, where she recorded many of her biggest hits including "I'd Rather Go Blind" and "Tell Mama."

Although successful on the rhythm and blues charts, James did not manage to catch on with wider audiences in the 1960s. With Chess through 1975, James continued to record with moderate success in the gray region between blues, soul, rhythm and blues, and rock. After a recording lapse lasting for much of the 1980s, she recorded the album *The Seven Year Itch* for Island Records in 1988. Despite her inability to establish herself as a mainstream superstar, James has been a major

influence on many singers who did attain that status including Diana Ross and Janis Joplin.

Quincy Jones (1933–)
Trumpeter, Arranger, Producer

Winner of twenty Grammy Awards and the writer of more than 52 film scores, Quincy Jones is popular music's quintessential musician/producer. Aside from performing trumpet with the likes of jazzmen Lionel Hampton and Dizzy Gillespie, Jones has produced for artists from Frank Sinatra to Michael Jackson.

Quincy Jones was born on March 14, 1933, in Chicago, Illinois. At age ten, Jones moved to Bremerton, Washington. As a member of Bump Blackwell's Junior Orchestra, Jones performed at local Seattle social functions. In 1949, Jones played third trumpet in Lionel Hampton's band in the local Seattle club scene. After befriending jazz bassist Oscar Pettiford, Jones established himself as an able musician and arranger.

From 1950 to 1953, Jones became a regular member of Hampton's band, and, subsequently, toured the United States and Europe. During the mid-1950s, Jones began to record jazz records under his own name. In 1956, he toured the Middle East and South America with the U.S. State Department Band headed by Dizzy Gillespie.

In 1961, Jones was appointed musical director at Mercury Records. In search of new musical horizons, Jones began producing popular music including Leslie Gore's 1963 hit "It's My Party." Jones's growing prestige at Mercury led to his promotion to vice president of the company, marking the first time an African American had been placed in an executive position at a major label. During this time, Jones also began to write and record film scores. In 1967, he produced the music score for the movie *In the Heat of the Night*. He also produced the music score for Alex Haley's television miniseries "Roots" and co-produced the film adaptation of Alice Walker's *The Color Purple* with Steven Spielberg.

After his production of the 1978 Motown-backed film *The Wiz*, Jones went on to produce the film's star, Michael Jackson, on such recordings as the 1979 release *Off the Wall* and the 1985 record-breaking hit *Thriller*. Jones's 1989 release *Back on the Block*, a Grammy winner, was praised by critics and was no doubt a sign of Jones's continuing role in the future development of African American popular music. Two years later, Jones sat down with his old buddy Miles Davis. The musical encounter was recorded and released in 1993 as *Miles & Quincy Live at Montreux*, along with a video documentary of the same name. In 1995, Jones released his album *Q's Juke Joint*, featuring updated versions of tunes popularized in post-slavery roadhouses.

Quincy Jones (AP/Wide World Photos, Inc.)

Jones is also influential in the media industry. He is chairman of Quest Broadcasting; in 1994, the group partnered with Chicago's Tribune Co. to buy television stations in Atlanta and New Orleans. His joint venture with Time Warner—*Vibe* magazine, which Jones founded—has been very successful. The publication covers urban music and culture and has a high readership among African Americans and Latinos. In the late 1990s, Jones turned to exploring the multimedia realm. He released a CD-ROM, *Q's Juke Joint*, which, such as his album of the same name, is an examination of African American music.

Louis Jordan (1908–1975)
Singer, Alto Saxophonist, Bandleader

Louis Jordan led one of the most popular and influential bands of the 1940s. The shuffle boogie rhythm of his jump blues ensemble, the Tympany Five, had a profound impact on the emergence of rhythm and blues. As guitarist Chuck Berry admitted, "I identify myself with Louis Jordan more than any other artist." For it was Jordan's swinging rhythms, theatrical stage presence, and songs about everyday life that made him a favorite among musicians and listeners throughout the 1940s.

Born in Brinkley, Arkansas, July 8, 1908, Jordan was the son of a bandleader and music teacher. He received his music education in the Brinkley public schools and the Baptist College in Little Rock. Jordan's early music career as a clarinetist included stints with the Rabbit Foot Minstrels and Ruby Williams's orchestra. Soon after moving to Philadelphia in 1932, Jordan joined Charlie Gains's group; sometime around 1936, he joined drummer Chick Webb's band.

After Webb's death in 1938, Jordan started his own group. Because Jordan performed for both white and black audiences, he, to use his own words, learned to "straddle the fence" by playing music ranging from blues to formal dance music. Signing with Decca records during the same year, Jordan began a recording career which, by the early 1940s, produced a string of million selling recordings such as "Is You Is or Is You Ain't (My Baby)," "Choo Choo Ch'Boogie," "Saturday Night Fish Fry," and "Caledonia." Aside from working with artists such as Louis Armstrong, Bing Crosby, and Ella Fitzgerald, Jordan appeared in several films such as the 1949 release *Shout Sister Shout*.

Although failing to achieve the success he experienced during the 1940s, Jordan fronted a big band in the early 1950s. During the 1960s and 1970s, he continued to tour the United States, Europe, and Asia. His career came to an end in 1975 when he suffered a fatal heart attack in Los Angeles. Jordan was inducted into the Rock and Roll Hall of Fame in 1987. He was further celebrated in 1990 in the hit stage production of *Five Guys Named Moe*.

Eddie Kendricks (1939–1992)
Singer

As a member of the Temptations in the 1960s, Eddie Kendricks's articulate soulful falsetto provided Motown with a number of pop music classics. Kendricks's gospel music background "enabled him to bring an unusual earnestness to the singing of love lyrics," wrote music historian David Morse. "He can be compared only with Ray Charles in his ability to take the most threadbare ballad and turn it into a dramatic and completely convincing statement."

Born on December 17, 1939, in Birmingham, Alabama, Kendricks grew up with close friend and Temptations's member Paul Williams. In 1956 Kendricks and Williams quit school and traveled northward to become singing stars in the tradition of their idols Clyde McPhatter and Little Willie John. In Detroit, Kendricks and Williams formed the doo wop singing group the Primes which performed at talent contests and house parties. In 1961 the Primes recorded the songs "Mother of Mine" and the dance tune "Check Yourself" for Berry Gordy's short-lived Miracle label.

Upon the suggestion of Berry Gordy, the Primes changed their name to the Temptations and after adding David Ruffin as lead vocalist, they set out to become one of the most successful groups on the Motown label. Throughout the decade, Kendricks sang lead on several songs including the classics "My Girl" in 1965, "Get Ready" in 1966, and "Just My Imagination (Running Away With Me)" in 1972.

In June of 1971, Kendricks pursued a solo career and eventually recorded two disco-influenced hits "Keep on Truckin" in 1973 and "Boogie Down" in 1974. Kendricks's career soon fell into decline. Unable to find material to suit his unique artistic sensibility, Kendricks switched record labels several times before reuniting with the Temptations in 1982. After the reunion, Kendricks performed with the Temptations on the Live Aid broadcast and on the album *Live at the Apollo Theater with David Ruffin and Eddie Kendricks*. In 1987 Ruffin and Kendricks signed a contract with RCA and recorded the aptly titled LP *Ruffin and Kendricks*. Stricken by lung cancer, Kendricks died in October 1992.

Chaka Khan (1953–)
Singer

Born in Great Lakes Naval Training Station, Illinois, in 1953, Chaka Khan (neé Yvette Marie Stevens) changed her name after attending the Yuruba Tribe African Arts Center in Chicago, her hometown. She sang with a number of groups including Lyfe, Lock and Chains, Baby Huey and the Babysitters and Ask Rufus, which shortened its name to Rufus and signed to ABC in 1973. After a modest selling debut album, Rufus's sophomore project featured Stevie Wonders's composition "Tell Me Something Good" on the *Rags to Rufus* album (1974). Soon, Khan earned the billing "featuring Chaka Khan," and the group produced a string of successful projects including *Rufusized* (1974), *Rufus featuring Chaka Khan* (1975), and *Ask Rufus* (1977).

Khan embarked on a solo career in 1978. During this time she collaborated with industry giants Quincy Jones ("Stuff Like That") and Joni Mitchell ("Don Juan's Reckless Daughter"). Her efforts as a solo artist featured collaborations with such luminaries as George Benson, The Average White Band, The Brecker Brothers, and Phil Upchurch. Throughout the 1980s, Khan expanded her reputation by recording in eclectic situations including jazz standards, rock, and hard hitting soul. She collaborated with a dizzying mix of musicians such as Prince, Freddie Hubbard, Chick Corea, and Grandmaster Melle Mel. In the 1990s, the music of her earlier career remained staples in the both the rhythm and blues and smooth jazz radio formats. Her 1998 release *Come 2 My House* is collaborative project with "the artist formerly known as Prince" and features Khan's signature vocal

Chaka Khan (AP/Wide World Photos, Inc.)

style: a wide range, intense musicality, clarion tone, and sensual feeling.

Gladys Knight (1944–)
Singer

Born May 28, 1944, in Atlanta, Georgia, Gladys Knight was raised in a family which valued education and the sounds of gospel music. At age four, Knight began singing gospel music at the Mount Moriah Baptist Church. When she was eight, Knight won first prize on the television program "Ted Mack's Amateur Hour" for a rendition of the song "Too Young." Between the years 1950 and 1953, Knight toured with the Morris Brown Choir of Atlanta, Georgia. Around this same time, Knight joined her sister Brenda, brother Merald, and cousins William and Eleanor Guest to form a local church singing group. In 1957 the group took the name the Pips upon the suggestion of cousin and manager James "Pips" Woods.

Two years later Langston George and Edward Patten replaced Brenda Knight and Eleanor Guest. Though Gladys periodically left the group, she rejoined in 1964. After recording for several record labels, the Pips finally signed with Motown's subsidiary, Soul. Despite the lack

Gladys Knight and the Pips (Corbis Corporation [Bellevue])

of commercial success, the group released a number of fine recordings under the supervision of Motown's talented production staff including Norman Whitfield and Ashford and Simpson. In 1967 the group released the single "I Heard It Through the Grapevine" which reached number two on the Billboard charts. Following a long string of hits on Motown, the Pips signed with the Buddah label in 1973, releasing the album *Imagination*, which provided the group with two gold singles "Midnight Train to Georgia" and "I've Got to Use My Imagination."

By the late 1970s the group, faced with legal battles and contract disputes, began to fall out of popular vogue. For three years the group was barred from recording or performing together. As a result of an out-of-court settlement in 1980, the Pips signed a new contract with CBS, where they remained until 1985. Joined by Dionne Warwick and Elton John, Knight recorded the Grammy Award-winning gold single "That's What Friends Are For" in 1986. Released in 1988, the title cut of the Pip's *Love Overboard* album became their biggest selling single in decades. That same year, Knight recorded the theme for the James Bond film *License To Kill*. Released on the MCA label, Knight's 1991 album *Good Women* features guest stars Patti Labelle and Dionne Warwick. Knight released another album *Just For You* in 1994. In 1995, Gladys Knight and the Pips were inducted into the Rock and Roll Hall of Fame.

Suge Knight (1966–)
Music Company Executive

Born Marion Knight, Jr. in 1966, Knight grew up in the rough neighborhood of Compton, California. Despite being surrounded by violence, Knight picked up the nickname "Suge"—short for "Sugar"—because of his basic good-natured temperament. While in high school, Knight devoted his time to playing football with the hopes of gaining an athletic scholarship to college.

Standing over 6 feet tall and weighing nearly three hundred pounds, Knight took his talents to the University of Nevada in Las Vegas. There he won several awards including the Rookie of the Year on defense and a spot on the dean's list for academics. After college, Knight was drafted by the NFL's Los Angeles Rams, but decided to pursue different avenues.

A string of run-ins with the law almost put an end to any hopes Knight had. Between the years of 1987 and 1990, Knight was arrested for several crimes including auto theft, battery, and attempted murder. His luck soon changed as he made a name for himself while working as a bodyguard for musicians. Eventually, Knight formed a publication company and made a significant amount of money from ownership rights to several of white rapper Vanilla Ice's songs.

Based on the success of his publishing company, Knight decided to venture into artist management. This led to Knight meeting Dr. Dre, formerly of N.W.A. At that time, Dre was managed by Ruthless Records, but Knight pulled some strings and signed Dre and two other Ruthless artists to new contracts. Controversy surrounded the transaction as Knight was accused of using force to finalize the deal. Together with Dr. Dre, Knight founded Death Row Records. Blistering success quickly followed as the label grossed more than $60 million in 1993. An already impressive artist roster including Dr. Dre, Snoop Doggy Dogg, and Warren G. quickly improved with the signing of Mary J. Blige and Jodeci. With three multi-platinum albums under his belt, Knight began to refer to Death Row Records as the Motown of the 1990s. In luring top artists to Death Row, Knight often doubles their royalty rates, offers more creative control for the musician, and upgrades their contracts. In 1995, Knight even bailed jailed rapper Tupac Shakur out of prison in order to add more talent to the Death Row cluster. In the late 1990s, Knight faced his own legal battles. In 1997, Knight was sentenced to nine years in state prison for conspiracy to illegally possess a firearm, after violating several state probations for weapons charges. This was followed by a federal prison term for his role in a drug case. Knight was granted a new hearing in 1998.

KRS-One (1965?–)
Rap Singer

A self-described teacher whose Boogie Down Productions (BDP) was an important influence on hardcore rap, KRS-One survived street life, prison, homelessness, the murder of a close friend, and negative criticism to emerge as one of rap's most powerful figures. Born as Lawrence Parker c. 1965 in Brooklyn, New York, KRS-One (initially representative of "Kris, Number One," later an acronym for Knowledge Reigns Supreme Over

Nearly Everyone") also went by Krishna Parker or Kris Parker. Leaving home at 13, he lived on the streets, taking odd jobs when available and hanging out in public libraries. Self-educated, he served a short stint in jail for selling marijuana. Upon his release, the 19-year-old met Scott Sterling, a social worker and DJ who worked under the name Scott LaRock. Together the two formed BDP.

BDP recorded one album *Criminal Minded* before LaRock was killed while trying to break up a fight. Persevering, KRS-One kept their music alive, recording several critically acclaimed works with the various musicians who comprised the BDP crew. In 1990, he created H.E.A.L., or Human Education Against Lies, an afrocentric, pro-educational organization. KRS-One also founded Edutainer Records that year. In 1991, he recorded *Live Hardcore Worldwide*, one of the first live rap albums ever, and produced such artists as Queen Latifah and the Neville Brothers. His 1992 album *Sex and Violence* returned to the earlier hardcore sound of BDP, while his 1997 recording *I Got Next* produced raw funk on tracks such as "The MC."

Patti LaBelle (1944–)
Singer

Born in Philadelphia, Pennsylvania, in 1944, Patti LaBelle (née Patricia Holt) has remained one of the most respected divas of the pop-soul tradition. Known for her dramatic vocalizations and stage presentations, LaBelle's career has lasted several decades by keeping up with popular trends without sacrificing her signature vocal gymnastics.

While still a teenager, Labelle formed the Bluebelles with Cindy Birdsong, Sarah Dash, and Nonah Henderson. They scored a hit in "I Sold My Heart to the Junkman" (1962) and "Down the Aisle" (1963) during the height of the girl group fad in popular music. Shortly thereafter, the group adopted the name Patti LaBelle and the Bluebelles, which was ultimately shortened to LaBelle, and they turned to a harder rock style in the early 1970s. The group scored a million seller hit with the energetic "Lady Marmalade." The group disbanded in 1976, and LaBelle embarked on a solo career.

In the mid-1980s, she recorded the hits "New Attitude" (1985) and "Oh People" (1986) and the Bayer Sayer-Burt Bacharach song "On My Own" (1986), which featured a duet with Michael McDonald of the Doobie Brothers. Labelle is the recipient of eight Grammy Award nominations and three Emmy Award nominations, and in 1992, she received a Grammy Award for best rhythm and blues vocal performance. While her entire body of recordings throughout the 1980s and 1990s were met with mixed commercial success, she has estab-

Patti LaBelle (Archive Photos, Inc.)

lished herself as a sentimental favorite among pop-soul audiences.

Little Richard (1932–)
Singer, Pianist

Flamboyantly dressed, with his hair piled high in a pompadour, Little Richard is a musical phenomenon, an entertainer hailed by pop superstar Paul McCartney as "one of the greatest kings of rock and roll." Richard's image, mannerisms, and musical talent set the trend for the emergence of modern popular music performers from Jimi Hendrix to Prince.

One of 12 children, Richard Wayne Penniman was born on December 5, 1932, in Macon, Georgia. As a child in Macon, Richard heard the sounds of gospel music groups, street musicians, and spiritual-based songs emanating from homes throughout his neighborhood. Nicknamed the "War Hawk" for his unrestrained hollers and shouts, Richard's voice projected with such intensity that he was once asked to stop singing in church. Richard's first song before an audience was with the Tiny Tots, a gospel group featuring his brothers Marquette and Walter. Later Richard sang with his family in a group called the Penniman Singers; they appeared at churches, camp meetings, and talent contests.

In high school, Richard played alto saxophone in the marching band. After school he took a part-time job at the Macon City Auditorium, where he watched the bands of Cab Calloway, Hot Lips Page, Lucky Millinder, and Sister Rosetta Thorpe. At age 14, Richard left home to become a performer in Doctor Hudson's Medicine Show. While on the road, he joined B. Brown's Orchestra as a ballad singer performing such compositions as "Good Night Irene" and "Mona Lisa." Not long afterward, he became a member of the traveling minstrel show of Sugarfoot Sam from Alabama.

Richard's first break came in 1951, when the RCA label recorded him live on the radio, producing the local hit "Every Hour." Traveling to New Orleans with his band the Tempo Toppers, Richard's group eventually played the Houston rhythm and blues scene, where he attracted the attention of Don Robey, president of Peacock Records. After cutting some sides for the Peacock label, Richard sent a demo tape to Art Rupe's Los Angeles-based Specialty label. Under the direction of Specialty's producer Bumps Blackwell, Richard recorded the 1956 hit "Tutti Frutti" at J&M Studios in New Orleans. Richard's subsequent sessions for Specialty yielded a long list of classic hits such as "Long Tall Sally," "Lucille," "Jenny, Jenny," and "Keep a Knocking." In 1957, Richard appeared in the films *Don't Knock Rock* with Billy Haley and *The Girl Can't Help It* starring Jane Mansfield.

In the following year, Richard quit his rock and roll career to enter the Oakland Theological College in Huntsville, Alabama. Between 1957 to 1959 Richard released several gospel recordings and toured with artists such as Mahalia Jackson. In 1962, Richard embarked on a tour of Europe with Sam Cooke. One year later Richard hired a then unknown guitarist, Jimi Hendrix, who went under the pseudonym of Maurice James. In Europe Richard played on the same bills as the Beatles and Rolling Stones.

By the 1970s, Richard pursued a career as a full-fledged evangelist and performer. In 1979, he set out on a nationwide evangelist tour. In the following decade, he appeared in the film *Down and Out in Beverly Hills* and recorded "Rock Island Line" on the tribute LP to Leadbelly and Woody Guthrie entitled *Folkways: A Vision Shared*.

Richard's continuing activity in show business represents the inexhaustible energy of a singer who had a profound impact on the careers of artists such as Otis Redding, Eddie Cochran, Richie Valens, Paul McCartney, and Mitch Ryder. Having earned special Grammy honors in 1993, Richard was honored with a lifetime achievement award by the Rhythm & Blues Foundation the

following year. Later that year, he headlined the 1994 New Orleans Jazz and Heritage Festival and he is a charter member of the Rock and Roll Hall of Fame and Museum. He was called upon by the House of Blues Foundation to assist in the organizations Blues School House program in 1995.

Master P (c. 1970–)
Music and Film Company Executive, Rap Singer, Actor

Born Percy Miller, Master P grew up in a housing project in New Orleans's Third Ward, an area with a reputation for a high crime rate and violence. His parents divorced when he was 11 years of age, and his mother moved to California. Though he shuttled back and forth between New Orleans and California, the teenaged Percy settled in the Crescent City, attended Booker T. Washington and Warren Eason high schools, and played basketball at both schools. After graduation, he reportedly earned a basketball scholarship to the University of Houston. However, he was sidelined by a leg injury and headed back home rather than sit out the season. After the death of his brother, Kevin, and with some junior college business courses to his credit, Master P moved to Richmond and opened a small record store, No Limits Records, financing the store with $10,000 that he received as part of a medical malpractice settlement related to the death of his grandfather.

Master P was soon able to turn his successful record store into a powerhouse producer of Southern-influenced gangsta rap albums. He self-produced his first album *The Ghetto's Tryin' to Kill Me* in 1994, selling 200,000 copies out of the trunk of his car. Master P then took the profits from this album and produced two collections of rap music: *Down South Hustlers, Vol. 1* and *West Coast Bad Boys, Vol. 1*. By 1997, the four-year label had a cluster of artists who, while not household names, were well-known to rap fans.

Master P next targeted the film industry. In 1997, he produced, directed, and acted in a low-budget semi-autobiographical film titled *I'm 'Bout It* without any outside backing. The success of this direct-to-video film spawned *I Got the Hook–Up* the following year. This time there was no problem signing Dimension Records as a distributor for the film. A third film *MP Da Last Don* soon followed.

No Limit then made a major move to Baton Rouge. It also undertook a number of new enterprises. A sports management company, No Limit Sports Management, was started in 1997 and represents such professional players as Ron Mercer of the Boston Celtics and Derek Anderson of the Cleveland Cavaliers. By 1998, No Limits Records had incorporated 12 businesses in Baton Rouge including a complex called "The Ice Cream Shop," which includes five recording studios, a dorm, a gym, a

Master P (AP/Wide World Photos, Inc.).

pool, an aquarium, a sun deck, a movie theater, a domed basketball court, and 15 Hummers for transportation. The Master P Foundation has also been a supporter of the Baton Rouge schools and community.

In 1998, Master P tried out for the Continental Basketball Association's Fort Wayne Furies and was signed as a free agent in October. His performance with the Furies brought an invitation to try out with the National Basketball Association's Charlotte Hornets. While Master P did not make the cut, he intends, as was the case with the other accomplishments in his life, to continue working until he succeeds.

Curtis Mayfield (1942–)
Singer, Songwriter, Music Producer

Born on June 3, 1942, in Chicago, Illinois, Curtis Mayfield learned to sing harmony as a member of the Northern Jubilee Singers and the Traveling Souls Spiritualist Church. In 1957, Mayfield joined the Roosters, a five-man doo wop singing group led by his close friend Jerry Butler. Renamed the Impressions, the group released the 1958 hit "Your Precious Love," featuring Butler's resonant baritone and Mayfield's wispy tenor. But in the following year, Butler left the group to pursue

a solo career. In search of material, Butler collaborated with Mayfield to write the hit songs "He Will Break Your Heart" and "I'm a-Telling You."

In 1960, Mayfield recruited Fred Cash to take Butler's place in the newly reformed Impressions. In the next year the Impressions hit the charts with the sensual soul tune "Gypsy Women." In collaboration with Butler, Mayfield also established the Curtom Publishing Company. With the loss of original members Richard Brooks and Arthur Brooks, the three remaining members of the Impressions, Mayfield, Cash, and Sam Goodman continued to perform as a trio. Under the direction of jazz musician/arranger Johnny Pate, the Impressions recorded "Sad Sad Girl" and the rhythmic gospel-based song "It's All Right," released in 1963.

During this time, Mayfield also wrote a number of songs for his Chicago contemporaries including "Monkey Time" for Major Lance, "Just Be True" for Gene Chandler, and "It's All Over Now" for Walter Jackson. Writing for the Impressions, however, Mayfield turned to more socially conscious themes reflecting the current of the civil rights era. Mayfield's finest "sermon songs" were "People Get Ready" (1965), "We're a Winner" (1968), and "Choice of Colors" (1969).

After leaving the Impressions in 1970, Mayfield released his debut album *Curtis*. On his 1971 LP *Curtis Live!*, Mayfield was accompanied by a tight four-piece backup group, which included guitar, bass, drums, and percussion. Mayfield composed the score for the 1972 hit film *Superfly*. The soundtrack became Mayfield's biggest commercial success, providing him two hits with the junkie epitaph "Freddie's Dead" and the wah-wah guitar funk classic "Superfly." Despite his commercial success, Mayfield spent the remainder of the decade in collaboration with other artists, working on such projects as the soundtrack for the film *Claudine*, featuring Gladys Knight and the Pips, and the production of Aretha Franklin's 1978 album *Sparkle*.

Throughout the next decade, Mayfield continued to record such albums as *Love is the Place* in 1981, and *Honesty* in 1982. Joined by Jerry Butler and newcomers Nate Evans and Vandy Hampton, the Impressions reunited in 1983, for a thirty-city anniversary tour. In 1983, Mayfield released the LP *Come in Peace With a Message of Love*. But in August 1990, while performing at an outdoor concert in Brooklyn, New York, Mayfield received an injury that left him paralyzed from the neck down. In the following year, Mayfield's contributions to popular music were recognized when the Impressions were inducted into the Rock and Roll Hall of Fame. In 1994, Mayfield was presented with the Grammy Legend Award. Earlier that year a number of his peers, including Aretha Franklin, got together to record *All Men Are Brothers: A Tribute to Curtis Mayfield*. Despite his

Notorious B.I.G. holding his Billboard Music Awards in 1995 (AP/Wide World Photos, Inc.).

injuries, Mayfield has triumphed, producing a Grammy nominated album *New World Order* in late 1996. Curtis Mayfield was inducted into the Rock and Roll Hall of Fame on April 5, 1999.

Notorious B.I.G. (1973–1997)
Rap Singer

Notorious B.I.G., also known as Biggie Smalls and B.I.G., was born Christopher Wallace in the Bedford-Stuyvesant section of Brooklyn in 1973. A self-described, former "100 percent hustler" and high school drop out, Notorious B.I.G. became within his short career one of most influential and respected talents in hip hop history.

Noted for his massive six foot three inch, over three hundred pound frame, a husky-voiced yet fluid, and rhythmically inventive delivery style and explicit lyrics, he began his career making amateur tapes for fun with the OGB (Old Gold Brothers), when his talents caught the attention of rapper Big Daddy Kane's DJ. He was soon featured in the rap trade magazine *The Source* in its "Unsigned Hype" column, a showcase for new rappers. A record deal with Uptown Records followed shortly thereafter, and he created "Party and Bullshit" for the film *Who's the Man?* After he signed with his business

associate and friend Sean "Puffy" Combs's Bad Boy label, Notorious B.I.G. recorded *Ready to Die* in 1994 and the project went platinum. He was named rap artist of year in 1995 at the *Billboard* Awards. Notorious B.I.G.'s star rose quickly within hip hop culture's inner circle, and he became a much sought after guest rapper on numerous recordings. His collaborations include Junior M.A.F.I.A, Mary J. Blige, Total, among others. In 1997 Notorious B.I.G. died a violent death after being shot in a Los Angeles parking lot. Another recording project, ironically titled *Life After Death . . . 'Til Death Do Us Part*, was released posthumously.

Teddy Pendergrass (1950–)
Singer

Born Theodore Pendergrass in 1950 in Philadelphia, the vocalist learned singing from his mother, who performed in nightclubs, and in his childhood apprenticeship in church. Although he became known as one of the most prominent soul balladeers of the late 1970s and 1980s, he began his professional career as a drummer for the group the Cadillacs.

In 1970 Pendergrass moved from his duties as drummer and began singing with Harold Melvin and the Blue

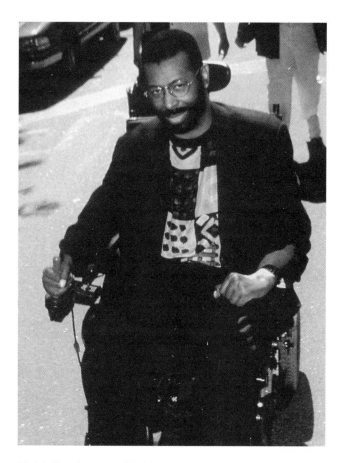

Teddy Pendergrass (Archive Photos, Inc.)

Notes, a group that had started as a doo wop group in the 1950s and which signed with the producers Gamble and Huff's label, Philadelphia International, in 1972. Pendergrass's powerful and passionate baritone presentation ultimately earned him the lead spot in the Blue Notes, and for six years his vocals became the group's signature sound. During this period the Blue Notes recorded such hits as "I Miss You" and "If You Don't Know Me By Now," among others, establishing themselves as one the premiere soul groups of the decade.

In 1976, Pendergrass left the group to pursue a successful solo career, remaining with Gamble and Huff and producing a string of hits, such as "I Don't Love You Anymore" (1976) and the number one rhythm and blues single "Close the Door" (1978). Pendergrass became a heartthrob among female fans, mounting successful tours with his Teddy Bear Orchestra and recording albums that were commercially profitable. His career path turned downward following a 1982 near-fatal car crash in Philadelphia that paralyzed him from the neck down. He has maintained a respectable recording career despite these challenges, releasing the album *You and I* in 1997, and some of his recordings over the last decade have done well on the charts.

Charley Pride (1939–)
Singer

The first African American superstar of country music, Charley Pride is a three-time Grammy Award winner whose supple baritone voice has won him international fame. He was the first African American to become a member of the Grand Ole Opry. A prolific artist, Pride has recorded more than thirty albums.

Born on March 18, 1938, in Slege, Mississippi, Charley Pride grew up listening to late night radio broadcasts of the Grand Ole Opry, country music's most famous showcase. Although he taught himself guitar at age 14, Pride soon turned his attention to a professional baseball career. At age 16, he left the cotton fields of Slege for a stint in the Negro American baseball league. During his baseball career, Pride sang on public address systems and in taverns. In 1963, country singer Red Sovine heard Pride and arranged for him to attend an audition in Nashville one year later. This led to a recording contract with the RCA label and produced the 1964 hit "Snakes Crawl at Night."

Throughout the 1960s, Pride toured incessantly, appearing at concert dates and state fairs, as well as on radio and television. In 1967, Pride debuted at the Grand Ole Opry and within the same year hit the charts with singles "Does My Ring Hurt Your Finger?" and "I Know One." With the release of *The Sensational Charley Pride* in 1969 and the subsequent year's *Just Plain Charley*, Pride found himself entering the decade of his greatest recognition. By the time he received the Country Music Award for entertainer of the year in 1970, Pride had already achieved tremendous success as a major figure in the popular cultural scene of the United States. Other honors included *Billboard*'s Trendsetter Award and the Music Operators of America's Entertainer of the Year Award.

In the 1980s, Pride not only continued to find success as a music star, he became a successful entrepreneur. Making his home on a 240-acre estate in North Dallas, Texas, Pride emerged as a majority stockholder in the First Texas Bank and part owner of Cecca Productions. Pride made more history in the 1993, when he became the first African American to join the cast of the Grand Ole Opry since DeFord Bailey's presence nearly 52 years earlier. The following year, Pride published his autobiography entitled *Pride: The Charley Pride Story*.

Prince (1958–)
Singer, Songwriter, Producer

The son of a jazz pianist, Prince Rogers Nelson was born on June 7, 1958, in Minneapolis, Minnesota. By age 14 Prince had taught himself to play piano, guitar, and drums. Drawn to many forms of rock and soul, Prince

Prince (AP/Wide World Photos, Inc.)

explained that he never grew up in one particular culture. "I'm not a punk, but I'm not an rhythm and blues artist either—because I'm a middle class kid from Minnesota."

It was his eclectic taste that led to Prince's creation of the Minneapolis sound. After forming the band Grand Central in high school in 1973, Prince renamed the group Champagne and eventually recruited the talents of Morris Day. In 1978 Prince signed with Warner Brothers and recorded his debut album *For You*. His follow-up album *Prince* featured the hit "I Wanna Be Your Lover." Rooted in the music of Sly and the Family Stone and Jimi Hendrix, Prince's third LP *Dirty Mind* was released in 1980.

Two years later, Prince achieved superstardom with his album *1999*, an effort which was followed by a spectacular tour comprised of Prince and the Revolution, the Time, and the bawdy girl trio Vanity 6. Prince's 1984 film soundtrack *Purple Rain*, which received rave reviews for Prince's portrayal of a struggling young musician, grossed $60 million at the box office in the first two months of its release. Near the end of 1985 Prince established his own record label Paisley Park, the warehouse/studio located in the wooded terrain of

Chanhassen, Minnesota. That same year, Prince released the album *Around the World in Day*, featuring the hit singles "Raspberry Beret," "Paisley Park," and "Pop Life."

Prince's next film project *Under the Cherry Moon*, filmed in France, was completed under his direction. The soundtrack *Parade Music From Under the Cherry Moon* produced a number of hit singles including "Kiss" and "Mountains." After reforming the Revolution, Prince released *SPIN of the Times* in 1987, which included a duet with Sheena Easton titled "I Could Never Take the Place of Your Man." Following the LP *Love Sexy*, Prince recorded several songs which appeared on the soundtrack for the film *Batman*. This was followed by another film soundtrack *Graffiti Bridge* in 1990.

In September 1992, Prince signed a six-album contract with Warner Brothers. Backed by his new first rate ensemble the New Power Generation, Prince embarked on a nationwide tour in April 1993 which proved the most impressive since his commercial breakthrough in the early 1980s. Prince has not only become an owner of his own nightclub, the Grand Slam, he has contributed a set of original music to the Joffery Ballet's production of "Billboards" which opened in January of 1993 to rave reviews.

That year, the eccentric performer also changed his name to an unpronounceable symbol and announced the retirement of "Prince" from recording. In 1994, The Artist Formerly Known as Prince (TAFKAP) debuted interactive CD-ROM software and New Power Generation retail establishments. Two years later, the long-time bachelor married on Valentine's Day and commissioned a symphony from his band to commemorate the occasion.

Public Enemy
Rap Group

As spokesmen of racial pride and proponents of militant public activism, Public Enemy have redefined the sound and the lyrical message of rap music. The formation of Public Enemy centered around Adelphi University in Long Island, New York, where the group's founder Carlton Ridenhour a.k.a Chuck D., a graphic design major, joined fellow students Hank Shocklee and Bill Stephney at radio station WBAU. First appearing on Stephney's radio show, Ridenhour soon hosted his own three-hour program. Ridenhour's powerful rap voice attracted a number of loyal followers. Ridenhour soon recruited the talents of William Drayton a.k.a Flavor Flav, Norman Rodgers a.k.a Terminator X, and Richard Griffin a.k.a Professor Griff to form Public Enemy. Shocklee and his production-oriented peers in the group came to be known as the Bomb Squad and their talents were often sought by other artists.

In 1987, Public Enemy released the debut album *Yo! Bum Rush the Show*, which sold more than 400,000 copies. Two years later Professor Griff, the group's "minister of information," was fired by Chuck D. for making anti-Semitic comments. Under the leadership of Chuck D. the group went on to record the song "Fight the Power" for director Spike Lee's film *Do The Right Thing*. The group's second album *It Takes a Nation of Millions to Hold Us Back* became a million seller.

Public Enemy's 1990 release *Fear of a Black Planet* featured themes regarding a world struggle for the advancement of the black race. The controversial "911 Is a Joke" led to widespread discourse over the song's allegations that emergency personnel respond slower, if at all, to calls originating from inner city or predominantly African American areas. The follow-up album *Apocalypse '91: The Enemy Strikes Black* was a startling statement of social and racial consciousness and featured a collaboration with the heavy metal band Anthrax on "Bring the Noise," a track that originally appeared on *It Takes a Nation*. Another single "By the Time I Get to Arizona" sparked another nationwide debate over the refusal of Arizona state officials to recognize Martin Luther King, Jr.'s birthday as a legal holiday.

Greatest Misses, a hits compilation released in 1992, seemed to signal the end of an era for the Public Enemy camp. In a departure from their earlier work, 1994's *Muse Sick n Hour Mess Age* traded the sonic dissonances of the Bomb Squad for samples from classic soul recordings. Meanwhile, most of the members had established themselves as solo artists or developed other career directions in the early 1990s, but overall the group's popularity seemed to wane as gangsta rap commandeered the airwaves.

Queen Latifah (1970–)
Singer, Actress

Born Dana Owens, rap artist Queen Latifah grew up in East Orange, New Jersey, and began performing in high school as the human beat box for the rap group Ladies Fresh. In 1989, she launched her solo recording career with the album *All Hail the Queen*, an afrocentric, pro-woman work. Her other recordings include: *Nature of a Sista'* (1991), featuring the single "Latifah Had It Up 2 Here; *Black Reign* (1993), which spawned the feminist anthem "U.N.I.T.Y"; and 1998's *Order in the Court*, which *Entertainment Weekly* called "fun and funky."

Latifah manages the careers of other rap artists through her New Jersey-based Flavor Unit Records and Management Company, of which she is the CEO. In addition, she is a regular on the Fox network's *Living Single*, along with co-stars Kim Fields, Erika Alexander, and Kim Coles. She has also made appearances on *The Fresh Prince of Bel-Air* and in such films as the Hudlin brothers' *House Party II*, Spike Lee's *Jungle Fever*, Ernest Dickerson's *Juice*, and the movie *Set It Off*. In 1998, Latifah gave a bravura perfomance as a sultry jazz singer in the movie *Living Out Loud*. Latifah was named one of People Magazine's Fifty Most Beautiful People the following year.

Otis Redding (1941–1967)
Singer, Songwriter

Born on September 9, 1941, in Dawson, Georgia, Otis Redding moved with his parents at age three to the Tindall Heights housing project in Macon. In grade school Redding played drums and sang in a church gospel group. A few years later he learned the vocals and piano style of his idol Little Richard. Quitting school in the tenth grade, Redding went on the road with Little Richard's former band, the Upsetters. But Redding's first professional break came when he joined Johnny Jenkins and the Pinetoppers. Redding's debut single was a Little Richard imitation tune "Shout Bamalama." Accompanying Jenkins to a Stax studio session in Memphis, Redding was afforded some remaining recording time. Backed by Jenkins on guitar, Steve Cropper on piano, Lewis Steinburg on bass, and Al Jackson on drums, Redding cut "Hey Hey Baby" and the hit "These Arms of Mine."

Signed to the Stax label, Redding released the 1963 album *Pain in My Heart*. Backed by members of Booker T. and the MGs, Redding's follow-up LP *Otis Blue (Otis Redding Sings Soul)* featured the 1965 hit "Respect." In the next year, Redding broke attendance records at shows in Harlem and Watts. After releasing a cover version of the Rolling Stones's song "Satisfaction" in 1966, Redding embarked on a European tour which included his appearance on the British television show "Ready Steady Go!"

In August 1966, Redding established his own record company, Jotis, which was distributed through the Stax label. Following a few commercially unsuccessful ventures, Redding recorded singer Arthur Conley who provided the label with the million-selling single "Sweet Soul Music." Redding's recordings "Try a Little Tenderness" and the vocal duet "Tramp," featuring Carla Thomas, hit the charts in 1967. On June 16, Redding, backed by the MGs, performed a stunning high-paced set at the Monterey Pop Festival. On December 10, Redding's career came to an tragic end when the twin engine plane carrying him to a concert date in Wisconsin crashed in Lake Monona, just outside Madison. As if in tribute, Redding's song "Sitting on the Dock of the Bay," re-

Otis Redding (Corbis Corporation [Bellevue])

leased a few weeks after his death, became his first gold record.

Lionel Richie (1949–)
Singer, Songwriter, Pianist

Lionel Brockman Richie was born on June 20, 1949, on the campus of Tuskegee Institute in Alabama. Richie's grandmother Adelaide Foster, a classical pianist, became his music instructor, introducing him to the works of Bach and Beethoven. While a freshman at the Tuskegee Institute, Richie formed the Mighty Mystics who, along with members of the Jays, became the Commodores. Combining gospel, classical, and country-western music, the Commodores emerged as a formidable live act throughout the 1960s and 1970s. After signing with the Motown label, the group landed its first hit in 1974 with the song "Machine Gun." In 1981 Richie recorded the hit theme song for Franco Zefferelli's film *Endless Love.*

A year later, Richie released his first solo album *Lionel Richie*, which featured the hits "Truly," "You Are," and "My Love." His follow-up release *Can't Slow Down* produced five more hits: "All Night Long (All Night)," "Running with the Night," "Hello," "Stuck on

You," and "Penny Lover." In collaboration with Michael Jackson, Richie co-wrote "We Are the World" for USA for Africa, the famine relief project organized and produced by Quincy Jones. In 1985 Richie received an Oscar nomination for "Best Original Song" for his composition "Say You, Say Me." A year later, Richie's third album *Dancing on the Ceiling* provided him with the hits "Dancing on the Ceiling," "Love Will Conquer All," "Ballerina Girl," and "Se La."

After taking a hiatus from recording, Richie released *Back to Front* in 1992, which yielded the hit "Do It to Me." This album was followed up by the recording *Time* in 1998. Richie was inducted into the Songwriters Hall of Fame in 1994.

Teddy Riley (1967–)
Producer, Songwriter, Musician

Born of October 8, 1967, Teddy Riley grew up in Harlem, New York. By age ten he could play guitar, bass, several horns, and keyboards. In his early twenties Riley merged aspects of hip hop, pop, and soul to create a new kind of music called "new jack swing." In the mid-1980s Riley formed his first band, Wreckx-N-Effect, with brothers Markell and Brandon Mitchell, which produced the hit single "New Jack Swing" (1984).

In 1987 he formed Guy with Aaron Hall and Timmy Gatling. Their first effort on the Uptown/MCA label, *Guy*, (1988) topped *Billboard*'s rhythm and blues chart and sold over two million copies. The group toured, selling out many venues. With their second album *1990s The Future*, Guy had more of a pop feel. *The Future* went platinum and received brilliant reviews.

Success was followed by difficult times. After his younger brother, Brandon Mitchell, was killed in gunfire, Riley decided to move to Virginia Beach. Then Riley and his longtime manager, Gene Griffen, split over a money dispute. Finally, Guy disbanded.

Next Riley formed Blackstreet with Chauncey "Black" Hannibal, Dave Hollister, and Levi Little. After the release of their first album, Hollister and Little left the group and were replaced by Eric Williams and Mark Middleton. They see themselves as role models and keep their music and image clean. The single "No Diggity" (1997) went platinum and topped the charts. Blackstreet won a Grammy Award for the best rhythm and blues performance in 1998.

Throughout his career Riley has written and produced 10 platinum albums, 22 platinum singles, and 11 gold singles for a variety of artists including Michael Jackson, Keith Sweat, Wreckx-N-Effect, Bobby Brown, and Kool Moe Dee. In 1990 Riley founded Future Records Recording Studio, LOR Records & Management, and Future Entertainment Group Ltd. in Virginia Beach.

Teddy Riley (Corbis Corporation [Bellevue])

Smokey Robinson (1940–)
Singer, Songwriter, Producer

Proclaimed by Bob Dylan as one of America's greatest poets, Smokey Robinson is a pop music legend. He has risen to fame as a brilliant songwriter, producer, and singer. His instantly recognizable falsetto voice continues to bring Robinson gold records and a legion of loyal fans.

William Robinson, Jr. was born in Detroit, on February 19, 1940. After his mother died when he was ten years old, Robinson was raised by his sister. Nicknamed "Smokey" by his uncle, Robinson was a bright student who enjoyed reading books and poetry. A reluctant saxophone student, Robinson turned his creative energy to composing songs that he collected in a dime store writing tablet. While attending Detroit's Northern High School in 1954, Robinson formed the vocal group the Matadors, which performed at battle-of-the-band contests and at recreation centers.

Robinson's introduction to Berry Gordy in 1957 resulted in the Matadors's first record contract with George Goldner's End label. Upon joining the newly formed Motown label in 1960, the group changed their name, at Gordy's suggestion, to the Miracles. Although the Miracles's debut album failed to attract notice, they provided Motown with its first smash hit "Shop Around" in 1961, a song written and co-produced by Robinson.

In close collaboration with Gordy, Robinson spent the following decade as one of Motown's most integral singers and producers. With the Miracles he recorded

such hits as "You Really Got a Hold On Me" in 1963, "Tracks of My Tears" in 1965, "I Second That Emotion" in 1967, and "Tears of a Clown" in 1970. As a writer he provided the label with hits such as "My Guy" for Mary Wells, "I'll Be Doggone" for Marvin Gaye, and "My Girl" for the Temptations.

In 1972, Robinson left the Miracles to launch a solo career. Despite the moderate success of his records during the disco craze of the 1970s, Robinson continued to perform and record. In 1979, Robinson experienced a comeback with the critically acclaimed hit "Cruisin." Three years later, Robinson appeared on the NBC-TV special *Motown 25: Yesterday, Today, and Tomorrow.* Between 1986 and 1991, Robinson released five more albums including *Smoke Signals, One Heartbeat,* and *Love, Smokey.* He was inducted into both the Rock and Roll Hall of Fame and the Songwriters Hall of Fame in 1986, and in 1987, he won a Grammy for his vocal performance on "Just to See Her." In 1995, Robinson was signed by Music by Design, a U.K. company that solicits artists to create original music for television and radio commercials.

Diana Ross (1944–)
Singer, Actress

One of six children, Diane Ross was born in Detroit, on March 26, 1944. An extremely active child, Ross swam, ran track, and sang in church. In 1959, she joined the Primettes, a group comprised of Mary Wilson, Florence Ballard, and Barbara Martin. After failing to attract the attention of the Lupine label, the group auditioned for Berry Gordy, Jr. who signed them to Motown. Upon the suggestion of Berry, the group changed its name to the Supremes. Released in 1961, the group's song "I Want a Guy," featuring Ross on lead vocals, failed to chart. Not long afterward, following Martin's departure, the trio continued to record with Ross on lead vocal.

The Supremes did not find commercial success on the Motown label until 1964, when they were placed under the guidance of the Holland-Dozier-Holland production team. In 1964, H-D-H turned out the Supreme's first smash hit "Where Did Our Love Go?" followed by numerous hits such as "Baby Love" in 1964, "I Hear a Symphony" in 1965, "You Can't Hurry Love" in 1966, and "Reflections" in 1967. With preferential treatment by Gordy, Ross became the dominant figure of the group. By the mid-1960s Ross's emerging talent prompted Gordy to bill the group as Diana Ross and the Supremes.

In 1970, Ross left the Supremes to launch her solo career. Her debut album *Diana Ross* featured the writing and production talents of Ashford & Simpson, an effort that included the hit "Reach Out and Touch (Somebody's Hand)." One year later she made her film debut in the Motown-sponsored movie *Lady Sings the*

Salt 'n' Pepa (AP/Wide World Photos, Inc.)

Blues in which she won an Oscar nomination for her biographical portrayal of jazz singer Billie Holiday. Her role in the 1975 Motown-backed film *Mahogany* brought her not only an Oscar nomination, but the number one selling single "Do You Know Where You're Going To." In 1978, Ross starred in the film version of *The Wiz*, the last full-scale motion picture to be backed by Motown.

After leaving Motown in 1981, Ross signed a $20 million contract with the RCA label. Her debut album *Why Do Fools Fall in Love?* went platinum. This was followed by four more LP's for RCA including *Silk Electric* in 1982, *Swept Away* in 1984, and *Eaten Alive* in 1985. Two years later, Ross left RCA to sign with the London-based EMI label, which produced the albums *Red Hot Rhythm 'n Blues* in 1987, *Working Overtime* in 1987, and *Greatest Hits, Live* in 1990. Meanwhile, Ross had returned to Motown Records as a recording artist and partial owner in 1989, one year after being inducted into the Rock and Roll Hall of Fame.

In the 1990s, the Grammy and Tony Award-winning Ross continued to enjoy popularity around the world; She achieved tremendous success as the owner of her own multi-million dollar corporation Diana Ross Enterprises. Her autobiography *Secrets of a Sparrow: Mem-*

oirs was published in 1993, and a compilation called *Diana Extended/The Remixes.* hit the stores in 1994. Ross continues to occasionally act, appearing as a schizophrenic in the television movie "Out of the Darkness" (1994) and alongside the young star Brandy in "Double Platinum" (1999).

Salt-N-Pepa
Rap Group

Salt-N-Pepa includes Salt (Cheryl James), Pepa (Sandy Denton), Spinderella (Deidre "Dee Dee" Roper), and former Spinderella, Latoya Hanson, and was formed in 1985 in Queens, New York. They were the first female rap group to go platinum and are widely recognized as paving the way for the present generation of female rap stars. Originally named Super Nature, they changed their name to Salt-N-Pepa in 1987.

Salt-N-Pepa's debut project *Hot Cool and Vicious* went platinum, setting the stage for a decade of mega hits for the group including "Push It" (1987); *A Salt with a Deadly Pepa* (1988), which was nominated for a Grammy; the single "Expressions" (1989); and *Black Magic* (1990). Their single "Let's Talk About Sex" was used a public service video education the youth commu-

Tupac Shakur (Archive Photos, Inc.)

nity about the dangers of AIDS. The project *Very Necessary* produced the hits "Whatta Man" and "Shoop." They released their fifth album *Brand New* in 1997.

Tupac Shakur (1971–1996)
Rap Singer

Born Tupac Amaru Shakur in the Bronx in 1971, Shakur was a multi-talented rap artist and actor who became a powerhouse in hip hop culture. He made his acting debut in an Apollo Theater production of *A Raisin in the Sun* in 1984 as a benefit for Jesse Jackson's unsuccessful presidential campaign. After his family moved to Baltimore, Shakur attended the High School of the Performing Arts and wrote his first rap song following the violent death of a friend. He dropped out of high school, moved to California, and began circulating tapes of his music until he landed a job as a roadie with the group Digital Underground, eventually working his way to a guest spot as a rapper in their stage show.

In 1991 he signed with Interscope Records and released his debut project *2Pacalypse Now*. A string of commercially successful and critically acclaimed projects followed, including *Strictly 4 My N.I.G.G.A.Z.* (1993), *Me Against the World* (1995), and *All Eyez On Me* (1996). Shakur's rap style was celebrated for its versatile vocal inflection, rhythmically subtle delivery, and the range of lyrical topics, although the latter was also the source of much criticism because of its frequently explicit content. Shakur also received accolades for his acting in the films, among them, *Juice* (1992), *Poetic Justice* (1993), *Above the Rim* (1994), and *Gang Related* (1997). Shakur career's was marred by controversies, which included intermittent trouble with the law for which he spent time incarcerated. Like his contemporary Notorious B.I.G., Shakur died in Las Vegas drive-by shooting in 1996.

Russell Simmons (1957?–)
Music Company Executive, Producer, Music Promoter

Hollis, Queens, in New York City was the birth place of Russell Simmons. Although he grew up in a middle class neighborhood, Simmons got involved with gangs in his teens. The 1970s brought change to Simmons's life, however, as he enrolled in classes at the Harlem branch of City College of New York. While studying sociology, Simmons began noticing the influence rap music had on young inner-city African Americans. The boasting and story telling skills of various rappers drew crowds on street corners and in neighborhood parks. Simmons found himself in the middle of a movement that would shape the sound of the music, particularly the rap genre.

Simmons left college to promote local rap artists. Hard work and perseverance led to the formation of Def Jam Records in 1984. Simmons and his partner, Rick Ruben, signed a deal with CBS Records to distribute their material. Simmons was primarily interested in promoting rap images that displayed the life and style of tough urban streets. Acts such as the Beastie Boys, L.L. Cool J, and Run-DMC pushed Def Jam Records to early success. Other groups such as Public Enemy enjoyed Simmons's input as their careers developed.

The music Simmons involved himself with not only revolutionized hip hop but helped bring fashion to forefront as well. High-top Adidas tennis shoes, black leather jackets, and t-shirts displaying the Def Jam Recording logo flooded the streets. These influences laid a foundation for Simmons own line of clothing called Phat Pharm. Simmons furthered his own professional growth by getting involved in film production. He contributed to *Krush Groove* and *Tougher Than Leather* in the late 1980s. Simmons is CEO of Rush Communications, which in 1992 was the nation's second largest African American-owned entertainment company. Rush is comprised of record labels, management companies, and clothing, radio, film and television divisions. In 1998, Simmons launched an hour-long syndicated series "Oneworld's Music Beat with Russell Simmons."

Donna Summer (1948–)
Singer

One of the biggest stars of the disco era, Donna Summer first gained notice with a pulsatingly, erotic Euro-hit, then moved on to mainstream popularity. She ruled the charts through the late 1970s, though the fading of disco left her with no choice but to streamline her style. Although her popularity declined in the ensuing years, she became one of the few stars of the era to transcend the kitsch that surrounded it.

Born Donna Gaines in Boston, the singer got her first break when she was cast in a traveling production of a rock musical. While in Germany she met Helmut Sommer, whom she married; she later made the acquaintance of Italian producer Giorgio Moroder, who produced her first hit, the throbbingly sexual "Love to Love You Baby." Summers's moans and groans were her initial route to stardom. Through the late 1970s, however, she continually expanded her range. Her hits included a cover version of the pop standard "Macarthur Park," as well as "On the Radio," "Bad Girls," "Hot Stuff," and "Last Dance."

Summer became a born-again Christian in the early 1980s, and gradually turned toward inspirational music. She earned Grammy Awards for best inspirational performance in 1984 and 1985, but she surfaced less and less frequently in the pop world. Summer continued to produce, and in 1999, she inked a multi-album deal with Epic Records with a live greatest hits collection planned as of this writing.

Tina Turner (1939–)
Singer

With a music career spanning more than thirty years, Tina Turner has come to be known as the "hardest working woman in show business." From soul music star to rock goddess, Turner's vocal style and energetic stage act remain a show-stopping phenomenon.

Born Annie Mae Bullock on November 25, 1939, in Brownsville, Tennessee, Turner moved to Knoxville with her parents at age three. Turner first sang in church choirs and at local talent contests. After moving with her mother to St. Louis at age 16, Turner met pianist Ike Turner, leader of the R and B group the Kings of Rhythm. Hired by the band to sing at weekend engagements, Annie Bullock married Ike Turner in 1958 and took the stage name Tina Turner. When the band's scheduled session singer failed to appear at a recording session in 1960, Tina stepped into record the R&B song "Fool in Love" which became a million seller.

With a major hit behind them, the Turners formed the Ike and Tina Turner Revue, complete with the Ikettes. Major international success came for the Turners in 1966 when producer Phil Spector combined his "wall of sound" approach with a R&B sound to record the hit "River Deep, Mountain High." Subjected to years of physical abuse by her husband, Turner divorced Ike in 1976 and set out on a solo career. That same year she co-starred in The Who's rock opera film *Tommy* as the Acid Queen.

In 1984 Turner's career skyrocketed with the commercial success of the album *Private Dancer*, which featured the hit singles "What's Love Got to Do With It?" and "Better Be Good." Turner's sensuously vibrant image soon appeared on high budget videos, magazine covers, and in films such as the 1985 release *Mad Max 3: Beyond the Thunderdome* in which she played the tyrannical Aunty Entity. With the immense commercial success of her 1989 album *Foreign Affair*, Turner closed out the decade as one of the most popular singers on the international music scene.

In 1991, Tina and Ike Turner were inducted into the Rock and Roll Hall of Fame. That same year, Turner

Tina Turner performing in 1997 (AP/Wide World Photos, Inc.).

Luther Vandross holding an American Music Award in 1992 (Archive Photos, Inc.).

released the album *Simply The Best* and, in 1993 a movie based on her life and starring Angela Bassett was released. Due to the movie's popularity, Turner returned to touring in 1997.

Luther Vandross (1951–)
Singer, Composer, Producer

One of the premier pop artists of the 1980s, Luther Vandross was responsible for the emergence of a new school of modern soul singers. Born in New York City on April 20, 1951, Vandross was the son of a gospel singer and a big band vocalist. Vandross received his musical education by listening to recordings of Aretha Franklin and the Supremes. In high school Vandross formed numerous singing groups. Throughout the 1970s, he was great as a background singer, performing with such artists as David Bowie, Carly Simon, and Ringo Starr. He also sang advertising jingles such as AT&T's theme "Reach Out and Touch."

Following the release of his first album *Never Too Much* in 1981, Vandross was called upon to sing duets with a number of pop artists including Aretha Franklin and Dionne Warwick. As a successful writer and pro-

ducer, Vandross has released eight million-selling albums including the 1990 release *Best of Love*, which went multi-platinum.

Mary Wells (1943–1992)
Singer

Born in 1943 and raised in Detroit, Michigan, Mary Wells started her music career as a featured soloist in her high school choir. At age 17 Wells signed a contract with Motown. With Smokey Robinson as her main producer and writer, Wells scored a number of hits such as "I Don't Want to Take a Chance" in 1961, "You Beat Me to the Punch" in 1962, and "My Guy" in 1964. In the same year, she recorded the album *Together* with Marvin Gaye and toured England with The Beatles.

At the peak of her career, Wells left the Motown label to become an actress. After relocating in Los Angeles, she signed a contract with the Twentieth Century Fox records. Unfortunately, Wells could never find a producer who equaled Robinson's ability to record her material. Her debut single in 1965 "Use Your Head" achieved only modest commercial success. In the 1970s Wells left music to raise her children. For a brief period she was married to Cecil Womack, brother of the rhythm and blues great Bobby Womack.

During the 1980s, Wells returned to music performing on the oldies circuit. In 1985 she appeared in "Motown's 25th Anniversary" television special. Diagnosed as having cancer of the larynx in August 1990, Wells, without medical insurance to pay for treatment, lost her home. Not long afterward, the Rhythm and Blues Foundation raised over $50,000 for Wells's hospital costs. Funds were also sent by artists such as Bruce Springsteen, Rod Stewart, and Diana Ross. Despite chemotherapy treatments, Wells died on July 26, 1992 and was buried at Forest Lawn Memorial Park in Los Angeles.

Jackie Wilson (1934–1984)
Singer

Between 1958 and 1963, Jackie Wilson reigned as one of the most popular rhythm and blues singers in the United States. Dressed in sharkskin suits and sporting a process hairstyle, Wilson exhibited a dynamic stage performance and a singing range which equaled his contemporaries James Brown and Sam Cooke.

Jack Leroy Wilson was born on June 9, 1934, in Detroit, Michigan. Wilson's mother sang spirituals and gospel songs at Mother Bradley's Church. As a youngster, he listened to the recordings of the Mills Brothers, Ink Spots, and Louis Jordan. In high school he became a boxer, and at age 16 he won the American Amateur Golden Gloves Welterweight title. But upon the insistence of his mother, Wilson quit boxing and pursued a career in music. While a teenager, Wilson sang with the Falcons in local clubs, and at talent contests held at the Paradise Theater. He also worked in a spiritual group with later members of Hank Ballard's Midnighters.

In 1953 Wilson replaced Clyde McPhatter as lead singer of the Dominoes. Wilson's only hit with the Dominoes was the reworking of the religious standard "St. Theresa of the Roses." Upon the success of the recording, Wilson signed a contract as a solo artist with the Brunswick label. Wilson's 1957 debut album *Reet Petite* featured the hit title track song which was written by songwriters Berry Gordy, Jr. and Billy Taylor. The songwriting team of Gordy and Taylor also provided Wilson with the subsequent hits "To Be Loved" in 1957, "Lonely Teardrops" in 1958, and "That's Why I Love You So" and "I'll Be Satisfied" in 1959.

During the early 1960s, Wilson performed and recorded numerous adaptations of classical music compositions in a crooning ballad style. This material, however, failed to bring out the powerful talent of Wilson's R&

Jackie Wilson (AP/Wide World Photos, Inc.)

B vocal style. Although Wilson's repertoire contained mostly supper club standards, he did manage to produce the powerful pop classics "Dogging Around" in 1960 and "Baby Workout" in 1963. Teamed with writer/producer Carl Davis, Wilson also recorded the hit "Whispers" and the rhythm and blues masterpiece "Higher and Higher" in 1967.

Following Wilson's last major hit "I Get the Sweetest Feeling" in 1968, he performed on the oldies circuit and on Dick Clark's "Good Ol' Rock 'n' Roll Revue." In 1975 Wilson suffered a serious heart attack on stage at the Latin Casino in Cherry Hill, New Jersey. Forced into retirement, Wilson spent his last eight years in a nursing home until his death on January 21, 1984.

Mary Wilson (1944–)
Singer

As a member of the Motown supergroup the Supremes, Mary Wilson's musical career represents an American success story. Born on March 6, 1944, in Greenville, Mississippi, Wilson moved to Detroit at age 11. Raised in the Brewster-Douglas housing project on the city's east side, Wilson learned to sing by imitating the falsetto voice of Frank Lyman. Along with Barbara Martin and Betty Travis, Wilson formed the Primettes. Upon the departure of Travis, another neighborhood girl named Diana Ross joined the group. Appearing at talent shows and sock hops, the Primettes went on to win first prize at the 1960 Detroit/Windsor Freedom Festival talent contest. Although the Primettes cut two singles on the Lupine label featuring Wilson on lead vocal, they failed to achieve commercial success.

On January 15, 1961, the 16-year-old Wilson and fellow Primette members Diana Ross, Florence Ballard and Barbara Martin signed with the Motown label as the Supremes. Wilson's effort to win the lead vocal spot, however, soon gave way to the dominance of Diana Ross. Released in 1964, the group's first gold single "Where Did Our Love Go?" made Wilson and the Supremes overnight celebrities. Between 1964 and 1968 Wilson sang background vocals on a number of hits including "Baby Love," "You Can't Hurry Love," and "Reflections." Before leaving the group in 1976, Wilson also sang such recordings as "Love Child," "I'm Living in Shame," and "Someday We'll Be Together."

In 1983 Wilson was briefly reunited with the Supremes on the "Motown's 25th Anniversary" television special. Making her home in Los Angeles, Wilson occasionally appears on the oldies circuit and at small Supremes revival shows.

Nancy Wilson (1937–)
Singer

Nancy Wilson was born in Chillicothe, Ohio, in 1937. Her musical talents were first noticed when, as a child, she performed for her family at various gatherings. The performances continued as Wilson became a member of her church choir. Influence from artists such as Billy Eckstine and Nat "King" Cole helped Wilson determine that singing would be her career. As a teen, Wilson and her family moved to Columbus, Ohio. Wilson soon became the host of her own radio show, Skyline Melody, during which she performed phoned in requests.

In 1955, Wilson enrolled in classes at Ohio's Central State College to pursue teaching credentials. Her stint in school was short lived, however, as Wilson dropped out to pursue her singing career. She spent the next three years touring the country as a member of Rusty Byrant's Carolyn Club Band. The experience Wilson gained while touring gave her the courage to go solo. New York City became Wilson's new home as her career skyrocketed.

Shortly after her arrival in the Big Apple, Wilson obtained permanent work at a local night club. Word of her masterful performances soon spread all over the city prompting a recording session with Capitol Records. 1960 marked the release of her debut album *Like*

in Love and the recording of her first major hit entitled "Save Your Love for Me." *How Glad I Am* won a Grammy in 1964, beginning a thirty-year streak of acclaim.

Wilson's blend of rhythm and blues, jazz, and pop styles captivated thousands of fans around the world. Television executives began to take advantage of Wilson's talents, giving her a weekly variety show. The Emmy Award-winning "The Nancy Wilson Show" was merely the beginning of Wilson's television appearances. Guest spots on "The Tonight Show," "The Merv Griffin Show," and "The Today Show" soon followed.

During the late 1970s and early 1980s, technology began to influence the fashion in which studio recordings were made. Wilson continued to record and tour despite differences with various recording companies over issues of sound. Nonetheless, she was named Global Entertainer of the Year in 1986 by the World Conference of Mayors and the NAACP bestowed upon her its Image Award that year as well.

Just as much heralded in the 1990s, Wilson's fifty-fifth full-length recording was completed in 1997. With a star on the Hollywood Walk of Fame, an Essence Award, a Martin Luther King Center for Social Change Award, and a Trumpet Award to her name, Wilson's bevy of honors is symbol of her timelessness and a testimony to the loyalty of her fans.

Stevie Wonder (1950–)
Singer, Pianist, Composer

Popular music's genius composer and singer Stevie Wonder has remained at the forefront of musical change. His colorful harmonic arrangements have drawn upon jazz, soul, pop, reggae, and rap-derived new jack rhythms. Wonder's gift to pop music is his ability to create serious music dealing with social and political issues while at the same time revealing the soulful and deeply mysterious nature of the human experience.

Steveland Morris Judkins was born on May 13, 1950, in Saginaw, Michigan. Raised in Detroit, Wonder first sang in the church choir. He was most attracted to the sounds of Johnny Ace and B. B. King that he heard on late night radio programs. By age eight Wonder learned to play piano, harmonica, and bongos. Through the connections of Miracles member Ronnie White, Wonder auditioned for Berry Gordy, Jr. who, immediately signing the 13-year-old prodigy, gave him the stage name of Little Stevie Wonder. After releasing his first singles "Thank You (For Loving Me All the Way)" and "Contract of Love" in 1963, "Fingertips, Pt. 2" became the first live performance of a song to reach the top of the pop charts. That year Wonder also became the first recording artist to hold number one slots on the *Billboard* Hot 100, R&B Singles, and album charts, simultaneously. In the fol-

Stevie Wonder (AP/Wide World Photos, Inc.)

long succession of hits including Bob Dylan's "Blowing in the Wind" in 1966, "I Was Made to Love Her" in 1967, and "For Once in My Life" in 1968. In 1969, President Richard Nixon gave Wonder a Distinguished Service Award from the President's Committee on Employment of Handicapped People. That year, *My Cherie Amour* generated a single of the same name.

After recording the 1970 album *Signed, Sealed & Delivered*, featuring the title track, Wonder moved to New York City, where he founded Taurus Production Company and Black Bull Publishing Company, both of which were licensed under Motown. With complete control over his musical career, Wonder began to write lyrics addressing social and political issues. Through the technique of overdubbing, he played most of the instruments on his recordings including the guitar, bass, horns, percussion, and brilliant chromatic harmonica solos. *Music From My Mind*, *Talking Book*, and *Inversions* all feature Wonder distinctive synthesizer accompaniment.

Released in 1979, Wonder's *Journey Through the Secret Life of Plants* was an exploratory musical soundtrack for a film documentary. In 1984, Wonder's soundtrack for the film *Woman in Red* won him an Academy Award for best song with "I Just Called To Say I Love You." One year later, Wonder participated in the recording of "We Are the World" for U.S.A for Africa, the famine relief project. He also teamed up with Paul McCartney for "Ebony and Ivory." Wonder's 1985 album *Square Circle* produced the hit singles "Part Time Lover" and "Overjoyed" and won a Grammy. After the 15-time Grammy Award winner was inducted into the Rock and Roll Hall of Fame in 1989, he composed material for the soundtrack to Spike Lee's film *Jungle Fever*. Eight years in the making, 1995's *Conversation Piece* hit fans the same year as did the double-live recording *Natural Wonder*. He also contributed to the tribute recording *Inner City Blues: The Music of Marvin Gaye* and to Quincy Jones's *Q's Jook Joint*. He won an *Essence* Award that year. Wonder has also founded the SAP/Stevie Wonder Vision Awards, which are given to research and products that enable visually-impaired people to enter the workforce.

lowing year, Wonder hit the charts with the song "Hey Harmonica Man."

With the success of his recording career, Wonder began touring more frequently. Motown assigned Wonder a tutor from the Michigan School for the Blind, allowing him to continue his education while on the road. In 1964, he performed in London with the Motown Revue, a package featuring Martha and the Vandellas, the Supremes, and the Temptations. Wonder's subsequent recording of the punchy rhythm and blues single "Uptight (Everything's Alright)" became a smash hit in 1966. Wonder's growing commercial success at Motown brought him greater artistic freedom in the studio. In collaboration with Clarence Paul, Wonder produced a

Visual and Applied Arts

◆ The African Roots of African American Art ◆ The Formation of an Arts Tradition
◆ The African Legacy Endures in Colonial America ◆ Rise of the Professional Artists
◆ African American Arts in the Twentieth Century ◆ Arts–Related Support Professions
◆ Exhibiting African American Art ◆ Visual and Applied Artists
◆ Museums and Galleries Exhibiting African American Art
by Phyllis J. Jackson

Africans and their descendants have been making objects and creating works of art since the first indentured Africans arrived on the North American continent in 1619. Black artists in the United States have created an extraordinary and distinctive visual tradition despite the social, political, and cultural odds confronting them. Some are such well-known historical figures as Henry Ossawa Tanner, Jacob Lawrence, Elizabeth Catlett, Romare Bearden, Faith Ringgold, and Martin Puryear. Others including Scipio Moorehead, Mary Edmonia Lewis, James Presley Ball, Robert Duncanson, and Meta Warrick Fuller are only familiar to art specialists. Still, thousands of other artists and their works have gone unrecorded or unheralded despite contributing to America's rich visual legacy. Whether formally trained or self-taught, crafting objects for their personal use or fulfilling public commissions, African American artists and artisans have applied all possible media and styles to express themselves aesthetically.

Art produced by African American artists over the centuries includes innumerable drawings, designs, paintings, sculptures, carvings, ceramics, architecture, photographs, prints, cartoons, computer graphics, web pages, furniture, clothing, jewelry, utensils, site-specific installations, performance pieces, films, and videos. In all its variants, African American art appeals to aesthetic sensibilities, inspires confidence, raises awareness, and challenges long-standing assumptions of viewers. Thus, African American art stands as one of the most important bodies of creative works shaping aesthetic, intellectual, and visual culture throughout the world.

◆ THE AFRICAN ROOTS OF AFRICAN AMERICAN ART

Of the millions of Africans who were brought to the Americas, the majority came from West and Central Africa. Transported by British, French, Dutch, Spanish, and Portuguese slave traders, Africans in the Americas originated from cultures as disparate as the Akan, Bambara, Edo, Igbo, Kongo, Mandinka, Mende, Twi, Wolof, Fante, and Yoruba. These ethnic groups, cultures, kingdoms, and nation-states had varying levels of social, political, and economic accomplishment. Within each of these societies, there was a common language, cosmology, spiritual practices, and political-economic history that shaped the related art-making practices. Consequently, a diverse artistic legacy emerged across the African continent, with each society developing its own unique arts traditions (i.e., subjects, forms, styles, materials and usage). For example, the stylized abstract copper reliquary figures from Gabon differ sharply from the naturalistic Ile Ife terracotta and bronze sculptures.

Despite this ethnic variety, Westerners use the sloppy generic term "tribe" to describe all African social systems. Generally speaking, this is a misleading term/concept because it obscures the structural complexity, diversity, and long histories of African societies. The term also distorts and diminishes the historical significance of the artistic, aesthetics, and patronage traditions that arose within each society. Under the American institution of slavery with its forced stripping of African cultural expressions and mixing together of African ethnic groups, most people of African descent in the United States lost knowledge of the unique qualities that distinguish one group of African people from another. Since most African Americans lack concrete connection to a specific ethnic group, culture, or region, they symbolically lay claim to the entire continent as an ancestral homeland.

Initially, however, Africans brought an appreciation for their culture's language, cosmology, spiritual beliefs, ceremonies, rituals, ancestry, and political history. In addition, they brought knowledge of the aesthetic values, artistic practices, and visual customs of their individual cultures. Many carried skills and talents from working as artists and artisans in one of the many gender-segregated workshops and guilds. African art guilds produced objects as varied as sculpture, jewelry, textiles, and pottery, all made from materials as diverse as gold, bronze, wood, ivory, cotton, silk, fur, raffia, clay, beads, and shells. For example, the Edo artists that cast the world-renowned "Benin bronzes" for the Edo royal courts of the fourteenth to eighteenth centuries worked within a very different artistic and political tradition than the ivory carvers of saltcellars that were exported from the Kongo to Europe. Some art forms, styles, and techniques have survived, retained in modified versions and adapted to American cultural milieu. With increasing frequency, twentieth century African American artists are self-consciously reclaiming African aesthetics and art practices.

◆ THE FORMATION OF AN ARTS TRADITION

Synthesis and resistance are the cultural and creative hallmarks of African American art. Culturally, African American art is a hybrid tradition of the aesthetic values and artistic practices of Africa, the African Diaspora, Western Europe, and Euro-America. Each of these cultural groups within their historical era has its own set of prevailing social values, economic conditions, and political relations, as well as individual and collective artistic interests. These factors combine to affect the changing proportion of African or European influence on black artists' work. The most formative influence arises from the fusion of so many African ethnic heritages into the revitalized amalgam now known as African American culture.

African and African Diasporic visual arts traditions are dramatically different from Western traditions in both form (medium/material, style/technique)and content (subject/themes, motifs/meaning). The ultimate tension is that Western traditions are based on principles that radically conflict in their regard for African life, art, and culture. African visual tradition assumes the hu-

manity, beauty, intelligence, and worth of African and African -descended people. Conversely, white-European tradition has exploited and manipulated the authority of Western philosophy, aesthetics, social theory, and science to associate full human potential with only people of European descent, especially male.

Necessarily, black art is a resilient representational practice that resists cultural oppression. From the colonial period of enslavement to the present day, black artists have had to work within and against a mainstream visual culture that customarily demonizes blackness and devalues all things African. As a result, black artists' work, self-consciously and by its mere existence, undermines European racial mythologies along with the social, political, and economic hierarchies that those European-derived myths justify. Black art, therefore, is an artistic and aesthetic heritage that works to value blackness and black people, particularly as worthy subject matter, while simultaneously redeeming the diverse cultural heritages of Africa.

◆ THE AFRICAN LEGACY ENDURES IN COLONIAL AMERICA

Africans in colonial America created art and artifacts that revealed their indebtedness to Africa's myriad cultural traditions. For the most part, black artists during the seventeenth and eighteenth centuries were enslaved. Works created under this adverse condition fall into two broad categories. First, Africans with technical skills were required to direct most of their time and creative talents to making items for the use and benefit of slaveholders. Enslaved Africans built many of the plantation manors along with the interior furnishings. Their metal crafting skills helped produce beautiful decorative arts as well as the shackles used for bondage. Second, since enslaved Africans were forced to work from sunup to sundown, they only occasionally found time or resources to apply their creative energies to benefit themselves, families, or friends. A standing, wrought iron figure and a decorated wooden drum made in the style of the Akan are the earliest known pieces of art made for themselves, uncovered through archaeological excavations of Virginia plantations.

Generally, early black artists did not have the liberty to make such art as painting and sculpture, nor did they have resources to work in such precious materials as canvas oil, marble, or gold. Rather, they adapted skills and techniques once employed to make objects for daily use, sacred ceremonies, or African royal courts. Artistic and aesthetic Africanisms can be found embedded in the details of architectural ornaments, building designs, handcrafted furniture, quilts, clothing, and tools. African carpenters designed and built their one-room quarters using styles and techniques originating in Africa. These techniques and motifs testify to the cultural and historic difficulties that surface when trying to draw concrete boundaries between what are black arts and what are Euro-American arts.

Early Black Artists Secure Compensation for Their Efforts

Black women and men were often sold and purchased based on their skills. They were often hired out by slaveholders and permitted to keep a small portion of the earned income. In this way, some slaves were able to save enough money to buy their own and family members' freedom. They often worked as anonymous apprentices and journeyman in occupations as varied as pottery, silversmithing, cabinet making, and tailoring.

The proportion of emancipated or even free-born black people and artists was higher in the North than the South. Yet, they too lived and labored within all the legal and cultural oppression of white supremacist culture. To secure monetary or material compensation for their work, free black artisans made objects that appealed to the aesthetic sensibilities of the patron class—whites with discretionary funds. Some of what has been preserved and celebrated as Euro-American art and architecture, in many instances, may have been produced by enslaved or free black people.

Prominent Black Artists in Early America

There are, however, art and artisans whose names and works are part of the historical record. Scipio Moorehead is the first black painter with an attributed work. Moorehead was an enslaved African who learned drawing and painting from his slaveholder's wife. He created a 1773 ink drawing *Portrait of Phillis Wheatley.* —of which an engraving of Moorehead's portrait served as the frontispiece of her celebrated book of poetry *Poems on Various Subjects, Religious and Moral.* The young poet paid homage to Moorehead's painting skills in a poem titled "To S. M., A Young African Painter, On Seeing His Work." Since none of Moorehead's paintings are extant, Wheatley's description serves to describe them.

Dave Drake (c. 1780s–1864) was one of the most prolific potters in the Edgefield District of South Carolina. Dave's slaveholder taught him the craft, but Dave quickly developed his own distinctive style for making large, glazed stoneware jars. It is unclear how Dave learned to read and write, but he did so even though it was a violation of South Carolina law. Dave left his own enduring legacy because he signed his name on dozens of pots. He also enhanced his renown work by compos-

This engraving was derived from a 1773 ink drawing entitled *Portrait of Phillis Wheatley* by early African American artist Scipio Moorehead (The Library of Congress).

ing such short, prophetic verses as "this noble jar will hold 20/fill it with silver then you'll have plenty" (March 31, 1858) that he inscribed around the exterior surface of over twenty pots.

Much later, Harriet Powers (1837–1911), a former slave made two appliquéd quilts in 1886 and 1898 that are highly regarded creative statements that reveal her retention of African design qualities. They are sometimes referred to as Bible quilts because most of the individual panels represent Old and New Testament scenes. Power's quilts are representative of the innovative character of black quilters, both female and male. These self-taught or informally trained artisans produced an important segment of nineteenth-century black arts and crafts.

◆ RISE OF THE PROFESSIONAL ARTISTS

In the late eighteenth and nineteenth centuries, many black people had aspiration to express themselves creatively in the fine arts of painting and sculpture. Among these early black artists, some were born free and others emancipated, but all accepted work when and where they could find it. Generally, these artists worked independently and without the support of artist collectives or the encouragement of black arts movements. More often than not, only Euro-Americans possessed the financial resources to purchase or commission hand-painted portraits, still life studies, history pictures, landscapes, mythological or genre scenes, monumental public sculpture, private garden sculpture, elaborate cemetery markers, or delicate decorative arts. As a result, for black artists working in the fine arts, financial success and artistic accomplishment depended upon a repression of African-derived forms or aesthetics and the avoidance of subject matter that celebrated or respected the humanity of African people and their descendants.

Historical records indicate that Joshua Johnston (1765–1830) was the earliest artist of African descent to work as a professional portrait painter. After being freed in 1796, Johnston worked as a "limner" or self-taught artist. He advertised his services in the newspapers and painted quaint, modest portraits of prosperous merchants and their families in the Baltimore, Maryland area. There are now eighty paintings signed by or attributed to Johnston. This relatively large body of work suggests that Johnston's simplistic and conservative style met with the puritanical aesthetic tastes of affluent whites in the early American republic. Only two portraits are of men of African descent and both wear clerics collars. These portraits link Johnston to a class of free-black, anti-slavery activists in his home city. Historians suggest that one painting *Portrait of a Cleric* is of Daniel Coker, a black abolitionist and forefather of the African Methodist Episcopal (A.M.E.) Church. As a founding father of black art, Johnston created works that met the needs of patrons in conflicting classes—a paradoxical legacy that continues today.

Black artists infused their representations of historical figures as well as fictional ones with a dignity and strength of character foreign to white artists' works. Before and after the Civil War, James Ball turned his camera on his own family, capturing polished images of free black people with access to the middle-class comforts. Although the family shots are a small percentage of Ball's pictures, they stand in sharp contrast to the tattered and unkempt look customarily used to represent black people by white artists. Patrick H. Reason's engraving of Henry Bibb's portrait is another exquisite example. It is a dignified portrayal of the anti-slavery lecturer and celebrated slave narrative author. Book in hand, Henry Bibb stares boldly out at the viewer. The pose refers to his command of the art of writing and his courage to resist oppression. It is an image that under-

mines the pro-slavery myths that black people were docile creatures who happily accepted positions of servitude and lacked the capacity to reason.

Professional African American Artists Depict Their Culture

In terms of subject and style, it is often difficult to distinguish the work of nineteenth-century black painters, sculptors, or photographers from that of their white counterparts. Robert Duncanson's Ohio River style landscape paintings, capturing the grandeur of the American wilderness, provide no indication that the artist is of African ancestry. This is also true for the daguerreotypes and photographs by James Presley Ball, as nearly all of his portraits are of Euro-Americans. The most notable and important exception occurs in the small percentage of professional African American artists' work that portrays black people.

Edward Mitchell Bannister's *Newspaper Boy* (1869) is an engaging portrait of an industrious black lad. This seemingly uncomplicated portrait is exceptional because white artists either represented black youth as ingratiating servants, or they depicted them as lazy, mischievous, and troublesome thieves. In this and other works, black artists rejected the demeaning facial caricatures and stereotypical scenes favored by Euro-American artists and collectors.

In the aftermath of the Civil War and Reconstruction, white Americans developed so many representations of grinning, deferential black male banjo players that the pictorial theme became a defaming and humiliating staple in the visual vocabulary of American culture. In 1893, however, Henry O. Tanner took up the banjo subject in *Banjo Lesson*, one of his three "genre" paintings portraying African Americans. Tanner's painting of an aged man passing on a cherished skill to a young boy turned a convention of gross caricature into a sensitive representation that respects rather than ridicules black musical talent and familial relations. Under risky circumstances, nineteenth century artists therefore used the visual arts as an arena to exercise their creativity while simultaneously struggling to undermine and rebuke hostile cultural imagery that perpetuated African American oppression.

African American Artists Study in Europe

The most ambitious African American artists throughout the nineteenth century and the first half of the twentieth century sought critical acclaim, patronage, and financial success working as formally trained fine artists. To work in the academic or avant-garde styles of their day, African American artists who had the neces-

Newspaper Boy. Edward Mitchell Bannister, 1869 (Art Resource).

sary financial resources or social connections traveled to France, England, German and Italy to train in the academies and studios of prominent painters and sculptors. In many cases, black artists such as the neoclassical sculptor Mary Edmonia Lewis (c.1850–1911) and Henry Ossawa Tanner (1859–1937) preferred to live and work in Europe. Black expatriates found more opportunities and greater acceptance living with racial prejudice in Europe than in segregated America.

◆ AFRICAN AMERICAN ARTS IN THE TWENTIETH CENTURY

During the twentieth century more and more creative African Americans swelled the ranks of formally trained and professional artists. They built upon the scattered personal efforts of their predecessors, fashioning a modern art tradition as individuals, art collectives, and participants of broad cultural movements. Various intellectual trends, political ideologies, and aesthetic values emerged during the century to demonstrate the look and significance of African American art. Influences as varied as pan-Africanism, modernist primitivism, Black power, feminism, Afrocentrism, and post-modernism

presented the work of artists as dissimilar as Augusta Savage, Palmer Hayden, Elizabeth Catlett, Norman Lewis, Faith Ringgold, Charles Searles, John Biggers, Renee Stout, Lorna Simpson, and David Hammons.

Twentieth century creative visionaries expanded the form of African American art by working in styles, techniques, and materials considered experimental, innovative, and avant-garde, as well as those deemed conservative and derivative. By broadening the parameters for acceptable subject matter to include representations of black people and black life, these artists dramatically transformed the power of American visual culture. In addition, African American artists and their supporters have engaged in century-long dialogues regarding the role of black artists, the purpose of their work, black artists' relationship to black communities, and their responsibility to try and improve the conditions under which black people live.

The "New Negro" Era

African American artists, who came of age at the turn of the twentieth century, emerged during an era that supported artistic sensibilities and creative concerns focusing on the cultivation and uplift of the "New Negro." As a concept or term, the "New Negro" came to designate an ideology of resistance and a form of progressive social activism that stood against all forms of oppression. This new attitude prompted hundreds of thousands of African Americans to migrate from the rural agrarian South to the urban industrial North to escape dire economic circumstances, the horrors of Jim Crow segregation, white supremacist nightriders, and lynch mob culture. The resulting surge in political organizing, social mobilization, and cultural renewal is referred to as the "New Negro" movement or the Negro Renaissance.

"New Negro" intellectuals and political leaders embraced a form of race consciousness that allowed them to value black culture and arts, actually celebrating them as integral to America's contemporary richness and future greatness. Their activism gave birth to a generation of modern African American artists with twentieth century, rather than nineteenth-century, artistic concerns. These artists worked in diverse media and styles, yet their aesthetic convictions rested on the assumption that black people and culture were worthy and significant subjects for modern art.

W. E. B. Du Bois routinely urged such African American artists as Henry Ossawa Tanner and Meta Warrick (1877–1968) to develop visual imagery that would rehabilitate the image of black people in the public imagination. He urged artists to produce paintings and sculptures that challenged the European and Euro-American tradition of representing black people in a litany of fine arts servants and advertising stereotypes. Some accepted the call to create art in service of social uplift, while others only wanted to make art as an individual form of expression. Whatever their creative inspiration, "New Negro" era artists' works are revered icons that serve as the collective cornerstone of the twentieth-century African American art and aesthetics.

Meta Warrick Fuller's 1914 bronze sculpture *Ethiopia Awakening* is a landmark artistic statement. It is the earliest example of African American art to overtly validate African arts and cultures. The near life-size personification of Africa wears the headdress of an ancient Egyptian queen. She appears to be emerging from her mummy-like wrapping, though the lower portion of her body remains bound. *Ethiopia Awakening* directly challenged a favored Western visual theme called The Four Continents (Europe, Asia, America and Africa). By convention many white artists portrayed the African continent as asleep, contributing nothing to the development of human civilization with the exception of slave labor. Throughout the twentieth century, however, many artists have become more knowledgeable about Africa and its cultures, allowing them to completely abandon Western-derived assertions that the continent of Africa laid dormant.

James VanDerZee's (1886–1983) photographs captured the vitality of Harlem in its heyday as the "mecca" of African American life and culture. For example, his individual and group portraits of Marcus Garvey and Universal Negro Improvement Association-sponsored parades are meaningful historical documents and creative aesthetic statements. He also permanently fixed the image of thousands of Harlemites whose names have been lost, although their upwardly mobile images continue to testify to the cultural energy of urban life. In addition, such painters as Edward Harleston, Malvin Gray Johnson, William Edouard Scott, and Laura Wheeler Warring captured the vibrancy of black culture in their portraits and pictorial scenes.

The Harlem Renaissance and the Works Progress Administration

The "New Negro" era sparked an intense flowering of artistic creativity among African American writers, musicians, singers, theater performers, and fine artists. When World War I ended in 1918, Harlem, an uptown section of Manhattan, was home to the largest black population in urban America and the cultural heart of this artistic activity. Frequently referred to as the Harlem Renaissance, it was a national and international movement in black arts and culture encompassing other

Famed photographer James VanDerZee took this portrait of black nationalist leader Marcus Garvey.

urban centers such as Chicago, Cleveland, and Washington, DC, as well as in the Caribbean and Europe.

Alain Locke (1885–1954), a Howard University philosophy professor and Rhodes scholar, was a prominent architect of the Harlem-based arts revival. He believed that if black artists demonstrated their creative and intellectual mastery of literature and the fine arts to the American public, they would garner respect for the black race and thereby change white attitudes and improve race relations. To stimulate critical and financial support for black artists, Locke served as guest editor for "Harlem: Mecca of the New Negro," a special issue of the journal *Survey Graphic* (1925). Contributing essayists theorized and celebrated the aesthetics of African art and the achievements of African American arts and culture.

Locke's essay "The Legacy of the Ancestral Arts" urged black artists to draw upon the artistic and cultural legacies of Africa in the creation of their art. Locke maintained that if the stylized abstraction of West African sculpture could inspire avant-garde artists (e.g. Pablo Picasso, George Braque, or Emile Nolde) to create important modern styles such as cubism or German

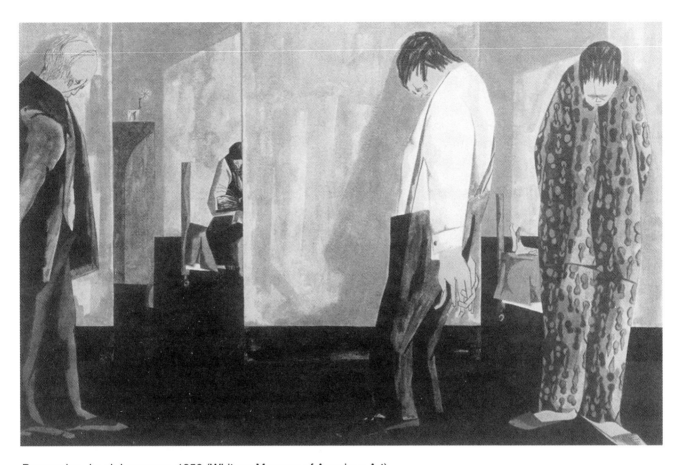

Depression. Jacob Lawrence, 1950 (Whitney Museum of American Art).

expressionism, it certainly should lead "New Negro" artists to develop a unique visual vocabulary. Locke's and his contributors' ideas were culturally progressive at the time. Yet, they rested on two concepts refuted today: the existence of biologically determined racial essences and a form of romantic primitivism. The later not only cast Africa and Africans as primitive, but as the polar opposite of civilized Europe and Europeans.

Nonetheless, artists as diverse as Aaron Douglas, Palmer Hayden, Sargent Claude Johnson, Archibald Motley, Jr. James Lesesne Wells, and Augusta Savage, temporarily or permanently abandoned the conventions of their European style training to experiment with African-inspired styles or subjects. Aaron Douglas is the artist most frequently highlighted as the quintessential Harlem Renaissance artist. A trained portrait painter, Douglas abandoned the realist style, developing instead a stylized Egyptian form of figurative painting that graces numerous Harlem Renaissance publications, including illustrations and designs in Alain Locke's book *The New Negro* and James Weldon Johnson's *God's Trombones: Seven Negro Sermons in Verse* (1927).

The movement generated an unprecedented level of patronage from private individuals and organizations.

For example, the National Association for the Advancement of Colored People (NAACP) and the National Urban League instituted important art awards. Their respective publications *Crisis* and *Opportunity* became venues for artists and for critical reviews of "New Negro" art exhibitions. The principal sponsorship of Harlem Renaissance art came from the Harmon Foundation, established by the real estate investor William E. Harmon. The foundation awarded prizes and sponsored juried exhibitions and shows that traveled around the United States. The foundation exercised creative control over the type of art produced or promoted. As a result, the foundation, shows, awards, and even the artists have been subject to social and critical controversy.

Occurring during the high point of the Harlem Renaissance, the stock market crash of 1929 cast the United States into the Great Depression. The Federal Arts Project (1935–1943) was one of the "New Deal" relief programs sponsored by Franklin D. Roosevelt's Works Progress Administration (WPA). The Federal Arts Project (FAP) paid artists to produce works celebrating America and American art styles for the public. The FAP promoted an environment where figuration and social realism were valued over abstraction and allegory. In many ways, FAP funding contributed to black artists' turning away from the stylistic Africanisms encouraged by Locke and the Harmon Foundation, focusing instead on African American folk culture.

A Federal Arts Project assignment employed a young Jacob Lawrence and provided him early support in his career. He subsequently became one of America's most celebrated black artists. Lawrence titled a series of sixty paintings *The Migration of the Negro* (1940–1941). The series secured him critical acclaim, a feature in *Fortune* magazine, a one-man show at the prestigious Downtown Gallery, and the purchase of several of his panels by the Museum of Modern Art. In Chicago, the Southside Community Art Center (SCAC) provided early careers opportunities for such artists as Archibald Motley, Jr., Charles Sebree, and Gordon Roger Parks. In addition, Hughie Lee-Smith and Charles Sallee found teaching opportunities and support at Karamu House Artist Association in Cleveland (established 1935). The Karamu House and SCAC are still in operation today.

Clearly, the Federal Arts Project and the Works Progress Administration were important for the development of African American art. Yet, black artists complained that the program administrators routinely discriminated against them. The Harlem Artists Guild (1935–1941), a collective founded by Augusta Savage, Elba Lightfoot, Charles Alston and Arthur Schomburg, made the redressing of the problems an important organizational goal.

African American Artists Explore Modernistic Art Forms

By the late 1930s and early 1940s, such artists as William H. Johnson, Charles Alston, Hale A. Woodruff, and Norman Lewis were less inspired by social realism and more interested in the formalist concerns of European modernism, especially expressionism and abstraction. Eldzier Cortor and Hughie Lee Smith, for instance, explored the visual power of surrealism in paintings. They preferred the challenge of working in styles that most Americans considered foreign and experimented with such a range of approaches that in some abstract paintings the subject is recognizable while in other paintings the subjects are completely non-presentational. Romare Bearden (1911–1988) was an African American artist that began working with representational abstraction. During the 1940s, however, he moved on to become an early practitioner of abstract expressionism, a modern art movement that catapulted New York onto the world art scene, effectively displacing Paris as the leading center of the art world.

The modernist disdain for realism took hold among American avant-garde artists, critics, and patrons. Thus, an arts environment was cultivated in which Euro-

American collectors could "discover" and champion the art of such self-trained African American artists as the painter Horace Pippen and the sculptor William Edmondson, because they did not employ the conventions of representation realism. Collectors believed these self-taught artisans found modernist expression without the struggle of rejecting formal training or attempting to surpass tradition. White collectors and curators commonly referred to these self-taught artists as "folk artists,'" "native artists," and "Negro-primitives," frequently preferring and promoting them over professionally trained African American artists. Despite the criticism that this was a racist and patronizing practice, twentieth-century self-taught artists have continued to be important contributors to African American art.

From "Black Art" to "Afrocentrism"

The Black Art movement, also referred to as the Black Aesthetic movement, developed during the tumultuous 1960s in defiant opposition to Western or Eurocentric aesthetic values that continued to regulate the appreciation and production of art and culture in the United States. Proponents of the Black Art movement challenged members of the black creative community to redefine the roles of the artist and art in light of an increasingly radicalized black political agenda. Black aestheticism championed the belief that the first step towards black liberation required black people to construct a new world view. It insisted that black people needed to develop a black consciousness or perspective that is Africa-centered rather than Europe-centered as a form of intellectual growth and personal empowerment.

The Black Art debates were heated and polemic. Definitions and interpretations of black aestheticism were conflicting. Addison Gayle's anthology *The Black Aesthetics* (1971) captured the theoretic diversity among literary and visual artists. Yet, proponents universally embraced some qualities. First and foremost, they rejected the notion that art and politics were separate domains of human activity. The late critic and poet Larry Neal, one of the movements most influential theorists, proclaimed, "the artist and the political activist are one." He maintained that the difference between the Black Arts and Black Power concepts is that "one is concerned with the relationship between art and politics; the other with the art of politics."

Under this theoretic formation, art was not a luxury, but a basic and necessary weapon in black people's struggle against the social and political order of the United States. In theory and practice, those embracing black aestheticism rejected the idea that art was destined for the pedestals and walls of private galleries, public museums, and homes of the affluent. They attacked the modernist doctrine of "art for art's sake" as false and misleading, asserting that art must support and promote a black revolution. Black visual artists across the United States heeded the call, creating a body of paintings, sculptures, prints, assemblages, and public murals that sought to inform and inspire black people to aggressively resist oppression. One stream of black aesthetic artists created works that were inspired by the revolutionary idealism of African liberation struggles against European colonialism. Another stream of Black Arts visionaries de-emphasized the political and focused on celebrating the glory of ancient and contemporary African cultures.

An example of the evolution of community art and its accessibility was represented by the emergence of a group called COBRA: the Coalition of Black Revolutionary Artist. Members of the group collaborated on a community mural project in Chicago, Illinois, creating the Wall of Respect (1967), painting portraits of historical black figures including Frederick Douglas, Marcus Garvey, and Malcolm X. Their celebration of ethnic heritage and identity became beacons for black consciousness murals in Detroit and Boston. COBRA later became known as the AFRI-COBRA: the African Commune of Bad Relevant Artists.

Prior to this period, affluent Euro-Americans were the main collectors, patrons, and consumers of black artists' work. Therefore, black artists' solicitation of a black audience marks a critical turning point in the development of the African American artistic tradition. These artists did not define their work as protest art, because by black aesthetic definitions, protest art plays to the moral conscience of a liberal white audience. Theoretically, the Black Art movement spoke to those who lived the black social and cultural experience.

In 1967 the Faith Ringgold's painting titled *US Postage Stamp to Commemorate the Advent of Black Power* indicated her general support for the more militant tendencies of the organized struggle for black human rights over those of the Civil Rights movement. Elizabeth Catlett aligned herself with specific political activists and a particular political organization in her 1969 prints entitled *Malcolm Speaks for Us* and *Homage to the Panthers*. Dana Chandler's paintings *(4)00 More Years* and *Molotov Cocktail* are representative of a group of works that launch a pictorial assault against American cultural symbols such as the United States flag. Other works such as Betye Saar's *The Liberation of the Aunt Jemima* (1972) attack the negative pictorial stereotypes that plague black men, women, and children. Saar revises the "mammy" image with a pistol, rifle, and broom. However, not in her old role as caretaker to the world, but in a new position as an urban warrior. Such artists as Saar, Murry DePillars, Jeff Donaldson, and Joe Overstreet created pieces that rob established

Faith Ringgold (Courtesy of Faith Ringgold)

visual clichés as Aunt Jemima of their widespread cultural currency.

The other stream of artists focused on cultural reclamation rather than political agitation. As more and more African countries gained their independence, beginning with Ghana in 1957, black artists began traveling to the African continent. They produced art honoring legendary African kings and queens, colorful scenes of African villages, and busy marketplaces. They learned about African art and culture from first-hand experience rather than books written by Europeans or Euro-Americans. They produced works such as Thomas Feeling's *Senegalese Woman* and John Bigger's *Ghanian Harvest Festival*, which capture the strength and beauty of African women while emphasizing the vibrancy of their traditional dress. In contrast to this document quality, such artists as Charles Searles and Faith Ringgold created colorful, African-inspired paintings and sculptures, borrowing African formal elements and materials and reworking them into generic stylized visions.

Since the so-called streams were never hard and fast, numerous artists worked in both, self-consciously attempting to balance the formal and the political. The Civil Rights and Black Power movements generated tremendous debates and activity among creative artists, and some critics dismissed the art as angry, romantic, or mere propaganda. As organized activism waned in the mid- to late 1970s, the Black Art movement lost much of it collective momentum. Many artists who emerged during the era are still creating, exhibiting, or teaching art today. Their artistic theories, artistic strategies, and aesthetic concerns helped lay the foundation for African American contemporary arts.

Contemporary Arts

During 1980s and 1990s, there has been a virtual explosion in the number of self-taught and formally trained African Americans who create, exhibit, and market their art. Contemporary artists have opportunities to work with a diverse array of materials, media, new technologies, and critical concepts. They are able to employ styles, techniques, and approaches unimagined by their creative predecessors.

During this time period, individual African American artists received critical recognition, increased gallery representation, greater inclusion in group and solo museum shows, and became the subject of academic scholarship. Such artists as Emma Amos, Jean-Michel Basquiat , Robert Colescott, Houston Conwill, Lyle Ashton Harris, Glenn Ligon, Renee Green, Lorraine O'Grady, Howardena Pindell, Alison Saar, and Fred Wilson have produced visually engaging art work. African American visual artists have been the recipients of prestigious prizes and awards. In 1987, Romare Bearden was awarded the Presidential Medal of Honor. In recent years, MacArthur Fellowships have been awarded to Robert Blackburn, David Hammons, Kerry James Marshall, Martin Puryear, John T. Scott, and Kara Walker.

Contemporary African American art manifests as multiple aesthetic and artistic trends, not as a single, consciously-constructed art movement. Afrocentricity, feminism, postmodernism are a few of the influential intellectual and cultural currents shaping the work of painters, sculptors, photographers, and video, mixed-media installation, and performance artists. Additionally, individual artists have the insight and liberty to have a multiplicity of interests. They explore issues of race, gender, sexuality, sexual orientation, and class as intersecting rather than mutually exclusive concerns. This stands in contrast to the Harlem Renaissance or Black Arts movement which primarily challenged racism, with the latter movement frequently dismissing feminists' calls to end sexism as hampering racial unity. Today, works by artists such as Lorna Simpson, Carrie Mae Weems, or Adrian Piper build on the groundbreaking feminist work of such artists as Elizabeth Catlett and Faith Ringgold who are themselves still producing.

Carrie Mae Weems and Lorna Simpson combine written text with photographic or figurative imagery. This contemporary practice allows them to create art that can challenge the viewer, pose questions, and offer devastating culture critiques that focus on dismantling racial and sexual mythologies. Simpson is the first African American woman to have a solo exhibit at the Museum of Modern Art, while Weems is the first African American woman to have a major exhibition at the National Museum for Women in the Arts.

Other contemporary artists such as Dawoud Bey, Renee Cox, Anthony (Tony) Gleaton, Fern Logan, and Coreen Simpson use the medium of photography in innovative and profoundly illuminating ways. Following the lead of Roy DeCarava and Gordon Parks, this new generation of artists turns their cameras on people, scenes, and cityscapes, transforming documentary photography into aesthetically stimulating art.

Additionally, there is an important contingent of contemporary African American painters and sculptors who consider abstraction and the emphasis on the skillful manipulation of materials far more rewarding than figuration or overt cultural criticism. Barbara Chase-Riboud, Melvin Edwards, Sam Gilliam, Richard Hunt, Marian Hassinger, Alvin D. Loving, Jr., Martin Puryear, Raymond Saunders, and William T. Williams continue to follow the abstractionist path paved by such artists as Alma Thomas (1891–1978), Hale Woodruff (1900–1980), and Norman Lewis (1909–1979).

Charles Bibbs, Varnetta Honeywood, Synthia Saint James are representative of a group of artists who celebrate African American culture in their work. They create symbolic images about love, strength, fortitude, survival, spirituality, and vitality. Their colorful, figurative works pay tribute to historical figures as well as daily activities that are the heart and soul of African American life and culture. They are heartwarming, esteem-building scenes that recall church and family gatherings, children playing, men laboring, women quilting or braiding hair, people dancing, or lovers embracing. Artists working in this trend self-consciously cultivate an appreciation for African-inspired aesthetics, design principles, forms, concerns, and some subject matter. The National Black Arts Festival, founded in 1988, is a citywide, biannual event held in Atlanta, Georgia, that showcases art of this type.

In many instances, these artists specifically create for popular culture rather than the so-called fine art market where collectors pay high prices for the unique art object. The celebratory images easily translate into accessibly priced reproductions, such as print, posters, cards, mugs, T-shirts, book illustrations, and even Internet pages that cater to an African American buying public. It was virtually impossible to find reproductions of African American art in the mid-1980s. Today, however, they can be purchased from galleries, frame shops, mail order, or web pages.

With the arrival of the twenty-first century, computer technology, public media, and visual images have emerged as important forms of expression. Such artists as Leah Gilliam are creating and appropriating visual images to make computer-generated art for distribution on CD-ROM or display on the Internet. Artists such as Renee Cox and Alonzo Adams even maintain their own Internet sites, allowing them to take African American art directly to a global audience.

◆ ARTS-RELATED SUPPORT PROFESSIONS

Historically, black artists have not had equal and unrestricted access to institutions that support the making, exhibiting, and collecting of art. Despite the modernist myth that art and aesthetics are separate and distinct from the political arena, the making and consuming of art are deeply enmeshed in it. Many arts schools, museums, galleries, as well as private and public patrons followed the Jim Crow and gender segregation dictated by U.S. laws or social customs. Thus, black men and women have not had equal access to training, severely limiting the number of people who could become artists. Moreover, in the arena of creative expression, whites males have had and continue to receive privileges not extended to women of all races or men of color. Fortunately, opportunities increased dramatically during the post-civil rights era, and this exponentially increased the number of black people who chose to train and define themselves as artists and independent craftspeople. Consequently, there has been an unprecedented flowering of African American arts and culture during the last three decades of the twentieth century, as countless black women and men opt to use the visual arts as a form of expression.

Despite the upsurge, the majority of African American artists still struggle to find support and encouragement from teachers, curators, dealers, collectors, critics, and historians. There is a need to increase the intelligently informed support for black artists and their work. Black artists must depend upon support from arts-related professionals to promote widespread knowledge and appreciation of their work. These arts-related professionals include art critics who evaluate the merit of art and art shows; curators who acquire, preserve, and exhibit art for public museums and private collectors; commercial art dealers who promote interest in specific artists, sell their original art, and market more accessibly priced reproductions; and art historians who study the types of art that creative people make. Necessarily, art historians are interested in providing insight about the beliefs and philosophies underpinning aesthetic preferences, criticism, patronage, collection, use, and exhibition patterns. They also chronicle the emergence of forms, subjects, styles, conventions, and techniques and try to account for their transformation and change over time.

These arts-related professionals are necessary forces in the development of scholarly and critical commentary (i.e., books, catalogues, and journal articles), and exhibitions that showcase black art. Black artists and their work will begin to gain more scholarly and critical attentions, exhibitions, gallery space, and sales as the number of art-related professionals with formal training in African American art expand.

Books and exhibition catalogues are an important source for stimulating interest in African American art. Presently, four illustrated surveys provide comprehensive and up-to-date accounts of African American visual arts. Samella Lewis' *African American Art and Artists* (1994) provides brief historical overviews and artists biographies. Crystal A. Britton's *African American Art: The Long Struggle* (1996) is a narrative of a collective visual tradition. Richard J. Powell's *Black Art and Culture in the Twentieth Century* (1997) is a more theoretical analysis of themes, trends, and high moments uniting black cultural production. Written as a new addition to the multi-volume series *World of Art* published by Thames and Hudson, Powell's book is the first in the collection to focus on African American artists.

In 1998, Oxford University Press released Sharon F. Patton's *African American Art* as an historic addition to its series the *Oxford History of Art*. It is a textbook that includes glossaries, timelines, and penetrating analyses. As the first African American art surveys by major mainstream publishing houses, Powell's and Patton's books are landmark and potentially trendsetting, scholarly publications. In addition, Hampton University Museum publishes a quarterly periodical *The International Review of African American Art*. A recent volume has been published as a collector's handbook.

◆ EXHIBITING AFRICAN AMERICAN ART

The decades of the 1970s through the 1990s gave birth to a group of influential exhibitions dedicated to resurrecting, presenting, and discussing African American art and artists. Curators organized these special focus exhibits to fill the void left by the institutionalized exclusion of black artists and their work in mainstream shows by public museums or private galleries. Initially, these shows possessed a strong archaeological quality. Curators mined the collections of a wide variety of public and private patrons, excavating and assembling images by artists working in diverse media from many historical eras and stylistic periods.

The first wave of shows and catalogues had a documentary character, focusing on demonstrating the existence of black professional fine artists. Art that had languished in storerooms for generations was made available for public viewing in such shows and catalogues as: *Forever Free: Art by African-American Women, 1862–1980*, an exhibition organized by Arna Bontemps and Jacqueline Fonvielle-Bontemps; Lynda R. Hartigan's *Sharing Traditions: Five Black American Artists in Nineteen-Century America* (1985); Keith Morrison's *Art in Washington and Its Afro-American Presence: 1940–1970* (1985); *Bucknell University's Since the Harlem Renaissance: Fifty Years of Afro- American Art* (1984); David Driskell's *Hidden Heritage: Afro-American Art, 1800–1950* (1985); Edmund Barry Gaither's *Massachusetts Masters: Afro-American Artists* (1988); and *African-American Artists 1880–1987: Selections from the Evans-Tibbs Collection* (1989). These catalogues broke new ground simply in the quality of the richly illustrated color publications. Since exhibitions are temporary, making the reproductions available to a relatively wide audience allowed students and scholars the opportunity to continue to study works that had been hidden from both the contemporary and historical view. The majority of the artists featured are male, yet the works of a few women, such as Edmonia Lewis, Lois Mailou Jones, or Alma Thomas, also appear.

Another group of exhibits focused on the crafts art made by enslaved Africans, as well as those forms of creative expressions made by self-taught artists after the abolition of slavery. John Michael Vlach organized *The Afro-American Tradition in Decorative Arts* (1978), and the catalogue is a foundational text on the arts produced by enslaved people. The exhibited objects and collection of essays edited by Edward Campbell Jr. and Kym S. Rice in *Before Freedom Came: African-American Life in the Antebellum South* are extremely valuable for understanding the material production as well as its archaeological to ideological contexts. In addition, Jane Livingston and John Beardsley's *Black Folk Art in America, 1930–1980* (1982), William Ferris' *Afro-American Folk Arts and Crafts* (1983), and *Baking in the Sun:Visionary Images from the South, Selections from the Collection of Sylvia and Warren Lowe* (1987) discuss folk arts practices through the first half of the twentieth century.

The years leading to the 1976 U.S. Bicentennial gave birth to a recovery movement championing American art and culture. Although primarily celebrating white artists, the recovery movement brought legitimacy to American folk arts, especially female quilting traditions. In the following decade, the folk arts revival converged

Edmonia Lewis (New York Public Library)

with the growing interest in African American arts, paving the way for such exhibitions and catalogues as Gladys-Marie Fry's *Stitched From the Soul: Slave Quilts From the Ante-Bellum South*, Cuesta Benberry's *Always There: The African American Presence in American Quilts*, Maude Wahlman's *Signs and Symbols: African Images in African-American Quilts* and Moira Roth's *Faith Ringgold: Change, Painted Story Quilts*, which showcased quilts made by women of African descent from the period of enslavement to the present. These shows placed an important body of art before the public for appreciation and scholarly study. It is worth noting that non-black museums, galleries, and curators supported these quilt shows at a higher rate than they did shows by formally trained, professional black women artists. Furthermore, the curators who created the most conceptually challenging study of African American art organized exhibitions that explored themes, movements, or styles.

A series of exhibitions mounted in the 1980s advanced the scholarship on African American artists. The Studio Museum of Harlem, while under the directorship of Mary Schmidt Campbell, took the lead in the development of such creative, thought-provoking, and historically-based shows as *New York/Chicago: WPA and the Black Artists* (1978); *Ritual and Myth: A Survey of African American Art* (1982); *An Ocean Apart: American Artists Abroad* (1983); *Tradition and Conflict: Images of a Turbulent Decade, 1963–1973* (1985); and the richly illustrated *Harlem Renaissance: Art of Black America* (1987). The catalogues are collaborative efforts, containing sets of essays from a wide range of contributors. Essayists do not explore issues impacting women artists or contrast any of the formal or thematic concerns of women with those of men. The strength of these publications is that the writers discuss the art critically and historically, moving beyond the formula of recounting biographical information and describing the art's formal qualities.

In 1989, a large number of well-financed exhibitions and catalogues appeared after decades of little activity. Gary A. Reynolds and Beryl J. Wright organized *Against the Odds: African-American Artists and the Harmon Foundation*. Richard Powell organized *The Blues Aesthetic: Black Culture and Modernism*. Alvia Wardlow curated *Black Art Ancestral Legacy: The African Impulse in African-American Art*. The California Afro-American Museum opened *Introspectives: Contemporary Art by Americans and Brazilians of African Descent* and *1960s: A Cultural Awakening Re-evaluated 1965– 1975;* Deborah Willis and Howard Dodson curated *Black Photographers Bear Witness: 100 Year of Social Protest*. Leslie King-Hammond curated *Black Printmakers and the WPA* for the Lehman College Art Gallery in the Bronx. The catalogues accompanying these shows also reveal tremendous depth in the archival research, the resurrection of buried histories, and the production of historical analyses.

In connection with the 1990 biannual National Black Arts Festival in Atlanta, the Nexus Contemporary Art Center mounted *Africobra: The First Twenty Years*. Regina A. Perry published her long awaited *Free Within Ourselves: African-American Artists in the Collection of the National Museum of American Art* in 1992. *Dream Singers, Story Tellers: An African-American Presence* (1992) with essays and text in both English and Japanese provided a refreshingly new approach for an international audience. Bomani Gallery's *Paris Connections: African American Artists in Paris* (1992) examined production from an international perspective. Curator Thelma Golden organized *Black Male: Representations of Masculinity in Contemporary American Art* for the Whitney Museum of American Art. The art selected for the show examined notions of race and gender in the minds of artists of different races and the public at large. Beryl Wright's catalogues for *African-American Art Twentieth Century Masterworks,*

(1993) and Richard J. Powell's *Exultations: African-American Art Twentieth Century Masterworks, II* (1995) were unapologetically focused on canon building.

These exhibits and catalogues demonstrate that African American artists have been and continue to be important agents in the struggle for social, political, and economic justice in the United States. African American artists stand among the legions of incredibly resilient, courageous, and visionary black people who acted on their beliefs that the life that they wanted for themselves and others must be free of racial, economic, cultural, and visual barriers. The core of what artists have to say on canvas, in stone or on video, join what artists in literature, music, or theater have been thinking and verbalizng for centuries. In spirit, however, African American visual artists add another dimension to the chorus of voices that celebrate the ways that people of African descent thrive in the United States.

◆ VISUAL AND APPLIED ARTISTS

(To locate biographical profiles more readily, please consult the index at the back of the book.)

Charles Alston (1907–1972)
Painter, Sculptor, Muralist

Born in Charlotte, North Carolina, in 1907, Alston received his B.A. and M.A. from Columbia University in New York. He was later awarded several fellowships and grants to launch his painting career.

Alston's paintings and sculpture are in such collections as those of IBM and the Detroit Institute of Arts. His murals depicting the history of medicine adorn the facade of Harlem Hospital in New York, and he was a member of the National Society of Mural Painters. Notable works include: *Exploration and Colonization* (1949); *Blues with Guitar and Bass* (1957); *Blues Song* (1958); *School Girl* (1958); *Nobody Knows* (1966); *Sons and Daughters* (1966); and *Frederick Douglass* (1968).

Benny Andrews (1930–)
Painter

Born in Madison, Georgia, on November 13, 1930, Andrews studied at Fort Valley State College in Georgia and later at the University of Chicago. He was awarded a B.F.A. from the Art Institute of Chicago in 1958. During his career, he has taught at the New York School of Social Research, New York City University, and Queens College in New York. His works have appeared in exhibitions around the country including the Boston Museum of Fine Arts, The Martha Jackson Gallery in New York City, and other museums and galleries.

Andrews directed the Visual Arts Program for the National Endowment for the Arts from 1982 to1984. He has directed the National Arts Program since 1985, offering children and adults an opportunity to exhibit and compete for prizes in many cities across the United States.

Other honors include an honorary doctorate from the Atlanta School of Art, 1984; John Hay Whitney Fellowship, 1965 to 1967; New York Council on The Arts Grantee, 1971; NEA Fellowship, 1974; Bellagie fellow, Rockefeller Foundation, 1987; and a National Endowment for the Arts Painting Fellowship, 1986. Notable works include: *The Family; The Boxer; The Invisible Man; Womanhood; Flora;* and *Did the Bear.*

Edward Mitchell Bannister (1828–1901)
Painter

Born in Nova Scotia in 1828, Bannister was the son of a West Indian father and African American mother. Both parents died when he was very young. Bannister moved to Boston in the early 1850s, where he learned to make solar plates and worked as a photographer.

Influenced by the Barbizon style popular at the time, Bannister's paintings convey his own love of the quiet beauty of nature and his pleasure in picturesque scenes with cottages, cattle, dawns, sunsets, and small bodies of water. In 1871, Bannister moved from Boston to Providence, Rhode Island, where he lived until his death in 1901. He was the only nineteenth-century African American artist who did not travel to Europe to study art, believing that he was an American and wished to paint as an American. Bannister became one of the leading artists in Providence in the 1870s and 1880s, and in 1880 he became one of seven founders of the Providence Art Club, which later became known as the Rhode Island School of Design. Notable works include: *After the Storm; Driving Home the Cows;* and *Narragansett Bay.*

Ernie Barnes (1938–)
Painter

Barnes attended North Carolina Central College (now North Carolina Central University) from 1957 to 1960, where he majored in art and played on the football team. Barnes left school without graduating when the Washington Redskins drafted him. After playing for other NFL teams and a Canadian Football League team, Barnes retired due to an injury.

However, Barnes had continued to paint throughout his football career, and his teammates dubbed him "Big Rembrandt." With his experience as a player and his painterly talents, Barnes became a sports artist. He secured a contract to paint for the American Football League and New York Jets owner Sonny Werblin.

He was the official artist for the 1984 Olympic Games in Los Angeles. Barnes paints in a colorful and lively style. He exaggerates the muscularity and physical attributes of his figures. He received national attention when his paintings were used on the 1970s television show *Good Times.* In 1997, he completed his commission for the Naismith Memorial Basketball Hall of Fame in Springfield, Massachusetts.

Richmond Barthé (1901–1989)
Sculptor

Born on January 28, 1901, in Bay St. Louis, Mississippi, Barthé was educated at the Art Institute of Chicago from 1924 to 1928. He studied under Charles Schroeder and Albin Polasek. Barthé's first love was painting, but it was through his experiments with sculpture that he began to gain initial critical attention in 1927. His first commissions were busts of Henry Ossawa Tanner and Toussaint L'Ouverture. The acclaim resulting from them led to a one-man show in Chicago and a Rosenwald Fellowship for study in New York City.

Barthé's work has been exhibited at several major American museums. The Metropolitan Museum of Art in New York City purchased *The Boxer* in 1943. In 1946, he received the first commission given to an African American artist for a bust of Booker T. Washington for New York University's Hall of Fame. A year later he was one of the committee of fifteen artists chosen to help modernize sculpture in the Catholic churches of the United States.

Barthé held membership in the National Academy of Arts and Letters. He died March 6, 1989, at his home in Pasadena, California, at the age of eighty-eight. Notable works include: *Singing Slave; Maurice Ens; Lot's Wife;* and *Henry O. Tanner.*

Jean–Michel Basquiat (1960–1988)
Painter

In a brief, tragic career, Jean-Michel Basquiat gained attention from wealthy collectors as a young artist discovered by Andy Warhol and promoted by other art consultants. He was raised in Brooklyn and attracted the New York art world with his trendy personal appearance (tangled dreadlocks) as a musician and artist at the age of eighteen. His works are autobiographical and deliberately "primitive" in style. In February 1985 he was a featured artist on the cover of the *New York Times Magazine,* shoeless in a suit, shirt, and tie.

Richmond Barthé with his Lincoln bust in 1941 (AP/Wide World Photos, Inc.).

Roots Odyssey. Romare Bearden, 1976 (VAGA).

The Whitney Museum of American Art in New York City owns many of the six hundred works this artist produced, reportedly valued in the tens of millions of dollars.

Basquiat began his career illegally painting images on buildings throughout the city. SAMO (slang for "same old s___") was his signature and trademark. He often used it in his paintings to preserve his reputation as a street artist. Basquiat was quoted as saying that his subject matter was, "[r]oyalty, heroism, and the streets."

He reportedly died of a drug overdose. Notable works include: *Self Portrait as a Heel #3; Untitled (History of Black People); Hollywood Africans;* and *CPRKR* (in honor of Charlie Parker).

Romare Bearden (1914–1988)
Painter, Collagist

Romare Bearden was born on September 2, 1914, in Charlotte, North Carolina. His family moved to Pittsburgh and later to Harlem. Bearden studied with George Grosz at the Art Students League and, later on the G.I. Bill, went to Paris where he met Henri Matisse, Joan

Miro, and Carl Holty. A product of the new generation of African Americans who had migrated from the rural areas of the South to the urban cities of the North, Bearden's work reflected the era of industrialization. His visual images would reflect the city life, jazz, and city people. Bearden's earlier works belonged to the school of social realism, but after his return from Europe his images became more abstract.

In the 1960s, Bearden changed his approach to his picture-making and began to make collages, soon becoming one of the best known collagists in the world. His images are montages of his memories of past experiences and of stories told to him by other people. They are for Bearden "an attempt to redefine the image of man in terms of the black experience." Notable works include: *Street Corner; He Is Arisen; The Burial; Sheba;* and *The Prevalence of Ritual.*

John Biggers (1924–)
Painter

Born in Gastonia, North Carolina, in 1924, Biggers has derived much of his subject matter from the contributions made by African Americans to the development of the United States. As a teacher at Texas Southern University, Biggers has become a significant influence on several young African American painters.

Some of his most powerful pieces have been created as a result of his study trips to Africa including *The Time of Ede, Nigeria*, a series of works done in the 1960s. Notable works include: *Cradle; Mother and Child; The Contributions of Negro Women to American Life and Education;* and *Shotgun, Third Ward, #1.*

Camille Billops (1933–)
Sculptor, Photographer, Filmmaker

A noted sculptor in art and retailing, Camille Billops was born in California in 1933, graduated from California State College in 1960, and then studied sculpture under a grant from the Huntington Hartford Foundation. In 1960, she had her first exhibition at the African Art Exhibition in Los Angeles, followed in 1963 by an exhibit at the Valley Cities Jewish Community Center in Los Angeles. In 1966, she participated in a group exhibition in Moscow. Since then, her artistic talents, which include poetry, book illustration, and jewelry making, have earned the praise of critics throughout the world, particularly in Sri Lanka and Egypt, where she also has lived and worked.

Billops has also taught extensively. In 1975, she was active on the faculties of the City University of New York and Rutgers at Newark, New Jersey. In addition, she has conducted special art courses in the Tombs, a New York City jail. She lectured in India for the United States Information Service on African American artists in 1972. She participated in an exhibit at the New York Cultural Center in 1973.

Billops is a printmaker, filmmaker, and photographer who has also been active in the mail-art movement which has made art more accessible to the public. She has written articles for the *New York Times, Amsterdam News* and *Newsweek.*

Her grants for film include the New York State Council on the Arts, 1987 and 1988; NYSCA and New York Foundation for the Arts, 1989; Rockefeller Foundation, 1991; and National Endowment for the Arts, 1994.

In 1992, Billops won the prestigious Grand Jury Prize for best documentary at the Sundance Film Festival for *Finding Christa*, an edited combination of interviews, home movies, still images, and dramatic acting. Notable works include: *Tenure; Black American; Portrait of an American Indian* (all three are ceramic sculptures); *Year after Year* (painting). *Older Women and Love* (film); *Suzanne, Suzanne* (film); *A String of Pearls* (film); and *The K.K.K. Boutique Ain't Just Rednecks* (film).

Billops is also the author of *The Harlem Book of the Dead,* with James VanDerZee and Owen Dodson.

Robert Blackburn (1921–)
Printmaker

Robert Blackburn was born in New York City in 1921. He studied at the Harlem Workshop, the Art Students League, and the Wallace Harrison School of Art. His exhibits include *Art of the American Negro, 1940,* Downtown Gallery, New York and Albany Museum; *Contemporary Art of the American Negro, 1966;* and numerous print shows in the United States and Europe. His work is represented in the Library of Congress, the Brooklyn and Baltimore museums, and the Atlanta University Collections. He is a member of the art faculty of Cooper Union.

Along with his other accomplishments, he founded The Printmaking Workshop as an artist-run cooperative in 1949. In 1971, it was incorporated as a nonprofit printmaking studio for work in lithography, etching, relief, and photo-processes. The workshop, a magnet for Third World and minority artists that reflects Mr. Blackburn's personalty, remains a haven for artists "to turn out prints for the love of it" and to do anything from experimental hodgepodge to polished pieces. In 1988, Bob Blackburn and the Printmaking Workshop were given the Governor's Art Award for making "a significant contribution to the cultural life of New York State." Notable works include *Boy with Green Head* and *Negro Mother.*

Selma Burke (1900–1995)
Sculptor, Educator

Selma Burke was an artist whose career spanned more than sixty years. She was born in Mooresville, North Carolina, on December 31, 1900. She received a B.A. from Winston-Salem University, a R.N. from St. Augustine College in 1924, an M.F.A from Columbia University in 1941, and a Ph.D. from Livingston College in 1970. Burke received her training as a sculptor at Columbia University in New York. She also studied with Maillol in Paris and with Povoley in Vienna.

Burke worked as an instructor in art and sculpture at Friends School/George's School/Forrest House in New York City from 1930 until 1949. From 1963 until 1976, she served as an instructor in art & sculpture at the Sidwell School, Haverford College, Livingston College, and Swarthmore College. The A.W. Mellon Foundation hired Burke as a consultant from 1967 until 1976. Burke founded New York City's Selma Burke School of Sculpture in 1940 and the Selma Burke Art Center in Pitts-

Robert Blackburn in his art studio (AP/Wide World Photos, Inc.).

burgh in 1968, where she taught and supported many young artists.

In 1987, Burke received the Pearl S. Buck Foundation Women's Award. She also received honorary degrees from Livingston College, the University of North Carolina, and Moore College of Art.

Burke is best known for her relief sculpture rendering of Franklin Delano Roosevelt that was minted on the American dime. On August 29, 1995, she died of cancer.

The Pearl S. Buck Foundation Woman's Award was given to her in 1987 for her professional distinction and devotion to family and humanity. Notable works include: *Falling Angel; Peace;* and *Jim.*

Stephen Burrows (1943–)
Fashion Designer

Stephen Burrows was born on September 15, 1943, in Newark, New Jersey. He observed his grandmother as a boy and started making clothes at a young age. He later studied at the Philadelphia Museum College of Art and the Fashion Institute of Technology in New York City.

With a partner, he opened a boutique in 1968. He worked for Henri Bendel from 1969 to 1973 and re-

turned to Bendel's in 1977. From 1974 to 1977 he tried, with a partner, to run a Seventh Avenue firm.

Known for his unique color combinations, he used patches of cloth for decorative motifs in the 1960s. Top-stitching of seams in contrasting threads, top stitched hems, known as "lettuce hems" because of their fluted effect, were widely copied. He preferred soft, clinging, easy-moving fabrics such as chiffon and matte jersey. He also liked asymmetry. His clothes were adopted readily by disco dancers, for whom he designed using natural fabrics with non-constricting, light and airy qualities. He won a Coty American Fashion Critics' Award in 1974 and a special Coty Award in 1977.

Elizabeth Catlett (1919–)
Sculptor, Painter

Elizabeth Catlett was born on April 15, 1919. The granddaughter of North Carolina slaves, Catlett was raised in the northwest district of Washington, DC. As a young woman she attempted to gain admission into a then all-white art school, the Carnegie Institute of Technology in Pittsburgh, Pennsylvania. She was refused entry and instead went to Howard University and gradu-

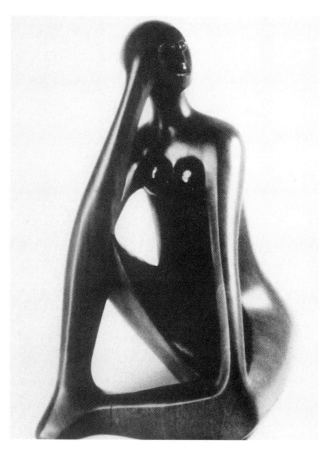

Woman Resting. Elizabeth Catlett.

ated as an honor student in 1935. In 1940, she went on to study at the University of Iowa, where she became the first of their students to receive an M.F.A.

Her exhibition history dates back to 1937 and includes group and solo presentations at all the major American art museums as well as institutions in Mexico City, Moscow, Paris, Prague, Tokyo, Beijing, Berlin, and Havana. Catlett's public sculpture can be found in Mexico City; Jackson, Mississippi; New Orleans; Washington, DC; and New York. Her work is represented in the permanent collection of over twenty museums throughout the world. The artist resides in Cuernavaca, Mexico.

Catlett accepted teaching positions at various African American colleges in order to earn a living, but by 1946 she had moved to Mexico, where she eventually settled. Always a promoter of human struggle—visually concerned with the recording of economic, social, and political themes—Catlett became involved with the Civil Rights movement so deeply that it contributed greatly to her philosophy of life and art. Between 1941 and 1969, Catlett won eight prizes and honors, four in Mexico and four in America. Notable works include: *Black Unity* (1968); *Target Practice* (1970); *Mother and Child* (1972); and *Woman Resting* (1981). In 1993, Catlett worked

with James Weldon Johnson on the book *Lift Every Voice and Sing.*

Catlett was presented with an honorary doctorate of human letters from Morgan State University in 1993. In 1995, the New School for Social Research presented her with an honorary doctorate of fine arts.

Dana Chandler (1941–)
Painter

Dana Chandler is one of the most visible African American painters in the United States. Chandler's huge, colorful black power murals can be spotted throughout the ghetto area of Boston, a constant reminder of the resolve and determination displayed by the new breed of young African American urban dwellers.

Chandler's easel works are bold and simple. One piece *The Golden Prison* shows an African American man with a yellow and red striped flag "because America has been yellow and cowardly in dealing with the black man." *Fred Hamton's Door* shows a bullet-splintered door bearing a stamp of U.S. government approval.

Born in Lynn, Massachusetts, in 1941, Chandler received his B.S. from the Massachusetts College of Art in 1967. Chandler has worked as a critic of African American art for Simmons College in Boston, an assistant professor of art and art history at Bay State Banner, and an artist in residence at Northeastern University. Notable works include: *Fred Hamton's Door; Martin Luther King, Jr. Assassinated; Death of Uncle Tom; Rebellion '68; Dynamite; Death of a Bigot;* and *The Golden Prison.*

Chandler is a member of the National Conference of Black Artists, Boston Black Artists Association, National Conference of Artists, Boston Union of Visual Artists, and the American Association of University Professors.

Barbara Chase-Riboud (1936–)
Sculptor, Author

Barbara Chase-Riboud was born in Philadelphia, Pennsylvania, in 1936. She received a B.F.A. from Temple University in 1956 and a M.F.A. from Yale University in 1960. Chase-Riboud grew up encouraged to express herself artistically by her jazz musician mother and a father she describes as a "frustrated painter." Enrolled in the Fletcher Art School at the age of seven, she studied piano and ballet as a child. Building on this early training, she majored in art at Temple University in Philadelphia. She then used a fellowship from the John Hay Whitney Foundation to study in Rome for one year. Chase-Riboud returned to the United States and attended Yale School of Art and Architecture.

After moving to Europe, Barbara Chase married the French photojournalist, Marc Riboud. She has lived and worked in Europe as a sculptor and writer since 1961.

Chase-Riboud's mixed-media sculptures combine "soft" and "hard" materials, such as silk cords, juxtaposed to metals, usually bronze cast, in the lost-wax technique. She uses contrasting materials to explore formal concerns and metaphorically comment on issues regarding race and society. Chase-Riboud's work has been exhibited in numerous one-woman shows and group shows such as *Three Generations of African-American Women Sculptors: A Study in Paradox* (1997) and *Explorations in the City of Light: African-American Artists in Paris, 1945–1965* (1996).

In addition to making visual arts, Chase-Riboud writes historical novels and poetry. Her publications include: *The President's Daughter* (1994); *Sally Hemmings; Valide; Echo of Lions; From Memphis to Peking*; and *Portrait of a Nude Woman as Cleopatra, a Meloloque.*

Robert Colescott (1925–)
Painter

Robert Colescott was born in California in 1925. He received his B.A. from the University of California in 1949 and later his M.A. in 1952. In 1953, Colescott studied in Paris with Fernand Leger. His exhibitions include: The Whitney Museum of American Art 1983 Biennial; the Hirshorn Museum and Sculpture Garden in Washington, DC, 1984; and the Institute of Contemporary Art at the University of Pennsylvania in 1985. His works are in the Metropolitan Museum of Art, the Portland Art Museum, the Delaware Museum of Art, the Baltimore Museum of Art, and the University of Massachusetts' fine art collection.

A controversial artist criticized by both African American groups and traditionalists, Colescott's work questions the "heroic" and "pushes the standards of taste." He has substituted black figures in place of white figures in famous European paintings as he explores racism and sex in his works, along with other taboos and stereotypes. Notable works include: *Homage to Delacroix: Liberty Leading the People; Eat Dem Taters; Shirley Temple Black and Bill Robinson White*; and *The Power of Desire, The Desire for Power.*

Houston Conwill (1947–)
Performance Artist, Environmental Artist

Born in Kentucky in 1947, Conwill spent three years studying for the priesthood. His strong Catholic upbringing and Catholic ritual play a part in his art that draws from both American and African myths and religions. In his explorations, he mostly uses non-traditional materials such as replacing canvas with latex. The environments that he builds, paints, and fills with real chalices, candlesticks, carpets, or sand are works to which he adds his own personal iconography as well as some ancient symbols. Notable works include: *The*

Cakewalk Manifesto; Passion of St. Matthew; East Shout; and *JuJu Funk.*

Emilio Cruz (1938–)
Painter

Emilio Cruz was born in New York City in 1938. His education includes work at the Art Students' League under Edwin Dickinson, George Grosz and Frank J. Reilly. Cruz has exhibited widely since 1959. Recent exhibits have included the Anita Shapolsky Gallery, 1986, 1991; The Studio Museum in Harlem, 1987; the Portland Museum of Art in 1987; the Rhode Island School of Design, 1987; the Gwenda Jay Gallery, Chicago, 1991; and the G.R. N'amdi Gallery, Birmingham, Michigan, 1991.

An artist whose works are narrative and formalistic (emphasizing color and forms as the dominant elements), he combines these two theoretical approaches often with figurative subjects.

His awards include: the Cintas Foundation Fellowship, 1965–1966; John Hay Whitney Fellowship, 1964–1965; Walter Gutman Foundation Award, 1962. Notable works include: *Silver Umbrella; Figure Composition 6*; and *Striated Voodoo.*

Roy DeCarava (1919–)
Photographer

Roy DeCarava's existence in New York City prepared him for his work as a photographer. He began as a commercial artist in 1938 by studying painting at Cooper Union. This was followed by classes at the Harlem Art Center from 1940 to 1942, where he concentrated on painting and printmaking. By the mid-1940s, he began to use photography as a convenient method of recording ideas for his paintings. In 1958, DeCarava gave up his commercial work and became a full-time freelance photographer. Edward Steichen began to study his work and suggested that he apply for a Guggenheim Fellowship. Winning this award allowed DeCarava the financial freedom to take his pictures and tell his story. One of DeCarava's photographs from this body of work appeared in Steichen's exhibition *Family of Man* at the Museum of Modern Art. Later, Langston Hughes worked with DeCarava to create the book *Sweet Flypaper of Life.*

DeCarava has worked as a photographer for *Sports Illustrated* and taught photography at Hunter College, New York. His work can be found in many important collections throughout the United States including: Andover Art Gallery, Andover-Phillips Academy, Massachusetts; Art Institute of Chicago, Chicago, Illinois; Atlanta University, Atlanta, Georgia; Belafonte Enterprises, Inc., New York; Center for Creative Photography, University of Arizona; the Corcoran Gallery of Art, Washington, DC; Harlem Art Collection, New York State Office Building, New York; Lee Witkin Gallery, New York; Menil Foundation, Inc., Houston, Texas; Metropolitan Museum of Fine Arts, Houston, Texas; The Museum of Fine Arts, Houston, Texas; Museum of Modern Art, New York; Olden Camera, New York; Joseph E. Seagram & Sons, Inc., New York; and Sheldon Memorial Art Gallery, University of Nebraska, Nebraska.

DeCarava received a Distinguished Career in Photography Award in 1991 from the Friends of Photography. That same year, the American Society of Magazine Photographers presented him with a special citation for photographic journalism. DeCarava has also received honorary doctorates from The Maryland Institute, Rhode Island Institute of Fine Arts, and Wesleyan University.

Beauford Delaney (1910–1979)
Painter

Born in Knoxville, Tennessee, in 1910, Beauford Delaney was described by his elder brother Samuel as a "remarkably dutiful child." For Beauford Delaney, recognition came by way of an elderly white artist of Knoxville named Lloyd Branson. Branson gave him lessons and, after a time, urged him to go to a city where he might study and come into contact with the art world.

In 1924, Beauford Delaney went to Boston to study at the Massachusetts Normal School, later studying at the Copley Society, where he took evening courses while working full-time at the South Boston School of Art. From Boston, Delaney moved on to New York.

It was in New York that Delaney took on the life of a bohemian, living in the village in coldwater flats. Much of his time was spent painting the portraits of the personalities of the day, such as Louis Armstrong, Ethel Waters, and Duke Ellington. In 1938, Beauford Delaney gained national attention when *Life Magazine* , in an article on "negroes," featured a photograph of him surrounded by a group of his paintings at the annual outdoor exhibition in Washington Square in New York. In 1945, Henry Miller wrote the essay "The Amazing and Invariable Beauford Delaney," which was later reprinted in *Remember to Remember*. The essay describes Delaney's bohemian lifestyle in New York during the 1940s and 1950s.

In the 1950s, Delaney left New York with the intention of studying in Rome. Taking the *Ile de France*, , he sailed to Paris, next visiting Greece, Turkey, Northern Italy—but he never got to Rome. Returning to Paris for one more visit, Delaney began to paint, make new friends, and create a new social life filled with other artistic figures. Paris was to become Beauford Delaney's permanent home.

By 1961, Delaney was producing paintings at such an intense rate that the pressure began to wear upon his strength, and he suffered his first mental collapse. He was confined to a clinic in Vincennes, and his dealer and close friends began to organize his life, hoping to help relieve some of the pressure. However, the rest of his life, Delaney was to suffer repeated breakdowns and by 1971 was back in a sanitarium, where he was to remain until his death in 1979.

Beauford Delaney's numerous exhibitions took place in such venues as Artists Gallery, New York in 1948; Roko Gallery, New York, 1950–1953; Musée d'Art Moderne, Paris, 1963; American Negro Exposition, Chicago, 1940; and Newark Museum, 1971. His work can be found in the collections of the Whitney Museum of American Art, New York; the Newark Museum, New Jersey; and Morgan State College in Baltimore, Maryland. Notable works include: *Greene Street; Yaddo; Head of a Poet;* and *Snow Scene*.

Aaron Douglas (1899–1988)
Painter, Illustrator

Born in Topeka, Kansas, in 1899, Aaron Douglas achieved considerable eminence as a muralist, illustrator, and academician. As a young man, Douglas studied at the University of Nebraska, Columbia University Teachers College, and l'Academie Scandinave in Paris. He had one-person exhibits at the Universities of Kansas and Nebraska and also exhibited in New York at the Gallery of Modern Art. In 1939, Douglas was named to the faculty of Fisk University and later became head of its department of art.

Douglas died on February 2, 1988. In 1992, Fisk University opened a new gallery in his memory. Douglas is considered one of the most important painter and illustrator of the "Negro Renaissance," now known as the Harlem Renaissance. Notable works include: murals at Fisk University and in the Countee Cullen branch of the New York City Public Library; illustrations in books by Countee Cullen, James Weldon Johnson, Alain Locke, and Langston Hughes. Alexander Dumas, Marion Anderson, and Mary McLeod Bethune are among the many African Americans he painted or rendered in charcoal.

David Clyde Driskell (1931–)
Painter, Historian

Born in Eatonton, Georgia, in 1931, Driskell studied at Howard University and earned his M.A. from the Catholic University of America in 1962. He also studied at the Skowhegan School of Painting and Sculpture and the Netherlands Institute for History of Art. He has taught at Talladega College, Fisk University, Institute for African Studies of the University of Ife in Nigeria, and the University of Maryland at College Park.

Immediately after the death of Alonzo Aden, Driskell was asked to direct the Barnett-Aden collection of African American Art. He has curated and mounted important exhibitions of African American art including *200 Years of African American Art*, shown at major museums to audiences across the United States.

A recipient of many awards including the John Hope Award and prizes from the Danforth Foundation, American Federation of Arts, and Harmon Foundation, Driskell has exhibited at the Corcoran Art Gallery, National Museum, and Rhodes National Gallery in Salisbury, Rhodesia. Notable works include: *Movement; The Mountain; Still Life With Gateleg Table;* and *Shango Gone.*

Robert Duncanson (1817–1872)
Painter

Robert Duncanson was the son of an African American mother and a Scottish-Canadian father. Born in upstate New York in 1817, he spent much of his childhood in Canada. During his youth, he and his mother moved to Mt. Healthy, Ohio, where in 1840 the Western Freedom's Aid Society, an anti-slavery group, raised funds to send him to Glasgow, Scotland, to study art. Returning to Cincinnati three years later, Duncanson advertised in the local newspaper as the proprietor of a daguerreotype studio. He continued to work at his daguerreotype studio until 1855, when he began to devote all of his time to his painting. Similar to many landscape artists of this time, Duncanson traveled around the United States drawing his compositions from the images of nature before him. In 1853, he made his second trip to Europe—this time to visit Italy, France, and England.

Although Duncanson was active during and after the Civil War, with the exception of his painting of *Uncle Tom and Eva*, he made no attempts to present the turmoil that was taking place within the United States or the social pressures that he experienced. In September 1872, Duncanson suffered a severe mental breakdown and committed suicide in Detroit, Michigan. Notable works include murals in the Taft Museum and *Bishop Payne.*

William Edmonson (1882–1951)
Sculptor

William Edmonson was a stonecutter and self-taught sculptor. Born in Nashville, Tennessee, in 1882, he supported himself working as a hospital orderly and other menial jobs. His work was discovered by Mrs. Meyer Dahl-Wolfe, who had an extensive private collection and brought Edmonson to the attention of the Museum of Modern Art. His work was received extremely well in an exhibition of self-taught artists. In 1937 he was the first African American to have a one-person exhibit at the museum. Private collectors and museums have purchased his few sculptures.

Inspired by biblical passages, Edmonson worked on tombstones and his sculpture, which he did in limestone, at the home he shared with his mother and sister until their deaths. He continued to live alone and work there until his own death in 1951. Notable works include: *Choir Girls; Lion;* and *Crucifixion.*

Elton Clay Fax (1909–1993)
Illustrator, Writer

Born in Baltimore in 1909, he graduated from Syracuse University with a B.F.A., in 1931. He taught at Claflin University from 1935 to 1936 and was an instructor at the Harlem Community Art Center from 1938 to 1939. His work has been exhibited at the Baltimore Art Museum, 1939; American Negro Exposition, 1940; the Metropolitan Museum of Art; and Visual Arts Gallery, New York, 1970. Examples of his work are included in some of the nation's university collections including Texas Southern, the University of Minnesota, and Virginia State University.

Publications by Fax include: *Africa Vignettes; Garvey; Seventeen Black Artists;* and *Black Artists of the New Generation. The Portfolio Black and Beautiful* features his art work, and he has written *Hashar,* a book about the life of the peoples of Soviet Central Asia and Kazakhstan. Notable works include: *Steelworker; Ethiopia Old and New; Contemporary Black Leaders;* and *Through Black Eyes.*

Elton Fax died in Queens, New York, in May, 1993.

Tom Feelings (1933–)
Illustrator

Born in Brooklyn, New York, on May 19, 1933, Thomas Feelings grew up in the Bedford-Stuyvesant neighborhood. He began to draw cartoons at the age of four, and his art work flourished under the guidance of an African American artist named Thipadeux who encouraged Feelings to draw the people in his neighborhood. After high school, he attended the Cartoonists and Illustrators' School in New York City on a three-year scholarship. Feelings's art studies were interrupted by four years of service for the U.S. Air Force in England, but upon completion of his military service, he continued his art studies at the New York School of the Visual Arts.

While in art school, Feelings produced "Tommy Traveler in the World of Negro History," a comic strip published in *New York Age,* a Harlem newspaper. Completing art school in 1961, Feelings marketed his portfolio to earn freelance assignments and began to get work with magazines of primarily African American readership.

Elton Fax drawing a sketch in 1974.

In 1964, Feelings traveled to Tema, a city in Ghana, with other African Americans enlisted by the Kwame Nkrumah, then head of Ghanian government, to help direct the newly independent country toward the future. Africa changed Feelings's art on a spiritual and stylistic level. In 1966, he was forced to leave when the Nkrumah government fell.

Feelings returned to the United States hungry for work. There was a huge demand for works by and depicting African Americans, especially children's books.

In this new climate, Feelings illustrated such books as *To Be A Slave* (1968) and *Moja Means One: A Swahili Counting Book*, which won a Caldecott Honor Award in 1972. From 1971 to 1974, Feelings administered the Guyanese Ministry of Education's children's book project while living in Guyana. There he wrote his autobiography *Black Pilgrimage* published in 1972. After returning to the United States, Feelings illustrated more books spread over the next ten years including *Now Sheba Sings the Song* (1987), a collaboration with the poet/ writer Maya Angelou.

While serving as an artist in residence at the University of South Carolina, Feelings has completed illustrations for two books. In 1993, he finished illustrations for *Soul Looks Back In Wonder*, a book compiling the poems of many African American authors. Two years later, he completed *The Middle Passage*, which portrays the passage of slave ships from Africa to the Western hemisphere. Both books received Coretta Scott King Awards from the American Library Association.

Feelings has earned many awards for his illustrations including two outstanding achievement awards from the New York School of Visual Arts, Visual Artists Fellowship and National Endowment for the Arts grants, and Distinguished Service to Children Through Art Award from the University of South Carolina (1991). Feelings has earned three Coretta Scott King Awards.

Meta Vaux Warrick Fuller (1877– 1968)
Sculptor

Meta Vaux Warrick Fuller was a part of the transitional period between the artists who chose to simulate Euro-American subjects and styles and the later artistic periods. Her African American subjects of *The Wretched*, exhibited at the Paris Salon in 1903 and 1904, did not suit popular tastes.

Born in 1877, in Philadelphia and educated at the School of Industrial Art and the Pennsylvania Academy, Fuller's interest in sculpture led her to study with Charles Grafly and at the Academie Colarossi in Paris with Rodin. She was the first African American woman to become a professional artist.

She married and settled in the Boston area, where in 1910, most of her works were destroyed by fire. The Boston Art Club and the Harmon Foundation exhibited her works, and representative pieces of her sculpture can be found in the Cleveland Museum of Art today.

Sam Gilliam (1933–)
Painter

Born in Mississippi in 1933, Sam Gilliam produces hanging canvases that are laced with pure color pigments rather than shades or tones. The artist bunches these pigments in different configurations on drooping, drape-like canvases, giving the effect, in the words of *Time* Magazine, of "clothes drying on a line." His canvases are said to be "like nobody else's, black or white."

Gilliam received his M.A. from the University of Louisville and was awarded National Endowment of Humanities and Arts grants. He has had one-man and group shows at the Washington Gallery of Modern Art; Jefferson Place Gallery; Adams-Morgan Gallery in Washington, DC; the Art Gallery of Washington University, St.

Louis, Missouri; the Speed Museum, Louisville; the Philadelphia Museum of Art; the Museum of Modern Art; the Phillips Collection and Corcoran Gallery of Art, both in Washington, DC; the San Francisco Museum of Art; the Walker Art Center, Minneapolis, and the Whitney Museum of American Art. He is represented in the permanent collection of over forty-five American museums.

Gilliam has also been represented in several group exhibitions including the First World Festival of Negro Arts in Dakar, Senegal (1966), "The Negro in American Art" at UCLA (1967), and the Whitney Museum's American Art Annual (1969).

From 1968 through 1970, his work was displayed in one-man shows at Washington, DC's Jefferson Place, and in 1971 he was featured in a one-man show at New York City's Museum of Modern Art.

In 1980, Gilliam was commissioned, with thirteen other artists, to design work for installation in the Atlanta, Georgia Airport Terminal, one of the largest terminals in the world and the first to install contemporary artwork on its walls for public viewing. Notable works include: *Watercolor 4* (1969); *Herald* (1965); *Carousel Change* (1970); *Mazda* (1970); *Plantagenets Golden* (1984); and *Golden Element Inside Gold* (1994).

Tyree Guyton (1955–)
Multimedia Artist

Born in Detroit on August 24, 1955, Tyree Guyton has transformed the blighted urban pocket in which he has spent much of his life into an enormous ongoing art project that utilizes the debris of the abandoned cityscape. Interested in the arts from a young age, after high school Guyton served in the U.S. Army and then worked at Ford Motor Company for several years. He also began a family and in his spare time took art classes.

In 1984, Guyton left his firefighting job to become a full- time artist. He started transforming the small city block in which he and wife, Karen Smith, and their several children lived. His grandfather, a former housepainter, was both a source of early inspiration and an integral contributor to Guyton's artistic project. Using ordinary housepaint, old toys, bicycles, and other found objects they salvaged from the junk piles that plague the city, Guyton transformed Heidelberg Street into a dynamic and unique art installation. A crack house, one of the many abandoned residences on the street, was painted in wild colors that discouraged the drug sales that even narcotics squad raids had not been able to stop. A tree was nailed several yards high with vintage bicycles. Polka dots decorated the street, Guyton's own home, and nearly every other available surface. The combination of dots, stripes, lively patterning, and re-invention of discarded objects had been inspired by

Tyree Guyton standing in front of his controversial Heidelberg Project (AP/Wide World Photos, Inc.).

the style in which Guyton's mother had decorated their home on a tight budget when he was growing up.

Long heralded by the international artistic community, Guyton's art has periodically come under criticism, however. Other residents of the eastside Detroit neighborhood dismiss the out-of-town visitors and laudatory praise heaped on the Heidelberg Project by the art critics and harken for the days of a neatly manicured lawn and more placid environs. In the fall of 1991, city bulldozers demolished several of the houses that Guyton had transformed, one of which had been slated for inclusion on a tour of local artistic sites. Ironically, that year he was named the Michiganian of the Year and the following year earned the Governor's Arts Award. Guyton sued the city—with the support of prominent members of Detroit's artistic community—but dropped the suit when a more sympathetic mayoral administration came into power in 1994. However, action by the Detroit City Council led to partial dismantling of the project by 1999.

Richard Hunt (1935–)
Painter, Sculptor

Richard Hunt was born in Chicago in 1935 and began his formal career after studying at the School of the Art

Institute of Chicago, where he received a number of awards.

After graduating in 1957, Hunt was given the James Nelson Raymond Traveling Fellowship. He later taught at the School of the Art Institute of Chicago and at the University of Illinois. From 1962 to 1963, he pursued his craft under a Guggenheim Fellowship.

Hunt's solo presentations have appeared at the Cleveland Museum of Art; Milwaukee Art Center; Museum of Modern Art; Art Institute of Chicago; Springfield Art Museum, Massachusetts; Indianapolis Museum of Art; and a U.S.I.S.-sponsored show throughout Africa, which was organized by the Los Angeles Museum of African American Art. Hunt sits on the board of governors at the School of the Art Institute of Chicago and the Skowhegan School of Painting and Sculpture; is a commissioner at the National Museum of American Art, Washington, DC; and serves on the advisory committee at the Getty Center for Education in the Arts, Malibu.

His works are in the Museum of Modern Art, New York; Cleveland Museum of Art, Ohio; Art Institute of Chicago; Milwaukee Art Center; Baltimore Museum of Art; Martin Gallery, Washington, DC; National Museum of American Art, Washington, DC; Hirshhorn Museum,

Washington, DC; Museum of Twentieth Century Art, Vienna, Austria; the Albright Knox Gallery, Buffalo, New York; National Museum of Israel, Jerusalem; Terry Dintenfass Gallery, New York; Dorsky Gallery, New York; Whitney Museum of American Art, New York; and Howard University. He has had many other commissions. Notable works include: *Man on a Vehicular Construct* (1956); *Linear Spatial Theme* (1962); *The Chase* (1965); and *Arching* (1986).

Joshua Johnston (1765–1830)
Painter

Active between 1789 and 1825, Joshua Johnston is the first known African American portrait painter from the Baltimore area. At least two dozen paintings have been attributed to this artist who was listed as a "free house-holder of colour, portrait painter". He was listed in the Baltimore directories in various studio locations.

It is believed Johnston may have been a former slave of Charles Wilson Peale, the artist who is also known for having started a drawing school in Maryland in 1795; or Johnston may have simply known the artist and his works. In either case, Johnston was most likely self-taught. A portraitist in the style of the period, his work now seems quaint. Only one black subject has been attributed to him, *Portrait of a Cleric*. Notable works include *Portrait of Adelia Ellender*, *Portrait of Mrs. Barbara Baker Murphy* and *Portrait of Sea Captain John Murphy*.

Larry Johnson (1949–)
Painter, Illustrator, Editorial Cartoonist

Born in Boston, Massachusetts, in 1949, Larry Johnson attended the School of the Boston Museum of Fine Arts. He became a staff illustrator at *The Boston Globe* in 1968, where he covered many assignments including courtroom sketches, sports events, entertainment, editorial sports cartoons and drawings, and other features. Johnson is now nationally syndicated through Universal Press Syndicate.

Barry Gaither, director of the National Center of African American artists in Boston, says, "Johnson's works can be divided horizontally between commercial illustration and fine art, and vertically between drawings and paintings in acrylics and watercolor." In addition to working for the *Globe*, Johnson worked for the now defunct *National Sports Daily*, has designed book jackets for Little Brown, and has been commissioned by Pepsi-Cola, the *Old Farmer's Almanac* , the National Football League, and *Fortune* , among others. He later left the *Globe* to freelance and run his own company,

Johnson Editions, producer of fine arts prints and other multiples, such as greeting cards. Johnson was awarded the Associated Press Editorial Cartoon Award in 1985. Notable works include *Island Chisel; Rainbow;* and *Promises*.

In 1995, several of Johnson's photographs were included in the six-artist exhibition entitled *New Testament*, which was hosted by the Marc Foxx Gallery in Santa Monica, California. The Margo Leavin Gallery in Los Angeles also hosted an exhibition of Johnson's art work in 1995.

Lester L. Johnson (1937–)
Painter, Educator

Born in Detroit, Michigan, in 1937, Johnson attended the University of Michigan, where he received a B.F.A. in 1973, and a M.F.A. in 1974. He teaches at the Center for Creative Studies, College of Art and Design, in Detroit, Michigan.

His works are in many collections including: the Detroit Institute of Arts; Osaka University Arts, Japan; Johnson Publishers and The Masonite Corp., Chicago; Sonnenblick-Goldman Corp., New York; Taubman Co., Inc., Bloomfield Hills, Michigan; and St. Paul Co., St. Paul, Minnesota.

Commissions have included: *Urban Wall Murals*, Detroit, 1974; New Detroit Receiving Hospital, 1980; and Martin Luther King Community Center. Johnson has exhibited at major institutions including the Whitney Museum of American Art Biennial, 1973; National African American Exhibit, Carnegie Institute, Pittsburgh, Pennsylvania; the National Academy of Design, Henry Ward Ranger National Invitational, 1977; and the Edward Thorp Gallery in New York City, 1994.

Among his awards are the Andrew W. Mellon Foundation Grant, 1982 and 1984; and a Recognition Award, African American Music Art Association.

Sargent Johnson (1888–1967)
Sculptor

Sargent Johnson, who three times won the Harmon Foundation's medal as the nation's outstanding African American artist, worked in stylized idioms, heavily influenced by the art forms of Africa in sculpture, mural bas-reliefs, metal sculpture, and ceramics.

Born in Boston in 1888, he studied at the Worcester Art School and moved to the San Francisco Bay area in 1915, where his teachers were Beniamino Bufano and Ralph Stackpole. He exhibited at the San Francisco Artists Annual, 1925 to 1931; Harmon Foundation, 1928 to 1931, 1933; Art Institute of Chicago, 1930; Baltimore Museum, 1939; and the American Negro Exposition,

Chicago, 1940. He was the recipient of numerous awards and prizes.

From the beginning of his career he spoke of his sculpture as an attempt to show the "natural beauty and dignity of the pure American Negro" and wished to present "that beauty not so much to the white man as to the Negro himself. Unless I can interest my race, I am sunk." Notable works include: *Sammy; Esther; Golden Gate Exposition Aquatic Park murals;* and *Forever Free.* He died in 1967.

William Henry Johnson (1901–1970)
Painter

William H. Johnson was a pioneer African American modernist whose work went from abstract expressionist landscape and flower studies influenced by Vincent Van Gogh, to studies of black life in America, and finally to abstract figure studies in the manner of Rouault.

Born in Florence, South Carolina, on March 18, 1901, he studied at the National Academy of Design; Cape Cod School of Art, under Charles Hawthorne; in southern France, 1926 to1929, and Denmark and Norway, 1930 to 1938. Exhibits include Harmon Foundation (Gold Medal in 1929); Aarlins, Denmark, 1935; Baltimore Museum, 1939; American Negro Exposition, Chicago, 1940. He produced one-person shows in Copenhagen in 1935, and at the Artists Gallery, New York, in 1938. Notable works include: *Booker T. Washington; Young Man in Vest; Descent from the Cross;* and *On a John Brown Flight.* He died on April 13, 1970.

Ben Jones (1942–)
Painter, Sculptor

Ben Jones was born in Patterson, New Jersey, in 1942, and studied at the School of Visual Arts; New York University, where he received an M.A.; the Pratt Institute; the University of Science and Technology, Ghana; and the New School of Social Research.

Jones is a professor of fine arts at Jersey City State College. As a sculptor, his works made during the height of the Black Arts movement in 1970 were cast in plaster from living models and painted in brightly colored patterns, resembling traditional African symbols. Masks, arms, and legs arranged in multiples or singly seem to have roots in African ceremony ritual and magic.

His pieces are in such collections as: the Newark Museum; Studio Museum in Harlem; Howard University; and Johnson Publications, Chicago. His exhibits have included: The Museum of Modern Art; Studio Museum in Harlem; Black World Arts Festival, Lagos, Nigeria; Newark Museum; Fisk University, Nashville, Tennessee, and others.

Jones's awards have included grants from the National Endowment for the Arts; the New Jersey Arts Council; Delta Sigma Theta Sorority, and others. Notable works include: *Five Black Face Images; High Priestess of Soul;* and *Untitled (6 Arms).*

Karl Kani (1968?–)
Fashion Designer

Born Carl Williams, Kani was preoccupied with style as a youth. His fashion sense first became noticed on the streets of Flatbush, a neighborhood of Brooklyn, New York. While his peers were buying the latest clothes, Williams was busy purchasing material he would later bring to various tailors, instructing them to make garments exactly how he wanted for a relatively small price. As time passed, people who had seen Williams in one of his "originals" wanted their own made-to-order clothes. Williams began taking orders and supplying the demand.

While working at Seasons Sportswear in south central Los Angeles, Williams developed the name Kani, based on the question "Can I?" as in "Can I do it?" In 1989, Kani met Carl Jones, co-founder of Threads 4 Life. Jones, who had already proven his ability to sell clothes with his Cross Colours line, agreed to help Kani get his designs out to the public. By 1992, the Kani line of clothing had added roughly $35 million dollars to the Threads 4 Life profit margin. Disagreements with Threads 4 Life eventually led Kani to venture off on his own.

Kani began "Karl Kani Infinity" in 1994. While competition for hip hop clothing had become fierce, Kani saw potential in the previously ignored market. Rap stars such as Tupac Shakur began wearing his designs, spreading the Kani name. In 1995, his designs were sold in more than three hundred stores nationwide.

Jacob Lawrence (1917–)
Painter

Born on September 7, 1917, in Atlantic City, New Jersey, Jacob Lawrence received his early training at the Harlem Art School and the American Artist School. He worked under the guidance of such artists as Charles Alston, Henry Bannarn, Anton Refregier, Sol Wilson, Philip Reisman, and Eugene Moreley. His rise to prominence was ushered in by his painting of several series of biographical panels commemorating important episodes in African American history. A narrative painter, Lawrence creates the "philosophy of Impressionism" within his work. Capturing the meaning and personality behind the natural appearance of a historical moment, Lawrence creates a formal series of several dozen small

Going to Church. William H. Johnson, c. 1940 (Art Resource).

paintings that relate to the course of a particular historic event in American history, such as *The Migration Series* (". . . and the Migrants keep coming"), which traces the migration of the African American from the South to the North, or the discussion on the course of a man's life (e.g., Toussant L'Ouverture and John Brown).

Lawrence is a visual American historian. His paintings record African American in trade, theater, mental hospitals, neighborhoods, or running in Olympic races. Lawrence's works are found in collections at the Metropolitan Museum of Art, Museum of Modern Art, Whitney Museum of American Art, the National Museum of American Art, and the Wadsworth Atheneum in Hartford, Connecticut.

Lawrence lives in Seattle, Washington. His notable works include: *The Life of Toussaint L'Ouverture* (forty

one panels, 1937); *The Life of Harriet Tubman* (forty panels, 1939); and *The Negro Migration Northward in World War* (sixty panels, 1942). He has also produced commissioned book and magazine illustrations, murals, posters, drawings, and prints. Among these are a 1976 print for the U.S. Bicentennial, illustrations for a 1983 special edition of John Hersey's book *Hiroshima* and a 1984 poster for the National Urban League.

In 1970, Lawrence was awarded the NAACP's Spingarn Medal. He received an invitation to paint the 1977 presidential inauguration of Jimmy Carter. President George Bush bestowed on Lawrence the National Medal of Arts in 1990. He is also the recipient of numerous honorary degrees.

Lawrence wrote and illustrated the book *The Great Migration: An American Story* in 1993.

Hughie Lee-Smith (1915–)
Painter

Hughie Lee-Smith was born on September 20, 1915, in Eustis, Florida. He studied at the Cleveland Institute of Art and Wayne State University, where he received his B.S. in art education in 1953.

From childhood, Lee-Smith was encouraged to pursue his art, and he has enjoyed a long career. He worked for the Ohio Works Progress Administration and the Ford Factory at River Rouge during the 1930s and 1940s. He did a series of lithographic prints and painted murals at the Great Lakes Naval Station in Illinois. He taught art at Karamu House in Cleveland, the Grosse Pointe War Memorial in Michigan, Princeton Country Day School, Howard University, the Art Students League, and other institutions.

Lee-Smith's works can be seen in museums, schools, galleries, and collections across the United States including the American Negro Exposition, Chicago; Southside Community Art Center; Snowden Gallery; Detroit Artists Market; Cleveland Museum of Art; Whitney Museum of American Art; Museum of Modern Art; the June Kelly Gallery, New York City, and the Evans-Tibbs Collection, Washington, DC. His painted environments are often of decaying or ghetto environments in a state of revitalization peopled by a single or sometimes double-figured occupant. His subjects suggest desolation or alienation, but waving banners or balloons in the scene counter the expression in their symbolism of hope and gaiety.

Lee-Smith's one-person shows and exhibitions are numerous. He has received more than a dozen important prizes including the Founders Prize of the Detroit Institute of Arts (1953), Emily Lowe Award (1957, 1985), Ralph Fabri Award, Audubon Artists, Inc. (1982), Binny and Smith Award (1983), and Len Everette Memorial Prize, Audubon Artists, Inc. (1986). He is a member of the Allied Artists of America, the Michigan Academy of the Arts, Sciences & Letters, and the Artists Equity Association. Notable works include: *Portrait of a Sailor; Old Man and Youth; Waste Land; Little Diana;* and *Aftermath.*

Edmonia Lewis (1845–1890)
Sculptor

Edmonia Lewis was America's first black female artist and also the first of her race and sex to be recognized as a sculptor. Born on July 4, 1845 in Albany, New York, she was the daughter of a Chippewa Indian

Hagar in the Wilderness. Edmonia Lewis.

woman and a free African American man. From 1859 to 1863, under the patronage of a number of abolitionists, she was educated at Oberlin College.

After completing her schooling, Lewis moved to Boston, where she studied with Edmund Brackett and did a bust of Colonel Robert Gould Shaw, the commander of the first black regiment organized in the state of Massachusetts during the Civil War. In 1865, she moved to Rome, where she soon became a prominent artist. Returning to the United States in 1874, she fulfilled many commissions including a bust of Henry Wadsworth Longfellow that was executed for the Harvard College Library.

Her works are fine examples of the neo-classical sculpture that was fashionable during her lifetime. It is believed that she died in Rome in 1890. Notable works include *Hagar in the Wilderness, Forever Free,* and *Hiawatha.*

Norman Lewis (1909–1979)
Painter

Norman Lewis was born in New York City in 1909. He studied at Columbia University and under Augusta Savage, Raphael Soyer, Vaclav Vytacil, and Angela Streater. During the Great Depression he taught art through the Federal Art Project from 1936 to 1939 at the Harlem Art Center. He received a Carnegie International Award in Painting in 1956 and has had several one-person shows at the Willard Gallery in New York.

As one of the artists to develop the abstract movement in the United States, Lewis participated in many group shows in such institutions as the Whitney Museum of American Art, the Metropolitan Museum of Art, and the Art Institute of Chicago. Notable works include *Arrival and Departure* and *Heroic Evening.*

Geraldine McCullough (1928–)
Sculptor

Geraldine McCullough's steel and copper abstraction *Phoenix* won the George D. Widener Gold Medal at the 1964 exhibition of the Pennsylvania Academy of Fine Arts. In earning this award, she added her name to a roster of artists who have already won the same honor including Jacques Lipchitz and Theodore Roszak.

A native of Arkansas, McCullough has lived in Chicago since she was three years old and is a 1948 graduate of the city's Art Institute. She also studied at the University of Chicago, DePaul University, Northwestern University, and the University of Illinois.

McCullough taught at Wendell Phillips High School from 1950 to 1964 in Chicago and at Rosary College in River Forest, Illinois. Currently, she works and resides in Oak Park, Illinois. She has received many awards and commissions. Her works are represented in collections at Howard University; in Oak Park, Illinois; the Oakland, California museum, and many others. Notable works include: *Bessie Smith; View from the Moon; Todd Hall Front; Atomic Rose; Phoenix;* and *Martin Luther King.*

Ionis Bracy Martin (1936–)
Painter, Printmaker, Educator

Born on August 27, 1936, in Chicago, Illinois, Ionis Bracy Martin attended the Junior School of the Art Institute of Chicago before going to Fisk University, where she studied with Aaron Douglas and earned her B.S. in 1957. Martin received an M.Ed. degree from the University of Hartford (1969) and an M.F.A. from Pratt Institute, Brooklyn, New York (1987). She is a trustee of the Wadsworth Atheneum, 1977, co-founder of the Artists Collective (with Jackie McLean, Dollie McLean, Paul Brown, and Cheryl Smith), 1972, co-trustee and chairperson of the Ella Burr McManus Trust for the Alfred E. Burr Sculpture Mall, 1985, and a member of the advisory board of the CRT Craftery Gallery, Hartford, 1973.

Exhibiting in the Hartford area, Martin has also been exhibited in New York; Springfield, Boston, and Northampton, Massachusetts; Fisk University, Nashville, Tennessee; and the University of Vermont, Burlington, Vermont. Among her many prizes and honors are a grant from the Connecticut Commission on the Arts (1969); a graduate fellowship in Printmaking, Pratt Institute (1981); a Summer-Six Fellowship from Skidmore College (1987); and a fellowship with the W.E.B. Du Bois Institute, Harvard University (1994).

Martin has been a teacher at Weaver and Bloomfield High Schools since 1961 and lecturer in African American art at Central Connecticut State University since 1985. Martin also lectures on and demonstrates serigraphy. Notable works include: *Mother and Child; Allyn's Garden; Gran' Daddy's Garden;* and *Little Women of the Amistad: Series.*

Evangeline J. Montgomery (1933–)
Jeweler, Photographer, Sculptor

Evangeline Montgomery was born in New York City on May 2, 1933. She received an associate's degree from Los Angeles City College in 1958 and her B.F.A. from the California College of Arts and Crafts in 1969 and also studied at the University of California, Berkeley and California State University.

Montgomery has worked as a freelance artist; an art consultant to museums, community organizations, and colleges for EJ Associates; and program director for Arts America. Known primarily for her metal boxes, incense burners, and jewelry, Montgomery has also been awarded prizes for her photography. Her works are in collections at the Oakland Museum and the University of Southern Illinois.

Active with many organizations, Montgomery has served on the San Francisco Art Commission, the advisory board of Parting Ways Ethnohistory Museum, and the board of directors of the Museum of the National Center of Afro-American Artists. She is currently a member of the Michigan Chapter of the National Conference of Artists, the College Art Association, the

Archibald Motley posing with one of his paintings in 1932 (Corbis Corporation [Bellevue]).

American Museums Association, and the Women's Art Caucus. Montgomery is also on the board of directors of the District of Columbia Arts Center.

Her awards have included a Smithsonian Fellowship and a museum grant from the National Endowment for the Arts. In 1989, Montgomery was presented with a Special Achievement Award from Arts America. Notable works include *Ancestor Box 1* and *Justice for Angela Davis*.

Archibald Motley (1891–1980)
Painter

Born in New Orleans in 1891, Motley's artistic talent was apparent by the time he attended high school. His father wanted him to become a doctor, but Archibald insisted on art and began formal education at the Art Institute of Chicago. During this time he worked as a laborer, coming into contact with the drifters, scavengers, and hustlers who are now immortalized in his street scenes. His genre scenes are highly stylized and colorful and are often associated with the *Ash-Can* school of art, a popular style in the 1920s.

In 1928, Motley had a one-person show in downtown New York and became the first artist, black or white, to make the front page of the *New York Times*. He was awarded a Guggenheim Fellowship in 1929 and studied in France. He was the recipient of a Harmon Foundation award for an earlier, more literal portrait. Notable works include: *The Jockey Club; The Plotters; Parisian Scene; Black Belt;* and *Old Snuff Dipper*. Motley died in 1980.

John Wilfred Outterbridge (1933–)
Sculptor

John Wilfred Outterbridge was born in Greenville, North Carolina, on March 12, 1933. He studied at North Carolina A&T University in Greensboro; the Chicago Art Academy; the American Academy of Art, Chicago; and the Art Center School of Design, Los Angeles.

From 1964 until 1968, Outterbridge worked as an artist/designer for the Traid Corporation. He worked as artistic director and co-founder of the Communicative Arts Academy from 1969 until 1975. He has also taught at California State University and Pasadena Art Museum. Outterbridge was director of the Watts Towers Art Center, Los Angeles, from 1976 until 1992.

Outterbridge's sculptures are assemblages constructed from discarded materials. Some of his works are tributes to African ancestors and their descendants in Los

Gordon Parks (Corbis Corporation [Bellevue])

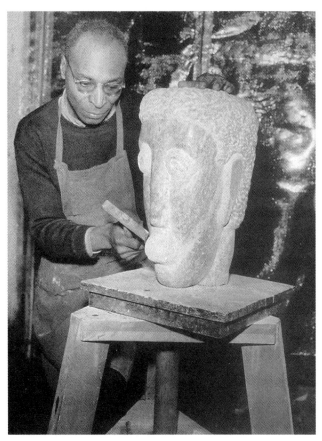

Marion Perkins working on a sculpture of an African head (AP/Wide World Photos, Inc.).

Angeles and in other communities. Outterbridge is known for making and helping create "Street Art," a combination of painting, relief sculpture, and construction that incorporates words and symbols expressing community goals and social ideas.

Outterbridge was featured in *Black Artists on Art* , Volume I (Selma Lewis/Ruth Waddy, Los Angeles Contemporary Crafts, 1971, 1976). Notable works include: *Shoeshine Box; Mood Ghetto;* and *Ethnic Heritage Group.*

In 1990, Outterbridge was presented with the Malcolm X Freedom Award by the New Afrikan People's Organization and the Lifetime Achievement Award from the First Annual King Blvd. Memorial Project. The National Endowment for the Arts awarded Outterbridge with its Visual Arts Fellowship in 1994. That same year, he was presented with an honorary doctorate of fine arts by the Otis College of Arts and Design and the J. Paul Getty Visual Arts Fellowship.

Gordon Parks (1912–)
Photographer, Composer, Writer, Director

Parks was born on November 30, 1912, in Fort Scott, Kansas. After the death of his mother, Parks went to St.

Paul, Minnesota to live with relatives. He attended Central and Mechanical Arts high schools. Despite having fond childhood memories of his father on the family farm, Parks had a dysfunctional upbringing. He worked at a variety of jobs including janitor, busboy, and semi-pro basketball player. Always interested in the arts, Parks also tried sculpting, writing and touring with a band, but these artistic endeavors were largely without focus.

In 1933, Parks joined the Civilian Conservation Corps and in the late 1930s, while working as a railroad porter, he became interested in photography as a medium on which he could finally concentrate his artistic interests. After purchasing a used camera, Parks worked as a freelance photographer and as a photojournalist. In 1942, he became a correspondent for the Farm Security Administration, and from 1943 to 1945 he was a correspondent for the Office of War Information. After the war he worked for Standard Oil Company of New Jersey, and in 1948 he became a staff photographer for *Life* magazine. He soon achieved national acclaim for his photographs and in the mid-1950s he began doing consulting work on Hollywood productions. In the 1960s

Parks began doing television documentaries, and in 1966 he published his biography *A Choice of Weapons.*

Parks is also the author of the following titles: *Flash Photography* (1947); *Camera Portraits: The Techniques and Principals of Documentary Portraiture* (1948); *The Learning Tree* (1963); *A Poet and His Camera* (1968); *Born Black* (1971); *Gordon Parks: Whispers of Intimate Things* (1971); *Moments without Proper Names* (1975); *Flavio* (1977); *To Smile in Autumn* (1979); *Shannon* (1981); *Voices in the Mirror* (1990); and *Arias in Silence* (1994). In 1968 Parks produced, directed, and wrote the script and music for the movie production of *The Learning Tree.* Parks also directed and scored the following movies: *Shaft* (1971); *Shaft's Big Score* (1972); *The Super Cops* (1974); *Leadbelly* (1976); *Odyssey of Solomon Northrup* (1984); and *Moments Without Proper Names* (1986).

Parks is a recipient of the NAACP's Spingarn Award (1972), the Rhode Island School of Design's Presidents Fellow Award (1984), and Kansan of the Year (1986). In 1988 President Ronald Reagan presented him with the National Medal for the Arts. That same year, Parks won the World Press Photo Award. In 1989, he was awarded the Library of Congress National Film Registry Classics film honor for *The Learning Tree.* He was also presented with the New York Mayor's Award and the Artist of Merit Josef Sudek Medal in 1989.

Parks is a member of the NAACP, Urban League, Newspaper Guild, Association of Composers and Directors, Writer's Guild, AFTRA, ASCAP, International Mark Twain Society, American Film Institute, Academy of Motion Pictures Arts and Sciences, and the American Society of Magazine Photographers.

On July 7, 1995, the Library of Congress announced that it had acquired the archives of Gordon Parks. The archives include roughly 15,000 manuscript pages of Parks's poems, novels and screenplays, as well as several thousand photographs and negatives.

Marion Perkins (1908–1961)
Sculptor

Born in Marche, Arkansas, in 1908, Perkins was a self-taught artist. His early works were composed while he tended a newspaper stand on Chicago's South side. He later studied privately with Simon Gordon as the two men became close friends.

Perkins's work has been exhibited at the Art Institute of Chicago, American Negro Exposition (1940), Xavier University, and Rockland College, Illinois (1965). As artist in residence at Jackson State College in Mississippi, where much of his sculpture is housed, Perkins founded a scholarship fund for art students. Perkins died in 1961.

Howardena Pindell (1943–)
Painter

Born in Philadelphia on April 14, 1943, Howardena Pindell received a B.F.A. from Boston University in 1965 and a M.F.A. from Yale University in 1967. She first gained national recognition for her 1969 exhibition "American Drawing Biennial XXIII" at the Norfolk Museum of Arts and Sciences in Virginia. By the mid-1970s, Pindell's work began appearing in such exhibitions as "Eleven Americans in Paris," Gerald Piltzer Gallery, Paris, 1975; "Recent Acquisitions; Drawings," Museum of Modern Art, New York, 1976; and "Pindell: Video Drawings," Sonja Henie Onstad Foundation, Oslo, Norway, 1976.

Pindell began to travel around the world as a guest speaker. Some of her lectures included "Current American and Black American Art: A Historical Survey" at Madras College of Arts and Crafts, Madras, India, 1975; and "Black Artists, U.S.A.," Academy of Art, Oslo, Norway, 1976. She is currently a professor of art at State University of New York at Stony Brook.

Her work is part of the permanent collection in over thirty museums including the Brooklyn Museum, High Museum in Atlanta, Newark Museum, Fogg Museum in Cambridge, Massachusetts, Whitney Museum of American Art, Museum of Modern Art, and the Metropolitan Museum of Art. Pindell has received two National Endowment for the Arts Fellowships and a Guggengeim Fellowship.

Pindell has received numerous awards throughout her career. In 1990, she won the College Art Association Award for Best Exhibitor. She received the Studio Museum in Harlem Award and Joan Mitchell Fellowship in 1994. In 1996, the Women Caucus for Art presented Pindell with its Distinguished Contribution to the Profession Award.

Jerry Pinkney (1939–)
Illustrator

Born in Philadelphia on December 22, 1939, Jerry Pinkney studied at the Philadelphia Museum College of Art. Pinkney has exhibited in illustrator shows throughout the country and is best known for his illustrations for children's and text books.

From his studio in his home in Croton-on-Hudson, New York, Pinkney has been a major contributor to the U.S. Postal Service's stamps in the Black Heritage Series. Benjamin Banneker, Martin Luther King, Jr., Scott Joplin, Jackie Robinson, Sojourner Truth, Carter G. Woodson, Whitney Moore Young, Mary McLeod Bethune, and Harriet Tubman stamps were designed by Pinkney.

A recipient of many honors, he has created illustrations in children's books such as *The Talking Eggs* , written by Robert San Souci; earned a Caldecott Honor of Medal (Pinkney's second such honor) in 1989, received a Coretta Scott King Honor Book Award; was named an American Library Association Notable Book; and won the Irma Simonton Black Award from the Bank Street College of Education. In 1994, Pinkney won the Caldecott Medal for his illustrations in the book *John Henry*. That same year, he won two Parent's Choice Awards for the books *John Henry* and *The Sunday Outing*.

Pinkney has worked in Boston as a designer and illustrator. He is one of the founders of Kaleidoscope Studio in Boston, where he also worked for the National Center of Afro-American Art. He also was a visiting critic for the Rhode Island School of Design. He has taught at Pratt Institute, the University of Delaware, and in the Art Department at the State University of New York at Buffalo. Notable works include: *The Tales of Uncle Remus*, published by Dial Brooks; *Call It Courage*, written by Armstrong Sperry and published by Aladdin Books; *Self Portrait*; and *Back Home*, written by his wife, Gloria Jean Pinkney.

Horace Pippin (1888–1946)
Painter

Horace Pippin has been ranked in the company of Henri Rousseau due to his accomplishment as a self-taught artist. Born on February 22, 1888, in West Chester, Pennsylvania, Pippin began painting in 1920, and continued until his death on July 6, 1946. Among his most vivid works are battle scenes that he remembered from his own experience in World War I.

Pippin's earliest works are designs burned into wood with a hot poker. He did not make his first oil painting until 1930. This task was complicated by his wartime injury; he had to guide his right arm with his left hand in order to paint. He painted family reunions, Biblical stories, and historical events. Notable works include: *John Brown Goes to a Hanging; Flowers with Red Chair; The Den; The Milk Man of Goshen;* and *Dog Fight Over the Trenches.*

James A. Porter (1905–1971)
Art Historian, Painter

James A. Porter was a painter who also earned acclaim as a writer and educator. Born in Baltimore in 1905, he studied at Howard University receiving a B.S. in 1927; Art Students League, New York; Sorbonne; and received a M.A. from New York University. He was awarded numerous travel grants that enabled him to study African and European art firsthand.

Among his ten one-person shows are exhibits at Port-au-Prince, Haiti, 1946; Dupont Gallery, Washington, DC,

1949; and Howard University, 1965. His works are in the collections of Howard University; Lincoln University, Missouri; Harmon Foundation; IBM; and others. The first African American art historian, he wrote *Modern Negro Art* (1943), as well as numerous articles.

In 1953, he became chairman of the Department of Art and director of the Gallery of Art at Howard University, a position he held until his death. He was a delegate to the UNESCO Conference on Africa held in Boston in 1961, and to the International Congress of African Art and Culture in Salisbury, Southern Rhodesia, 1962. In 1965, at the twenty-fifth anniversary of the founding of the National Gallery of Art, he was named "one of America's Most Outstanding Men of the Arts." His notable works include: *On a Cuban Bus; Portrait of F. A. as Harlequin; Dorothy Porter;* and *Nude.*

Martin Puryear (1941–)
Sculptor

Martin Puryear was born in Washington, DC, in 1941. He attended Catholic University of America and received an M.F.A. from Yale University in 1971. He has studied in Sweden and worked in Sierra Leone with the Peace Corps from 1964 to 1966.

Representing the United States in the 1989 São Paulo Bienal in Brazil, he received first prize. His work has been described as post-minimalist, but it really defies categorizing. Puryear executes his own large pieces in wood and metal.

Puryear was the only African American artist in the contemporary section of the exhibit "Primitivism in Twentieth-Century Art: Affinity of the Tribal and Modern" at the Museum of Modern Art 1984; his other exhibits include Brooklyn Museum, 1988 to 1989, the Whitney Biennal, 1989, and New York Galleries, since 1987.

Puryear studied in Japan in 1987 on a Guggenheim Fellowship. Notable works include: *For Beckwith; Maroon Desire; and Sentinel.* His works since 1985 have been untitled.

Faith Ringgold (1930–)
Painter, Fiber Artist

Committed to a revolutionary perspective both in politics and in aesthetics, Faith Ringgold is a symbolic expressionist whose stark paintings are acts of social reform directed toward educating the consciousness of her audience. Her most intense focus has been upon the problems of being black in America. Her works highlight the violent tensions which tear at American society including the discrimination suffered by women. Ringgold is also known for her distinctive story quilts. These quilts feature paintings on canvas that are bordered with quilted textiles and handwritten strips of white fabric that contain fanciful stories.

Born in Harlem on October 8, 1934, she was raised by parents who made sure she would enjoy the benefits of a good education. She received her B.S. in 1955 and her M.F.A. in 1959 from the City College of New York. She is a professor of Art at the University of California at San Diego.

Ringgold's boldly political work has been widely shown. Since 1968 she has had several one-person shows and her paintings are included in the collections of the Chase Manhattan Bank, New York City; the Museum of Modern Art, the Bank Street College of Education, New York City; and the Solomon R. Guggenheim Museum.

In 1972, Ringgold became one of the founders of the Women Students and Artists for Black Liberation, an organization whose principal goal is to make sure that all exhibitions of African American artists give equal space to paintings by men and women. In line with her interest in sexual parity, she has donated a large mural depicting the roles of woman in American society to the Women's House of Detention in Manhattan.

Her first quilt *Echoes of Harlem, Tar Beach* was completed in 1980. Other quilts produced by Ringgold include *The Sunflower Quilting Bee at Arles*, and *Who's Afraid of Aunt Jemima*. In 1991, she illustrated and wrote a children's book *Tar Beach*. This book was followed in 1992 by *Aunt Harriet's Underground Railroad in the Sky*. Notable artistic works include: *The Flag Is Bleeding; Flag for the Moon; Die Nigger; Mommy & Daddy*; and *Soul Sister, Woman on a Bridge*.

Ringgold has received several awards for her work including honorary doctorates from Moore College of Fine Art, Wooster College, Massachusetts College of Art, and City College of Art. In 1996, she received an award from the National Museum of Women in the Arts.

Betye Saar (1926–)
Painter, Sculptor

Betye Saar was born in California on July 30, 1926. She went to college, got married, and raised her children—all while creating artwork built upon discarded pieces of old dreams, postcards, photographs, flowers, buttons, fans, and ticket stubs. Her motifs range from the fetish to the everyday object. In 1978, Saar was one of a select group of American female artists to be discussed in a documentary film entitled *Spirit Catcher: The Art of Betye Saar*. It appeared on WNET-13 in New York as part of "The Originals: Women in Art" series. Her exhibitions include an installation piece especially designed for The Studio Museum in Harlem in 1980, and several one-person exhibitions at the Monique Knowlton Gallery in New York in 1981.

Saar studied at Pasadena City College, University of California where she received a B.F.A. in 1949, as well as Long Beach State College, University of Southern California, San Fernando State College, Valley State College, California, and the American Film Institute. She was a teacher-in-residence at Hayward State College, California. She has exhibited throughout the United States. In 1994, Saar's works were displayed with over two hundred other artists at Brazil's Bienal, a biannual art exhibition featuring the works of artists from over 71 countries. Notable works include: *The Vision of El Cremo; Africa; The View from the Sorcerer's Window*; and *House of Gris Gris*, a mixed-media installation created with daughter Alison Saar.

Synthia Saint James (1949–)
Illustrator, Author

Saint James was born in 1949 in Los Angeles, California. She is a self-taught illustrator and author whose work has been exhibited internationally in Stockholm, Sweden, Paris, France, Seoul, Korea, Quebec, Canada, Los Angeles, New York City, and Salt Lake City, as well as the National Museum of Women in the Arts, Washington DC.

Saint James's colorful figurative images celebrate the daily life and culture of African Americans in her paintings. The stylized silhouettes take shape through the use of broad sweeps of contrasting color. Her pictures grace the covers of over fifty books including those by Terry McMillan, Iyanla Vanzant, and Alice Walker. Dozens of corporations, organizations, and individuals have commissioned Saint James to design work for their licensed products, event, and commemorative posters. The United States Postal Service, commissioned her to create the first Kwanzaa Stamp, made available on October 22, 1997.

Saint James is an award-winning author and illustrator of children's books including *The Gift's of Kwanzaa* and *Sunday*. She received a 1997 Coretta Scott King Honor for her illustrations in *Neeny Coming. . . Neeny Going*. Saint James's eighth children's book *No Mirrors In My Nana's House* (1998) was written by Ysaye Barnwell, and her ninth book *Girls Together* (1999) was written by Sherley Anne Williams.

Augusta Savage (1900–1962)
Sculptor

A leading sculptor who emerged during the Harlem Renaissance, Augusta Savage was one of the artists represented in the first all-black exhibition in America, sponsored by the Harmon Foundation at International

Gamin. Augusta Savage (Art Resource).

House in New York City. In 1939, her symbolic group piece *Lift Every Voice and Sing* was shown at the New York World's Fair Community Arts Building.

Savage was born in Green Cove Springs, Florida, on February 29, 1900, and studied at Tallahassee State Normal School at Cooper Union in New York City, as well as France as the recipient of Carnegie and Rosenwald fellowships. She was the first African American to win acceptance in the National Association of Women Painters and Sculptors.

In the 1930s she taught in her own School of Arts and Crafts in Harlem and helped many of her students take advantage of Works Progress Administration projects for artists during the Depression. Notable works include: *Lift Every Voice and Sing; The Chase; Black Women; Lenore; Gamin; Marcus Garvey;* and *W.E.B. Du Bois.*

Charles Searles (1937–)
Painter, Educator

Born in Philadelphia, Pennsylvania, in 1937, Searles studied at Fleicher Art Memorial, and the Penn Academy of Fine Arts (1968 to 1972). His works have been exhibited at the Dallas, the Brooklyn, Philadelphia,

Reading, High, Milwaukee, Whitney, and Harlem Studio Museums; Columbia University; and many other galleries and museums.

Searles has traveled to Europe and Africa. He has taught at the Philadelphia College of Art, the Philadelphia Museum Art Studio Classes, University of the Arts, Brooklyn Museum Art School, Jersey State College, and Bloomfield College in New Jersey.

He was commissioned to execute several murals including the U.S. General Service Administration interior; *Celebration* (1976) for the William J. Green Federal Building; *Play Time* (1976) for the Malory Public Playground; Newark, New Jersey Amtrak Station wall sculpture (1985); and the Dempsey Service Center wall sculpture (1989).

His works are in the collections of the Smithsonian Institute, Washington, DC; New York State Office Building; Philadelphia Museum of Art; Federal Railroad Administration; Ciba-Gigy, Inc.; Dallas Museum of Art; Montclair Art Museum; Phillip Morris, Inc.; and Howard University.

The human figure, color, and rhythmic patterns dominate his paintings. Notable works include: *Cultural Mix; Rhythmic Forms; Play Time;* and *Celebration.*

Lorna Simpson (1960–)
Photographer, Conceptual Artist

Simpson was born in Brooklyn, New York, on August 13, 1960, and attended the School of Visual Arts, where she earned her B.F.A. in 1982. She received her M.F.A. from the University of California, San Diego, in 1985. Her works are concerned with language and words, especially those with double and contradictory meanings, as well as stereotypes and cliches about gender and race.

Simpson is among the new young photographers who have broken into the mainstream of conceptual based art. Her work has been shown at the Museum of Modern Art and the Wadsworth Atheneum. She is on the advisory board of the New Museum, New York City, and also on the board of Artists Space.

In 1990, Simpson became the first African American woman to have her work featured in the Venice Biennale, an international art exhibition. Her work has been shown in exhibitions throughout the United States, Europe, Latin America, and Japan. Several institutions have offered exhibitions of her work, among them the Ansel Adams Center in San Francisco, the Whitney Museum of American Art in New York City, and the Milwaukee Art Museum. Her works have also been exhibited in the Just Above Mid-Town Gallery, Mercer Union (Toronto), and the Wadsworth Atheneum Museum's Matrix Gallery.

Norma Sklarek (Courtesy of Norma Sklarek)

Willi Smith (Corbis Corporation [Bellevue])

Notable works include: *Outline; Guarded Conditions; Easy for Who to Say; Flipside; Bio; Untitled ("prefer/refuse/decide");* and the interactive multimedia composition *Five Rooms.*

Norma Merrick Sklarek (1928–)
Architect

Sklarek was born on April 15, 1928, in New York City, and received a B.A. in architecture from the Barnard College of Columbia University in 1950. In 1954, she became the first African American woman to be licensed as an architect in the United States. In 1966, Sklarek became the first African American woman to be named a fellow of the American Institute of Architects.

Sklarek's career began at Skidmore, Owens, Merrill, where she worked as an architect from 1955 until 1960. She also served on the faculty of New York City College from 1957 until 1960. In 1960, she took a position with Gruen and Associates in Los Angeles, California, where she worked for the next twenty years. She also served as a faculty member at UCLA from 1972 until 1978. Sklarek became vice president of Welton Becket Associates in 1980 and worked there until 1985. From 1985 until 1989, Sklarek was a partner in the firm Siegel, Sklarek, and

Diamond, the largest female-owned architectural firm in the United States. In 1989, she began working as a principal for The Jerde Partnership before retiring in 1992.

Among the notable structures designed by Sklarek are the U.S. Embassy in Tokyo; Courthouse Center, Columbus, Indiana; City Hall, San Bernardino, California; and Terminal One, Los Angeles International Airport.

Moneta Sleet, Jr. (1926–)
Photographer

Moneta Sleet was born on February 14, 1926, in Owensboro, Kentucky. He studied at Kentucky State College under Dr. John Williams, a family friend, dean of the college, and an accomplished photographer. In 1947, he received his B.A. from Kentucky State College. He earned a master's degree from New York University in 1950.

Sleet taught photography at Maryland State College from 1948 until 1949. He moved to New York City in 1950 to work as a sportswriter for *Amsterdam News.* He also worked as a photographer for *Our World* from 1951 until 1955. Sleet moved to Chicago and took a job with the Johnson Publishing Company, where he has been staff photographer for *Ebony* and *Jet* magazines since 1955.

Abraham's Oak. Henry Ossawa Tanner, 1905 (Art Resource).

In 1969, Moneta Sleet became the first African American to win a Pulitzer Prize in Photography. Although employed by *Ebony*, he was eligible for the award because his photograph of Coretta Scott King at her husband's funeral was picked up by a wire service and published in daily newspapers throughout the country. He has also received awards from the Overseas Press Club of America, National Urban League, and the National Association of Black Journalists. In 1989, the University of Kentucky inducted Sleet into its Kentucky Journalism Hall of Fame.

His work has appeared in several group exhibitions at museums including The Studio Museum in Harlem and Metropolitan Museum of Art. In 1970, solo exhibitions were held at the City Art Museum of St. Louis and at the Detroit Public Library. Other solo exhibitions of Sleet's work have been held at the New York Public Library, Newark Public Library, Chicago Public Library Cultural Center, Milwaukee Public Library, Martin Luther King Jr. Memorial Library, Albany Museum of Art, New York State Museum, and the Schomberg Center for Research in Black Culture.

Sleet is a member of the NAACP and the Black Academy lof Arts and Letters.

Willi Smith (1948–1987)
Fashion Designer

Born on February 29, 1948, in Philadelphia, Pennsylvania, Willi Smith studied at the Parsons School of Design on a scholarship and became popular during the 1960s. He was known for his designer wear in natural fibers, that were cross-seasonal and affordable. His clothes were sportswear pieces that mixed readily with Willi-wear from previous years as well as other clothes. Smith was innovative in mixing and matching plaids, stripes, and vivid colors. He designed for both men and women. Smith had his clothes manufactured in India, traveling there several times a year to supervise the making of his functional and practical collections.

In 1983 Willi Smith received the Coty American Fashion Critics Award for Women's Fashion. He died in 1987.

Nelson Stevens (1938–)
Muralist, Painter, Graphic Artist

Born in Brooklyn, New York, in 1938, Stevens received a B.F.A. from Ohio University in 1962 and a M.F.A. from Kent State University in 1969.

An active member of AFRI-COBRA—a group exploring the aesthetics of African American art, which includes the use of the human figure, bright colors, African inspired patterns, text, letters and other symbols relating to the African American experience. He is also a member of the National Conference of Artists.

Stevens is a professor of art at the University of Massachusetts in Amherst, Massachusetts. He has exhibited at the National Center of Afro-American Artists, Boston; The Studio Museum in Harlem; Howard University; Kent State University. Notable works include: *Madonna and Child*, for a 1993 calendar; *Art in the Service of the Lord; Malcolm—King of Jihad;* and *A Different Kind of Man.*

Henry Ossawa Tanner (1859–1937)
Painter

Alain Locke called Henry Ossawa Tanner the leading talent of the "journeyman period" of African American art. Born in Pittsburgh on June 21, 1859, Tanner chose painting rather than the ministry as a career, overcoming the objections of his father, an African Methodist Episcopal bishop. After attending the Pennsylvania Academy of Fine Arts, he taught at Clark University in Atlanta while working as a photographer. Some of Tanner's most compelling work, such as *The Banjo Lesson* (1890), was produced during this period in which he emerged as the most promising African American artist of his day.

In 1891, Tanner abandoned black subject matter and left the United States for Paris, where he concentrated on religious themes. In 1896, his *Daniel in the Lion's Den*, a mixture of realism and mystical symbolism, won honorable mention at the Paris Salon. The following year, the French government purchased his *Resurrection of Lazarus*. In 1900, Tanner received the Medal of Honor at the Paris Exposition and the Lippincott Prize.

Tanner died in 1937. Notable works include: *Flight into Egypt; The Annunciation; Thankful Poor;* and *The Sabot Makers.*

Alma W. Thomas (1891–1978)
Painter

Born in Columbus, Georgia, in 1891, Alma Thomas moved to Washington, DC, as a teenager. She enrolled at Howard University and was the first graduate of its art department in 1924. In 1934 she received her M.A. from Columbia University and later studied at American University.

Retiring after a thirty-eight-year teaching career in public schools, Thomas concentrated solely on her painting. She is best known for her non-objective, mosaic-like works that emphasize color, pattern, and space.

The optical relationships of her colors in flat shapes create three-dimensional forms, enlivening the painted surfaces with movement and pulsating rhythms. It is this later work that brought her many prizes and awards.

Her works are in the collections of the National Museum of American Art at the Smithsonian Institute, Howard University, Concord Gallery, Metropolitan Museum, La Jolla Museum, and private corporations. Notable works include: *The Eclipse; Arboretum Presents White Dogwood; Elysian Fields; Red Sunset;* and *Old Pond Concerto.*

Bob Thompson (1937–1966)
Painter

Born in Louisville, Kentucky, in 1937, Thompson studied at the Boston Museum School in 1955 and later spent three years at the University of Louisville. In 1960, Thompson participated in a two-person show at Zabriskie Gallery and two years later received a John Hay Whitney Fellowship. For the next several years, Thompson had several one-person exhibitions in New York and Chicago. His work was also seen in Spain. He died in Rome at the age of twenty-nine.

Thompson's work is in several permanent collections around the country including the Chrysler Museum in Provincetown, Massachusetts. In 1970, Thompson's work was featured in the *African-American Artist* exhibition at the Boston Museum of Fine Arts. Notable works include: *Ascension to the Heavens; Untitled Diptych; The Dentist* (1963); and *Expulsion and Nativity* (1964).

James VanDerZee (1886–1983)
Photographer

James VanDerZee was born on June 29, 1886, in Lenox, Massachusetts. His parents had moved there from New York in the early 1880s after serving as maid and butler to Ulysses S. Grant. The second of six children, James grew up in a family filled with creative people. Everybody painted, drew, or played an instrument, so it was not considered out of the ordinary when, upon receiving a camera in 1900, VanDerZee became interested in photography.

By 1906 VanDerZee had moved to New York, married, and took odd jobs to support his growing family. In 1907, he moved to Phoetus, Virginia, where he worked in the dining room of the Hotel Chamberlin in Old Point Comfort, Virginia. During this time he also worked as a photographer on a part-time basis. In 1909, he returned to New York.

By 1915, VanDerZee had his first photography job as assistant in the Gertz Department Store in Newark, New

James VanDerZee (AP/Wide World Photos, Inc.)

Jersey. With the money he saved from this job, he was able to open his own studio in 1916. Over the course of a half century, James VanDerZee would record the visual history of Harlem. His subjects included Marcus Garvey, Sweet Daddy Grace, Father Divine, Joe Louis, Madame Walker, and many other famous African Americans.

In 1969, the exhibition *Harlem On My Mind* produced by Thomas Hoving, then director of the Metropolitan Museum of Art, brought James VanDerZee international recognition. He died in 1983.

Laura Wheeler Waring (1887–1948)
Painter

Born in 1887 in Hartford, Connecticut, Waring received her first training at the Pennsylvania Academy of Fine Arts, where she studied for six years. In 1914, she won the Cresson Memorial Scholarship, which enabled her to continue her studies at the Academie de la Grande Chaumiere in Paris.

Waring returned to the United States as an art instructor at Cheyney State Teachers College in Pennsylvania. Eventually she became head of the art department. Her work, particularly portraiture, has been exhibited at several leading American art galleries. In 1927, she received the Harmon Award for achievement in fine art. With Betsy Graves Reyneau, Waring completed a set of twenty-four re-paintings of a variety of their works titled *Portraits of Outstanding Americans of Negro Origin* for the Harmon Foundation in the 1940s.

Waring was also the director in charge of the African American art exhibits at the Philadelphia Exposition in 1926 and was a member of the national advisory board of Art Movements, Inc. She died in 1948. Notable works include: *Alonzo Aden; W.E.B. Du Bois; James; Weldon Johnson;* and *Mother and Daughter.*

Carrie Mae Weems (1953–)
Photographer, Conceptual Artist

Carrie Mae Weems was born in Portland, Oregon, in 1953. She received her B.F.A. from the California Institute of the Arts in 1981 and a M.F.A. from the University of California at San Diego in 1984. She also received an M.A. in African American folklore from the University of California at Berkeley.

A young artist who explores stereotypes, especially those of African American women, Weems has been widely exhibited in the last few years. Formerly a photo documentarian, Weems also teaches filmmaking and photography at Hampshire College in Amherst, Massachusetts. Her new works are "about race, gender, class and kinship."

She has exhibited at the Rhode Island School of Design and Wadsworth Atheneum, Hartford, Connecticut. Notable works include: *Mirror, Mirror; Black Woman With Chicken; High Yella Girl; Colored People; Family Pictures and Stories;* and *Ain't Jokin'.*

Edward T. Welburn (1950–)
Automobile Designer

Edward T. Welburn is the chief designer of automobiles for the Oldsmobile Studio of General Motors. In 1992, his design for the Olds Achieva was honored as one of the outstanding designs of the model year.

Welburn began his career with the GM Design Staff as a creative designer in 1972, advancing to the positions of senior creative designer and assistant chief designer. While a member of the GM Design Staff, he designed the Cutlass Supreme, Cutlass Ciera, and the Oldsmobile Calais. In 1989, he moved to the Oldsmobile Studio as chief designer.

In 1985, the Indianapolis 500 pace car was designed by a team on which Welburn served. He was named Alumni of the Year in 1989 by the Howard University

1993 Oldsmobile Achieva SC designed by Edward Welburn (General Motors Corp.)

Student Association. Welburn won the Industrial Designers Society of America Award for Design Excellence for his part in the design for *Oldsmobile Aerotech* in 1992.

Welburn is a member of The Cabinet and the Founders Society of the Detroit Institute of Arts.

James Lesesne Wells (1902–1993)
Artist

Born on November 2, 1902, in Atlanta, James Lesesne Wells was a pioneer of modern American printmaking. After graduating from high school, Wells lived with relatives in New York City and worked for two years to earn money for college. He studied drawing at the National Academy of Design for one term from 1918 to 1919. Wells spent one year at Lincoln University before transferring to Teachers College at Columbia University in 1923 and earned a B.S. in 1927. He received an M.S. from Columbia in 1938.

Immediately after earning his undergraduate degree, Wells created African American print illustrations for magazines. He also made connections with art dealer and gallery owner J. D. Neumann, who included Wells's work in a 1929 exhibition of *International Modernists*. These projects captured the attention of Howard University's James V. Herring, who invited Wells to join the prestigious school's art faculty that year. Thus began a 39-year career at the university, during which Wells established a graphics arts department and taught several soon to be well-known artists including Charles Alston and Jacob Lawrence. Wells taught clay modeling, ceramics, sculpture, metals, and block printing.

During the Great Depression, Wells devoted himself to printmaking involving African American history and industrial themes. Despite a lack of critical recognition, Wells's work won numerous art competitions throughout the 1930s including the George E. Haynes Prize in 1933. At this time, he also served as the director of a summer art workshop that preceded the Harlem Community Art Center.

After World War II, Wells spent a sabbatical year working at Stanley Hayter's famous Atelier 17, then the most innovative center of etching and printmaking in the United States. Wells continued to teach and win awards for his artwork in the 1950s and 1960s. He moved the Washington, DC, and joined his brother-in-law Eugene Davidson, president of the local NAACP, in segregation protests. The harassment Wells suffered as a result of his outspokenness—a cross was burned in his yard in 1957—may have inspired the religious themes of much of his work from the era. He took first prize in a religious art exhibition sponsored by the Smithsonian in 1958.

After retiring from Howard in 1968, Wells continued to paint and make prints in the 1980s. In 1980, then-U.S. president Jimmy Carter bestowed Wells with a presidential citation for lifelong contributions to American art. Four years later, Washington, DC, had a "James L. Wells Day." Designated a "living legend" by the National Black Arts Festival in 1991, Wells's work was featured in a retrospective exhibition by the Harmon Foundation, which had recognized him for his artwork as early as 1916, when he took a first prize in painting and second prize in woodworking. He died of congestive heart failure at the age of ninety.

Charles White (1918–1979)
Painter

White was born in 1918 in Chicago and was influenced as a young boy by Alain Locke's critical review of the Harlem Renaissance, *The New Negro*. At the age of twenty-three, White won a Rosenwald Fellowship which enabled him to work in the South for two years, during which time he painted a celebrated mural depicting the black people's contribution to American democracy. It is now the property of the Hampton Institute in Virginia.

The bulk of White's work is done in black-and-white, a symbolic motif which he felt gave him the widest possible purview. Notable works include: *Let's Walk Together; Frederick Douglass Lives Again; Women;* and *Gospel Singer*.

Paul Revere Williams (1894–1980)
Architect

Williams was born in Los Angeles, California, on February 18, 1894, and graduated from the University of California at Los Angeles. He later attended the Beaux Arts Institute of Design in Paris and received honorary degrees from Howard, Lincoln, and Atlanta Universities as well as Hampton Institute.

Williams became a certified architect in 1915. After working for Reginald Johnson and John Austin, he opened his own firm in 1923. Williams designed some four hundred homes and a total of three thousand buildings including homes for Cary Grant, Barbara Stanwyk, William Holden, Frank Sinatra, Betty Grable, Bill "Bojangles" Robinson, and Bert Lahr.

In 1926 he was the first African American to become a member of the American Institute of Architects. He served on the National Monument Commission, an appointee of President Calvin Coolidge. Notable works include: *Los Angeles County Airport; Palm Springs Tennis Club;* and *Saks Fifth Avenue at Beverly Hills*. He died on January 23, 1980.

William T. Williams (1942–)
Painter

William T. Williams was born in Cross Creek, North Carolina, on July 17, 1942. He received his B.F.A. from Pratt Institute in 1966 and his M.F.A. from Yale University in 1968.

In 1970, Williams taught painting classes at Pratt Institute and at the School of Fine Arts. Since 1971, he has been a professor of art at City University of New York, Brooklyn College. He also served as a visiting professor of art at Virginia Commonwealth University.

Williams has been the recipient of several awards. In 1992, the Studio Museum in Harlem presented him with its Annual Award for Lifetime Achievement. He was also awarded the Mid-Atlantic Foundation Fellowship in 1994.

Exhibitions of Williams's work have been presented at, among others, The Studio Museum in Harlem, Wadsworth Atheneum, Art Institute of Chicago, and The Whitney Museum of American Art. Notable works include: *Elbert Jackson L.A.M.F. Port II; Big Red for N.C.;* and *Buttermilk*.

John Wilson (1922–)
Painter, Printmaker

Born in Boston on April 14, 1922, John Wilson studied at the Boston Museum of Fine Arts; Fernand Leger School, Paris; El Instituto Politecnico, Mexico City; and the Escuela de las Artes del Libro, Mexico City. In 1947, Wilson received a B.A. from Tufts University. He has been a teacher at Boston Museum, Pratt Institute, and Boston University.

His numerous exhibits include: the Albany Institute; the Library of Congress National (and International) Print Exhibit(s); Smith College; Carnegie Institute; and the American International College, Springfield, Massachusetts. His work is represented in the collections of the Museum of Modern Art; Schomburg Collection; Department of Fine Arts, French Government; Atlanta University; and Bezalel Museum, Jerusalem. Notable works include: *Roxbury Landscape* (oil, 1944); *Trabajador* (print, 1951); and *Child with Father* (graphic, 1969).

Wilson created the Dr. Martin Luther King Jr. Monument in Buffalo, New York, in 1983 and the Dr. Martin

Luther King Jr. Commemorative Statue at the U.S. Capitol in Washington, DC. In 1987, he completed the monument *Eternal Presence*, which resides at the Museum of the National Center of Afro-American Artists, Boston, Massachusetts.

Hale Woodruff (1900–1979)
Painter, Muralist

Hale Woodruff's paintings were largely modernist landscapes and formal abstractions, but he has also painted rural Georgia scenes evocative of the "red clay" country. Born in Cairo, Illinois, in 1900, he graduated from the John Herron Art Institute in Indianapolis. Encouraged by a bronze award in the 1926 Harmon Foundation competition, Woodruff went to Paris to study at both the Academie Scandinave and the Academie Moderne, as well as with Henry Ossawa Tanner.

In 1931, he became art instructor at Atlanta University and later accepted a similar post at New York University. In 1939, he was commissioned by Talladega College for *The Amistad Murals*, an episodic depiction of a slave revolt.

In 1948, Woodruff teamed with Charles Alston to work on the Golden State Mutual Life Insurance Company Murals in California, which presented the contribution of African Americans to the history of the development of California. Woodruff's last mural assignment came in 1950 when he developed the series of mural panels for Atlanta University entitled *The Art of the Negro*. Other notable works include: *Ancestral Remedies; The Little Boy;* and *The Amistad Murals*.

Richard Yarde (1939–)
Painter

Richard Yarde was born in Boston, Massachusetts, on October 29, 1939. He studied at the School of the Museum of Fine Arts and at Boston University, where he received a B.F.A. in 1962 and an M.F.A. in 1964. He has taught at Boston University, Wellesley College, Amherst College, Massachusetts College of Art, Mount Holyoke College, and the University of Massachusetts.

Yarde has received numerous awards for his art including Yaddo fellowships in 1964, 1966, and 1970, McDowell Colony awards in 1968 and 1970, and the Blanche E. Colman Award in 1970.

The Boston Museum of Fine Arts, Wadsworth Atheneum, Rose Art Museum, National Museum of African-American Artists, and Studio Museum in Harlem have all exhibited his works. He has held one-person shows at numerous galleries and universities. His works are in many collections, such as the Wadsworth

Atheneum in Hartford, Connecticut. Notable works include: *The Stoop;Passage Edgar and I; The Corner; Paul Robeson as Emperor Jones; Head and Hands I; Josephine's Baffle Triptych;* and *Richard's Cards.*

◆ MUSEUMS AND GALLERIES EXHIBITING AFRICAN AMERICAN ART

Alabama

George Washington Carver Museum
1212 Old Montgomery Rd.
PO Drawer 10
Tuskegee Institute, AL 36087-0010
(205) 727-3200
Fax:(205) 727-4597

California

African American Historical and Cultural Society
Fort Mason Center Bldg. C, No. 165
San Francisco, CA 94123
(415) 441-0640

California Afro-American Museum
Exposition Park
600 State Dr.
Los Angeles, CA 90037
(213) 744-7432
Fax:(213)744-2050
www.caam.ca.gob

DeYoung Museum
Golden Gate Park
San Francisco, CA 94118
(415) 863-3330
www.thinker.org/fam/

Ebony Museum of Art
30 Jack London Village, Stes. 208 and 209
Oakland, CA 94607
(510) 763-0745

Museum of African-American Art
4005 S. Crenshaw Blvd., 3rd Fl.
Los Angeles, CA 90008
(323) 294-7071

Wilson Brown Gallery
255 G St., Ste. 147
San Diego, CA 92101
(619) 232-8377
www.africanamericanart.net/

Colorado

Black American West Museum and Heritage Center
3091 California St.
Denver, CO 80207
(303) 292-2566
www.coax.net/people/lws/vawm.us.htm

Connecticut

Artists Collective, Inc.
35 Clark St.
Hartford, CT 06120
(860) 527-3205

Connecticut Afro-American Historical Society
444 Orchard St.
New Haven, CT 06511
(203) 776-4907

Delaware

Afro-American Historical Society of Delaware
512 E. 4th St.
Wilmington, DE 19801
(302) 571-9300

District of Columbia

Anacostia Museum
1901 Fort Pl., SE
Washington, DC 20020
(202) 287-3306
Fax:(202) 287-3183

Bethune Museum-Archives, National Historic Society
1318 Vermont Ave., NW
Washington, DC 20005
(202) 332-1233
Fax:(202) 332-6319

Evans-Tibbs Collection
1910 Vermont Ave., NW
Washington, DC 20001
(202) 234-8164

Howard University Gallery of Art
2455 6th St., NW
Washington, DC 20059
(202) 806-7070
Fax:(202) 806-6503

Sign of the Times Cultural Workshop and Gallery, Inc.
605 56th St., NE
Washington, DC 20019
(202) 399-3400
members@aol.com/signtimes

Smithsonian Institute, National Museum of African Art
950 Independence Ave., SW
Washington, DC 20560
(202) 357-4600
Fax:(202) 357-4879
www.si.edu/nmasa

Florida

Appleton Museum of Art/The Appleton Cultural Center
4333 E. Silver Springs Blvd.
Ocala, FL 32670
(352) 236-7100
www.fsu.edu/˜svad/Appleton/AppletonMuseum.html

Black Archives Research Center and Museum, Florida A and M University
c/o Florida A and M University
PO Box 809
Tallahassee, FL 32307
(850) 599-3020

Black Heritage Museum
PO Box 570327
Miami, FL 33257-0327
(305) 252-3535

Gallery Antiqua
5138 Biscayne Blvd.
Miami, FL 33137
(305) 759-5355

Georgia

Apex Museum
135 Auburn Ave., NE
Atlanta, GA 30303
(404) 521-2739
www.apexmuseum.org

Clark Atlanta University Art Galleries
223 James P. Brawley Dr., SW
Atlanta, GA 30314
(404) 880-6102
www.cau.edu/artgalleries

Hammonds House Galleries
503 Peeples St., SW
Atlanta, GA 30310
(404) 752-8730

Herndon Home
587 University Pl., NW
Atlanta, GA 30314
(404) 581-9813

High Museum of Art
1280 Peachtree St.
Atlanta, GA 30309
(404) 733-4422
www.high.org

King-Tisdell Cottage of Black History Museum
502 E. Harris St.
Savannah, GA 31401
(912) 234-8000

Martin Luther King Jr. Center, Cultural Affairs Program
449 Auburn Ave., NE
Atlanta, GA 30312
(404) 524-1956

McIntosh Gallery
One Virginia Hill
587 Virginia Ave.
Atlanta, GA 30306
(404) 892-4023
www.artnet.com/mcintosh.html

National Black Arts Festival
236 Forsyth St., Ste. 405
Atlanta, GA 30303
(404) 730-7315

Uncle Remus Museum
PO Box 184
Eatonton, GA 31024
(706) 485-6856

U.S. National Park Service, Martin Luther King Jr. National Historic Site and Preservation District
522 Auburn Ave., NE
Atlanta, GA 30312
(404) 331-5190

Illinois

Afro-American Genealogical and Historical Society, Du Sable Museum of African American History
740 E. 56th Pl.
Chicago, IL 60637
(773)947-0600
www.dusable.org

Art Institute of Chicago
111 S. Michigan Ave.
Chicago, IL 60603
(312) 357-1052
www.artic.edu/aic/

Indiana

Indiana University Art Museum
1133 E. 7th St.
Bloomington, IN 47405-7309
(812) 855-5445
Fax:(812) 855-1023
www.indiana.edu/~iuam

Kansas

First National Black Historical Society of Kansas
601 N. Water
Wichita, KS 67201
(316) 262-7651

Maryland

African-American Visual Arts
P.O. Box 31677
Baltimore, MD 21207
(410) 664-1946
members.tripod.com/~AVAA/

Alliance of African-American Artists
4936-3 Columbia Rd.
Columbia, MD 21044-2176
(410) 740-0033
Fax:(410)740-0223
www.artists4a.com

Baltimore's Black American Museum
1765 Carswell St.
Baltimore, MD 21218
(410) 243-9600

Great Blacks in Wax Museum
1601-03 E. North Ave.
Baltimore, MD 21213
(410) 563-3404
Fax:(410) 675-5040
www.gbiw.org

Maryland Museum of African Art
5430 Vantage Point Rd.
Columbia, MD 21044-0105
(410) 730-7105
Fax:(410) 715-3047

Massachusetts

National Center of Afro-American Artists
300 Walnut Ave.
Boston, MA 02119
(617) 442-8614

Wendell Street Gallery
17 Wendel St.
Cambridge, MA 02138
(617) 864-9294

Michigan

Black Folk Arts
425 W. Margaret
Detroit, MI 48203
(313) 865-4546

Charles H. Wright Museum of African-American History
315 E. Warren Ave.
Detroit, MI 48201-1443
(313) 494-5800
www.maah-detroit.org

Detroit Institute of Arts
5205 Woodward Ave.
Detroit, MI 48202
(313) 833-7900
www.dia.org

G.R. N'namdi Gallery
161 Townsend
Birmingham, MI 48009
(313) 642-2700

University of Michigan Art Museum
525 S. State St.
Ann Arbor, MI 48109
(734) 764-0395
www.umich.edu/~umma/

Your Heritage House
110 E. Ferry
Detroit, MI 48202
(313) 871-1667

Minnesota

Pillsbury House/Cultural Arts
3501 Chicago Ave. S.
Minneapolis, MN 55407
(612) 824-0708

Mississippi

Smith Robertson Museum and Cultural Center
PO Box 3259
Jackson, MS 39207
(601) 960-1457

Missouri

Black Archives of Mid-America
2033 Vine St.
Kansas City, MO 64108
(816) 483-1300
Fax:(816) 483-1341
www.blackarchives.org

Vaughn Cultural Center
4321 Semple
St. Louis, MO 63120
(314) 381-5280

Nebraska

Great Plains Black Museum
2213 Lake St.
Omaha, NE 68110
(402) 345-2212

New Jersey

African Art Museums of the SMA Fathers
23 Bliss Ave.
Tenafly, NJ 07670
(201) 567-0450
www.smafathers.org

Newark Museum
49 Washington St.
Newark, NJ 07101-0540
(973) 596-6550
Fax:(201) 642-0459

New York

African-American Cultural Center of Buffalo
350 Masten Ave.
Buffalo, NY 14209
(716) 884-2013

African-American Culture and Arts Network
2090 Adam Clayton Powell, Jr. Blvd.
New York, NY 10027
(212) 749-0827

African-American Institute Museum
380 Lexington Ave.
New York, NY 10168
(212) 949-5666
Fax:(212) 682-6174

African American Museum of Nassau County
110 Franklin St.
Hempstead, NY 11550
(516) 572-0730

Bedford-Stuyvesant Restoration Center for Arts and Culture
1368 Fulton, Ste. 4G
Brooklyn, NY 11216
(718) 636-6948

Black Filmmaker Foundation
670 Broadway, Ste. 304
New York, NY
(212) 253-1690
Fax:(212) 253-1689

Black Spectrum Theater Co.
Roy Wilkens Park
119-07 Merrick Blvd.
Jamaica, NY 11434
(718) 723-1800
www.blackspectrum.com

Brooklyn Museum of Art
200 Eastern Parkway
Brooklyn, NY 11238-6052
(718) 638-5000
Fax:(718) 638-3731
www.brooklynart.org/

Cinque Gallery
560 Broadway
New York, NY 10012
(212) 966-3464

Community Folk Art Gallery
2223 Genessee St.
Syracuse, NY 13210
(315) 424-8487

Grinnell Gallery
800 Riverside Dr.
New York, NY 10032
(212) 927-7941

Harlem Institute of Fashion
157 W. 126th St.
New York, NY 10027
(212) 666-1320

Harlem School of the Arts
645 St. Nicholas Ave.
New York, NY 10030
(212) 926-4100
www.erols.com/nsoa

Hatch-Billops Collection, Inc.
491 Broadway
New York, NY 10012
(212) 966-3231

International Agency for Minority Artists Affairs Inc.
163 W. 125th St.
New York, NY 10027
(212) 749-5298
www.harlem.cc

June Kelly Gallery
591 Broadway, 3rd Fl.
New York, NY 10012
(212) 226-1660
www.junekellygallery.com

Museum of African and African-American Art and Antiquities
11 E. Utica St.
Buffalo, NY 14209
(716) 862-9260

Schomburg Center For Research in Black Culture
515 Malcolm X Blvd.
New York, NY 10037-1801
(212) 491-2200
www.nypl.org/research/sc/

Studio Museum in Harlem
144 W. 125th St.
New York, NY 10027
(212) 864-4500
Fax:(212) 666-5753
www.studentmuseuminharlem.ark

North Carolina

African-American Atelier
Greensboro Cultural Center
200 N. Davie St.
Greensboro, NC 27401
(336) 333-6885

Afro-American Cultural Center
401 N. Meyers St.
Spirit Square
Charlotte, NC 28202
(704) 374-1565

Biggers Art Sales Traveling Gallery
1404 N. Oakwood St.
Gastonia, NC 28052
(704) 867-4525

Black Artists Guild
400 N. Queen St.
P.O. Box 2162
Kinston, NC 28501
(252) 523-0003

Diggs Art Gallery
Winston-Salem State University
601 Martin Luther King, Jr. Dr.
Winston-Salem, NC 27110
(336) 750-2458

Duke University Museum of Art
PO Box 90732
Durham, NC 27708-0732
Fax:(919) 681-8624
www.duke.edu/web/dumal/

Huff's Art Studio
2846 Patterson Ave.
Winston-Salem, NC 27105
(336) 724-7581

NCCU Art Museum
PO Box 19555
Durham, NC 27707
(919) 560-6211
Fax:(919) 560-5012

St. Augustine's College Art Gallery
Dept. of Art
Saint Augustine's College
Raleigh, NC 27611
(919) 516-4026

Shaw University Art Center
Shaw University Dept. of Art
Raleigh, NC 27602
(919) 546-8420

Weatherspoon Art Gallery
North Carolina A and T State University
P.O. Box 26170
Greensboro, NC 27402-6170
(336) 334-5770

Ohio

African American Museum
1765 Crawford Rd.
Cleveland, OH 44106
(216) 791-1700

Afro-American Cultural Center
Cleveland State University
Black Studies Program
2121 Euclid Ave., UC 103
Cleveland, OH 44115
(216) 687-3655

Allen Memorial Art Museum
Oberlin College
Oberlin, OH 44074
(440) 775-8665
www.oberlin.edu/~allenart/

Cincinnati Art Museum
953 Eden Park Dr.
Cincinnati, OH 45202-1596
(513) 721-5204
Fax:(513) 721-0129
www.cincinnatiartmuseum.org

Karamu House
2355 E. 89th St.
Cleveland, OH 44106
(216) 795-7070
www.karamu.com

Malcolm Brown Gallery
20100 Chagrin Blvd.
Shaker Heights, Ohio 44122
(216) 751-2955
www.malcolmbrowngallery

National Afro-American Museum and Cultural Center
1350 Brush Row Rd.
PO Box 578
Xenia, OH 45384
(937) 376-4944
Fax: (937) 376-2007
www.ohiohistory.org

Resident Art and Humanities Consortium
1515 Linn St.
Cincinnati, OH 45214
(513) 381-0645

Oklahoma

Kirkpatrick Center Museum Complex
2100 N.E. 52nd
Oklahoma City, OK 73111
(405) 602-6664
www.omniplex.org

NTU Art Association
2100 N.E. 52nd St.
Oklahoma City, OK 73111
(405) 424-1655

Pennsylvania

African Cultural Art Forum
237 S. 60th St.
Philadelphia, PA 19139
(215) 476-0680

Afro-American Historical and Cultural Museum
701 Arch St.
Philadelphia, PA 19106
(215) 574-0380
www.aampmuseum.org

Minority Arts Resource Council
1421 W. Girard Ave.
Philadelphia, PA 19130
(215) 236-2688

Rhode Island

Rhode Island Black Heritage Society
202 Washington St.
Providence, RI 02905
(401) 751-3490

South Carolina

Avery Research Center for Afro-American History and Culture
125 Bull St.
College of Charleston
Charleston, SC 29424
(842) 953-7609
www.cofc.edu/~averyrsc

I.P. Stanback Museum and Planetarium
South Carolina State University
300 College St., NE
Orangeburg, SC 29117
(803) 536-7174

Mann-Simons Cottage: Museum of African-American Culture
1403 Richland St.
Columbia, SC 29201
(803) 252-1770

Rice Museum
Intersection of Front and Screven Sts.
PO Box 902
Georgetown, SC 29442
(843) 546-7423
Fax:(843) 545-9093
www.thestrand.com/rice

Tennessee

Black Cultural Exchange Center
1927 Dandridge Ave.
Knoxville, TN 37915
(423) 524-8461

Blues City Cultural Center
39 Carnes Ave.
Memphis, TN 38114
(901) 327-7060

Carl Van Vechten Gallery of Fine Arts
Fisk University
Dr. D. B. Todd Blvd. and Jackson St. N.
Nashville, TN 37203
(615) 329-8720

Chattanooga African American Museum
200 E. Martin Luther King, Jr. Blvd.
Chattanooga, TN 37203
(423) 267-1076

Memphis Black Arts Alliance
985 S. Bellevue
Memphis, TN 38106
(901) 948-9522
www.webspawner.com/users/mbaa/

Tennessee State University Institute for African Studies
Tennessee State University
PO Box 828
Nashville, TN 37209
(615) 963-5561

Texas

African American Museum
3536 Grant Ave.
Dallas, TX 75315
(214) 565-9026
Fax:(214) 421-8204

Black Art Gallery
5408 Almeda Rd.
Houston, TX 77004
(713) 529-7900

Utah

Utah Museum of Fine Arts
370 South 1530 East, Rm. 101
Salt Lake City, UT 84122
(801) 581-7332
Fax:(801) 585-5198
www.utah.edu/umfa

Virginia

Alexandria Black History Resource Center
220 N. Washington St.
Alexandria, VA 22314
(703) 838-4356

Black Historical Museum and Cultural Center
00 Clay St.
Richmond, VA 23220
(804) 780-9093
members.spree.com/education/bhmv/

Hampton University Museum
Hampton University
Hampton, VA 23668
(757) 727-5308
www.hamptonu.edu

Harrison Museum of African American Culture
523 Harrison Ave., NW
Roanoke, VA 24016
(540) 345-4818

Science and Technology

◆ Early African American Inventors ◆ Early African American Scientists
◆ African Americans in Medicine ◆ African Americans in Air and Space
◆ Modern Contributions to Science and Technology ◆ Popular African American Internet Sites
◆ Engineers, Mathematicians, Inventors, Physicians, and Scientists
by Kristine Krapp

Perhaps in science more than in other areas, African Americans have been afforded few sanctioned opportunities to offer contributions. However, will and intelligence helped individuals bring their ideas and dreams into the light. The Industrial Revolution swept African Americans along just as dramatically as it did the rest of the world. Though not all of them became household names, African Americans have made their mark in science and technology. For example, when Alexander Graham Bell invented the telephone, he chose Lewis Latimer to draft the plans. Later, Latimer became a member of the Edison Pioneers, a group of inventors who worked for Thomas Edison from 1884 to 1912.

One of the earliest African American stars of science was Benjamin Banneker, a free African American who lived in the 1700s. Considered the first African American scientist, Banneker was an expert in mathematics and astronomy, both of which he studied during his friendship with an influential white Quaker neighbor. In 1754, Banneker constructed what has been considered the first grandfather clock made in the United States. Later, Banneker and the Quaker's son were selected to lay the plans for the city of Washington, DC. Thus, not only was Banneker the first African American to receive a presidential appointment, he was one of the first African American civil engineers. In the early 1790s, his almanac—a year-long calendar loaded with weather and astronomical information that was especially useful to farmers—was published with much success. New editions were issued for several years.

In 1790, the U.S. government passed the U.S. Patent Act, legislation that extended patent rights to inventors including free blacks. Slaves would not have this right until the passage of the Fourteenth Amendment. In one of history's most absurd bureaucratic fiats, slaves could neither be granted patents nor could they assign patents to their masters. The underlying theory was that since slaves were not citizens they could not enter into contracts with their owners or the government. As a result, the efforts of slaves were dismissed or credited to their masters. One can only speculate on the extent to which slaves were active in invention. For example, Joe Anderson, a slave, was believed to have played a major role in the creation of a grain harvester, or reaper, that his master Cyrus McCormick was credited with inventing, but available records are insufficient to determine the degree to which Anderson was involved. Similarly, Benjamin Montgomery, a slave belonging to Confederate President Jefferson Davis, is thought to have concocted an improved boat propeller. Since the race of patent-seekers was rarely noted and other African American inventions such as ice cream, created by Augustus Jackson of Philadelphia in 1832, were simply never patented, one cannot be sure how many inventions were made by free blacks either.

The first free blacks to have their inventions recorded were Thomas L. Jennings, whose dry-cleaning methodology received patent protection in 1821, and Henry Blair who invented a seed planter in 1834. Free black Norbert Rillieux patented his sugar refining evaporator, thus revolutionizing the industry. The son of a French planter and a slave woman, Rillieux left his home in New Orleans to study engineering in Paris. After teaching mathematics there and experimenting with steam evaporation, he created his vacuum pan evaporator. With his invention, a single person could do work that once required several people working at once. He returned to the United States and became wealthy as the device was implemented in sugar refineries in his home state and abroad in Cuba and Mexico. However, racial tensions in the United States wore on him, and in 1854, he moved to France, where he spent the remainder of his life.

In 1848, free black Lewis Temple invented the toggle harpoon for killing whales, a major industry at the time. Temple's invention almost completely replaced the type of harpoon formerly used as it greatly diminished the mammal's ability to escape after being hooked. Prior to the Civil War, Henry Boyd created an improved bedframe, and James Forten, one of the few African Americans from that era to gain extreme wealth from an invention, produced a device that helped guide ship sails. He used the money he earned to expand his sail factory.

The Reconstruction era opened the door to creativity that had been suppressed in African Americans. Between 1870 and 1900, a time when nearly eighty percent of African American adults in the United States were illiterate, African Americans were awarded several hundred patents. Elijah McCoy worked as a locomotive fireman on a Michigan line lubricating the hot steam engines during scheduled train stops. After years of work, in 1872, McCoy perfected and patented an automatic lubricator that regularly supplied oil to the engine as the train was in motion. The effect on the increasingly important railway system was profound as conductors were no longer forced to make oiling stops. McCoy adapted his invention for use on ships and in factories. When copycats tried to steal his invention, the phrase "the real McCoy" came into vogue.

In 1884, Granville T. Woods invented an improved steamboiler furnace in his Cincinnati electrical engineering shop. Three years later, Woods patented an induction telegraph or "Synchronous Multiplex Railway Telegraph," that allowed train personnel to communicate with workers on other trains while in motion. He was also responsible for what later became known as the trolley when he produced an overhead electrical power supply system for streetcars and trains. A prolific inventor, Woods, known as "The Black Edison," patented more than sixty valuable inventions including an airbrake, which he eventually sold to George Westinghouse, and an incubator.

Jan Matzeliger came to the United States from South America in 1877. Living in Lynn, Massachusetts, he obtained work in a shoe factory. There he witnessed the tedious process by which shoe soles were attached to shoe uppers by workers known as hand lasters. For six months he secretly labored at inventing a machine to automate the work. Unsatisfied with his original design, he spent several more years tweaking and perfecting his

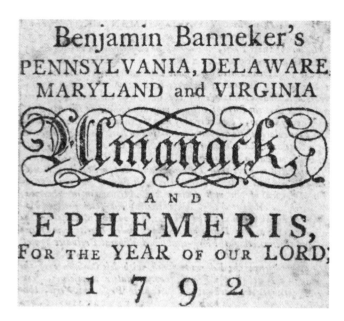

The title page from Benjamin Banneker's 1792 *Almanack* (The Library of Congress).

creation so that by the time he was granted a patent in 1883, the equipment was so successful that manufacturers the world over clamored for the gadgetry.

Progress has been a gift from women as well as men. For example, Sarah Goode is credited with creating a folding cabinet bed in 1885; Sarah Boone invented the ironing board in 1892; and photographer Claytonia Dorticus was granted several patents that were concerned with photographic equipment and developing solutions as well as a shoe dye. But Madame C. J. Walker, often regarded only as an entrepreneur, was one of the most successful female inventors. She developed an entire line of hair care products and cosmetics for African Americans, claiming that her first idea had come to her in a dream.

During the next few years, Garrett Morgan patented a succession of products including a hair straightening solution that was still a bestseller in as late as the 1970s; a gas mask, or "breathing device" for firefighters; and an improved traffic signal. Morgan tried to pass himself off as Native American. However, once his identity as an African American was discovered, several of his purchase orders were canceled.

Nonetheless, the early inventors paved the way for future African Americans. These men and women, as well as the countless unknown ones, were forced to endure the byproducts of racism. Whites were oftentimes hesitant to buy African American inventions unless the smell of eventual monetary gains was too strong. McCoy, Woods, and several others died poor, although their creations sold extremely well.

◆ EARLY AFRICAN AMERICAN SCIENTISTS

The contributions of African American scientists are better known than those of African American inventors, partly because of the recognition awarded to George Washington Carver, an agriculturalist, who refused to patent most of his inventions. Born into slavery in 1864, Carver was the first African American to graduate from Iowa Agricultural State College, where he studied botany and agriculture. One year after earning a master's degree, Carver joined Tuskegee Institute's Agriculture Department. In his role as department head, he engineered a number of experimental farming techniques that had practical applications for farmers in the area. Through his ideas, from crop rotation to replenish nutrient-starved soil to his advocacy of peanuts as a cash crop, Carver left an indelible mark in his field. An inventor at heart, he was behind the genesis of innumerable botanical products, by-products, and even recipes. Recognition of his efforts came in several forms including induction into England's Royal Society of Arts and Manufacturing and Commerce in 1916. In 1923, he received an NAACP Spingarn Medal. Six years after his death, in 1949, Carver was the subject of a U.S. postal stamp.

Born approximately ten years before Carver earned his bachelor's degree, Ernest Everett Just was a pioneering marine biologist who had graduated *magna cum laude* from Dartmouth College in 1907. The first-ever recipient of a Spingarn Medal in 1915, his first paper was published as "The Relation of First Cleavage Plane to the Entrance Point of the Sperm" in 1912. The work showed how the location of cell division in the marine worm *Nereis* is determined by the sperm's entry point on an egg. Just did the majority of his research at the Marine Biological Laboratory in Woods Hole, Massachusetts, where he spent many summers. Teaching at Howard for many years, he had a tenuous relationship with the school, paving the way for him to accept an offer to conduct research at the Kaiser Wilhelm Institute for Biology in Berlin, Germany. The first American to be invited to the internationally respected institution and remained there from 1929 to 1933, at which point the Nazi regime was surging to power. Because he preferred working abroad to being shut out of the best laboratories in the United States on the basis of race, Just spent the rest of his career in France, Italy, Spain, and Portugal.

African Americans have had successes in the hard sciences, engineering, and mathematics as well. In 1876, Edward Bouchet became the first African American to earn a doctorate from a university in the United States, when he acquired a Ph.D. in physics from Yale. In the twentieth century, Elmer Samuel Imes, husband of Harlem Renaissance writer Nella Larsen, received a

George Washington Carver (Corbis Corporation [Bellevue])

Ph.D. in physics from the University of Michigan in 1918. In his dissertation, Imes took the works of white scientists Albert Einstein, Ernest Rutherford, and Niels Bohr, one step further, definitively establishing that quantum theory applied to the rotational states of molecules. His efforts would later play a role in space science.

Chemist Percy Julian carved a brilliant career for himself after obtaining a doctorate from Switzerland's University of Vienna in 1931. His specialty was creating synthetic versions of expensive drugs. Much of his work was conducted at his Julian Research Institute in Franklin Park, Illinois. In the 1940s, another scientist, Benjamin Peery, switched his focus from aeronautical engineering to physics while still an undergraduate at the University of Minnesota. After garnering a Ph.D. from the University of Michigan, Peery went on to a lengthy career teaching astronomy at Indiana University, the University of Illinois, and Howard University.

Between 1875 and 1943, only eight African Americans were awarded doctorates in pure mathematics. David Blackwell became the first tenured African American professor at the University of California at Berkeley in 1955. An expert in statistics and probability, he was a trailblazer despite a racially motivated setback he incurred soon after completing his doctoral work at the University of Illinois. Nominated for a Rosenwald Fellowship from the Institute for Advanced Study at Princeton University, Blackwell was rejected because of his race. Undaunted, he went on to become the only African American mathematician to be elected into the National Academy of Sciences.

◆ AFRICAN AMERICANS IN MEDICINE

The medical profession has yielded a number of African Americans of high stature. As early as the 1860s, African Americans had entered medical schools in the North and had gone on to practice as full-fledged physicians. In fact, during the Civil War, Dr. Alexander T. Augusta was named head of a Union army hospital and Rebecca Lee Crumpler became the first female African American doctor by graduating from the New England Female Medical College in Boston. She was able to attend on a scholarship that she received from Ohio Sen. Benjamin Wade, an abolitionist. She used her schooling to provide health care to former slaves in the former confederate capital of Richmond, Virginia. Her 1883 *Book of Medical Discourses* taught women how to address their own health issues, as well as those of their children.

Rebecca J. Cole was the second African American woman to become a physician and the first African American graduate of the Women's Medical College of Pennsylvania. For over fifty years, she devoted her life to improving the lot of the poor. Her positions included performing a residency at the New York Infirmary for Women and Children and running Washington, DC's Government House for Children and Old Women and Philadelphia's Woman's Directory, a medical aid center.

In 1867, Susan McKinney Steward began studying at the New York Medical College for Women. Three years later she earned the distinction of being the third African American female physician in the United States and the first in New York State. She specialized in homeopathic treatments and had black and white patients of both genders as clients. After opening a second office in New York City, she helped co-found the Brooklyn Women's Hospital and Dispensary. She also served at the Brooklyn Home for Aged Colored People. Steward vigorously supported women's suffrage movement and conducted missionary work with her second husband, a chaplain for the Buffalo Soldier regiment. She ended her career by taking on the role of school doctor at Wilberforce University.

In 1868, Howard University opened its College of Medicine, the first African American medical school in

the country. The school nearly failed five years later when monetary problems arose and salaries for faculty were unavailable. Thanks to the efforts of Dr. Charles Purvis, who convinced the school to let him and his peers continue teaching on a non-paid basis, the school survived the crisis. Purvis was later appointed chief surgeon of Washington, DC's Freedman's Hospital by U.S. President Chester Arthur. Purvis was thus the first African American to run a civilian hospital. He did so until 1894, when he began a private practice.

Meanwhile, in 1876, Nashville's Meharry Medical College was founded. Despite the decidedly low number of jobs for African American physicians who were routinely turned away from nearly every facility other than Freedman's Hospital, the school was another sign of the slowly developing progress by African American physicians including Dr. Daniel Hale Williams, who replaced Purvis at Freedman's. Williams advanced Freedman's through internships, better nurses' training, and the addition of horse-drawn ambulances.

Williams had graduated from the Chicago Medical College in 1883 and entered into private practice almost immediately. Business was slow until 1890, when he met Emma Reynolds, an aspiring African American nurse, whose skin color had kept her from gaining admission to any of the nursing schools in Chicago. Inspired by her unfortunate dilemma, Williams decided to operate his own hospital in hopes of initiating his own program for aspiring nurses. With 12 beds, Provident Hospital became the first African American operated facility in the United States, and Reynolds was the first to enroll in Williams's classes. Near the end of his career, Williams was appointed the first African American associate surgeon at Chicago's St. Luke Hospital and later was the only African American charter member of the American College of Surgeons. During his career, Williams helped convince forty hospitals to treat African American patients.

African Americans in the South also received improved care in the late 1890s, thanks to Alice Woodby McKane and her spouse who was also a doctor. In 1893, they founded the first training school for African American nurses—in Savannah, Georgia. McKane had obtained her medical degree one year earlier from the Women's Medical College of Pennsylvania. In 1895 the couple set up their first hospital in Monrovia, Liberia, before establishing the McKane Hospital for Women and Children in Georgia the following year.

Progress moved westward as another African American woman used her training to benefit the region's African American population, though her patients transcended all racial barriers. Beginning in 1902, Denver's

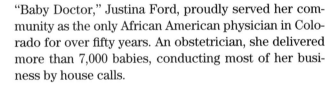

Daniel Hale Williams (Corbis Corporation [Bellevue])

Charles Richard Drew (AP/Wide World Photos, Inc.)

"Baby Doctor," Justina Ford, proudly served her community as the only African American physician in Colorado for over fifty years. An obstetrician, she delivered more than 7,000 babies, conducting most of her business by house calls.

Back in the East, Freedman's Hospital was the training ground for future head trauma authority, Dr. Louis Wright, a Harvard Medical School graduate whose high academic standing meant nothing to Boston area hospitals that refused to hire African Americans. When World War I erupted, Wright enlisted and found himself in charge of his unit's surgical ward. After the war, Wright, who had received a Purple Heart, became the first African American physician to work in a New York City hospital when he was appointed to Harlem Hospital in 1919. Later he became director of surgery, president of the medical board, and was admitted to the American College of Surgeons. Four years before his death in 1952, he founded the Cancer Research Foundation at Harlem Hospital. The son of two physicians, his father and his stepfather, the latter of whom was the first African American graduate of Yale Medical School, Wright had two daughters who continued the family legacy by becoming doctors.

An almost legendary legacy was created by Dr. Charles R. Drew, a star high school athlete whose interest lay in medicine. A pathologist and expert on blood transfusions, Drew discovered that blood plasma was easier to store than whole blood and was compatible with all blood types. His experiments helped him receive a M.D. in 1940. During World War II, he helped Great Britain develop a national blood collection program and was later asked to do the same for the U.S. Armed Forces. Unfortunately racism reared its ugly head again—African American donors were first completely excluded from the program and later were only allowed to donate to other African American servicemen. Frustrated, Drew withdrew from the program, briefly resuming his teaching career at Howard before joining the staff of Freedman's Hospital as medical director.

Howard continued developing new talents. Dr. Roland Scott, a physician at Howard University's College of Medicine, became a pioneer in the study and treatment of sickle cell anemia. His research was pivotal in drawing public attention to the disorder and prompting the U.S. government to devote money to more extensive study. Under the Sickle Cell Anemia Control Act passed in 1972, Congress forced the National Institutes of Health to set up treatment centers for patients. Scott was named director of the program that involved screening as well as treatment for those already afflicted.

◆ AFRICAN AMERICANS IN AIR AND SPACE

In 1920, Texan Bessie Coleman was accepted at the French flying school, École d'Aviation des Freres, following a string of rejections from aviation schools in the United States. Having completed seven months of instruction and a rigorous qualifying exam, she earned her international aviator's license from the Federation Aeronautique Internationale the following year and went on to study further with aircraft designer Anthony H. G. Fokker. Known to an admiring public as "Queen Bess," Bessie Coleman was the first African American woman ever to fly an airplane, the first American to earn an international pilot's license, and the first African American female stunt pilot. During her brief yet distinguished career as a performance flier, she appeared at air shows and exhibitions across the country, earning wide recognition for her aerial skill, dramatic flair, and tenacity. The tragic demise of the professional aviatrix occurred in 1926, when she was scheduled to parachute jump from a speeding plane at 2,500 feet. Ten minutes after takeoff, however, the plane careened wildly out of control, flipping over and dropping Coleman, who plunged 500 feet to her death. Though he remained in the aircraft, the pilot was instantly killed when the plane crashed to the ground. Later a service wrench mistakenly left behind in the engine was found to have been the cause of the accident.

Six years later, in 1932, pilot James Herman Banning and mechanic Thomas C. Allen flew from Los Angeles to New York City in 41 hours and 27 minutes. The transcontinental flight was followed by the first round-trip transcontinental flight the next year. That feat was accomplished by Albert Ernest Forsythe and Charles Alfred Anderson, who flew from Atlantic City to Los Angeles and back in 11 days, foreshadowing the advent of commercial flight.

Willa B. Brown became the first African American woman to hold a commercial pilot's license in the United States in 1934. She also the first African American woman to ascend to the rank of lieutenant in the Civil Air Patrol Squadron. Brown later founded the National Airmen's Association of America, the first aviators group for African Americans. With her husband, Cornelius R. Coffey, she established the first African American-owned flying school—Coffey School of Aeronautics—and the first African American-owned school to receive certification from the Civil Aviation Authority. Brown became the first African American member of the Federal Aviation Agency's Women's Advisory Council in 1972.

The second African American woman to earn a full commercial pilot's license was Janet Harmon Bragg, a Georgian nurse who took an interest in flying when she began dating Johnny Robinson, one of the first African American aviation instructors. The first woman of any race to be admitted to Chicago's Curtiss Wright Aeronautical University, she was initially denied her commercial license despite having successfully fulfilled all preliminary requirements including the airborne portion of the test. Her white instructor from the Federal Aviation Administration made it quite clear, however, that he would not grant a license to an African American woman. Rather than give up, Bragg merely tested again with another instructor the same year and was granted her license in 1942. Along with a small group of African American aviation devotees, she formed the Challengers Air Pilots Association (CAPA). Together, members of CAPA opened an airport in Robins, Illinois, the first owned and operated by African Americans.

Other African American notables in the field of aviation include: Perry H. Young, who, in 1957 became the first African American pilot for a scheduled passenger commercial airline, New York Airways; Otis B. Young, Jr., who, in 1970, was the first African American pilot of a jumbo jet; and former naval pilot Jill Brown, who became the first African American female to pilot for a major airline in 1987.

Military men were the first African Americans to enter into the line of space exploration. In 1961, U.S. Air Force Captain Edward Dwight was invited by Pres. John F. Kennedy to apply to test-pilot school. Two years later, Dwight was in the midst of spaceflight training when Kennedy was assassinated. Without the president's support, Dwight was pretty much ignored by National Aeronautics and Space Administration (NASA). Air Force Major Robert H. Lawrence thus became the first African American astronaut a few years later. A doctor of physical chemistry, Lawrence was killed in a plane crash in December of 1967, just six months after his selection by NASA. African Americans would not make inroads in space until the genesis of the Space Shuttle program.

African American scientists were, however, prevalent. For example, Katherine Johnson joined the National Advisory Committee on Aeronautics, the precursor to NASA, in 1953. Initially all she was asked to do was basic number crunching, but she spent a short period filling in at the Flight Research Division. There her valued interpretation of data helped in the making of prototype spacecraft, and she soon developed into an aerospace technologist. She developed trajectories for the Apollo moon-landing project and devised emergency navigational methods for astronauts. She retired in 1986.

Emergencies of another sort have been tackled by air force flight surgeon Vance Marchbanks, whose research showed that adrenaline levels could affect the exhaustion level of flight crews. His work brought him to the attention of NASA, and he became a medical observer for NASA's Project Mercury. Along with several other personnel scattered about the globe, Marchbanks, stationed in Nigeria, was responsible for monitoring pioneering astronaut John Glenn's vital signs as he orbited the earth in 1962. Later, Marchbanks received the civilian post of chief of environmental health services for United Aircraft Corporation, where he had a hand in designing the space suit and medical monitoring systems used in the Apollo moon shot.

Also specializing in design, aeronautical test engineer Robert E. Shurney spent nearly his entire career, from 1968 to 1990, at the Marshall Space Flight Center, specializing in design utility. His products included refuse disposal units that stored solids in the bottom and liquid in tubes to prevent any materials from floating openly and contaminating an entire cabin. The units were used in the Apollo program, Skylab, and on the first space shuttle missions. He also crafted strong, yet lightweight, aluminum tires for the lunar rover. Much of his experimentation was conducted on KC-135 test planes in order to achieve the condition of weightlessness.

Assertiveness enabled O. S. Williams to bring forth his own achievements. In 1942, Williams talked his way into employment at Republic Aviation Corporation as part of the technical staff. Better known as "Ozzie," he took the experience he earned there to NASA contractor Grumman Corporation. The small rocket engines that he co-developed saved the lives of the Apollo 13 astronauts when the ship's main rocket exploded during flight in 1970.

Three missions later, George Carruthers, a Naval Research Laboratory astrophysicist, designed the far-ultraviolet camera/spectograph for use on Apollo 16. The semiautomatic device was able to photograph deep space—regions too far to be captured by regular cameras—once set up on the surface of the moon. Carruthers, who earned a Ph.D. in aeronautical and astronautical engineering from the University of Illinois in 1964 and was granted his first patent in 1969 for an electromagnetic radiation image converter.

With a 1965 Ph.D. in atomic and molecular physics from Howard University, Carruther's contemporary, George E. Alcorn, has been one of the most prominent people working with semiconductors and spectrometers.

Working for private industry, including IBM and NASA, Alcorn has over 25 patents to his name including secret projects concerning missile systems.

In a less clandestine fashion, aerospace engineer Christine Darden has been a leading NASA researcher in supersonic and hypersonic aircraft. Her main goal has been the reduction of sonic boom, a phenomenon that creates an explosive burst of sound that can traumatize those on the ground. Darden works at manipulating an aircraft's wing or the shape of its nose, to try to control the feedback produced by air waves resulting from a plane's flight.

Dealing with people rather than machinery, director of psychophysiology at NASA's Ames Research Center, Patricia Cowings's post-doctoral work has touched upon such fields as aerospace medicine and bioastronautics. Since the late 1970s, she has assisted astronauts by teaching them biofeedback techniques—how to impose mind over matter when zero gravity wreaks havoc with one's system. By studying physical and emotional problems that arise in such a setting, she can seek the cause and prescribe a therapy to alleviate stress. She was also the first woman of any race in the United States to receive astronaut training.

These individuals are joined by numerous others in the field of aviation and space flight including chemical engineer Henry Allen, Jr., a liquid and solid rocket fuel specialist; missile expert and inventor extraordinaire Otis Boykin; health services officer Julian Earls; aerospace technologist Isabella J. Coles; astrodynamicist Robert A. Gordon; and operations officer Isaac Gillam, IV, to name a few. Once the Space Shuttle program began in earnest, however, African Americans also took to the skies.

Traveling in the Space Shuttle *Challenger*, U.S. Air Force Colonel Guion "Guy" Bluford was the first African American to fly in space, where he coordinated experiments and was in charge of deploying satellites. After his first mission in 1983, Bluford participated in three more. Astronaut Ronald McNair was aboard the tragic *Challenger* flight of 1986, his second trip on the shuttle. The vehicle exploded 73 seconds after liftoff, killing all seven crew members. Charles Bolden's first mission was aboard the 1986 flight of the Space Shuttle *Columbia*. He has also flown on the *Discovery*. The first African American to pilot a space shuttle was Frederick Drew Gregory, who did so in 1985, on his first journey to outer space. A veteran pilot of both helicopters and airplanes, Gregory became an astronaut in 1979. Gregory also made history on his fourth flight, when he commanded the first mission comprised of Russians and Americans. Mae Jemison went into space as a science specialist in 1992's joint U.S.-Japanese project on the shuttle *Endeavor.* The following year, Bernard Harris took off in the Space Shuttle *Columbia.* He served as a mission specialist in Spacelab-D2, alongside Germans and Americans.

◆ MODERN CONTRIBUTIONS TO SCIENCE AND TECHNOLOGY

The achievements of African American inventors and scientists of the mid- to late twentieth century have been obscured by reasons more complex than blatant racial prejudice. The main reasons include the advent of government and corporate research and development teams. Such work, whether contracted or direct, often precludes individual recognition, regardless of a person's race. Nonetheless, in the corporate world as well as in academia, African American scientists and engineers play a substantial role in the development of solid state devices, high-powered and ultra-fast lasers, hypersonic flight—two to three thousand miles per hour—and elementary particle science. African American engineers employed by NASA in managerial and research positions have made and continue to make considerable contributions.

African American manufacturing and servicing firms in various computer and engineering areas have been established. For example, African American entrepreneur Marc Hannah has made a niche for himself in the field of computer graphics as cofounder of Silicon Graphics Incorporated. Chief scientist and vice president of the company, Hannah has adapted his electrical engineering and computer science know-how to a variety of applications including military flight simulators and CAT scan devices. In addition, his computer-generated, 3-D special effects have been featured in such major films as *Terminator 2* (1991), *Aladdin* (1992), and *Jurassic Park* (1993).

Academia has more African American science and technology faculty members, college presidents, and school of engineering deans than in the past. Many of these academics are serving in the country's most prestigious institutions. However, this progress has not continued, and there is cause for concern in the future. The seventies was a decade of tremendous growth for minorities in science and engineering. In the eighties, though, there was a progressive decline in the production of African American scientists, even though the numbers of Asian American and women scientists were still growing. In 1977, for example, people of color earned 13 percent of science and engineering doctorates, with Asian Americans at three percent of those. By 1993, 16 percent of the degrees went to people of color, and Asian Americans earned seven percent of those

degrees. In addition, women earned 40 percent of science and engineering doctorates in 1993, up from 25 percent in 1977. The numbers of African Americans entering scientific fields has slowly increased since the late 1980s, although they continue to be grossly underrepresented. Another area in which African Americans have been faltering is medicine.

In the mid to late 1990s, the number of African American applicants to medical school was declining at a high rate. The search for potential African American physicians has been nearing crisis-level status. The repercussions of this shortage includes difficulty for the poor and elderly in finding African American attendants if they so desire. Primary care specialists—internists, pediatricians, obstetricians, gynecologists, etc.—were particularly in demand.

The health care profession began responding to this problem in 1991, when the Association of American Medical Colleges initiated Project 3000 by 2000—the primary aim being to graduate 3,000 minorities by the year 2000. As of 1996, the program was well on its way to success. In particular, Xavier University was the top school in the country for African American placement into medical school, gaining a reputation for placing an average of seventy percent of its pre-med seniors into medical schools each year. Meanwhile, African American doctors already in practice were forming cooperatives amongst themselves in order to serve those African American patients who were discriminated against by Health Maintenance Organizations (HMOs) that considered them too poor or sick to be participants.

The situation is not as dire in engineering, perhaps due in part to a mentoring program established in 1975, by the National Action Council for Minorities in Engineering (NACME). With industry backing, the council has focused on youngsters as early as the fourth-grade level. More than 4,700 of their students have acquired engineering degrees and their graduates make up ten percent of all engineers from minority groups. However, there is some indication that fewer African Americans are entering engineering fields since 1980. As of 1996, about 29 percent of the college-age population was made up of African Americans, Latinos, and Native Americans. This same group, though, accounted for less than three percent of engineering doctoral recipients.

Still, the importance of role models with names and faces can not be overlooked. Some African American scientists have entered into the public consciousness; for example, in 1973, Shirley Ann Jackson became the first African American woman in the United States to earn a Ph.D. in theoretical particle physics as well as the first female African American to earn a Ph.D. from the prestigious Massachusetts Institute of Technology (MIT). She has had a distinguished career, culminating with her appointment as chair of the Nuclear Regulatory Commission by President Bill Clinton in 1995.

Another African American rose to the position of National Science Foundation (NSF) director, the highest science-related administrative post in the United States. Holder of a physics Ph.D. from St. Louis' Washington University, Walter Massey was able to create a number of programs to provide science-oriented training to young African Americans. During his two-year stint at the NSF, from 1991 to 1993, Massey repeated the kind of success he had when he began the Inner City Teachers Science program while teaching at Brown University.

In the field of medical research, Charles Whitten founded the National Association for Sickle Cell Disease in 1971. His work has been complemented more recently by Griffin Rodgers, chief of the Molecular Hematology Unit at the National Institutes of Health. In the 1990s, Rodgers was working on an experimental anti-cancer drug that could possibly provide benefits for sickle cell anemia patients.

Patients with prostate cancer have been encouraged by the work of Detroit-based urologist and oncologist Isaac Powell. In 1995, the Centers for Disease Control and Prevention named his screening program as the outstanding community health project of the year. Powell has been pursuing the idea of advanced diagnostic testing for African American men. Through a partnership with the Karmanos Cancer Institute and area churches, nurses, and hospitals, Powell has been able to educate the public about the importance of undergoing prostate cancer screening. Benefitting from a prostate-specific antigen test, patients have had their cancer caught early enough to undergo successful surgery. In 1996, Powell's program was being exported to other cities in the United States.

The cancer research of a young African American biologist, Jill Bargonetti, has garnered much attention. She discovered a correlation between a specific gene's ability to bind with the genetic matter known as DNA and its ability to suppress tumors. In 1996, she received a $300,000, three-year grant from the American Cancer Society and a $200,000, four-year award from the Department of Defense to pursue her study of breast cancer.

Outside of medical research, one-time Olympic athlete and engineering physicist Meredith Gourdine earned a Ph.D. from the California Institute of Technology in 1960. The Olympic medalist then formed Gourdine Systems, a research and development firm geared towards patenting inventions that use state-of-the-art power sources developed from advanced research in physics. Though blinded by diabetes in 1973, Gourdine went on to launch

Energy Innovations the next year. An inventor at heart, he has more than seventy patents in his name and was inducted into the Black Inventors Hall of Fame.

The energy of earthquakes motivates geophysicist Waverly Person. His interest in seismology paid off when he was named director of the U.S. Geological Survey's National Earthquake Information Center in 1977. The first African American earthquake scientist, Person is also the first African American in more than thirty years to hold such a prominent position in the U.S. Department of the Interior.

Similarly, meteorologist Warren Washington has been concerned with the earth's climate. Since 1987, the greenhouse effect expert has been director of the Climate and Global Dynamics Division of the National Center for Atmospheric Research. After seven years there, he was elected to a one-year term as the first African American president of the American Meteorological Society. Afterwards, Washington co-founded the Black Environmental Science Trust, introducing African American children to science.

Along with hundreds of other notable African Americans, scientists have been working towards restoring scientific education at all levels. Their presence, whether inside or outside of the public eye, is felt. Younger African Americans who learn of their endeavors are thus encouraged to free their creative science minds.

Rainbow/PUSH Coalition Seeks Greater Minority Representation in Silicon Valley

Having addressed the lack of employment opportunities for African Americans on Wall Street, the Reverend Jesse Jackson used the same policy during 1999 towards the Silicon Valley—a segment of the economy where whites hold more than ninety percent of the chief executive officer jobs and board seats at the top 150 public corporations. Seeking greater African American representation in this prominent high-tech region of California, Jackson's Rainbow/PUSH Coalition purchased approximately $100,000 worth of stock in fifty of the largest high-tech corporation and announced future plans of opening a staffed office in San Jose, assembling an advisory board of influential Silicon Valley executives to suggest methods of increasing African American and Hispanic American participation in the region's workforce, and hosting a conference that will address methods to effectively educate minorities for high-tech careers.

While acknowledging that nearly 31 percent of the high-tech industry's engineers and professionals are Asian American and that Silicon Valley is a major employer of immigrants, Jackson is exerting pressure on corporations to reach beyond their usual networks to work with minority-owned businesses in order to widen their pool of money and talent. With the support of a number of African American chief executive officers—Frank S. Greene of New Vista Capital, Robert E. Knowling of Covad Communications, Roy Clay of Rod-L Electronics; and Kenneth L. Coleman of Silicon Graphics Inc.—Jackson hopes to end the so-called "color-blind" hiring practices that high-tech corporate executives claim to apply which, in Jackson's opinion, prevents them from recognizing minority markets. (According to *Target Market News*, African Americans annually spend $3.8 billion on computer and consumer electronic gear.)

◆ POPULAR AFRICAN AMERICAN INTERNET SITES

An increasing number of African Americans—5.6 million, according to a 1999 Nielsen-CommerceNet study—are using the Internet at home, work, school, and at libraries. This represents an increase of more than fifty percent from just one year ago. Comparatively though, the 24 percent of blacks using the Internet is far below the estimated 36 percent for whites. In addition, a recent survey of college freshmen revealed a great disparity in Internet usage among students enrolled at prestigious private colleges—80 percent of whom stated that they use computers regularly—and those attending traditionally African American public institutions—41 percent of whom stated the same.

Although this digital divide between blacks and whites remains wide, studies show that it is narrowing for the first time since Internet use significantly rose in the early 1990s. Among the reasons suggested are the falling prices of personal computers, rising spending power, a growing belief among parents that computers are crucial to their children's future, and an increasing number of African American web sites.

Some of the most popular African American web sites offering valuable information on the various subjects covered in this reference work are listed below, along with their Internet addresses.

Chronology

The African-American Mosaic: A Library of Congress Resource Guide for the Study of Black History and Culture
lcweb.loc.gov/exhibits/african/intro.html

Black Facts Online!
www.blackfacts.com

Charles H. Wright Museum of African American History
www.maah-detroit.org

Florida Black Heritage Trail
www.flheritage.com/magazine/bht

African American Firsts

Black History: Virginia Profiles
www.gatewayva.com/pages/bhistory/profiles.shtml

The Internet African American History Challenge
www.brightmoments.com/blackhistory

The MUNIRAH Chronicle of Black Historical Events and Facts
maelstrom.stjohns.edu/archives/Munirah.html

Significant Documents in African American History

Featured Document: The Emancipation Proclamation
www.nara.gov/exhall/featured-document/eman/emanproc.html

FindLaw: Brown v. Board of Education
caselaw.findlaw.com/scripts/getcase.pl?court=US&navby=case&vol=347&invol=483

Freedmen's Bureau Records
www.freedmensbureau.com

African American Landmarks

National Park Service African-American Civil War Sites
www.itd.nps.gov/cwss/aa-sites.html

The National Underground Railroad Freedom Center
www.undergroundrailroad.org

Our Sacred History: Celebrating African American History & Culture
www.cr.nps.gov/aahistory

African and the Black Diaspora

Africa Online
www.africaonline.com

Africa Online's African Women Page
www.africaonline.com/AfricaOnline/coverwomen.html

More African American parents are realizing the benefits of acquiring personal computers for their children (Index Stock Imagery).

AfricaNews Online
www.africanews.org

PanAfrican News Agency
www.africanews.org/PANA/index.html

The Universal Black Pages
www.ubp.com

World African Network Online
www.worldafricannet.com

Africans in America: 1600–1900

Africans in America
www.pbs.org/wgbh/aia/home.html

American Slave Narratives: An Online Anthology
xroads.virginia.edu/~HYPER/wpa/wpahome.html

NYPL Digital Schomburg Images of 19th Century African Americans
digital.nypl.org/schomburg/images_aa19

Civil Rights

African American Odyssey
memory.loc.gov/ammem/aaohtml/exhibit/aointro.html

National Civil Rights Museum
www.midsouth.rr.com/civilrights

Black Nationalism

Encyclopaedia Africana: A Dictionary of African Biography
www.ulbobo.com/eap/index.html

Nation of Islam Online
www.nationofislam.org

National Organizations

Dr. Huey P. Newton Foundation/The Black Panther Party
www.blackpanther.org

NAACP Online
www.naacp.org

National Society of Black Engineers
www.nsbe.org

National Urban League
www.nul.org

Law

The Minority Business Enterprise Legal Defense and Education Fund
www.mbeldef.org

NARA Exhibit: American Originals, Part 2: Dred Scott Decision
www.nara.gov/exhall/originals/scott.html

The National Bar Association
www.nationalbar.org

Politics

Blacks in Government
bigserve.mettersmedia.net

Congressional Black Caucus Foundation Online
www.cbcfonline.org

Minority On-Line Information Service (MOLIS)
web.fie.com/molis

Population

African-American Population as a Percentage of Total Population
www.lmic.state.mn.us/dnet/maplib/demogs/race/us/pages/africanu.htm

U.S. Census Bureau: The Black Population in the U.S.
www.census.gov/population/www/socdemo/race/black.html

Employment and Income

Coalition of Black Investors
www.cobinvest.com

North Carolina Institute of Minority Economic Development, Inc.
www.ncimed.com

The State of Black Male America: 1998
www.ritesofpassage.org/genstb98.htm

Entrepreneurship

blackenterprise.com: The Virtual Desktop for African Americans
www.blackenterprise.com

The Network Journal: **Black Professional and Small Business News**
www.tnj.com

The Family

African American Web Connection
www.aawc.com

African Wedding Guide
www.melanet.com/awg/start.html

Black Family Network
www.blackfamilynet.net

BlackFamilies.com: Keeping Our Families Whole
www.blackfamilies.com

The BlackStripe
www.blackstripe.com

Kwanzaa Information Center
www.melanet.com/kwanzaa/

BLK **Homie Pages**
www.blk.com

SistahNet
demeter.hampshire.edu/~sistah

Education

The Amistad Research Center
www.tulane.edu/~amistad

The Carter G. Woodson Institute for Afro-American and African Studies
minerva.acc.virginia.edu/~woodson

Morehouse College
www.morehouse.edu

Religion

Black Catholic Information Mall
www.bcimall.org

National Baptist Convention, U.S.A.
www.nbcusa.org

Literature

African American Literature Book Club
aalbc.com

Black Women in Publishing
www.bwip.org

The Harlem Renaissance
harlem.eb.com

Voices from the Gaps: Women Writers of Color
voices.cla.umn.edu

Media

Black Voices
www.blackvoices.com

The Black World Today
www.tbwt.com

MSBET
www.msbet.com

NetNoir Online: The Black Network
www.netnoir.com

The World of *Essence* Online
www.essence.com

Film and Television

Black Film Center/Archive Home Page
www.indiana.edu/~bfca

CyberSoul City
www.hbo.com/soul

UniWorld Films Online
www.uniworldfilms.com

Drama, Comedy, and Dance

It's Showtime at the Apollo!
www.apolloshowtime.com

Jomandi Productions, Inc.
www.jomandi.com

Soul in Motion Players, Inc.
www.us.net/simpinc

Classical Music

African American Art Song Alliance
www.uni.edu/taylord/alliance.html

Afrocentric Voices in "Classical" Music
mailer.fsu.edu/~rljones/afrovoice

**Still Going On: An Exhibit Celebrating the Life
and Times of William Grant Still**
scriptorium.lib.duke.edu/sgo/start.html

Sacred Music Traditions

Black Gospel Music
members.tripod.com/~JCBlom/index.html

The Black Gospel Music Clef
www.blackgospel.com

GospelForce.com
www.gospelforce.com

Blues and Jazz

The Blue Highway
www.thebluehighway.com

Blue Note Records
www.bluenote.com/

The Blues Foundation
www.blues.org

Jazz Central Station.com
www1.jazzcentralstation.com

Popular Music

EURWEB: The Urban Cyberstation
www.eurweb.com

Malaco Music Group
www.malaco.com/

**Peeps Republic-The Source for Hip-Hop
Culture News**
www.peeps.com

The R&B Page
www.rbpage.com

***Vibe* Online**
www.vibe.com

The Visual and Applied Arts

ArtNoir Showcase
www.artnoir.com

California African-American Museum
www.caam.ca.gov

Genesis Art Line: Where Art & Technology are Picture Perfect
www.genesisartline.com

Living Under Enslavement: African Americans on Hermitage Plantation
www.hfmgv.org/smartfun/hermitage/open.html

The Museum of African Slavery
jhunix.hcf.jhu.edu/~plarson/smuseum/welcome.htm

National Museum of African Art
www.si.edu/nmafa

Science and Technology

The African World Community Network
www.tawcnet.com

The Conduit: The Definitive Technological Guide for the African in America
www.theconduit.com

EverythingBlack.com
www.everythingblack.com

The Faces of Science: African Americans in the Sciences
www.lib.lsu.edu/lib/chem/display/faces.html

Sports

BlackBaseball's Negro Baseball Leagues
www.blackbaseball.com

Harlem Globetrotters
www.harlemglobetrotters.com

National Association of Black Scuba Divers
www.nabsdivers.org

National Brotherhood of Skiers
www.nbs.org

Negro League Baseball Online
www.negroleaguebaseball.com/

Urban Sports Network
www.urbansportsnetwork.com

Military

African-American Civil War Memorial Freedom Foundation
www.afroamcivilwarmemorial.org

366th Infantry Homepage
www.wiz-worx.com/366th

◆ ENGINEERS, MATHEMATICIANS, INVENTORS, PHYSICIANS, AND SCIENTISTS

(To locate biographical profiles more readily, please consult the index at the back of the book.)

George E. Alcorn (1940–)
Physicist

George Edward Alcorn was born on March 22, 1940. He graduated with a B.A. in physics in 1962 and a M.A. in nuclear physics from Howard University in 1963. In 1967 he earned his Ph.D. from Howard University in atomic and molecular physics. After earning his Ph.D., Alcorn spent twelve years working in industry.

Alcorn left IBM, where he had worked as a Second Plateau Inventor, to join NASA in 1978. While at NASA, Alcorn invented an imaging x-ray spectrometer using thermomigration of aluminum, for which he earned a patent in 1984, and two years later devised an improved method of fabrication using laser drilling. His work on imaging x-ray spectrometers earned him the 1984 NASA/Goddard Space Flight Center (GSFC) Inventor of the Year Award. During this period he also served as deputy project manager for advanced development and was responsible for developing new technologies required for the space station *Freedom*. He also managed the GSFC Evolution Program, concerned with ensuring that over its thirty-year mission the space station develops properly while incorporating new capabilities. Since 1992, Alcorn has served as chief of Goddard's Office of Commercial Programs, supervising programs for technology transfer, small business innovation research, and the commercial use of space programs. He managed a shuttle flight experiment that involved Robot Operated Material Processing System, or ROMPS, in 1994.

Alcorn holds over 25 patents. He is a recognized pioneer in the fabrication of plasma semiconductor devices, and his patent "Process for Controlling the Slope of a Via Hole" was an important contribution to the process of plasma etching. This procedure is now used by many semiconductor manufacturing companies. Alcorn was one of the first scientists to present a computer-modeling solution of wet etched and plasma etched structure, and has received several cash prizes for his inventions of plasma-processing techniques.

Archie Alexander (1888–1958)
Civil Engineer

Born in 1888 in Ottumwa, Iowa, Archie Alphonso Alexander graduated from the University of Iowa with a B.S. in civil engineering in 1912. During his collegiate years he was a star football player who earned the nickname "Alexander the Great" on the playing field. His first job was as a design engineer for the Marsh Engineering Company that specialized in building bridges. Two years later, in 1914, Alexander formed his own company, A. A. Alexander, Inc. Most of the firm's contracts were for bridges and sewer systems. So successful was he that the NAACP awarded him its Spingarn Medal in 1928. The following year, he formed Alexander and Repass with a former classmate. Alexander's new company was also responsible for building tunnels, railroad trestles, viaducts, and power plants. Some of Alexander's biggest accomplishments include the Tidal Basin Bridge and K Street Freeway in Washington, DC; a heating plant for his alma mater, the University of Iowa; a civilian airfield in Tuskegee, Alabama; and a sewage disposal plant in Grand Rapids, Michigan.

A member of Kappa Alpha Psi, Alexander was awarded their "Laurel Wreath" for great accomplishment in 1925. Alexander received honorary civil engineering degrees from the University of Iowa in 1925 and Howard University in 1946. The following year, Alexander was named one of the University of Iowa's outstanding alumni and "one of the first hundred citizen of merit." Politically active, Alexander was appointed Governor of the Virgin Islands in 1954 by President Dwight Eisenhower, though he was forced to resign one year later due to health problems. He died at his home in Des Moines, Iowa in 1958.

Benjamin Banneker (1731–1806)
Mathematician/Statistician, Astronomer, Surveyor/Explorer, Publisher

Benjamin Banneker was born on November 9, 1731, on a tobacco farm near Baltimore, Maryland. His mother was a free woman and his father was her slave, whom she purchased and married. At the age of 21, Banneker became interested in watches and later constructed a grandfather clock based upon a pocket watch he had seen, calculating the ratio of the gears and wheels and carving them from wood. The clock operated for more than forty years.

Banneker's aptitude for mathematics and knowledge of astronomy enabled him to accurately predict the solar eclipse of 1789. By 1791, he began publishing an almanac which contained tide tables, weather information, data on future eclipses, and a listing of useful medicinal products and formulas. The almanac, which was the first scientific book published by an African American, appeared annually for more than a decade. Banneker sent a copy to Thomas Jefferson, and the two corresponded, debating the subject of slavery.

Banneker served as a surveyor on the six-person team that helped lay out the base lines and initial boundaries for Washington, DC. When the chairman of the committee, Major Pierre Charles L'Enfant, abruptly resigned and returned to France with his plans, Banneker was able to reproduce the plans from memory in their entirety. He died on October 25, 1806.

Andrew J. Beard (1849–1921)
Railroad Porter, Inventor

Inventor Andrew Jackson Beard was born a slave in Eastlake, Alabama. While working in an Alabama railroad yard, Beard had seen men lose hands, arms, legs, and even their lives in accidents occurring during the manual coupling of railroad cars. The system in use involved the dropping of a metal pin at exactly the right moment when two cars met. Men were often caught between cars and crushed to death during this split-second operation. Beard's invention, the "Jenny Coupler," was an automatic device which secured two cars by merely bumping them together. In 1897 Beard received $50,000 for an invention that has since prevented the death or maiming of countless railroad workers.

Guion S. Bluford, Jr. (1942–)
Space/Atmospheric Scientist, Aerospace Engineer, Air Force Officer, Airplane Pilot

Guy Bluford was born November 22, 1942, in Philadelphia. He graduated with a B.S. from Pennsylvania State University in 1964. He then enlisted in the U.S. Air Force and was assigned to pilot training at Williams Air Force Base in Arizona. Bluford served as a fighter pilot in Vietnam and flew 144 combat missions, 65 of them over North Vietnam. Attaining the rank of lieutenant colonel, Bluford received an M.S. from the Air Force Institute of Technology in 1974 and a Ph.D. in aerospace engineering in 1978.

In 1979, Bluford was accepted in NASA's astronaut program as a mission specialist. On August 30, 1983, with the liftoff of the *Challenger* shuttle Bluford became the first African American in space. He flew three other space shuttle missions, aboard *Challenger* in 1985 and aboard *Discovery* in 1991 and 1992, for a total of 688 hours in space. Bluford retired from NASA in 1993 to pursue a career in private industry.

Bluford has won numerous awards including the Distinguished National Science Award given by the National Society of Black Engineers (1979), NASA Group Achievement Award (1980, 1981), NASA Space Flight Medal (1983), and the NAACP Image Award in 1983.

Some of his military honors include the National Defense Service Medal (1965), Vietnam Campaign Medal (1967), Air Force Commendation Medal (1972), Air Force Meritorious Service Award (1978), the USAF Command Pilot Astronaut Wings (1983), and the NASA Distinguished Service Medal (1994).

Charles F. Bolden, Jr. (1946–)
Airplane Pilot, Space/Atmospheric Scientist, Marine Officer, Operations and Systems Researcher/Analyst

Born in Columbia, South Carolina and a graduate of the U.S. Naval Academy and the University of Southern California, Charles Bolden, Jr., has a B.S. in electrical science and a M.S. in systems management. Bolden began his career as a second lieutenant in the U.S. Marine Corps, becoming a naval aviator by 1970. In 1973, he flew more than one hundred sorties while assigned in Thailand. Upon return to the United States, Bolden began a tour as a Marine Corps selection and recruiting officer. In 1979, he graduated from the U.S. Naval Test Pilot School and was assigned to the Naval Test Aircraft Directorates.

Bolden was selected as an astronaut candidate by NASA in May of 1980, and, in July of 1981, completed the training and evaluation program—making him eligible for assignment as a pilot on space shuttle flight crews. A veteran of four shuttle missions, Bolden has served as pilot for the Hubble Space Telescope deployment mission and was commander of the first joint American-Russian space shuttle mission. In 1994, he accepted a position at the Naval Academy. Bolden has been awarded the Defense Superior Service Medal, the Defense Meritorious Service Medal, the Air Medal, the Legion of Merit, and the Strike/Flight Medal. His current rank is major general.

Marjorie L. Browne (1914–1979)
Mathematician/Statistician, Educator

Browne was born September 9, 1914, in Memphis, Tennessee. She received a B.S. in mathematics from Howard University in 1935, an M.S. from the University of Michigan in 1939, and a Ph.D. in mathematics, again from the University of Michigan, in 1949. Browne was one of the first two African American women to earn a Ph.D. in mathematics. She taught at the University of Michigan in 1947 and 1948. She accepted the post of professor of mathematics at North Carolina Central University in 1949 and became department chairperson in 1951. In 1960, she received a grant from IBM to establish one of the first computer centers at a minority university.

Browne's doctoral dissertation dealt with topological and matrix groups, and she was published in the *American Mathematical Monthly*. She was a fellow of the

Major Charles Bolden (AP/Wide World Photos, Inc.)

National Science Foundation in 1958–1959 and again in 1965–1966. Browne was a member of the American Mathematical Society, the Mathematical Association of America, and the Society for Industrial and Applied Mathematics. She died in 1979.

George E. Carruthers (1939–)
Astrophysicist

Dr. George Carruthers is one of the two naval research laboratory people responsible for the *Apollo 16* lunar surface ultraviolet camera/spectrograph, which was placed on the lunar surface in April 1972. It was Carruthers who designed the instrument while William Conway adapted the camera for the lunar mission. The spectrographs, obtained from 11 targets, include the first photographs of the ultraviolet equatorial bands of atomic oxygen that girdle the earth. The camera was also used on *Skylab* in 1974.

Carruthers, who was born in Cincinnati, Ohio in 1939, grew up on Chicago's South Side. He built his first telescope at the age of ten. He received his Ph.D. in aeronautical/astronautical engineering from the University of Illinois in 1964, the same year that he started employment with the Navy. Carruthers is the recipient of the NASA Exceptional Scientific Achievement medal for his work on the ultraviolet camera/spectrograph. He also won the Arthur S. Fleming Award in 1971.

Ben Carson (1951–)
Neurosurgeon

Born Benjamin Solomon Carson on September 18, 1951, in Detroit, Michigan, Dr. Carson has been recognized throughout the medical community for his prowess in performing complex neurosurgical procedures, particularly on children with pediatric brain tumors his main focus. Among his accomplishments are a number of successful hemispherectomies, a process in which a portion of the brain of a critically ill seizure victim or other neurologically diseased patient is removed to radically reduce the incidence of seizures. Carson's most famous operation took place in 1987, earning him international acclaim. That year he successfully separated a pair of West German Siamese or conjoined twins, who had been attached at the backs of their heads. The landmark operation took 22 hours; Carson led a surgical team of seventy doctors, nurses, and technicians.

Carson was raised in Detroit. A problem student—he almost killed a peer during a knife fight when he was 14 years old—and a failing student, his mother imposed a reading program on him and limited his television viewing until his grades improved. In high school, he continued to excel and was accepted at Yale University in 1969 with a scholarship. With a B.A. from that Ivy League institution, Carson entered the University of Michigan, where he obtained his M.D. in 1977. For one year he served as a surgical intern at the Johns Hopkins Hospital, later doing his residency there. From 1983 to 1984, Carson practiced at the Sir Charles Gairdner Hospital in Perth, Australia. In 1984, at 33 years of age, he became the youngest chief of pediatric neurosurgery in the United States. Then, in 1985, Johns Hopkins named him director of pediatric neurosurgery. In the mid-1990s, he was an associate professor neurosurgery, plastic sur-

Ben Carson examines a model of the human brain (AP/Wide World Photos, Inc.).

gery, and oncology at the Johns Hopkins School of Medicine, in addition to his duties at the hospital. In 1996, Carson, whose autobiography was called *Gifted Hands*, was in the midst of establishing a scholarship fund, USA Scholars Program, with the aid of his wife.

George Washington Carver (1861?–1943)
Educator, Agricultural/Food Scientist, Farmer

George Washington Carver devoted his life to research projects connected primarily with Southern agriculture. The products he derived from the peanut and the soybean revolutionized the economy of the South by liberating it from an excessive dependence on cotton.

Born a slave in 1865 in Diamond Grove, Missouri, Carver was only an infant when his mother was abducted from her owner's plantation by a band of slave raiders. His mother was sold and shipped away, and Carver was raised by his mother's owners, Moses and Susan Carver. Carver was a frail and sickly child, and he was assigned lighter chores around the house. Later he was allowed to attend high school in a neighboring town.

Carver worked odd jobs while he pursued his education. He was the first African American student admitted at Simpson College, Indianola, Iowa. He then attended Iowa Agricultural College (now Iowa State University) where, while working as the school janitor, he received a degree in agricultural science in 1894. Two years later he received a master's degree from the same school and became the first African American to serve on its faculty. Within a short time his fame spread, and Booker T. Washington offered him a post at Tuskegee Institute. It was at the Institute's Agricultural Experimental Station that Carver did most of his work.

Carver revolutionized the southern agricultural economy by showing that three hundred products could be derived from the peanut. By 1938, peanuts had become a $200 million industry and a chief product of Alabama. Carver also demonstrated that one hundred different products could be derived from the sweet potato.

Although he did hold three patents, Carver never patented most of the many discoveries he made while at Tuskegee, saying "God gave them to me, how can I sell them to someone else?" In 1940 he established the George Washington Carver Foundation and willed the rest of his estate to the organization, so his work might be carried on after his death. He died on January 5, 1943.

Jewel Plummer Cobb (1924–)
Cell Biologist

Born in 1924, Cobb grew up exposed to a variety of African American professionals through her parents. By 1950, she had completed her M.S. and Ph.D. in biology. As a cell biologist, her focus was the action and interaction of living cells. She was particularly interested in tissue culture, in which cells are grown outside of the body and studied under microscopes. Among her most important work was her study with Dorothy Walker Jones of how new cancer-fighting drugs affected human cancer cells. Cobb also conducted research into skin pigment. She was particularly interested in melanoma, or skin cancer, and melanin's ability to protect skin from damage caused by ultraviolet light.

Cobb noted the scarcity of women in scientific fields, and she wrote about the difficulties women face in a 1979 paper "Filters for Women in Science." In this piece, Cobb argued that various pressures, particularly in the educational system, act as filters that prevent many women from choosing science careers. The socialization of girls has tended to discourage them from pursuing math and the sciences from a very early age, and even those women who got past such obstacles have struggled to get university tenure and the same jobs (at equal pay) as men.

Cobb has been president emeritus of California State University in Fullerton since 1990. She has been active in her community, recruiting women and minorities to

the sciences and founding a privately funded gerontology center.

W. Montague Cobb (1904– 1990)
Anthropologist, Organization Executive/Founder, Medical Researcher, Educator, Editor

William Montague Cobb was born on October 12, 1904, in Washington, DC. For over forty years he was a member of the Howard University Medical School faculty and thousands of medical and dental students studied under his direction. At Howard, he built a collection of more than six hundred documented skeletons and a comparative anatomy museum in the gross anatomy laboratory. In addition to a B.A. from Amherst College, an M.D. from Howard University, and a Ph.D. from Case Western Reserve, he received many honorary degrees. Cobb died on November 20, 1990, in Washington, DC.

As editor of the *Journal of the National Medical Association* for 28 years, Cobb developed a wide range of scholarly interests manifested by the nearly seven hundred published works under his name in the fields of medical education, anatomy, physical anthropology, public health and medical history. He was the first African American elected to the presidency of the American Association of Physical Anthropologists and served as the chairman of the anthropology section of the American Association for the Advancement of Science. Among his many scientific awards is the highest award given by the American Association of Anatomists. For 31 years he was a member of the board of directors of the NAACP and served as the president of the board from 1976 to 1982.

Price M. Cobbs (1928–)
Psychiatrist, Author, Management Consultant

Cobbs was born in Los Angeles, California, in 1928, and followed in his father's path when he enrolled in medical school after earning a B.A. from the University of California at Berkeley. He graduated from Meharry Medical College in 1958 And, within a few years, had established his own San Francisco practice in psychiatry.

With his academic colleague at the University of California, William H. Grier, Cobbs authored the groundbreaking 1968 study *Black Rage*. In it, the authors argued that a pervasive social and economic racism had resulted in an endemic anger that stretched across all strata of African American society, from rich to poor; this anger was both apparent and magnified by the social unrest of the 1960s. Cobbs and Grier also coauthored a second book *The Jesus Bag* (1971) that discussed the role of organized religion in the African American community.

A seminar Cobbs held in 1967 with other mental health care professionals eventually led him to found his own diversity training company, Pacific Management Systems. Since its inception, the company has been instrumental in providing sensitivity training for Fortune 500 companies, community groups, law enforcement bodies, and social service agencies. A member of numerous African American professional and community organizations as well as an assistant clinical professor at the University of California at San Francisco, Cobbs continues to guide PMS well into its third decade. The firm has pioneered the concept of ethnotherapy, which uses the principles of group therapy to help seminar participants rethink their attitudes toward members of other ethnic groups, the disabled, and those of alternative sexual orientations.

Elbert F. Cox (1895–1969)
Educator, Mathematician/Statistician

Cox was born in Evansville, Indiana on December 5, 1895. He received his B.A. from Indiana University in 1917 and his Ph.D. from Cornell University in 1925. His dissertation dealt with polynomial solutions and made Cox the first African American to be awarded a Ph.D. in pure mathematics. Cox was an instructor at Shaw University (1921–1923), a professor in physics and mathematics at West Virginia State College (1925–1929), and an associate professor of mathematics at Howard University from 1929 to 1947. In 1947, he was made full professor and retired in 1966.

During his career, Cox specialized in interpolation theory and differential equations. Cox was a Brooks fellow (1924, 1925) and an Erastus Brooks fellow. He belonged to the Mathematical Society and the Physical Society. Cox died in 1969.

Ulysses G. Dailey (1885–1961)
Editor, Health Administrator, Surgeon, Diplomat

From 1908 to 1912, Ulysses Grant Dailey served as surgical assistant to Dr. Daniel Hale Williams, founder of Provident Hospital and noted heart surgeon. Born in Donaldsonville, Louisiana, in 1885, Dailey graduated in 1906 from Northwestern University Medical School, where he was appointed a demonstrator in anatomy. He later studied in London, Paris, and Vienna, and in 1926 set up his own hospital and sanitarium in Chicago. Dailey was associated with Provident Hospital after his own hospital closed in 1932, and he retained a position there until his death.

A member of the editorial board of the *Journal of the National Medical Association* for many years, Dailey traveled around the world in 1933 under the sponsorship of the International College of Surgeons, of which he was a founder fellow. In 1951, and 1953, the U.S. State Department sent him to Pakistan, India, Ceylon, and Africa. One year later he was named honorary consul to Haiti, moving there in 1956 when he retired.

Charles R. Drew (1904–1950)
Educator, Medical Researcher, Health Administrator, Surgeon/Physician

Using techniques already developed for separating and preserving blood, Charles Drew pioneered further into the field of blood preservation and organized procedures from research to a clinical level, leading to the founding of the world's two largest blood banks just prior to World War II. Born on June 3, 1904 in Washington, DC, Drew graduated from Amherst College in Massachusetts, where he received the Messman Trophy for having brought the most honor to the school during his four years there. He was not only an outstanding scholar but the captain of the track team and a star halfback on the football team.

After receiving his medical degree from McGill University in 1933, Drew returned to Washington, DC, to teach pathology at Howard. In 1940, while taking his D.Sc. degree at Columbia University, he wrote a dissertation on "banked blood" and soon became such an expert in this field that the British government called upon him to set up the first blood bank in England. He also initiated the use of "bloodmobiles," trucks equipped with refrigerators to transport blood and plasma to remote locations.

During World War II, Drew was appointed director of the American Red Cross blood donor project. Later, he served as chief surgeon at Freedmen's Hospital in Washington, DC, as well as professor of surgery at Howard University Medical School from 1941–1950. A recipient of the 1944 Springarn Medal, Drew was killed in an automobile crash on April 1, 1950.

Joycelyn Elders (1933–)
Physician, Endocrinologist, Former U.S. Surgeon General

Dr. Joycelyn Elders was born Minnie Joycelyn Jones, on August 13, 1933, in Schaal, Arkansas. The first of eight children, she grew up working in cotton fields. An avid reader, Jones earned a scholarship to Philander Smith College in Little Rock. Jones studied biology and chemistry in hopes of becoming a lab technician. She was inspired towards greater ambitions after meeting Edith Irby Jones (no relation), the first African American woman to study at the University of Arkansas School of Medicine. After obtaining her B.A., Jones served as a physical therapist in the U.S. Army in order to fund her post-graduate education. She was able to enroll in the University of Arkansas School of Medicine herself in 1956. However, as the only African American woman and one of only three African American students, she and the other two African Americans were forced to use a separate university dining facility—the one provided for the cleaning staff.

Having married Oliver B. Elders in 1960, the newly dubbed Joycelyn Elders fulfilled a pediatric internship at the University of Minnesota, then returned to Little Rock in 1961 for a residency at the University of Arkansas Medical Center. Her success in the position led her to be appointed chief pediatric resident, in charge of the all-white, all-male battery of residents and interns. During the next twenty years, Elders forged a successful clinical practice, specializing in pediatric endocrinology, the study of glands. She published more than 100 papers in that period and rose to professor of pediatrics, a position she maintained from 1976 until 1987, when she was named director of the Arkansas Department of Health.

Over the course of her career, Elders's focus shifted somewhat from diabetes in children to sexual behavior. At the Department of Health, Elders was able to pursue her public advocacy in regards to teenage pregnancy and sexually transmitted diseases. In 1993, U.S. president Bill Clinton nominated Elders for the U.S. surgeon general post, making her the second African American and the fifth woman to hold the cabinet position. Though her confirmation was not unchallenged—many decried her liberal stance—she was formally voted into approval for the position by the Senate on September 7, 1993.

During her tenure, Elders attacked Medicaid for failing to help poverty-stricken women prevent unwanted pregnancies and faulted pharmaceutical companies for overpricing contraceptives. Between 1993 and December of 1994, she spoke out in support of the medicinal use of marijuana, in favor of studying drug legalization, family planning, and against toy guns for children. The biggest flak occurred when Elders was reported to have recommended that masturbation be discussed in schools as part of human sexuality. She was forced to resignation by Clinton in December of 1994.

Elders returned to the University of Arkansas Medical School, though the state's General Assembly budget committee tried to block her return and resumed teaching. In 1995, she was hosting a daily talk show on AM stations KYSG in Little Rock and WERE in Cleveland. That same year, she joined the board of the American Civil Liberties Union. In 1996, her autobiography was published.

Solomon C. Fuller (1872–1953)
Neurologist, Psychiatrist

Born on August 11, 1872, in Monrovia, Liberia, Fuller was the son of Solomon Fuller, a coffee planter and government official whose father had been a slave in Virginia. In 1889, he sailed to the United States and earned his M.D. from Boston University School of Medicine in 1897.

By 1900, he had started his own study of mental patients and, four years later, traveled to Germany to study with Emil Kraepelin and Alois Alzheimer, the discoverer of the disease that bears his name. During his stay in Germany, Fuller had an opportunity to spend an afternoon with Paul Ehrlich, who in 1908 would win the Nobel Prize for his research in immunology.

Fuller's most significant contribution was in the study of Alzheimer's disease. By the latter part of the twentieth century, scientists still had not reached full agreement as to its cause. At the time of Fuller's work, the prevailing belief was that arteriosclerosis, or hardening of the arteries, caused Alzheimer's. Fuller disagreed and put forth this opinion in the course of diagnosing the ninth documented case of Alzheimer's. Proof of his ideas came in 1953, the year he died, when other medical researchers would confirm the lack of any linkage between arteriosclerosis and Alzheimer's.

Helene D. Gayle (1955–)
Epidemiologist, AIDS Researcher

Helene Gayle was born in 1955 in Buffalo, New York, the third of five children of an entrepreneur father and social worker mother. After graduating from Barnard College in 1976, she then won acceptance to the University of Pennsylvania's medical school.

Having once heard a speech on the cure of smallpox had inspired Gayle to pursue public health medicine, and her direction would prove a significant one in the years to come as the plague of AIDS came to decimate communities across the globe. She received her M.D. from University of Pennsylvania as well as a master's degree in public health from Johns Hopkins, both in 1981. After a residency in pediatrics, she was selected to enter the epidemiology training program in 1984 at the Centers for Disease Control in Atlanta, Georgia, the nation's top research center for infectious diseases.

For much of the 1980s Gayle was intensely involved in the CDC's research into AIDS and HIV infection through her work first in the center's Epidemic Intelligence Service and later as a chief of international AIDS research, a capacity in which she oversaw the scientific investigations of over three hundred CDC researchers. Gayle has been instrumental in raising public awareness about the disease and is especially driven to point out how devastating AIDS has been to the African American community. Sex education, better health care for the poor, and substance abuse prevention are some of the proposals Gayle has championed that she believes will help reduce deaths from AIDS.

In 1992 Gayle was hired as a medical epidemiologist and researcher for the AIDS division of the U.S. Agency for International Development, cementing her reputation as one of the international community's top AIDS scientists. She is currently the director of the Centers for Disease Control.

Evelyn Boyd Granville (1924–)
Author, Educator, Lecturer

Born in 1924, Granville attended Smith College from 1941 to 1946 and earned an A.B. and a M.A. in mathematics. She received a Ph.D. from Yale University in 1949, making her one of the first two African American women to be awarded a Ph.D. in pure mathematics. Granville's first teaching position was as an instructor at New York University (1949–1950). She moved to Fisk University where she was an assistant professor (1950–1952), and then to the University of Southern California as a lecturer (1961–1973). Since then she has been an associate professor at California State University. Granville is the author of *Theory of Applications of Math for Teachers*.

Frederick D. Gregory (1941–)
Airplane Pilot, Astronaut

Gregory was born January 7, 1941 in Washington, DC. He is the nephew of the late Dr. Charles Drew, noted African-American blood plasma specialist. Under the sponsorship of United States Representative Adam Clayton Powell, Gregory attended the U.S. Air Force Academy and graduated with a B.S. in 1964. In 1977, he received an M.S.A. from George Washington University.

Gregory was a helicopter and fighter pilot for the USAF from 1965 to 1970 and a research and test pilot for the USAF and National Aeronautics and Space Administration (NASA) in 1971. In 1978 he was accepted into NASA's astronaut program, making him the second African American astronaut in NASA's history. In 1985 he went into space aboard the *Challenger* Space Shuttle as a pilot, a first for an African American. Currently, Gregory is with NASA's Office of Safety and Mission Assurance at the Johnson Space Center in Houston, Texas, and he is a colonel in the USAF.

Gregory belongs to the Society of Experimental Test Pilots, the Tuskegee Airmen, the American Helicopter Society, and the National Technical Association. He has won numerous medals and awards including the Meritorious Service Medal, the Air Force Commendation Medal, and two NASA Space Flight Medals. He has twice received the Distinguished Flying Cross and is also the recipient of George Washington University's Distin-

guished Alumni Award, NASA's Outstanding Leadership Award, and the National Society of Black Engineers' Distinguished National Scientist Award.

Lloyd A. Hall (1894–1971)
Research Director, Chemist

Grandson of the first pastor of Quinn Chapel A.M.E. Church, the first African American church in Chicago, Lloyd Augustus Hall was born in Elgin, Illinois, on June 20, 1894. A top student and athlete at East High School in Aurora, Illinois, he graduated in the top ten of his class and was offered scholarships to four different colleges in Illinois. In 1916, Hall graduated from Northwestern University with a B.S. in chemistry. He continued his studies at the University of Chicago and the University of Illinois.

Hall served during World War I as a lieutenant inspecting explosives at a Wisconsin plant. After the war, Hall joined the Chicago Department of Health Laboratories, where he quickly rose to senior chemist. In 1921, he took employment at Boyer Chemical Laboratory before becoming president and chemical director of the Chemical Products Corporation the following year. In 1924, he was offered a position with Griffith Laboratories. Within one year he was chief chemist and director of research.

There Hall discovered curing salts for the preserving and processing of meats, thus revolutionizing the meatpacking industry. He also discovered how to sterilize spices and researched the effects of antioxidants on fats. Along the way, he registered more than one hundred patents for processes used in the manufacturing and packing of food, especially meat and bakery products.

In 1954, Hall became chairman of the Chicago chapter of the American Institute of Chemists. The following year, he was elected a member of the national board of directors, becoming the first African American man to hold that position in the institute's 32-year history. Upon his retirement from Griffith in 1959, Hall continued to serve as a consultant to various state and federal organizations. In 1961, he spent six months in Indonesia, advising the Food and Agricultural Organization of the United Nations. From 1962 to 1964, he was a member of the American Food for Peace Council, an appointment made by President John F. Kennedy.

Marc R. Hannah (1956–)
Computer Scientist

Hannah, a native Chicagoan, was born on October 13, 1956. In high school, he took a computer science course that kindled his interest in this relatively new field. Inspired, too, by the example of an older brother, he earned high grades that would qualify him for a Bell Laboratories-sponsored scholarship to engineering school. He would eventually earn a Ph.D. from Stanford University in 1985.

While at Stanford, he met James Clark, an engineering professor who was a pioneer in computer graphics, having invented a special computer chip that was the heart of an imaging process. Hannah redesigned the chip to operate five times faster, an advance that impressed Clark enough to invite Hannah to join him in founding a computer graphics company. The deal was soon struck, and in 1981 Silicon Graphics was born.

Silicon Graphics' technology has been used to enhance many devices, such as military flight simulators and medical CAT scans. Among the most lucrative areas for this technology, and certainly the one best-known, is that of video and film animation. The special effects made possible by three-dimensional imaging in films, such as *Star Wars*, *Terminator II*, and *Jurassic Park*, that have thrilled millions. Hannah is now vice president and chief scientist of the company's Entry Systems Division.

Matthew A. Henson (1866–1955)
Seaman, Explorer/Surveyor, Author

Matthew Henson was born August 6, 1866, in Charles County, Maryland near Washington, DC. He attended school in Washington, DC, for six years but at the age of thirteen signed on as a cabin boy on a ship headed for China. Henson worked his way up to seaman while he sailed over many of the world's oceans. After several odd jobs in different cities, Henson met U.S. Navy surveyor Robert Edward Peary in Washington, DC. Peary, who was planning a trip to Nicaragua, hired Henson on the spot as his valet. Henson was not pleased at being a personal servant but nonetheless felt his new position held future opportunities.

Peary eventually made seven trips to the Arctic starting in 1893. He became convinced that he could become the first man to stand at the North Pole. Henson accompanied Peary on these trips to Greenland and became an integral part of Peary's plans. The pair made four trips looking for a passageway to the North Pole. In 1909, Peary and Henson made their final attempt at reaching the Pole. Although Peary was undoubtedly the driving force of these expeditions, he was increasingly reliant on Henson. Henson's greatest asset was his knowledge of the Inuit language and his ability to readily adapt to their culture. He was also an excellent dog driver and possessed a physical stamina that Peary lacked due to leukemia. Henson felt that he was serving the African American race by his example of loyalty, fortitude, and trustworthiness.

By the end of March of 1909, they were within 150 miles of their goal. Henson, because of his strength,

Matthew Henson (The Library of Congress)

would break trail and set up camp for the night, while Peary followed. On April 6th, Henson thought he had reached the Pole. When Peary arrived later he asserted that they had indeed reached the North Pole. Henson then had the honor of planting the U.S. flag.

In 1912, Henson wrote *A Negro at the North Pole*, but the book aroused little interest. By the 1930s, however, Henson began receiving recognition for his contributions to arctic exploration. In 1937 he was the first African American elected to the Explorers Club in New York. In 1944 he and other surviving members of the expedition received Congressional medals. In 1954 Henson received public recognition for his deeds from President Eisenhower. Henson died in 1955 and was buried in New York. In 1988 his remains were exhumed and buried with full military honors at Arlington National Cemetery, next to the grave of Robert Peary.

William A. Hinton (1883–1959)
Lecturer, Medical Researcher, Educator

Long one of the world's authorities on venereal disease, Dr. William A. Hinton is responsible for the development of the Hinton test, a reliable method for detecting syphilis. He also collaborated with Dr. J. A. V. Davies on what is now called the Davies-Hinton test for the detection of this same disease.

Born in Chicago on December 15, 1883, Hinton graduated from Harvard in 1905. In 1912, he finished his medical studies in three years at Harvard Medical School. After graduation he was a voluntary assistant in the pathological laboratory at Massachusetts General Hospital. This was followed by eight years of laboratory practice at the Boston Dispensary and at the Massachusetts Department of Public Health. In 1923, Hinton was appointed lecturer in preventive medicine and hygiene at Harvard Medical School where he served for 27 years. In 1949, he was the first person of color to be granted a professorship there.

In 1931, at the Boston Dispensary, Hinton started a training school for poor girls so that they could become medical technicians. From these classes of volunteers grew one of the country's leading institutions for the training of technicians. Though he lost a leg in an automobile accident, Hinton remained active in teaching and at the Boston Dispensary Laboratory, which he directed from 1916 to 1952. He died in Canton, Massachusetts on August 8, 1959.

Shirley Ann Jackson (1946–)
Lecturer, Physicist

Born in Washington, DC, on August 5, 1946, Shirley Ann Jackson graduated as valedictorian of her class from Roosevelt High School in 1964. In 1968, she received a B.S. degree from Massachusetts Institute of Technology. In 1973 she became the first African American woman in the United States to earn a Ph.D. in physics, which she also earned from Massachusetts Institute of Technology.

Jackson's first position—as a research associate at the Fermi National Accelerator Laboratory in Batavia, Illinois where she studied large subatomic particles—reflected her interest in the study of subatomic particles. Jackson has worked as a member of the technical staff on theoretical physics at AT&T Bell Laboratories, as a visiting scientist at the European Center for Nuclear Research in Geneva, and as a visiting lecturer at the NATO International Advanced Study Institute in Belgium.

In 1995, President Bill Clinton named Jackson as chair of the Nuclear Regulatory Commission (NRC). Under Jackson's direction, the NRC has become more aggressive about inspections and has forced some top officials out of office because of their lax enforcement of safety regulations. Jackson is a professor at Rutgers University and is active in many organizations including the National Academy of Sciences, the American Association for the Advancement of Science, and the National Science Foundation.

Mae Jemison (AP/Wide World Photos, Inc.)

Mae C. Jemison (1956–)
Physician/Surgeon

Mae Jemison was born October 17, 1956, in Decatur, Alabama, but her family moved to Chicago when she was three years old. She attended Stanford University on a National Achievement Scholarship and received a B.S. in chemical engineering and a B.A. in Afro-American studies in 1977. She then enrolled in Cornell University's medical school and graduated in 1981. Her medical internship was at the Los Angeles County/University of Southern California Medical Center in 1982. She was a general practitioner with the INA/Ross Loos Medical Group in Los Angeles until 1983, followed by two years as a Peace Corps medical officer in Sierra Leone and Liberia. Returning to the United States in 1985, she began working for CIGNA Health Plans, a health maintenance organization in Los Angeles, and applied for admission into NASA's astronaut program.

In 1987, Jemison was accepted in NASA's astronaut program. Her first assignment was representing the astronaut office at the Kennedy Space Center in Cape Canaveral, Florida. On September 12, 1992, Jemison became the first African American woman in space on the shuttle *Endeavor*. She served aboard the *Endeavor* as a science specialist. As a physician, she studied the effect of weightlessness on herself and other crew members. Jemison resigned from NASA in 1993 to pursue personal goals related to science education and health care in West Africa. In 1994 Jemison founded the International Science Camp in Chicago to help young people become enthusiastic about science.

In 1988, Jemison won the Science and Technology Award given by *Essence* magazine and in 1990 she was Gamma Sigma Gamma's Woman of the Year. In 1991 she earned a Ph.D. from Lincoln University. She also served on the board of directors of the World Sickle Cell Foundation from 1990 to 1992.

Frederick M. Jones (1893–1961)
Mechanic

In 1935, Frederick McKinley Jones built the first automatic refrigeration system for long haul trucks. Later, the system was adapted to various other carriers including railway cars, ships, and trucks. Previously, foods were packed in ice so slight delays led to spoilage. Jones' new method instigated a change in eating habits of the entire nation and allowed for the development of food production facilities in almost any geographic location. Refrigerated trucks were also used to preserve and ship blood products during World War II.

Jones was born in Kentucky in 1893. His mother left the family when he was a baby, and his father left him at age five to be raised by a priest until he was 16 years of age. There Jones received a sixth grade education. When he left the rectory, he worked as a pin boy, mechanic's assistant, and finally, as chief mechanic on a Minnesota farm. He served in World War I and, in the late 1920s, his mechanical fame spread when he developed a series of devices to adapt silent movie projectors into sound projectors.

Jones also developed an air conditioning unit for military field hospitals, a portable x-ray machine, and a refrigerator for military field kitchens. During his life, a total of 61 patents were issued in Jones's name. He died in 1961.

Percy L. Julian (1899–1975)
Educator, Medical Researcher, Research Director

Born on April 11, 1899 in Montgomery, Alabama, Julian attended DePauw University in Greencastle, Indiana. He graduated Phi Beta Kappa at DePauw University and was valedictorian of his class after having lived during his college days in the attic of a fraternity house where he worked as a waiter. For several years, Julian taught at Fisk, West Virginia State College, and Howard University where he was associate professor and head of the chemistry department. He left to attend Harvard

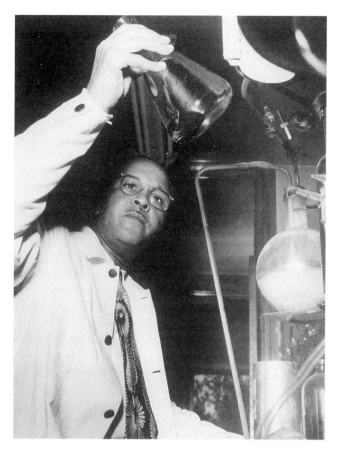

Percy Julian conducting an experiment in his laboratory in 1947 (AP/Wide World Photos, Inc.).

and the University of Vienna, where he earned a Ph.D. in 1931. Julian then continued his research and teaching duties at Howard.

In 1935, Julian synthesized the drug physostigmine, which is used today in the treatment of glaucoma. He later became director of research, chief chemist and did soybean research at the Glidden Company, where he specialized in the production of sterols, which he extracted from the oil of the soybean. The method perfected by Julian in 1950 eventually lowered the cost of sterols to less than 20 cents a gram and, ultimately, enabled millions of people suffering from arthritis to obtain relief through the use of cortisone, a sterol derivative. Later, Julian developed methods for manufacturing sex hormones from soya bean sterols: progesterone was used to prevent miscarriages, while testosterone was used to treat older men for diminishing sex drive. Both hormones were important in the treatment of cancer.

In 1954, after serving as director of research for the Glidden Company, he founded his own company, the Julian Laboratories, in Chicago and Mexico. Years later, the company was sold to Smith, Kline, and French. In

1947, Julian was awarded the Spingarn Medal and, in 1964, he founded Julian Institute and Julian Associates Incorporated in Franklin Park, Illinois. He was awarded the Chemical Pioneer Award by the American Institute of Chemists in 1968. Julian died on April 19, 1975.

Ernest E. Just (1883–1941)
Editor Zoologist, Marine Biologist

Born in Charleston, South Carolina, on August 14, 1883, Ernest Just received his B.A. in 1907 with high honors from Dartmouth and his Ph.D. in 1916 from the University of Chicago. His groundbreaking work on the embryology of marine invertebrates included research on fertilization—a process known as parthenogenesis—but his most important achievement was his discovery of the role protoplasm plays in the development of a cell.

Just began teaching at Howard University in 1907 and started graduate training at the Marine Biological Laboratory in Woods Hole, Massachusetts in 1909. He performed most of his research at this site over the next twenty summers. Between 1912 and 1937, he published more than fifty papers on fertilization, parthenogenesis, cell division, and mutation. He also published a textbook in 1939 that was the result of his research in cell functioning and the structure and role of protoplasm within a cell.

A member of Phi Beta Kappa, Just received the Spingarn Medal in 1914 and served as associate editor of *Physiological Zoology*, *The Biological Bulletin*, and *The Journal of Morphology*. In 1930 Just was one of 12 zoologists to address the International Congress of Zoologists and he was elected vice president of the American Society of Zoologists. Just left the United States in 1929 because of racist attitudes that prevented his career from advancing. He died on October 27, 1941.

Samuel L. Kountz (1930–1981)
Physician/Surgeon, Medical Researcher

Born in 1930 in Lexa, Arkansas, Samuel Kountz graduated third in his class at the Agricultural, Mechanical and Normal College of Arkansas in 1952, having initially failed his entrance exams. He pursued graduate studies at the University of Arkansas, earning a degree in chemistry. Senator J. W. Fulbright, whom he met while a graduate student, advised Kountz to apply for a scholarship to medical school. Kountz won the scholarship on a competitive basis and was the first African American to enroll at the University of Arkansas Medical School in Little Rock, graduating with his M.D. in 1958. Kountz was responsible for finding out that large doses of the drug methylprednisolone could help reverse the acute rejection of a transplanted kidney. The drug was used for a number of years in the standard management of kidney transplant patients.

While he was still an intern, Kountz assisted in the first West Coast kidney transplant. In 1964, working with Dr. Roy Cohn, one of the pioneers in the field of transplantation, Kountz again made medical history by transplanting a kidney from a mother to a daughter—the first transplant between humans who were not identical twins. At the University of California in 1967, Dr. Kountz worked with other researchers to develop the prototype of a machine that is now able to preserve kidneys up to fifty hours from the time they are taken from the body of a donor. The machine, called the Belzer Kidney Perfusion Machine, was named for Dr. Folker O. Belzer, who was Kountz's partner. Kountz went on to build one of the largest kidney transplant training and research centers in the nation. He died in 1981 after a long illness contracted on a trip to South Africa in 1977.

Lewis H. Latimer (1848–1928)
Draftsperson, Electrical Engineer

Lewis Howard Latimer was employed by Alexander Graham Bell to make the patent drawings for the first telephone, and later he went on to become chief draftsman for both the General Electric and Westinghouse companies. Born in Chelsea, Massachusetts, on September 4, 1848, Latimer enlisted in the Union Navy at the age of 15 and began studying drafting upon completion of his military service. In 1881, he invented a method of making carbon filaments for the Maxim electric incandescent lamp and later patented this method. He also supervised the installation of electric light in New York, Philadelphia, Montreal, and London for the Maxim-Weston Electric Company. In 1884, he joined the Edison Company.

Theodore K. Lawless (1892–1971)
Physician, Philanthropist

Theodore Kenneth Lawless was born on December 6, 1892, in Thibodeaux, Louisiana. He received his B.S. from Talladega College in 1914 and continued to further his education at the University of Kansas and Northwestern University, where he received his M.D. in 1919. He then pursued a master's in dermatology, which he finished at Columbia University. From there he furthered his studies at Harvard University, the University of Paris, the University of Freiburg, and the University of Vienna.

Lawless started his own practice in the Chicago's predominantly African American South Side upon his return in 1924, which he continued until his death in 1971. He soon became one of the premiere dermatologists in the country and earned great praise for researching treatments and cures for a variety of skin diseases including syphilis and leprosy. During the early years of his career, he taught dermatology at Northwestern University Medical School, where his research was instrumental in devising electropyrexia, a treatment for those suffering cases of syphilis in its early stages. Before he left his role at Northwestern in 1941, he aided in building the university's first medical laboratories.

After leaving Northwestern, Lawless entered the business world beginning as president of 4213 South Michigan Corporation, which sold low-cost real estate, and later as president of the Service Federal Savings and Loan Association. And by the 1960s, he was well-known as one of the 35 richest African American men in the United States. During his lifetime, Lawless served on dozens of boards of directors and belonged to countless organizations. He served on the Chicago Board of Health, as senior attending physician at Provident hospital, as associate examiner in dermatology for the National Board of Medical Examiners, as chairman of the Division of Higher Education, and as consultant to the Geneva Community Hospital in Switzerland. He was also recognized with many awards for his exemplary breakthroughs in medicine, public service, and philanthropy including the Harmon Award in Medicine in 1929, the Churchman of the Year in 1952, the Springarn Medal from the NAACP in 1954, and the Daniel H. Burnham Award from Roosevelt University in 1963. He died in 1971.

Robert H. Lawrence, Jr. (1935–1967)
Astronaut, Airplane Pilot

Air Force Major Robert H. Lawrence, Jr. was the first African American astronaut to be appointed to the Manned Orbiting Laboratory. Lawrence was a native of Chicago, and while still in elementary school he became a model airplane hobbyist and a chess enthusiast. Lawrence became interested in biology during his time at Englewood High School in Chicago. As a student at Englewood, Lawrence excelled in chemistry and track. When he graduated, he placed in the top ten percent of the class.

Lawrence entered Bradley University, joining the Air Force Reserve Officer's Training Corps and attaining the rank of lieutenant colonel, making him the second highest ranking cadet at Bradley. Lawrence was commissioned a second lieutenant in the United States Air Force in 1956 and soon after received his bachelors degree in chemistry. Following a stint at an air base in Germany, Lawrence entered Ohio State University through the Air Force Institute of Technology as a doctoral candidate, earning his Ph.D. in 1965. Law-

Major Robert H. Lawrence, Jr. (AP/Wide World Photos, Inc.)

rence's career came to an end in 1967 when his F-104D Starfighter jet crashed on a runway in a California desert.

Elijah McCoy (1843–1929)
Inventor, Machinist

Born in Canada, McCoy traveled to Scotland at age 16. There he was apprenticed to a master mechanic and engineer. After the Civil War, he moved to Ypsilanti, Michigan, where he sought work as an engineer. However, he was only able to obtain employment as a fireman and oiler for Michigan Central Railroad.

McCoy's first invention was a lubricating cup that used steam pressure to drive oil into channels that brought it to a steam engine's moving parts. It was patented in 1872. Before this invention, these parts had to be oiled at the car's intermittent stops, slowing the pace of rail travel considerably. In addition, the automatic device kept the engine better lubricated than was possible with the old method. Variations of this cup came to be used on many types of heavy machinery. Although McCoy received at least 72 patents in his lifetime, little money would reach his pockets as a result of his ideas. Because he lacked the capital to invest in manufacturing, he sold most of his patents for modest sums of money while the manufacturers made millions. Later in his life, he helped found the Elijah McCoy Manufacturing Company, but he died just a few years later.

Ronald E. McNair (1950–1986)
Astronaut

Ronald McNair was born on October 21, 1950, in Lake City, South Carolina. He was a graduate of North Carolina A&T State University with a B.S. degree in physics. He also received a Doctor of Philosophy in Physics from Massachusetts Institute of Technology. He was presented an honorary Doctorate of Laws from North Carolina A&T in 1978.

McNair was working on the use of lasers in satellite communications when he was selected by NASA in 1978 to train as an astronaut. In August 1979, he completed a one-year training and evaluation period that made him eligible for assignment as mission specialist on Space Shuttle flight crews. He presented papers in the areas of lasers and molecular spectroscopy and gave many presentations in the United States and Europe. He was the second African American to orbit the earth on a NASA mission.

Despite the rigorous training in the NASA program, he taught karate at a church, played the saxophone, and found time to interact with young people. McNair was aboard the shuttle *Challenger* that exploded shortly after liftoff from Cape Kennedy and plunged into the waters off the Florida coast on January 28, 1986. The shuttle had a crew of seven persons including two women, a mission specialist, and a teacher-in-space participant.

Walter E. Massey (1938–)
Physicist

Walter Eugene Massey was born in Hattiesburg, Mississippi, on April 5, 1938. At the end of tenth grade, he accepted a scholarship to Morehouse College. He almost quit after a few weeks, but graduated four years later with a B.S. in physics. He completed his Ph.D. in physics in 1966.

Massey's research interests have included solid state theory (study of properties of solid material) and theories of quantum liquids and solids. While still a graduate student, he studied the behavior of both solid and liquid helium-3 and helium-4, publishing a series of papers on this work in the early 1970s. He became a full professor at Brown University in 1975 and was named dean of the college in the same year. Massey's best-known accom-

Ronald McNair (AP/Wide World Photos, Inc.)

plishment at Brown was his development of the Inner City Teachers of Science (ICTOS) program, a program for the improvement of science instruction in inner city schools. He was awarded the American Association for the Advancement of Science's Distinguished Service Citation for his development of ICTOS.

In 1979 the University of Chicago invited Massey to become professor of physics and director of the Argonne National Laboratory, which the university operates for the U.S. Department of Energy. The facility was beset by financial troubles at the time, and Massey has been credited with its successful recovery. In the fall of 1990, Massey was chosen by Pres. George Bush to head the National Science Foundation (NSF), a position he held until 1993. He was only the second African American to hold that post. Massey has been president of Morehouse College since 1995.

Jan Matzeliger (1852–1889)
Inventor, Shoemaker/Leather Worker

Born in 1852 in Paramaribo, Dutch Guiana, Matzeliger found employment in the government machine works at the age of 10. Nine years later, he left home and eventually immigrated to the United States, settling in Philadelphia, where he worked in a shoe factory. He later moved to New England, settling permanently in Lynn, Massachusetts in 1877. The Industrial Revolution had by this time resulted in the invention of machines to cut, sew, and tack shoes, but none had been perfected to last a shoe, which involved stretching the leather over a model foot. Observing this, Matzeliger designed and patented a device, one which he refined over the years to a point where it could last the leather, arrange the leather over the sole, drive in the nails, and deliver the finished product—all in one minute's time.

Matzeliger's patent was subsequently bought by Sydney W. Winslow, who established the United Shoe Machine Company. The continued success of this business brought about a fifty percent reduction in the price of shoes across the nation, doubled wages for unskilled workers, and improved working conditions for millions of people dependent on the shoe industry for their livelihood. Between 1883 and 1891, Matzeliger received five patents on his inventions, all which contributed to the shoe making revolution. His last patent was issued in September 1891, two years posthumously.

Matzeliger died of tuberculosis in 1889 at the age of 37, long before he had the chance to realize a share of the enormous profit derived from his invention. He never received any money. Instead, he was issued stock in the company that did not become valuable until after his death.

Garrett A. Morgan (1877–1963)
Inventor

Born in Paris, Kentucky, in 1877, Morgan moved to Cleveland at an early age. Although he was most famous for his invention of the gas inhalator, an early gas mask, he also invented an improvement on the sewing machine that he sold for $150, as well as a hair refining cream that straightened human hair. The cream remained in use for over forty years. In 1923, having established his reputation with the gas inhalator, he was able to command a price of $40,000 from the General Electric Company for his automatic traffic signal.

In 1912, Morgan developed his "safety hood," a gas inhalator that was a precursor to the gas mask. The value of his invention was first acknowledged during a successful rescue operation of several men trapped by a tunnel explosion in the Cleveland Waterworks, some two hundred feet below the surface of Lake Erie. During the emergency, Morgan, his brother, and two other volunteers were the only men able to descend into the smoky, gas-filled tunnel and save several workers from asphyxiation.

Orders for the Morgan inhalator soon began to pour into Cleveland from fire companies all over the nation,

Garrett Morgan (AP/Wide World Photos, Inc.)

but as soon as Morgan's racial identity became known, many of them were canceled. In the South, it was necessary for Morgan to utilize the services of a white man to demonstrate his invention. During World War I the Morgan inhalator was transformed into a gas mask used by combat troops. Morgan died in 1963 in Cleveland—the city that had awarded him a gold medal for his devotion to public safety.

Waverly J. Person (1927–)
Geophysicist

Waverly J. Person, born in 1927, is the first African American to hold the prominent position of director of the United States Geological Survey's National Earthquake Information Center. A respected geophysicist and seismologist, he was also one of the first African Americans in his field. He also currently encourages minority students to consider the earth sciences as a career.

While a technician at the National Information Earthquake Center, he took up graduate studies. From 1962 to 1973, he held that position and simultaneously completed graduate work at American University and George Washington University. His supervisors increasingly assigned him more challenging tasks that he performed well, gaining notice among his peers. Soon he was qualified as a geophysicist and transferred to the United States Geological Survey's National Earthquake Information Center in Colorado. In 1977, Person was named director of the Colorado National Earthquake Information Center and in 1994 was named director of the National Earthquake Information Center.

Norbert Rillieux (1806–1894)
Inventor, Mechanical Engineer

Norbert Rillieux's inventions were of great value to the sugar refining industry. The method formerly used called for gangs of slaves to ladle boiling sugarcane juice from one kettle to another—a primitive process known as "the Jamaica Train." In 1845, Rillieux invented a vacuum evaporating pan (a series of condensing coils in vacuum chambers) that reduced the industry's dependence on gang labor and helped manufacture a superior product at a greatly reduced cost. The first Rillieux evaporator was installed at Myrtle Grove Plantation, Louisiana, in 1845. In the following years, factories in Louisiana, Cuba, and Mexico converted to the Rillieux system.

A native of New Orleans, Rillieux was the son of Vincent Rillieux, a wealthy engineer, and Constance Vivant, a slave on his plantation. Young Rillieux's higher education was obtained in Paris, where his extraordinary aptitude for engineering led to his appointment at the age of twenty-four as an instructor of applied mechanics at L'Ecole Centrale. Rillieux returned to Paris permanently in 1854, securing a scholarship and working on the deciphering of hieroglyphics.

When his evaporator process was finally adopted in Europe, he returned to inventing with renewed interest—applying his process to the sugar beet. In so doing, he cut production and refining costs in half. Rillieux died in Paris on October 8, 1894, leaving behind a system that is in universal use throughout the sugar industry, as well as in the manufacture of soap, gelatin, glue, and many other products.

Mabel K. Staupers (1890–1989)
Nursing Executive, Civil Rights/Human Rights Activist

Staupers was born in Barbados in 1890 and moved with her family to Harlem as a teenager. She graduated from Washington, DC's Freedmen's Hospital School of Nursing in 1917, returned to Harlem, and, by 1920, had co-founded a tuberculosis clinic for African American sufferers. She served as the director of nursing at the clinic named after Booker T. Washington before deciding she could better serve in the profession as an educator.

The racism that Staupers witnessed while at Jefferson Hospital Medical College in Philadelphia convinced her to work toward eradicating prejudice in the profession. Returning to New York, she served as executive secretary of the Harlem Committee of the New York Tuberculosis and Health Association from 1922 to 1934 before taking on a post of the same title at the National Association of Colored Graduate Nurses (NACGN), an organization that worked to improve working conditions for and erase racism toward African American nurses. With the outbreak of World War II, Staupers began enjoining the military branches to accept African American nurses into its medical Corps units.

The U.S. Army Nurse Corps was the first to integrate, but only grudgingly, with a quota system in place. Staupers fought with the help of First Lady Eleanor Roosevelt to end the quotas and win these African American nurses wishing to serve their country more equal assignments. By the war's end, the quota system had been eliminated and the Navy Nurse Corps had also been integrated. She urged the group to disband in 1949, shortly after serving as its president, because as she said, at the time, overly racist policies had been eliminated. In 1951, Staupers was awarded the NAACP's distinguished Spingarn Medal. She recounted her life in the 1961 autobiography *No Time for Prejudice: A Story of the Integration of Negroes in Nursing in the United States*. Staupers died in 1989, a few months short of what would have been her one hundredth birthday.

Lewis Temple (1800–1854)
Inventor

The toggle harpoon invented by Lewis Temple improved the whaling methods of the nineteenth century, leading to a doubling of the annual catch. Little is known of Temple's early background, except that he was born in Richmond, Virginia, in 1800 and had no formal education. As a young man he moved to New Bedford, Massachusetts, then a major whaling port. Finding work as a metal smith, Temple modified the design of the whaler's harpoon and, in 1848, manufactured a new version of the harpoon with a barbed and pivoting head, making it much harder for a harpooned whale to escape. Using the "toggle harpoon," the whaling industry soon entered a period of unprecedented prosperity. Temple, who never patented his harpoon, died destitute.

Vivien Thomas (1910–1985)
Surgical Research Technician

Born in Nashville, Tennessee, in 1910, Thomas had dreamed of a career as a physician since childhood. As a teenager, he worked as a carpenter and as an orderly to earn money for college and enrolled in Tennessee Agricultural and Industrial College in 1929. The stock market crash later that year eradicated Thomas's savings, and he was forced to quit school.

The following year, he was hired for a research assistant post at Vanderbilt University Medical School; he would become trauma researcher and surgeon Alfred Blalock's assistant. For the next decade, Thomas worked long hours in the lab, conducting medical experiments for Blalock that eventually led to lifesaving advances in medicine during World War II, especially in the use of blood transfusions.

When Blalock was hired by the prestigious medical school at Johns Hopkins University in 1940, he would accept the post only if they hired Thomas as well. One of their most significant achievements together was a surgical procedure that restructured the blood vessels around an infant's heart if the child was in danger of death due to poor circulation of blood into the lungs.

Thomas became a well-known, and well-regarded figure on the campus of Johns Hopkins. He remained at the institution even after his mentor passed away in 1964 and, in 1971, was honored by graduates of its medical school for his achievements. He became a medical school faculty member in 1977 and received an honorary degree in 1976. He retired in 1979. Thomas passed away in 1985, the same year a recounting of his life was published titled *Pioneering Research in Surgical Shock and Cardiovascular Surgery: Vivien Thomas and His Work with Alfred Blalock.*

Margaret E. M. Tolbert (1943–)
Analytical Chemist

Margaret E. Mayo Tolbert was born on November 24, 1943, the third of six children raised by their grandmother. She obtained a M.S. in analytical chemistry in one year and, in 1970, she was recruited to join the doctoral program in chemistry at Brown University. Her research on biochemical reactions in liver cells was partially funded by a scholarship from the Southern Fellowship Fund.

In 1979, Tolbert spent five months in Brussels, Belgium, studying how different drugs are metabolized in rat liver cells at the International Institute of Cellular and Molecular Pathology. After, she was appointed director of the Carver Research Foundation. During her tenure, Tolbert was able to bring several large scientific research contracts to the university from the federal government—contracts that expanded the research capabilities of the entire school. From 1990–1993, Tolbert directed the Research Improvement in Minority Institutions Program for the National Science Foundation (NSF), which works to strengthen the infrastructure of research programs at minority colleges and universities.

In 1996, Tolbert was appointed the director of the New Brunswick Laboratory at Argonne National Laboratories. As only the third director in the laboratory's almost fifty-year history, Tolbert's position allows her to help the entire country by enhancing nuclear security nationally as well as support international nonproliferation efforts.

Levi Watkins, Jr. (1945–)
Surgeon, Educator

Levi Watkins was born in Kansas in 1945 but grew up in Montgomery, Alabama, where through his involvement in local churches became acquainted with civil rights leaders Dr. Ralph David Abernathy and the Rev. Martin Luther King, Jr. Both were prominent members of the Montgomery community, as was Watkins's own father, a college professor. The teenager's participation in civil rights issues did not stop him from excelling academically as he graduated as valedictorian of his high school class and went on to earn a 1966 honors degree from Tennessee State University.

Watkins's awareness of issues of racial inequality led him to apply to Vanderbilt University Medical School, and he first learned of his acceptance as its first African American student by reading the newspaper headline announcing the breakthrough. He graduated in 1970 and began his internship and surgical training at the prestigious medical school at Johns Hopkins University. Watkins also studied at Harvard University Medical School for a time and conducted research that led to the lifesaving practice of prescribing angiotensin blockers for patients susceptible to heart failure.

In 1978, Watkins became Johns Hopkins's first African American chief resident in cardiac surgery and became a faculty member that year as well. Two years later, he made medical history with the first successful surgical implantation of an AID (Automatic Implantable Defibrillator) device, which has been credited with saving countless lives by its ability to restore a normal heartbeat during an attack of arrhythmia. In 1991 he became a full professor of cardiac surgery at Johns Hopkins, another first for the institution. For several years, however, Watkins had been working to increase minority presence at this elite medical school, and he instituted a special minority recruiting drive when he was appointed to the medical school's admissions committee in 1979. He is currently dean of the school.

Daniel H. Williams (1856–1931)
Surgeon/Physician

A pioneer in open heart surgery, Daniel Hale Williams was born in Hollidaysburg, Pennsylvania, on January 18, 1856. In 1878 he apprenticed to a prominent physician, giving him the training to enter the Chicago Medical College in 1883.

Williams opened his office on Chicago's South Side at a time when Chicago hospitals did not allow African American doctors to use their facilities. In 1891, Dr. Williams founded Provident Hospital, which was open to patients of all races. At Provident Hospital on July 10, 1893, Williams performed the operation upon which his later fame rests. A patient was admitted to the emergency ward with a knife wound in the pericardium, or the membrane enclosing the heart. With the aid of six staff surgeons, Williams made an incision in the patient's chest and successfully repaired the tear. The patient fully recovered and was able to leave the hospital, scarred but cured.

In 1894, Pres. Cleveland appointed Williams surgeon-in-chief of Freedmen's Hospital in Washington, DC. He completely reorganized and updated procedures at the hospital, adding specialty departments, organizing a system horse-drawn ambulances, and initiating more sanitary medical practices. After some political infighting at Freedmen's, he resigned his post in 1897 to return to Provident.

Williams was instrumental in the forming of the Medico-Chirurgical Society and the National Medical Association. In 1913, he was inducted into the American Board of Surgery at its first convention. Over the course of his career, Williams helped establish over forty hospitals in twenty states to serve African American communities. He died on August 4, 1931, after a lifetime devoted to his two main interests—the NAACP and the construction of hospitals and training schools for African American doctors and nurses.

O. S. Williams (1921–)
Aeronautical Engineer

Oswald S. "Ozzie" Williams was born on September 2, 1921, in Washington, DC. He was the second African American to receive a degree in aeronautical engineering in 1943, and he earned his master's in the field in 1947.

In 1950, Williams took an engineering position at Greer Hydraulics, Inc. There he was responsible for the development of the first experimental airborne radio beacon, which was used to locate crashed airplanes. However, it was never produced commercially. At Grumman International, where he was hired on as a propulsion engineer in 1961, Williams managed the development of the *Apollo* Lunar Module reaction control subsystem. He was fully responsible for the $42 million effort for eight years. He managed the three engineering groups that developed the small rocket motors that guided the lunar module, the part of the *Apollo* spacecraft that actually landed on the moon. Williams went on to a career in marketing at Grumman, culminating in his election as a company vice president in 1974.

Sports

◆ Baseball ◆ Football ◆ Boxing ◆ Basketball ◆ Other Sports ◆ Women in Sports
◆ Athletes, Coaches, and Sports Executives

Despite the prejudices of the nineteenth and twentieth centuries, African Americans have excelled in various sports. In addition to accomplishing a multitude of athletic feats, many of the exploits of African American athletes have helped to spur societal changes. The integration of baseball in 1947 by Jackie Robinson and the legacy of heavyweight champion Joe Louis helped to launch the Civil Rights movement. Additionally, the rise in black nationalism of the 1960s and 1970s was projected by the words and deeds of African American athletes, such as Muhammad Ali, Wilt Chamberlain, and Curt Flood.

Professional and some amateur sports have also given African Americans the opportunity for instant fame and wealth afforded by few other venues. For some, success on the athletic field carries over into the private sector, as many African American athletes have used their wealth and clout to start businesses and give back to the community. As the twenty-first century begins, however, a major obstacle exists—few African Americans have been given employment in front office positions or been granted ownership of professional sports teams.

◆ BASEBALL

Professional baseball began in Hoboken, New Jersey, in 1846. The game was dominated by amateurs and roving semi-professionals until the National League was formed in 1876. Initially, there was no prohibition against African Americans playing in the National League or its rivals—the American Association, the Union League, and the Players League. Moses Fleetwood Walker was the first prominent African American professional baseball player during the 1880s for the Toledo Mud Hens of the American Association. However, in an exhibition

game with a National League team, the Chicago White Stockings, the "color line" was drawn in baseball for the first time. White Stockings player/manager Cap Anson refused to play on the same field with Walker. Later, when Anson heard an African American was about to be signed in the National League, he used his influence to initiate a "gentlemen's agreement" among the teams not to sign any African American players. This agreement became the standard in organized baseball.

Efforts to sneak African Americans into the major leagues under the guise of being Cuban or American Indians failed. Until the 1920s, the only way for African Americans to play baseball was as semi-professionals touring and playing wherever they got the chance. As the 1920s dawned, an organized, professional Negro League was established by Rube Foster and others to give African Americans the chance to play big league baseball. The Negro League featured teams such as the Detroit Stars, Homestead Grays, New York Elite Giants, and others that played wherever they could find a stadium and funding. They frequently filled Major League Baseball stadiums when given the chance and the quality of their product was evidenced by such Hall of Fame players such as Satchel Paige, Josh Gibson, Ray Dandridge, "Cool Papa" Bell, Oscar Charleston, Buck Leonard, and Judy Johnson.

However, the Negro League was never financially stable, and teams frequently folded. Many players earned money be playing in Cuba and the Dominican Republic. Despite efforts by Major League Commissioner Judge Kenesaw Mountain Landis to stop them, many exhibition games were arranged between Negro League and Major League All-Star teams. The exhibitions were competitive and the Negro League players demonstrated their skill by winning many of the contests. However, as long as Landis was commissioner of Major League Baseball, integration was impossible.

In 1945, following the death of Landis and the appointment of Happy Chandler as commissioner, Brooklyn Dodger general manager and part-owner Branch Rickey began a search for an African American to integrate Major League Baseball. He settled on UCLA alumnus Jackie Robinson. In 1946, Robinson played for the Dodgers top minor league team in Montreal. In 1947, he integrated baseball despite virulent opposition from players, teammates, and all of the other Major League Baseball owners. Robinson was named the National League's Rookie of the Year in 1947 and won the Most Valuable Player award in 1949. The Cleveland Indians integrated the American League in 1947 with Larry Doby.

By 1958, all Major League Baseball teams had integrated their rosters and African American players became stars in both leagues. In 1975, Frank Robinson became the first African American manager of a Major League Baseball team with the Cleveland Indians. However, baseball's front office positions remained closed to African Americans as the game features few African American managers or general managers. The power structure changed slightly in the 1988 when former player Bill White became the first African American to be president of the National League. White was succeeded in 1994 by another African American, Leonard Coleman.

In addition, many of baseball's top stars have been African American. Hank Aaron became baseball's all-time home run leader and drove in more runs than anyone in history. Rickey Henderson holds the record for most steals, and Lee Smith has more saves than any other player. Additionally, African American players have been the recipients of the Most Valuable Player Award in the American or National League over 35 percent of the time during the last half century.

Curt Flood also changed the face of baseball. In 1969, Flood decided to challenge his trade from the St. Louis Cardinals to the Philadelphia Phillies on the grounds that baseball's reserve clause—binding players to their existing teams—was in violation of federal antitrust laws. A lawsuit brought by Flood was eventually heard by the U.S. Supreme Court, which ruled against Flood and decided that baseball could retain its posture as the only professional sport exempted from federal antitrust legislation. Shortly after the decision, an agreement between the players and management ended the reserve system and established free agency.

The percentage of African American players in Major League Baseball has declined since its peak in the 1970s. One factor responsible for this change is the streamlin-

Jackie Robinson (Archive Photos, Inc.)

ing of inner city baseball programs and urban little leagues due financial problems. The economic situation has become such in some American cities that even scholastic athletic programs are threatened with cutbacks or dissolution. However, many of the games top players are African American including Ken Griffey, Jr.; Barry Bonds; Derek Jeter; Mo Vaughn; and Kenny Lofton.

In 1997, the fiftieth anniversary of the integration of baseball by Jackie Robinson, Major League Baseball took action to honor Robinson's feat. Commissioner Bud Selig retired Robinson's number 42 from use by any baseball team. President Bill Clinton offered remarks on Robinson's legacy at a ceremony in New York's Shea Stadium. That summer, Robinson's widow, Rachel, took part in a ceremony at the Baseball Hall of Fame dedicating a wing to African Americans.

◆ FOOTBALL

Unlike the other major American sports, professional football was integrated from its inception. Beginning in 1919 with Fritz Pollard of the Akron Indians of the American Professional Football League, African Americans participated in professional football until the 1930s.

In 1933, however, the National Football League, expelled its African American players.

The NFL was bereft of African American players until the Los Angeles Rams signed Kenny Washington in 1946. Cleveland Browns fullback Marion Motley, who debuted later that year, was the earliest African American star. Syracuse University's Jim Brown began his career with the Browns shortly after the retirement of Motley and became the top running back in the league. Brown led the league in rushing for eight of his nine years and held the career yardage mark for 19 years after his retirement.

By the end of Brown's career in the mid-1960s, several other African American stars had emerged. New York Giants safety Emlen Tunnel set the record for career interceptions while Chicago Bears running back Gale Sayers was considered one of the most exciting running backs of the era. Blacks excelled at every position except quarterback, which was reserved for white players.

African American stars continued to proliferate in the 1960s and 1970s. Charley Taylor was the first African American to lead the league in receptions twice. Willie Wood was the first to lead the NFL in interceptions. In 1973, the Buffalo Bills' O. J. Simpson became the first player to rush for more than 2,000 yards in a single season. The visibility of African Americans in the NFL was demonstrated with the popularity of certain teams's defensive lines and their familiar nicknames. The Minnesota Vikings offered the "Purple People Eaters," including Carl Eller, Alan Page and Jim Marshall. David "Deacon" Jones and Rosey Grier were mainstays on the Los Angeles Rams' "Fearsome Foursome." The great Pittsburgh Steeler defenses of the 1970s were known as the "Steel Curtain" and included "Mean" Joe Greene.

During the 1980s, the Giants' Lawrence Taylor revolutionized the position of outside linebacker. In 1984, Walter Payton of the Bears eclipsed Jim Brown's record for career rushing yards and concluded his brilliant career in 1987 with more than 16,700 yards. In 1988, the Washington Redskins' Doug Williams became the first African American to quarterback his team to a Super Bowl victory. The 1990s have been dominated by three running backs who have won Most Valuable Player Awards: the Detroit Lions' Barry Sanders, the Dallas Cowboys' Emmitt Smith, and the Denver Broncos' Terrell Davis. The San Francisco 49ers' record setting wide receiver Jerry Rice holds the record of most touchdowns scored in league history. The Cowboys' flamboyant cornerback Deion Sanders has become one of the games most visible and dominant defensive players.

African Americans currently represent approximately 70 percent of those playing in the NFL. However,

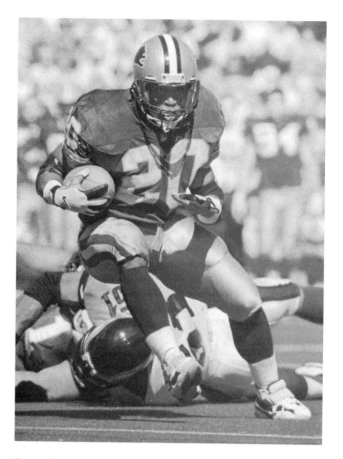

Barry Sanders (AP/Wide World Photos, Inc.)

African American representation in the coaching ranks and the front office has not grown at the same pace as it has on the playing field. African Americans make up less than 20 percent of the head coaches in the league and none of the upper level management positions.

This is a similar problem in college football, as most coaching jobs are still held by whites. Historically, the major avenue for African Americans in coaching and at one time in playing was through historically African American colleges. Grambling's former head coach Eddie Robinson produced several NFL stars as did other predominately African American colleges. However, the integration of major Southern universities has weakened the influence of African American colleges.

◆ BOXING

African American athletes have been boxing professionally since colonial times. In 1886 George "Little Chocolate" Dixon became the first African American to win a world boxing title. In 1908, Jack Johnson became the first to win the heavyweight title. Joe Walcott captured the world lightweight and welterweight titles. African Americans have dominated the sport since the

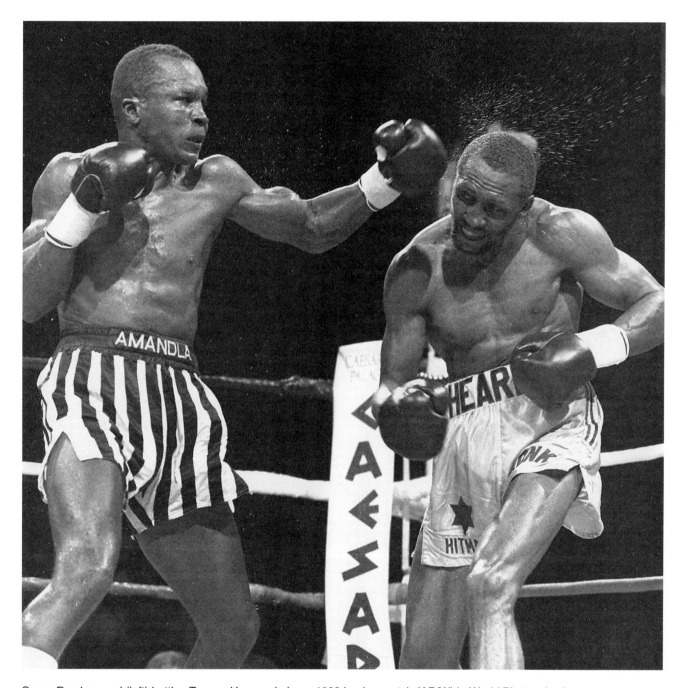

Sugar Ray Leonard (left) battles Tommy Hearns during a 1989 boxing match (AP/Wide World Photos, Inc.).

1930s, especially the heavyweight division. Joe Louis held the world heavyweight title for a record 11 years and eight months in the 1930s and 1940s. Middleweight champion Sugar Ray Robinson is considered by many to be "pound for pound" the greatest boxer of all time. Henry Armstrong held three world titles at once—featherweight, lightweight, and welterweight—during the Great Depression.

Louis, Robinson, and Armstrong were stars in what is considered the first golden age of African Americans in

boxing. A new golden age was ushered in on March 8, 1971, when Muhammad Ali and Joe Frazier drew the sport's first multimillion-dollar gate. Ali, a national figure since winning an Olympic gold medal in 1960, was one of the first athletes to comment on American political and social events.

Other divisions have featured African American stars. During the 1970s and 1980s attention shifted to talented fighters in the middle and welterweight divisions including Sugar Ray Leonard, Marvin Hagler, and Thomas

Hearns. When Ali was no longer able to defend his heavyweight crown, new challengers such as Larry Holmes and Michael Spinks ascended to the championship ranks.

As purses for major boxing events reached the $100 million mark in the mid-1980s, a new generation of fighters arose. Mike Tyson, became the best known heavyweight champion since Ali and the wealthiest boxer of all time. His tumultuous reign was ended with a knockout by James "Buster" Douglas, who in turn lost the title to Evander Holyfield. Tyson, however, continued to be the most visible figure in boxing. In 1992, he was convicted of sexual assault and sentenced to jail. After his release, he quickly regained his title until Holyfield won it from him in 1996. In a 1997 rematch Tyson bit Holyfield twice during the early rounds of the fight, earning a disqualification. Tyson was subsequently suspended from boxing. Despite the lifting of that suspension, legal troubles and prison time have clouded the career of boxing's most famous figure.

Other fighters, including Pernell Whitaker and Roy Jones, Jr., have shone brightly in recent years; however, none has the public appeal of Tyson. Many expert see the lack of a popular champion as a sign of the death of the sport of boxing.

Top boxers can conceivably earn as much as $100 million for less than a dozen major ring events. The advent of pay-per-view television and cable network sponsorship has lead to soaring profits for the sport and its practitioners, although declining ratings and public interest threaten this trend. Colorful entrepreneur Don King is the most famous, wealthy, and controversial boxing promoter of the modern era. His powerful position in boxing's ranks and his hold on Tyson have allowed him to control championship boxing, despite frequent troubles with the Internal Revenue Service and complaints from former fighters who worked under King.

◆ BASKETBALL

African American presence in basketball dates to the early days of the sport. College basketball dominated the first half of the twentieth century as no major professional league existed until the late 1940s. In 1916, educators, coaches, and faculty members from Hampton Institute, Shaw, Lincoln, Virginia Union, and Howard University formed the Central Interscholastic Athletic Association, the first African American collegiate conference. Others soon followed, including the Southeastern Athletic Conference, Southwestern Athletic Conference, and Southern Intercollegiate Athletic Conference.

Much of the legacy of African American basketball history lies in its pioneers. Bob Douglas, who founded the Harlem Renaissance in the 1920s, is considered the "Godfather of black basketball." His innovations included monthly player contracts, a custom designed team bus, and tours in the South. John McLendon, a coach during the 1950s and 1960s, is recognized as the strategic architect of the fast break and was the first African American to publish a book detailing his coaching philosophy. He was also the first to coach a professional team. Additionally, McLendon was a prominent advocate of the desegregation of intercollegiate athletics.

For years most top college African American players signed with the Harlem Globetrotters, an internationally known barnstorming team. From their inception in 1926, the Globetrotters have delighted basketball fans worldwide with their unique combination of skill and humor. Famous Globetrotters include "Meadowlark" Lemon, "Curly" Neal, "Goose" Tatum, and Marques Haynes.

Professional basketball organized in the late 1940s as the National Basketball Association and was integrated in 1950. In the same year Chuck Cooper of Duquesne University was the first African American to be drafted in the league. Nat "Sweetwater" Clifton was the first signed to a professional contract. However, on October 31, 1950, when Earl Lloyd of the then Washington Capitols took the court, he became the first African American to actually participate in an NBA game.

Basketball grew in the 1950s and 1960s as African American players such as Bill Russell, Wilt Chamberlain, Elgin Baylor, and Oscar Robertson enjoyed success in both college and then as professionals. In 1966, Texas Western University became the first college team to win the NCAA National Championship with an all-African American starting five. They beat the favored and all-white University of Kentucky, a milestone that began the end of segregated basketball teams.

The late 1960s and 1970s featured the rise of two of the great stars of the game—Kareem Abdul-Jabbar and Julius Erving. Abdul-Jabbar starred at UCLA and led the Bruins to three straight NCAA crowns. He then became a professional star with the Milwaukee Bucks and Los Angeles Lakers. Along with Earl Monroe, Willis Reed, Elvin Hayes, and others, African American players began to dominate the league. The rival American Basketball Association began the slam dunk competitions which dominate the NBA All-Star Weekend. Julius Erving became the most popular player in the ABA due to his dunks and acrobatics.

The 1980s and 1990s featured the growth of basketball into one of the most popular sports in the United States and around the world. The huge success of the NCAA Final Four has led to large financial revenues for colleges. In 1982 John Thompson of Georgetown Uni-

Wilt Chamberlain (right) and Bill Russell—two of the most dominant centers in the history of professional basketball (Corbis Corporation [Bellevue]).

Alonzo Mourning (AP/Wide World Photos, Inc.)

versity became the first African American to coach in the Final Four. Two years later his team won the tournament. The talents of Magic Johnson, Isiah Thomas, Charles Barkley, Karl Malone, Alonzo Mourning, and others led to large growth of the college game and the NBA. These players became celebrities as well as athletes, endorsing a wide variety of products and becoming celebrities.

The most famous player of both decades is Michael Jordan. Considered the greatest basketball player of all time, Jordan's success and personality have made him one of the most famous people in the world. He led the University of North Carolina to an NCAA title in 1982 and led the Chicago Bulls to six NBA titles. His endorsements established Nike athletic shoes as one of the largest apparel companies in the world.

African Americans now occupy more than 80 percent of the spots on NBA rosters including such young stars as Shaquille O'Neal, Kobe Bryant, Kevin Garnett, Grant Hill, Allen Iverson, and Tim Duncan. Other areas, especially coaching and management positions, have less representation. The Atlanta Hawks' Lenny Wilkens has won more games than any other coach in history, with more than 1,000 victories. Approximately 15 percent of top management and administrative positions are held by African Americans. In 1990, Bertram Lee and Peter C. B. Bynoe became the first African American owners of a professional sports franchise with the purchase of the Denver Nuggets.

The end of the 1990s saw two incidents dent the popularity and rapid growth of professional basketball. In 1997, Latrell Sprewell, an All–Star player, attempted to strangle his coach, P.J. Carlesimo, at a practice. Sprewell claimed Carlesimo's harsh coaching style inspired the attack, and the fact that Sprewell is black and Carlesimo white further added to the tense situation. The NBA suspended Sprewell for one year and his team terminated his contract. Sprewell countered with a lawsuit against the league and against his team. Eventually, his contract was reinstated and the league terminated his suspension. In the summer of 1998, Sprewell's lawsuit was dismissed. That fall, Sprewell returned to the NBA as a player for the New York Knicks.

Sprewell's return was delayed along with the NBA season by a labor dispute which resulted in a lock out by NBA owners. The players were led by union representative Patrick Ewing and by union head Billy Hunter, both African American. The dispute centered around the players's efforts to loosen restrictions on salaries for rookies and limits on free agency. The owners countered with demands of reducing salaries and preserving free agent restrictions. The lockout finally ended in early January with the owners winning most of their demands. The NBA is the first professional sports league in the modern era to have restrictions on the maximum salary a player can earn. In addition, most free agent restrictions are still in place. The rookie salary cap, however, was discarded. Play resumed for the league with an abbreviated schedule.

◆ OTHER SPORTS

African American athletes have excelled in track and field, winning medals at various Olympiads and other competitions. This tradition began at the 1908 London Olympics, when John Baxtor Taylor became the first African American to capture a gold medal as part of the 4-by-400-meter relay team.

Jesse Owens was the star of the first half of the twentieth century. Owens is best known for his four gold medal performance at the 1936 Olympics in Berlin, Germany. However, it was on May 25, 1935, at Ann Arbor, Michigan, that Jesse Owens provided the greatest performance in track and field history at the Big Ten Championships as a member of Ohio State University. Owens began this day by equalling the world record in the 100-yard dash. He then proceeded to set the world records in the broad jump, 220-yard dash, and 220-yard low hurdles.

Owens began a string of medal-winning performances by African Americans in track and field. At the 1960 Olympics, Ralph Boston broke Owens's long jump record to win the gold medal. In so doing, he also became one of only two track stars to break a world record on six separate occasions. Rafer Johnson won the decathlon in the same Olympics. Bob Beamon, at the 1968 Mexico City Games, jumped nearly 29', 2 1/2" in the long jump to break his own world record by approximately two feet. Beamon's record would stand for a quarter of a century, until finally topped by Mike Powell. In 1984, in Los Angeles, Carl Lewis became the first athlete since Owens in 1936 to win four gold medals. Edwin Moses became the greatest 400- meter hurdler in history, winning gold medals in 1976 and 1984 as well as winning 122 straight races. At the 1992 Olympic Games, Michael Johnson became the next African American star, winning the 400-meter dash. At the 1996 Olympics in Atlanta, Johnson became the first man to win the 200-meter and 400-meter races in the same games.

One of the most controversial events in Olympic history occurred in 1968 during an awards ceremony. After finishing first and third respectively, in the 200-meter dash, Tommie Smith and John Carlos, while on the victory stand, raised their arms in unison with black gloves on their clenched fists. This became known as the "Black power salute." Their protest caused them to lose their medals.

Michael Johnson holding the gold medal that he won at the 1996 Olympic Games in Atlanta (Archive Photos, Inc.).

The professional tennis community was largely devoid of African Americans through World War II, as they were not welcome by the U.S. Lawn Tennis Association (USLTA). In a sport primarily associated with the upper class, the only avenues of competition open for African Americans were universities and colleges, clubs and various minor tournaments. Shortly after the war, the USLTA loosened its discrimination policy and, in 1948, Oscar Johnson became the first African American player to win a USLTA-sanctioned event.

Arthur Ashe, a classy and congenial champion, won the Australian Open in 1970 and the Wimbledon title in 1975, along with several less celebrated tournaments during his career. He represented the United States as a member of the Davis Cup team ten times and was its captain from 1981 to 1984. Ashe also made contributions off the court. He made significant contributions as a human rights activist and retained a dignity and grace during his battle with AIDS. In 1996 MaliVai Washington became the first African American since Ashe to reach the Wimbledon finals.

African Americans's attempts to break into golf prior to World War II paralleled those of their tennis counter-

Arthur Ashe holding the Wimbledon Trophy above his head in 1975 (AP/Wide World Photos, Inc.).

Tiger Woods (AP/Wide World Photos, Inc.)

parts. However, the Professional Golfers Association (PGA) did not rescind its white-only policy until 1959, when Charlie Sifford became the first African American to be issued a PGA card as an "approved player." In 1967 Renee Powell became the first African American female to be issued a LPGA card. Sifford was the best known of the initial participants on the tour. He was the first to win a predominantly white event with his victory at the 1957 Long Beach Open. In 1975 Lee Elder became the first African American to compete at the Masters tournament. In the 1980s Calvin Peete enjoyed success on the tour and competed in the 1983 Ryder Cup.

However, not until the arrival of Tiger Woods in the mid-1990s did an African American golfer become a superstar. Woods was a child prodigy, winning several junior tournaments before he was a teenager. In 1994 Woods became the first African American to win the U.S. Amateur title. He repeated this feat the next two years, becoming the first man to win the amateur title three years in a row. In 1997, after becoming a professional, Woods won the Masters tournament with a record score. He also rose to the ranking of the world's top player. These accomplishments indicate the level of

fame Woods has achieved. He has become the preeminent African American athlete with the retirement of Michael Jordan and has several endorsement deals.

African American luminaries exist in other sports. By winning the Brunswick Memorial World Open, George Branam became the first African American bowler to win a Professional Bowling Association (PBA) title. The weightlifter John Davis was the first athlete of any race to win eight consecutive World and Olympic Championships, during a career spanning three decades. Superlative bodybuilder Lee Haney reached the top of his field by winning eight consecutive Mr. Olympia titles from 1984 to 1991. Chris Dickerson won this award in 1982. At the turn of the nineteenth century, cyclist Marshall Taylor, was among the three most celebrated African American athletes in the world. During the same era, jockey Isaac Murphy, viewed as the greatest in the world at his craft, was part of a triumphant half century of African American jockeys. Oliver Lewis won the inaugural Kentucky Derby aboard Aristedes, in 1875. However, no African American has ridden in the Derby since 1911.

One sport that African Americans have had a negligible influence is auto racing. Willie T. Ribbs is the only

African American to drive at the Indianapolis 500 and has failed in his efforts to put together a successful NASCAR team. Julius Erving and former football star Joe Washington are the first African American owners of a NASCAR team but race with a white driver. Wendell Scott is the only African American to win a NASCAR race, with that win coming in the 1960s.

◆ WOMEN IN SPORTS

Although not provided with the same opportunities that have been traditionally afforded to men, African American women have made a significant contribution to the sports world. African American women are on the vanguard of the new opportunities, achieving success in sports as varied as tennis to basketball.

In 1948, Alice Coachman became the first African American woman to capture an Olympic gold medal in the high jump. Wilma Rudolph overcame debilitating childhood illnesses to win three golds at the 1960 Olympiad in Rome. Her teammate, 15-year-old Barbara Jones, became the youngest female to win a gold medal in track and field. In the 1968 games, Wyomia Tyus became the second African American to win more than one gold medal in one Olympiad as well as the first to set world records in two different events. In 1988, Debi Thomas became the first African American woman to win an Olympic medal in figure skating. Florence Griffith Joyner won four medals during the 1988 Olympiad, including three gold medals. Jackie Joyner-Kersee, owner of two Olympic gold medals and Gail Devers, who has overcome the effects of Graves' disease to win a gold medal at the 1992 Olympic Games, are recent stars.

The first female African American athlete to dominate her sport was tennis's Althea Gibson. A superb athlete, Gibson was named 1957's female athlete of the year during which she captured the prestigious Wimbledon singles title and U.S. Lawn Tennis Association championship. She won both titles again in 1958 and was the undisputed number one women's player in the world during those years. She became the first African American woman to capture a Grand Slam event in 1956 with her singles and doubles championships at the French Open. Zina Garrison-Jackson was the next prominent female African American tennis player, eventually reaching a top-ten ranking. She was also named Female Athlete of the Year in 1981.

In the late 1990s the Williams sisters, Venus and Serena, entered the international tennis scene, bringing new attention to the sport among African Americans. Venus, the eldest reached the finals of the 1997 U.S. Open before losing to Martina Hingis. Serena came along slower, but in 1999 reached the finals of the Lipton

Althea Gibson holding the Kent Trophy in 1957 (AP/Wide World Photos, Inc.).

Championships only to lose to her older sister. In 1999, Venus and Serena Williams, both top-ten players, won the French Open women's doubles title.

Basketball has been a major outlet for African American female athletes. Cheryl Miller is one of the most famous female basketball players. She was named All-American at the conclusion of each of her four years at the University of Southern California, was national player of the year three times, and was inducted in the Basketball Hall of Fame in 1994. The decade of the 1970s featured the great center Lusia Harris, the first woman to be inducted into the Basketball Hall of Fame. Others who have left their marks in basketball annals include University of Kansas star Lynette Woodard, perhaps best known as the first female member of the Harlem Globetrotters in 1985.

In 1997 two professional basketball leagues for women were established. The WNBA, supported by the men's NBA, and the ABL. Both leagues allowed stars such as Cynthia Cooper, Lisa Leslie, Sheryl Swoopes, and Chamique Holdsclaw the chance to exhibit their skills beyond the college level. The ABL folded before it could launch its third season.

Lisa Leslie (AP/Wide World Photos, Inc.)

Dominique Dawes performing at the 1996 Olympic Games in Atlanta (AP/Wide World Photos, Inc.).

Other notables in sports include the late volleyball player Flo Hyman; bodybuilder Lenda Murray, who won the Ms. Olympia title six times; Lyle (Toni) Stone who was the first African American woman to play professional baseball with the Indianapolis Clowns of the Negro American League in 1953; and Olympic gymnast Dominique Dawes. In 1978, Wendy Hilliard became the first African American member of the U.S. National Rhythmic Gymnastics Team.

Unfortunately, very few of the above mentioned women ever had the opportunity to display their talents on a professional level. Women's athletics has long been hamstrung by the lack of non-amateur forums in which African American female athletes could participate. For many, the Olympic Games or intercollegiate athletics have been the final step of their careers.

Women's athletics received a boost with the enactment of Title IX of the Education Amendment Act of 1972, which stipulated that any university receiving federal funds was obligated to provide an equal or proportionate number of scholarships for women. While the law provides opportunities to women, it has been criticized in its implementation as many universities have cut men's programs to fund scholarships for women.

◆ ATHLETES, COACHES, AND SPORTS EXECUTIVES

(To locate biographical profiles more readily, please consult the index at the back of the book.)

Henry "Hank" Aaron (1934–)
Baseball Player, Sports Executive

Henry "Hank" Aaron was born in Mobile, Alabama, on February 5, 1934. He played sandlot ball as a teenager and later played for a local team named the Black Bears. He first played professional baseball with the Indianapolis Clowns of the Negro American League.

In June of 1952, Aaron's contract was purchased by the Boston Braves. The following season, playing for their minor league team in Jacksonville, his .362 average led the South Atlantic League. In 1954 he was promoted to the Braves, then based in Milwaukee.

Aaron enjoyed perhaps his finest season in 1957, when he was named Most Valuable Player and led his team to a world championship. He batted .322, with 44 homers, 132 RBIs, and scored 118 runs.

In 1974 Aaron became the all-time home run leader when he hit his 715th home run, breaking Babe Ruth's mark of 714 home runs. He then finished his career in Milwaukee with the American League's Brewers. He completed his career with a total of 755 home runs.

During his career, Aaron won a pair of batting titles and hit over .300 in 12 seasons. He won the home run and RBI crowns four times apiece, hit 40 or more homers eight times, and hit at least 20 home runs for twenty consecutive years, a National League record. In addition, he was named to twenty consecutive All-Star teams.

In January of 1982, Aaron was elected by the Baseball Writers Association to the Baseball Hall of Fame. Since the mid-1990s, he has served as vice president/assistant to the president for the Braves.

Kareem Abdul-Jabbar (1947–)
Basketball Player

Abdul-Jabbar was born Ferdinand Lewis Alcindor, Jr. on April 16, 1947, in New York City. In high school, at 7' 1/2" tall, he established a New York City record of 2,067 points and 2,002 rebounds, leading Power Memorial High School to three straight championships. Power won 95 and lost only six games during his years with the team.

Abdul-Jabbar combined great height with catlike moves and a deft shooting touch to lead UCLA to three consecutive NCAA Championships. Twice, as a sophomore and a senior, he was chosen as the top collegiate player in the country. He finished his career at UCLA as the ninth all-time collegiate scorer, accumulating 2,325 points in 88 games for an average of 26.4 points per game. After leading UCLA to its third consecutive NCAA title, Abdul-Jabbar signed a contract with the Milwaukee Bucks for $1.4 million.

In his rookie season, 1969–1970, he led the Bucks, a recently established expansion club, to a second place finish in the Eastern Division. After being voted Rookie of the Year, he went on to win the scoring championships in 1971 and 1972. He won a world championship in 1971. In 1973, he finished second in scoring with a 30.2 point average, but became dissatisfied with life in Milwaukee. At the end of the 1974–1975 season he was traded to the L.A. Lakers. Abdul-Jabbar enjoyed a very successful career with the Lakers, leading the team to NBA championships in 1980, 1982, 1985, 1987, and 1988.

Abdul-Jabbar converted to the Hanafi sect of Islam while in college. Greatly influenced by the life and struggles of Malcolm X, he believes that the Islamic religion is distinct from the nationalistic Black Muslims.

Kareem Abdul-Jabbar shooting his patented "sky hook" (AP/Wide World Photos, Inc.).

Abdul-Jabbar announced that his retirement after the 1988–1989 season, one year after the Lakers had won back-to-back World Championships. He was elected into the Basketball Hall of Fame in 1994.

Muhammad Ali (1942–)
Boxer

Born Cassius Clay, in Louisville, Kentucky, on January 17, 1942, Ali started boxing as a youth. After winning

Muhammad Ali (Corbis Corporation [Bellevue])

the 1960 Olympic gold medal as light-heavyweight, Clay turned pro. In 1963 he converted to Islam, and changed his name to Muhammad Ali. A year later, Ali won the world heavyweight championship by knocking out Sonny Liston.

After nine successful title defenses, Ali refused to serve in the armed forces during the Vietnam War. He maintained that it was contrary to Muslim beliefs. Stripped of his title and banned from boxing in the United States, Ali was jailed, but he refused to back down and was finally cleared on a technicality by the U.S. Supreme Court in 1970.

Coming back to the ring after a three and one-half year layoff, he was defeated by heavyweight champion Joe Frazier. In 1974 when neither held a title belt, Ali defeated Frazier to earn a shot at regaining the title.

Few fans gave Ali a chance against heavyweight champion George Foreman when they met in Zaire on October 30, 1974. A 4–1 underdog at ring time, Ali amazed the boxing world and knocked out his stronger, younger opponent. After regaining the crown, Ali defeated Frazier in their third fight in Manilla. Ali then lost his title to Leon Spinks in 1978, briefly regained it, and then retired.

In 1980 Ali came out of retirement to fight his former sparring partner, heavyweight champion Larry Holmes. He was defeated by Holmes and after a 1981 loss to Trevor Berbick, retired.

Forced to fight when he was past his prime, Ali took tremendous beatings late in his career. This led to the former champion being diagnosed with Parkinson's disease late in the 1980s. Despite the disease, Ali has maintained a public presence, being chosen to light the Olympic torch at the 1996 Summer Olympics in Atlanta.

Henry Armstrong (1912–1988)
Boxer

The only fighter ever to hold three titles at the same time is Henry Armstrong, who accomplished this feat on August 17, 1938, when he added the lightweight championship to his featherweight and welterweight titles.

Armstrong was born on December 12, 1912, in St. Louis, Missouri. In 1929, while fighting under the name of Melody Jackson, he was knocked out in his professional debut in Pittsburgh. Two weeks later he won his first fight. For the next eight years he traveled from coast to coast, fighting until he was finally given a shot at the featherweight title on October 20, 1937. He won the title when he defeated Petey Sarron.

Less than a year later, on May 31, 1938, Armstrong picked up his second title with a decision over welterweight champion Barney Ross. Within three months he added the lightweight crown, winning a decision over Lou Ambers.

Armstrong was inducted into the Black Athletes Hall of Fame in 1975 and died in 1988.

Arthur Ashe (1943–1993)
Tennis Player, Television Commentator

Born in Richmond, Virginia, Ashe learned the game of tennis at the Richmond Racket Club, which had been formed by local African American enthusiasts. Dr. R. W. Johnson, who had also served as an advisor and benefactor to Althea Gibson, sponsored Ashe's tennis.

By 1958, Ashe reached the semifinals in the under-15 division of the National Junior Championships. In 1960 and 1961, he won the Junior Indoors Singles title. In 1961, Ashe entered UCLA on a tennis scholarship.

While still an amateur, Ashe won the United States Amateur Tennis Championship and the U.S. Open Tennis Championship and became the first African American ever named to a Davis Cup Team.

In 1975, Ashe defeated Jimmy Connors to win Wimbledon and won the World Championship Tennis singles title over Bjorn Borg.

In 1979, at the age of 35, Ashe suffered a heart attack. Following quadruple bypass heart surgery, Ashe retired from active tennis. He began writing a nationally syndicated column and contributed monthly articles to *Tennis Magazine*. He wrote a tennis diary *Portrait in Motion*, his autobiography *Off the Court*, and the book *Advantage Ashe*. In addition, he compiled the historical work *A Hard Road to Glory: A History of the African-American Athlete*.

Ashe was named captain of the U.S. Davis Cup team in 1981. He was a former president and active member of the board of directors of the Association of Tennis Professionals, and a co-founder of the National Junior Tennis League. Late in his career, he also served as a television sports commentator.

In April of 1992, Ashe announced that he had contracted AIDS as the result of a tainted blood transfusion received during heart bypass surgery. He died on February 6, 1993.

Ernie Banks (1931–)
Baseball Player, Banking Executive, Community Activist

Born in Dallas, Banks was slightly built at 6'1", 180 pounds, but his powerful wrists help him produce a career total of 512 home runs. His 44 homers and five grand slams in 1955 were single season records for shortstops. His best season was 1958, during which he led the National League in at-bats (617), home runs (47), runs batted in (129), and slugging percentage (.614). He was named the league's Most Valuable Player after the 1958 and 1959 seasons.

Banks, who was moved to first base during the 1961 season and played in 717 consecutive games, may have the somewhat dubious distinction of being the greatest player to never play in a World Series, as his Cubs rarely produced winning ballclubs during his tenure.

Banks, along with second baseman Gene Baker, formed the majors' first all-African American double play combination. He was the second African American to play for the Cubs, after Baker. Banks was elected to the Baseball Hall of Fame in 1977, and is also a member of the Texas Sports Hall of Fame.

After his playing career, Banks became a bank executive with Seaway National Bank. He remained visible in the community, becoming a board member of the Chicago Transit Authority, the Chicago Metropolitan YMCA, and the Los Angeles Urban League.

Elgin Baylor (1934–)
Basketball Player, Basketball Coach, Sports Executive

Born on September 16, 1934, in Washington, DC, Elgin Baylor first attracted attention while attending Spingarn High School. He became an All-American at Seattle University, leading the Chieftains to the Final Four in 1958. In 1959, Baylor made his professional debut with the Minneapolis Lakers, becoming the first rookie to be named Most Valuable Player in the All-Star Game. He also was named to the All-League team, setting a scoring record of 64 points in a single game.

After five years as a superstar, Baylor injured his knee during a 1965 playoff game against the Bullets and never played at the same level again. His career point total of 23,149 is fourth highest in NBA history, and his scoring average of 27.4 is the second highest. His best year was 1961–1962, when he averaged 38.2 points a game. When he retired in 1968, Baylor had been an All-Pro nine times and had played in eight consecutive All-Star games.

Baylor was inducted into the Black Athletes Hall of Fame in 1975, and the Basketball Hall of Fame in 1976. He was head coach of the New Orleans Jazz in 1978–1979. Since 1986, Baylor has been executive vice president of basketball operations for the Los Angeles Clippers.

Barry Bonds (1964–)
Baseball Player

Barry Bonds was born on July 24, 1964, in Riverside, California. He was exposed to baseball heavily during childhood. Bonds's father, Bobby, and his godfather, Hall of Famer Willie Mays, were Major League outfielders. Bonds played three sports in high school—baseball, basketball, and football. Although he was offered a contract to play with the San Francisco Giants upon graduation, he opted to attend college at Arizona State University.

After success at the collegiate level, Bonds was selected by the Pittsburgh Pirates as the sixth selection in the 1985 baseball draft. He spent a brief time in the minor leagues before being called up by the National League club at the age of 21. During his rookie season, he led all first-year players in home runs, runs batted in, stolen bases, and walks.

In 1990 Bonds earned Most Valuable Player (MVP) honors. He hit 32 home runs, stole 52 bases, batted in 114 runs, scored 104 runs, and earned his first of four consecutive Gold Gloves for defensive play during the year. With Bonds's support the Pirates won the Eastern Division of the National League but ended up losing to the Cincinnati Reds in a postseason series.

The Pirates entered the playoffs during the next two seasons, but met with postseason frustration both years. The 1992 campaign was notable because Bonds earned his second MVP award for his stellar performance. Regardless of his success during the regular season, however, Bonds was unable to contribute in the same fashion during the playoffs.

After the completion of the 1992 season, Bonds signed a lucrative deal with the San Francisco Giants. The contract provided him with $43.75 million over the course of six years, making him the highest paid player at the time. Although some critics doubted that any player was worth such a salary, Bonds quieted them by earning another MVP award on the strength of a season that featured 46 home runs and 123 RBIs. The Giants failed to make the playoffs, though, losing the honor to the Atlanta Braves on the last day of the season.

Although Bonds has continued to post strong numbers through the remainder of the 1990s, his team has made the playoffs only once, in 1997. That year they lost to the Florida Marlins. Bonds's continued success during the regular season is remarkable in light of the fact that opposing pitchers do not often offer him decent pitches. They would rather walk Bonds than risk giving up an extra base hit against him.

Bonds is one of only a handful of players, including his father, who have hit more than three hundred home runs and have stolen more than three hundred bases.

Lou Brock (1939–)
Baseball Player, Baseball Coach, Business Executive

Born in El Dorado, Arkansas, Lou Brock is one of the greatest base stealers in baseball history. He stole 938 bases during his 19-year career with the Chicago Cubs and St. Louis Cardinals. In 1977, Brock collected his 893rd steal, eclipsing the mark that had been held by Ty Cobb for 49 years. In 1974, at the age of 35, Brock's 114 steals broke Maury Wills's single season record. Brock registered at least 50 steals in 12 consecutive seasons and at the time of his retirement was the only player to hold both the Major League single season and career record in any major statistical category.

In 1967, Brock led the league in at-bats, runs scored, and steals. The following season he set the pace in triples and steals, leading the Cardinals to pennants both seasons. With Brock, St. Louis also won World Championships in 1964 and 1967.

Brock went on to become a coach and business executive and was presented with the Jackie Robinson Award by *Ebony* magazine. He won the Roberto Clemente Award in 1975. He was also the recipient of the B'nai B'rith Brotherhood Award and was voted Man of the Year by the St. Louis Jaycees. Brock was inducted into the Baseball Hall of Fame in 1985.

Jim Brown (AP/Wide World Photos, Inc.)

Jim Brown (1936–)
Football Player, Actor, Community Activist

James Nathaniel Brown was born February 17, 1936, on St. Simon Island, Georgia, but moved to Manhasset, Long Island, New York, when he was seven. While at Manhasset High School he became an outstanding competitor in baseball, football, track and field, basketball, and lacrosse and following graduation had a choice of 42 college scholarships, as well as professional offers from both the New York Yankees and the Boston Braves. Brown chose to attend Syracuse University. An All-American performer in both football and lacrosse, he turned down the opportunity to compete in the decathlon at the 1956 Olympic games because it would have conflicted with his football schedule. He also spurned a three-year $150,000 offer to become a professional fighter.

In 1957 Brown began his professional football career with the Cleveland Browns. In his rookie season, he led the league in rushing, helped Cleveland to a division championship, and was unanimously named Rookie of the Year. Brown broke the single season and lifetime rushing and scoring records and was an All-League fullback. His records include most yards gained, lifetime (12,312), and most touchdowns, lifetime (106). He was voted Football Back of the Decade for 1950–1960.

Brown announced his retirement in the summer of 1966, deciding to devote his attention to his movie and business careers. He has made several films including *Rio Conchos, The Dirty Dozen,* and *100 Rifles.* In addition to his film activities., he is president and founder of Amer-I-can and an outspoken activist in issues relating to African Americans and sports.

Roy Campanella (1921–1993)
Baseball Player

Roy Campanella was born on November 19, 1921, in Philadelphia, and began playing semi-professional baseball at the age of 15 with the Bacharach Giants. In 1946, Campanella was signed by the Brooklyn Dodgers. Over the next eight years, the Dodger catcher played with five National League pennant winners and one world championship team. He played on seven consecutive National League All-Star teams (1949 to 1955) and won three Most Valuable Player Awards (1951, 1953, and 1955).

In January 1958, Campanella's career was ended by an automobile accident which left him paralyzed and confined to a wheelchair. In 1969, he was inducted into the Baseball Hall of Fame and into the Black Athletes Hall of Fame in 1975. Campanella died in 1993.

Wilt Chamberlain (1936–)
Basketball Player, Actor, Entrepreneur, Community Activist

Wilt Chamberlain was born in Philadelphia on August 21, 1936. By the time he entered high school, he was already 6'11". When he graduated from high school, he had his choice of 77 major colleges, and 125 smaller schools. He chose Kansas University, but left after his junior year despite being a two-time All-American and playing in the 1957 Final Four.

Before entering the NBA in 1959, Chamberlain played with the Harlem Globetrotters. Although dominating the sport statistically from his rookie season, Chamberlain was a member of only two championship teams, the 1967 Philadelphia 76ers and the 1972 Los Angeles Lakers. For his efforts in defeating the Knicks in the 1972 series, including playing the final game with both hands painfully injured, he was voted MVP. At the start of the 1974 season, he left the Lakers to become player-coach of the San Diego Conquistadors (ABA) for a reported $500,000 contract.

Wilt Chamberlain holds most major records for a single game including most points (100); field goals made (36); free throws (28); and rebounds (55). His season records include: highest scoring average (50.4); highest field goal percentage (.727); and most rebounds (23,924).

Chamberlain was inducted into the Basketball Hall of Fame in 1978 and has owned various businesses since he left professional basketball. He is involved with various charitable groups and has appeared in several motion pictures.

Alice Coachman (1923–)
Track and Field Athlete

Alice Coachman, who attended both the Tuskegee Institute and Albany State University, was the first African American woman to win an Olympic gold medal and the only American woman to earn a gold medal at the 1948 Games, winning the medal in the high jump. She was also an outstanding basketball player, earning All-American honors as a guard at Tuskegee.

Born in Albany, Georgia, on November 9, 1923, Coachman made a name for herself when, as a seventh grader, she high jumped 5'4 1/2", less than an inch from the world record. She also won the Amateur Athletic Union (AAU) Outdoor 50-meter title four times; 100-meters three times; and the high jump ten times. Coachman won the 50-meter twice and the high jump three times during indoor meets.

Coachman's ten victories without a loss, between 1939 and 1948, is an AAU record. She is a member of eight different halls of fame including the National Track and Field Hall of Fame, the Black Athletes Hall of Fame, the Tuskegee Hall of Fame, and the Georgia State Hall of Fame.

Leonard S. Coleman, Jr. (1949–)
National League of Professional Baseball Clubs President, State Government Official, Business Executive

Leonard Coleman, Jr. was born in Newark, but he grew up in Montclair, New Jersey. At Montclair High School, Coleman played baseball and football. He was named all-state and all-American during his senior year. He continued playing baseball and football as an undergraduate at Princeton University, becoming the first African American to score a touchdown for that prestigious Ivy League school. As a sophomore, he joined two other African American players in a protest, charging the Princeton football program with violations of the university's policy of equal opportunity for minorities. When the complaints drew national attention, Coleman and his two friends were dismissed from the team, but a panel charged with investigating the incident urged greater sensitivity toward minority students in the ath-

Cynthia Cooper (AP/Wide World Photos, Inc.)

baseball after they leave the Little Leagues. In 1994, Coleman was unanimously chosen to succeed Bill White as president of the National League.

During his tenure, he has carried out his vision for professional baseball—less drug abuse among players including the discouragement of chewing tobacco usage; less fighting during games; and more promotion of baseball as entertainment for the whole family. Coleman has also been a crusader for the rights of African American baseball players, especially former Negro League participants and their spouses.

Cynthia Cooper (1963–)
Basketball Player

Cynthia Cooper was born in Chicago, Illinois, in 1963. She played college basketball at the University of Southern California. Her team at USC is one of the greatest in the history of women's college basketball. It included Hall of Famer Cheryl Miller and won NCAA titles in 1983 and 1984.

Following college, Cooper spent many years playing professional basketball in Europe. In 1988 she was on the U.S. Olympic team that captured a gold medal at the Seoul Olympiad. She was also a member of the bronze medal team in 1992 at the Barcelona Olympiad.

With the formation of the Women's National Basketball Association in 1997, Cooper had the chance to compete professionally in the United States. The 5'10" guard is a member of the Houston Comets. Cooper has become one of the most prominent players in the league, winning the WNBA's first two MVP awards. In addition, she led the Comets to the first two league titles and was named the MVP of the 1997 championship game.

Willie Davis (1934–)
Football Player, Television Analyst, Business Executive

Willie Davis was born in Lisbon, Louisiana. After he played college football at Grambling, he was signed by the Cleveland Browns as an offensive lineman during the first two years of his NFL career (1958–1959). Moving to the Green Bay Packers for the 1960 season, Davis played for ten more seasons and enjoyed a success on a team that won several championships.

Davis was an All-Pro in 1962 and from the 1964 to the 1967 seasons. He was part of a Packers dynasty which included championships in 1961, 1962, 1965, 1966, and 1967, and did not miss a single game during his career with Green Bay. Following the conclusion of his career, Davis earned a M.B.A. from the University of Chicago which helped him to launch a career in business and community relations.

Davis is the president and owner of All-Pro Broadcasting, Inc., and had served on the Board of Directors

letic program. Coleman attributes that experience to helping him develop a keen social consciousness.

After earning his bachelor's degree from Princeton in 1971, Coleman moved on to Harvard University, where he pursued dual master's degrees in public administration and education. In 1976, he accepted a position as a missionary to Africa for the Protestant Episcopal Church. All told he spent four years in Africa, serving in 17 different countries and cultivating a close friendship with South African Archbishop Desmond Tutu.

Returning to the United States in 1980, Coleman first served as president of the Greater Newark Urban Coalition. In 1982, he was appointed commissioner of the New Jersey Department of Energy. In 1986, Coleman was named commissioner of the New Jersey Department of Community Affairs. In 1988, he left the public sector for a job as an investment banker with Kidder, Peabody & Co. Eventually, he was named vice president of municipal finance.

In 1991, Coleman accepted his first position with Major League Baseball as director of marketing development. In that position, he was credited with further encouraging Reviving Baseball in the Inner Cities (R.B.I.), an initiative aimed at keeping city teenagers active in of the Joseph Schlitz Brewing Company. Additionally, he is on the advisory board of the Black Peace Officers Association and president and director of the Los Angeles Urban League.

Formerly a football analyst for NBC television, Davis has done public relations and promotional work for the Chrysler Corporation. He was named "Man of the Year" by the NAACP in 1978. Davis was elected to the Football Hall of Fame in 1981 and is also a member of the NAIA Hall of Fame.

Dominique Dawes (1976–)
Gymnast, Actress

Dawes was born in Silver Spring, Maryland, in 1976. She is the first African American to excel in gymnastics, becoming only the second African American to qualify for the U.S. Olympic team for gymnastics in 1992.

Dawes began competing in gymnastics at the age of five, eventually becoming a national and Olympic champion. In 1992 at the Barcelona Olympiad she was a member of the U.S. team awarded the bronze medal. At the U.S. National Championships in 1994, Dawes became the first African American to win the all-around title as best gymnast. In 1996 at the Atlanta Olympiad she won two individual bronze medals as well as being a member of the U.S. team awarded the gold medal.

In the fall of 1995 Dawes entered Stanford University. She also appeared in the Broadway musical *Grease* in 1996.

Lee Elder (1934–)
Golfer, Entrepreneur

Lee Elder was born in Washington, DC, on July 14, 1934. He first was involved with golf as a caddie at the age of fifteen. After his father's death during World War II, Elder and his mother moved to Los Angeles, where he met the famed African American golfer Ted Rhodes. He was later drafted by the U.S. Army, where he sharpened his skills as captain of the golf team.

Following his discharge from the army, he began to teach golf. In 1962, he debuted as a professional, winning the United Golf Association (an African American organization) national title. Elder had played seventeen years with the United Golf Association, prior to his participation in the PGA. He debuted with the PGA in November of 1967, finishing one stroke out of the money. In thirty PGA tournaments, Elder earned $38,000. He was the first African American professional golfer to reach $1 million in earnings and, in 1975, was the first to play at the Masters.

In 1997, when Tiger Woods became the first African American to win the Masters, Elder was present and

Lee Elder (AP/Wide World Photos, Inc.)

was thanked by Woods for his pioneering efforts in the integration of the PGA Tour and the Masters. Elder owns a public relations firm.

Julius Erving (1950–)
Basketball Player, Television Analyst

Julius Erving was born in Hempstead, Long Island, on February 22, 1950. As a player at Roosevelt High School, Erving made the All-County and All-Long Island teams. He was awarded an athletic scholarship to the University of Massachusetts, and after completing his junior year, signed a $500,000, four-year contract with the Virginia Squires of the ABA. Voted Rookie of the Year in 1972, he eventually signed with the New Jersey Nets for $2.8 million over four years.

In his first season with the Nets, Erving led the league in scoring for the second consecutive year and led his team to the ABA championship. After being traded to the Philadelphia 76ers, Erving became a favorite with fans, leading the team to the NBA championship in 1983. He became the 13th player to score 20,000 points. Erving retired following the 1986–1987 season. He is credited with popularizing the slam dunk and the vertical game in basketball. He is presently a broadcaster for NBC. He

George Foreman (AP/Wide World Photos, Inc.)

was elected to the National Basketball Hall of Fame in 1992.

George Foreman (1948–)
Boxer, Minister

Born in Marshall, Texas, George Foreman has emerged as one of boxing's most endearing figures. During his childhood in Houston, Foreman was a truant, snatching purses and participating in petty larcenies. His early success in boxing included a gold medal performance at the 1968 summer Olympic Games. After turning pro, he quickly became a top contender, recording 42 knockouts in his first 47 bouts.

Foreman captured the heavyweight title with his victory over Joe Frazier, in Kingston, Jamaica, on January 22, 1973. Having twice defended his belt successfully, he prepared to face Muhammad Ali on October 30, 1974, in Kinshasa, Zaire. The fight became known as the "Rumble in the Jungle." Despite being a 4–1 favorite, Foreman was out-fought by Ali who used his "rope-a-dope" tactic to tire Foreman and knock him out in the eighth round.

Foreman soon retired to become a minister and transformed his image into that of a congenial and very

popular ex-champion. He initiated a comeback and recaptured the heavyweight crown when he defeated Michael Moorer on November 5, 1994. Foreman, thereby, became the oldest man in history to win the heavyweight championship of the world. He retired shortly thereafter to his gym in Houston.

Althea Gibson (1927–)
Tennis Player, Community Activist, Sports Consultant, Author

Althea Gibson was born on August 25, 1927, in Silver, South Carolina, but was raised in Harlem. She began her tennis career when she entered and won the Department of Parks Manhattan Girls' Tennis Championship. In 1942, she began to receive professional coaching at the Cosmopolitan Tennis Club, and a year later, won the New York State Negro Girls Singles Title. In 1945 and 1946, she won the National Negro Girls Singles championship, and in 1948 won the title in the Women's Division.

A year later Gibson entered Florida A&M, where she played tennis and basketball. In 1950, she was runner-up for the National Indoor Championship, and became the first African American to play at the U.S. Open at the

Forest Hills Country Club. The following year she became the first African American to play at Wimbledon.

In 1957 Gibson won the Wimbledon singles crown, and teamed with Darlene Hard to win the doubles championship. In 1957 and 1958, Gibson won the U.S. Open Women's Singles title.

Gibson has served as a recreation manager, a member of the New Jersey State Athletic Control Board, on the Governor's Council on Physical Fitness, and as a sports consultant. She is also the author of the book *I Always Wanted to be Somebody.*

Bob Gibson (1935–)
Baseball Player, Baseball Coach, Radio Announcer

Bob Gibson was born in Omaha, Nebraska, into poverty. Fatherless, he was one of seven children who lived in a four-room wooden shack. Denied a spot on Omaha Technical High School's baseball team because he was African American, he was permitted to join the track and field and basketball teams. He attended Creighton University in Omaha and became the first African American athlete to play both basketball and baseball.

Gibson's skill at basketball allowed him to play with the Harlem Globetrotters. While with them, he accepted an offer to join the St. Louis Cardinals minor league team at Omaha for a salary of $3,000 and a $1,000 bonus. Gibson debuted with the Cardinals in 1959, beginning a Hall of Fame career that lasted 17 seasons and included 5 twenty-victory seasons and 13 consecutive winning seasons. His highlights include a 1968 campaign in which he recorded a remarkable 13 shutouts, 22 victories, 268 strikeouts and an Earned Run Average of 1.12, still a National League record in 1996.

During his career, Gibson recorded 3,117 strikeouts and finished with an ERA of 2.91. He won seven and lost two games in three World Series appearances, with an ERA of 1.89. In Game 1 of the 1968 series he struck out 17 Detroit Tigers. Gibson pitched the Cardinals to World Championships in 1964 and 1967.

Gibson has served as pitching coach with the New York Mets and Atlanta Braves and has been a special pitching consultant to many teams. He has also broadcast for the St. Louis Cardinals.

Josh Gibson (1911–1947)
Baseball Player

Josh Gibson was a catcher whose entire 16-year career was spent in the Negro League. His career began in 1929 and with the exception of a stint with the Pittsburgh Crawfords, between 1934 and 1936, and one

Josh Gibson was reputed to be the greatest hitter ever in the Negro Baseball League (Corbis Corporation [Bellevue]).

season in Mexico in 1941, Gibson played with the Homestead Grays.

Gibson was born in Buena Vista, Georgia, in 1911, and moved to Pittsburgh, where he left school at the age of 14 to work for Gimbels Department store. Gimbels had a baseball team, which is where Gibson first attracted attention. His first game with Homestead took place on July 25, 1929, when, as a spectator, he was called out of the stands to replace an injured starter in a game against the Kansas City Monarchs.

Gibson was known for his legendary power. Playing at Yankee Stadium, he once hit a home run over the left field bullpen and out of the stadium. Gibson also hit a 580-foot home run over the top of the bleachers.

Gibson died in 1947, from a stroke thought to be brought on by his alcoholism. He was elected to the Hall of Fame in 1972.

Ken Griffey, Jr. (1969–)
Baseball Player

Ken Griffey, Jr. is one of the most famous professional athletes in America at the turn of the century. Griffey's

Ken Griffey, Jr. (AP/Wide World Photos, Inc.)

talents and flair have made him one of the most popular baseball players in today's game as evidenced by his nine All-Star Game appearances.

Griffey was drafted first overall in 1987 by the Seattle Mariners while still in high school in Cincinnati. He broke into Major League Baseball in 1989 at the age of 19. He has won nine gold gloves for his play in centerfield for the Mariners and has driven in more than 100 runs six times. In 1998, Griffey accomplished the rare feat of hitting fifty home runs in back-to-back years. His chase of the single season home run record with Mark McGwire and Sammy Sosa in the summer of 1998 caught the attention of the entire nation.

Griffey's skills on the field have translated into many corporate sponsorships, making him one of the nation's most visible athletes.

Lusia Harris (1955–)
Basketball Player, Basketball Coach, Motivational Speaker

Lusia Harris was born in 1955, in Minter City, Mississippi, and participated on the silver medal-winning Olym-

pic basketball team in 1976. She was high scorer at the Olympics and at the 1975 World University and Pan American Games. In college, she led Delta State University to three Association for Intercollegiate Athletics for Women titles from 1975 to 1977. She was named Mississippi's first amateur athlete of the year in 1976. Harris was selected as Delta State's homecoming queen, the first African American so honored.

Harris, the dominant female player of her era, broke hundreds of records and won countless American and international awards. As a graduate student, she became assistant basketball coach and admissions counselor at Delta State. She played briefly with the Houston Angels of the new Women's Professional League in 1980.

In the 1990s, Harris has been coaching basketball and teaching physical education in Mississippi. In 1992, along with Nera White, Harris became the first woman inducted into the Basketball Hall of Fame. She is also a motivational speaker.

Chamique Holdsclaw (1977–)
Basketball Player

Holdsclaw was born in 1977 in Queens, New York. Holdsclaw left New York to attend the University of Tennessee and play for coach Pat Summitt.

At Tennessee, Holdsclaw became the most honored female basketball player since Cheryl Miller. Holdsclaw was a three-time All-American, two-time player-of-the-year award winner, and winner of three NCAA titles. In 1998 Holdsclaw became the first African American female basketball player to win the Sullivan Award. This award is given to the top amateur athlete in America.

Holdsclaw, a 6'2" forward, has been compared to both Cheryl Miller and Michael Jordan. She is being viewed as the commercial and athletic star to increase the visibility of the WNBA. Holdsclaw was the first pick in the 1999 WNBA draft by the Washington Mystics.

Larry Holmes (1949–)
Boxer

Holmes was born in Cuthberth, Georgia, and turned professional at the age of twenty-four after serving as sparring partner for Muhammad Ali. On June 9, 1978, he won the World Boxing Council heavyweight title from Ken Norton. On October 2, 1980, in Las Vegas, he defeated Ali by a technical knockout.

Holmes defended his title 12 times until losing to Michael Spinks on September 22, 1985, and again on April 19, 1986, in 15-round decisions. In all, Holmes held the heavyweight title for seven years, three months, and 13 days. A brief comeback attempt ended in a knockout by Mike Tyson on February 22, 1988. Holmes, who was voted one of the ten Most Outstanding Men in America by the Junior Chamber of Commerce, has continued to fight due to monetary difficulties stemming from his relationship with his former promoter Don King.

Evander Holyfield (1962–)
Boxer

Evander Holyfield is known for his championship boxing ability and his devout religious faith and humble demeanor. In boxing, a sport dominated by braggadocio and large egos, Holyfield has become a popular champion due to his talent and humility.

Holyfield was born and still resides in Atlanta, Georgia. In 1984 he won the bronze medal in the light heavyweight division after a controversial disqualification in a preliminary bout. He immediately turned professional and in 1986 won the cruiserweight title from Dwight Muhammad Qawi. By 1989 he was the undisputed cruiserweight champion.

Holyfield entered the heavyweight division that same year and in 1990 defeated Buster Douglas to win the heavyweight title. After several defenses of his title, Holyfield was defeated by Riddick Bowe in 1992 and retired due to health problems.

Holyfield, a natural light heavyweight, has always undergone strenuous training to be able to fight against the bigger fighters in the heavyweight division. In 1993 he came out of retirement to defeat Bowe and regain his title. After losing his title to Michael Moorer, Holyfield finally fought heavyweight champion Mike Tyson in 1996. Holyfield upset Tyson to regain the heavyweight title and then defeated Tyson the next year when Tyson bit Holyfield twice and was disqualified.

Reggie Jackson (1946–)
Baseball Player, Television Analyst, Sports Executive

Because of his outstanding performance in postseason play, Reggie Jackson became known as "Mr. October." During his years with the Oakland Athletics and New York Yankees, Jackson captured or tied 13 World Series records to become baseball's top record holder in series play.

Born in Wynecote, Pennsylvania, on May 18, 1946, he followed his father's encouragement to become an all-around athlete while at Cheltenham High School. He ran track, played halfback in football, and was a star hitter on the school baseball team. An outstanding football and baseball player at Arizona State University, he left after his sophomore year to join the Athletics (then located in Kansas City).

In 1968, his first full season with the Athletics, Jackson hit 29 homers and batted in 74 runs, but made 18 errors and struck out 171 times, the second worst seasonal total in baseball history. After playing a season of winter ball under Frank Robinson's direction, his performance continued to improve, and, in 1973, he batted .293, led the league in home runs (32), RBIs (117), and slugging average (.531), and was selected Most Valuable Player.

While with Oakland, Jackson helped the Athletics to three straight World Series championships, from 1972 to 1974. Later, with the New York Yankees, Jackson won the World Series in 1977 and 1978. The Yankees also won the American League pennant in 1981. In 1977, he was named Series MVP, after hitting five home runs—including three on three consecutive pitches, in the sixth and deciding game.

The first of the big money free agents, Jackson hit 144 homers, drove in 461 runs, and boosted his total career home runs to 425 while with the Yankees. Jackson retired as an active player in 1987 and has occasionally served as a commentator during baseball broadcasts. His tumultuous relationship with Yankees owner George Steinbrenner has continued through the various jobs Jackson has held with the organization. He was elected to the Baseball Hall of Fame in 1993.

Earvin "Magic" Johnson, Jr. (1959–)
Basketball Player, Basketball Coach, Sports Executive, Talk Show Host, Entrepreneur

Earvin Johnson, Jr. was born August 14, 1959, in Lansing, Michigan, and attended Everett High School. While playing for Everett he picked up the nickname "Magic" because of his ball-handling abilities. While in high school, Johnson made the All-State Team and for three years was named the United Press International Prep-Player of the Year in Michigan.

In 1977, Johnson enrolled at Michigan State University and led the Spartans to the national championship in 1979. He then turned professional and was selected by

Reggie Jackson (AP/Wide World Photos, Inc.)

the Los Angeles Lakers in the National Basketball Association draft. He led the Lakers to five NBA titles in the 1980s. Johnson played with the Lakers until his retirement in 1991 when he tested positive for the HIV virus.

Johnson was the recipient of many awards and was chosen to play on many postseason all-star teams. He was named to the All-Big Ten Team in 1977 and chosen as the NCAA Tournament-Most Valuable Player. He was also a consensus All-American selection (1979). During his professional career, he was named to the NBA All-

Rookie Team (1980) and the All-NBA Team (1982 to 1989, 1991). He was also recognized as the NBA Finals Most Valuable Player (1987) and the NBA All-Star Game Most Valuable Player (1990, 1992).

During his retirement, Johnson played on the U.S. Olympic Basketball Team in 1992 and in the 1992 NBA All-Star game, where he won another Most Valuable Player award. He also coached the Lakers briefly at the end of the 1994 season, became team vice president, and had an ownership stake in the Lakers, which he was

Earvin "Magic" Johnson celebrating his gold medal at the 1992 Olympics Games in Barcelona (Corbis Corporation [Bellevue]).

forced to surrender upon his short-lived return in 1996 as a player. Johnson hosted a late night talk show in 1998, but it was cancelled shortly afterwards. Johnson currently owns and operates the nationwide MJR theater franchise.

Jack Johnson (1878–1946)
Boxer

Jack Johnson became the first African American heavyweight champion by winning the crown from Tommy Burns in Sydney, Australia, on December 26, 1908.

Johnson was born in Galveston, Texas, on March 31, 1878. He was so tiny as a boy that he was nicknamed "Li'l Arthur," a name that stuck with him throughout his career. As a young man, he drifted around the country, making his way through Chicago, Boston, and New York. He learned to box by working out with veteran professionals whenever he could. When he finally got his chance at the title, he had already been fighting for nine years and had lost only 3 of 100 bouts.

With his victory over Burns, Johnson became the center of a bitter racial controversy, as his flamboyant lifestyle and outspokenness aroused white resentment. Public pressure forced former champion Jim Jeffries to come out of retirement and challenge Johnson for the title. When the two fought on July 4, 1910, in Reno, Nevada, Johnson knocked out Jeffries in the 14th round.

In 1913, Johnson left the United States due to legal difficulties. Two years later he defended his title against Jess Willard in Havana, Cuba, and was knocked out in the 26th round. His career record was 107 wins, 6 losses.

Johnson died on June 10, 1946, in an automobile crash in North Carolina. He was inducted into the Boxing Hall of Fame in 1954.

Michael Jordan (1963–)
Basketball Player

Michael Jordan was born in Brooklyn, New York, on February 17, 1963, and attended the University of North Carolina. He won the national championship as a freshman with the Tar Heels. As a rookie with the Chicago Bulls in 1985, Jordan was named to the All-Star team. A skilled ball handler and a slam dunk artist, he became the second NBA player in history to score more than 3,000 points in a single season in 1986.

Jordan was the NBA's individual scoring champ from 1987 through 1993. He was also named the NBA's Most Valuable Player at the end of the 1987–1988 season. In 1991, Jordan led the Chicago Bulls to their first NBA Championship and was the league's Most Valuable Player. Under Jordan's leadership, the Bulls repeated as championships in 1992 and 1993. In 1992 Jordan played for the U.S. Olympic basketball team, which captured the gold medal in Barcelona.

In October of 1993, Jordan announced his retirement from basketball to pursue another lifelong dream—to become a professional baseball player. Jordan began his professional baseball career in 1994 with the Chicago White Sox's Class A team, the Birmingham Barons. Despite having only a .202 batting average for the year, Jordan was voted the most popular man in baseball in a national poll and remained at the top of *Forbes* magazine's list of the world's top paid athletes for the third consecutive year.

In March of 1995, Jordan returned to the NBA with the Bulls. He was named the 1996 All-Star game MVP. Jordan led the Bulls to three straight titles from 1996 to 1998. The 1996 team set a record for best record in NBA history. After hitting the shot that won the 1998 NBA Championship, Jordan retired. In 1999 he joined a bid to purchase the NBA's Charlotte Hornets.

Michael Jordan (AP/Wide World Photos, Inc.)

Florence Griffith Joyner (AP/Wide World Photos, Inc.)

Florence Griffith Joyner (1959–1998)
Track and Field Athlete

Born in Los Angeles on December 21, 1959, Florence Griffith started in track at an early age. She first attended California State University-Northridge, but later transferred with her coach Bob Kersee when he moved to UCLA. In 1987 she married 1984 Olympic gold medalist Al Joyner.

At the 1984 Olympic games she won a silver medal. She returned to the Olympic games in 1988, winning a gold medal in the 100-meter, 200-meter, 400-meter relay, and 1600-meter relay races. She set the world record for the 100-meter and 200-meter races that year.

Nicknamed "Flo-Jo," she was inducted into the Track and Field Hall of Fame in 1995. In 1998, she died suddenly in her sleep of an apparent heart seizure.

Jackie Joyner-Kersee (1962–)
Track and Field Athlete, Community Activist, Sports Agent

Often touted as the world's greatest female athlete, Jackie Joyner-Kersee won two gold medals at the 1988

Olympic games and a gold and a bronze medal at the 1992 games.

Joyner-Kersee was born on March 3, 1962, in East St. Louis, Illinois. Prior to winning the 1988 gold medal, she participated in the 1984 Olympics and won the silver medal for the heptathlon despite a torn hamstring muscle.

The only woman to gain more than 7,000 points in the heptathlon four times, she set a world record with 7,215 points at the 1988 Olympic trials. Joyner-Kersee also earned another gold medal in the heptathlon and a bronze medal in the long jump at the 1992 Olympics in Barcelona, Spain. In 1996 at the Atlanta Olympics she won a bronze medal in the long jump, her sixth medal, the most in the history of U.S. women's track and field.

Joyner-Kersee briefly played in the ABL, before retiring from sports to devote time to charitable causes. In addition, Joyner-Kersee is one of the few female sports agents in the United States.

Dick "Night Train" Lane (1928–)
Football Player, Football Coach, Community Activist

Born in Austin, Texas, on April 16, 1928, Dick "Night Train" Lane became one of the NFL's best free agent

Jackie Joyner-Kersee holds the gold medal that she won at the 1992 Olympic Games in Barcelona (AP/Wide World Photos, Inc.).

finds. After attending Scottsbluff Junior College, Lane's spent his 14-year NFL career with three teams, the Los Angeles Rams (1952 to 1953), Chicago Cardinals (1954 to 1959), and Detroit Lions (1960 to 1965), during which he earned All-Pro honors six times.

A cornerback, Lane twice led the NFL in interceptions including a record 14 as a rookie. His 68 career interceptions place him third on the all-time NFL list. Lane, who was chosen as an all-time NFL All-Pro in 1969 and was voted All-Time Player of the Century in 1968, was inducted into the Pro Football Hall of Fame in 1974 and the Black Athletes Hall of Fame in 1977.

Lane coached at Southern University and Central University in the early to mid-1970s. He was also an assistant NFL coach. Lane became the Detroit Police Athletic League Athletic Director in 1975. He is the founder of the Michigan Youth Development Foundation and is past President of the Detroit Varsity Club. He has been involved with the Boy's Club of Metro Detroit as well as the Booker T. Washington Businessmen's Association. During his playing days, Lane had directed youth programs in Chicago and Detroit.

"Sugar" Ray Leonard (1956–)
Boxer, Television Analyst

One of the flashiest and most popular fighters of the modern era, Sugar Ray Leonard brought fame to the lighter divisions of boxing which traditionally have not garnered the attention the heavyweight division draws. Leonard was born in Wilmington, North Carolina, and won the gold medal in the light welterweight division at the 1976 Montreal Olympics.

Leonard rose through the professional ranks, winning the welterweight title from Wilfred Benitez in 1979. His fights with Roberto Duran and Tommy Hearns established his fame. After losing his first fight and his title to Duran, Leonard used a taunting style and flamboyant ring persona to force Duran to quit in the middle of their second fight. In 1981 he defeated Hearns in the fourteenth round by technical knockout, rallying from a point deficit. He retired shortly thereafter due to a detached retina.

In 1987, Leonard made a comeback by upsetting middleweight champion Marvelous Marvin Hagler. The upset prolonged his career; however, he was unable to fight at his former level and retired shortly after the upset.

Leonard's public persona has led to many sponsorship deals. In addition, he serves as a boxing analyst for HBO and ESPN Classic Sports.

Carl Lewis (1961–)
Track and Field Athlete

Carl Lewis was born on July 1, 1961, in Birmingham, Alabama. In the 1984 Olympics in Los Angeles, Lewis became the first athlete since Jesse Owens in 1936 to win four gold medals in Olympic competition.

An often controversial track and field performer, the New Jersey native went into the 1984 competition with the burden of tremendous expectations as the result of intense pre-Olympic publicity. He did not set any Olympic records, and despite his four gold medals, found himself criticized in the media.

Lewis went to the 1988 Olympics in Seoul, South Korea, hoping to duplicate his four gold medal wins. He was the subject of interest as he faced off against his archrival Canadian Ben Johnson.

Lewis won gold medals in the long jump and the 100-meter dash (after Johnson was disqualified for steroid use) and a silver medal in the 200-meter dash. At the 1992 Olympics in Barcelona, Lewis won a gold medal for the long jump. He won his final gold medal at the 1996 Atlanta Olympiad in the long jump.

Carl Lewis (AP/Wide World Photos, Inc.)

Joe Louis (1914–1981)
Boxer

Joe Louis held the heavyweight championship for the longest stretch in history—more than 11 years, and defended the title more often than any other heavyweight champion. His 25 title fights were more than the combined total of the eight champions who preceded him.

Born on May 13, 1914, in a sharecropper's shack in Lexington, Alabama, Louis moved to Detroit as a small boy. Taking up boxing as an amateur, he won 50 out of 59 bouts (43 by knockout), before turning professional in 1934.

In 1935 Lewis fought Primo Carnera, a former boxing champion. Louis knocked out Carnera in six rounds, earning his nickname, "The Brown Bomber." After knocking out ex-champion Max Baer, Louis suffered his lone pre-championship defeat at the hands of Max Schmeling, who knocked him out in the twelfth round. Less than a month later, Louis knocked out another former champion, Jack Sharkey, in three rounds. He later won a rematch with Schmeling in a racially charged fight that earned him national attention. After defeating a number of other challengers, he was given a title fight with Jim

Joe Louis (Corbis Corporation [Bellevue])

Braddock on June 22, 1937. He stopped Braddock in the eighth round to gain the title.

After winning a disputed decision over Joe Walcott in 1947, Louis knocked out Walcott six months later, and then went into retirement. Monetary problems forced Louis into several comebacks that resulted in losses to new heavyweight champions Ezzard Charles and Rocky Marciano. These monetary difficulties were a problem for Louis for the rest of his life. He died April 12, 1981 at the age of 67.

Willie Mays (1931–)

Baseball Player, Baseball Coach, Entrepreneur

During his 21 seasons with the Giants, Willie Mays hit more than 600 home runs. Besides being a solid hitter, Mays also was one of the game's finest defensive outfielder and baserunners.

Born in Fairfield, Alabama, on May 6, 1931, Mays made his professional debut on July 4, 1948, with the Birmingham Black Barons. He was signed by the New York Giants in 1950 and reached the major leagues in 1951. He was named the National League's Rookie of the Year for his 20 home runs, 68 RBIs, and fielding which contributed to the Giants pennant victory.

After two years in the U.S. Army, Mays returned to lead the Giants to the World Championship in 1954, gaining recognition as the league's Most Valuable Player for his 41 homers, 110 RBIs, and .345 batting average.

When the Giants moved to San Francisco, Mays continued his home run hitting, and led his team to a 1962 pennant. A year later, *Sport* magazine named him "the greatest player of the decade." He won the MVP award again in 1965, after hitting 52 home runs and batting .317.

Traded to the New York Mets before the 1972 season, he continued to play outfield and first base. At the end of the 1973 season, his statistics included 2,992 games, 3,283 hits, and 660 home runs. Willie Mays is one of only seven ballplayers to have hit four home runs in one game. After acting as a coach for the Mets, Mays left baseball to pursue a business career. He was elected to the Baseball Hall of Fame in 1979.

Cheryl Miller (1964–)

Basketball Player, Television Analyst, Basketball Coach, Sports Executive, Community Activist

Cheryl Miller was born and raised in Riverside, California. She has occasionally been overshadowed by her brother, Reggie, a guard with the Indiana Pacers. Another brother, Darrell, played baseball professionally with the California Angels in the late 1980s.

The 6'3" Cheryl Miller began attracting notice in high school, having once scored 105 points in a game at Polytechnic High School. Miller was offered nearly 250 scholarships before deciding to enroll at the University of Southern California (USC). There she led the Trojans to two national titles, was All-American four times, and was named National Player of the Year three times.

Miller was a member of numerous national teams including the U.S. Junior National Team in 1981 and the National Team the following year. She participated in the World Championships and the Pan American Games in 1983. In 1984, she won an Olympic gold medal.

Following her playing career, Miller worked for ABC and ESPN as a broadcaster. In 1993, she became the women's head basketball coach at her alma mater, USC, but announced her retirement in 1995. In the previous year, she was elected into the Basketball Hall of Fame. Currently, Miller is the head coach and general manager of the WNBA's Phoenix Mercury.

Edwin Moses (1955–)

Track and Field Athlete, Business Consultant, Olympic Committee Chairperson

Born in Dayton, Ohio, in 1955, Edwin Moses became an internationally known track star in hurdles. Having attended Morehouse College, he was the top ranked intermediate hurdler in the world by 1976. That same year he earned a gold medal at the Olympic Games, a feat to be duplicated eight years later. Moses also won a bronze medal at the 1988 Games. A world record holder in the 400-meter hurdles, he recorded 122 consecutive victories in competition. *Sports Illustrated* presented Moses with its Athlete of the Year award in 1984, one year after he won the Sullivan Award, given annually to the best amateur athlete.

Moses received his M.B.A. from Pepperdine University in 1994 and is currently a financial consultant. He is the chairperson of the U.S. Olympic Committee Substance Abuse Center and serves on the International Olympic Committee Athletes Commission.

Shaquille O'Neal (1972–)

Basketball Player, Rap Artist, Actor

Born in Newark, New Jersey in 1972 to a military family, Shaquille O'Neal has become one of the most famous athletes in America. O'Neal has also appeared in movies and has released his own rap albums.

O'Neal's size and talent attracted attention while he was in high school, and he attended Louisiana State University. He was named All-American in 1992 and left school to pursue a professional basketball career. He was the first pick of the 1992 NBA draft by the Orlando Magic and starred for them until 1996. He led the Magic to the 1995 NBA finals. In 1996 he signed a free agent contract with the Los Angeles Lakers. O'Neal has been an All-Star every season he has played in the NBA.

O'Neal has recorded several rap albums and appeared in various movies. In 1996 he was the star of the film *Kazaam*.

Jesse Owens (1913–1980)

Track and Field Athlete, Entrepreneur

The track and field records Jesse Owens set have all been eclipsed, but his reputation as one of the first great

Shaquille O'Neal (AP/Wide World Photos, Inc.)

Jesse Owens (center) salutes the American flag while standing atop the podium at the 1936 Olympic Games in Berlin (AP/ Wide World Photos, Inc.).

athletes with the combined talents of a sprinter, low hurdler, and broad jumper has not diminished.

Born James Cleveland Owens in Danville, Alabama, on September 12, 1913, Jesse and his family moved to Ohio when he was still young. In 1932, while attending East Technical High School in Cleveland, Owens was clocked at 10.3 seconds in the 100-meter dash. Two years later, Owens entered Ohio State University and became known as "The Ebony Antelope." While competing in the Big Ten Championships at Ann Arbor, Michigan, on May 25, 1935, Owens had what has been called "the greatest single day in the history of man's athletic achievements." In the space of about seventy minutes, he tied the world record for the 100-yard dash and surpassed the world record for five other events including the broad jump, the 220-yard low hurdles, and the 220-yard dash.

In 1936, at the Berlin Olympics, Owens won four gold medals, at that time the most universally acclaimed feat in the history of the games. However, he still faced discrimination in the United States after his victories. He never graduated from Ohio State but did eventually found his own public relations firm.

Leroy Robert "Satchel" Paige (1906–1982)
Baseball Player, Baseball Coach

Long before Jackie Robinson broke the color barrier of "organized baseball," Satchel Paige was the most famous African American baseball player. As an outstanding performer in the Negro Leagues, Paige had become a legendary figure whose encounters with Major League Baseball players added considerably to his athletic reputation.

Paige was born in Mobile, Alabama, on July 7, 1906. He began playing semi-professional ball while working as an iceman and porter. In the mid 1920s, he became a professional player with the Birmingham Black Barons, and later, while playing at Chattanooga, acquired the sobriquet "Satchel" because of his "Satchel-sized feet."

For the next two decades, Paige was the dominant pitcher in Negro League baseball. In 1933, he won 31 games and lost 4. Paige also dominated winter ball in Latin America during the 1930s. In 1942, Paige led the Kansas City Monarchs to victory in the Negro World Series, and four years later he helped them to the pennant by allowing only two runs in 93 innings, a performance which included a string of 64 straight scoreless innings.

In 1948, he was brought up to the major leagues. Despite being well past his prime, he still was able to contribute six victories in Cleveland's pennant drive and pitched in the World Series. Four years later, while pitching for the St. Louis Browns, he was named to the American League All-Star squad.

Until the 1969 baseball season, Paige was active on the barnstorming circuit with the Harlem Globetrotters and a host of other exhibition teams. In 1969 the Atlanta Braves, in an attempt to make Paige eligible for baseball's pension plan, signed him to a one-year contract as coach. Paige died in June of 1982.

Walter Payton (1954–)
Football Player, Entrepreneur

Walter Payton was born on July 25, 1954, in Columbia, Mississippi. When he retired as a running back for the Chicago Bears after the 1986 season, he was the National Football League's all-time leading rusher, breaking a record held for many years by Jim Brown.

A graduate of Jackson State University, Payton played his entire career in Chicago, receiving numerous awards and helping to lead the Bears to a victory in Super Bowl XX. He broke O. J. Simpson's single game rushing record after gaining 275 yards during a game with the Minnesota Vikings in 1977. Seven years later, during a game against the New Orleans Saints, he surpassed Jim Brown's career rushing record and concluded his career with a total of 16,726.

Following his retirement, Payton funded several auto racing teams and fronted a group of businessmen in an attempt to bring a professional football team to the city of St. Louis. In 1998 Payton was diagnosed with a potentially fatal liver disease.

Calvin Peete (1943–)
Golfer

Calvin Peete was born in Detroit, on July 18, 1943. During World War II, Peete moved with his family to Pahikee, Florida. One of 19 children, as a youth he was a farm laborer and itinerant peddler, selling wares to farmers along the East Coast.

He began golfing at the age of 23 and soon realizing that he possessed some aptitude for the sport. Unlike other African American golfers of his era who were forced into caddying as a means of gaining entrance into the sport, Peete was able to move directly toward a professional career. Peete did, however, face the handicap of a left arm that he was unable to completely straighten, leading experts to tell him that he would never be successful.

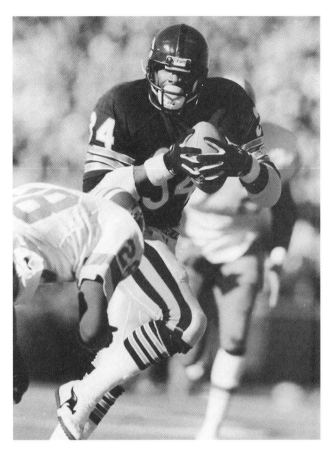

Walter Payton (AP/Wide World Photos, Inc.)

After turning pro in 1971, Peete struggled. In 1978, he placed 108th in total money winnings on the PGA tour. Peete's first tour victory came at the 1979 Greater Milwaukee Open, which he won again in 1982, along with the Anheuser-Busch Classic, BC Open, and the Pensacola Open. In 1981 and 1982, he finished first on the tour in the categories of driving accuracy and greens reached in regulation.

Despite his success, Peete was not considered fully accredited because the PGA does not recognize a golfer unless he has obtained a high school diploma. This was a requirement toward obtaining a spot on the prestigious Ryder Cup team. In 1982, with the assistance of his wife, Peete passed the Michigan General Equivalency examination 24 years after leaving high school. *Ebony* magazine rewarded him with a Black Achievement award, and, in 1983, Peete was presented with the Jackie Robinson Award.

Peete captured two more PGA titles in 1983—the Georgia-Pacific Atlanta Classic and the Anheuser-Busch Classic. He was also asked to represent the United States as a member of the Ryder Cup team. That same year, he won the Ben Hogan Award. The following year,

Peete had the best scoring average on the PGA tour. He is now a member of the PGA's Senior Tour.

Willis Reed (1942–)
Basketball Player, Sports Executive

Willis Reed was born in Bernice, Louisiana, on June 25, 1942. He attended Grambling College, where he was discovered by Red Holtzman of the New York Knicks. Reed led the Knicks in scoring and rebounding on his way to becoming Rookie of the Year in 1965.

In 1970, the Knicks won their first NBA Championship. Reed won three MVP awards that season-one for the regular season, one for the All-Star game, and one for the playoffs.

He was named to the All-Star team his first seven seasons. In 1973, he led the Knicks to their second NBA title and was again named MVP for the second time. Knee problems then ended his career. In 1981, Reed was elected to the Basketball Hall of Fame. He has worked as an executive with the New Jersey Nets.

Jerry Rice (1962–)
Football Player

Jerry Rice was born in Starkville, Mississippi, on October 13, 1962. At a collegian at Mississippi Valley State, Rice set 18 Division II records. Drafted in the first round by the 49ers in 1985, Rice combined with quarterbacks Joe Montana and Steve Young to form the most elite pass-catching combination in pro football history.

Rice currently holds the career record for touchdowns. His ten straight seasons with more than 1,000 receiving yards is also a league record. His best season was the strike-shortened 1987 campaign, during which he scored 22 touchdowns in only 12 regular season games. In that same year, Rice scored touchdowns in 13 straight games. In a 1990 contest with the Atlanta Falcons, Rice scored five touchdowns. He was named to the Pro Bowl every season until slowed by an injury in 1997. He was named the NFL's Player of the year by the *Sporting News* in 1987 and 1990. Rice was Most Valuable Player in the 49ers' Super Bowl XXIII victory over the Cincinnati Bengals.

Rice helped lead the 49ers to Super Bowl victories after the 1988, 1989, and 1994 seasons. He traces the development of his superb hands to his childhood, during which his father would toss him bricks during construction work.

Oscar Robertson (1938–)
Basketball Player, Business Executive, Community Activist

Oscar Robertson was born in Charlotte, Tennessee, in 1938, before moving to Indiana and attending Indian-

apolis' Crispus Attucks High School. He led his team to the prestigious Indiana state basketball title on two occasions and shortly thereafter became the first African American to play at the University of Cincinnati. He helped Cincinnati reach the Final Four in 1959 and 1960, was named the United Press International college player of the year for three consecutive seasons, and set 14 major collegiate records. He also became the first to lead the NCAA in scoring for three consecutive seasons.

In 1960, and after participating on the U.S. gold medal winning Olympic basketball team as co-captain, Robertson signed a $100,000 contract with the Cincinnati Royals, earning Rookie of the Year honors during his initial season in the NBA. At 6'5", 210 pounds, he would become the NBA's first true "big guard." The multi-dimensional Robertson, known as the "Big O," was a textbook fundamental player and unyieldingly physical. During the 1962 season he led the NBA in assists, at 11.4 per game. His best season was the 1964 campaign in which he averaged 31.4 points per game and was named the league's Most Valuable Player.

Over the course of five separate seasons, Robertson, averaged more than 20 points and 10 assists per game, something no other player in NBA history has accomplished. He was the Most Valuable Player of the 1961, 1964, and 1969 All-Star games. Late in his career, Robertson joined the Milwaukee Bucks and led Milwaukee to its only NBA championship in 1971.

Robertson became the president of the NBA Players Association. Under his leadership, the NBAPA established collective bargaining with the league's owners. He was elected to the Basketball Hall of Fame in 1979, and was named to the NBA's 35th anniversary all-time team in 1980. Robertson was also elected to the Olympic Hall of Fame in 1984.

Robertson has remained visible off the court, becoming a successful chemical company executive as president/CEO of ORCHEM, Inc. in 1981, and starting Oscar Robertson and Associates in 1983. He is a member of the NAACP Sports Board, a trustee of the Indiana High School and Basketball Halls of Fame, the National Director of the Pepsi-Cola Hot Shot Program, and the President of the NBA Retired Players Association. Robertson was also the developer of affordable housing units in Cincinnati and Indianapolis. He served in the U.S. Army for eight years.

Eddie G. Robinson (1919–)
College Football Coach

Eddie G. Robinson was born on February 13, 1919, in Jackson, Louisiana. As a gifted athlete in high school, Robinson earned a scholarship to Leland College in Louisiana. A star quarterback, Robinson got involved in

Eddie Robinson (AP/Wide World Photos, Inc.)

his first coaching clinic there. After obtaining his bachelor's degree, Robinson took his first college coaching job in 1941. Though only 22 years old at the time, Grambling State gave Robinson the opportunity to coach.

The early success of Grambling State's football team established Robinson as a fixture at Grambling State. He coached numerous NFL stars and successful teams during his tenure as coach. In 1985, Robinson had surpassed Bear Bryant as the career leader in victories by a head coach. He retired following the 1997 season.

Frank Robinson (1935–)
Baseball Player, Baseball Manager, Sports Executive

Born in Beaumont, Texas, in 1936, Frank Robinson moved to Oakland, California, at the age of five. During his teens, he was a football and baseball star at McClyronds High School. After graduation in 1953, he signed with the Cincinnati Reds.

In 1956, Robinson debuted in Major League Baseball, hitting 38 homers and winning Rookie of the Year honors. During the next eight years, he hit 259 homers and had 800 RBIs. In 1961, Robinson was named Most Valuable Player for leading Cincinnati to the National League pennant. Five years later, Robinson won the

American League's Triple Crown and became the first player to win the MVP in both leagues. He retired as an active player after the 1976 season with a lifetime batting average of .294 in 2,808 games along with 2,943 hits, 1,829 runs, and 1,812 RBIs. His 586 home runs rank fourth all-time.

Frank Robinson was Major League Baseball's first African American manager. He was named to the head post of the Cleveland Indians in 1975. Robinson left the Indians in 1977, and became the manager of the Rochester Red Wings, a minor league team, in 1978. In 1981, Robinson was hired by the San Francisco Giants, where he managed the team until 1984. He also managed the Baltimore Orioles during the late 1980s. He later became the assistant general manager of that team. He is currently the special projects assistant to the commissioner's office. Robinson was elected to the National Baseball Hall of Fame in 1982.

Jackie Robinson (1919–1972)
Baseball Player, Business Executive, Community Activist

Born in Cairo, Georgia, on January 31, 1919, Robinson was raised in Pasadena, California. At UCLA he gained All-American honorable mention as a halfback, but he left college in his junior year to play professional football for the Los Angeles Bulldogs. After serving as a U.S. Army lieutenant during World War II, Robinson returned to civilian life with the hope of becoming a physical education coach. He began to play in the Negro Baseball League to establish himself.

In 1945, while he was playing with the Kansas City Monarchs, Branch Rickey of the Brooklyn Dodgers signed him to a contract. In 1946 he played for the Dodgers top minor league in Montreal. On April 10, 1947, the Dodgers announced that they had purchased Robinson's contract and the following day he began his Major League Baseball career. During a 10-year career, he hit .311 in 1,382 games with 1,518 hits, 947 runs, 273 doubles, and 734 RBIs. He won the National League's Most Valuable Player award in 1949, and played on six National League pennant winners, as well as one world championship team. Robinson was inducted into the National Baseball Hall of Fame in 1962.

After his retirement from baseball, Robinson became a bank official, president of a land development firm, and a director of programs to combat drug addiction. He died on October 24, 1972 in Stamford, Connecticut.

"Sugar Ray" Robinson (1921–1989)
Boxer

Born Walker Smith, in Detroit on May 3, 1921, he took the name Robinson from the certificate of an amateur boxer whose identity enabled him to meet the age requirements for getting a match in Michigan.

As a youth, Robinson had watched a Detroit neighbor, Joe Louis, train for an amateur boxing career. When Robinson moved to New York two years later, he began to spend most of his time at local gyms in preparation for his own amateur career. After winning all 89 of his amateur bouts and the 1939 Golden Gloves featherweight championship, he turned professional in 1940 at Madison Square Garden.

Robinson beat Tommy Bell in an elimination title bout in December 1946 to win the welterweight title. He successfully defended the title for five years, and on February 14, 1951, took the middleweight crown from Jake LaMotta.

In July of 1951, he lost the title to Randy Turpin, only to win it back two months later. Retiring for a time, Robinson subsequently fought a series of exciting battles with Carl "Bobo" Olsen, Carmen Basilio, and Gene Fullmer before retiring permanently on December 10, 1965, having won six titles.

Suffering from diabetes, hypertension, and Alzheimer's disease, Robinson died of natural causes at the Brotman Medical Center in Culver City, California, on April 12, 1989. Over his career, he won 174 of 201 professional bouts and titles in three weight classes.

Wilma Rudolph (1940–1994)
Track and Field Athlete, Track and Field Coach, Community Activist, Lecturer

Rudolph was born on June 23, 1940, in St. Bethlehem, Tennessee, the 17th of 19 children. At an early age, she survived polio and scarlet fever. Through daily leg massages administered in turn by different members of her family, she progressed to the point where she was able to walk with the aid of a special shoe. Three years later, however, she discarded the shoe, and began joining her brother in backyard basketball games. At Burt High School in Clarksville, Rudolph broke the state basketball record for girls. As a sprinter, she was undefeated high school track meets.

In 1957, Rudolph enrolled at Tennessee State University and began training for the Olympic games in Rome. She gained national recognition in college meets, setting the world record for 200-meters in July of 1960. In the Olympics, she earned the title of the "World's Fastest Woman" by winning gold medals for the 100-meter dash, the 200-meter dash (setting an Olympic record), and for anchoring the 400-meter relay (setting a world record). She was named by the Associated Press as the U.S. Female Athlete of the Year for 1960 and also won United Press Athlete of the Year honors.

Rudolph served as a track coach, an athletic consultant, and assistant director of athletics for the Mayor's Youth Foundation in Chicago. She was also the founder of the Wilma Rudolph Foundation. Rudolph also was a talk show hostess and active on the lecture circuit. On November 12, 1994, Wilma Rudolph died at her home in Brentwood, Tennessee, of a brain tumor.

Bill Russell (1934–)
Basketball Player, Basketball Coach, Sports Executive, Television Commentator

Bill Russell, who led the Boston Celtics to eleven titles including eight in a row, is regarded as the finest defensive basketball player in the game's history. The 6'10" star is also the first African American to coach a National Basketball Association team.

Russell was born on February 12, 1934, in Monroe, Louisiana. The family settled in Oakland, California, when Russell was a youth. At McClyronds High School, Russell proved to be an awkward but determined basketball player who eventually received a scholarship to the nearby University of San Francisco.

In his sophomore year he became the most publicized athlete on the West Coast. Over the next two years, his fame spread across the nation as he led his team to a record sixty consecutive victories and two straight NCAA titles.

The Celtics had never won an NBA Championship before Russell's arrival in 1957. With the help of Russell's defensive capabilities, the Celtics became the most successful team in the history of professional sports, winning the world championship eight years in a row. Russell himself was named Most Valuable Player on five separate occasions (1958, 1961 to 1963, 1965). In 1966, Russell became the Celtics player/coach.

After the 1968–1969 season, having led the Celtics to their eleventh NBA crown, Russell retired as both coach and player. He left the game as its all-time leader in minutes played (40,726). In 1980, the Professional Basketball Writers Association of America selected Russell as the greatest player in NBA history.

After retirement, Russell was a color commentator on NBC-TV's NBA Game of the Week. In 1974, he accepted a lucrative contract to become head coach and general manager of the Seattle Supersonics and was inducted into the Basketball Hall of Fame. He remained at Seattle's helm through 1977 and returned to the coaching ranks ten years later for a one-year stint with the Sacramento Kings. He also served as the team's director of player personnel in 1988.

Deion Sanders (AP/Wide World Photos, Inc.)

Deion Sanders (1967–)
Football Player

Deion Sanders was born in Fort Myers, Florida, and first achieved fame as an All-American defensive back at Florida State University. Sanders was also a baseball star at the school, and after leaving college in 1989 pursued professional careers in both sports.

Sanders was drafted by the football Atlanta Falcons and has also played for the San Francisco 49ers and the Dallas Cowboys. He has been an All-Pro seven times and was named the top defensive player in the league in 1994. He also won Super Bowls with San Francisco in 1994 and Dallas in 1995.

Sanders baseball career has also been successful. He was drafted and played with the New York Yankees until traded to the Atlanta Braves in 1991. He played in two World Series with the Braves and has also played with the San Francisco Giants and Cincinnati Reds. Sanders's baseball career has been cut short by injuries suffered while playing football.

Sanders is known for his fun-loving image, evidenced by his nickname, "Prime Time." Known for flashy clothing and on-field theatrics, Sanders has become one of the most visible athletes in the United States. However, a brush with depression caused him to change his image and rediscover his Christian faith in 1998.

Gale Sayers (1943–)
Football Player, Athletic Director, Community Activist, Entrepreneur

Gale Sayers was born in Wichita, Kansas, on May 30, 1943. He participated in football and track while in high school and enrolled at Kansas University. He signed with the Chicago Bears before graduating but returned to finish and also earned a master's degree.

Sayers garnered All-Pro honors in his rookie season of 1965 and three of the next four seasons. Sayers led the league in rushing in 1969. In a 1965 game against the San Francisco 49ers, he tied an NFL record by scoring six touchdowns.

Sayers's career was ended after the 1971 season due to a knee injury. His final totals included 56 touchdowns—39 rushing, 9 receiving, six on kickoff returns (including a 103 yarder in 1967), and two on punt returns. He was named to the "All-NFL 1960–1984 All-Star Team" as a kick returner. Despite his brief career, he was inducted into the Pro Football Hall of Fame in 1977.

Following his playing career, Sayers was named assistant to the athletic director at Kansas and in 1981, became the athletic director at Southern Illinois University. Active in the community, Sayers has been the commissioner of the Chicago Park District; the co-chairperson of the Legal Defense Fund for Sports, NAACP Coordinator; and an honorary chairman of the American Cancer Society in addition to his involvement in the Reach Out Program. In 1982, Sayers founded his own computer company.

Charlie Sifford (1922–)
Golfer

Charlotte, North Carolina, native Charlie Sifford was the first African American to participate in a predominately white golf event, the 1957 Long Beach Open. Sifford's entry into golf began as a caddie at the age of nine. At 13, he won a caddie tournament shooting a 70. After moving to Philadelphia, Sifford worked as a teaching professional and chauffeur.

Sifford became the first African American to be awarded a PGA card as an approved player in 1959 when the tour lifted its "Caucasian only" clause. He was also the first to win a PGA event, the Los Angeles Open, in 1969. On the Seniors Tour, Sifford triumphed at the PGA Seniors Open (1975), and the Suntree Seniors Open (1980). He also won the Negro National Title six times.

O.J. Simpson (AP/Wide World Photos, Inc.)

O.J. Simpson (1947–)
Football Player, Television Commentator, Actor

Born in San Francisco on July 9, 1947, Simpson starred at the University of Southern California, winning the Heisman Trophy in 1968. One year prior to that, he was a member of the USC relay team that set a world record of 38.6 seconds in the 440-yard run. ABC Sports voted him College Player of the Decade. He signed with the Buffalo Bills in 1969, and three years later won his first rushing title.

Simpson enjoyed his finest season in 1973. On opening day, he rushed for 250 yards against the New England Patriots, breaking the record of 247 yards held by Willie Ellison. His yardage total of 2,003 for the entire season surpassed the previous mark of 1,863 held by Jim Brown. In addition, he scored 12 touchdowns, averaged six yards per carry, and had more rushing yardage than 15 other NFL clubs. He was named Player of the Year and won the Jim Thorpe Trophy.

Simpson retired from football in 1978. He has appeared in several feature films and worked as a sports commentator for ABC-TV and NBC-TV. In 1995, a jury found Simpson not guilty of charges that he had brutally slain his ex-wife and a male friend. The decision was

rejected by most Americans, and Simpson has since been forced to live a reclusive lifestyle.

Lawrence Taylor (1959–)
Football Player

Born in Williamsburg, Virginia, Lawrence Taylor revolutionized the linebacker position in the NFL by virtue of his strength and speed.

After an outstanding career at the University of North Carolina where he was named Atlantic Coast Conference Player of the Year in 1980, Taylor was taken by the New York Giants with the second pick of the 1981 draft. Taylor amassed 132 1/2 career sacks and was an integral part of two Giants Super Bowl championships, following the 1986 and 1990 seasons. He was named to the NFL's All-Decade team for the 1980s. Problems with substance abuse and taxes have marked his post-football career, leading him to attempt a professional wrestling career in order to earn money.

Marshall W. "Major" Taylor (1878–1932)
Cyclist

Marshall W. "Major" Taylor became America's first African American U.S. National Champion in 1899. Born in Indianapolis in 1878, the son of a coachman, he worked at a bicycle store part-time as a teen. After attending his first race, his boss suggested that Major enter a couple of races. He won a 10-mile race and proceeded to compete as an amateur.

By the time he was 16, he went to work in a factory owned by a former champion and, with his new boss's encouragement, competed in races in Canada, Europe, Australia and New Zealand. During nearly 16 years of competition, he won numerous championships and set several world records. Taylor is a member of the Bicycle Hall of Fame. He died in 1932.

Debi Thomas (1967–)
Figure Skater

Born in Poughkeepsie, New York, Debi Thomas was the first African American figure skater to win a major championship. Thomas was the winner at the 1985 National Sports Festival in Baton Rouge. The following year she captured the U.S. and World figure skating titles, becoming the first African American to capture an international singles meet. Having attended Stanford, she was a bronze medalist at the 1988 Olympic Games.

John Thompson (1941–)
College Basketball Coach

John Thompson was born in Washington, DC, in 1941. He played college basketball at Providence Col-

John Thompson announcing his resignation as head coach of the Georgetown University basketball team in 1999 (AP/Wide World Photos, Inc.).

lege and graduated in 1964. Thompson played with the Boston Celtics of the NBA from 1964 to 1966. He won NBA titles each season and played behind Hall of Fame center Bill Russell.

In 1966 Thompson began coaching St. Anthony's High School in Washington, DC. In 1972 he was offered the head coaching job at Georgetown University. Thompson turned Georgetown into a national powerhouse. In 1982 he led the Hoyas to the national championship game, becoming the first African American to coach in the Final Four. The Hoyas won the championship in 1984 and were runner-up the next season. Thompson's Hoyas won six Big East titles and he developed star players such as Patrick Ewing, Alonzo Mourning, Dikembe Mutombo, and Allen Iverson.

In 1988, Thompson coached the U.S. Olympic basketball team to a bronze medal at the Seoul Olympiad. He frequently criticized the NCAA for tighter academic standards which he felt discriminated against African Americans. Several times he walked off the court before games to protest increasing test scores for freshman students. Thompson resigned in the middle of the 1999

season due to personal problems. He was elected to the National Basketball Hall of Fame in 1999.

Gene Upshaw (1945–)
Football Player, Executive Director of the NFLPA, Community Activist

Born in Robstown, Texas, Upshaw attended Texas A & I University. He was named All-Pro eight times and inducted into the Pro Football Hall of Fame in 1987.

Upshaw is currently the executive director of the National Football League Players Association, a post he has held since 1982. Under his leadership, the organization has expended considerable resources on education and rehabilitation for substance abuse. Upshaw is also the president of the Federation of Professional Athletes AFL-CIO, as well as a member on the California Governor's Council on Wellness and Physical Fitness. He is the coordinator for voter registration and fund-raising in Alameda County (California) and has served as the planning commissioner for that same county.

Upshaw was the recipient of the Byron (Whizzer) White Humanitarian award as voted by the NFL players in 1980. In 1982, he was presented with the A. Philip Randolph Award.

Bill White (1934–)
Baseball Player, Baseball Announcer, Former National League of Professional Baseball Clubs President

William DeKova White was born in Lakewood, Florida, on January 28, 1934. He began his Major League Baseball career with the New York Giants in 1956 and spent thirteen years as a player with the San Francisco Giants, St. Louis Cardinals, and the Philadelphia Phillies. During his career, White was named to the National League All-Star team six times and won seven Gold Gloves. He retired from baseball in 1969 and in 1971 joined Phil Rizzuto as a television announcer for the New York Yankees.

On April 1, 1989, Bill White became the first African American president of the National League. He held the post until he was succeeded in 1994 by another African American, Leonard Coleman.

Lenny Wilkins (1937–)
Basketball Player, Basketball Coach

Lenny Wilkins was born in 1937 in New York City. He developed his game on the city's streets and then starred at Providence College. Wilkins was drafted by the St. Louis Hawks of the NBA in 1960. Wilkins was named to All-Star teams and was MVP of the 1971 game while a member of the Seattle SuperSonics.

Wilkins returned to Seattle as coach in 1978 and led the Sonics to the NBA championship in 1979. He coached

Lenny Wilkins (AP/Wide World Photos, Inc.)

with the Sonics until 1986, when left to coach the Cleveland Cavaliers. In 1993, Wilkins was named coach of the Atlanta Hawks and in 1995 broke Red Auerbach's record for most victories by an NBA head coach.

Wilkins was inducted into the Basketball Hall of Fame as a player (1988) and as a coach (1998). In 1996, he coached the men's basketball team that won the gold medal at the Atlanta Olympiad.

Venus (1980–) and Serena (1981–) Williams
Tennis Players

The Williams sisters were tennis prodigies in the mid-1990s under the coaching of their father Richard. Featured in various articles and televisions shows, Richard Williams refused to let his daughters join the professional tennis tour until he thought they were ready. In 1997, Venus, the eldest by fifteen months, made her pro debut, followed the next year by her sister.

Venus achieved fame by advancing to the finals of the 1997 U.S. Open. Her game has steadily improved and she is one of the top ten players in women's professional tennis. Her sister Serena cracked the top ten in the spring of 1999. The two sisters played against each other in the finals of the 1999 Lipton Championships with Venus emerging victorious.

Tiger Woods (1975–)
Golfer

Tiger Woods is the most successful African American golfer in history despite his youth. Woods was born in Long Beach, California, and was a child prodigy in golf. He became the first player to win the U.S. Amateur title three straight years, from 1994 to 1996, while a student at Stanford University.

In 1996, Woods turned professional. In the spring of 1997, Woods won the Masters tournament, becoming the first African American to win a major title in golf. Woods set the course record in his victory and made the cover of several national magazines. His victory propelled him to the ranking of the world's top player, the youngest man and first African American to hold that title.

Military

◆ The Colonial Period ◆ The Revolutionary War (1775–1783) ◆ The War of 1812 (1812–1815)
◆ The Civil War (1861–1865) ◆ The Indian Campaigns (1866–1890)
◆ The Spanish–American War (1898) ◆ World War I (1914–1918)
◆ The Interwar Years (1919–1940) ◆ World War II (1941–1945)
◆ The Desegregation of the Military (1946–1949) ◆ The Korean War (1950–1953)
◆ The Vietnam War (1964–1973) ◆ Military Participation in the 1970s and 1980s
◆ The Persian Gulf War (1991) ◆ The Military Moving into the New Millennium
◆ Outstanding Military Figures ◆ Military Statistics
by Kevin C. Kretschmer

As with other aspects of U.S. society, the role of African American in the nation's armed forces has been evolutionary. It was shaped by the white majority of an infant republic that embraced and then rejected slavery. Then came an adolescent "separate but equal" era of racial segregation. Finally, the United States matured—as an increasingly multicultural society—in its understanding of race and racism.

Sadly, a nation's history is often shaped by its wars. Insofar as African Americans and the U.S. military are concerned, the historic linkage extends from before the Revolutionary War to the most recent military expeditions involving United States troops.

◆ THE COLONIAL PERIOD

Based on European experiences, the early American colonists were wary of the military. As a result, much of early U.S. military history revolves around the locally recruited militia—now the National Guard of the states and territories.

Fearful of Indian warfare and slave insurrection, colonial governments sought to reduce the risk of a confederation between Indians and slaves. Some colonial governments promised freedom and various other inducements to African American slaves willing to help fight the Indians, and they paid Indians to hunt down and return escaped slaves. As early as 1703, South

Carolina authorities began to enlist slaves into its colonial militia. The Massachusetts Bay government required that African American men, free and slave alike, undergo militia training. Less concerned with an Indian attack than a slave uprising, Virginia forbid the arming of slaves. Though few in number, both enslaved and free African Americans served in colonial militias and fought in the French and Indian War, 1754–1763.

As tensions mounted between Great Britain and the American colonies, confrontation led to bloodshed in the Boston Massacre of March 5, 1770. In protest against the manner of taxation and British authority, a crowd of angry Boston residents confronted a group of British soldiers . One of the soldiers fired on the crowd and an escaped slave named Crispus Attucks was struck. Attucks fell dead at the feet of the British soldiers, followed by four white citizens who, with him, became martyrs to the cause of American independence.

◆ THE REVOLUTIONARY WAR (1775–1783)

In 1775, African American men joined whites in fighting the British during the battles of Lexington and Concord, the first battles of the Revolutionary War. An African American, Salem Poore, fought in the Battle of Bunker Hill. Credited with firing the shot that killed Major John Pitcairn, commander of the British force,

Poore received a commendation for gallantry. He would later serve with George Washington at Valley Forge.

Although a number of African Americans were serving in New England units and proving themselves both capable and brave, Southern slaveholders objected to their presence. In response to these critics, General Washington and his principal officers agreed to reject all slaves and bar free African American veterans from reenlisting, a policy quickly ratified by the Continental Congress.

French and Spanish forces allied with the American colonists did not hesitate to enlist African Americans into their ranks. The English also did not object to this valuable source of military manpower. When Lord Dunmore, the royal governor of Virginia, promised freedom to slaves who joined His Majesty's troops, he was able to organize an Ethiopian Regiment composed of approximately three hundred men.

As it became increasingly difficult for the colonial militias and the Continental Army to meet recruiting needs, George Washington began to reconsider his earlier agreement to prohibit African Americans from serving. The success of the British in attracting African American volunteers seeking to earn their freedom was a matter of concern. With troop strength dangerously low following the brutal winter at Valley Forge, Washington reversed his earlier policies and welcomed both free and enslaved African Americans into the Continental Army.

By 1778, the Continental Army was racially integrated. On average, each brigade contained 42 African American soldiers. In the naval service, African American sailors were engaged in nearly every phase of shipboard operations. In addition to cooking and cleaning, African American seamen manned guns, joined boarding parties, and served as sharpshooters in Marine detachments. Ultimately, 5,000 African Americans served in the war for American independence. Some won their freedom, while others gained respect in their communities and a measure of economic security.

The Revolutionary War presented the idea that through military service African Americans could secure freedom and liberty. The War also established the trend of government promises to African Americans in times of military need, which were forgotten when the crisis ended. The only places in which African Americans obtained any form of freedom were those that abolished slavery.

A memorial to the African Americans who served the American cause during the Revolutionary War will be erected on the Mall in Washington, DC. Ironically it will be dedicated after similar recognition of the twentieth-century Tuskegee Airmen at the U.S. Air Force Academy and the nineteenth-century "Buffalo Soldiers" at Fort Leavenworth, Kansas.

◆ THE WAR OF 1812 (1812–1815)

Following the Revolutionary War, the exclusion of African Americans from military service was reinstated. In 1792, Congress restricted military service to "free able-bodied white males." Six years later, the Secretary of War ordered the commandant of the Marine Corps that "no Negro, mulatto or Indian is to be enlisted." However, when the need arose for recruits during the War of 1812, African American sailors made up approximately twenty percent of Navy crews. Commodore Oliver Hazard Perry welcomed African American sailors who served in his armada, which defeated the British on Lake Erie.

While the Army and Marine Corps continued to exclude African Americans, the Louisiana legislature authorized enlistments of free African American landowners. The combat bravery of these African American troops was a key factor in the U.S. victory at the Battle of New Orleans. As African Americans were not authorized to serve in the Army, their contributions went unrecognized by the U.S. Army.

◆ THE CIVIL WAR (1861–1865)

Only weeks after the Confederate assault on Fort Sumter in 1861, which initiated the Civil War, African Americans from Ohio's Wilberforce College answered Abraham Lincoln's call for volunteers to help subdue the Confederacy. Similar offers quickly came from Washington, DC, and New York, where the governor was offered three African American regiments to serve for the duration of the war, with their weapons, clothing, equipment, pay and provisions all to be provided by the African American population of the state. These and other such requests to serve were rejected because the war was expected to be short.

Although some Union leaders such as Major General John C. Fremont wanted to recruit African Americans as soldiers, the Lincoln administration refused permission to proceed with the effort. Fearful that such action would antagonize slave-holding border states loyal to the Union, President Lincoln made it clear that this was a war to preserve the Union, not to free the slaves. Union General Benjamin Butler, who would later command African American troops, offered Union soldiers to suppress a rumored slave uprising in Maryland. Meanwhile, the Confederacy enjoyed the fruits of slave labor in constructing fortifications and related combat service-support roles. As early as June of 1861, some Southern states recruited free African Americans for military service.

Service records have revealed that over 18,000 African Americans served as seamen during the Civil War (The Library of Congress).

Though prohibited from enlisting African Americans for military duty as troops, some Union generals began using African American fugitives from slave territory as teamsters, cooks, and laborers. Only after important military setbacks, as well as considerable debate in the press and Congress, did the legislature authorize the employment of African American soldiers with the Militia Act of July 17, 1862. The War Department had not yet given permission to recruit African American soldiers when General Jim Lane organized and trained the 1st Kansas Colored Volunteers and sent them into action against Confederate troops near Butler, Missouri, in late October of 1862. The success of African American troops in their first engagements in as part of the Union Army, helped to reduce opposition to their recruitment.

U.S. Colored Troops (USCT)

Following the Emancipation Proclamation of September 22, 1862, systematic recruitment of African Americans began throughout the country. Massachusetts organized the 54th and 55th Massachusetts Infantry Regiments. Raised by Colonel Robert Gould Shaw, the 54th led the Union attack on Fort Wagner, South Caroli-

na on July 18, 1863. This strategically-located Confederate position on Morris Island dominated the shipping channel leading into the harbor at Charleston. Although access to Fort Wagner was restricted to a narrow road, and subject to fire from three Confederate forts and batteries nearby, Union General Truman Seymour boasted that he could take it in one night. A reporter for the *New York Tribune* quoted the general as saying that he would have General George C. Strong's brigade take the lead and ". . . put those damned niggers from Massachusetts in the advance; we might as well get rid of them one time as another."

Under intense fire, the 54th made their charge with Shaw urging his men over an earthwork and into the fort. The African American soldiers were met with a barrage of artillery, rifle fire, and grenades. As he crossed the fort's parapet, Shaw was shot dead. Half of the officers and men of his regiment were killed, wounded, or captured in the battle. Although eventually driven away from the fort, the 54th Massachusetts Infantry came to symbolize the courage and determination of African American troops.

Despite repeated demonstrations of their ability and courage, skepticism regarding the usefulness of African American soldiers remained. General Benjamin Butler was determined to prove the African American troops under his command were fit to bear arms. On the dawn of September 29, 1864, Butler ordered his troops of the XVII Corps to storm a fortified Confederate position at New Market Heights, Virginia. The bayonet attack drove the Confederates from their position on the high ground at great cost. Butler recorded in his memoirs that "the capacity of the Negro race for soldiers had then and there been fully settled forever."

By July of 1863, over thirty African American regiments were being organized or were already on the field. These units and others previously organized, except for the 54th and 55th Massachusetts, were designated as U.S. Colored Troops (USCT). Following the establishment of USCT regiments, African Americans fought and died in every major Civil War action. For a period, they did so with substantially less pay than white troops. While white privates received $13 per month plus $3.50 in clothing allowance, African American troops of any rank were paid only $10 per month. In some units, African American soldiers would not accept the lesser pay. Several men from an African American Rhode Island artillery unit on duty in Texas were sentenced to hard labor for refusing their pay. When Sergeant William Walker persuaded the men of his South Carolina regiment company to refuse to perform any duty unless they received pay equal to that of white troops, he was brought up on charges of mutiny and executed by firing squad. After vigorous protests by prominent officers of

Union military camp of the "Colored Battery" in Jacksonville, Tennessee (The Library of Congress).

African American troops, newspaper editors, and legislators, the 1864 Army Appropriation Act was enacted to provide identical pay scales for all soldiers.

The passions of the Civil War resulted in the ignoring of the then-emerging doctrines of land warfare on such issues as treatment of noncombatants and prisoners of war. The most serious documented breaches of land warfare standards were committed by the Confederacy. African American soldiers who fell into Confederate hands were either reenslaved or summarily killed. One of the bloodiest such events was the Confederate butchery at Fort Pillow, Tennessee. Congressional Report No. 65, "Fort Pillow Massacre" (April 24, 1864), identified the Confederate leader responsible as General Nathan Bedford Forrest, who would later organize the Ku Klux Klan. According to the report:

> . . . the rebels commenced an indiscriminate slaughter, sparing neither age nor sex, white or black, soldier or civilian. The officers and men seemed to vie with each other in the devilish work; men, women, and even children, wherever found, were deliberately shot down, beaten, and hacked with sabers; some of the children not more than ten years old were forced to stand up and face

their murderers while being shot; the sick and wounded were butchered without mercy, the rebels even entering the hospital building and dragging them out to be shot or killing them as they lay there unable to offer the least resistance.

Although somewhat exaggerated in the interest of propaganda, the report clearly established that African American troops were murdered while attempting to surrender. The slaughter at Fort Pillow and the murder of captured and wounded African American troops at the Battle of Poison Spring, Arkansas, would not go unanswered. African American troops assaulted their Confederate enemy with ferocious intensity as they shouted their battle cry, "Remember Fort Pillow!" and "Remember Poison Spring!"

Many African American men served in the Union cause, but very few were permitted to do so as officers. Despite strident public opposition and War Department policy unfavorable to the appointment of African American officers, nearly one hundred African American men held commissions during the course of the Civil War. Over three-fourths of these commissions were awarded in General Butler's Louisiana regiments. Many African Americans gained their appointment as officers in state militias. A few African American surgeons and a large number of chaplains also received appointments. After Martin R. Delany, a Harvard-trained physician, had an audience with Abraham Lincoln, the president directed his secretary of war to meet this "most remarkable black man." On February 26, 1865, Martin R. Delany was commissioned a Major of Infantry, making him the highest-ranking African American field officer during the war. Before Delany had an opportunity to organize and command an *armee d'Afrique*, the Civil War ended. He retained the rank of major until 1868.

One African American officer, Robert Smalls, was commissioned in the U.S. Colored Troops, but served with the Navy. Smalls earned his commission by stealing the Confederate ship he was serving on as a slave-sailor. Aided by seven fellow slave-sailors, Smalls took the helm of the three hundred-ton side-wheel steamer *Planter* in the early morning of May 13, 1862, and sailed it out of Charleston Harbor, delivering it to the U.S. Navy's blockade offshore. Fitted with two guns and carrying four others as cargo, the *Planter* was a welcome addition to the Union fleet. Having demonstrated his ability and leadership, Smalls served as pilot of the *Planter* for a time before piloting the gunboat *Keokuk*. During Reconstruction, the former slave was elected to the United States Congress as a representative from the state of South Carolina and was made a major general in the state militia.

While not accepted into the Union forces, African American women also played an important role during the War. Many endured great hardships in their efforts to keep their families together as their husbands, fathers, and sons marched off to war. While some African American women served as volunteer nurses, others took a more aggressive role in support of the Union cause. Both Sojourner Truth and Harriet Tubman used their knowledge of Underground Railroad routes to guide federal forces operating in hostile territory. In one such instance, Tubman led three hundred Union cavalrymen on a raid in South Carolina that freed eight hundred slaves and destroyed cotton valuable to the Confederacy.

The Medal of Honor

America's highest decoration for valor was established during the Civil War when Congress authorized issuance of a Medal of Honor on December 21, 1861. Issuance was initially limited to enlisted men of the Navy and the Marine Corps, but the award was expanded to include the Army on July 12, 1862. On March 3, 1863, commissioned officers also became eligible for the Medal of Honor. During the Civil War, 1,523 Medals of Honor were awarded, 23 to African American servicemen. The first African American recipient was Sergeant William H. Carney of the 54th Massachusetts Infantry for combat valor on July 18, 1863 at Fort Wagner, South Carolina. Thirteen of the medals were awarded to African American soldiers who fought in the battle of New Market Heights, Virginia on September 29–30, 1864.

Although the Union did not actively recruit African Americans until 1863, their numbers proved significant during the Civil War. U.S. Colored Troops constituted 13 percent of the Army, while African American sailors accounted for about 8 percent of the Union Navy. By the end of the war, more than 37,000 African American servicemen had died, constituting nearly 35 percent of all African Americans who served in combat.

◆ THE INDIAN CAMPAIGNS (1866–1890)

Post-Civil War America acquired a new appreciation for the importance of military power. In 1866, the 39th Congress passed legislation to "increase and fix the Military Establishment of the United States." The peacetime army would have five artillery regiments, ten cavalry regiments and forty-five infantry regiments. This legislation also stipulated "That to the six regiments of cavalry now in service shall be added four regiments, two of which shall be composed of colored men . . . . " Consequently, the nation gained its first African American regular Army regiments: The 9th and 10th Cavalry, and the 24th and 25th Infantry, which would become known as the "Buffalo Soldiers." This nickname was bestowed upon the soldiers by Plains Indians who saw a resemblance between their hair and that of the buffalo, an animal the Indians considered sacred. Although the term "Buffalo Soldiers" initially denoted those four post-Civil War regiments, it was later proudly adopted by veterans of all racially segregated African American Army ground units of the 1866–1950 era.

The general perception today of the makeup of the U.S. Army during the post-Civil War westward expansion does not reflect its true composition. Approximately twenty percent of army soldiers on duty in the West were African American. The mythology of the cavalry riding to rescue of endangered settlers does not reflect that many of these armed horsemen were African American. Despite often working with rejected horses, inadequate rations, and deteriorating equipment—compounded by the hostility often shown them by many white settlers, as well as some of their own officers—the African American regiments enjoyed the lowest desertion rates of all Army units.

The heroism of African American soldiers is attested to by the 18 Medals of Honor they earned during what historians term both "The Indian Campaigns" and "The Plains War." However, as 370 Medals of Honor were awarded during that era of military history, the 18 given

Christian A. Fleetwood received the Congressional Medal of Honor during the Civil War (The Library of Congress).

to African American soldiers certainly does not reflect a number proportional to those received by whites, when considering their percentage of all soldiers serving. The first Medal of Honor awarded to an African American soldier during the period was presented to First Sergeant Emanuel Stance of Company F, 9th Cavalry for actions occurring on May 20, 1870, in the battle of Kickapoo Springs, Texas.

African American participation in the war against Native Americans was embedded in historical ironies, both in terms of fighting another race subjugated by Anglo-Americans, and in terms of anti-African American sentiment within the United States military itself. One of many painful episodes for the original "Buffalo Soldiers" was the case of Second Lieutenant Henry Ossian Flipper. Born in Thomasville, Georgia on March 21, 1856, Flipper was the first African American to graduate from the U.S. Military Academy at West Point, New York. He ranked fiftieth among the seventy-six members of the Class of 1887 and became the only African American commissioned officer in the regular Army. Assigned initially to Fort Sill, Oklahoma Territory, Lieutenant Flipper was eventually sent to Fort Davis, Texas.

He was assigned the duties routine to a newly-commissioned officer, such as surveying and supervising construction projects. Flipper also acquired some combat experience fighting Apache Indians led by Chief Victoria.

In August of 1881, Lieutenant Flipper was arrested and charged with failing to mail $3,700.00 in checks to the Army Chief of Commissary. The young lieutenant was tried for embezzlement and conduct unbecoming an officer. He was acquitted of the first charge (the checks were found in his quarters), but convicted of the second. Upon confirmation of his sentence by President Chester Arthur, Flipper was dismissed from the service on June 30, 1882. Returning to civilian life, Flipper used his West Point education as a surveyor and engineer in working for mining companies. He also published his memoirs as well as technical books dealing with both Mexican and Venezuelan laws. Additionally, Flipper served as a translator for the Senate Committee on Foreign Relations, and became a special assistant to the Secretary of the Interior.

Nearly a century after Flipper left West Point, a review of his record indicated that he had been framed by his fellow officers. His records were corrected, and he was granted an honorable discharge from the Army. On the 100th anniversary of his graduation, a memorial bust and alcove were dedicated in his honor in the cadet library at the U.S. Military Academy.

There were only two other nineteenth-century African American graduates of West Point: John H. Alexander (1864–1894), in the Class of 1887, and Charles A. Young (1864–1922), in the Class of 1889. It would be 47 years before another African American cadet graduated from the U.S. Military Academy.

◆ THE SPANISH-AMERICAN WAR (1898)

America's "Ten Week War" with Spain marked the nation's emergence as a global colonial power. Although the United States had just completed its own "Indian Campaigns," the tension between the two nations arose from Spain's treatment of Cuba's indigenous population. In 1885, open rebellion by the Cuban people resulted in brutal suppression by the Spanish. The battleship *USS Maine* was sent to Cuba to protect U.S. interests there and as a reminder of America's intention to enforce the Monroe Doctrine.

On the evening of February 15, 1898, a gigantic explosion rocked the warship. It sank rapidly in Havana harbor, killing 266 U.S. sailors—22 of them African Americans. The cause of the Maine's sinking was undetermined, but inflamed American passions were demonstrated by the slogan, "Remember the Maine, to hell with Spain."

Lieutenant Henry O. Flipper (National Archives and Records Administration)

On March 29, the United States issued an ultimatum to Spain, demanding the release of Cubans from brutal detention camps, the declaration of an armistice, and preparations for peace negotiations mediated by President McKinley. The Spanish government did not comply and, on April 19, the United States Congress proclaimed Cuba free and independent. In its proclamation, Congress authorized the president to use U.S. troops to remove Spanish forces from Cuba.

In the annals of U.S. military history, the Spanish-American War was of special significance for the African American officer. It was the first time that African American men served in every Army grade below general officer. This opportunity arose because of a geographically-determined national security strategy. Separated from both Europe and Asia by oceans, the United States understood that those waters also provided a mobilization time cushion. Any perceived threat from either direction had to overcome United States naval power before touching the mainland. Thus, the Navy became the "first line of defense." The small U.S. Army was really a cadre force. Time would permit recruitment, training, and deployment of volunteers or draft-

ees who would fight on United States soil led by experienced regulars. An additional mobilization asset was the various state militias comprised of part-time citizen soldiers.

The war with Spain was an expeditionary campaign requiring maritime deployment to foreign soil. Instead of a mobilize-and-defend situation, the United States had to mobilize and transport before deploying on foreign soil. It was the nation's first large-scale exposure to the complex logistics of overseas operations, an experience that would evolve into occupation duty and related counterinsurgency warfare.

The regular Army of only 28,000 men included the African American 9th and 10th Cavalry Regiments, and the 24th and 25th Infantry Regiments. On June 24, 1898, one squadron of the 10th Cavalry, two squadrons of Rough Riders, which were a regiment of U.S. cavalry volunteers recruited by Theodore Roosevelt, and a squadron from the regular Army's 1st Cavalry, attacked and defeated twice their number of Spanish soldiers. When Rough Riders were pinned down by Spanish fire while crossing open ground near Las Guasimas, 10th Cavalry troops and soldiers from the 1st Cavalry regiment arrived and relieved the pressure. John J. "Black Jack" Pershing, the 10th Cavalry's regimental quartermaster, credited his men with "relieving the Rough Riders from the volleys that were being poured into them from that portion of the Spanish line."

The 25th Infantry also took part in the action, storming the village of El Caney on the morning of July 1. Armed with a battery of Hotchkiss automatic guns, the 10th Cavalry figured prominently in taking Kettle Hill, while the 24th Infantry, along with the 71st New York Volunteers, stormed San Juan Hill. African American soldiers also manned trenches around Santiago de Cuba, which capitulated in mid-July, ending the war in Cuba. The end of the war, however, did not end the danger to the occupying troops.

Although hostilities between the United States and Spain were officially ended, U.S. troops in Cuba faced a challenge more deadly than the Spanish forces. More than three of every four deaths among U.S. troops were attributed to disease, particularly typhoid and yellow fever. In the mistaken belief that peoples of African descent had a natural immunity to tropical disease, troops of the 24th Infantry were assigned work details at a hospital treating victims of typhoid and yellow fever. Roughly half of the African American troops assigned to the hospital contracted the illnesses. Many of the African American female volunteer nurses who cared for the sick and dying also became victims.

African Americans also served in the U.S. Volunteer Infantry (USVI), a manpower augmentation of 175,000

The 24th Negro Infantry distinguished itself during Spanish-American War campaigns (The Library of Congress).

troops from the federalized national guard reserves. The USVI was to include the nation's oldest African American national guard unit, which had its organizational roots in Chicago, Illinois. Formed in the wake of the 1871 Chicago fire, it was originally known as the Hannibal Guards. It became an Illinois militia unit on May 5, 1890 as the 9th Battalion, commanded by Major Benjamin G. Johnson, an African American. When the Spanish-American War erupted, other African American militia regiments were organized: the 3rd Alabama, the 23rd Kansas, the 3rd North Carolina, the 9th Ohio, and the 6th Virginia.

Until converted into artillery battalions in World War II, the 8th Illinois USVI was always commanded by an African American officer; Colonel John R. Marshall was the highest-ranking African American officer of the Spanish-American War and commanded the 8th Illinois until 1914. Marshall was born on March 15, 1859, in Alexandria, Virginia. After attending public schools in Alexandria and Washington, DC, he became an apprentice bricklayer. After moving to Chicago, he was appointed deputy clerk of Cook County. Marshall joined the Illinois National Guard, organized a battalion, and served in it as a lieutenant and major. In June of 1892, he

was commissioned a colonel and assumed command of the 8th Illinois USVI Regiment. He led the regiment to Cuba where it joined with the 23rd Kansas and 3rd North Carolina in occupation duty.

The Spanish-American War provided a small increase in the number of African American regular Army officers. Benjamin O. Davis served as a lieutenant in the 8th Illinois USVI. Upon his discharge, he enlisted in the regular Army on June 14, 1899, as a private in the 9th Cavalry. He was promoted to corporal and then to sergeant major. Davis was commissioned a U.S. Army second lieutenant of cavalry on February 2, 1901. Also commissioned as regular Army officers that year were John R. Lynch and John E. Green. As the twentieth century began, the U.S. Army had four African American commissioned officers (excluding chaplains): Captain Charles Young, and Lieutenants Davis, Green, and Lynch. In 1940, Davis would become the nation's first African American general officer.

Although only ten weeks long, the Spanish-American War produced fifty-two Medal of Honor recipients, among them six African Americans. Five were from the 10th Cavalry, which fought as infantry in Cuba, while the sixth was a African American sailor stationed aboard the *USS Iowa*, which saw action in the waters off Santiago, Cuba.

◆ WORLD WAR I (1914–1918)

The nation's entry into World War I raised the question of how to utilize African American troops. The Army's existing African American units were kept on patrol in the Southwest or sent for duty in the Philippines. The majority of African American draftees or enlistees were assigned to stevedore units at ports or to labor units as quartermaster troops. Of the more than 400,000 African American soldiers who served during the war, only about ten percent saw combat duty, assigned to either of two infantry divisions: the 92nd Infantry Division and the 93rd Infantry Division (Provisional). The 92nd was mainly comprised of draftees, while the 93rd had three regiments made up of National Guard units from Connecticut, Illinois, Maryland, Massachusetts, New York, Ohio, Tennessee and the District of Columbia, with a fourth regiment made up of draftees. Neither infantry division trained together as a unit in the United States. As many white citizens feared arming a substantial number of African Americans in a single location, the Army stationed the individual regiments of each division in widely-separated areas of the country. The regiments did not link up together as divisions until they reached France.

The most difficult problem for the War Department was the demand that African Americans be trained as commissioned officers. Initially, the idea was dismissed as ludicrous as it was said to be "common knowledge" that African Americans inherently lacked leadership qualities. Only the persistence of the NAACP, the Urban League and such African American newspapers as *The Chicago Defender*, helped change War Department policy. An African American Officer Training School was established at Fort Des Moines, Iowa. On October 14, 1917, the school graduated and commissioned the first class of 639 African American officers. By the close of the war, 1,200 African American officer candidates had earned commissions from the school. Although that number was far greater than had been commissioned in prior wars, it still represented only seven-tenths of one percent of the officer corps. By comparison, African American troops accounted for 13 percent of the total active duty force. In addition, the War Department had an ironclad rule that no African American officer could command white officers or enlisted men.

To comply with this rule, the War Department needed to find a way of skirting the problem posed by Lieutenant Colonel Charles Young, the Army's highest-ranking African American officer and a West Point graduate. Young had trained African American troops for combat and led them in action, causing some white officers to fear that he would assume command of the 10th Cavalry, which was otherwise commanded by whites. Pressured by these officers, the United States senators who represented them in Congress, and President Wilson, the War Department developed a strategy to eliminate Young from consideration. Young, who had contracted Bright's disease, but whose physical health appeared excellent otherwise, was given a medical examination in July of 1917. The medical report was forwarded to a retiring board that recommended that he be removed from active duty due to ill health; the War Department concurred.

To prove his fitness for active duty, Colonel Young rode on horseback (walking a quarter of the distance for good measure) from Xenia, Ohio to Washington, DC. Starting on June 6, 1918, he covered the 497-mile distance in 16 days, taking just one day off to rest. While Young received support from the African American press and many powerful friends, the War Department relented only five days before the end of World War I. Though he was promoted to full colonel while in retirement, he was called to active service to command a company of trainees at Camp Grant, Illinois—an assignment usually given to officers at the rank of captain. Young never was given the opportunity to command troops in Europe, which likely would have resulted in his promotion to brigadier general. Though he remained on active duty until his death on January 8, 1922, Young never received another promotion.

One solution used by the military to solve the issue of utilizing African American officers and soldiers during the war was to offer African American regiments to foreign forces. The 93rd Infantry Division was attached to the allied French Army and used French weapons, wore French helmets, and ate French rations—only their uniforms were provided by the U.S. Army. Colonel William Hayward, commander of New York's 369th Infantry Regiment that constituted one of the four regiments of the 93rd, criticized General John J. Pershing for this decision. Colonel Hayward charged that Pershing "simply put the black orphan in a basket, set it on the doorstep of the French, pulled the bell, and went away."

Despite this status, it was the 369th Infantry Regiment (15th New York) that established the best World War I record of any U.S. Army infantry regiment. Attached to the French 4th Army, the 369th served for 191 consecutive days in the trenches, longer than any other U.S. unit. In that time they never lost a foot of ground to the enemy, nor had a single soldier taken prisoner by the Germans. The 369th gathered many nicknames. They called themselves the "Black Rattlers," while the French

A group of African American World War I sailors (National Archives and Records Administration).

dubbed them the "Men of Bronze" and the Germans labeled them the "Harlem Hell Fighters."

In 1919, Columbia University President Nicholas Murray Butler gave *Harper's Weekly* his assessment of the 369th Infantry Regiment, "No American soldier saw harder or more constant fighting and none gave better accounts of themselves. When fighting was to be done, this regiment was there."

Unlike the 93rd Infantry Division, which only came together as a unit in France before being broken up and parceled out to various French commands, the 92nd Infantry Division remained intact. Unfortunately, the 92nd did not fare nearly as well as did the 93rd. The commander, Major General Charles C. Ballou, shared the prejudices of many white officers and rarely stood up for his African American troops. Ballou seldom insured that the soldiers of the 92nd were provided with proper training, equipment, and support services. Upon their arrival in France, the ill-prepared African American soldiers under his command were immediately sent into the fray. Led by white senior officers and unseasoned African American junior officers, the disorganized regiments suffered heavy casualties during several key offenses late in the war.

Ballou's response to the failings of the 92nd was to blame his junior officers, bringing thirty up for court-martial on charges of cowardice. Several officers were convicted by an all-white court-martial board and given harsh sentences before the trials were suspended with the transfer of the 92nd to the command of Lieutenant General Robert L. Bullard. Under Bullard, the morale and training of the 92nd increased, as did its fighting effectiveness. Nevertheless, the damage was done. Bullard was unhappy with the general performance of the division and worried about its reflection on him as a leader. As soon as the war ended, he recommended the immediate transfer of the division back to the United States. The result of the 92nd Infantry's substandard performance was to bolster the already negative opinions of critics of African American units.

Despite the "Jim Crow" atmosphere, African American soldiers still earned an impressive number of awards for combat bravery in defeating German troops. Sergeant Henry Johnson and Private Needham Roberts of New York's 369th Infantry Regiment were the first Americans, black or white, to receive the French Croix de Guerre. France awarded its Croix de Guerre to 34 African American officers and 89 African American enlisted men during the war. In the 92nd Infantry, 14 African American officers and 43 African American enlisted men earned the U.S. Army's Distinguished Service Cross (DSC). Some 10 officers and 34 enlisted men of the 93rd Infantry were DSC recipients.

The African American presence in the U.S. Navy during World War I was negligible. Restricted to ratings in the messmen branch (cooks, stewards, mess attendants), few African Americans enlisted in the Navy. Of a total naval strength of 435,398, only 5,328 were African American by June 30, 1918. Thus, African Americans accounted for only 1.2 percent of the Navy. Continuing its policy of preventing African Americans from earning commissions, the naval officer corps remained completely white. In addition, some naval captains refused to transport African American army troops home after the war.

Although they were not permitted to serve in the Armed Forces, African American women contributed to America's efforts in World War I. They made bandages, worked in hospitals and troop centers, and promoted the purchase of Liberty Bonds to finance the war effort. They also served in the Red Cross, YWCA, and other relief organizations.

Posthumous Medal of Honor Awarded

No Medal of Honor was awarded to an African American serviceman during World War I. In 1988, the Department of the Army researched the National Archives to determine whether racial barriers had prevented the awarding of the nation's highest decoration for valor to an African American. The archives search produced evidence that Corporal Freddie Stowers of Anderson County, South Carolina, had been recommended for the award. For "unknown reasons," the recommendation had not been processed. Stowers was a squad leader in Company C, 371st Infantry Regiment, 93rd Infantry Division. On September 28, 1918, he led his squad through heavy machine-gun fire and destroyed the gun position on Hill 188 in the Champagne Marne Sector, France. Mortally wounded, Stowers led his men through a second trench line. Unable to proceed any further, Stowers continued to yell encouragement to his comrades until dying on the field of battle. On April 24, 1991, President George Bush belatedly presented Stowers's Medal of Honor to his surviving sisters in a White House ceremony.

◆ THE INTERWAR YEARS (1919–1940)

With the end of the war, the nation generally returned to applying the *Plessy v. Ferguson* doctrine. Some senior white Army officers advocated barring enlistment or reenlistment of African Americans altogether, an action that would have eventually abolished the four African American regular Army regiments by attrition.

A focal point of the Army's discriminatory sentiment was the African American commissioned officer. Despite countless well-documented cases of superb combat leadership, most African American officers were eliminated from active duty following World War I. An effective tool against retaining African American officers was their alleged poor performance that was buttressed by criticism of the African American Officer Training School (OTS) at Des Moines, Iowa. One of the severest critics was Major General Ballou, commander of the 92nd Infantry Division during World War I. Ballou emphasized that while white candidates were required to be college graduates, "only high school educations were required for . . . the colored . . . and in many cases these high school educations would have been a disgrace to any grammar school. For the parts of a machine requiring the finest steel, pot metal was provided."

However, there were combat-experienced white officers who held a decidedly different view of African American officer training, such as Major Thomas A. Roberts. "As I understand the question," Roberts wrote in April of 1920, "what the progressive Negro desires today is the removal of discrimination against him; that this can be accomplished in a military sense I believe to be largely possible, but not if men of the two races are segregated." Noting his appreciation of the "tremendous force of the prejudice against association between Negroes and whites," Roberts declared "my experience has made me believe that the better element among the Negroes desires the removal of the restriction rather than the association itself."

The exclusionary campaign was also evident in the Army's civilian components, the National Guard and Officers Reserve. New York's 369th Infantry Regiment was maintained at full strength, though the 8th Illinois lost one battalion.

As for commissioned officers, the Reserve Officers Training Corps (ROTC) detachments at Howard and Wilberforce Universities provided the bulk of new African American second lieutenants. With no allocations for African American officers to attend service schools, the lack of opportunity to maintain proficiency caused considerable attrition in the number of African American reserve officers. To retain their commissions, other officers took advantage of correspondence and specially-organized seminar courses.

◆ WORLD WAR II (1941–1945)

Less than two months after war began in Europe, the nation's preeminent African American organizations, the NAACP and the National Urban League, mobilized in an effort to defeat U.S. racial segregation as well as Axis fascism. The African American community foresaw that the United States would eventually ally itself with Britain and France in war against Germany, Italy, and Japan.

Military mobilization began on August 27, 1940, with the federalizing of the National Guard and activation of the Organized Reserve. When Japan attacked Pearl Harbor on December 7, 1941, there were 120,000 officers and 1,523,000 enlisted men on active duty in the Army and its air corps. On September 16, 1940, the nation began its first peacetime draft. By the end of World War II, the Selective Service System had inducted 10,110,104 men, of which 1,082,539 (10.7 percent) were African American.

America's war effort required rapid expansion of both military and industrial power. Victory depended on the constant provision of ammunition, guns, planes, tanks, naval vessels, and merchant ships. The nation would have to unite to survive. A minority number of African Americans, including Nation of Islam founder Elijah Muhammad, openly favored a Japanese victory; Muhammad's stance led to a four-year term in the U.S. Penitentiary at Milan, Michigan.

Essential to the desegregation activism of both the NAACP and the Urban League was the impact of African American-owned weekly newspapers, such as Robert S. Abbott's *Chicago Defender* and Robert Vann's *Pittsburgh Courier*. The rallying slogan was the "Double V"—victory against fascism abroad and racial discrimination at home. The goal was equal opportunity in the armed services and within the civilian defense industries.

Soon, the NAACP and the Urban League were joined by the African American activists of the March on Washington movement, led by A. Philip Randolph of the Brotherhood of Sleeping Car Porters and Maids. Randolph predicted that upwards of 100,000 African Americans would march on Washington demanding equal employment opportunities in defense plant employment. On June 25, 1941, a week before the scheduled march, President Franklin D. Roosevelt forestalled the event by issuing Executive Order 8802. The President's order established a Committee on Fair Employment Practice "to provide for the full and equitable participation of all workers in defense industries, without discrimination." Of course, the executive order did not apply to the armed services.

The necessity of winning the war opened the economy to millions of African American men and women who surged into defense plants and earned the same wages as their white counterparts. Thus, the war years brought economic upward mobility to many African American civilians. The postwar benefits of the G.I. Bill of Rights also played a major role, causing the number of African American college graduates and home owners to increase dramatically.

The U.S. Army had actually taken its first steps toward racial integration early in World War II. The obvious waste of duplicated facilities caused the Army to operate all of its 24 officer candidate schools as racially-integrated institutions, where the primary quality sought was proven leadership capacity. The "ninety-day wonders," who survived the standard three-month course, were commissioned as second lieutenants from each of the 24 Army branches, ranging from the Army Air Forces Administrative School (Miami, Florida) to the Tank Destroyer School (Camp Hood, Texas). However, upon graduation, African American officers were only assigned to African American units.

The Army Air Force (AAF)

The exception in racially-integrated Army officer procurement during World War II was the Army Air Force Aviation Cadet program, which trained pilots, bombardiers, and navigators. Ironically, African American non-flying officers graduated from the integrated AAF Officer Candidate School at Miami Beach.

A total of 926 African American pilots earned their commissions and wings at the segregated Tuskegee Army Air Field (TAAF) near Chehaw, Alabama. The 673 single-engine TAAF pilot graduates would eventually form the four squadrons of the 332nd Fighter Group.

Led by Lieutenant Colonel Benjamin O. Davis, Jr., a 1936 West Point graduate, the 99th Fighter Squadron was assigned to the 33rd Fighter Group commanded by Colonel William M. Momyer. The 99th's first operational mission was a June 2, 1943, strafing attack on the Italian island of Pantelleria. On that date, Captain Charles B. Hall scored the squadron's first air victory by shooting down an FW-190 and damaging an ME-109. The 99th then settled into normal operations.

In September, Colonel Davis was recalled to take command of the 332nd Fighter Group. It was at that point that he and the African American community discovered that the "Tuskegee Experiment" was about to be labeled a failure. To that effect, Colonel Momyer submitted an extremely negative appraisal of the 99th Fighter Squadron:

> "Based on the performance of the 99th Fighter Squadron to date, it is my opinion that they are not of the fighting caliber of any squadron in this group. They have failed to display the aggressiveness and daring for combat that are necessary to a first class fighting organization. It may be expected that we will get less work and less operational time out of the 99th Fighter Squadron than any squadron in this group."

Members of the 92nd Division marching in Ponsacco, Italy during World War II.

On October 16, 1943, squadron commander Davis appeared before the War Department's Committee on Special [Negro] Troop Policies to answer his group commander's allegations. In his 1991 autobiography, written after his retirement as an Air Force lieutenant general, Davis described the problem he faced at the Pentagon as a lieutenant colonel. He wrote, "It would have been hopeless for me to stress the hostility and racism of whites as the motive behind the letter, although that was clearly the case. Instead, I had to adopt a quiet, reasoned approach, presenting the facts about the 99th in a way that would appeal to fairness and win out over ignorance and racism."

Davis presented such a convincing factual case that Army Chief of Staff General George C. Marshall ordered a G-3 [operations] study of the African American squadron. The study's title "Operations of the 99th Fighter Squadron Compared with Other P-40 Squadrons in the Mediterranean Theatre of Operations" precisely describes its contents. In his book, General Davis described the G-3 study: "It rated the 99th according to readiness, squadron missions, friendly losses versus enemy losses, and sorties dispatched." The opening statement in the report was the clincher: "An examina-

tion of the record of the 99th Fighter Squadron reveals no significant general difference between this squadron and the balance of the P-40 squadrons in the Mediterranean Theatre of Operations."

On October 13, 1942, the Army had activated the 100th, 301st, and 302nd Fighter Squadrons. Combined with the 99th, the four squadrons became the 332nd Fighter Group. Colonel Robert R. Selway, Jr., a white pilot, was its initial commanding officer. With the 99th vindicated by the G-3 study, Davis assumed command of the Fighter Group at Selfridge Army Air Field, Michigan. The three squadrons of the 332nd previously based in the United States departed for Italy on January 3, 1944, absorbing the 99th as its fourth squadron upon arrival.

During the period that the 99th was deployed and the 332nd was organizing, the TAAF program expanded to training two-engine B-25 pilots. While the fighter pilot fought alone, the B-25 "Mitchell" medium bomber required a five to six-man crew that included two pilots, a bombardier, and a navigator. The 253 medium bomber pilots trained at TAAF, as well as 393 African American navigators and bombardiers from Hondo and Midland Fields in Texas, formed the nation's second African American flying organization when the Army Air Force

Trained in Tuskegee, Alabama, and later based in southern Italy, the Tuskegee Airmen flew sorties into southern Europe and North Africa during World War II (The Library of Congress).

activated the four-squadron 477th Bombardment Group (Medium) in June of 1943.

The 477th was plagued from the start by a shortage of enlisted aircrew members, ground technicians, and even airplanes. Fifteen months after activation, the 477th was still short 26 pilots, 43 copilots, 2 bombardier-navigators, and all of its authorized 288 gunners. Moving from base to base for "operational training," the 477th logged 17,875 flying hours in one year without a major accident. Although finally earmarked for duty in the Pacific, the war ended before the 477th was deployed overseas.

As for the 332nd Fighter Group, it became a famous flying escort for heavy bombers. It was the only AAF fighter group that never lost an escorted bomber to enemy planes. The wartime record of the 332nd Fighter Group was 103 enemy aircraft destroyed during 1,578 combat missions. In addition to more than 100 Distinguished Flying Crosses, the 332nd also earned three Distinguished Unit Citations.

The "Tuskegee Experiment" thus proved that African American could fly advanced aircraft and could also conduct highly successful combat operations meeting

AAF standards. The fruit of the Tuskegee Airmen's efforts would be harvested in less than three years—the 1948 racial desegregation of the U.S. Armed Forces.

The Ground War

During World War II, the U.S. Army fielded two major African American combat organizations: the 92nd Infantry Division in Europe, and the 93rd Infantry Division in the Pacific.

Just as in World War I, the 93rd Infantry Division suffered from fragmentation. Major General Raymond G. Lehman's headquarters sailed from San Francisco on January 11, 1944, while the artillery and infantry battalions and division headquarters assembled on Guadalcanal at the end of February. This would be the last time all the components of the division would be in the same place. The division would spend the rest of the war island-hopping, relieving units that had defeated Japanese troops. World War II casualties sustained by the 93rd were 12 killed in action, 121 wounded in action and five who died of wounds. The usual after-action comments were made concerning the lack of initiative by junior officers, but overall, the 93rd was described as well-disciplined and with morale.

The 92nd Infantry Division, in contrast, gained a reputation as a chaotic outfit. During its preparation for deployment overseas, portions of the 92nd were sprinkled across the United States. While the division headquarters were at Fort Huachuca, Arizona, subordinate units were stationed at Fort McClellan, Alabama; Camp Robinson, Arkansas; Camp Breckinridge, Kentucky; and Camp Atterbury, Indiana. The division's World War II casualty figures were vastly different from those of the 93rd: 548 killed in action, 2,187 wounded in action, and 68 who died of wounds. From its training in the United States through combat in Europe, the division's main problem seemed to be its commander, Major General Edward M. Almond. Many veterans of the 92nd continue to blame General Almond for the division's reputation and casualties.

It appears that "Ned" Almond was racist. In a 1984 interview, retired Lieutenant General William P. Ennis, Jr. gave a "warts and all" description of Almond. As a World War II brigadier general, Ennis had commanded the corps artillery that supported the 92nd Infantry Division. According to Ennis, Almond and many white Southern officers in the division were selected because "in theory, they knew more about handling Negroes than anybody else, though I can't imagine why because [Almond] just despised the ground they walked on." One African American officer, Captain Hondon B. Hargrove, was a 1938 Wilberforce University ROTC graduate. After his wartime service in the division's 597th Field Artillery Battalion, he commented that Almond did not believe "any black, no matter what his file showed, or how much training he had, was able in an officer's position . . . . He firmly believed only white officers could get the best out of [Negro troops] . . . [and] just could not countenance black officers leading them."

While Almond denigrated the competence of African American officers, Officer Candidate School (OCS) commandants generally held opposite views. For example, Brigadier General H. T. Mayberry, who commanded the Tank Destroyer OCS, observed in a 1945 interview that "a considerable number of young, potentially outstanding Negro officers were graduated. It was surprising—to me, at least—how high the Negroes (those who graduated) stood in the classes." Lieutenant Colonel Robert C. Ross, a field artillery battalion commander in the 92nd Infantry Division, reported to Almond on five African American officers who completed the basic artillery course. Three were made course instructors, while two were selected "as outstanding students from the entire forty-eight officers, both white and colored, from the first Officers Basic School."

General Almond established his headquarters at Viareggio, Italy on October 5, 1944. Two days later, the division's 370th Infantry Regiment began its assault on Massa. Professor Lee described the 92nd Infantry Division's major weakness: "It was a problem in faith and lack of it—the wavering faith of commanders in the ability and determination of subordinates and enlisted men, and the continuation in the minds of enlisted men of training period convictions that they could not trust their leaders." Thus, the Massa attack degenerated into chaos. In what was to be a major charge against the division, the men began to "melt away" from the fighting. After Massa, there were increasing cases of mutinous behavior toward both black and white officers.

In February 1945, the 92nd became the focus of serious Pentagon scrutiny. Truman K. Gibson, Jr., an African American insurance company lawyer from Chicago and Civilian Aide to Secretary of War Henry L. Stimpson, examined the situation. In his assessment, Gibson refused to generalize about the capabilities of African American soldiers based on the performance of General Almond's division. In a March 14 news conference in Rome, Gibson maintained that "If the division proves anything, it does not prove that Negroes can't fight. There is no question in my mind about the courage of Negro officers or soldiers and any generalization on the basis of race is entirely unfounded."

On May 14, 1945, a week after Germany surrendered, Lieutenant Colonel Marcus H. Ray wrote a letter to Gibson. A Chicagoan, as was Gibson, Colonel Ray was a National Guard officer of the 8th Illinois when it mobilized in 1940, and ended the war as commanding officer of the 600th Field Artillery Battalion of the 92nd Infantry Division. Colonel Ray closed his letter to Gibson by observing that "those who died in the proper performance of their assigned duties are our men of the decade and all honor should be paid them. They were Americans before all else. Racially, we have been the victims of an unfortunate chain of circumstances backgrounded by the unchanged American attitude as regards the proper 'place' of the Negro. . . . I do not believe the 92nd a complete failure as a combat unit, but when I think of what it might have been, I am heartsick. . . ."

The 761st Tank Battalion

The most highly acclaimed African American ground combat unit of World War II was the 761st Tank Battalion. As an organization, it enjoyed substantially better circumstances than the 92nd Infantry Division. Before the United States entered World War II, some white U.S. Army officers favored opening opportunities for black soldiers. They rejected the dogma of their colleagues who declared that modern weaponry was "too technical" for African Americans. One such officer, Lieutenant General Lesley James McNair, became the commanding general of Army ground forces. In that post he spent most of his time visiting the nationwide array of ground forces training camps. When he visited the 761st at Camp Claiborne, Louisiana, he openly praised and encouraged the Army's first African American tankers. When the 761st went ashore in France on October 10, 1944, the men believed, rightly, that their outfit's existence was due mainly to McNair. (General McNair was killed by United States "friendly fire" on July 25, 1944, in France. The Joint Chiefs of Staff National Defense University is located at Fort Lesley J. McNair, named in his honor, in Washington, DC.)

The 761st joined the 26th Division on October 31 and was welcomed by the division commander, Major General Willard S. Paul: "I am damned glad to have you with us. We have been expecting you for a long time, and I am sure you are going to give a good account of yourselves." Two days later, Lieutenant General George S. Patton visited and welcomed the 761st. Equipped with Sherman Tanks, the 761st saw its initial combat experience on November 8, 1944 at Athaniville, France—the first of 183 continuous days of combat for the battalion. The battalion is credited with killing 6,266 enemy soldiers and capturing 15,818. Despite its outstanding combat record, the 761st did not receive a Presidential Unit Citation until January 24, 1978.

One veteran of the 761st Tank Battalion, Company A, was posthumously awarded the Medal of Honor in January of 1997. Staff Sergeant Ruben Rivers, of Tecumseh, Oklahoma, was severely wounded on November 16, 1944, when his tank hit a German mine at a railroad crossing outside of Guebling, France. With his lower thigh sliced to the bone, Rivers declined a morphine injection and refused evacuation. Instead, he took command of another tank at the head of the column and led the advance toward their next objective, Bourgaltroff. Three days later, fierce fighting ensued when Company A was met at Bourgaltroff by enemy tanks and anti-tank weapons. Under heavy fire, his company commander ordered his tanks to pull back below the crest of a hill. Rivers, however, had spotted the enemy positions and radioed his commander that he would press the fight. Rivers continued firing until the tank was hit in the turret by an armor-piercing round, killing him and wounding the other members of the crew.

Smaller African American combat units made significant contributions in combat operations in both Europe and the Pacific. Fire from African American artillerymen helped dislodge German troops as U.S. forces fought to cross the Rhine River. For its defense of Bastogne, a strategic city in Belgium, the 969th Field Artillery Battalion received a Distinguished Unit Citation for meritorious service performed while attached to a white organization. Company C of the 614th Tank Destroyer Battalion became the first African American ground unit to win that honor in World War II for driving off a German force that blocked the 411th Infantry in its advance on Climbach, Germany. African American anti-aircraft outfits protected outposts in the Pacific and shot down German aircraft in Europe.

Because of a policy of racial segregation and discrimination, most of the one million African Americans in uniform during World War II were not assigned combat duty. Instead, they were assigned duty in the Service of Supply (SOS). In this capacity, they proved instrumental in the outcome of the war by operating bulldozers and cranes, setting up communications systems, and transporting essential supplies to the front. More than seventy percent of the truck companies in the Army's Motor Transport Service were African American. Their role was critical in Europe because the railroads in France were destroyed by retreating German forces. Therefore, Allied forces had to be supplied by truck. The "Red Ball Express" was formed to meet this need in August of 1944, with an original route between Saint Lo and Paris. On a normal day, 899 vehicles on the Red Ball Express traveled 1,504,616 miles on the trip that took an average time of 54 hours.

The White Ball Route replaced the Red Ball Express in November of 1944. Four of the nine truck companies transporting supplies from Le Havre and Rouen to forward areas were African American. They also saw duty on the Antwerp-Brussels-Charleroi Route and the Green Diamond Route between Normandy and the Brest peninsula. The 3917th Gasoline Supply Company supplied the Third Army with up to 165,000 gallons of gas a day. African American truckers were also well represented among the twelve amphibian truck companies. Though assigned transport duty, African American truckers were subject to hostile fire and were called upon to fight in emergencies. A number received military honors from both the United States and France for courage and meritorious service in combat.

The Women's Auxiliary Army Corps

With the creation of the Women's Auxiliary Army Corps on May 14, 1942, African American women could serve in the U.S. military in greater numbers than ever before. Many of the 4,000 black volunteers, however, were assigned duties unlike their white counterparts. While white women typically typed in offices, most African American women were assigned to cleanup details, laundry, and mess duty. Nevertheless, there were notable exceptions in the branch that would soon be renamed the Women's Army Corps. Overseas, the 6888th Postal Battalion was commanded by African American Major Charity Adams, who arrived in England in 1945. The unit was later sent to the European mainland where it improved the mail delivery system, a system invaluable to troop morale.

African American women also served in the Army Nurse Corps. Initially, African American nurses were only permitted to care for African American patients, but that policy proved impractical. The resentment generated when African American women were assigned to care for German prisoners of war ultimately led to a change in policy, enabling African American nurses to care for wounded Americans, regardless of race.

The Sea Services

Following a decade of excluding African Americans from enlistment, the U.S. Navy decided upon a separate African American branch in 1932. The branch was known as the Stewards' Service, though it was referred to in the African American community as the "sea-going bell hops." In 1940, the Navy consisted of 170,000 men, of whom 4,007 (or 2.3 percent) were African Americans in the Stewards' Service. In addition to African Americans, Navy stewards were also recruited from among Filipinos and other Asian American populations.

The advent of World War II transformed the situation. President Franklin D. Roosevelt had served as assistant secretary of the Navy during World War I and considered it "his branch" of the armed services. Therefore, his January 9, 1942, memo to the Navy had tremendous impact. The president noted to Secretary of the

Navy Frank Knox: "I think that with all the Navy activities, Bureau of Navy might invent something that colored enlistees could do in addition to the rating of messman." The Navy relented on April 7, 1942, by announcing it would accept 14,000 African American enlistees in all ratings and branches. The initial training of African American sailors was conducted at the Great Lakes Naval Training Station, north of Chicago, Illinois.

It was at the station that the Navy finally made a breakthrough in regard to African American personnel. In January of 1944, 16 African American petty officers began a special and intensive course of instruction that was conducted without public announcement. Three months later, the Navy announced the commissioning of 12 African American ensigns and one warrant officer, the Navy's "Golden Thirteen."

Shortly after the "Golden Thirteen" were commissioned, the Navy opened the V-12 officer training programs to African American. Among the V-12 graduates who became Navy officers in World War II were Samuel L. Gravely, Jr. and Carl T. Rowan. Gravely became the Navy's first African American admiral while Rowan is a syndicated columnist and broadcaster.

By the end of World War II, 165,000 African Americans had served in the Navy; 17,000 in the Marine Corps; 5,000 in the Coast Guard; 12,000 in Construction Battalions (Sea Bees); and 24,000 in the Merchant Marine. These African American soldiers served with distinction. Notable among them was mess steward Dorie Miller, who on December 7, 1941, manned a machine gun aboard the *USS West Virginia* as Japanese aircraft attacked Pearl Harbor. Miller was credited with destroying four planes before being ordered to abandon the sinking ship. After some delay, Miller was personally awarded the Navy Cross by Admiral Chester W. Nimitz. He was also promoted to mess attendant first class. Miller died when the escort aircraft carrier *USS Liscombe Bay* was sunk on November 24, 1943. Three other African American mess attendants received the Navy Cross during World War II: Eli Benjamin (*USS Intrepid*); Leonard Harmon (*USS San Francisco*); and William Pinkney (*USS Enterprise*). Dorie Miller is memorialized by one of three Navy warships named for African Americans: the frigates *USS Miller* and *USS Jesse L. Brown* and the missile submarine *USS George Washington Carver*.

Belated Recognition for African American Heroes

Despite their many accomplishments, African American soldiers were not sufficiently honored for their heroics during World War II. Even though 1.2 million African Americans served in the U.S. Armed Forces during war, not one received the nation's highest military award at the time, the Medal of Honor. Additionally, only nine were awarded the military's second highest honor, the Distinguished Service Cross. This was scant recognition, considering that more than 142,000 African Americans died in the war.

In 1992, the U.S. Army contracted with Shaw University for a group of professional military historians to comb the nation's archives and the memories of its veterans, both black and white, to discover why no African Americans had received a Medal of Honor during World War II and to determine whether some deserved the honor. After a 15-month study, the historians cited the racist climate of the Army for the lack of African American recognition and identified ten soldiers who might be deserving of that ultimate military honor. They passed the list of names onto a special Army Senior Officer Awards Board, which narrowed the list to nine, then to the Joint Chiefs of Staff, who reduced it to seven. The Pentagon then sent those seven names to the U.S. Congress and to The White House. As the time limit for awarding the medal had expired in 1952, Congress included a waiver for the seven in the 1997 defense authorization bill. Congress approved a resolution to honor the nominees and sent it on to the president.

At a White House ceremony on January 13, 1997, President Bill Clinton presented Medals of Honor to the families of Staff Sergeant Edward A. Carter, Jr., First Lieutenant John R. Fox, Private First Class Willy F. James, Jr., Staff Sergeant Ruben Rivers, First Lieutenant Charles L. Thomas, Private George Watson, and to the lone survivor, First Lieutenant Vernon J. Baker. The 76-year-old Baker, a 28-year Army veteran, was most gracious in accepting the honor, stating that he had long ago resolved any bitterness that he had felt towards the Army for its past racial discrimination.

◆ THE DESEGREGATION OF THE MILITARY (1946–1949)

As the Allied victory of World War II approached, the highest levels of the United States government recognized that a new era of domestic racial relations had emerged. The war to defeat Fascism had, indeed, involved the entire U.S. population.

One impetus for a change in military policy regarding African Americans was an August 5, 1945 letter from Colonel Noel F. Parrish, commander of Tuskegee Army Air Field, to Brigadier General William E. Hall, Headquarters Army Air Forces. Colonel Parrish recommended "that future policy, instead of retreating defensively further and further, with more and more group concessions, openly progress by slow and reasonable but definite steps toward the employment and treatment of Negroes as individuals which law requires and military efficiency demands."

Although Secretary of War Henry L. Stimson often revealed racist tendencies, his assistant, John R. McCloy, was considerably more liberal. When Robert P. Patterson succeeded Stimson, he adopted McCloy's suggestion for a study on the future use of African Americans in the military. A board of three Army generals conducted the study: Lieutenant General Alvan C. Gillem, Jr., a former corps commander; Major General Lewis A. Pick, who built the Ledo Road in Burma; and Brigadier General Winslow C. Morse of the Army Air Force. During a six-week period, the "Gillem Board" took testimony from more than fifty witnesses in forming the Army's postwar racial policy. Two key individuals who worked with the Gillem Board were the two African American Chicagoans who served sequentially as civilian aide to the secretary of war: Truman K. Gibson, Jr. and the recently discharged Lieutenant Colonel Marcus H. Ray.

The Gillem Board's findings leaned toward more efficient use of African American manpower, but did not advocate actual desegregation. That ambiguity reactivated the prewar coalition of the NAACP, the National Urban League, and the grassroots labor forces led by A. Philip Randolph.

The advent of the Cold War led to the National Security Act of 1947. The new law provided for the establishment of the Department of Defense (DOD), with the subordinate departments of Army, Navy, and Air Force. The act also created the Central Intelligence Agency (CIA).

In the continuing movement toward desegregation of the Armed Forces, 1947 brought two important African American personnel shifts within the Department of Defense: Lieutenant Colonel Marcus H. Ray returned to active duty as senior advisor on racial matters in Europe, and in the Pentagon, Dr. James C. Evans, a Howard University professor and Department of Army official, moved to the new post of special assistant to the secretary of defense. As the highest-ranking African American civilian in the Department of Defense, Dr. Evans served under ten secretaries of defense until his retirement in 1970.

The demand for desegregation of the military became a key political issue in black America. As preparations for the 1948 presidential election intensified, President Harry Truman faced a campaign against Republican Thomas E. Dewey, states rights segregationist Strom Thurmond, and the Progressive Party of former Vice

President Henry A. Wallace. In such a fragmented situation, the African American vote became crucial. By May of 1948, President Truman had decided to desegregate the Armed Forces by executive order. However, the decision required two political concessions. First, no deadlines would be imposed. Second, the order would not denounce racial segregation. On July 26 President Truman issued Executive Order 9981, which signaled an end to segregation in the military.

In June of 1949, Wesley A. Brown became the first African American ever to graduate from the U.S. Naval Academy in Annapolis, Maryland. Brown, who had excelled as a student at Washington, DC's Dunbar High School, was appointed to the academy by New York Congressman Adam Clayton Powell, Jr. in June of 1945. Since Annapolis had opened in 1850, only five African Americans had been admitted to the school. All had either resigned or had been dismissed for alleged academic or disciplinary reasons. Despite harassment by classmates and hostility from instructors, Brown became the 20,699th midshipman to earn a commission from the naval academy.

◆ THE KOREAN WAR (1950–1953)

On June 25, 1950, North Korean forces surged across the 38th parallel and invaded South Korea. They routed U.S. ground forces in Korea and drove them south. At the start of the Korean War, the Air Force was the only completely desegregated branch of the military.

The first victory by U.S. troops in the Korean War occurred on July 20, 1950, at Yechon thanks to the African American soldiers of the 24th Infantry Regiment. Group commander Captain Charles M. Bussey, a World War II Tuskegee Airman, earned a Silver Star for his role in the battle. Two African American soldiers received posthumous Medals of Honor during the Korean War: Private First Class William Thompson and Sergeant Cornelius H. Charlton, both of the 24th Infantry Regiment.

Thompson distinguished himself by bravery and determination above and beyond the call of duty in action on August 6, 1950, near Haman, Korea. While his platoon was reorganizing under cover of darkness, enemy forces overwhelmed the unit with a surprise attack. Johnson set up his machine gun in the path of the onslaught and swept the enemy with fire, momentarily halting their advance and thus permitting the remainder of his platoon to withdraw to a more secure position. Although hit repeatedly by grenade fragments and small-arms fire, he resisted his comrades's efforts to induce him to withdraw. Steadfast at his machine gun, he

African American members of the 2nd Infantry Division crouching in a foxhole during the Korean War.

continued to deliver fire until he was mortally wounded by an enemy grenade.

Charlton, a member of Company C, distinguished himself in action on June 2, 1951, near Chipo-Ri, Korea. During an attack on heavily defended positions on an enemy-held ridge line, his platoon leader was wounded and evacuated. Charlton assumed command, rallied the men, and spearheaded the assault up the hill. Personally eliminating two hostile positions and killing six of the enemy with rifle fire and grenades, he continued up the slope until the unit stalled with heavy casualties. Regrouping the men, he led them forward, only to be forced back again by a shower of grenades. Despite a severe chest wound, Charlton refused medical attention and led a third charge that advanced to the crest of the ridge. He then charged a remaining enemy position on a nearby slope alone and, though hit by a grenade, raked the position with fire that routed the defenders. He died of wounds received during his daring exploits.

The first African American naval officer to lose his life in combat during the Korean War was Ensign Jesse L. Brown, who was also the first African American to earn naval aviator's wings. Brown, a Navy pilot, was shot down shortly after takeoff from the aircraft carrier *USS Leyte* on December 4, 1950. He crash-landed his plane on a snow-covered mountain near North Korea's Chosin Reservoir, but was unable to remove himself from the wreckage. A white pilot landed his aircraft near Brown's, but failed to pull him free. Other flyers radioed for help and, though a rescue helicopter, made it to the location, the tangled metal could not be cut away quickly enough to save the life of the injured airman. Brown, who had previously flown twenty air combat missions, was posthumously awarded a Distinguished Flying Cross and a Purple Heart. On March 18, 1972, the U.S. Navy launched the destroyer escort *USS Jesse L. Brown*, marking the first time a Navy ship was ever named in honor of an African American naval officer.

The Korean War Evolution

The early defeats that the U.S. forces experienced in Korea prompted President Truman to replace his close friend, Secretary of Defense Louis A. Johnson with retired General of the Army George C. Marshall, who had been Truman's secretary of state during from 1947 to 1949. One of Marshall's first acts as secretary of defense was the creation of a new entity: the Office of Assistant Secretary of Defense for Manpower and Reserves (OASD MPR). Marshall appointed Anna M. Rosenberg, a 48-year-old New York City labor and public relations consultant, as head of the office. In 1944, she had persuaded President Franklin D. Roosevelt to have Congress enact the education provisions of the World War II G. I. Bill of Rights. Dr. James C. Evans's Office of Special Assistant became a part of the OASD (MPR), which brought together two individuals knowledgeable in the rigors of discrimination—a Hungarian Jewish immigrant and an African American college professor. Known affectionately in the Pentagon as "Aunt Anna," Rosenberg's OASD (MPR) was responsible for industrial and military manpower including Selective Service System policies. Secretary Rosenberg viewed military desegregation as an impetus for societal reform observing that, "In the long run, I don't think a man can live and fight next to one of another race and share experiences where life is at stake, and not have a strong feeling of understanding when he comes home."

The effective implementation of Executive Order 9981 turned on how well African American military personnel used their opportunities. Many African American generals and admirals owe their stars to the wise counsel of Dr. James C. Evans, who often mentored young African American officers by suggesting advantageous career paths in the military. By the close of the Korean War, racial segregation had been totally removed from the U.S. Armed Forces. In the years preceding the Vietnam War, African Americans entered the military and opted for full careers in increasing numbers. Between 1953 and 1961, there was a slow increase in the number of African American career officers in each branch of the service.

◆ THE VIETNAM WAR (1964–1973)

During the brief cease-fire period between the end of the Korean War and the heightening of conflict in Vietnam, the Kennedy Administration—prompted by Congressman Adam Clayton Powell, Jr., and others—sought to end any remaining discrimination in the U.S. Armed Forces. Through Secretary of Defense Robert McNamara, Kennedy stressed to military leaders the need for fostering equal opportunities for African American servicemen, both on and off base.

Extensive U.S. involvement in Vietnam began during the summer of 1964 following an attack on the *USS Maddox* by North Vietnamese naval vessels in the Gulf of Tonkin. Within four months, the United States had 23,000 soldiers fighting in Vietnam. Shortly thereafter, the Army, Navy, and Marine Corps were all engaged in the action in ever-increasing numbers. While the U.S. fighting force in Vietnam was comprised of all the

nation's racial and ethnic groups, African Americans were disproportionately represented. Furthermore, they were more likely to be placed in combat units. Although African Americans constituted about 10.5 percent of the Army, they accounted for nearly 13 percent of those killed or wounded. By 1965, the conflict in Vietnam had escalated into a full-scale war, mounted to support the democracy of South Vietnamese and to protect U.S. interests in Southeast Asia. The Vietnam War proved deadlier than the Korean War and lasted longer than any other war in U.S. history.

The uncertain objectives of the Vietnam War, the high casualty rates, and the disproportionate number of African American soldiers in Vietnam caused tremendous controversy in the African American community. In 1965, Malcolm X claimed that the U.S. government was "causing American soldiers to be murdered every day, for no reason at all." Martin Luther King, Jr. criticized African American involvement in Vietnam, remarking that "we are taking young black men who have been crippled by our society and sending them 8,000 miles away to guarantee liberties in Southeast Asia which they have not found in southwest Georgia or East Harlem."

With the assassinations of Dr. King and Senator Robert Kennedy in 1968, some African American soldiers became increasingly demoralized and disenchanted. Their anger intensified as racial prejudice remained common in Vietnam, on stateside military bases, and aboard the aircraft carriers *USS Kitty Hawk*, *USS Constellation*, and *USS Franklin D. Roosevelt*. One of the most famous African American protesters of the Vietnam War was heavyweight champion Muhammad Ali. An African American Muslim, Ali declared himself a conscientious objector in 1968 on religious grounds. He was convicted of violating the Selective Service Act, stripped of his heavyweight boxing championship, and threatened with an extensive jail term. In 1970, the U.S. Supreme Court overturned his conviction.

Still, most young African American men were willing to answer the draft board's call. Private First Class Milton Olive of Chicago was typical of African Americans who risked, and sometimes lost, their lives during the war. Olive was killed by an exploding grenade on which he had fallen in order to save the lives of his comrades; the government acknowledged his heroism by awarding him a posthumous Medal of Honor. By mid-1969, nine other African Americans had joined Olive as recipients of the Medal of Honor: Private First Class James Anderson, Jr., Sergeant Rodney M. Davis, Specialist Five Lawrence Joel, Specialist Five Dwight H. Johnson, Sergeant Matthew Leonard, Sergeant Donald R. Long, Captain Riley L. Pitts, First Lieutenant Ruppert

During the Vietnam War, African Americans increasingly entered the armed services and opted for full careers (AP/Wide World Photos, Inc.).

L. Sargent, Specialist Five Clarence E. Sasser. According to *New York Times* reporter Thomas Johnson, officers in the Military Assistance Command said that the 173rd Airborne Brigade, a crack outfit with a heavy African American representation, was "the best performing unit in Vietnam." In such elite combat units, one out of every four soldiers was an African American man.

In 1973, the United States withdrew all troops from Vietnam and South Vietnam collapsed in 1975.

◆ MILITARY PARTICIPATION IN THE 1970s AND 1980s

In 1972, a year before the final withdrawal of U.S. troops from Vietnam, the Defense Department issued the report "The Search for Military Justice." This report recognized that discrimination still existed in the military. In particular, it found that a disproportionate number of disciplinary incidents involved African Americans and Hispanics who were often punished more severely than whites. In the 1970s, African Americans represented about 13 percent of discharged servicemen, but received 33 percent of dishonorable discharges, 21 percent of bad conduct discharges, 16 percent of undesirable discharges and 20 percent of general discharges. Less than honorable discharges can negatively affect a person for life, threatening one's civilian career, earning ability, and level of veterans benefits.

High ranking government and military officials moved to eliminate racial prejudices and barriers. Unquestionably, this became easier as African Americans, despite their relatively low numbers in the officer ranks, rose to the highest levels of the military. In 1975, Daniel "Chappie" James became the first African American to be promoted to full general in the U.S. Air Force. Two years later, President Jimmy Carter appointed lawyer/politician Clifford L. Alexander, Jr. to be secretary of the Army, making him the first African American to hold that post. Alexander had previously served in the administrations of John F. Kennedy, Lyndon B. Johnson, and Richard Nixon. As Army secretary, Alexander was responsible for 1.9 million soldiers and a budget of $34 billion. He served in the post until 1980.

By the 1980s, the military was demonstrably less discriminatory than civilian life. The decade also saw increasing numbers of women joining the military, working side-by-side with men in many jobs. These advancements facilitated the breakdown of gender, as well as racial, obstacles to success in the military. By the end of the decade, African Americans represented 28 percent of the total enlisted Army force, while African American women numbered nearly 45 percent of enlisted women in the Armed Forces' largest branch. However, recruiting African American officer candidates continued to be difficult, due, in part to competition from industry and from private sector jobs that offered talented African American men and women higher salaries than were available in the military.

In August of 1989, President George Bush appointed General Colin L. Powell, U.S. Army, to be chairman of the Joint Chiefs of Staff, the nation's highest military post. Powell became the first African American in U.S. Armed Forces history to hold that title as well as the youngest.

◆ THE PERSIAN GULF WAR (1991)

African Americans divided over U.S. involvement in the Gulf War, with almost fifty percent of those polled at the time opposed to it. Several African American leaders, including Representative Charles Rangel of New York, were especially concerned about the high number of African Americans fighting to liberate Kuwait from Iraq. General Colin Powell, himself, initially favored economic sanctions (embargoes) over military action, until war became the stated policy of President George Bush. From then on, Powell drafted and put into action a brilliant military campaign—beginning with a large-scale air attack—that minimized the loss of U.S. lives. U.S. military objectives were met in just a few weeks time.

About 104,000 of the 400,000 troops serving in the Persian Gulf War were African American. According to the Department of Defense, African Americans accounted for 30 percent of Army, 21 percent of Navy, 17 percent of Marine Corps, and 14 percent of Air Force personnel stationed in the Persian Gulf (in 1991, African Americans comprised only 12.4 percent of the U.S. population). For Powell, the high participation of African Americans, as shown by the Gulf War numbers, is a positive, rather than a negative: "To those who question the proportion of blacks in the armed services, my answer is simple. The military of the United States is the greatest equal opportunity employer around."

◆ THE MILITARY MOVING INTO THE NEW MILLENNIUM

During the 1990s, African Americans continued to make strides in rising to the highest military ranks. The percentage of African American officers in the U.S.

General Colin Powell with Brigade Commander Kristin Baker at a West Point graduation ceremony (AP/Wide World Photos, Inc.).

Armed Forces remained on an upward trend, rising above seven percent by 1994. In 1993, Togo D. West, Jr. became the second African American to hold the president-appointed post of secretary of the Army. West served in that position until late 1997, when President Bill Clinton tabbed him to replace Jesse Brown as secretary of veterans affairs. Brown, who had vacated the post in July of 1997, was the first African American to serve as the department's secretary. A decorated Marine who served in Vietnam, Brown held the post for more than four years. The Department of Veterans Affairs is the presidential Cabinet's second-largest department, with 215,000 employees and an annual budget of $41 billion. Another important African American first was the selection of Command Sergeant Major Gene C. McKinney to become the sergeant major of the Army in 1995. That singular post represents the highest-ranking noncommissioned officer in the U.S. Army. McKinney, the former command sergeant major of the U.S. Army Europe, became the tenth enlisted man to hold the title. The sergeant major of the Army's job is to advise the Army chief of staff on issues concerning the organization's 420,000 enlisted personnel.

Since the end of the Persian Gulf War, African American military men and women have been well-represented in peacekeeping missions in Somalia, Haiti, and the republics of the former Yugoslavia. Polls of African American service personnel indicate that the vast majority regard the U.S. Armed Forces as the U.S. institution most free of racism and discrimination, while offering the greatest opportunity for career advancement. Statistical evidence bears out these assertions.

However, a pair of scandals chiefly involving African American enlisted men rocked the Army during the latter half of the decade, causing some to question the fairness of military justice. The first of the two scandals took place at the Aberdeen Proving Ground, Maryland, and involved eleven African American enlisted men and one African American officer accused of sexual misconduct in multiple incidents with white female recruits. All of the enlisted men were drill sergeants, who allegedly took advantage of the recruits under their direct supervision during basic training. The charges included both consensual sex and rape. The first charges came out in September of 1996, though a number of the recruits were slow to point fingers and admitted willing participation in the acts. Army investigators later found allegations that they tried to influence recruits to make the more serious charge of rape.

The NAACP and the Congressional Black Caucus criticized the Army's handling of the case and claimed that the charges were more serious than they would have been had they involved white soldiers. Eventually, at an NAACP press conference, five of the women admitted that the sex had been consensual. However, in the military consensual sex between soldiers of unequal rank in cases involving direct subordinates is still a crime for both parties. Though some of the rape charges were dropped, several of the men were convicted and sentenced, while others had their military careers effectively ended.

The second scandal involved Sergeant Major of the Army Gene C. McKinney. The scandal became public in February of 1997 when McKinney's former public relations aide, retired Sergeant Major Brenda Hoster, charged him with sexual harassment. Eventually, five other women four subordinates and one officer—came forward to accuse McKinney of additional sexual abuse charges. All of the women were white.

On March 13, 1998, a military jury of four Army officers (including two women) and four enlisted men acquitted McKinney of 18 of the 19 charges including all of the sexual misconduct charges. McKinney was found guilty on an obstruction of justice charge relating to a phone call he had made to one of his accusers. However, tapes of that phone call revealed no improper "coaching" on his part. Uncontradicted evidence presented at trial established that the government had manipulated McKinney into calling the accuser, who was permitted to lie to him about her prior contacts with Army investigators. In fact, in exchange for their testimony, several of the women were granted immunity for crimes they had previously committed and were rewarded with plum duty assignments. McKinney, on the other hand, was demoted one rank, though he was not given prison time.

Many in the media concluded that the Pentagon had allowed a "show trial" in an effort to declare to the country its policy of "zero tolerance" of sexual harassment. Others conjectured that McKinney had been singled out, as white defendants in other Army sexual abuse cases occurring concurrently had been quietly slapped on the wrist. Social researchers claim that there are credible reasons for the prevalence of reported sexual assault cases against African Americans in the military, noting that one cannot abuse power if one do not possess it. In any case, the U.S. Army embarrassed itself by taking a weak case to trial that could not address the problem of sexual harassment, while bringing down one of its most important and visible members.

The U.S. Armed Forces enters the new millennium as a primary avenue of upward mobility for those who are ambitious and willing to apply themselves. The overall percentage of African Americans in the military indicates that many have chosen to take that road to success. As of 1995, the combined personnel strength of the Army, Navy, Marine Corps and Air Force was 1,518,000, of which 298,000 (or 19.6 percent) were African American. African American officers and enlisted personnel combined for 26.9 percent of the Army, 17.2 percent of the Navy, 16.0 percent of the Marine Corps and 14.5 percent of the Air Force; African Americans accounted for 12.6 percent of the United States population in 1995.

◆ OUTSTANDING MILITARY FIGURES

(To locate biographical profiles more readily, please consult the index at the back of the book.)

Ensign Jesse L. Brown (1926–1950)
Naval Aviator

Jesse Leroy Brown was born on October 13, 1926, in Hattiesburg, Mississippi. He graduated from Eureka High School in 1944 and studied engineering at Ohio State University from 1944 to 1947. In 1946, he joined the U.S. Naval Reserve and became an aviation cadet the following year.

Brown's flight training accused at Pensacola, Florida, and in 1948 he became the first African American to fly for the Navy. In 1949, Brown worked aboard the aircraft carrier *USS Leyte*, earning an Air Medal and a Korean

Service Medal for his twenty air combat missions. On December 4, 1950, while flying air support for Marines at the Battle of the Chosin Reservoir, his plane was hit by enemy fire. He crash-landed his aircraft, but was trapped inside and died before rescue efforts could cut through the wreckage to extract him. He was posthumously awarded a Purple Heart and a Distinguished Flying Cross for exceptional courage, airmanship, and devotion to duty. Brown was the first African American naval officer to lose his life in combat during the Korean War.

In March of 1972, a destroyer escort, the *USS Jesse L. Brown*, was named in his honor and launched at the Avondale Shipyards at Westwege, Louisiana. It marked the first time that a ship was named for an African American naval officer.

Sharian G. Cadoria (1940–)
Military Officer

Born to a poor rural family on January 26, 1940, in Marksville, Louisiana, Sharian Grace Cadoria credits her mother with instilling within her the qualities of discipline, honesty, and perseverence. From an early age, she helped supplement the family income by picking cotton, lugging 100-pound capacity bags through the fields. To attend school, she and her two siblings walked five miles each way, passed daily by a "whites only" school bus that traveled the same route. After high school, Cadoria attended Southern University in Baton Rouge. During her junior year she was recruited for a four-week Women's Army Corps (WAC) training program. Though she was actually more interested in joining the navy, she attended the WAC program, which was conducted at Fort McClellan, Alabama, during the summer of 1960. After graduating with a B.S. in Business Education in 1961, she decided to make the Army her career.

It wasn't long before Cadoria realized that, to many in the Army, she had two strikes against her: being African American and being female. At Fort McClellan in the early 1960s, she suffered numerous indignities and missed out on several advancement opportunities as a result of her race. As she progressed through the ranks, however, she faced greater resistance because of her gender, than because of her race. Cadoria was not content to take either of the typical paths open for female advancement-administration and nursing. Instead, she rose through the ranks of the military police.

From 1967–1969, while U.S. involvement in Vietnam was at its peak, Cadoria spent 33 months in the Southeast Asian country. The severity of the experience almost caused Cadoria to give up her military career and she gave seriously considered joining a convent on her return. The turning point came in December of 1969 when she was selected to attend the Command and

General Staff College, becoming the first African American woman to be chosen for the school.

Even the dissolution of the WAC in 1978 and the integration of its members into the regular Army did not slow her ascent. Among her marks of distinction, Cadoria was the first woman to command a male battalion; the first African American director of manpower and personnel for the Joint Chiefs of Staff (a position that required her to fill openings in all branches of the armed services, both active and reserve); and the first woman to achieve the rank of general apart from the nursing corps. She also graduated from the U.S. Army War College and the National Defense University. Cadoria even managed to find enough time outside her busy career to attend the University of Oklahoma, where she earned an M.A. in social work in 1974. In 1985, Cadoria was promoted to brigadier general, becoming only the second African American female, and the first in the regular U.S. Army, to attain the rank. Cadoria retired from the military in 1990.

During nearly three decades of service, Cadoria was awarded an Air Medal, four Army Commendation Medals, three Bronze Stars, a Defense Superior Service Medal, a Distinguished Service Medal, and two Meritorious Service Medals.

Sergeant William H. Carney (1840–1908)
First African American Medal of Honor Recipient

William H. Carney was born in Norfolk, Virginia in 1840. At 14, he attended a secret school run by a local minister. In 1856, his father moved the family to New Bedford, Massachusetts. Carney, a man of growing religious conviction, considered becoming a minister, but the Civil War disrupted his plans. Instead, he enlisted in the 54th Massachusetts Colored Infantry Regiment on February 17, 1863.

As a member of Company C of the 54th, Sergeant Carney was part of the force assigned to lead the advance on Fort Wagner, South Carolina, on July 18, 1863. Fort Wagner, a vital Confederate position in the defense of Charleston, was heavily fortified. Led by Colonel Robert Gould Shaw, a white commander, the African American troops attempted a valiant, but ultimately disastrous, assault in the late afternoon. During the attack, the flag bearer was wounded, but before the stars and stripes fell to the ground, Carney grabbed the staff and continued onward. With most of his comrades falling around him, Carney led the charge. He wound up at the fort's entrance—alone. Hiding in the shadows of the fort, Carney avoided rounds and shells falling around him, while clutching the flag. Eventually, a Confederate squad stumbled upon his position and he was forced to flee. Shot twice, he still managed to escape, later joining up with a white soldier who bandaged his wounds. Together, they retreated to the safety of the Union lines, but not before another shot grazed Carney's head. After further medical treatment, Carney returned to his regiment, where his fellow troops cheered his return, flag in hand. "Boys, the old flag never touched the ground," he proclaimed proudly. Unfortunately, approximately half of Carney's comrades, as well as Colonel Shaw, met their end in the unsuccessful undertaking. For his actions, Carney was awarded the Medal of Honor. Among African American soldiers or sailors who were awarded a Medal of Honor for actions during the Civil War, Carney's occurred earliest, though he was not issued his medal until May 23, 1900.

On June 30, 1864, Sergeant Carney was discharged from the infantry at Black Island, South Carolina. He was granted disability for lingering medical problems resulting from the wounds he received in the famed battle. After a short sojourn to California, Carney returned to New Bedford, where he served as a mail carrier for 32 years. After retirement, he moved to Boston to accept a job as a messenger in the State House. He was injured in an elevator accident on November 23, 1908 and died on December 9. Carney was buried in New Bedford.

General Benjamin O. Davis, Jr. (1912–)
First African American Brigadier General in the U.S. Air Force

Born in Washington, DC, on December 18, 1912, Benjamin Oliver Davis, Jr., son of a career U.S. Army officer, moved often in his early years. Stops included Alabama (where his father taught military science at Tuskegee Institute) and Cleveland, where he graduated as president of his high school class. Davis attended both Western Reserve University and the University of Chicago before accepting an appointment to the U.S. Military Academy in 1932, having been nominated by longtime Chicago Congressman Oscar DePriest.

When Davis entered West Point, no African American had graduated from the academy in 43 years. In an attempt to get Davis to resign, his fellow cadets forced him to endure four years of "silencing." That behavior, encouraged by superiors who also wanted Davis to fail, consisted of no one speaking to him (except to issue an order), room with him (though he lived in a two-man room), or eat with him. Nevertheless, Davis excelled, graduating 35th in a class of 276 in 1936. Though the Army generally allowed West Point graduates with high class rank to choose their branch of preference, Davis was denied his choice, the U.S. Army Air Corps. Instead,

Lieutenant General Benjamin O. Davis, Jr. (AP/Wide World Photos, Inc.)

he was assigned to Fort Benning, Georgia as an infantry officer, where he experienced further institutional and de facto racism.

After five years in the infantry and following a stint at Fort Riley, Kansas, Davis finally got his wish when just months before the United States entered World War II in 1941, he was allowed to transfer to the Army Air Corps. The transfer was part of a daring military experiment championed by President Franklin D. Roosevelt: the creation of an African American flying unit. The 66th Air Force Training Detachment was based at the Tuskegee, Alabama Army Air Field, and Davis was in the first training class. On September 2, 1941, he became the first African American to officially fly solo as an Army Air Corps officer. Shortly after graduation in 1942, Davis—as the only previously commissioned officer—became commander of the African American 99th Pursuit Squadron (later renamed the 99th Fighter Squadron). Davis quickly earned promotions, rising to the rank of lieutenant colonel by the time the 99th arrived in French Morocco for combat duty on April 24, 1943.

In late August of 1943, Davis returned to the U.S. to command the African American 332nd Fighter Group, made up of three squadrons and later the 99th. In April of 1944, the 332nd arrived in Italy, where it flew missions deep into France and Germany. The sterling record of the 332nd contributed to Davis's promotion to full colonel just a few months later. In two hundred escort missions, the unit never lost a bomber to Nazi aircraft fire. During World War II, Davis flew sixty missions and logged 224 combat hours. For individual heroism, he was honored with several decorations including a Silver Star (pinned to his uniform by his father, Brigadier General Benjamin O. Davis, Sr.) and a Distinguished Flying Cross, the Corps' highest award.

Davis's post-World War II career may not have been as glamorous, but it was no less significant. He played a leading role in the integration of the military in 1949. During the Korean War, he commanded the 51st Fighter Interceptor Wing, later serving as director of operations and training for the Far East Air Forces. His promotion to brigadier general in 1954 made him the first African American general in U.S. Air Force history, as well as the highest-ranking African American in the U.S. military at the time. Other notable assignments included being named deputy chief of staff of the U.S. Air Force in Europe in 1957; director of manpower and organization for the U.S. Air Force headquarters in 1961; and chief of staff of the United Nations Command and U.S. Forces in Korea in 1965. Davis became a major general in 1957 and a lieutenant general in 1965, becoming the first African American to hold either rank in the U.S. Armed Forces. Named to command the Philippines-based 13th Air Force in August of 1967, Davis was responsible for all Air Force units in Southeast Asia, which included those serving in the Vietnam War. Davis retired from active duty in 1970.

After retiring from the military, Davis served in several high ranking posts in the U.S. Department of Transportation through the mid-1970s. On December 9, 1998, President Bill Clinton bestowed upon Davis a fourth star, bringing his rank to full general. He currently lives in Arlington, Virginia.

Among Davis's many military decorations are three Distinguished Service Medals, an Army and an Air Force Silver Star, a Distinguished Flying Cross, three Legions of Merit, and an Air Medal with five Oak Leaf Clusters.

Brigadier General Benjamin O. Davis, Sr. (1877–1970)
First African American Brigadier General in the U.S. Armed Forces

Born in Washington, DC, on June 1, 1877, Benjamin Oliver Davis, Sr. came from a middle-class family largely employed in the civil service. Benjamin, however, was not interested in pursuing a career in the federal bureaucracy. Instead, he wanted to become a soldier. In high

Brigadier General Benjamin O. Davis, Sr.

school, he was a member of the Cadet Corps, an extracurricular organization that introduced him to military training and procedure. Following high school, Davis attended classes at Howard University, but despite his parents' objections, he left college in 1898 for an opportunity to fight in the Spanish-American War.

Hoping to see action in Cuba, Davis bounced from the District of Columbia National Guard, in which he was elected a second lieutenant of Company D, to the 8th U.S. Volunteer Infantry, where he accepted a temporary commission as a First Lieutenant in Company G. However, neither unit ever made it out of the states. After the conclusion of the war, Davis sought an Army commission through other avenues. Despite his failure to accomplish his goal at the time, he did not give up his dream of becoming an Army officer.

On June 14, 1899, he enlisted as a private in the Troop I, 9th U.S. Cavalry, an African American regular Army unit. Though openly discouraged by most whites and African Americans, in August of the following year he submitted an application to take the competitive officer candidate examination. A few months later he took the battery of tests and finished among the top candidates. On February 2, 1901, he was commissioned a second lieutenant in the regular Army. His first assignment was with Troop F, 10th U.S. Cavalry, then stationed in the Philippines.

Over the next three decades, Davis received a number of assignments designed to keep him from being in a position to command white soldiers. He served as a military attache to Liberia from 1909 to 1911, commanding officer of a supply troop in the Philippines from 1917 to 1920, and instructor of the 372nd Infantry of the Ohio National Guard from 1924 to 1929. Between such service assignments, he taught military science and tactics at Wilberforce and Tuskegee Universities. Promotions for African American officers were rare in those years, but Davis rose through the ranks until he became a full colonel on February 18, 1930. In 1938, Davis took command of the African American 369th Cavalry, New York National Guard.

Davis's promotion to brigadier general on October 25, 1940, marked the first time an African American had been promoted to general in the history of the U.S. Armed Forces. The promotion was seen by many detractors as a political ploy by President Franklin D. Roosevelt to garner African American votes in an election year. However, Davis had spent a forty-year military career in assignments that offered him few opportunities to shine. The promotion was a capping to a difficult career marred by perpetual discrimination. Davis retired just a few months later, having reached the official retirement age of 64.

The ink was not yet dry on Davis's retirement paperwork when he was called back to active service in early 1941 to supervise the introduction of 100,000 African American soldiers into the Army, an institution rampant with unofficial but effective policies of segregation. During World War II, Davis inspected African American units, heard racial complaints, and handled public relations duties throughout the European military theater as a member of the Washington-based inspector general's staff. Davis's strenuous efforts on behalf of African American servicemen made the normally publicity-shy officer a very visible figure in the African American press.

After the war, Davis served as assistant to the inspector general of the Army from 1945 to 1947, then as special assistant to the secretary of the Army from 1947 to 1948. His focus throughout that period was the orderly integration of units in the military's largest branch (President Harry Truman's Executive Order 9981, the historic order that led to the integration of the entire military, was issued six days after Davis's retirement). On July 20, 1948, Davis retired from the Army a second and final time at a special White House ceremony during which his career was lauded by President Truman himself.

Among his later activities, Davis was a member of the American Battle Monuments Commission. Deteriorating eyesight and health problems brought his public life to an end in 1960. Davis died of leukemia on November 26, 1970, in North Chicago, Illinois, and was buried in Arlington National Cemetery. Davis's military honors included a Bronze Star and a Distinguished Service Medal, as well as such foreign decorations as the Croix de Guerre with Palm (from France) and the Grade of Commander of the Order of the Star of Africa (from Liberia).

Lieutenant Colonel Charity Adams Earley (1918–)

First African American Woman Commissioned in the Women's Auxiliary Army Corps

Charity Edna Adams was born in Columbia, South Carolina, in 1918. She was valedictorian of her high school class and continued her studies at Ohio's Wilberforce University, where she was awarded a B.A. in 1938. Back in Columbia, she taught high school math while studying for a master's degree in psychology.

In the fall of 1941, the War Department began considering ways in which women could be used in support roles so that soldiers in non-combat specialties could be freed up for combat. The result of their brainstorming was the creation of an organization they named the Women's Auxiliary Army Corps (WAAC). By early 1942, recruitment for the new branch was underway. One method used to recruit officer candidates was to ask colleges to compile lists of names for consideration. Wilberforce University submitted a list on which the name Charity E. Adams appeared. In June of that year, Adams filled out and mailed back the application sent her.

Within a month, Adams was at Fort Des Moines, Iowa, as a member of the first WAAC officer candidate school class. Though Adams and the 38 other African American officer candidates trained alongside white officer candidates, they were surprised to find all non-training facilities rigidly segregated, such as housing assignments and mess hall seating. Adams graduated from basic training on August 30, 1942, and became the first African American woman to be commissioned in the WAAC. She was then appointed commander of the basic training company for enlisted females, where her administrative abilities quickly impressed the post's commanding officer.

Adams was soon promoted to captain and was assigned to Fort Des Moines' Plans and Training Section. Her new responsibilities included supervising and training recruits in such skills as office administration, photography, and radio operation. As part of her job, she made frequent trips to duty stations in other states including Massachusetts, New Jersey, and North Carolina. She even had occasion to visit the newly-completed Pentagon, located just outside Washington, DC. By mid-1943, the WAAC was renamed the Women's Army Corps (WAC), and Adams had received a promotion to major.

Despite Adams's stellar record, neither she nor any other African American WACs were being posted overseas. Finally, in December of 1944, Adams became the first African American WAC to be selected for overseas duty. She flew to Birmingham, England, to command the newly-formed 6888th Central Postal Battalion. The 800-woman unit was responsible for directing all incoming and outgoing mail for the seven million U.S. Armed Forces personnel, Seabees, and American Red Cross workers serving in the European Theater of Operations. Several months of backed-up mail awaited the new arrivals. Adams quickly organized her command into five companies, then set the women into eight-hour, round-the-clock shifts. She also created lists to track units, sought means to differentiate between persons with similar names, and traced persons whose whereabouts were unknown. In May of 1945, as the war in Europe ended, the 6888th was moved to France, where it continued its duties with reduced personnel. Adams was relieved of command in December and sent back to the U.S. for discharge. At the separation center, Adams was promoted to lieutenant colonel just days before leaving the service. Such promotions were a courtesy to service personnel who were deemed deserving of elevated rank, had not been promoted on active duty. At separation, Adams was the highest-ranking African American officer in the WAC.

Within months of her discharge, Adams enrolled at Ohio State University, where she earned a master's degree in psychology in 1946. She married Dr. Stanley A. Earley, M.D. in 1949, at which point she took the name Charity Adams Earley. Among her postwar positions were registration officer at the Cleveland office of the Veterans Administration, personnel officer at both Tennessee A&I University, in Nashville, and Georgia State College, in Savannah, and employment and personnel counselor, YWCA, New York City. Earley recalled her wartime experiences in the book *One Woman's Army: A Black Officer Remembers the WAC*. In 1991, Earley received honorary doctorates from Wilberforce University and the University of Dayton.

Lieutenant Henry O. Flipper (1856–1940)
First African American Graduate of the U.S. Military Academy

Henry Ossian Flipper was born a slave in Thomasville, Georgia, on March 21, 1856. After the Civil War, his father moved the family to Atlanta. Flipper's father was a skilled shoemaker who created a successful business

that allowed him to educate his two sons. In 1866, Flipper began attending schools established by the American Missionary Association and, in 1869, he started taking classes at Atlanta University. In 1873, he received an appointment to the U.S. Military Academy at West Point, New York. Though Flipper was the fifth African American to enter the academy, he was the first to withstand the intense discriminatory practices of the institution, graduating 50th in a class of 76 in June of 1877. He also has the distinction of being the first African American graduate of an engineering school in the United States. A year after graduation his surprisingly restrained memoir of the experience was published as *The Colored Cadet at West Point.*

Upon graduation, Flipper was commissioned a second lieutenant and received his assignment of choice: the African American 10th U.S. Cavalry. The regiment was one of two units that Native Americans had nicknamed "Buffalo Soldiers." Flipper served at various frontier installations in the Southwest during the next few years including Fort Sill, Oklahoma, and Fort Concho, Texas. An incident that occurred at the latter duty station may have played a role in ending Flipper's military career a short time later: he was seen riding with an attractive white woman. Racist white officers, incensed that Flipper might have been focusing his attentions on a white female, sought ways to remove him from the Army. In 1882, while serving as Commissary Officer at Fort Davis, Texas, Flipper was brought up on charges by his commander, who accused him of embezzling funds and of conduct unbecoming an officer and a gentleman. At the court-martial trial, Flipper was acquitted of the former charge, but was found guilty of the latter and dismissed from the Army, as was required by the conviction.

To his death, Flipper protested his innocence, and he constantly attempted to clear his name. His battle went all the way to the halls of Congress, where he hoped a bill introduced by Wisconsin Congressman Michael Griffen in 1898 would restore him to the duty, grade, rank, pay, and station in the Army he would have attained had he not been unjustifiably turned out. This and numerous other trips to Washington to vindicate himself met with failure.

However, his dismissal from the Army did not cause Flipper to fail in civilian life. After the Army, Flipper went on to become a notable figure in the American Southwest and in Mexico, working as a civil and military engineer. He became much sought after by both private and governmental bodies as a surveyor, engineer, and consultant. He later became a translator of Spanish land grants. His work *Spanish and Mexican Land Laws: New Spain and Mexico* was published by the Department of Justice in 1895. As his reputation spread, job opportunities increased. He served as consulting engineer to the builders of one of the earliest railroads to be constructed in the Alaska Territory, worked for an oil company pioneering the industry in Venezuela, and was an aide to the United States Senate Committee on Foreign Relations. In the course of his career, he befriended such prominent Washington officials as Senator A.B. Fall of New Mexico. When Fall became secretary of the interior, Flipper became his assistant until the infamous Teapot Dome scandal severed their relationship in the mid-1920s. Flipper returned to Atlanta at the close of his career, living with his brother, until his death on May 3, 1940.

In 1978, Flipper's body was disinterred and moved from Atlanta to Thomasville, where he was given a full military funeral attended by nearly five hundred people. In 1997, the Texas Christian University Press published *Black Frontiersman: The Memoirs of Henry O. Flipper, First Black Graduate of West Point*, which was compiled and edited from Flipper's papers by Theodore D. Harris.

Though Flipper died before he could be absolved, others took up his fight. In 1976, descendants and supporters approached the Army Board for the Correction of Military Records on his behalf. Although the board stated that it did not have the authority to overturn Flipper's conviction, it found the penalty imposed "unduly harsh and unjust" and recommended that Flipper's dismissal be commuted to a good conduct discharge. Subsequently, with other appropriate approvals, the Department of the Army issued an honorable discharge in Flipper's name, dated June 30, 1882, the date he had been dismissed from the Army. On October 21, 1997, a private law firm filed an application of pardon in Flipper's name with the secretary of the Army. After several months of review by U.S. Army and Department of Justice personnel, President Bill Clinton pardoned Flipper on February 19, 1999.

Vice Admiral Samuel L. Gravely, Jr. (1922–)
First African American Admiral

Samuel Lee Gravely, Jr. was born in Richmond, Virginia, on June 4, 1922. Enrolled at Virginia Union University when the U.S. entered World War II, Gravely quit school to enlist in the U.S. Naval Reserve on September 15, 1942. He received recruit training at Great Lakes (Illinois) Naval Training Center and skill training at the Service School, Hampton (Virginia) Institute. To become an officer he attended the Officer Training Camp at the University of California, Los Angeles, the Pre-Midshipmen School in Asbury Park, New Jersey, and the Midshipmen School at Columbia University in New York City, where he trained from August to December of 1944. The first African American graduate of a midshipman school, Gravely was commissioned an ensign in the U.S. Naval Reserve, on December 14, 1944.

Grandy's initial assignment was as the assistant battalion commander at the Great Lakes Naval Training Center. Later, he became the first African American officer to be assigned shipboard duty when he held such titles as communications officer, electronics officer, executive officer, and personnel officer aboard the submarine chaser *USS PC-1264*. After a brief stint as communications watch officer with the Fleet Training Group, in Norfolk, Virginia, Gravely was released from active duty on April 16, 1946. He then returned to college and received a B.A. in history from Virginia Union University in 1948. Though he had plans of becoming a teacher and coach, he took a job in Richmond as a railway postal clerk following graduation.

In 1948, Harry Truman's historic Executive Order 9981 forced the U.S. Armed Forces to integrate and the military began increasing the recruitment of African Americans. On August 30, 1949, Gravely returned to duty as assistant to the officer in charge of recruiting at the Naval Recruiting Station, Washington, DC. After attending the Communications Officers Short Course, Gravely saw active duty aboard a pair of ships that engaged the enemy during the Korean War: first as radio operator on the battleship *USS Iowa* and later as communications officer on the cruiser *USS Toledo*. His reputation as a communications expert played a vital role in subsequent assignments. After more than a decade in the military, Gravely finally decided to make the navy his career and he formally transferred from the Naval Reserve to the regular Navy on August 16, 1955. From that point on, Gravely frequently shifted between land-based administrative positions and shipboard assignments, occasionally punctuated by training course instruction.

Steadily promoted through the ranks, Gravely was the touchstone for African American achievement in the Navy. He became the first African American officer to command a U.S. Navy ship on January 15, 1961, when he assumed temporary command of the destroyer *USS Theodore E. Chandler*. When he accepted command of the destroyer escort *USS Falgout* on January 31, 1962, he became the first African American to command a fighting ship. From August of 1963 to June 1964, Gravely attended the senior course in naval warfare at the Naval War College in Newport, Rhode Island. He was then tabbed program manager for the National Command Center and the National Emergency Airborne Command Post at the Defense Communications Agency in Arlington, Virginia. In 1966, when Gravely guided the *USS Taussig* into direct offensive action during the Vietnam War, he became the first African American naval officer to command a U.S. warship under combat conditions since the Civil War.

On June 2, 1971, the day he was relieved of command of the guided missile frigate *USS Jouett*, Gravely became the first African American to be promoted to the rank of rear admiral. In mid-July of that year, he was made commander of the Naval Communications Command and director of the Naval Communications Divisions under the chief of naval operations, dual posts he held for two years. On August 28, 1976, he was promoted to vice admiral, another first as an African American naval officer. The next month, he was placed in command of the U.S. Navy's Third Fleet, making him the first African American to command a U.S. Navy fleet. As commander of the Third Fleet, Gravely was in charge of one hundred ships and 60,000 officers overseeing fifty million miles of ocean (approximately a quarter of the earth's surface). His final naval assignment was as director of the Defense Communications Agency, a post he held from September 15, 1978, until his retirement on August 1, 1980.

After retiring from the U.S. Navy, Gravely worked for several private sector companies. He was senior corporate advisor for Potomac Systems Engineering; director of the Command Support Division for Automated Business Systems and Services, Inc., and a member of the board of directors for Draper Laboratory. In 1991, he was named an aide-de-camp to then-Virginia Governor L. Douglas Wilder. Gravely lives on a rural, two-acre estate in Haymarket, Virginia.

While in the Navy, Gravely received numerous decorations including a Legion of Merit with gold star, a Bronze Star, a Meritorious Service Medal, a Joint Service Commendation Medal, a Navy Commendation Medal, a World War II Victory Medal, a Naval Reserve Medal, an American Campaign Medal, a Korean Presidential Unit Citation, a National Defense Medal with one bronze star, a China Service Medal, a Korean Service Medal with two bronze stars, a United Nations Service Medal, an Armed Forces Expeditionary Medal, a Vietnam Service Medal with six bronze stars, and an Antarctic Service Medal. He has also received numerous civilian awards including Savannah State College's Major Richard R. Wright Award of Excellence (1974), the Prince Hall Founding Fathers Military Commanders Award (1975), and the Virginia Press Association's Virginian of the Year (1979). Gravely received an honorary doctor of laws degree from his alma mater, Virginia Union University, in 1979.

Major General Marcelite Harris (1943–)
Two-Star General, U.S. Air Force

Marcelite Harris was born on January 16, 1943, in Houston, Texas. She attended Houston public schools,

Marcelite J. Harris (AP/Wide World Photos, Inc.)

graduating from Kashmere Gardens Junior-Senior High School in 1960. At Spelman College in Atlanta, Harris studied speech and drama in hopes of becoming an actress. During college she took part in a USO tour of Germany and France. The experience gave her an opportunity to find out about the military, but it did not spark any career interest within her at the time. After earning a B.A. in 1964, she struggled to find stage work. She took a job with a Headstart program at a Houston YMCA, while taking law classes at night. Finding it difficult to maintain that pace, Harris decided to look into other career options and chose the U.S. Air Force.

Harris began at the Officer Training School at Lackland Air Force Base in Texas in September of 1965 and was commissioned a second lieutenant on December 21 of that year. Her first assignment was as assistant director for administration with the 60th Airlift Wing at California's Travis Air Force Base. In January of 1967, she received her first promotion and transferred to Bitburg Air Base in West Germany. At Bitburg, Harris served as administrative officer of the 71st Tactical Missile Squadron for two years. Then, in May 1969, at the suggestion of a superior, she changed career tracks to maintenance. She was reassigned as maintenance analysis officer of the 36th Tactical Fighter Wing, also based at Bitburg. As the first female Air Force officer in a "man's field," Harris faced hostility from many of the men under her command. In order to gain credibility with the maintenance crews that she supervised, Harris decided to learn more about aircraft engineering. She applied for the Aircraft Maintenance Officer Course, but was turned down at first. Harris persisted and was later accepted to the eight-month course, graduating in May 1971.

Harris's next assignment took her to Thailand's Korat Royal Thai Air Force Base, where she was maintenance supervisor of the 49th Tactical Fighter Squadron from August of 1971 to May of 1972. Despite initial resistance from the maintenance crews under her command, Harris forged a cooperative relationship with her personnel. The result was a superb performance record for the aircraft piloted by a tactical fighter squadron flying sorties over Vietnam.

Harris returned to Travis Air Force Base for a three-year stint before accepting a very visible assignment in Washington, DC, in September 1975. For more than two and a half years, Harris served as personnel staff officer and White House social aide during the Ford and Carter administrations. A late 1970s stop at the U.S. Air Force Academy in Colorado Springs, Colorado was followed by a transfer to McConnell Air Force Base in Kansas. On November 29, 1980, in the midst of three consecutive assignments at McConnell, Harris married Maurice Anthony Harris. Harris's last assignment on foreign soil was a three and a half year stretch as director of maintenance at the Pacific Air Forces Logistic Support Center at Kadena Air Base in Japan starting in November of 1982. While in Japan, Harris earned a B.S. in business management from the University of Maryland's Asian Division in 1986.

Returning to the United States in March of 1986, Harris became deputy commander of maintenance at Keesler Air Force Base in Mississippi. Meanwhile, she continued her climb up the career ladder, reaching full colonel on September 1, 1986. In December of 1988 she was named commander of the 3300th Technical Training Wing at Keesler, becoming the third female to attain that level in the history of the U.S. Air Force. On May 1, 1991, while stationed at Tinker Air Force Base in Oklahoma, Harris became the first African American woman to attain the rank of brigadier general in the Air Force. Following a short stint at Randolph Air Force Base in Texas, she became director of maintenance at U.S. Air Force Headquarters, Washington, DC, in September of 1994. On May 25, 1995, Harris became the first African American female to be promoted to the rank of major general. Her promotion not only made her the highest-ranking African American woman in the Air Force, but in the Department of Defense as a whole. In her role as

director of maintenance and deputy chief of staff, logistics, she was accountable for the maintenance operations of every Air Force installation, commanding a workforce of more than 125,000 and a large budget. Harris retired from the U.S. Air Force on February 22, 1997.

Among the decorations awarded to Harris during her 31-year career are a Legion of Merit with oak leaf cluster, a Bronze Star, a Meritorious Service Medal with three oak leaf clusters, an Air Force Commendation Medal with oak leaf cluster, a National Defense Service Medal with oak leaf cluster, and a Vietnam Service Medal with three oak leaf clusters. Among her civilian honors are *Dollars and Sense* magazine's Most Prestigious Individual (1991), Journal Recording Publishing Co.'s Woman of Enterprise (1992), the National Federation of Black Women Business Owners' Black Woman of Courage (1995), the Ellis Island Medal of Honor (1996), and the Women's International Center's Living Legacy Patriot Award (1998).

General Daniel James, Jr. (1920–1978)
First African American Four-Star General, U.S. Air Force

Daniel James, Jr. was born on February 11, 1920, in Pensacola, Florida. The youngest boy in a large family, he grew up in a home with strict parents who stressed education, hard work, and honesty as means to success. At an early age, James borrowed the nickname "Chappie" from an older brother, a star athlete whom he idolized. James was educated in the private school run by his mother until secondary school age, when he attended Washington High. At Tuskegee (Alabama) Institute, James worked for the college in exchange for credit hours. A physical education major, he was expelled for fighting just two months before he would have graduated in 1941.

During his senior year of college, James enrolled in the Civilian Pilot Training Program. Indirectly sponsored by the War Department, the program operated at six African American colleges to train African American pilots under segregated conditions. James quickly earned his pilot's license and proved himself among the more capable flyers. Upon expulsion from college, he was hired to train the first class of cadets selected for the "Tuskegee Experiment;" among that first class of flyers was Benjamin O. Davis, Jr., who would become the first African American Air Force general. Captivated by flying, James turned his attention away from academics to focus on becoming an Air Force officer. He applied for the Aviation Cadet Program and was accepted in January of 1943. Graduating in July of that year, James was commissioned a second lieutenant in the U.S. Air Force. He was then assigned to the 617th Bombardment Squad-

Daniel James, Jr. (AP/Wide World Photos, Inc.)

ron, 477th Bombardment Group at Selfridge Field, Michigan, for combat training on B-25 bombers. During World War II, however, racially-motivated bureaucratic waffling kept most African American pilots from being assigned overseas, and James never left the United States.

In the fall of 1949, James received his first overseas assignment. He became flight leader of the 12th Fighter Bomber Squadron, 18th Fighter Wing at Clark Air Force Base in the Philippines. During the Korean War, the 12th was based in Japan and Korea. Usually in F-51 Mustangs, James flew 101 combat missions during the war, most during the early days of the conflict. One such mission, in support of United Nations ground forces, resulted in James being awarded a Distinguished Flying Cross. Leading four bombers through heavy enemy fire and low visibility on October 15, 1950, James was credited with personally killing more than one hundred enemy troops.

Following Korea, James was assigned to a base near Rome, New York, where a racist commanding officer boasted he would rid the unit of the African American flyer. Despite the forced integration of the military, which had begun several years earlier, racism still played a major role in duty assignments at the time. Subsequently, James was reassigned to Otis Air Force Base on Cape Cod, Massachusetts. Among his assignments at Otis, James was given command of the all-white 437th Fighter Interceptor Squadron in the Air Defense Command in April of 1953. His loyal and supportive leadership style, as well as his insistence on excellence, earned his mens'

allegiance and his superiors' respect. In 1957, he graduated from the Air Command and Staff College at Maxwell Air Force Base in Alabama. His next assignment was at the Pentagon in the Air Defense Division, a job he admitted not particularly enjoying though he understood the importance of it.

James spent the early 1960s at the Royal Air Force Base at Bentwaters, England, where he held three assignments with the 81st Fighter Wing. He returned to the U.S. in the fall of 1964 and held several command positions at Davis-Monthan Air Force Base in Arizona, during which time he was promoted to colonel. In 1966, during the early stages of the Vietnam War, James was assigned to the 8th Tactical Fighter Wing at Thailand's Ubon Royal Thai Air Force Base. He flew 78 missions over Vietnam in F-4C Phantom jets as deputy commander for operations, then vice commander, of the unit, popularly known as the "Wolf Pack." His next assignment brought him just fifty miles from his hometown to Florida's Eglin Air Force Base. After Eglin, he was sent out of the country once again, assuming command of the 7272nd Fighter Training Wing at Wheelus Air Base in Libya. His stay there was shortened, however, when Colonel Moammar Khadafy deposed King Idris and pushed for the closing of the base. Despite James's objections, the U.S. Embassy in Libya decided to shut Wheelus down. James then distinguished himself by overseeing an orderly removal of U.S. personnel and equipment from the base.

Upon his return to the U.S., James was quickly promoted through the upper echelons of the U.S. Air Force. On March 31, 1970, he was sworn in as a deputy assistant of defense for public affairs by Secretary of Defense Melvin R. Laird. James quickly became a much-in-demand speaker and the Pentagon eagerly used his talents by sending him around the country to make speeches in support of military policies. James was rewarded for his willingness to appear before the public, especially since some of that public used his appearances as a venue to demonstrate against the Vietnam War. He was promoted to brigadier general that summer and his rise through the general ranks proved exceedingly swift. He was made a major general on August 1, 1972, and less than a year later, on June 1, 1973, he was elevated to lieutenant general.

James left the Pentagon in August of 1974 and became vice commander of Military Airlift Command the next month. James earned his final promotion on August 29, 1975, when he became the first African American to become a four-star general. The next day he took command of the North American Air Defense Command (NORAD), the bi-national defense force of 65,000 servicemen assigned the task of protecting the United States and Canada from surprise nuclear attack, and NORAD's

American subunit, the U.S. Air Force Aerospace Defense Command, both of which are headquartered at Colorado Springs, Colorado. In September of 1977, James suffered a heart attack. After 35 years of service, he retired from the U.S. Air Force on January 26, 1978. One month later, on February 25, 1978, he suffered a second, fatal heart attack. James was buried with highest military honors at Arlington National Cemetery, in Arlington, Virginia.

One of the most highly-decorated servicemen in Air Force history, among the awards James received were a Distinguished Service Medal with oak leaf cluster, a Legion of Merit with oak leaf cluster, a Distinguished Flying Cross with two oak leaf clusters, a Meritorious Service Medal, an Air Medal with thirteen oak leaf clusters, an American Defense Service Medal, an American Campaign Medal, a World War II Victory Medal, a Korean Service Medal with four service stars, and a Vietnam Service Medal with four service stars. James received awards from an astounding number of civilian organizations including the Arnold Air Society, the Phoenix Urban League, Kappa Alpha Psi Fraternity, the American Legion, the Veterans of Foreign Wars, the Capital Press Club, and the United Negro College Fund, to name a few. He also received honorary degrees from the University of West Florida, the University of Akron, Virginia State College, Delaware State College, and St. Louis University.

General Hazel W. Johnson (1927–)
First Female African American Brigadier General, U.S. Army

Hazel Winifred Johnson was born on October 10, 1927, in West Chester, Pennsylvania. She grew up on a farm near Malvern in Chester County and attended high school in nearby Berwyn. She received her registered nurse diploma at New York City's Harlem Hospital in 1950 and enlisted in the U.S. Army Nurse Corps in 1955. Johnson used civilian educational opportunities to rapidly advance through the ranks of the nurse corps. She earned a bachelor's degree in nursing from Villanova University in 1959 and was commissioned a second lieutenant by direct appointment on May 11, 1960. Three years later she earned a master's degree in nursing education from Columbia University.

Johnson was a staff member of the U.S. Medical Research and Development Command in Washington, DC, from 1967 to 1973, and dean of the Walter Reed Army Institute of Nursing at the famed Walter Reed Army Medical Center also in Washington, DC, from 1976 to 1978. She earned a Ph.D. in educational administration from Catholic University of America in 1978 before a brief assignment as chief nurse with the U.S. Army Medical Command in Korea. On September 1, 1979,

General Hazel Johnson (AP/Wide World Photos, Inc.)

Johnson became the first African American female in U.S. military history to advance to the rank of brigadier general. At that time, she was also made chief of the Army Nurse Corps, Office of the Surgeon General in Washington, DC. She held that post until August 31, 1983, when she retired from the U.S. Army.

Johnson served as director of the government affairs division of the American Nursing Association from 1983 until 1986, when she joined the faculty of Virginia's George Mason University as a professor of nursing. Her military decorations include a Distinguished Service Medal, a Legion of Merit, a Meritorious Service Medal, and an Army Commendation Medal with oak leaf cluster.

Sergeant Henry Johnson (1897?–1929)
369th Infantry Regiment, 93rd Division, U.S. Army

Henry Johnson was born around 1897 in Winston-Salem, North Carolina, and grew up in Albany, New York. Upon America's entrance into World War I, Johnson enlisted in the Army on June 5, 1917. He was mustered into Company C, 15th National Guard of New York (later renamed the 369th Infantry Regiment) as a private on July 25. The unit received its training at Camp Wadsworth in Spartanburg, South Carolina.

The 369th landed in Brest, France on January 1, 1918. In March, the 369th was attached to the 16th Division of the French Army, making it the first African American unit to reach the war zone. According to his muster roll, Johnson was promoted to the rank of sergeant on May 1. Several days later, U.S. troops captured a German-held bridge near the Aisne River, and Johnson's unit was assigned to guard it. In the early morning hours of May 14, a force of about 32 Germans tried to retake the bridge. Johnson and fellow soldier Needham Roberts were on sentry duty at the time, armed with pistols and a few hand grenades. The two groups exchanged fire, and Johnson was wounded three times, while Roberts was injured twice. After the pair ran out of ammunition, the Germans rushed them, capturing Roberts. Johnson pulled a bolo knife and, along with the butt of his pistol, fought hand-to-hand, rescuing his badly wounded compatriot. The startled Germans retreated, preventing them from launching a surprise attack that would likely have inflicted heavy casualties on the regiment. When the skirmish was over, Johnson was credited with killing at least four Germans and wounding ten or more others.

Johnson was hospitalized for several weeks with serious wounds to his back, left arm, face and feet, most of which were inflicted by knives or bayonets. For his heroics, the government of France awarded him a Croix de Guerre with gold leaf, while Roberts also received a Croix de Guerre. In the process, they became the first two Americans to receive the French medal for individual heroism in combat. Johnson was cited by the French as a "magnificent example of courage and energy." The U.S. Army did not award Johnson any decoration for his part in the incident—not even a purple heart.

Despite his injuries, Johnson received no disability allowance when he was discharged from the Army on February 14, 1919. On his return to Albany he received a hero's welcome. New York Governor Alfred E. Smith and other state officials greeted Johnson's arrival at the Albany train station with a homecoming reception. For a while after the war, Johnson's celebrity allowed him to tour the country promoting the sale of Liberty Bonds. Afterwards, however, his injuries proved too disabling for him to return to regular work. Johnson died in poverty at Walter Reed Army Hospital in Washington, DC, on July 2, 1929. He was buried with full military honors in Arlington National Cemetery in Arlington, Virginia.

Doris (Dorie) Miller (1919–1943)
Mess Attendant, First Class, U.S. Navy

The son of sharecroppers, Doris Miller was born on a farm near Waco, Texas, on October 12, 1919. Working in the fields with his parents, Miller grew into a solidly-built young man. He went on to become a star fullback on the football team at Waco's Moore High School. At 19 years of age, Miller enlisted in the U.S. Navy as a messman, the only job open to African American naval recruits at the time.

Assigned to the battleship *USS West Virginia*, Mess Attendant Second-Class Miller was nearing the end of

Dorie Miller (Schomburg Center for Research in Black Culture)

his first hitch when, on December 7, 1941, he was thrust into one of the most important events in U.S. history: Japan's surprise attack on the U.S. naval base at Pearl Harbor on Oahu Island, Hawaii. At 7:55 a.m. on that typically quiet Sunday morning, Miller was below deck collecting laundry. Suddenly, the crew heard a midship explosion. The blast knocked Miller down. Sirens soon called the crew to their battle stations. Miller arrived on deck to witness Japanese planes in full attack on the U.S. Pacific Fleet. Bombing runs were supplemented by machine-gun fire as Japanese aircraft swooped down on virtually undefended ships. In the confusion, sailors ran in all directions, many of them jumping overboard to avoid strafing runs by the enemy flyers. Amid walls of smoke and flame, Miller made his way to his assigned post on the signal bridge. When he arrived, Miller found the ship's commander lying on deck, bleeding from his stomach and chest. He dragged the mortally-wounded officer out of direct fire to a place where a medic and other sailors attempted to treat him. Miller then fought his way back to the bridge, where he spotted an un-manned machine gun. Without any prior weaponry training, Miller started firing the anti-aircraft gun. He brought down four Japanese planes before exhausting the gun's ammunition and being ordered to abandon the sinking ship. For his heroism, Miller was awarded the Navy Cross, which was conferred on him by the commander in chief of the Pacific Fleet, Admiral Chester W. Nimitz. Miller was commended for "distinguished devotion to duty, extreme courage, and disregard of his personal safety during attack." He also received a Purple Heart and was subsequently promoted to mess attendant first class.

Miller became the first African American hero of the war and traveled around the nation to promote the sale of war bonds. After that tour of duty ended, he was sent to Bremerton, Washington, to qualify as a cook. Though he had shown enormous ability as a gunner, navy policy still restricted African Americans to the Stewards Branch. Miller later served as a mess attendant on the light aircraft carrier *USS Liscombe Bay*. A Japanese submarine torpedoed the vessel on November 24, 1943. The resulting explosion killed most of the crew including Miller before the vessel sank in the South Pacific.

After the war, legislation was introduced on two occasions to posthumously award Miller the Congressional Medal of Honor for his Pearl Harbor heroics, but it was defeated both times. However, the Navy honored Miller in succeeding years by naming several things after him, most notably, the destroyer escort *USS Miller*, which was christened in 1973. In so doing, the Navy made Miller the first African American enlisted man to have a ship named after him.

General Frank E. Petersen (1932–)
First African American General in the U.S. Marine Corps

Frank Emmanuel Petersen, Jr. was born March 2, 1932, in Topeka, Kansas, where he attended public schools and graduated from Topeka High School in 1949. He attended Topeka's Washburn University for a year before dropping out to enlist in the U.S. Navy Reserve in June of 1950 as an apprentice seaman, serving as an electronics technician. While attending the Navy's electronics school, he applied for admission to the Naval Aviation Cadet Program. He was accepted and, while in flight training at the U.S. Naval Air Station in Pensacola, Florida, applied for a commission in the U.S. Marine Corps. Petersen earned his wings and accepted a second lieutenant's commission in the Corps on October 22, 1952, becoming the branch's first African American aviator.

Petersen received further training at the Marine Corps Air Station El Toro in Santa Ana, California, before being sent to Korea in 1953. Petersen flew a total of 64 combat missions during the latter stages of the Korean War, building a reputation as a superb fighter pilot. In July of 1954, he returned to the Marine Corps' Santa Ana, California facility, where he remained until January of

General Frank E. Petersen (Corbis Corporation [Bellevue])

1960. In February of 1955, Petersen formally transferred from the U.S. Navy Reserve to the U.S. Marine Corps. During the 1960s and 1970s, Petersen took advantage of many civilian and military educational opportunities. He twice attended George Washington University, where he earned a B.S. in 1967 and an M.S. in 1973. He also attended several service schools including the Marine Corps Amphibious Assault School, the Aviation Safety Officers' Course, and the National War College. Petersen has the distinction of being the first African American corpsman to attend the latter school.

At the height of the Vietnam War, Petersen became the first African American officer to command a squadron in the U.S. Navy or Marine Corps. In June of 1968, he took command of VMF-314, Marine Aircraft Group 13, Republic of Vietnam. The unit, popularly known as the "Black Knights," excelled with Petersen as commander, being named the most outstanding fighter squadron in the entire Marine Corps during the year he was in charge. Petersen also was a fighter pilot and flew more than two hundred missions in F-4 Phantom jets.

Earlier in the 1960s, during a short stay at the Marine Corps Air Station in Iwakuri, Japan, Petersen took on the role of "race counselor" to calm the racial tensions existing not only between black and white Marines, but between white Americans and the native Japanese. After Vietnam, he performed a similar function, only on a much larger scale, as special assistant for minority affairs to the Marine commandant. In this role Petersen traveled to Germany and Japan to investigate racial conditions among corps members. His straightforward report nearly destroyed his career when senior officers would not accept its damning contents. Events occurring in the U.S. at large, however, lent credence to his findings, and the Corps soon adopted changes.

In February of 1979, Petersen became the first African American to reach the rank of brigadier general in the U.S. Marine Corps. While assigned to Marine Corps headquarters in Washington, DC, during the early to mid-1980s, promotions to major general and lieutenant general followed. Starting in 1985, Petersen served as senior ranking pilot in the U.S. Navy and U.S. Marine Corps, and was the senior pilot of the entire U.S. Armed Forces from 1986 until his retirement in 1988. In all, he flew more than 350 combat missions covering 4,000 hours in the air.

Petersen is a recipient of more than twenty individual medals for combat valor including a Distinguished Flying Cross, an Air Medal with silver star, a Meritorious Service Medal, a Legion of Merit with Combat V, a Navy Commendation Medal with Combat V, a National Defense Service Medal with bronze star, an Air Force Commendation Medal, and a Purple Heart.

In 1989, Petersen became a vice president at DuPont. He is a member of the Tuskegee Airmen and the Business Executives for National Security. He is also on the board of directors of the National Bone Marrow Foundation and the Higher Education Assistance Foundation. In 1998, *Into the Tiger's Jaw: America's First Black Marine Aviator*, Petersen's autobiography, was written with assistance from J. Alfred Phelps.

General Colin L. Powell (1937–)

First African American Chairman of the Joint Chiefs of Staff

Colin Luther Powell was born in New York City on April 5, 1937, and graduated from Morris High School in the South Bronx in 1954. In 1958, he received a B.S. in geology from City College of New York, where he was very active in the ROTC program, from which he graduated first in his class. He also attained the highest ROTC rank of cadet colonel.

On June 9, 1958, Powell was commissioned a second lieutenant in the U.S. Army. He attended Infantry Officers Basic Training, as well as the Airborne and Ranger schools at Fort Benning, Georgia, before receiving his first regular duty assignment. In 1959, he went to West

Germany, where he was a platoon leader, executive officer, and a rifle company commander during his three-year stay. In 1962, he was assigned as a military advisor to a South Vietnamese infantry battalion. In the second year of that tour he was wounded by a Vietcong booby trap and was awarded a Purple Heart. Powell returned to Vietnam in 1968 as an infantry officer, serving in such capacities as battalion executive officer and division operations officer. That tour ended prematurely when he was injured in a helicopter crash, in which he rescued two fellow soldiers from the burning wreckage.

Returning to the United States, Powell enrolled in the M.B.A. program at George Washington University and graduated in 1971. In 1972, he was named a White House fellow and served as assistant to the deputy director of the Office of Management and Budget. From 1973 to 1975, he commanded the 1st Battalion, 32nd Infantry in South Korea. Powell was already receiving relatively high-profile assignments before graduating from the National War College in June of 1976, but from that point on his career accelerated. He next commanded the 2nd Brigade, 101st Airborne Division (Air Assault) at Fort Campbell, Kentucky from 1976 to 1977. Several appointments in Washington, DC, followed. He was executive to the special assistant to the secretary and deputy secretary of defense starting in 1977, executive assistant to the secretary of energy for several months in 1979 and senior military assistant to the deputy secretary of defense later that year. Powell he was promoted to brigadier general on June 1 of that same year.

Powell served as assistant commander of the 4th Infantry Division at Fort Carson, Colorado, from 1981 to 1983. He then returned to the nation's capital as senior military adviser to the secretary of defense from 1983 to 1985. Powell went back to West Germany in 1986 to become commanding general of the U.S. V Corps. In 1987, he returned to Washington, DC, first as deputy to the national security adviser, then as national security adviser himself. In April of 1989, he was promoted to four-star general. In August of that year, Powell was named chairman of the Joint Chiefs of Staff, the highest military post in the United States. Powell not only became the first African American in U.S. Armed Forces history to hold that title, but also the youngest. From that position, Powell received international recognition as one of the chief architects of the successful 1989 assault on Panamanian dictator Manuel Noriega and the 1991 Persian Gulf War against Iraq. Both military actions achieved swift and thorough victories with minimal U.S. casualties, while arousing little opposition domestically. Powell retired from the U.S. Army on September 30, 1993.

The public acclaim Powell received for those one-sided military victories opened to him the possibility of a future in nationally-elected political office. Powell wrote his memoir *My American Journey* and embarked on a nationwide tour to promote the book in 1995. During the tour, there was widespread speculation that he would seek the nomination for president the next year. However, on November 9, 1995, Powell held a press conference to announce that he would not enter the presidential race.

In 1996, Powell was named to the board of trustees at Howard University. He devotes a great deal of time to America's Promise—The Alliance for Youth, for which he is chairman. Founded in April of 1997, the Arlington, Virginia-based nonprofit organization works to improve the lives of at-risk youths by increasing their employability. He also remains active as a lecturer and guest speaker.

During his tenure in the military, Powell was a recipient of numerous decorations including a Purple Heart, a Bronze Star, a Legion of Merit with oak leaf cluster, a Soldier's Medal, an Air Medal, a Distinguished Service Medal, a Defense Superior Service Medal, a Joint Service Commendation Medal, and an Army Commendation Medal. He has received many civilian honors as well. In 1993, former President Ronald Reagan presented Powell with the Ronald Reagan Freedom Award. That same year, he received an honorary doctorate from Yeshiva University.

J. Paul Reason (Department of the Navy)

Admiral J. Paul Reason (1943–)
First African American Four-Star Admiral, U.S. Navy

Joseph Paul Reason was born on March 22, 1943, in Washington, DC, where he attended primary and secondary school. After high school, he attended Howard University for three years before receiving nomination to the U.S. Naval Academy from Michigan Congressman Charles Diggs.

While at the Naval Academy, Reason applied to the Navy's nuclear propulsion program, run by Vice Admiral Hyman G. Rickover, "father" of the nuclear submarine. Rickover interviewed Reason and accepted him into the program. Rickover, the first Jewish admiral, took a special interest in Reason as an officer, monitoring Reason's progress from behind the scenes and ensuring that he received fair treatment during his career. Reason's initial assignment was on the destroyer escort *USS J.D. Blackwood* but after completing the nuclear propulsion program in 1968, he transferred to the nuclear-powered missile cruiser *USS Truxtun*. In 1970, he earned a master's degree in computer systems management.

In 1971, Reason began a four-year stint on the nuclear-powered aircraft carrier *USS Enterprise*, during which

he was twice deployed to the Southeast Asia/Indian Ocean region during the Vietnam War. He rejoined the *USS Truxtun* in 1975 as the combat systems officer. From there, he became an assignment officer at the Bureau of Naval Personnel. In late 1976, Reason was named naval aide to the White House for the Gerald Ford administration, a position he kept after Jimmy Carter assumed the presidency in January of 1977. In 1979, he was assigned to the *USS Mississippi* as the ship's executive officer. After a six-year stay aboard that ship, Reason was given command of his own ship, the *USS Coontz*, in 1985. Shortly afterward, he became commander of a nuclear-powered guided missile cruiser, the *USS Bainbridge*.

From 1986 to 1988, Reason was commander of Naval Base Seattle, where he was responsible for all naval activities in Oregon, Washington, and Alaska. His next assignment put him in command of Cruiser-Destroyer Group One, which he led from 1988 to 1994. During that time, he also commanded Battle Group Romeo through operations in the Pacific and Indian Oceans, as well as in the Persian Gulf. Reason was promoted to vice admiral in early 1994 and put in charge of the Naval Surface Force of the U.S. Atlantic Fleet. In August of that year, he was made deputy chief of naval operations for plans, policy, and operations, a post he held for two years.

In May 1996, President Bill Clinton nominated Reason for a promotion and assignment as commander in chief of the U.S. Atlantic Fleet, based in Norfolk, Virginia. His promotion in December of 1996 made him the U.S. Navy's first African American four-star admiral. As chief of the Atlantic fleet, Reason commands roughly half of the U.S. Navy, or more than 124,000 service personnel. He oversees an annual budget of $19.5 billion and the operations of 195 warships and 1,357 aircraft based at 18 major shore facilities.

Among Reason's many military decorations are a Distinguished Service Medal, a Legion of Merit, a Navy Commendation Medal, a National Defense Service Medal, an Armed Forces Expeditionary Medal, a Sea Services Deployment Ribbon, a Republic of Vietnam Honor Medal, and a Republic of Vietnam Campaign Medal.

General Roscoe Robinson, Jr. (1928–1993)
First African American Four Star General, U.S. Army

Roscoe Robinson, Jr. was born on October 28, 1928, in St. Louis, Missouri, where he graduated from Charles Sumner High School. He received an appointment to the U.S. Military Academy at West Point, New York and graduated with a B.S. in military engineering in 1951.

On June 1, 1951, Robinson was commissioned a second lieutenant in the U.S. Army. He attended the Associate Infantry Officer Course and the Basic Airborne Course at Fort Benning, Georgia, before joining the 11th Airborne Division at Fort Campbell, Kentucky. In October of 1952, he was assigned to the 31st Infantry Regiment, 7th Infantry Division in Korea. During the Korean War, his unit saw combat action and Robinson received a bronze star for bravery as commander of a rifle company. Among his assignments in the late 1950s was a tour with the U.S. military mission to Liberia.

From 1965 to 1967, Robinson was the personnel management officer of the Infantry Branch, Officer Personnel Directorate, Office of Personnel Operations, U.S. Army, in Washington, DC. Starting in 1968, Robinson commanded the Second Battalion, Seventh Cavalry, the historic African American unit that was part of the regular Army in 1866 as Company B, Seventh Cavalry. The unit, part of the First Cavalry Division (Airmobile), U.S. Army Pacific, Vietnam, engaged in fighting during the war with Robinson being awarded a silver star for valor. In the early 1970s, Robinson served with the at U.S. Pacific Command in Hawaii, including executive to the chief of staff.

In addition to battlefield heroics, Robinson helped his career by expanding his education. He earned a master's degree in international affairs from the University of Pittsburgh and received further military training at the U.S. Army Command and General Staff College at Fort Leavenworth, Kansas, and at the National War College in Washington, DC.

In 1972, Robinson became commanding officer of the 2nd Brigade, 82nd Airborne Division at Fort Bragg, North Carolina. He was promoted to the rank of brigadier general on July 1, 1973, and was made deputy commander of the U.S. Army Garrison, Okinawa Base Command. Robinson became a two-star general on July 1, 1976, and, in November of that year, returned to Fort Bragg to become commanding general of the 82nd Airborne Division. In 1978, he was made deputy chief of staff for operations, U.S. Army Europe and the Seventh Army. On June 1, 1980, he was promoted to lieutenant general and became commanding general of the U.S. Army, Japan IX Corps. Robinson became the first African American four-star general in the history of the U.S. Army and the second in the U.S. Armed Forces on August 30, 1982. From 1982 to 1985, he served as the United States representative to the North Atlantic Treaty Organization, becoming the nation's first African American to serve in that capacity. Robinson retired from active military service in 1985.

After his retirement from the Army, Robinson served on the boards of several companies including Comsat, Giant Food, Metropolitan Life, and the parent company of Northwest Airlines. In 1987, he was named to oversee the work of a panel designated with the task of reviewing the Korean War performance records of certain African American Army units that had been criticized at the time. On July 22, 1993, Robinson died of leukemia at the Walter Reed Army Medical Center in Washington, DC. He is buried in Arlington National Cemetery in Arlington, Virginia.

During his 34-year career, Robinson was the recipient of numerous military awards including a Silver Star with oak leaf cluster, a Legion of Merit with two oak leaf clusters, a Distinguished Flying Cross, a Bronze Star, ten Air Medals, a Defense Distinguished Service Medal, and an Army Commendation Medal.

Roderick K. von Lipsey (1959–)
Fighter Pilot, U.S. Marine Corps

Roderick K. von Lipsey was born on January 13, 1959, in Philadelphia, Pennsylvania. Beginning in third grade, he was educated in private schools, first at Norwood Academy, then at La Salle College High School. He attended the U.S. Naval Academy in Annapolis, Maryland, majoring in English literature. Upon graduation, von Lipsey joined the U.S. Marine Corps and was commissioned a second lieutenant in May of 1980.

In January of 1981, after completing basic Marine Corps training, von Lipsey went to Pensacola, Florida, and Kingsville, Texas, to master aircraft that would earn him the "naval aviator" designation. Then, starting in September of 1982, he spent an additional six months at the Marine Corps base at Yuma, Arizona, to become combat ready on the F-4 Phantom fighter jet.

In 1983, von Lipsey was assigned to Fort Beaufort, South Carolina, to gain experience in aircraft maintenance and maintenance quality assurance. The following year, he became the officer in charge of aircraft maintenance for F-4 Phantoms at the base. Von Lipsey began training on the F/A-18 Hornet fighter jet in 1985. In 1986, he was deployed to NATO exercises in Europe and the Mediterranean, for which he was awarded a Navy Commendation medal for his performance of logistics responsibilities. In January of 1987, von Lipsey was sent to the prestigious Navy Fighter Weapons School at Naval Station Miramar in California. Informally known as TOPGUN, the grueling six-week training program hones the technique of experienced fighter pilots and teaches them how to use newly-developed skills to instruct others. In 1989, von Lipsey was stationed at the Marine Fighter Attack Squadron at Kaneohe Bay, Hawaii.

On August 2, 1990, Iraq invaded Kuwait. Von Lipsey was quickly sent to Saudi Arabia to take part in Operation Desert Shield, a measure designed to prevent further Iraqi aggression. While in the Middle East, von Lipsey joined Marine Fighter/Attack Squadron 235. On January 20, 1991, at the start of Operation Desert Storm against Iraqi forces in Kuwait, von Lipsey led an attack of 35 aircraft from the Third Marine Aircraft Wing. The six hundred-mile journey to a secret air base in eastern Iraq resulted in the demolition of the base's maintenance and repair hangars, as well as the network of railroad tracks that were its supply lines. All of the planes under von Lipsey's command returned safely. For his meritorious service in the execution of this highly successful mission, he was awarded the Distinguished Flying Cross. That attack was just one of more than forty sorties flown by von Lipsey during the Gulf War.

Following his return from the Middle East in 1991, von Lipsey was chosen as one of two aides-de-camp to Chairman of the Joint Chiefs of Staff General Colin L. Powell. Initially the junior aide, and later the senior, von Lipsey helped orchestrate the general's busy travel schedule, which included trips to such countries as Belgium, Czechoslovakia, Hungary, Jamaica, Poland, and Somalia. He remained in that assignment until 1993, when he was awarded a White House fellowship, serving as a special assistant in the areas of foreign and security policy to White House Chief of Staff Thomas F. McLarty III. Often traveling on Air Force One as a member of President Clinton's entourage, von Lipsey provided national security updates and background information for McLarty at high-level meetings with foreign political leaders. Von Lipsey was awarded a second fellowship in 1994 with the Council on Foreign Relations. When the fellowship ended in mid–1995, he was assigned to Marine Corps Air Squadron El Toro, based in Santa Ana, California. He received a promotion to lieutenant colonel shortly afterward.

Von Lipsey received additional military training at the Amphibious Warfare School in Quantico, Virginia. He also earned a master of arts degree in international affairs from Catholic University. Von Lipsey was honored by *Time* magazine as one of America's most promising leaders under forty years of age in the December 1994 special report "Fifty for the Future." He is a member of the Council on Foreign Relations, as well as the International Institute for Strategic Studies. In 1997, he edited and co-authored the book *Breaking the Cycle*, which presented new ways of dealing with conflict resolution in countries plagued by violent, intergroup disputes.

In addition to the Distinguished Flying Cross with Combat V, von Lipsey has received a Defense Meritorious Service Medal with Combat V, a Single Mission Air Medal, a Strike/Flight Air Medal, a Joint Service Commendation Medal, and two Navy Commendation Medals.

◆ MILITARY STATISTICS

Ready Reserve Personnel Profile—Race, and Sex: 1990 to 1997

ITEM	RACE					PERCENT DISTRIBUTION			
	Total	White	Black	Asian	American Indian	White	Black	Asian	American Indian
1990	1,641,475	1,289,367	271,470	14,616	7,695	78.5	16.5	0.9	0.5
1993	1,840,650	1,425,255	309,699	21,089	9,068	77.4	16.8	1.1	0.5
1994	1,779,436	1,366,387	297,519	22,190	8,870	76.8	16.7	1.2	0.5
1995	1,633,497	1,254,592	273,847	21,792	8,591	76.8	16.8	1.3	0.5
1996	1,522,451	1,166,628	249,114	21,240	8,226	76.6	16.4	1.4	0.5
1997, total [1]	**1,437,722**	**1,102,234**	**229,950**	**21,412**	**8,115**	**76.7**	**16.0**	**1.5**	**0.6**
Male	1,214,511	956,215	170,425	18,224	6,580	78.7	14.0	1.5	0.5
Officers	187,339	160,468	12,729	2,370	469	85.7	6.8	1.3	0.3
Enlisted	1,027,172	795,747	157,696	15,854	6,111	77.5	15.4	1.5	0.6
Female	223,080	145,992	59,519	3,185	1,535	65.4	26.7	1.4	0.7
Officers	42,988	32,516	6,715	549	112	75.6	15.6	1.3	0.3
Enlisted	180,092	113,476	52,804	2,636	1,423	63.0	29.3	1.5	0.8

[1] Includes unknown sex.

Source: U.S. Dept. of Defense, *Official Guard and Reserve Manpower Strengths and Statistics,* annual.

Appendix

◆African American Recipients of Selected Awards
◆African American Federal Judges
◆African American Olympic Medalists

◆ AFRICAN AMERICAN RECIPIENTS OF SELECTED AWARDS

ACADEMY AWARD OF MERIT (OSCAR)— ACADEMY OF MOTION PICTURE ARTS AND SCIENCES

Best Performance by an Actor in a Leading Role

1963   Sidney Poitier, in *Lilies of the Field*

Best Performance by an Actor in a Supporting Role

1982   Louis Gossett, Jr., in *An Officer and a Gentleman*

1989   Denzel Washington, in *Glory*

1996   Cuba Gooding, Jr., in *Jerry Maquire*

Best Performance by an Actress in a Supporting Role

1939   Hattie McDaniel, in *Gone with the Wind*

1990   Whoopi Goldberg, in *Ghost*

Best Original Score

1984   Prince, for *Purple Rain*

1986   Herbie Hancock, for *'Round Midnight*

AMERICAN ACADEMY AND INSTITUTE OF ARTS AND LETTERS AWARD

Art

1946   Richmond Barthé

1966   Romare Bearden

1971   Norman Lewis

Literature

1946   Gwendolyn Brooks; Langston Hughes

1956   James Baldwin

1961   John A. Williams

1970   James A. McPherson

1971   Charles Gordone

1972   Michael S. Harper

1974   Henry Van Dyke

1978   Lerone Bennett, Jr.; Toni Morrison

1985   John Williams

1987   Ernest J. Gaines

1992   August Wilson

Music

1974   Olly Wilson

1981   George Walker

1988   Hale Smith

1991   Tania J. Leon

AUSTRALIAN OPEN

Men's Singles

1970 Arthur Ashe

Men's Doubles

1977 Arthur Ashe

Women's Doubles

1957 Althea Gibson, with Darlene Hard

CONGRESSIONAL GOLD MEDAL

1978 Marian Anderson

1990 Jesse Owens

1994 Colin L. Powell, Jr.

1998 Little Rock Nine: Jean Brown Trickey, Carlotta Walls LaNier, Melba Patillo Beals, Terrence Roberts, Gloria Ray Karlmark, Thelma Mothershed Wair, Ernest Green, Elizabeth Eckford, and Jefferson Thomas

1999 Rosa Louise McCauley Parks

EMMY AWARD—ACADEMY OF TELEVISION ARTS AND SCIENCES

Primetime Awards

Outstanding Lead Actor in a Drama Series

1966 Bill Cosby, in "I Spy" (NBC)

1967 Bill Cosby, in "I Spy" (NBC)

1968 Bill Cosby, in "I Spy" (NBC)

1991 James Earl Jones, in "Gabriel's Fire" (ABC)

1998 Andre Braugher, in "Homicide: Life on the Street" (NBC)

Outstanding Lead Actor in a Comedy, Variety, or Music Series

1959 Harry Belafonte, in "Tonight with Belafonte"

1985 Robert Guillaume, in "Benson" (ABC)

Outstanding Lead Actress in a Comedy, Variety, or Music Series

1981 Isabel Sanford, in "The Jeffersons" (CBS)

Outstanding Lead Actress in a Comedy or Drama Special

1974 Cicely Tyson, in "The Autobiography of Miss Jane Pittman" (CBS)

Outstanding Lead Actress in a Miniseries or Special

1991 Lynn Whitfield, in "The Josephine Baker Story" (HBO)

1997 Alfre Woodard, in "Miss Evers' Boys" (HBO)

Outstanding Supporting Actor in a Comedy, Variety, or Music Series

1979 Robert Guillaume, in "Soap" (ABC)

Outstanding Supporting Actor in a Miniseries or Special

1991 James Earl Jones, in "Heatwave" (TNT)

Outstanding Supporting Actress in a Drama Series

1984 Alfre Woodard, in "Doris in Wonderland" episode of "Hill Street Blues" (NBC)

1991 Madge Sinclair, in "Gabriel's Fire" (ABC)

1992 Mary Alice, in "I'll Fly Away" (NBC)

Outstanding Supporting Actress in a Comedy, Variety, or Music Series

1987 Jackee Harry, in "227"

Outstanding Supporting Actress in a Miniseries or Special

1991 Ruby Dee, in "Decoration Day," *Hallmark Hall of Fame* (NBC)

Outstanding Directing in a Drama Series

1986 Georg Stanford Brown, in "Parting Shots" episode of "Cagney & Lacey" (ABC)

1990 Thomas Carter, in "Promises to Keep" episode of "Equal Justice" (ABC)

1991 Thomas Carter, in "In Confidence" episode of "Equal Justice" (ABC)

1992 Eric Laneuville, in "All God's Children" episode of "I'll Fly Away" (NBC)

Outstanding Producing in a Miniseries or Special

1989 Suzanne de Passe, in "Lonesome Dove"

Outstanding Producing in a Variety, Music, or Comedy Special

1984 Suzanne de Passe, in "Motown 25: Yesterday, Today and Forever"

1985 Suzanne de Passe, in "Motown at the Apollo"

Outstanding Variety, Music, or Comedy Special

1997 "Chris Rock: Bring on the Pain" (HBO)

Outstanding Achievement in Music Composition

1971 Ray Charles, in "The First Nine Months Are the Hardest" (NBC)

1972 Ray Charles, in "The Funny Side of Marriage" (NBC)

Outstanding Achievement in Music Composition for a Series

1977 Quincy Jones and Gerald Fried, in "Roots" (ABC)

Outstanding Choreography

1981 Debbie Allen, for "Come One, Come All" episode of "Fame"

1982 Debbie Allen, for "Class Act" episode of "Fame"

1989 Debbie Allen, for "Motown 30: What's Goin' On!"

Daytime Awards

Outstanding Talk Show

1987 "The Oprah Winfrey Show"

1988 "The Oprah Winfrey Show"

1989 "The Oprah Winfrey Show"

1991 "The Oprah Winfrey Show"

1992 "The Oprah Winfrey Show"

1994 "The Oprah Winfrey Show"

1995 "The Oprah Winfrey Show"

1996 "The Oprah Winfrey Show"

1997 "The Oprah Winfrey Show"

Outstanding Talk Show Host

1987 Oprah Winfrey, "The Oprah Winfrey Show"

1991 Oprah Winfrey, "The Oprah Winfrey Show"

1992 Oprah Winfrey, "The Oprah Winfrey Show"

1993 Oprah Winfrey, "The Oprah Winfrey Show"

1994 Oprah Winfrey, "The Oprah Winfrey Show"

1995 Oprah Winfrey, "The Oprah Winfrey Show"

1996 Montel Williams, "The Montel Williams Show"

Sports Awards

Outstanding Sports Personality/Studio Host

1998 James Brown (Fox Sports Network)

Outstanding Sports Event Analyst

1997 Joe Morgan (ESPN/NBC)

Outstanding Sports Journalism

1995 "Broken Promises" and "Pros and Cons" episodes of "Real Sports with Bryant Gumbel"

1998 "Diamond Buck$" and "Winning at All Costs" episodes of "Real Sports with Bryant Gumbel"

Hall of Fame Award

1992 Bill Cosby

1994 Oprah Winfrey

FRENCH OPEN

Men's Doubles

1971 Arthur Ashe

Women's Singles

1956 Althea Gibson

Women's Doubles

1956 Althea Gibson

1999 Venus and Serena Williams

GRAMMY AWARDS—NATIONAL ACADEMY OF RECORDING ARTS AND SCIENCES

Record of the Year

1963 *I Can't Stop Loving You,* by Count Basie

1967 *Up, Up and Away,* by 5th Dimension

1969 *Aquarius/Let the Sun Shine In*, by 5th Dimension

1972 *The First Time Ever I Saw Your Face*, by Roberta Flack

1973 *Killing Me Softly with His Song*, by Roberta Flack

1976 *This Masquerade*, by George Benson

1983 *Beat It*, by Michael Jackson

1984 *What's Love Got To Do with It?*, by Tina Turner

1985 *We Are the World*, by USA For Africa; produced by Quincy Jones

1988 *Don't Worry, Be Happy*, by Bobby McFerrin

1991 *Unforgettable*, by Natalie Cole with Nat "King" Cole

1993 *I Will Always Love You*, by Whitney Houston

1995 *Kiss From a Rose* by Seal

Album of the Year

1973 *Innervisions*, by Stevie Wonder; produced by Stevie Wonder

1974 *Fulfillingness' First Finale*, by Stevie Wonder; produced by Stevie Wonder

1976 *Songs in the Key of Life*, by Stevie Wonder; produced by Stevie Wonder

1983 *Thriller*, by Michael Jackson; produced by Quincy Jones

1984 *Can't Slow Down*, by Lionel Richie; produced by Lionel Richie and James Anthony Carmichael

1990 *Back on the Block*, by Quincy Jones; produced by Quincy Jones

1991 *Unforgettable*, by Natalie Cole

1999 *The Miseducation of Lauryn Hill*, by Lauryn Hill; produced by Lauryn Hill

HEISMAN MEMORIAL TROPHY—DOWNTOWN ATHLETIC CLUB OF NEW YORK CITY, INC.

1961 Ernie Davis, Syracuse University, TB

1965 Michael Garrett, University of Southern California, TB

1968 O. J. Simpson, University of Southern California, TB

1972 Johnny Rodgers, University of Nebraska, FL

1974 Archie Griffin, University of Ohio State, HB

1975 Archie Griffin, University of Ohio State, HB

1976 Anthony (Tony) Dorsett, University of Pittsburgh, HB

1977 Earl Campbell, University of Texas, FB

1978 Billy Sims, University of Oklahoma, HB

1979 Charles White, University of Southern California, TB

1980 George Rogers, University of South Carolina, HB

1981 Marcus Allen, University of Southern California, TB

1982 Herschel Walker, University of Georgia, HB

1983 Mike Rozier, University of Nebraska, TB

1985 Bo Jackson, Auburn University, TB

1987 Tim Brown, University of Notre Dame, FL

1988 Barry Sanders, Oklahoma State University, HB

1989 Andre Ware, University of Houston, QB

1991 Desmond Howard, University of Michigan, WR

1993 Charlie Ward, Florida State University, QB

1994 Rashaan Salaam, Colorado, RB

1995 Eddie George, Ohio State, RB

1997 Charles Woodson, University of Michigan, DB/R

1998 Ricky Williams, University of Texas at Austin, TB

CLARENCE L. HOLTE LITERARY PRIZE (BIANNUAL)—CO-SPONSORED BY THE PHELPS-STOKES FUND AND THE SCHOMBURG CENTER FOR RESEARCH IN BLACK CULTURE OF THE NEW YORK PUBLIC LIBRARY

1979 Chancellor Williams, for *The Destruction of Black Civilization: Great Issues of a Race from 4500 B.C. to 2000 A.D.*

1981 Ivan Van Sertima, for *They Came Before Columbus*

1983 Vincent Harding, for *There Is a River: The Black Struggle for Freedom in America*

1985 No award

1986 John Hope Franklin, for *George Washington Williams: A Biography*

1988 Arnold Rampersad, for *The Life of Langston Hughes, Volume 1 (1902-1941): I, Too, Sing America*

KENNEDY CENTER HONORS—JOHN F. KENNEDY CENTER FOR THE PERFORMING ARTS

1978 Marian Anderson

1979 Ella Fitzgerald

1980 Leontyne Price

1981 William "Count" Basie

1983 Katherine Dunham

1984 Lena Horne

1986 Ray Charles

1987 Sammy Davis, Jr.

1988 Alvin Ailey

1989 Harry Belafonte

1990 Dizzy Gillespie

1991 Fayard and Harold Nicholas

1992 Lionel Hampton

1993 Arthur Mitchell; Marion Williams

1994 Aretha Franklin

1995 B. B. King; Sidney Poitier

1996 Benny Carter

1997 Jessye Norman

1998 Bill Cosby

MARTIN LUTHER KING, JR. NONVIOLENT PEACE PRIZE—MARTIN LUTHER KING, JR. CENTER FOR NONVIOLENT SOCIAL CHANGE, INC.

1973 Andrew Young

1974 Cesar Chavez

1975 John Lewis

1976 Randolph Blackwell

1977 Benjamin E. Mays

1978 Kenneth D. Kaunda; Stanley Levison

1979 Jimmy Carter

1980 Rosa Parks

1981 Ivan Allen, Jr.

1982 Harry Belafonte

1983 Sir Richard Attenborough; Martin Luther King, Sr.

1984 No award

1985 No award

1986 Bishop Desmond Tutu

1987 Corazon Aquino

1988 No award

1989 No award

1990 Mikhail Gorbachev

1991 No award

1992 No award

1993 Jesse Jackson

MISS AMERICA—MISS AMERICA ORGANIZATION

1984 Vanessa Williams (New York); Suzette Charles (New Jersey)

1990 Debbye Turner (Missouri)

MISS BLACK AMERICA—J. MORRIS ANDERSON PRODUCTION COMPANY

1968 Sandy Willliams (Pennsylvania)

1969 G. O. Smith (New York)

1970 Stephanie Clark (District of Columbia)

1971 Joyce Warner (Florida)

1972 Linda Barney (New Jersey)

1973 Arnice Russell (New York)

1974 Von Gretchen Sheppard (California)

1975 Helen Ford (Mississippi)

1976 Twanna Kilgore (District of Columbia)

1977 Claire Ford (Tennessee)

1978 Lydia Jackson (New Jersey)

1979 Veretta Shankle (Mississippi)

1980 Sharon Wright (Illinois)

1981 Pamela Jenks (Massachusetts)

1982 Phyllis Tucker (Florida)

1983 Sonia Robinson (Wisconsin)

1984 Lydia Garrett (South Carolina)

1985 Amina Fakir (Michigan)

1986 Rachel Oliver (Massachusetts)

1987 Leila McBride (Colorado)

1989 Paula Swynn (District of Columbia)

1990 Rosie Jones (Connecticut)

1991 Sharmelle Sullivan (Indiana)

1992 Marilyn DeShields

1993 Pilar Ginger Fort

1994 Karen Wallace

1995 Asheera Ahmad

MISS USA—MADISON SQUARE GARDEN TELEVISION PRODUCTIONS

1990 Carole Gist (Michigan)

1992 Shannon Marketic

1993 Kenya Moore (Michigan)

1994 Frances Louise "Lu" Parker

1995 Chelsi Smith (Texas)

1996 Ali Landry

MS. OLYMPIA WINNERS—INTERNATIONAL FEDERATION OF BODYBUILDERS, WOMEN'S BODYBUILDING CHAMPIONS

1983 Carla Dunlap

1990 Lenda Murray

1991 Lenda Murray

1992 Lenda Murray

1993 Lenda Murray

1994 Lenda Murray

1995 Lenda Murray

MR. OLYMPIA WINNERS—INTERNATIONAL FEDERATION OF BODYBUILDERS, MEN'S BODYBUILDING CHAMPIONS

1967 Sergio Oliva

1968 Sergio Oliva

1982 Chris Dickerson

1984 Lee Haney

1985 Lee Haney

1986 Lee Haney

1987 Lee Haney

1988 Lee Haney

1989 Lee Haney

1990 Lee Haney

1991 Lee Haney

1998 Ronnie Coleman

NATIONAL BASEBALL HALL OF FAME

1962 Jackie Robinson

1969 Roy Campanella

1971 Leroy R. "Satchel" Paige

1972 Josh Gibson; Walter "Buck" Leonard

1973 Roberto W. Clemente; Monte Irvin

1974 James T. "Cool Papa" Bell

1975 William "Judy" Johnson

1976 Oscar M. Charleston

1977 Ernest Banks; Martin Dihigo; John H. Lloyd

1979 Willie Mays

1981 Andrew "Rube" Foster; Robert T. Gibson

1982 Hank Aaron; Frank Robinson

1983 Juan A. Marichal

1985 Lou Brock

1986 Willie L. "Stretch" McCovey

1987 Ray Dandridge; Billy Williams

1988 Willie Stargell

1990 Joe Morgan

1991 Rod Carew; Ferguson Jenkins

1993 Reggie Jackson

1995 Leon Day

1996 Bill Foster

1997 Willie Wells

1998 Larry Doby

1999 Orlando Cepeda; Joe Williams

NATIONAL BASKETBALL HALL OF FAME

1972 Robert Douglass

1974 Bill Russell

1976 Elgin "The Big E" Baylor; Charles Cooper

1978 Wilt Chamberlain

1979 Oscar Robertson

1981 Clarence Gaines; Willis Reed

1983 Sam Jones

1984 Nate Thurmond

1986 Walt "Clyde" Frazier

1987 Wes Unseld

1988 William "Pop" Gates; K.C. Jones; Lenny Wilkins (player)

1989 Dave Bing; Elvin Hayes; Earl "The Pearl" Monroe

1990 Nate "Tiny" Archibald

1991 Lusia Harris-Stewart; Connie Hawkins; Bob Lanier

1992 Walt Bellamy; Julius "Dr. J" Erving; Calvin Murphy

1994 Kareem Abdul-Jabbar; Cheryl Miller

1995 George Gervin; David Thompson

1996 Alex English

1998 Marques Haynes, Lenny Wilkins (coach)

1999 Wayne Embry, John Thompson

NATIONAL BOOK AWARD—NATIONAL BOOK FOUNDATION

1953 Ralph Ellison, for *Invisible Man*, Fiction

1969 Winthrop D. Jordan, for *White over Black: American Attitudes toward the Negro, 1550-1812*, History and Biography

1983 Gloria Naylor, for *The Women of Brewster Place*, First Novel; Joyce Carol Thomas, for *Marked By Fire*, Children's Literature; Alice Walker, for *The Color Purple*, Fiction

1990 Charles Johnson, for *Middle Passage*, Fiction

1991 Melissa Fay Green, for *Praying for Sheetrock*, Nonfiction

1992 Edward P. Jones, for *Lost in the City*, Fiction

NATIONAL MEDAL OF ARTS—NATIONAL ENDOWMENT FOR THE ARTS

1985 Ralph Ellison (writer); Leontyne Price (singer)

1986 Marian Anderson (singer)

1987 Romare Bearden (artist); Ella Fitzgerald (singer)

1988 Gordon Parks (photographer and film director)

1989 Katherine Dunham (choreographer); Dizzy Gillespie (musician)

1990 Riley "B. B." King (musician)

1991 James Earl Jones (actor); Billy Taylor (musician)

1994 Harry Belafonte (singer)

1995 Gwendolyn Brooks (poet); Ossie Davis (actor); Ruby Dee (actress)

1996 The Harlem Boys Choir (chorale); Lionel Hampton (musician)

1997 Betty Carter (singer)

1998 Fats Domino (singer)

NATIONAL SOCIETY OF ARTS AND LETTERS GOLD MEDAL OF MERIT AWARD

1982 Andre Watts (music)

NATIONAL TRACK AND FIELD HALL OF FAME—THE ATHLETICS CONGRESS OF THE USA

1974 Ralph Boston; Lee Calhoun; Harrison Dillard; Rafer Johnson; Jesse Owens; Wilma Rudolph; Malvin Whitfield

1975 Ralph Metcalfe

1976 Robert Hayes; Hayes Jones

1977 Robert Beamon; Andrew W. Stanfield

1978 Tommie Smith; John Woodruff

1979 Jim Hines; William DeHart Hubbard

1980 Wyomia Tyus

1981 Willye White

1982 Willie Davenport; Eddie Tolan

1983 Lee Evans

1984 Madeline Manning Mims

1986 Henry Barney Ewell

1988 Gregory Bell

1989 Milt Campbell; Edward Temple

1990 Charles Dumas

1994 Cornelius Johnson; Edwin Moses

1995 Valerie Brisco; Florence Griffith Joyner

1997 Evelyn Ashford; Henry Carr; Renaldo Nehemiah

NEW YORK DRAMA CRITICS' CIRCLE AWARD

Best American Play

1959 *A Raisin in the Sun*, by Lorraine Hansberry

1975 *The Taking of Miss Janie*, by Ed Bullins

1982 *A Soldier's Play*, by Charles Fuller

1996 *Seven Guitars*, by August Wilson

Best New Play

1985 *Ma Rainey's Black Bottom*, by August Wilson

1987 *Fences*, by August Wilson

1988 *Joe Turner's Come and Gone*, by August Wilson

1990 *The Piano Lesson*, by August Wilson

NOBEL PEACE PRIZE—NOBEL FOUNDATION

1950 Ralph J. Bunche

1964 Martin Luther King, Jr.

NOBEL PRIZE IN LITERATURE—NOBEL FOUNDATION

1993 Toni Morrison

PRESIDENTIAL MEDAL OF FREEDOM—UNITED STATES EXECUTIVE OFFICE OF THE PRESIDENT

1963 Marian Anderson; Ralph J. Bunche

1964 John L. Lewis; Leontyne Price; A. Philip Randolph

1969 Edward Kennedy "Duke" Ellington; Ralph Ellison; Roy Wilkins; Whitney M. Young, Jr.

1976 Jesse Owens

1977 Martin Luther King, Jr. (posthumously)

1980 Clarence Mitchell

1981 James H. "Eubie" Blake; Andrew Young

1983 James Cheek; Mabel Mercer

1984 Jack Roosevelt "Jackie" Robinson (posthumously)

1985 William "Count" Basie (posthumously); Jerome "Brud" Holland (posthumously)

1987 Frederick Douglass Patterson

1988 Pearl Bailey

1991 Colin L. Powell

1992 Ella Fitzgerald

1993 Arthur Ashe, Jr. (posthumously); Thurgood Marshall (posthumously); Colin L. Powell

1994 Dorothy Height; Barbara Jordan

1995 William Thaddeus Coleman, Jr.; John Hope Franklin; A. Leon Higginbotham, Jr.

1996 John H. Johnson; Rosa Parks

1998 James Farmer

PROFESSIONAL FOOTBALL HALL OF FAME

1967 Emlen Tunnell

1968 Marion Motley

1969 Fletcher "Joe" Perry

1971 Jim Brown

1972 Ollie Matson

1973 Jim Parker

1974 Richard "Night Train" Lane

1975 Roosevelt Brown; Leonard "Lenny" Moore

1976 Leonard "Len" Ford

1977 Gale Sayers; Bill Willis

1980 Herb Adderley; David "Deacon" Jones

1981 Willie Davis

1983 Bobby Bell; Bobby Mitchell; Paul Warfield

1984 Willie Brown; Charley Taylor

1985 O. J. Simpson

1986 Ken Houston; Willie Lanier

1987 Joe Greene; John Henry Johnson; Gene Upshaw

1988 Alan Page

1989 Mel Blount; Art Shell; Willie Wood

1990 Junious "Buck" Buchanan; Franco Harris

1991 Earl Campbell

1992 Lem Barney; John Mackey

1993 Larry Little; Walter Payton

1994 Tony Dorsett; Leroy Kelly

1995 Lee Roy Selmon

1996 Charlie Joiner; Mel Renfro

1997 Mike Haynes

1998 Mike Singletary; Dwight Stephenson

1999 Eric Dickerson; Lawrence Taylor

PULITZER PRIZE—COLUMBIA UNIVERSITY GRADUATE SCHOOL OF JOURNALISM

Biography or Autobiography

1994 *W. E. B. Du Bois: Biography of a Race, 1968–1919*, by David Levering Lewis

Journalism: Commentary

1996 E. R. Shipp

Journalism: Feature Writing

1999 Angelo B. Henderson

Letters: Drama

1970 *No Place To Be Somebody*, by Charles Gordone

1982 *A Soldier's Play*, by Charles Fuller

1987 *Fences*, by August Wilson

1990 *The Piano Lesson*, by August Wilson

Letters: Fiction

1978 *Elbow Room*, by James Alan McPherson

1983 *The Color Purple*, by Alice Walker

1988 *Beloved*, by Toni Morrison

Letters: Poetry

1950 *Annie Allen*, by Gwendolyn Brooks

1987 *Thomas and Beulah*, by Rita Dove

Letters: Special Awards and Citations

1977 Alexander Palmer Haley, for *Roots*

Music: Special Awards and Citations

1976 Scott Joplin

1996 George Walker

1997 Wynton Marsalis

1999 Edward Kennedy "Duke" Ellington (posthmously)

ROCK AND ROLL HALL OF FAME

1986 Chuck Berry; James Brown; Ray Charles; Sam Cooks; Fats Domino; Little Richard; Robert Johnson; Jimmy Yancey

1987 The Coasters; Bo Diddley; Aretha Franklin; Marvin Gaye; Louis Jordan; B.B. King; Clyde McPhalter; Smokey Robinson; Big Joe Turner; T-Bone Walker; Muddy Waters; Jackie Wilson

1988 The Drifters; Barry Gordy, Jr.; The Supremes

1989 The Ink Spots; Otis Redding; Bessie Smith; The Soul Stirrers; The Temptations; Stevie Wonder

1990 Louis Armstrong; Hank Ballard; Charlie Christian; The Four Tops; Holland, Dozier, and Holland; The Platters; Ma Rainey

1991 La Vern Baker; John Lee Hooker; Howlin' Wolf; The Impressions; Wilson Pickett; Jimmy Reed; Ike and Tina Turner

1992 Blue Brand, Booker T. and the M.G.'s; Jimi Hendrix; Isley Brothers; Elmore James; Doc Pomus; Professor Longhair; Sam and Dave

1993 Ruth Brown; Etta James; Frankie Lymon and the Teenagers; Sly and the Family Stone; Dinah Washington

1994 Willie Dixon; Bob Marley; Johnny Otis

1995 Al Green; Martha and the Vandellas; The Orioles

1996 Little Willie John; Gladys Knight and the Pips; The Shirelles

1997 Mahalia Jackson; The Jackson Five; Parliament

1998 Jelly Roll Morton; Lloyd Price

1999 Charles Brown; Curtis Mayfield; The Staple Singers

SPRINGARN MEDAL—NATIONAL ASSOCIATION FOR THE ADVANCEMENT OF COLORED PEOPLE

1915 Ernest E. Just—head of the department of physiology at Howard University Medical School.

1916 Charles Young—major in the United States Army.

1917 Harry T. Burleigh—composer, pianist, singer.

1918 William Stanley Braithwaite—poet, literary critic, editor.

1919 Archibald H. Grimké—former U.S. Consul in Santo Domingo, president of the American Negro Academy, author, president of the District of Columbia branch of the NAACP.

1920 William Edward Burghardt DuBois—author, editor, organizer of the first Pan-African Congress.

1921 Charles S. Gilpin—actor.

1922 Mary B. Talbert—former president of the National Association of Colored Women.

1923 George Washington Carver—head of research and director of the experiment station at Tuskegee Institute.

1924 Roland Hayes—singer.

1925 James Weldon Johnson—former United States Consul in Venezuela and Nicaragua, author, editor, poet; secretary of the NAACP.

1926 Carter G. Woodson—editor, historian; founder of the Association for the Study of Negro Life and History.

1927 Anthony Overton—businessman; president of the Victory Life Insurance Company (the first African American organization permitted to do business under the rigid requirements of the State of New York).

1928 Charles W. Chesnutt—author.

1929 Mordecai Wyatt Johnson—the first African American president of Howard University.

1930 Henry A. Hunt—principal of Fort Valley High and Industrial School, Fort Valley, Georgia.

1931 Richard Berry Harrison—actor.

1932 Robert Russa Moton—principal of Tuskegee Institute.

1933 Max Yergan—secretary of the YMCA in South Africa.

1934 William Taylor Burwell Williams—dean of Tuskegee Institute.

1935 Mary McLeod Bethune—founder and president of Bethune Cookman College.

1936 John Hope—president of Atlanta University.

1937 Walter White—executive secretary of the NAACP.

1939 Marian Anderson—singer.

1940 Louis T. Wright—surgeon.

1941 Richard Wright—author.

1942 A. Philip Randolph—labor leader, international president of the Brotherhood of Sleeping Car Porters.

1943 William H. Hastie—jurist, educator.

1944 Charles Drew—scientist.

1945 Paul Robeson—singer, actor.

1946 Thurgood Marshall—special counsel of the NAACP

1947 Percy Julian—research chemist.

1948 Channing H. Tobias—minister, educator.

1949 Ralph J. Bunche—international civil servant, acting United Nations mediator in Palestine.

1950 Charles Hamilton Houston—chairman of the NAACP Legal Committee.

1951 Mabel Keaton Staupers—leader of the National Association of Colored Graduate Nurses.

1952 Harry T. Moore—state leader of the Florida NAACP.

1953 Paul R. Williams—architect.

1954 Theodore K. Lawless—physician, educator, philanthropist.

1955 Carl Murphy—editor, publisher, civic leader.

1956 Jack Roosevelt Robinson—athlete.

1957 Martin Luther King, Jr.—minister, civil rights leader

1958 Daisy Bates and the Little Rock Nine—for their pioneer role in upholding the basic ideals of American democracy in the face of continuing harassment and constant threats of bodily injury.

1959 Edward Kennedy "Duke" Ellington—composer, musician, orchestra leader.

1960 Langston Hughes—poet, author, playwright.

1961 Kenneth B. Clark—professor of psychology at the City College of the City University of New York, founder and director of the Northside Center for Child Development, prime mobilizer of the resources of modern psychology in the attack upon racial segregation.

1962 Robert C. Weaver—administrator of the Housing and Home Finance Agency.

1963 Medgar Wiley Evers—NAACP field secretary for Mississippi, World War II veteran.

1964 Roy Wilkins—executive director of the NAACP.

1965 Leontyne Price—singer.

1966 John H. Johnson—founder and president of the Johnson Publishing Company.

1967 Edward W. Brooke III—the first African American to win popular election to the United States Senate.

1968 Sammy Davis, Jr.—performer, civil rights activist.

1969 Clarence M. Mitchell, Jr.—director of the Washington Bureau of the NAACP, civil rights activist.

1970 Jacob Lawrence—artist, teacher, humanitarian.

1971 Leon H. Sullivan—minister.

1972 Gordon Alexander Buchanan Parks—writer, photographer, filmmaker.

1973 Wilson C. Riles—educator.

1974 Damon Keith—jurist.

1975 Hank Aaron—athlete.

1976 Alvin Ailey—dancer, choreographer, artistic director.

1977 Alexander Palmer Haley—author, biographer, lecturer.

1978 Andrew Young—United States Ambassador to the United Nations, diplomat, cabinet member, civil rights activist, minister.

1979 Rosa Parks—community activist.

1980 Rayford W. Logan—educator, historian, author.

1981 Coleman A. Young—mayor of the City of Detroit, public servant, labor leader, civil rights activist.

1982 Benjamin E. Mays—educator, theologian, humanitarian).

1983 Lena Horne—performer, humanitarian.

1984 Tom Bradley—government executive, public servant, humanitarian.

1985 William H. "Bill" Cosby—comedian, actor, educator, humanitarian.

1986 Benjamin Lawson Hooks—executive director of the NAACP.

1987 Percy Ellis Sutton—public servant, businessman, community leader.

1988 Frederick Douglass Patterson—doctor of veterinary medicine, educator, humanitarian, founder of the United Negro College Fund.

1989 Jesse Jackson—minister, political leader, civil rights activist.

1990 L. Douglas Wilder—governor of Virginia.

1991 Colin L. Powell—general in the United States Army, chairman of the Joint Chiefs of Staff.

1992 Barbara C. Jordan—educator, former congresswoman.

1993 Dorothy L. Height—president of the National Council of Negro Women.

1994 Maya Angelou—poet, author, performing artist.

1995 John Hope Franklin—historian.

1996 A. Leon Higginbotham, Jr.—jurist, judge.

1997 Carl T. Rowan—journalist.

1998 Myrlie Evers-Williams—former chair, board of directors, NAACP

1999 Earl G. Graves, publisher and media executive

SULLIVAN AWARD—AMATEUR ATHLETIC UNION

1961 Wilma Rudolph

1981 Carl Lewis

1983 Edwin Moses

1986 Jackie Joyner-Kersee

1988 Florence Griffith-Joyner

1991 Mike Powell

1993 Charlie Ward

1996 Michael Johnson

1998 Chamique Holdsclaw

TONY (ANTOINETTE PERRY) AWARD— LEAGUE OF AMERICAN THEATERS AND PRODUCERS

Actor (Dramatic)

1969 James Earl Jones, for *The Great White Hope*

1975 John Kani, for *Sizwe Banzi*; Winston Ntshona, for *The Island*

1987 James Earl Jones, for *Fences*

Supporting or Featured Actor (Dramatic)

1982 Zakes Mokae, for *Master Harold. . . and the Boys*

1992 Larry Fishburne, for *Two Trains Running*

1994 Jeffrey Wright, for *Angels in America*

1996 Ruben Santiago-Hudson, for *Seven Guitars*

Actor (Musical)

1970 Cleavon Little, for *Purlie*

1973 Ben Vereen, for *Pippin*

1982 Ben Harvey, for *Dreamgirls*

1992 Gregory Hines, for *Jelly's Last Jam*

Supporting or Featured Actor (Musical)

1954 Harry Belafonte, for *John Murray Anderson's Almanac*

1975 Ted Rose, for *The Wiz*

1981 Hinton Battle, for *Sophisticated Ladies*

1982 Cleavant Derricks, for *Dreamgirls*

1983 Charles "Honi" Coles, for *My One and Only*

1984 Hinton Battle, for *The Tap Dance Kid*

1991 Hinton Battle, for *Miss Saigon*

1997 Chuck Cooper, for *The Life*

Supporting or Featured Actress (Dramatic)

1977 Trazana Beverley, for *For Colored Girls Who Have Considered Suicide/When the Rainbow Is Enuf*

1987 Mary Alice, for *Fences*

1988 L. Scott Caldwell, for *Joe Turner's Come and Gone*

1997 Lynne Thigpen, for *An American Daughter*

Actress (Musical)

1962 Diahann Carroll, for *No Strings*

1968 Leslie Uggams, for *Hallelujah, Baby*

1974 Virginia Capers, for *Raisin*

1982 Jennifer Holliday, for *Dreamgirls*

1989 Ruth Brown, for *Black and Blue*

1996 Audra McDonald, for *Master Class*

Supporting or Featured Actress (Musical)

1950 Juanita Hall, for *South Pacific*

1968 Lillian Hayman, for *Halleluja, Baby*

1970 Melba Moore, for *Purlie*

1975 Dee Dee Bridgewater, for *The Wiz*

1977 Delores Hall, for *Your Arms's Too Short To Box with God*

1978 Nell Carter, for *Ain't Misbehavin*

1992 Tonya Pinkins, for *Jelly's Last Jam*

1994 Audra McDonald, for *Carousel*

1996 Ann Duquesnay, for *Bring in 'Da Noise, Bring in 'Da Funk*

1997 Lillias White, for *The Life*

Play

1974 *The River Niger*, by Joseph A. Walker

1987 *Fences*, by August Wilson

UNITED STATES MEDAL OF HONOR

Civil War

Army

William H. Barnes, Private, Company C, 38th United States Colored Troops.

Powhatan Beaty, First Sergeant, Company G, 5th United States Colored Troops.

James H. Bronson, First Sergeant, Company D, 5th United States Colored Troops.

William H. Carney, Sergeant, Company C, 54th Massachusetts Infantry, United States Colored Troops.

Decatur Dorsey, Sergeant, Company B, 39th United States Colored Troops.

Christian A. Fleetwood, Sergeant Major, 4th United States Colored Troops.

James Gardiner, Private, Company 1, 36th United States Colored Troops.

James H. Harris, Sergeant, Company B, 38th United States Colored Troops.

Thomas R. Hawkins, Sergeant Major, 6th United States Colored Troops.

Alfred B. Hilton, Sergeant, Company H, 4th United States Colored Troops.

Milton M. Holland, Sergeant, 5th United States Colored Troops.

Alexander Kelly, First Sergeant, Company F, 6th United States Colored Troops.

Robert Pinn, First Sergeant, Company I, 5th United States Colored Troops.

Edward Radcliff, First Sergeant, Company C, 38th United States Colored Troops.

Charles Veal, Private, Company D, 4th United States Colored Troops.

Navy

Aaron Anderson, Landsman, *USS Wyandank.*

Robert Blake, Powder Boy, *USS Marblehead.*

William H. Brown, Landsman, *USS Brooklyn.*

Wilson Brown, *USS Hartford.*

John Lawson, Landsman, *USS Hartford.*

James Mifflin, Engineer's Cook, *USS Brooklyn.*

Joachim Pease, Seaman, *USS Kearsarge.*

Interim Period

Navy

Daniel Atkins, Ship's Cook, First Class, *USS Cushing.*

John Davis, Seaman, *USS Trenton.*

Alphonse Girandy, Seaman, *USS Tetrel.*

John Johnson, Seaman, *USS Kansas.*

William Johnson, Cooper, *USS Adams.*

Joseph B. Noil, Seaman, *USS Powhatan.*

John Smith, Seaman, *USS Shenandoah.*

Robert Sweeney, Seaman, *USS Kearsage, USS Jamestown.*

Western Campaigns

Army

Thomas Boyne, Sergeant, Troop C, 9th United States Cavalry.

Benjamin Brown, Sergeant, Company C, 24th United States Infantry.

John Denny, Sergeant, Troop C, 9th United States Cavalry.

Pompey Factor, Seminole Negro Indian Scouts.

Clinton Greaves, Corporal, Troop C, 9th United States Cavalry.

Henry Johnson, Sergeant, Troop D, 9th United States Cavalry.

George Jordan, Sergeant, Troop K, 9th United States Cavalry.

William McBreyar, Sergeant, Troop K, 10th United States Cavalry.

Isaiah Mays, Corporal, Company B, 24th United States Infantry.

Issac Payne, Private (Trumpeteer) Seminole Negro Indian Scouts.

Thomas Shaw, Sergeant, Troop K, 9th United States Cavalry.

Emanuel Stance, Sergeant, Troop F, 9th United States Cavalry.

Augustus Walley, Private, Troop 1, 9th United States Cavalry.

John Ward, Sergeant, Seminole Negro Indian Scouts.

Moses Williams, First Sergeant, Troop 1, 9th United States Cavalry.

William O. Wilson, Corporal, Troop 1, 9th United States Cavalry.

Brent Woods, Sergeant, Troop B, 9th United States Cavalry.

Spanish-American War

Army

Edward L. Baker, Jr., Sergeant Major, 10th United States Cavalry.

Dennis Bell, Private, Troop H, 10th United States Cavalry.

Fitz Lee, Private, Troop M, 10th United States Cavalry.

William H. Thompkins, Private, Troop G, 10th United States Cavalry.

George H. Wanton, Sergeant, Troop M, 10th United States Cavalry.

Navy

Joseph B. Noil, Non-combatant Service, *USS Powhatan.*

Robert Penn, Fireman, First Class, *USS Iowa.*

World War I

Army

Freddie Stowers, Corporal, Company C, 371st Infantry Regiment, 93rd Infantry Division.

World War II

Army

Vernon Baker, First Lieutenant.

Edward A. Carter, Jr., Staff Sergeant.

John R. Fox, First Lieutenant.

Willy F. James, Jr., Private First Class.

Ruben Rivers, Staff Sergeant.

Charles L. Thomas, First Lieutenant.

George Watson, Private.

Korean War

Army

Cornelius H. Charlton, Sergeant, 24th Infantry Regiment, 25th Division.

William Thompson, Private, 24th Infantry Regiment, 25th Division.

Vietnam War

Army

Webster Anderson, Sergeant, Battery A, 2nd Battalion, 320th Artillery, 101st Airborne Division.

Eugene Ashley, Jr., Sergeant, Company C, 5th Special Forces Group (Airborne), 1st Special Forces.

William M. Bryant, Sergeant First Class, Company A, 5th Special Forces Group, 1st Special Forces.

Lawrence Joel, Specialist Sixth Class, Headquarters and Headquarters Company, 1st Battalion, 173d Airborne Brigade.

Dwight H. Johnson, Specialist Fifth Class, Company B, 1st Battalion, 69th Armor, 4th Infantry Division.

Garfield M. Langhorn, Private First Class, Troop C, 7th Squadron, 17th Cavalry, 1st Aviation Brigade.

Matthew Leonard, Platoon Sergeant, Company B, 1st Battalion, 16th Infantry, 1st Infantry Division.

Donald R. Long, Sergeant, Troop C, 1st Squadron, 4th Cavalry, 1st Infantry Division.

Milton L. Olive III, Private First Class, Company B, 2nd Battalion 503d Infantry, 173d Airborne Brigade.

Riley L. Pitts, Captain, Company C, 2nd Battalion, 27th Infantry, 25th Infantry Division.

Charles C. Rogers, Lieutenant Colonel, 1st Battalion, 5th Infantry, 1st Infantry Division.

Rupert L. Sargent, First Lieutenant, Company B, 4th Battalion, 9th Infantry, 25th Infantry Division.

Clarence E. Sasser, Specialist 5th Class, Headquarters Company, 3rd Battalion, 60th Infantry, 90th Infantry Division.

Clifford C. Sims, Staff Sergeant, Company D, 2nd Battalion, 501st Infantry, 101st Airborne Division.

John E. Warren, Jr., First Lieutenant, Company C, 2nd Battalion, 22d Infantry, 25th Infantry Division.

Marines

James A. Anderson, Jr. Private First Class, 2nd Platoon, Company F, 2nd Battalion, 3rd Marine Division.

Oscar P. Austin, Private First Class, Company E, 7th Marines, 1st Marine Division.

Rodney M. Davis, Company B, First Battalion, 5th Marines, 1st Marine Division.

Robert H. Jenkins, Jr., Private First Class, 3rd Reconnaissance Battalion, 3rd Marine Division.

Ralph H. Johnson, Private First Class, Company A, 1st Reconnaissance Battalion, 1st Marine Division.

UNITED STATES OPEN

Men's Singles

1968 Arthur Ashe

Women's Singles

1957 Althea Gibson
1958 Althea Gibson

Mixed Doubles

1957 Althea Gibson

UNITED STATES POET LAUREATE

1993 Rita Dove (served until 1995)

UNITED STATES POSTAL SERVICE STAMPS ON AFRICAN AMERICAN HISTORY

Louis Armstrong

Benjamin Banneker

William "Count" Basie

James Pierson Beckwourth

Mary McLeod Bethune

James Hubert "Eubie" Blake

Ralph Johnson Bunche

George Washington Carver

Nat "King" Cole

Bessie Coleman

John Coltrane

Allison Davis

Benjamin O. Davis, Sr.

Frederick Douglass

Charles Richard Drew

(W)illiam (E)dward (B)urghardt Du Bois

Jean Baptiste Pointe Du Sable

Paul Laurence Dunbar

Edward Kennedy "Duke" Ellington

Erroll Garner

(W)illiam (C)hristopher Handy

Coleman Hawkins

Matthew Alexander Henson

Billie Holiday

Mahalia Jackson

James Price Johnson

James Weldon Johnson

Robert Johnson

Scott Joplin

Percy Lavon Julian

Ernest Everett Just

Martin Luther King, Jr.

Joe Louis

Hudson William Ledbetter, "Leadbelly"

Roberta Martin

Jan E. Matzeliger

Clyde McPhatter

Charles Mingus

Thelonious Sphere Monk

Ferdinand "Jelly Roll" Morton

James Cleveland "Jesse" Owens

Charlie "Bird" Parker

Bill Pickett

Salem Poor

Gertrude "Ma" Rainey

(A)sa Philip Randolph

Otis Redding

John Roosevelt "Jackie" Robinson

James Andrew "Jimmy" Rushing

Bessie Smith

Henry Ossawa Tanner

Sonny Terry

Sister Rosetta Tharpe

Sojourner Truth

Harriet Tubman

Madame C. J. Walker

Clara Ward

Booker Taliaferro Washington

Dinah Washington

Ethel Waters

Muddy Waters

Ida Bell Wells-Barnett

Josh White

Howlin' Wolf

Carter Godwin Woodson

Whitney Moore Young

WIMBLEDON—ALL ENGLAND LAWN TENNIS AND CROQUET CLUB

Men's Singles

1975 Arthur Ashe

Ladies' Singles

1957 Althea Gibson

1958 Althea Gibson

Ladies' Doubles

1957 Althea Gibson, with Darlene Hard

1958 Althea Gibson, with Maria Bueno

◆ AFRICAN AMERICAN FEDERAL JUDGES

PRESIDENT FRANKLIN D. ROOSEVELT

1937	William H. Hastie*	District Court, Virgin Islands
1939	Harnian E. Moore*	District Court, Virgin Islands

PRESIDENT HARRY S TRUMAN

1945	Irvin C. Mollison*	United States Customs Court
1949	William H. Hastie*	Court of Appeals, Third Circuit
1949	Harnian E. Moore (a)*	District Court, Virgin Islands

PRESIDENT DWIGHT D. EISENHOWER

1957	Scovel Richardson*	United States Customs Court
1958	Walter Gordon*	District Court, Virgin Islands

PRESIDENT JOHN F. KENNEDY

1961	James B. Parsons**	Senior Judge, District Court, Illinois
1961	Wade M. McCree**	District Court, Michigan
1961	Thurgood Marshall**	Court of Appeals, Second Circuit

PRESIDENT LYNDON B. JOHNSON

1964	Spottswood Robinson**	District Court, District of Columbia
1964	A. Leon Higginbotham**	District Court, Pennsylvania
1965	William B. Bryant	Senior Judge, District Court, District of Columbia
1966	Wade H. McCree*	Court of Appeals, Sixth Court
1966	James L. Watson	United States Customs Court
1966	Constance B. Motley	Senior Judge, District Court, New York
1966	Spottswood Robinson	Senior Judge, Court of Appeals for the Federal Circuit
1966	Aubrey E. Robinson	Chief Judge, District Court, District of Columbia
1967	Damon Keith**	District Court, Michigan
1967	Thurgood Marshall*	Associate Justice, Supreme Court
1967	Joseph C. Waddy**	District Court, District of Columbia

PRESIDENT RICHARD M. NIXON

1969	Almeric Christian**	District Court, Virgin Islands
1969	David W. Williams	Senior Judge, District Court, California
1969	Barrington D. Parker	Senior Judge, District Court, District of Columbia
1971	Lawrence W. Pierce**	District Court, New York
1971	Clifford Scott Green	District Court, Pennsylvania
1972	Robert L. Carter	Senior Judge, District Court, New York
1972	Robert M. Duncan**	Military Court of Appeals
1974	Robert M. Duncan**	District Court, Ohio

PRESIDENT GERALD R. FORD

1974	Henry Bramwell**	Senior Judge, District Court, New York
1976	George N. Leighton**	Senior Judge, District Court, Illinois
1976	Matthew Perry**	Military Court of Appeals
1976	Cecil F. Poole**	District Court, California

PRESIDENT JIMMY CARTER

1978	Almeric Christian (a)**	Chief Judge, District Court, Virgin Islands
1978	U.W. Clemon	District Court, Alabama
1978	Robert F. Collins**	District Court, Louisiana

1978	Julian A. Cook, Jr.	District Court, Michigan
1978	Damon J. Keith	Court of Appeals, Sixth Circuit
1978	A. Leon Higginbotham*	Court of Appeals, Third Circuit
1978	Mary Johnson Lowe	District Court, New York
1978	Theodore McMillian	Court of Appeals, Eighth Circuit
1978	David S. Nelson	District Court, Massachusetts
1978	Paul A. Simmons**	District Court, Pennsylvania
1978	Jack E. Tanner	District Court, Washington
1979	Harry T. Edwards	Court of Appeals for the Federal Circuit
1979	J. Jerome Farris	Court of Appeals, Ninth Circuit
1979	Joseph W. Hatchett	Court of Appeals, Eleventh Circuit
1979	Terry J. Hatter	District Court, California
1979	Joseph C. Howard	District Court, Maryland
1979	Benjamin T. Gibson	District Court, Michigan
1979	James T. Giles	District Court, Pennsylvania
1979	Nathaniel R. Jones	Court of Appeals, Sixth Circuit
1979	Amalya L. Kearse	Court of Appeals, Second Circuit
1979	Gabrielle Kirk McDonald**	District Court, Texas
1979	John Garrett Penn**	District Court, District of Columbia
1979	Cecil F. Poole	Court of Appeals, Ninth Circuit
1979	Matthew J. Perry	District Court, South Carolina
1979	Myron H. Thompson	District Court, Alabama
1979	Anne E. Thompson	District Court, New Jersey
1979	Odell Horton	District Court, Tennessee
1979	Anna Diggs Taylor	District Court, Michigan
1979	Horace T. Ward	District Court, Georgia
1979	Alcee L. Hastings***	District Court, Florida
1980	Clyde S. Cahill, Jr.**	District Court, Missouri
1980	Richard C. Erwin	District Court, North Carolina
1980	Thelton E. Henderson	District Court, California
1980	George Howard, Jr.	District Court, Arkansas
1980	Earl B. Gilliam	District Court, California
1980	Norma Holloway Johnson	District Court, District of Columbia
1980	Consuela B. Marshall	District Court, California
1980	George White	District Court, Ohio

PRESIDENT RONALD REAGAN

1981	Lawrence W. Pierce	Court of Appeals, Second Circuit
1982	Reginald Gibson	United States Court of Claims
1984	John R. Hargrove	District Court, Maryland
1984	Henry Wingate	District Court, Mississippi
1985	Ann Williams	District Court, Illinois
1986	James Spencer	District Court, Virginia
1987	Kenneth Hoyt	District Court, Texas
1988	Herbert Hutton	District Court, Pennsylvania

PRESIDENT GEORGE BUSH

1990	Clarence Thomas**	Court of Appeals for the Federal Circuit
1990	James Ware	District Court, California
1991	Saundra Brown Armstrong	District Court, California
1991	Fernando J. Giatan	District Court, Missouri
1991	Donald L. Graham	District Court, Florida
1991	Sterling Johnson	District Court, New York
1991	J. Curtis Joyner	District Court, Pennsylvania
1991	Timothy K. Lewis	District Court, Pennsylvania

1991	Joe B. McDade	District Court, Illinois
1991	Clarence Thomas	Associate Justice, Supreme Court
1992	Garland E. Burrell, Jr.	District Court, California
1992	Carol Jackson	District Court, Missouri
1992	Timothy K. Lewis	Court of Appeals, Third Circuit

PRESIDENT BILL CLINTON

1993	Henry Lee Adams	District Court, Florida
1993	Wilkie Ferguson	District Court, Florida
1993	Raymond Jackson	District Court, Virginia
1993	Gary Lancaster	District Court, Pennsylvania
1993	Reginald Lindsay	District Court, Massachusetts
1993	Charles Shaw	District Court, Missouri
1994	Deborah Batts	District Court, New York
1994	Franklin Burgess	District Court, Washington
1994	James Beaty, Jr.	District Court, North Carolina
1994	David Coar	District Court, Illinois
1994	Audrey Collins	District Court, California
1994	Clarence Cooper	District Court, Georgia
1994	Michael Davis	District Court, Minnesota
1994	Raymond Finch	District Court, Virgin Islands
1994	Vanessa Gilmore	District Court, Texas
1994	A. Haggerty	District Court, Oregon
1994	Denise Page Hood	District Court, Michigan
1994	Napoleon Jones	District Court, California
1994	Blance Manning	District Court, Illinois
1994	Theodore McKee	Circuit Court, Third Circuit
1994	Vicki Miles‐LaGrange	District Court, Oklahoma
1994	Solomon Oliver, Jr.	District Court, Ohio
1994	Barrington Parker, Jr.	District Court, New York
1994	Judith Rogers	Circuit Court, District of Columbia
1994	W. Louis Sands	District Court, Georgia
1994	Carl Stewart	Circuit Court, Fifth Circuit
1994	Emmet Sullivan	Circuit Court, District of Columbia
1994	William Walls	District Court, New Jersey
1994	Alexander Williams	District Court, Maryland
1995	R. Guy Cole	Circuit Court, Sixth Circuit
1995	Curtis Collier	District Court, Tennessee
1995	Wiley Daniel	District Court, Colorado
1995	Andre Davis	District Court, Maryland
1995	Bernice B. Donald	District Court, Tennessee
1996	Charles N. Clevert, Jr.	District Court, Wisconsin
1996	Joseph A. Greenaway, Jr.	District Court, New Jersey
1997	Eric L. Clay	Circuit Court, Sixth Circuit
1997	Algenon L. Marbley	District Court, Ohio
1997	Martin J. Jenkins	District Court, California
1997	Henry H. Kennedy, Jr.	District Court, District of Columbia
1998	Gregory Sleet	District Court, Delaware
1998	Ivan L.R. Lemelle	District Court, Louisiana
1998	Sam A. Lindsay	District Court, Texas
1998	Johnnie B. Rawlinson	District Court, Nevada
1998	Margaret Seymour	District Court, South Carolina
1998	Richard Roberts	District Court, District of Columbia
1998	Gerald Bruce Lee	District Court, Virginia
1998	Lynn Bush	Court of Federal Claims

1998	Stephan P. Mickle	District Court, Florida
1998	Victoria Roberts	District Court, Michigan
1998	Raner Collins	District Court, Arizona
1998	Ralph Tyson	District Court, Louisiana
1999	William Hibbler	District Court, Illinois

(a) Reappointment

* Deceased

** No longer serving

*** Impeached and removed from the court

◆ AFRICAN AMERICAN OLYMPIC MEDALISTS

Place/Year	Athlete	Event	Place	Time/Distance
St. Louis, 1904	George C. Poag	200 M Hurdles	3rd	
	George C. Poag	400 M Hurdles	3rd	
London, 1908	J.B. Taylor	1600 M Relay	1st	3:29.4
Paris, 1924	Dehart Hubbard	Long Jump	1st	24' 5.125"
	Edward Gourdin	Long Jump	2nd	23' 10"
Los Angeles, 1932	Eddie Tolan	100 M Dash	1st	10.3
	Ralph Metcalfe	100 M Dash	2nd	10.3
	Eddie Tolan	200 M Dash	1st	21.2
	Ralph Metcalfe	200 M Dash	3rd	21.5
	Edward Gordon	Long Jump	1st	25' .75"
Berlin, 1936	Jesse Owens	100 M Dash	1st	10.3
	Ralph Metcalfe	100 M Dash	2nd	10.4
	Jesse Owens	200 M Dash	1st	20.7
	Matthew Robinson	200 M Dash	2nd	21.1
	Archie Williams	400 M Run	1st	46.5
	James DuValle	400 M Run	2nd	46.8
	John Woodruff	800 M Run	1st	1:52.9
	Fritz Pollard, Jr.	110 M Hurdles	3rd	14.4
	Cornelius Johnson	High Jump	1st	6'8"
	Jesse Owens	Long Jump	1st	26' 5.75"
	Jesse Owens	400 M Relay	1st	39.8
	Ralph Metcalfe	400 M Relay	1st	39.8
London, 1948	Harrison Dillard	100 M Dash	1st	10.3
	Norwood Ewell	100 M Dash	2nd	10.4
	Norwood Ewell	200 M Dash	1st	21.1
	Mal Whitfield	400 M Run	3rd	46.9
	Willie Steele	Long Jump	1st	25' 8"
	Herbert Douglass	Long Jump	3rd	25' 3"
	Lorenzo Wright	400 M Relay	1st	40.6
	Harrison Dillard	1600 M Relay	1st	3:10.4
	Norwood Ewell	1600 M Relay	1st	3:10.4
	Mal Whitfield	1600 M Relay	1st	3:10.4
	Audrey Patterson	200 M Dash	3rd	25.2
	Alice Coachman	High Jump	1st	5' 6.125"
Helsinki, 1952	Andrew Stanfield	200 M Dash	1st	20.7
	Ollie Matson	400 M Run	3rd	46.8
	Mal Whitfield	800 M Run	1st	1:49.2
	Harrison Dillard	110 M Hurdles	1st	13.7
	Jerome Biffle	Long Jump	1st	24' 10"
	Meredith Gourdine	Long Jump	2nd	24' 8.125"
	Harrison Dillard	400 M Relay	1st	40.1
	Andrew Stanfield	400 M Relay	1st	40.1
	Ollie Matson	400 M Relay	1st	40.1
	Bill Miller	Javelin	2nd	237
	Milton Campbell	Decathlon	2nd	6,975 pts.
	Floyd Patterson	Boxing: Middleweight	1st	
	Norvel Lee	Boxing: Light Heavyweight	1st	
	Nathan Brooks	Boxing: Flyweight	1st	
	Charles Adkins	Boxing: Light Welterweight	1st	
	Barbara Jones	400 M Relay	1st	45.9
Melbourne, 1956	Andrew Stanfield	200 M Dash	2nd	20.7
	Charles Jenkins	400 M Run	1st	46.7
	Lee Calhoun	110 M Hurdles	1st	13.5
	Charles Dumas	High Jump	1st	6' 11.25"
	Gregory Bell	Long Jump	1st	25' 8.25"
	Willye White	Long Jump	2nd	19' 11.75"
	Ira Murchison	400 M Relay	1st	39.5
	Leamon King	400 M Relay	1st	39.5
	Charles Jenkins	400 M Relay	1st	39.5
	Lou Jones	1600 M Relay	1st	3:04.8

Place/Year	Athlete	Event	Place	Time/Distance
	Milton Campbell	Decathlon	1st	7,937 pts.
	Rafer Johnson	Decathlon	2nd	7,587 pts.
	K.C. Jones	Men's Basketball	1st	
	Bill Russell	Men's Basketball	1st	
	James Boyd	Boxing: Light Heavyweight	1st	
	Mildred McDaniel	High Jump	1st	5′ 9.25″
	Margaret Matthews	400 M Relay	3rd	44.9
	Isabelle Daniels	400 M Relay	3rd	44.9
	Mae Faggs	400 M Relay	3rd	44.9
	Wilma Rudolph	400 M Relay	3rd	44.9
Rome, 1960	Les Carney	200 M Dash	2nd	20.6
	Lee Calhoun	110 M Hurdles	1st	13.8
	Willie May	110 M Hurdles	2nd	13.8
	Hayes Jones	110 M Hurdles	3rd	14
	Otis Davis	400 M Run	1st	44.9
	John Thomas	High Jump	3rd	7′ .25″
	Ralph Boston	Long Jump	1st	26′ 7.75″
	Irvin Robertson	Long Jump	2nd	26′ 7.25″
	Otis Davis	1600 M Relay	1st	3:02.2
	Rafer Johnson	Decathlon	1st	8,392 pts.
	Oscar Robertson	Men's Basketball	1st	
	Walt Bellamy	Men's Basketball	1st	
	Bob Boozer	Men's Basketball	1st	
	Wilbert McClure	Boxing: Light Middleweight	1st	
	Cassius Clay	Boxing: Light Heavyweight	1st	
	Edward Crook	Boxing: Middleweight	1st	
	Quincelon Daniels	Boxing: Light Welterweight	3rd	
	Earlene Brown	Shot Put	3rd	53′ 10.25″
	Wilma Rudolph	100 M Dash	1st	11
	Wilma Rudolph	200 M Dash	1st	24
	Martha Judson	400 M Relay	3rd	44.5
	Lucinda Williams	400 M Relay	3rd	44.5
	Barbara Jones	400 M Relay	3rd	44.5
	Wilma Rudolph	400 M Relay	3rd	44.5
Tokyo, 1964	Robert Hayes	100 M Dash	1st	9.9
	Henry Carr	200 M Dash	1st	20.3
	Paul Drayton	200 M Dash	2nd	20.5
	Hayes Jones	110 M Hurdles	1st	13.6
	Robert Hayes	400 M Relay	1st	39
	Paul Drayton	400 M Relay	1st	39
	Richard Stebbins	400 M Relay	1st	39
	John Thomas	High Jump	2nd	7′ 1.75″
	John Rambo	High Jump	3rd	7′ 1″
	Ralph Boston	Long Jump	2nd	26′ 4″
	Walt Hazzard	Men's Basketball	1st	
	Lucius Jackson	Men's Basketball	1st	
	Charles Brown	Boxing: Featherweight	3rd	
	Ronald Harris	Boxing: Lightweight	3rd	
	Joe Frazier	Boxing: Heavyweight	1st	
	Robert Carmody	Boxing: Flyweight	3rd	
	Wyomia Tyus	100 M Dash	1st	11.4
	Edith McGuire	100 M Dash	2nd	11.6
	Edith McGuire	200 M Dash	1st	23
	Wyomia Tyus	400 M Relay	2nd	43.9
	Edith McGuire	400 M Relay	2nd	43.9
	Willye White	400 M Relay	2nd	43.9
	Marilyn White	400 M Relay	2nd	43.9
Mexico City, 1968	Jim Hines	100 M Dash	1st	9.9
	Charles Greene	100 M Dash	3rd	10
	Tommie Smith	200 M Dash	1st	19.8
	John Carlos	200 M Dash	3rd	20
	Lee Evans	400 M Run	1st	43.8

Place/Year	Athlete	Event	Place	Time/Distance
	Larry James	400 M Run	2nd	43.9
	Ron Freeman	400 M Run	3rd	44.4
	Willie Davenport	110 M Hurdles	1st	13.3
	Ervin Hall	110 M Hurdles	2nd	13.4
	Jim Hines	400 M Relay	1st	38.2
	Charles Greene	400 M Relay	1st	38.2
	Mel Pender	400 M Relay	1st	38.2
	Ronnie Ray Smith	400 M Relay	1st	38.2
	Wyomia Tyus	400 M Relay	1st	42.8
	Barbara Ferrell	400 M Relay	1st	42.8
	Margaret Bailes	400 M Relay	1st	42.8
	Mildrette Netter	400 M Relay	1st	42.8
	Lee Evans	1600 M Relay	1st	2:56.1
	Vince Matthews	1600 M Relay	1st	2:56.1
	Ron Freeman	1600 M Relay	1st	2:56.1
	Larry James	1600 M Relay	1st	2:56.1
	Edward Caruthers	High Jump	2nd	7' 3.5"
	Bob Beamon	Long Jump	1st	29' 2.5"
	Ralph Boston	Long Jump	3rd	26' 9.25"
	Spencer Haywood	Men's Basketball	1st	
	Charlie Scott	Men's Basketball	1st	
	Michael Barrett	Men's Basketball	1st	
	James King	Men's Basketball	1st	
	Calvin Fowler	Men's Basketball	1st	
	John Baldwin	Boxing: Light Middleweight	3rd	
	Alfred Jones	Boxing: Middleweight	3rd	
	Albert Robinson	Boxing: Featherweight	2nd	
	Ronald Harris	Boxing: Lightweight	1st	
	James Wallington	Boxing: Light Welterweight	3rd	
	George Foreman	Boxing: Heavyweight	1st	
	Wyomia Tyus	100 M Dash	1st	11
	Barbara Ferrell	100 M Dash	2nd	11.1
	Madeline Manning	800 M Run	1st	2:00.9
Munich, 1972	Robert Taylor	100 M Dash	2nd	10.24
	Larry Black	200 M Dash	2nd	20.19
	Vince Matthews	400 M Run	1st	44.66
	Wayne Collett	400 M Run	2nd	44.80
	Rod Milburn	110 M Hurdles	1st	13.24
	Eddie Hart	400 M Relay	1st	38.19
	Robert Taylor	400 M Relay	1st	38.19
	Larry Black	400 M Relay	1st	38.19
	Gerald Tinker	400 M Relay	1st	38.19
	Randy Williams	Long Jump	1st	27' .25"
	Arnie Robinson	Long Jump	3rd	26' 4"
	Jeff Bennet	Decathlon	3rd	7,974 pts.
	Wayne Collett	400 M Dash	2nd	44.80
	Marvin Johnson	Boxing: Middleweight	3rd	
	Ray Seales	Boxing: Light Welterweight	1st	
	Cheryl Toussain	1600 M Relay	2nd	3:25.2
	Mable Fergerson	1600 M Relay	2nd	3:25.2
	Madeline Manning	1600 M Relay	2nd	3:25.2
Montreal, 1976	Millard Hampton	200 M Dash	2nd	20.29
	Dwayne Evans	200 M Dash	3rd	20.43
	Fred Newhouse	400 M Run	2nd	44.40
	Herman Frazier	400 M Run	3rd	44.95
	Willie Davenport	110 M Hurdles	3rd	13.38
	Edwin Moses	400 M Hurdles	1st	47.64
	Millard Hampton	400 M Relay	1st	38.83
	Steve Riddick	400 M Relay	1st	38.83
	Harvey Glance	400 M Relay	1st	38.83
	John Jones	400 M Relay	1st	38.83
	Herman Frazier	1600 M Relay	1st	2:58.7

Place/Year	Athlete	Event	Place	Time/Distance
	Benny Brown	1600 M Relay	1st	2:58.7
	Maxie Parks	1600 M Relay	1st	2:58.7
	Fred Newhouse	1600 M Relay	1st	2:58.7
	Arnie Robinson	Long Jump	1st	27' 4.75"
	Randy Williams	Long Jump	2nd	26' 7.25"
	James Butts	Triple Jump	2nd	56 8.5"
	Phil Ford	Men's Basketball	1st	
	Adrian Dantley	Men's Basketball	1st	
	Walter Davis	Men's Basketball	1st	
	Quinn Buckner	Men's Basketball	1st	
	Kenneth Carr	Men's Basketball	1st	
	Scott May	Men's Basketball	1st	
	Philip Hubbard	Men's Basketball	1st	
	Johnny Tate	Boxing: Heavyweight	3rd	
	Leo Randolph	Boxing: Flyweight	1st	
	Howard David	Boxing: Lightweight	1st	
	Sugar Ray Leonard	Boxing: Light Welterweight	1st	
	Michael Spinks	Boxing: Middleweight	1st	
	Leon Spinks	Boxing: Light Heavyweight	1st	
	Rosalyn Bryant	1600 M Relay	2nd	3:22.8
	Shelia Ingram	1600 M Relay	2nd	3:22.8
	Pamela Jiles	1600 M Relay	2nd	3:22.8
	Debra Sapenter	1600 M Relay	2nd	3:22.8
	Lusia Harris	Women's Basketball	2nd	
	Charlotte Lewis	Women's Basketball	2nd	
Los Angeles, 1984	Carl Lewis	100 M Dash	1st	9.9
	Sam Graddy	100 M Dash	2nd	10.19
	Carl Lewis	200 M Dash	1st	19.80
	Kirk Baptiste	200 M Dash	2nd	19.96
	Alonzo Babers	400 M Run	1st	44.27
	Antonio McKay	400 M Run	3rd	44.71
	Earl Jones	800 M Run	3rd	1:43.83
	Roger Kingdom	110 M Hurdles	1st	13.20
	Greg Foster	110 M Hurdles	2nd	13.23
	Edwin Moses	400 M Hurdles	1st	47.75
	Danny Harris	400 M Hurdles	2nd	48.13
	Sam Graddy	400 M Relay	1st	37.83
	Ron Brown	400 M Relay	1st	37.83
	Calvin Smith	400 M Relay	1st	37.83
	Carl Lewis	400 M Relay	1st	37.83
	Sunder Nix	1600 M Relay	1st	2:57.91
	Roy Armstead	1600 M Relay	1st	2:57.91
	Alonzo Babers	1600 M Relay	1st	2:57.91
	Antonio McKay	1600 M Relay	1st	2:57.91
	Michael Carter	Shot Put	1st	21.09 m
	Carl Lewis	Long Jump	1st	8.54 m
	Al Joyner	Triple Jump	1st	17.26 m
	Mike Conley	Triple Jump	2nd	17.18 m
	Evelyn Ashford	100 M Dash	1st	10.97
	Alice Brown	100 M Dash	2nd	11.13
	Valerie Brisco-Hooks	200 M Dash	1st	21.81
	Florence Griffith	200 M Dash	2nd	22.04
	Valerie Brisco-Hooks	400 M Run	1st	48.83
	Chandra Cheeseborough	400 M Run	2nd	49.05
	Kim Gallagher	800 M Run	2nd	1:58.63
	Benita Fitzgerald-Brown	100 M Hurdles	1st	12.84
	Kim Turner	100 M Hurdles	2nd	12.88
	Judi Brown	400 M Hurdles	2nd	55.20
	Valerie Brisco-Hooks	1600 M Relay	1st	3:18.29
	Chandra Cheeseborough	1600 M Relay	1st	3:18.29
	Lillie Leatherwood	1600 M Relay	1st	3:18.29
	Sherri Howard	1600 M Relay	1st	3:18.29

Place/Year	Athlete	Event	Place	Time/Distance
	Jackie Joyner	Heptathlon	2nd	6,386 pts.
	Tyrell Biggs	Boxing: Super Heavyweight	1st	
	Henry Tillman	Boxing: Heavyweight	1st	
	Frank Tate	Boxing: Light Middleweight	1st	
	Virgil Hill	Boxing: Middleweight	2nd	
	Evander Holyfield	Boxing: Light Heavyweight	3rd	
	Steven McCrory	Boxing: Flyweight	1st	
	Meldrick Taylor	Boxing: Featherweight	1st	
	Pernell Whitaker	Boxing: Lightweight	1st	
	Jerry Page	Boxing: Light Welterweight	1st	
	Mark Breland	Boxing: Welterweight	1st	
	Patrick Ewing	Men's Basketball	1st	
	Vern Fleming	Men's Basketball	1st	
	Michael Jordan	Men's Basketball	1st	
	Sam Perkins	Men's Basketball	1st	
	Alvin Robertson	Men's Basketball	1st	
	Wayman Tisdale	Men's Basketball	1st	
	Leon Wood	Men's Basketball	1st	
	Cathy Boswell	Women's Basketball	1st	
	Teresa Edwards	Women's Basketball	1st	
	Janice Lawrence	Women's Basketball	1st	
	Pamela McGee	Women's Basketball	1st	
	Cheryl Miller	Women's Basketball	1st	
	Lynette Woodard	Women's Basketball	1st	
Seoul, 1988	Carl Lewis	100 M Dash	1st	9.92
	Calvin Smith	100 M Dash	2nd	9.99
	Joe DeLoach	200 M Dash	1st	19.75
	Carl Lewis	200 M Dash	2nd	19.79
	Steve Lewis	400 M Run	1st	43.87
	Butch Reynolds	400 M Run	2nd	43.93
	Danny Everett	400 M Run	3rd	44.09
	Roger Kingdom	110 M Hurdles	1st	12.98
	Tonie Campbell	110 M Hurdles	3rd	13.38
	Andre Phillips	400 M Hurdles	1st	47.19
	Edwin Moses	400 M Hurdles	3rd	47.56
	Butch Reynolds	1600 M Relay	1st	2:56.16
	Steve Lewis	1600 M Relay	1st	2:56.16
	Antonio McKay	1600 M Relay	1st	2:56.16
	Danny Everett	1600 M Relay	1st	2:56.16
	Carl Lewis	Long Jump	1st	8.72 m
	Mike Powell	Long Jump	2nd	8.49 m
	Larry Myricks	Long Jump	3rd	8.27 m
	Florence Griffith-Joyner	100 M Dash	1st	10.54
	Evelyn Ashford	100 M Dash	2nd	10.83
	Florence Griffith-Joyner	200 M Dash	1st	21.34
	Shelia Echols	400 M Relay	1st	41.98
	Florence Griffith-Joyner	400 M Relay	1st	41.98
	Evelyn Ashford	400 M Relay	1st	41.98
	Alice Brown	400 M Relay	1st	41.98
	Jackie Joyner-Kersee	Long Jump	1st	24' 3.5"
	Jackie Joyner-Kersee	Heptathlon	1st	7,291 pts.
	Denean Howard-Hill	1600 M Relay	2nd	3:15.51
	Valerie Brisco	1600 M Relay	2nd	3:15.51
	Diane Dixon	1600 M Relay	2nd	3:15.51
	Florence Griffith-Joyner	1600 M Relay	2nd	3:15.51
	Kim Gallagher	800 M Run	3rd	1:56.91
	Andrew Maynard	Boxing: Light Heavyweight	1st	
	Ray Mercer	Boxing: Heavyweight	1st	
	Kennedy McKinney	Boxing: Bantamweight	1st	
	Riddick Bowe	Boxing: Super Heavyweight	2nd	
	Roy Jones	Boxing: Middleweight	2nd	
	Kenny Monday	Wrestling: Freestyle	1st	

Place/Year	Athlete	Event	Place	Time/Distance
	Nate Carr	Wrestling: Freestyle	3rd	
	Zina Garrison	Tennis: Doubles	1st	
	Zina Garrison	Tennis: Singles	3rd	
	Tom Goodwin	Baseball	1st	
	Ty Griffin	Baseball	1st	
	Cindy Brown	Women's Basketball	1st	
	Vicky Bullett	Women's Basketball	1st	
	Cynthia Cooper	Women's Basketball	1st	
	Teresa Edwards	Women's Basketball	1st	
	Jennifer Gillom	Women's Basketball	1st	
	Bridgette Gordon	Women's Basketball	1st	
	Katrina McClain	Women's Basketball	1st	
	Teresa Weatherspoon	Women's Basketball	1st	
	Willie Anderson	Men's Basketball	3rd	
	Stacey Augmon	Men's Basketball	3rd	
	Bimbo Coles	Men's Basketball	3rd	
	Jeff Grayer	Men's Basketball	3rd	
	Hersey Hawkins	Men's Basketball	3rd	
	Danny Manning	Men's Basketball	3rd	
	J.R. Reid	Men's Basketball	3rd	
	Mitch Richmond	Men's Basketball	3rd	
	David Robinson	Men's Basketball	3rd	
	Charles D. Smith	Men's Basketball	3rd	
	Charles E. Smith	Men's Basketball	3rd	
Barcelona, 1992	Dennis Mitchell	100 M Dash	3rd	10.04
	Gail Devers	100 M Dash	1st	10.82
	Mike Marsh	200 M Dash	1st	20.01
	Michael Bates	200 M Dash	3rd	20.38
	Gwen Torrence	200 M Dash	1st	21.81
	Quincy Watts	400 M Run	1st	43.50
	Steve Lewis	400 M Run	2nd	44.21
	Johnny Gray	800 M Run	3rd	1:43.97
	Mike Marsh	400 M Relay	1st	37.40
	Leroy Burrell	400 M Relay	1st	37.40
	Dennis Mitchell	400 M Relay	1st	37.40
	Carl Lewis	400 M Relay	1st	37.40
	Evelyn Ashford	400 M Relay	1st	42.11
	Esther Jones	400 M Relay	1st	42.11
	Carlette Guidry-White	400 M Relay	1st	42.11
	Gwen Torrence	400 M Relay	1st	42.11
	Tony Dees	110 M Hurdles	2nd	13.24
	Kevin Young	400 M Hurdles	1st	46.78
	Sandra Farmer	400 M Hurdles	2nd	53.69
	Janeene Vickers	400 M Hurdles	3rd	54.31
	Andrew Valmon	800 M Relay	1st	2:55.74
	Quincy Watts	800 M Relay	1st	2:55.74
	Michael Johnson	800 M Relay	1st	2:55.74
	Steve Lewis	800 M Relay	1st	2:55.74
	Natasha Kaiser	800 M Relay	2nd	3:20.92
	Gwen Torrence	800 M Relay	2nd	3:20.92
	Jearl Miles	800 M Relay	2nd	3:20.92
	Rochelle Stevens	800 M Relay	2nd	3:20.92
	Hollis Conway	High Jump	3rd	7' 8"
	Carl Lewis	Long Jump	1st	28' 5.5"
	Mike Powell	Long Jump	2nd	28' 4.25"
	Joe Greene	Long Jump	3rd	27' 4.5"
	Jackie Joyner-Kersee	Long Jump	3rd	23' 2.5"
	Mike Conley	Triple Jump	1st	59' 7.5"
	Charlie Simpkins	Triple Jump	2nd	57' 9"
	Jackie Joyner-Kersee	Heptathlon	1st	7,044 pts.
	Tim Austin	Boxing: Flyweight	3rd	
	Chris Byrd	Boxing: Middleweight	2nd	

Place/Year	Athlete	Event	Place	Time/Distance
	Kevin Jackson	Wrestling: Middleweight	1st	
	Charles Barkley	Men's Basketball	1st	
	Clyde Drexler	Men's Basketball	1st	
	Patrick Ewing	Men's Basketball	1st	
	Magic Johnson	Men's Basketball	1st	
	Michael Jordan	Men's Basketball	1st	
	Karl Malone	Men's Basketball	1st	
	Scottie Pippen	Men's Basketball	1st	
	David Robinson	Men's Basketball	1st	
	Vicky Bullett	Women's Basketball	3rd	
	Daedra Charles	Women's Basketball	3rd	
	Cynthia Cooper	Women's Basketball	3rd	
	Teresa Edwards	Women's Basketball	3rd	
	Carolyn Jones	Women's Basketball	3rd	
	Katrina McClain	Women's Basketball	3rd	
	Vickie Orr	Women's Basketball	3rd	
	Teresa Weatherspoon	Women's Basketball	3rd	
Atlanta, 1996	Dominique Dawes	Gymnastics: Floor Exercise	3rd	
	Dominique Dawes	Gymnastics: Team	1st	
	Michael Johnson	200 M Dash	1st	19.32
	Michael Johnson	400 M Run	1st	43.49
	Allen Johnson	110 M Hurdles	1st	12.95
	Mark Crear	110 M Hurdles	2nd	13.09
	Derrick Adkins	400 M Hurdles	1st	47.54
	Calvin Davis	400 M Hurdles	3rd	47.96
	Tim Harden	400 M Relay	2nd	38.05
	Jon Drummond	400 M Relay	2nd	38.05
	Michael Marsh	400 M Relay	2nd	38.05
	Dennis Mitchell	400 M Relay	2nd	38.05
	LaMont Smith	1600 M Relay	1st	2:55.99
	Alvin Harrison	1600 M Relay	1st	2:55.99
	Derek Mills	1600 M Relay	1st	2:55.99
	Anthuan Maybank	1600 M Relay	1st	2:55.99
	Dan O'Brien	Decathlon	1st	8,824 pts.
	Charles Austin	High Jump	1st	7' 10"
	Carl Lewis	Long Jump	1st	27' 10.75"
	Joe Greene	Long Jump	3rd	27' .50"
	Kenny Harrison	Triple Jump	1st	59' 4"
	Gail Devers	100 M Dash	1st	10.94
	Gwen Torrence	100 M Dash	3rd	10.96
	Kim Batten	400 M Hurdles	2nd	53.08
	Tonja Buford-Bailey	400 M Hurdles	3rd	53.22
	Gail Devers	400 M Relay	1st	41.95
	Chryste Gaines	400 M Relay	1st	41.95
	Gwen Torrence	400 M Relay	1st	41.95
	Inger Miller	400 M Relay	1st	41.95
	Rochelle Stevens	1600 M Relay	1st	3:20.91
	Maicel Malone	1600 M Relay	1st	3:20.91
	Kim Graham	1600 M Relay	1st	3:20.91
	Jearl Miles	1600 M Relay	1st	3:20.91
	Jackie Joyner-Kersee	Long Jump	3rd	22' 11"
	Floyd Mayweather	Boxing: Featherweight	3rd	
	Terrance Cauthen	Boxing: Lightweight	3rd	
	Rhoshii Wells	Boxing: Middleweight	3rd	
	Antonio Tarver	Boxing: Light Heavyweight	3rd	
	Nate Jones	Boxing: Heavyweight	3rd	
	David Reid	Boxing: Light Middleweight	1st	
	Teresa Edwards	Women's Basketball	1st	
	Ruth Bolton	Women's Basketball	1st	
	Lisa Leslie	Women's Basketball	1st	
	Katrina McClain	Women's Basketball	1st	
	Sheryl Swoopes	Women's Basketball	1st	

Place/Year	Athlete	Event	Place	Time/Distance
	Nikki McCray	Women's Basketball	1st	
	Dawn Staley	Women's Basketball	1st	
	Venus Lacey	Women's Basketball	1st	
	Carla McGhee	Women's Basketball	1st	
	Mitch Richmond	Men's Basketball	1st	
	Scottie Pippin	Men's Basketball	1st	
	Gary Payton	Men's Basketball	1st	
	Charles Barkley	Men's Basketball	1st	
	Hakeem Olajuwon	Men's Basketball	1st	
	David Robinson	Men's Basketball	1st	
	Penny Hardaway	Men's Basketball	1st	
	Grant Hill	Men's Basketball	1st	
	Karl Malone	Men's Basketball	1st	
	Reggie Miller	Men's Basketball	1st	
	Jacque Jones	Baseball	3rd	

Index

Personal names, place names, events, organizations, and various subject areas or keywords contained in the *Reference Library of Black America* are listed in this index with corresponding volume and page numbers indicating text references. Page numbers appearing in boldface indicate major treatments of topics, such as biographical profiles and organizational entries. Page numbers appearing in italics refer to photographs, illustrations, and maps found throughout the reference work.

E

U

W

X

Y